Selected
Black American, African,
and
Caribbean Authors

Selected
Black American, African,
and
Caribbean Authors

A Bio-Bibliography

Compiled by
JAMES A. PAGE
and
JAE MIN ROH

LIBRARIES UNLIMITED, INC.
Littleton, Colorado
1985

Originally published by G. K. Hall in 1977 as *Selected Black American Authors: An Illustrated Bio-Bibliography*. Copyright © by James A. Page.

The present edition has been revised and expanded.

LIBRARIES UNLIMITED, INC.
P.O. Box 263
Littleton, Colorado 80160-0263

Library of Congress Cataloging in Publication Data

Page, James A. (James Allen), 1918-
    Selected Black American, African, and Caribbean authors.

    Includes index.
    1. American literature--Afro-American authors--Bio-bibliography. 2. Afro-American authors--Biography--Dictionaries. 3. African literature--Black authors--Bio-bibliography. 4. Caribbean literature--Black authors--Bio-bibliography. 5. Authors, Black--Biography--Dictionaries. I. Roh, Jae Min, 1927-   . II. Title.
Z1229.N39P34   1985   016.81'09'896   85-5225
[PS153.N5]
ISBN 0-87287-430-3

Libraries Unlimited books are bound with Type II nonwoven material that meets and exceeds National Association of State Textbook Administrators' Type II nonwoven material specifications Class A through E.

Contents _____

Preface

Selected Black American, African, and Caribbean Authors: A Bio-Bibliography provides a study of African-descended authors and their works. This reference is a handy, compact, one-volume companion to Afro-American writings. It is concerned primarily with Afro-American literature of the United States, from its beginnings to the present. However, it also attempts to give some insight into the literary scene on the Mother Continent itself, as well as in the Caribbean diaspora.

This second edition represents a revision and an enlargement of *Selected Black American Authors: An Illustrated Bio-Bibliography* (Boston, G. K. Hall, 1977), compiled by myself. My fellow librarian, Jae Min Roh, has joined me in the task of not only supplementing and updating the first edition, but also making it more useful and meaningful to its ultimate users. The book is designed to be useful to a wide scope of readership, ranging from the junior high school level through the university research level. It meets the needs of schools and libraries, as well as those of individuals. It is also anticipated that it will be useful to students of Afro-American literature outside the United States.

We began the task of updating and compiling this work by sending questionnaires to both authors and publishers. More than 300 authors were sent questionnaires requesting full biographical and bibliographical information; the publishers of about 300 living and many deceased authors were sent similar questionnaires. This guide is a product, therefore, of information submitted by the authors themselves, and/or their publishers; as well as of information already available in a wide variety of published sources. In the case of conflicting information from different sources, our authority was first of all the authors or publishers themselves—where available. To unravel inconsistencies we consulted the *National Union Catalog* as our final authority. We also made comparisons with *Black American Writers Past and Present*, *Dictionary of Literary Biography*, *Dictionary Catalog of the Schomburg Collection of Negro Literature and History*, *Contemporary Authors*, and *Books in Print*, among others.

The end result of this effort has been an expansion of coverage from 453 authors in the first edition to 632 in this one. These writers are:

1. *Literary Writers.* The primary concern has been extended to this group of writers, which includes novelists, poets, playwrights, essayists, and critics.

2. *Non-Literary Writers.* We have concentrated a great deal on the social and the religious—perhaps more than in any other areas. Much, if not most, of the output of Afro-Americans down through the years has consisted of protest and Black Consciousness. Because of the conditions under which Blacks have labored for centuries, they have been more prone to protesting discrimination and segregation

than to producing more esoteric, "literary" works. However, our better writers have been successful in combining both the literary and the Black Consciousness areas. Due consideration has also been given to writers concerned with current events and civil rights, Black authors discussed by scholars and critics listed in references cited in the "Bibliography of Sources," and publishers or editors of newspapers and magazines that have an impact on writing.

3. *Writers Outside the United States.* In referring to the non-American writers, an effort has been made to represent East, West, and South Africa, as well as to give consideration to both Anglophone and Francophone elements of these societies. The same has been true in presenting Caribbean writers, although the work has been weighted more heavily in favor of the more prolific writers. One overruling criterion is that foreign writers covered here must have either lived, studied, or been published in the continental United States.

Our listings have included only published books. We have not entered works included only in anthologies or only in periodicals (except in rare occasions where they were not published elsewhere). We almost always give place, publisher, and date of publication. The exceptions to this rule have been made when a title was published long ago and full information is lacking. Even then we list it only if we have full reprint information, so that virtually every title has full publishing information. In some instances—for brevity—we do not cite the place of publication when we have given that information in a preceding entry on the same author. In other instances we have listed plays and poems without publishers, when that information was not available. At times plays were produced without being published. However, all of our major titles have full information. Paperback editions and foreign editions have been so indicated.

We have been selective in both authors and titles, and have made no attempt to be exhaustive. We have based this selectivity primarily upon the studied research and reasoned judgment of such renowned critics and teachers of Black literature as Houston A. Baker, Sterling A. Brown, Arthur P. Davis, James Weldon Johnson, J. Saunders Redding, Eugene B. Redmond, and Darwin T. Turner. In addition, we have updated our information in what seemed to us to be the most significant of the authors' works in the various genres. Finally, we have included some newer writers who show promise by having won major literary awards, having achieved best-seller status, or having received other unusual recognition.

Our criteria of selection are as follows: (1) *Authors* must have had at least one book published, preferably more. (2) *Authors* must have been included in other sources, i.e., anthologies, critical studies, handbooks, biographical references. (3) *Poets* must have had more than one book published—unless the poet is outstanding in another field. (4) *Playwrights* are usually included if they have had one or more plays either published or performed. (5) *Essayists* must have produced significant work in the arts, biography, criticism, history, sciences, social sciences, theology, or other areas.

Excluded from this selection are: (1) *Authors* who have published their own books; (2) *Authors* who have been published *only* in anthologies or other compilations; (3) *Authors* who have been published *only* in journals; (4) *Most Authors* who have published "as told to" works; and (5) *Sports and Entertainment Figures* except those of unusual prominence (or whose books were works of art).

The main body of this bio-bibliography is arranged alphabetically by author's last name. Each entry contains biographical information including birth and death dates and places, family, education, address, and career information (where accessible). Also included in each entry is a Writings section, spelling out the author's works; selected comments on his or her career; and a list of sources.

The writings are arranged in two categories, Fiction and Nonfiction. We have used *fiction* "in its widest sense, comprehending every literary product of the imagination, whether in prose or verse, or in a narrative or a dramatic form" (as defined in *Webster's Twentieth Century Dictionary*). Where possible, we indicate the genre or approximate subject matter of each title, such as novels, short stories, plays, poems, and essays. Under each category the titles are arranged in chronological order of publication.

A list of abbreviations used in the text follows the preface. The main body is succeeded by a Bibliography of Sources. Next there are nationality rosters for each of the non-American groups, followed by an Occupational Index and a Title Index which facilitate searching.

It is hoped that this work has sufficiently accomplished our objective of presenting a broad spectrum of what is being thought about, written, and spoken of in that vast, diverse world known as Black America. We shall be happy if this book can help its users to formulate a balanced view of Black experiences as expressed in writings by Blacks.

* * *

We are indebted to numerous works and authors. One book we found quite useful in our early searches was the *Author Biographies Master Index*, 2nd edition. Among the most important were *Books in Print*; *Contemporary Authors*; *Contemporary Novelists*; *Contemporary Poets*; *Current Biography*; *Dictionary of American Negro Biography*; *Dictionary of Literary Biography*; and *Who's Who among Black Americans*. Other important references were *Something about the Author*; *Reader's Encyclopedia of American Literature*; *Writers Directory*; and *Who's Who in America*.

For the African and Caribbean authors, we used, among others: *African Authors*; *Black Writers in French*; *Complete Caribbeana*; *Emerging African Nations and Their Leaders*; *International Authors and Writers Who's Who*; *Jamaican National Bibliography*; *A Reader's Guide to African Literature*; *West Indian Literature*; and *Who's Who in African Literature*.

I wish to acknowledge the assistance of Lois Phillips of Los Angeles County Public Library, Camille Carter of Los Angeles Public Library, and Millicent Hill, English Teacher, Los Angeles Unified School District. In addition, there are Nathaniel Davis of the Center for Afro-American Studies, University of California at Los Angeles; Mary Jane Hewitt of the Museum of Afro-American Art, Santa Monica, California, and Carolyn McIntosh of the University of Southern California. We received great stimulus and inspiration from " 'Of Our Spiritual Strivings': Recent Developments in Black Literature and Criticism," a conference held at the University of California, Los Angeles, April 22-23, 1983.

Much of our research has been conducted at the Doheny Library of the University of Southern California, and in the Literature, History, and Social Science Departments of Los Angeles Public Library. We also sought information at Los Angeles Southwest Community College, the University of California at Los Angeles, and California State University, Los Angeles. The entire project has been based on the work, support, and background which was rendered me in compiling the original volume. We hope we have avoided most errors; however, we will appreciate having any omissions or corrections called to our attention.

Finally, I wish to commend my daughter Anita for assistance in many ways over the course of the project; and my wife, Ethel, who always dedicates herself completely and makes every effort to back me wholeheartedly.

James A. Page

Abbreviations

A.A. — Associate in Arts
Acad. — Academy; academic
ACRL — Association of College & Research Librarians
ACTFL/SCOLT — American Council for Teaching of Foreign Languages/ Southern Conference on Language Teaching
admin. — administration; administrator
Ala. — Alabama
ALA — American Library Association
A&M — Agricultural & Mechanical
AME — African Methodist Episcopal
Amer. — American
apptd. — appointed
Apr. — April
Ariz. — Arizona
Ark. — Arkansas
ASCAP — American Society of Composers, Authors and Publishers
ASNLH — Association for Study of Negro Life and History
Assn. — Association
Assoc. — Associate; Associated
Asst. — Assistant
Aug. — August
autobiog. — autobiography
Ave. — Avenue
B.A. — Bachelor of Arts
Bap. — Baptist
BBC — British Broadcasting Corp.
bd. — board
B.D. — Bachelor of Divinity
B.F.A. — Bachelor of Fine Arts
biog. — biography
bk(s). — book(s)
bldg. — building
B. Phil. — Bachelor of Philosophy
Brit. — Britain; British

B.S. — Bachelor of Science
bull. — bulletin
bus. — business
Cal. — California
Can. — Canada
CEA — College English Association
chap. — chapter
c/o — care of
Co. — Company
Coll. — College
Colo. — Colorado
Com. — Committee; Commission
comp. — compiler
conf. — conference
Conn. — Connecticut
contrib. — contributor; contributing; contribution
co-op. — cooperative
CORE — Congress of Racial Equality
Corp. — Corporation
CUNY — City University of New York
d. — daughter
D.C. — District of Columbia
D.C.L. — Doctor of Civil Law
D.D. — Doctor of Divinity (honorary)
dec. — deceased
Dec. — December
Del. — Delaware
dept. — department
dir. — director
dist. — district
div. — division; divorced
Dr. — Doctor; Drive
e. — east, eastern
econ. — economic(s)
ed. — edited, editor; edition; editorial
educ. — education; educational; educator
encyl. — encyclopedia

Eng. — English; England
Feb. — February
Fed. — Federal
Fla. — Florida
Found. — Foundation
Ga. — Georgia
gen. — general
govt. — government
grad. — graduate
HARYOU — Harlem Youth Opportunities Unlimited
HEW — Health, Education and Welfare, Department of
H.H.D. — Doctor of Humanities
hist. — history; historical
hon. — honorary; honorable
Ill. — Illinois
ILO — International Labor Organization
Inc. — Incorporated
Ind. — Indiana
Inst. — Institute; institutional
instr. — instructor; instruction
Intnl. — international
Jan. — January
J.D. — Doctor of Jurisprudence
Jr. — Junior
juv. — juvenile
Kan. — Kansas
Ky. — Kentucky
La. — Louisiana
L.A. — Los Angeles
lab. — laboratory
lang(s). — language(s)
lect. — lecturer
legis. — legislature
L.H.D. — Doctor of Humane Letters; Doctor of Humanities
lib. — library
librn. — librarian
lit. — literature
Litt.D. — Doctor of Letters
LL.B. — Bachelor of Laws
LL.D. — Doctor of Laws
LL.M. — Master of Laws
Lt. — Lieutenant
M.A. — Master of Arts
mag(s). — magazine(s)
Mar. — March
Mass. — Massachusetts
Md. — Maryland
M.Ed. — Master of Education
mem. — member
M.F.A. — Master of Fine Arts

mgr. — manager
Mich. — Michigan
Minn. — Minnesota
Miss. — Mississippi
M.L.A. — Modern Language Association
M.L.S. — Master of Library Science
Mo. — Missouri
mod. — modern
M.S. — Master of Science
M.S.L.S. — Master of Science, Library Science
M.S.W. — Master of Social Work
Mt. — Mount
mus. — museum
Mus.B. — Bachelor of Music
n. — north; northern
NAACP — National Association for the Advancement of Colored People
natl. — national
N.C. — North Carolina
n.d. — not dated
N. Dak. — North Dakota
NDEA — National Defense Education Act
NEA — National Endowment for the Arts
Neb. — Nebraska
NEH — National Endowment for the Humanities
NET — National Educational Television
Nev. — Nevada
N.H. — New Hampshire
N.J. — New Jersey
N. Mex. — New Mexico
no. — number
Nov. — November
n.p. — no place or no publisher
N.Y. — New York
N.Y.C. — New York City
N.Y.U. — New York University
OBAC — Organization of Black American Culture
Oct. — October
OEO — Office of Equal Opportunity
Okla. — Oklahoma
Ore. — Oregon
org. — organization
Pa. — Pennsylvania
pam. — pamphlet
P.E.N. — Poets, Playwrights, Editors, Essayists and Novelists
Ph.D. — Doctor of Philosophy
Phila. — Philadelphia
Pl. — Place
polit. — political

Pres. — President
Presby. — Presbyterian
prin. — principal
prod. — producer; produced
Prof. — Professor
PTA — Parent Teachers Association
pub. — published; publisher; publishing
publ. — publication
PUSH — People United to Save Humanity
Rd. — Road
ref. — reference
relig. — religion; religious
rep. — representative
res. — research
rev. — revised
Rev. — Reverend
R.I. — Rhode Island
s. — south; southern
S.C. — South Carolina
sch. — school
sci. — science
S. Dak. — South Dakota
secy. — secretary
SEEK — Search for Education, Elevation
    and Knowledge
sem. — seminary
Sept. — September
ser. — series
serv. — service
Sgt. — Sergeant
SNCC — Student Nonviolent Coordinating
    Committee
soc. — society; social
sociol. — sociological; sociology
spec. — specialist; special
St. — Street; Saint
S.T.D. — Doctor of Sacred Theology
S.T.M. — Master of Sacred Theology

stud. — student
SUNY — State University of New York
supt. — superintendent
supvr. — supervisor
tchg. — teaching
tchr. — teacher
tech. — technical
Tenn. — Tennessee
Tex. — Texas
Th.D. — Doctor of Theology
theol. — theologian; theological
transl. — translated; translation
TV — television
U. — University
UCLA — University of California at Los
    Angeles
UN — United Nations
U.S. — United States
USIA — United States Information Agency
USIS — United States Information Service
USSR — Union of Soviet Socialist Republics
V. — Vice
Va. — Virginia
vol(s). — volume(s)
Vt. — Vermont
w. — west; western
Wash. — Washington
Wash., D.C. — Washington, D.C.
Wis. — Wisconsin
WPA — Works Progress Administration
W. Va. — West Virginia
Wyo. — Wyoming
YMCA — Young Men's Christian
    Association
YMHA — Young Men's Hebrew Association
YWCA — Young Women's Christian
    Association
yr(s). — year(s)

ABBOTT, ROBERT SENGSTACKE. Publisher.

Born on St. Simon's Island, off coast of Ga., Nov. 24, 1870. *Education:* Beach Inst., Savannah, Ga.; Claflin Inst., Orangeburg, S.C.; Hampton Inst., Va.; Kent Coll. of Law, Chicago. *Family:* Married 1st Helen Thornton Morrison in 1918 (div.); married 2nd Edna Brown Dennison. *Career:* Apprentice Printer, *Savannah News*; Founder-Pub., *Chicago Defender*, 1905- (grew from weekly to a daily). *Honors:* Apptd. mem., Ill. Race Relations Com., 1919; Pres., Hampton Inst. Alumni Assn.; Laurel Wreath for Distinguished Serv., Kappa Alpha Psi; hon. degrees from Morris Brown U., Ga., & Wilberforce U., Ohio. Died in 1940.

Writings:

Nonfiction

Chicago Defender, newspaper (1905-)

Sidelights: Abbott wrote near the end of his life, "I have endeavored to bring to the attention of the reading public all the inhuman treatment, discrimination, segregation, disfranchisement, peonage and all other injustice directed at my people." (*Negroes Who Helped Build America*)

Sources: *Famous American Negroes; The Lonesome Road; Negroes Who Helped Build America; They Showed the Way.*

ABDUL, RAOUL. Opera Singer.

Born in Cleveland, Ohio, Nov. 7, 1929. *Education:* Karamu House, Cleveland; Cleveland Inst. of Music; Cleveland Music Sch. Settlement; N.Y. Coll. of Music; New Sch. for Soc. Res.; Mannes Coll. of Music; (grad.) Acad. of Music & Dramatic Art, Vienna. *Family:* Single. *Career:* Public relations, Karamu House, Cleveland; Youth Ed., *Cleveland Call and Post*; Cultural Ed., *New York Age*; Ed. Asst. to Langston Hughes; Syndicated Columnist, "The Cultural Scene," Assoc. Negro Press; Organizer, coffee concerts (chamber music), Harlem, 1958-59. *Mailing address:* 360 W. 22nd St., N.Y., N.Y. 10011.

Writings:

Fiction

3000 Years of Black Poetry, co-ed. with Alan Lomax (N.Y., Dodd, 1970; Greenwich, Conn., Fawcett, 1971)

Magic of Black Poetry, ed. (Dodd, 1972)

Nonfiction

Famous Black Entertainers of Today (Dodd, 1974)

Blacks in Classical Music: A Personal History (Dodd, 1978)

Sidelights: Singer: Marlboro Music Festival, 1956; Vienna Music Festival, 1962; Nuremberg (opened Brotherhood Week, 1962); Schubert Cycle, Harvard, summer sch. (1966); German lieder recital, Carnegie Hall, 1967. Sang works from Karl Orff, Mozart, Menotti, and Darius Milhaud.

Sources: Pub. information; *3000 Years of Black Poetry.*

ABRAHAMS, PETER LEE [Peter Graham]. (South African). Novelist, Poet, Short Story Writer, Journalist.

Born in Vrdedorp, near Johannesburg, S. Africa, in 1919. *Family:* (Father, Ethiopian; mother, "Cape Coloured."); wife and 3 children. *Career:* Assigned by *London Observer* to S. Africa for ser. of articles, 1952; rerun in *N.Y. Herald Tribune*'s Paris ed. Wrote radio scripts for BBC's Third Programme in early 1950s. (Lived in Kingston, Jamaica) and worked as radio broadcaster-commentator for West India News and as free-lancer. Also ed. of *West Indian Economist. Mailing address:* c/o Macmillan Pub. Co., 866 Third Ave., N.Y., N.Y. 10022.

Writings:
Fiction

A Blackman Speaks of Freedom, poems (Durban, S. Africa, Universal Printing Works, 1941)

Dark Testament, short stories (London, Allen & Unwin, 1942)

Song of the City, novel (London, Dorothy Crisp, 1944)

Mine Boy, novel (Dorothy Crisp, 1946; reissue, London, Faber, 1954, 1966; N.Y., Knopf, 1955; London, Heinemann, African Writers Ser., 1963; reprint, 1965, 1966, 1968; N.Y., Macmillan, 1970; N.Y., Collier, 1970)

The Path of Thunder, novel (N.Y., Harper, 1948; Faber, 1948, 1952; reprint, Old Greenwich, Conn., Chatham, 1975)

Wild Conquest, novel (Faber, 1951; Harper, 1950; London, Penguin, 1966; Garden City, N.Y., Doubleday, 1971)

Tell Freedom, novel (Knopf, 1954; Faber, 1954; Allen & Unwin, 1963; Collier, 1970; Macmillan, 1970)

A Wreath for Udomo, novel (Faber, 1956, 1965; Knopf, 1956; Macmillan, African-Amer. Lib., 1971)

A Night of Their Own, novel (Faber, 1965; Knopf, 1965)

The Fury of Rachel Monette, novel (Macmillan, 1980)

Nonfiction

Return to Goli (Faber, 1953, 1957)

Jamaica: An Island Mosaic (London, Her Majesty's Stationary Office, 1957)

This Island Now (Faber, 1966; Knopf, 1967; Macmillan, 1971; Collier, 1971)

The Quiet Voice (Phila., Dorrance, 1966)

An Atlas of Radiological Anatomy, with Jamie Weir (Kent, Eng., Pitman Medical, 1978)

Sidelights: Bernth Lindfors informs us that Abrahams "is at his best when transcribing newsworthy events which have a basis in fact; his autobiographical and travel writings, for instance, are superb." (*Contemporary Novelists*)

Sources: *A Reader's Guide to African Literature*; *Books in Print*, 1980-81; *Contemporary Novelists*, 1972; *Who's Who in African Literature*.

ACHEBE, CHINUA. (Nigerian). Novelist, Short Story Writer.

Born in Agidi, near Onitsa, E. Central State, Nigeria, Nov. 15, 1930. *Family:* (Son of Ibo tchr.). *Education:* Govt. Coll., Umuahia, 1944; B.A., U. Coll., Ibadan, 1953. *Career:* Talks Producer, Nigerian Broadcasting Serv., 1954- ; Dir., External Broadcasting, "Voice of Nigeria," 1961- ; founded pub. co. with Christopher Okigbo (poet) in Enugu, 1967; Res. Fellow, Inst. of African Studies, U. of Nigeria, Nsukka, E. Central State; Ed. of "Nsukkascope" (campus mag.); Ed., "Okike," Nwamife pub.; Ed. Advisor, Heinemann's "African Writers Ser."; Ed. Advisor, Nwankwo Ifejika & Co.; Enugu. Tchr., U. of Mass. & U. of Conn. *Honors:* Visited E. Africa on Rockefeller

Found. Grant, 1960-62; Fellow for Creative Artists, UNESCO (traveled to U.S., Brazil, and Great Britain), 1963; Fellow, MLA of Amer.; (Doctorates) Stirling U.; Southampton U. Recently followed Heinrich Boll, Nobel Prize winner, as 2nd recipient of Scottish Arts Council's Neil Gunn Fellowship. Poems *Beware, Soul Brother*, won 1st Commonwealth Poetry Prize; hon. Doctorate of Letters, Dartmouth U., 1972 (for "unique contribution to the literature of the world"). *Mailing address:* U. of Nigeria, Nsukka, Nigeria.

Writings:
Fiction

Things Fall Apart, novel, transl. into 13 langs. (London, Heinemann, 1958; N.Y., Astor-Honor, 1959; N.Y., McDowell, Obolensky, 1959; Greenwich, Conn., Fawcett, 1959; Heinemann, African Writers Ser., 1962; N.Y., Fawcett, 1978; Heinemann, Guided Readers Ser., 1981)

No Longer at Ease, novel (Astor-Honor, 1960; Heinemann, 1960, 1966; McDowell, Obolensky, 1960; Greenwich, Conn., Fawcett, 1960; Garden City, N.Y., Anchor, Doubleday, 1967; Fawcett, 1977; Heinemann, African Writers Ser., 1981)

The Sacrificial Egg, short stories (Onitsha, Etudo, Ltd., 1962)

Arrow of God, novel (Heinemann, 1964, 1974; N.Y., John Day, 1964; paper, Doubleday, 1969)

A Man of the People, novel (Heinemann, 1966; John Day, 1966)

Chike and the River, juv. (Eng., Cambridge U. Press, 1966)

Beware, Soul Brother and Other Poems (Heinemann, African Writers Ser., 1972)

Girls at War and Other Stories (Doubleday, 1973; Fawcett, 1973)

How the Leopard Got His Claws, juv. with John Iroaganachi (N.Y., Okpaku, 1973)

Nonfiction

Morning Yet on Creation Day, essays (Garden City, N.Y., Anchor, 1975; Heinemann, 1975)

Sidelights: Chinua Achebe reveals: "I am a political writer. My politics is concerned with universal human communication across racial and cultural boundaries as a means of fostering respect for all people. Such respect can issue only from understanding. So my primary concern is with clearing the channels of communication in my own neighbourhood by hacking away at the thickets that choke them." (*Contemporary Novelists*)

Sources: *Bibliography of Creative African Writing; Books in Print*, 1980-81, 1981-82; *Contemporary Novelists*, 1972; *A Man of the People; Who's Who in African Literature.*

AIDOO, CHRISTINA AMA ATA. (Ghanaian). Novelist, Playwright, Short Story Writer.
Born in Abeadzi Kyiakor, Ghana, in 1942. *Education:* B.A. (honors), U. of Ghana, Legon, 1964; Stanford U. (Creative Writing). *Career:* Res. Fellow, Inst. of African Studies, U. of Ghana, Legon; Eng. Prof., U. of Ghana, Cape Coast. *Honors: No Sweetness Here* won prize from *Black Orpheus* mag. *Mailing address:* c/o Longman's, 5 Bentinck St., London WIM 5RN, Eng.

Writings:
Fiction

Dilemma of a Ghost, play (N.Y., Collier, 1965, 1971; N.Y., Macmillan, African-Amer. Lib., 1971)

No Sweetness Here, short stories (N.Y., Doubleday, 1970; N.Y., Harlow, Longman, 1970, 1972)

Anowa, play (N.Y., Longman, 1970)

Our Sister Killjoy or Reflections from a Black-Eyed Squint (N.Y., NOK Pub., Intnl., 1979)

Anowa, short stories (Wash., D.C., Three Continents, Sun-Lit. Ser., 1980)

Sources: *African Authors; Books in Print*, 1978-79; *Freedomways*, 1979; *No Sweetness Here.*

ALLEN, ROBERT L. Editor, Reporter.
Born in Atlanta, Ga., May 29, 1942. *Education:* B.S., Morehouse Coll., 1963; Columbia U., 1963-64. *Family:* Married Pamela Parker. *Career:* Asst. Prof., New Coll. & Black Studies Dept., San Jose State Coll., 1969-72; Staff Reporter, *Guardian* newsweekly, N.Y.C., 1967-69; Ed., *Black Scholar* (present). *Mailing address:* Black Scholar, P.O. Box 908, Sausalito, Cal. 94965.

Writings:
Nonfiction

Black Awakening in Capitalist America (N.Y., Doubleday, 1969)

A Guide to Black Power in America: An Historical Analysis (London, Gollancz, 1970)

Reluctant Reformers: Racism and Social Reform Movements in the United States, with Pamela P. Allen (Wash., D.C., Howard U. Press, 1974)

Sources: *Black Awakening in Capitalist America; Who's Who among Black Americans*, 1975-76.

ALLEN, SAMUEL W. [Paul Vesey]. Poet, Lawyer, Translator.
Born in Columbus, Ohio, Dec. 9, 1917. *Education:* A.B., Fisk U., 1938; J.D., Harvard Law Sch., 1941; grad. study, New Sch. for Soc. Res., 1947-48; Sorbonne, 1949-50. *Family:* d., Marie-Christine Allen. *Career:* Deputy Asst. Dist. Attorney, N.Y.C., 1946-47; Civilian Attorney, U.S. Armed Forces in Europe, 1952-55; practice of law, Brooklyn, N.Y., 1956-57; Assoc. Prof. of Law, Tex. S. U., Houston, 1958-60; Asst. Gen. Counsel, USIA, 1961-64; Chief Counsel, U.S. Community Relations Serv., 1965-68; Avalon Prof. of Humanities, Tuskegee Inst., 1968-70; Visiting Prof. of Eng. & Co-Dir., Afro-Amer. Inst., Wesleyan U., 1969-70; Prof. of Eng., Boston U., 1971-81. *Honors:* Poetry recording, Lib. of Congress, 1972; NEA Creative Writing Fellowship Award (Poetry), 1979-80. *Mailing address:* 145 Cliff Ave., Winthrop, Mass. 02152.

Writings:
Fiction

Elfenbein Zahne (Ivory Tusks), bilingual vol. under pen name Paul Vesey (Heidelberg, Wolfgang Rothe, 1956)

Ivory Tusks and Other Poems (Millbrook, N.Y., Kriya Press, 1968)

Poems from Africa, ed. (N.Y., Crowell, 1973)

Paul Vesey's Ledger, poems (London, Bremen, 1975)

Nonfiction

Orphee Noir, by Jean-Paul Sartre, transl. (London, Présence Africaine, 1960)

Pan-Africanism Reconsidered, co-ed. (Berkeley, Cal., U. of Cal. Press, 1962)

Sidelights: (Other works) "Africa," by Aime Cesaire, translated in *Voices in the Whirlwind and Other Essays*, ed. by Ezekiel Mphahlele (New York, Hill & Wang, 1972); "Elegy for Martin Luther King," by Leopold Senghor (translated, Benin City, Nigeria, *Benin Review*, 1974); "Attended Sorbonne ... Richard Wright introduced him to Présence Africaine circle.... An early awareness of what Cesaire dubbed 'Negritude' led him to translate Jean-Paul Sartre's *Orphee Noir*; 'Negritude and Its Relevance for the American Negro Writer,' a paper delivered at the 1959 New York Black Writers' Conference, has become the frequently reprinted classic text on the subject....
"Sam Allen's first published book of poems appeared in Germany.... Georg Dickenberger in Nigeria's "Black Orpheus" stated, 'It is a new consciousness that has found expression in (Allen's) language.... A consciousness whose imagery is both African and occidental but whose mixed heritage confronts us as a unit.' " (Author)

Sources: Author information; *Blackamerican Literature; Negroes in Public Affairs and Government; Poetry of Black America*.

AMERICA, RICHARD F. Business Professor.
Career: U.S. Dept. of Housing & Urban Development; Prof. of Industry, Wharton Sch., U. of Pa. *Mailing address:* c/o Wharton Sch., U. of Pa., 34th & Spruce Sts., Phila., Pa. 19104.

Writings:
Nonfiction

Developing the Afro-American Economy: Building on Strength (Lexington, Mass., Lexington Bks., 1977)

Moving Ahead: Black Managers in American Business, with Bernard E. Anderson (N.Y., McGraw-Hill, 1978)

Sidelights: *Moving Ahead* carries "interviews with 100 black men and women managers from a variety of businesses; the techniques they used to advance in their careers and the situations and personalities they encountered which sometimes stymied them." (*Freedomways*)

Sources: *Books in Print*, 1978-79; *Freedomways*, vol. 19, no. 1, 1979.

AMINI, JOHARI M. [Jewell Christine McLawler Latimore]. Poet, Teacher.
Born in Phila., Pa., Feb. 13, 1935. *Education:* A.A., Chicago City Coll., 1968; U. of Chicago, 1968-69; B.A., Chicago State Coll., 1970; M.A., U. of Chicago, 1972. *Family:* Widowed; d. Marciana; son Kim Allan. *Career:* Lect., Black Studies, U. of Ill., Chicago Circle Campus, 1972- ; Instr., Psychology, Black Lit., Soc. Sci., Kennedy-King Coll., Mini Campus, Chicago, 1970-72; Co-Instr., The Black Aesthetic, Ind. U., Bloomington, spring 1971; Treasurer, OBAC. *Honors:* U. of Chicago scholarship, 1968. *Mailing address:* c/o Third World Press, 7850 S. Ellis Ave., Chicago, Ill. 60619.

Writings:
Fiction

Images in Black, poems (Chicago, Third World, 1967, 1968, 1969)

Black Essence, poems (Third World, 1968)

"A Folk Fable," single poem issue (Third World, 1969)

Let's Go Somewhere, poems (Third World, 1970)

A Hip Tale in the Death Style, poems (Detroit, Broadside, 1972)

An African Frame of Reference, poems (Chicago, Inst. of Positive Educ., 1972)

Re-Definition: Concept as Being, poems (Third World, 1973)

Sources: Author information; *Black Arts; Broadside Authors and Artists; Poetry of Black America.*

ANDERSON, GARLAND. Playwright.
Born in Wichita, Kan., 1886. *Career:* Hotel switchboard operator; bellhop; playwright. Died in 1939.

Writings:
Fiction

Appearances, or *Don't Judge by Appearances*, play (N.Y., 1925)

Extortion, play (1929)

Nonfiction

From Newsboy and Bellhop to Playwright, autobiog. (San Francisco, Author, 1926-1927?)

Sidelights: *Don't Judge by Appearances* (1925) was the first full-length drama by a Black American on Broadway. Produced at Frolic Theater, New York, Oct. 1925. Also produced in West End of London, at Royalty Theatre, 1930.

Sources: *Black American Playwrights, 1800 to the Present: A Bibliography; Black American Playwrights, 1823-1977; More Black American Playwrights.*

ANDERSON, JERVIS. Journalist, Biographer.
Born in Jamaica, Brit. W. Indies. *Education:* N.Y.U. *Career:* Staff Writer, *New Yorker. Mailing address:* c/o Farrar, Straus & Giroux, 19 Union Square W., N.Y., N.Y. 10003.

Writings:
Nonfiction
A. Philip Randolph, a Biographical Portrait (N.Y., Harcourt, 1973)

This Was Harlem: A Cultural Portrait, 1900-1950 (N.Y., Farrar, 1982)

Sidelights: This book (*This Was Harlem*) has been serialized in four long parts in the *New Yorker* (June 29, July 6, 13, 20, 1981). The subtitles are: I. The Journey Uptown; II. Shaping a Black Metropolis; III. What a City!; IV. Hard Times and Beyond. (*Freedomways*)

Sources: *A. Philip Randolph; Books in Print*, 1980-81; *Freedomways*, 1983.

ANDERSON, MARIAN. Concert Singer.
Born in Phila., Pa., in 1902. *Education:* Phila. public schs.; Musical educ.: private study (Phila., N.Y., abroad); hon. degrees from 22 Amer. insts.; 1 Korean. *Family:* Married Orpheus H. Fisher, July 24, 1943. *Career:* Many concert tours of the U.S. and Europe. Retired in 1965. *Honors:* Career launched when she won 1st prize in competition with others at Lewisohn Stadium, 1925; $10,000 Bok Award, 1940; Finnish decoration, "probenignitate humana," 1940; decorations from Sweden, Philippines, Haiti, France, numerous cities and states in the U.S.; Rosenwald Fund scholarship for study in Germany; request for command performance by Brit. crown; Spingarn Medal; Order of African Redemption of Republic of Liberia; 1st Black to sing at Metropolitan Opera; Natl. Conf. of Christians & Jews Award, 1957, for autobiography; named one of world's ten most admired women by Amer. Inst. of Public Opinion poll, 1961. *Mailing address:* c/o Viking Press, 625 Madison Ave., N.Y., N.Y. 10022.

Writings:
Nonfiction
My Lord What a Morning, autobiog. (N.Y., Viking, 1956; London, Cresset Press, 1957)

Sidelights: One of the world's leading contraltos, Miss Anderson has appeared in all famous concert halls internationally. She has established a trust fund to aid talented American artists.
     In 1957, she published her autobiography, *My Lord What a Morning*. Her writing style is not vivid, but it gives a clear picture of herself as a simple, deeply religious woman who feels a strong obligation to use her talent for the benefit of others. (*American Women Writers*)

Sources: *American Women Writers; Historical Negro Biographies; Negro Handbook; Negroes in Public Affairs and Government.*

ANDREWS, BENNY. Artist, Art Instructor.
Born in Madison, Ga., Nov. 13, 1930. *Education:* Fort Valley State Coll., 1948-50; U. of Chicago, 1956-58; B.F.A., Chicago Art Inst., 1958. *Career:* Artist and Illustrator; Instr. in Art, New Sch. for Soc. Res., N.Y.C., 1967-68; Instr. in Art, Queens Coll., CUNY, 1968- ; Visiting Artist, Cal. State Coll., Hayward, 1969; Work presented in permanent collections: Mus. of African Art, Wash., D.C.; Slater Memorial Mus., Norwich, Conn.; Mus. of Mod. Art, N.Y.C.; Norfolk Mus., Norfolk, Va. *Honors:* John Hay Whitney Found. Fellow, 1965; N.Y. State Council Creative Arts Program award, 1971; Negro Art Collection award, Atlanta U., for "Educational Arts," 1971. *Mailing address:* c/o Freedomways, 799 Broadway, N.Y., N.Y. 10003.

Writings:
Nonfiction

Black Emergency Cultural Coalition (Attica Book), ed. with Rudolph Baranik (S. Hackensack, N.J., Custom Communications Systems, 1972?)

Between the Lines: 70 Drawings and 7 Essays (N.Y., Pella, 1978)

Sidelights: "The essays [in *Between the Lines*] address problems faced by the artistic community in confronting racism, sexism, and the selection and marketing of art." (*Freedomways*)

Sources: *Contemporary Authors*, vol. 106, 1982; *Freedomways*, vol. 19, 1979.

ANDREWS, RAYMOND. Novelist.
Born in Madison, Ga., June 6, 1934. *Education:* Mich. State U., 1956-58. *Family:* Married Adelheid Wenger (airline sales agent), Dec. 26, 1966. *Career:* Sharecropper, 1943-49; hospital orderly, 1949-51; postal mail sorter, 1956; stockroom clerk, 1957; Royal Dutch Airlines employee, 1958-66; photograph librn., 1967-72; messenger, telephone operator, night dispatcher, bookkeeper, Archer Courier, N.Y.C. *Honors:* Winner, James Baldwin Prize for Fiction. *Mailing address:* c/o Dial Press, One Dag Hammarskjold Plaza, 247 E. 47th St., N.Y., N.Y. 10017.

Writings:
Fiction

Appalachee Red (N.Y., Dial, 1978)

Rosiebelle Lee Wildcat Tennessee (Dial, 1980)

Sources: *Books in Print*, 1978-79; Pub. information; *Publishers Weekly*, May 2, 1980.

ANGELOU, MAYA [Marguerite Johnson]. Singer, Dancer, Biographer, Poet, Playwright.
Born in St. Louis, Mo., Apr. 4, 1928. *Education:* George Washington High Sch., San Francisco, Cal.; studied music 7 yrs.; studied dance with Pearl Primus, Martha Graham, Ann Halprin; drama with Frank Silvera, Gene Frankel. *Family:* Son, Guy Johnson. *Career:* Toured Europe and Africa for State Dept. in *Porgy and Bess* (singer and dancer); taught dance in Rome and Tel Aviv; prod., directed, and starred in *Cabaret for Freedom* (with Godfrey Cambridge) at N.Y.'s Village Gate; starred in Genet's *The Blacks*, St. Mark's Playhouse; Northern Coordinator, S. Christian Leadership Conf. (for Martin L. King, Jr.); Assoc. Ed., *Arab Observer*, Cairo, Egypt; Free-lance Writer, *Chanaian Times* and Ghanaian Broadcasting Corp., Accra; Asst. Admin., Sch. of Music and Dance, U. of Ghana; Feature Ed., *African Review* (Ghana); wrote and prod. 10-part TV ser. on African tradition in Amer. life; wrote original screenplay and musical score for film "Georgia, Georgia"; mod. version adaptation of Sophocles' *Ajax*, premiered at Mark Taper Forum, L.A., 1974; Reynolds Prof., Wake Forest U., Winston-Salem, N.C. *Mailing address:* c/o Random House, 201 E. 50th St., N.Y., N.Y. 10017.

Writings:
Fiction

The Clawing Within, play (1966-67)

Just Give Me a Cool Drink of Water 'Fore I Diiie, poems (N.Y., Random House, 1971)

Oh Pray My Wings Are Gonna Fit Me Well, poems (Random House, 1975)

And Still I Rise, poems (Random House, 1978)

Shaker, Why Don't You Sing?, poems (Random House, 1983)

Nonfiction

I Know Why the Caged Bird Sings, autobiog. (Random House, 1969; N.Y., Bantam, 1971)

Gather Together in My Name, autobiog. (Random House, 1974)

Singin' and Swingin' and Gettin' Merry Like Christmas, autobiog. (Random House, 1976)

The Heart of a Woman, autobiog. (Random House, 1981)

Sidelights: Miss Angelou has so far written four volumes of her autobiography. *I Know Why the Caged Bird Sings* is the story of childhood suffering in the 1930s; *Gather Together in My Name* describes the peacetime confusion and suffering after World War II; *Singin' and Swingin' and Gettin' Merry Like Christmas* tells of her unsuccessful marriage and the rise of her theatrical career; and *The Heart of a Woman* writes of her life in the late 1950s and 1960s.

Sources: *The First Time; Gather Together in My Name; Just Give Me a Cool Drink of Water 'Fore I Diiie;* Pub. information.

ANTHONY, MICHAEL. (Trinidadian). Novelist, Journalist, Short Story Writer.
Born in Mayaro, Trinidad, Feb. 10, 1932. *Education:* Jr. Tech. Coll., San Fernando, Trinidad. *Family:* Married Yvette Francesca; four children. *Career:* Staff, Reuters, London, 1964-68; Official, Ministry of Culture, San Fernando, Trinidad, 1970- ; Writer, Asst. Ed., Texaco, Trinidad, 1970- . *Mailing address:* c/o Publ. Dept., Texaco, Trinidad, Pointe-à-Pierre, Trinidad.

Writings:
Fiction

The Games Were Coming, novel (London, Deutsch, 1963; Boston, Houghton Mifflin, 1968; London, Heinemann, Caribbean Writers Ser., 1973)

The Year in San Fernando, novel (Deutsch, 1965; Heinemann, Caribbean Writers Ser., no. 1, 1970)

Green Days by the River, novel (Deutsch, 1967; Houghton Mifflin, 1967; Heinemann, 1973)

Sandra Street and Other Stories (Heinemann, Secondary Readers, 1973)

Cricket in the Road, short stories (Deutsch, 1973; Heinemann, Caribbean Writers Ser., no. 16, 1973)

Streets of Conflict, novel (Deutsch, 1976)

Folk Tales and Fantasies, short stories (Port-of-Spain, Trinidad, Columbus, 1976)

Nonfiction

Glimpses of Trinidad and Tobago: With a Glance at the West Indies (Port-of-Spain, Columbus, 1974)

Profile Trinidad; A Historical Survey from the Discovery to 1900 (London, Macmillan Caribbean, 1975)

Sidelights: Michael Anthony lived for 14 years in England and 2 years in Brazil.

Sources: *Caricom Bibliography; Complete Caribbeana, 1900-1975; Contemporary Novelists,* 2nd ed., 1976; *Modern Black Writers; Writers Directory,* 1982-84.

ARATA, ESTHER SPRING. Bibliographer, Teacher.
Born in Newark, Ohio, Feb. 5, 1918. *Education:* B.A., Coll. of St. Francis, Joliet, Ill.; M. Educ., St. Louis U., 1958; M.A., 1967. *Family:* Married John J. Arata (instr., photographer, artist). *Career:* Head, Home Economics Dept., Coll. of St. Francis, 1943-51; Eng. Tchr., private sch. (Maumee, Ohio), 1951-59; High schs., Columbus, Ohio, 1961-63 and E. St. Louis, Ill., 1963-66; Instr., Eng., St. Louis U., 1966-67; Instr., Eng., Mercy Jr. Coll., St. Louis, 1967-68; Asst. Prof., Eng., U. of Wis., Eau Clair, 1968- . *Mailing address:* c/o Scarecrow Press, 52 Liberty St., Box 656, Metuchen, N.J. 08840.

Writings:

Nonfiction

Black American Writers Past and Present: A Biographical and Bibliographical Dictionary, with Others (Metuchen, N.J., Scarecrow, 1975)

Black American Playwrights, 1800 to the Present: A Bibliography, with Nicholas J. Rotoli (Scarecrow, 1976)

More Black American Playwrights: A Bibliography, with Others (Scarecrow, 1978)

Sources: *Books in Print*, 1978-79; *Freedomways*, vol. 19, no. 1, 1979.

ARMAH, AYI KWEI. (Ghanaian). Novelist, Journalist.
Born in Takaradi, Ghana, in 1939. *Education:* Achimota Coll., U. of Ghana, Legon; Groton Sch., Mass.; B.A. (cum laude, Soc. Studies), Harvard U., 1963; M.F.A. (Lit.), Columbia U. *Career:* French-Eng. transl. for mag. *Revolution Africaine*, Algiers; TV scriptwriter, Ghana; Eng. Tchr., Ghana, 1966; Ed. and Transl., *Jeune Afrique* (new mag.), Paris, 1967-68; Writer, *The New African, Drum* mag., *Atlantic Monthly, N.Y. Review of Bks.*; Tchr., African Lit. and Creative Writing, U. of Mass. *Honors:* Farfield Found. Grant. *Mailing address:* c/o Heinemann, 48 Charles St., London WIX 8AH, Eng.

Writings:

Fiction

The Beautyful Ones Are Not Yet Born, novel (Boston, Houghton Mifflin, 1968; N.Y., Macmillan, 1969; N.Y., Collier, 1969)

Fragments, novel (Houghton Mifflin, 1969; Macmillan, African-Amer. Lib., 1971)

Why Are We So Blest? novel (N.Y., Doubleday, 1972)

Two Thousand Seasons, novel (Nairobi, E. African Pub. House, 1973; N.Y., Third World, 1980)

The Healers, novel (E. African Pub. House, 1978; London, Heinemann Educ. Bks., 1979)

Sidelights: W. H. New avers that "Ayi Kwei Armah has established himself as modern Africa's most controlled novelist." (*Contemporary Novelists*)

Sources: *The Beautyful Ones Are Not Yet Born; Black Books Bulletin; Books in Print*, 1979-80; *Contemporary Authors*, vols. 61-64, 1976; *Contemporary Novelists*, 1972; *The Novels of Ayi Kwei Armah; Who's Who in African Literature.*

ATKINS, RUSSELL. Poet, Composer, Editor.
Born in Cleveland, Ohio, Feb. 25, 1926. *Education:* Cleveland public schs.; Cleveland Inst. of Art; Cleveland Inst. of Music. *Family:* Single. *Career:* Ed.-Founder, *Free Lance* mag., 1950; Publ. Mgr. and Asst. to Dir., Sutphen Sch. of Music, 1957-60; Consultant, writers workshops; Opportunities Industrialization Center, Free-lance Poets, Muntu Poets, Karamu Poetry Workshop; affiliated with Iowa Workshop & Cleveland State U. Poetry Forum; Advisory Ed., *Ju Ju* mag. *Honors:* Scholarships: Mus. of Art & Karamu; Cleveland Music Sch. Settlement; *Free Lance* awarded grant, NEA; hon. doctorate from Cleveland State U., 1976; $5,000 Individual Artists Fellowship, Ohio Arts Council, 1978. *Mailing address:* 6005 Grand Ave., Cleveland, Ohio 44104.

Writings:

Fiction

Psychovisualism, poems (Cleveland, *Free Lance*, pam. ser., 1956-58)

Phenomena, poems (Wilberforce, Ohio, Wilberforce U. Press, 1961)

Objects, poems (Eureka, Cal., Hearse, 1963)

Two by Atkins, plays (*Free Lance*, 1963)

Objects 2, poems (Cleveland, Renegade, 1963)

Heretofore, poems (London, Bremen, 1968)

A Podium Presentation, poems (*Free Lance*, 1968)

The Nail, play (*Free Lance*, 1970)

Malefiction, fiction (*Free Lance*, 1971)

Here in The, poems (Cleveland, State U., Poetry Center, 1976)

Whichever, poems (*Free Lance*, 1978)

Sidelights: "Before too long, Atkin's scattered work will have to be collected in recognition of his being one of the most restlessly creative forces in U.S. poetry for two decades." (Publisher)

Sources: Author information; *Books in Print*, 1979-80; *Poetry of Black America*; Pub. information.

ATTAWAY, WILLIAM ALEXANDER. Novelist, Composer.
Born in Greenville, Miss., in 1911. *Education:* Chicago public schs.; U. of Ill. *Family:* Lives with wife in Barbados, W. Indies. *Career:* Seaman; salesman; labor organizer; actor (played in *You Can't Take It with You*). *Mailing address:* c/o Chatham Bookseller, 8 Green Village Rd., Madison, N.J. 07940.

Writings:
Fiction
Let Me Breathe Thunder, novel (N.Y., Doubleday, 1939; reprint, Chatham, N.J., Chatham, 1969)

Blood on the Forge, novel (Doubleday, 1941; reprint, Chatham, 1969; N.Y., Macmillan, paper, 1970; N.Y., Collier, 1970)

Nonfiction
Calypso Song Book (N.Y., McGraw-Hill, 1957)

Hear America Singing (N.Y., Lion, 1967)

Sidelights: Attaway was considered an interpreter of the Great Migration of the Thirties. In addition to writing, he has arranged songs for Harry Belafonte. He wrote the script for the screen version of Irving Wallace's *The Man*, as well as other scripts.

Sources: *Books in Print*, 1978-79; *Cavalcade; Current Biography*, 1941; *A Native Sons Reader; Negro Novel in America.*

AWOONOR, KOFI [George Awoonor-Williams]. (Ghanaian). English Professor, Poet.
Born in Wheta, District Anlo South, Volta Region, Ghana, Mar. 13, 1936. *Education:* Achimota Coll., Accra; B.A., U. Coll. of Ghana, Legon, 1960; M.A. (Mod. Eng.), London U., 1970; Ph.D. (Comparative Lit.), SUNY, Stony Brook, 1972. *Family:* Children: Sika, Dunyo, Kolepe. *Career:* Lect. & Res. Fellow, U. of Ghana, Accra, 1960-64; Ghana Ministry of Information, Dir. of Films, Accra, 1964-67; Asst. Prof., Eng., SUNY, Stony Brook, 1968-75; Asst. Prof., Eng., U. of Cape Coast, Ghana, 1976- . *Honors:* Longmans Fellow, U. of London, 1967-68. *Mailing address:* c/o Loretta Barrett, Doubleday Pub. Co., 177 Park Ave., N.Y., N.Y. 10017.

Writings:
Fiction
Rediscovery, poems (Evanston, Ill., Northwestern U. Press, 1964)

Ancestral Power and Lament, play (London, Heinemann, 1970)

Messages: Poems from Ghana, ed. with G. Adali-Mortty (Heinemann, 1970; N.Y., Humanities, 1971)

This Earth, My Brother: An Allegorical Tale of Africa, novel (N.Y., Doubleday, 1971; Garden City, N.Y., Anchor Bks., 1972)

Night of My Blood, poems (Doubleday, 1971)

Ewe Poetry (Doubleday, 1972)

Ride Me Memory, poems (Greenfield Center, N.Y., Greenfield Rev. Press, 1973)

The House by the Sea, poems (Greenfield, 1978)

Fire in the Valley: Ewe Folktales (N.Y., NOK, 1979)

Nonfiction
Guardians of the Sacred Wand, essays (NOK, 1974)

The Breast of the Earth: A Survey of the History, Culture and Literature of Africa South of the Sahara, criticism (N.Y., Anchor, 1975; NOK, 1980)

Sidelights: Awoonor was arrested for suspected subversion, charged with harboring a subversionist, served 1 yr. in prison in Ghana, 1975-76.

Sources: *Books in Print*, 1979-80, 1980-81, 1981-82; *Contemporary Authors*, vols. 29-32, 1978; *Who's Who in African Literature.*

AZIKIWE, BENJAMIN NNAMDI. (Nigerian). Autobiographer, Publisher, Journalist, Politician. Born in Zungeru, Northern Nigeria, Nov. 16, 1904; an Ibo. *Education:* Mission schs., Onitsha; Hope Waddell Inst., Calabar; Methodist Boys High Sch., Lagos; Storer Coll., W. Va.; Howard U., Wash., D.C.; B.A., Lincoln U.; grad. work in journalism, polit. sci., & hist., U. of Pa.; Master of Sci. & Master of Laws; Litt. D. & LL.D. *Career:* Ed., *Africa Morning Post*, Ghana (3 yrs.); Executive Com., Nigerian Youth Movement, 1939; Pub., Zik's Press, Ltd., chain of newspapers: *West African Pilot*, Lagos; *Eastern Nigerian Guardian*, Port Harcourt; *Nigerian Spokesman*, Onitsha; *Daily Comet*, Kano; *Eastern Sentinel*, Enugu; and *Nigerian Monitor*, Uyo. Organized Natl. Council of Nigeria & the Cameroons, 1947. Governor-Gen., Nigeria, 1959-64. *Mailing address:* c/o Greenwood Press, 88 Post Road W., P.O. Box 5007, Westport, Conn. 06881.

Writings:
Nonfiction
Liberia in World Affairs (London, Stockwell, 1935). Reprinted as *Liberia in World Politics* (Westport, Conn., Negro Universities Press, 1970)

Renascent Africa (Accra, Gold Coast, Author, 1937; Lagos, Nigeria, Cass, 1937; London, Cass, 1969; N.Y., Negro Universities Press, 1969; Atlantic Highlands, N.J., Africana Mod. Lib., Humanities, 1968)

Zik, a Selection from the Speeches of Nnamdi Azikiwe (Cambridge, Eng., Cambridge U. Press, 1961)

My Odyssey: An Autobiography (London, Hurst, 1970; N.Y., Praeger, 1970)

Sidelights: First President, 1963 (unanimously elected) until the first military coup against the federal government. Azikiwe went into isolation at his home in Nsukka, where he had been instrumental in establishing the University of Nigeria at Nsukka. In July 1966, he agreed to serve as political advisor to the military regime that had taken over the Eastern Region. When the Region seceded from the nation, Azikiwe exiled himself to London to teach and write. After the fall of the Biafran state, he returned to help in establishing a unified government.

Sources: *Black Collegian*, Dec. 1981/Jan. 1982; *Books in Print*, 1980-81; *Current Biography*, 1957; *My Odyssey*.

BAILEY, PEARL MAE. Singer, Comedienne, Actress.
Born in Newport News, Va., Mar. 29, 1918. *Education:* Coll. grad. *Family:* Married 1st John R. Pinkett, Jr. (div.), Mar. 20, 1952; married 2nd Louis Bellson, Jr. (drummer), in London, Nov. 19, 1952. *Career:* Vocalist with Cootie Williams & Count Basie bands. Made stage debut Mar. 30, 1946, when she shared top billing in Negro musical "St. Louis Woman" at Martin Beck Theatre. First film was *Variety Girl*; also in *Carmen Jones*; sang in theater operetta *Arms and the Girl*. Role of Madame Fleur in *House of Flowers*, which opened at New York's Alvin Theatre on Dec. 30, 1954. Was also a hit in *Hello Dolly* and had 1st full dramatic role as the cook in *Member of the Wedding*. *Honors:* Donaldson Award for most promising new performer of 1946 for her work in musical *St. Louis Woman*. *Mailing address:* P.O. Box 52, Northridge, Cal. 91324.

Writings:
Fiction
Duey's Tale (N.Y., Harcourt, 1975)

Nonfiction
Raw Pearl (Harcourt, 1968; N.Y., Pocket Bks., 1968)

Talking to Myself (Harcourt, 1971)

Pearl's Kitchen: An Extraordinary Cookbook (Harcourt, 1973)

Hurry Up, America, and Spit (HarBraceJ, 1976)

Sources: *Books in Print*, Supplement, 1975-76; *Current Biography*, 1955.

BAKER, AUGUSTA. Librarian, Juvenile Writer.
Born in Baltimore, Md., Apr. 1, 1911. *Education:* B.A., N.Y. State Coll., 1933; B.S. (Lib. Sci.), 1934, Albany. *Family:* Married 2nd Gordon Alexander, 1944; son (1st marriage), James Baker, III. *Career:* Children's librn., N.Y. Public Lib., 1937-53; Storytelling Spec., 1953-61; Coordinator of Children's Services, 1961-? Organized children's lib. serv. for Trinidad Public Lib., Port-of-Spain, 1953; Tchr., Sch. of Lib. Sci., Columbia U., 1956-? *Honors:* Dutton-Macrae Award of Amer. Lib. Assn. for advanced study in field of lib. work with children, 1953; *Parents* mag. medal for "outstanding service to the nation's children"; ALA Grolier Award, 1968, for "outstanding achievement in guiding and stimulating the reading of children and young people"; Women's Natl. Bks. Assn. Constance Lindsay Skinner Award, 1971. *Mailing address:* c/o R. R. Bowker Co., 1180 Ave. of the Americas, N.Y., N.Y. 10036.

Writings:
Fiction
Talking Tree, ed. juv. (Phila., Lippincott, 1955)

Golden Lynx, and Other Tales, ed. juv. (Lippincott, 1960)

Young Years, Best Loved Stories and Poems for Little Children, ed. juv. with Eugenia Gerson (N.Y., Home Library Press, 1960, 1963; N.Y., Parents' Magazine Enterprises, 1963)

Best Loved Nursery Rhymes and Songs, Including Mother Goose Selections (Parents' Magazine Enterprises, 1973)

Nonfiction
The Black Experience in Children's Books (N.Y., N.Y. Public Lib., 1971, 1974)

Storytelling Techniques for Children, with Ellin Green (N.Y., Bowker, n.d.)

Storytelling Art and Technique (Bowker, 1977)

Sidelights: Augusta Baker was founder of the James Weldon Johnson Collection (children's books about Negro life), located at Countee Cullen Regional Branch of the New York Public Library. Conducted series of weekly broadcasts, "The World of Children's Literature," on WNYC Radio, beginning in 1971.

Sources: *Freedomways*, vol. 19, 1979; *Something about the Author*, 1973.

BAKER, HOUSTON A., JR. English Professor, Critic.
Born in Louisville, Ky., Mar. 22, 1943. *Education:* B.A., Howard U., 1965; M.A., 1966, Ph.D., 1968, UCLA; U. of Edinburgh, Scotland (1 yr. of doctoral work), 1967-68. *Family:* Married Charlotte M. Pierce; son Mark Frederick. *Career:* Instr., Eng., Howard U., 1968; Instr., Eng., Yale U., 1968-69; Asst. Prof., Eng., 1969 (apptd. for 4-yr. term); Assoc. Prof. and Mem., Center for Advanced Studies, U. of Va., 1970 (for 3-yr. term); Prof. of Eng., U. of Va., 1973-74; Dir., Afro-Amer. Studies, and Prof. of Eng., U. of Pa., 1974-77; Prof. of Eng., U. of Pa., 1977 to present (Albert M. Greenfield Chair in Human Relations); Visiting Lect.: Yale U., U. of Wis., Fisk U., Hampton Inst., N. Mex. State U., U. of Akron, Hollins Coll., U. of Rochester, William & Mary, Morgan State Coll., U. of the W. Indies, Sorbonne, U. of Edinburgh, Sussex U.; Distinguished Visiting Prof., Cornell U., 1977; Visiting Prof., Haverford Coll., 1983. *Honors:* 4-yr. competitive scholarship, Howard U., 1961-65; John Hay Whitney Found. Fellow, 1965-66; 3-yr. NDEA Fellow, 1965-68; Magna Cum Laude and Phi Beta Kappa, Howard U., 1965; elected to Kappa Delta Pi; winner, Alfred Longueil Poetry Award, UCLA, 1966; Phi Beta Kappa Visiting Lect., 1975-76; Fellow, Center for Advanced Study in Behavioral Scis., Stanford, 1977; Guggenheim Fellow, 1978; Fellow, Natl. Humanities Center, 1982; Rockefeller Fellow, Minority-Group Scholars Program, 1982. *Mailing address:* c/o Eng. Dept., U. of Pa., Phila., Pa. 19104.

Writings:
Fiction
Renewal: A Volume of Black Poems, co-ed. with Charlotte Pierce-Baker (Phila., U. of Pa., 1977)

No Matter Where You Travel, You Still Be Black, poems (Detroit, Lotus, 1979)

Spirit Run, poems (Lotus, 1982)

Nonfiction
Black Literature in America, ed. (N.Y., McGraw-Hill, 1971)

Long Black Song: Essays in Black American Literature and Culture (Charlottesville, U. of Va., 1972)

Twentieth-Century Interpretations of Native Son, ed. (Englewood Cliffs, N.J., Prentice-Hall, 1972)

Many-Colored Coat of Dreams: The Poetry of Countee Cullen (Detroit, Broadside, 1974)

Singers of Daybreak: Studies in Black American Literature (Wash., D.C., Howard U. Press, 1974)

Reading Black: Essays in the Criticism of African, Caribbean and Black American Literature (Ithaca, N.Y., African Studies & Res. Center, Cornell U., 1976)

A Dark and Sudden Beauty: Two Essays in Black American Poetry by George Kent and Stephen Henderson, ed. (Phila., Afro-Amer. Studies Program, U. of Pa., 1977)

Journey Back (Chicago, U. of Chicago Press, 1980)

Three American Literatures: Essays in Chicano, Native American, and Asian American Literature for Teachers of American Literature, ed. (N.Y., MLA, 1982)

English Literature: Opening Up the Canon, co-ed. with Leslie Fiedler (Baltimore, Johns Hopkins U. Press, 1982)

Sources: Author information; *Freedomways*, vol. 19, 1979; *Twentieth-Century Interpretations of Native Son.*

BAKER, JOSEPHINE. Dancer, Singer, Biographer.
Born in St. Louis, Mo., June 3, 1906. *Family:* Married Jo Bouillon. *Career:* Performer, Folies-Bergère, Paris; nightclub and concert performer, worldwide. *Honors:* Two French decorations for wartime activities: Legion of Honor, Rosette of the Resistance. Died in 1975.

Writings:
Nonfiction

Josephine, with Jo Bouillon, transl. from the French by Mariana Fitzpatrick (N.Y., Harper, 1977)

Sidelights: Josephine Baker became a citizen of France in 1937. Her 300-acre estate, Les Milandes, a medieval château, was used to rear her 11 adopted children, all of diverse nationalities.

Sources: *Current Biography*, 1964; *Freedomways*, vol. 18, no. 2, 1978; *Josephine; Negro Almanac.*

BALDWIN, CLAUDIA A. Librarian, Bibliographer.
Born in Milwaukee, Wis., Jan. 19, 1950. *Education:* B.A., 1971, M.L.S., 1972, U. of Wis., Madison; M.A., UCLA, 1979. *Career:* Librn., Newark Public Lib., 1972-76; Librn., Cal. State U., Dominguez Hills, Carson, Cal., 1976- . *Mailing address:* c/o Cal. State U., Dominguez Hills, Carson, Cal. 90747.

Writings:
Nonfiction

Nigerian Literature: A Bibliography of Criticism, 1952-1976 (Boston, G. K. Hall, 1980)

Sources: Author information; *Books in Print*, 1981-82.

BALDWIN, JAMES. Essayist, Novelist, Playwright, Lecturer.
Born in N.Y.C., Aug. 2, 1924. *Education:* De Witt Clinton High Sch., N.Y.C.; D. Litt. (hon.), U. of Brit. Columbia, 1963. *Family:* Single. *Career:* Ed., De Witt Clinton High Sch. paper; won a Eugene Saxton Fellowship and lived in Europe 1948-56; active in civil rights movement in U.S.; Lect. *Mailing address:* c/o Edward J. Acton, Inc., 17 Grove St., N.Y., N.Y. 10014.

Writings:
Fiction

Go Tell It on the Mountain, novel (N.Y., Dial, 1952; N.Y., Knopf, 1953; N.Y., Grosset & Dunlap, 1961; N.Y., New American Library, 1954; N.Y., Dell, 1965, 1970)

The Amen Corner, play (produced 1953; Dial, 1968)

Giovanni's Room, novel (Dial, 1956, 1962; Dell, 1958, 1966)

Another Country, novel (Dial, 1962; Dell, 1963, 1970)

Blues for Mr. Charlie, play (Dial, 1964)

Going to Meet the Man, short stories (Dial, 1965; Dell, 1965)

Tell Me How Long the Train's Been Gone, novel (Dial, 1968; NAL, 1974; Dell, 1969, 1975)

If Beale Street Could Talk, novel (Dial, 1974; N.Y., NAL, 1975)

Little Man, Little Man; A Story of Childhood (Dial, 1976)

Just Above My Head, novel (Dial, 1979)

Nonfiction

Notes of a Native Son, essays (Boston, Beacon, 1955; Dial, 1950, 1957; N.Y., Bantam, 1955; 1971)

Nobody Knows My Name: More Notes of a Native Son, essays (Dial, 1961; Dell, 1961, 1962)

The Fire Next Time, essays (Dial, 1963; N.Y., Watts, 1963; Dell, 1964, 1970)

Nothing Personal, with Richard Avedon (N.Y., Atheneum, 1964; Dell, 1964, 1965, 1969)

Rap on Race, with Margaret Mead (Phila., Lippincott, 1971; Dell, 1972)

Black Antisemitism and Jewish Racism, with Others (N.Y., Baron, 1972)

A Dialogue, with Nikki Giovanni (Dial, 1972; Lippincott, 1973)

No Name in the Street (Dial, 1972; Dell, 1973)

One Day When I Was Lost; A Scenario (Dial, 1973)

The Devil Finds Work (Dial, 1976)

Sidelights: In the intensification of the civil rights movement during the early 1960s, Baldwin became an active participant. As various groups struggled to end discrimination and segregation, Baldwin became an increasingly ardent spokesman, enunciating in essays and speeches the agony of being Black in America. (*Dictionary of Literary Biography*)

James Emanuel writes, "James Baldwin, the most eloquently intense and morally insistent essayist in midcentury America...." (*Contemporary Novelists*)

Sources: *Afro-American Authors; Afro-American Literature: Fiction; Black American Literature: Fiction; Black Insights; Black Voices; Books in Print*, 1978-79; *Cavalcade; Contemporary Novelists; Dark Symphony; Dictionary of Literary Biography*.

BAMBARA, TONI CADE. Novelist, Juvenile Writer, Short Story Writer, English Professor.
Born in N.Y.C., Mar. 25, 1939. *Education:* B.A., Queens Coll., 1959; U. of Florence, Italy (Commedia dell'Arte), 1961; Ecole de Mime Etienne Decroux, Paris, 1961, & N.Y., 1963; M.A., CUNY, 1964; additional study: N.Y.U., New Sch. for Soc. Res., Katherine Dunham Dance Studio, Syvilla Fort Sch. of Dance, Clark Center of Performing Arts, 1958-69; Studio Mus. of Harlem Film Inst., 1970. *Career:* Reviewer of films, plays, & books; Soc. Investigator, N.Y. State Dept. of Welfare, 1959-61; Free-lance Writer, Venice Ministry of Museums, Venice, Italy, 1961-62; Dir. of Recreation, Psychiatry Dept., Metropolitan Hospital, N.Y.C., 1962-64; Eng. Instr., SEEK Program, City Coll., N.Y., 1965-69; Assoc. Prof., Eng., Rutgers U., Livingston Coll., 1965- . *Honors:* Award, Black Child Development Inst. for Serv. to Independent Black Sch. Movement. *Mailing address:* c/o Random House, Inc., 201 E. 50th St., N.Y., N.Y. 10022.

Writings:
Fiction

Tales and Short Stories for Black Folks (paper, N.Y., Doubleday, 1971)

Gorilla, My Love, short stories (N.Y., Random House, 1972; N.Y., Pocket Bks., 1973)

The Sea Birds Are Still Alive, novel (Random House, 1977, 1982)

The Salt Eaters, novel (Random House, 1980)

Nonfiction

The Black Woman, ed. (N.Y., New Amer. Lib., 1970)

Junior Casebook on Racism, juv. (N.Y., Bantam, 1973)

Sidelights: "*The Black Woman*" is "a collection of poems, stories, essays, formal, informal, reminiscent, that seem best to reflect the preoccupations of the contemporary Black woman in this country." (*The Black Woman*)

Sources: *The Black Woman; Books in Print*, 1978-79, 1982-83; *Contemporary Authors*, vols. 29-32, 1972.

BANNEKER, BENJAMIN. Mathematician, Astronomer, Surveyor.
Born in Baltimore, Md., Nov. 9, 1731. *Education:* Fundamentally educated and self-taught. *Family:* Single. *Career:* Inventor of first hour-striking clock in America. In 1787 George Ellicott, a neighbor, lent Banneker Ferguson's *Astronomy*, Mayer's *Tables*, and Leadbetter's *Lunar Tables*, with some astronomical instruments. Banneker thoroughly mastered the books, so much so that in 1789 he was commissioned for the surveying of the Federal Territory (District of Columbia). Died in Oct. 1806.

Writings:
Nonfiction

Almanac, Banneker began issuing in 1791 and continued annually until 1802 (a remarkable scientific achievement for a Black American in the 1790s)

Benjamin Banneker's Pennsylvania, Delaware, Maryland and Virginia Almanack and Ephemeris for the Year of Our Lord, 1792... (Baltimore, William Goddard & James Angell, 1792)

Sidelights: Thomas Jefferson, then Secretary of State, replied to Banneker, who had sent him a letter and a copy of his *Almanac*, as follows: "Nobody wishes more than I do to seek such proofs as you exhibit, that nature has given to our black brethren talents equal to those of the other colors of men." (*Early Negro American Writers*)

"Benjamin Banneker was ... [not just] a self-taught mathematician, astronomer, surveyor, poet, and mechanic. He was also a humanitarian. He cared ... [deeply] about the quality of life for black people in America. He spoke out boldly in his letters and conversations with the nation's leaders for the humane treatment of his people. He showed to a slaveholding nation that Blacks are a part of the human family. He used his own achievements as proof that the idea of the inferiority of black people of African descent should be destroyed. His life was ... just as much a search for independence ... as it was for the American colonies during the 1700's and the Revolutionary War." (*Seven Black American Scientists*)

Sources: *Early Negro American Writers; Seven Black American Scientists.*

BARAKA, IMAMU AMIRI [Everett LeRoi Jones]. Poet, Playwright, Revolutionary.
Born in Newark, N.J., Oct. 7, 1934. *Education:* B.A., Howard U., 1954; New Sch. for Soc. Res.; M.A. (German Lit.), Columbia U. *Family:* Married 1st Hettie Cohen, Oct. 13, 1958; d. Kellie Elizabeth, d. Lisa V. Chapman; div. Aug. 1965; married 2nd Amini Baraka (Sylvia Robinson), Aug. 1966; children: Obalaji, Ras, Shani, Amiri, Ahi. *Career:* Founder, *Yugen* (with 1st wife), 1958. Contrib.: *Evergreen Review, Poetry, Saturday Review, The Nation.* Ed.: ("little mags."), *Kulchur, The Floating Bear.* Jazz Critic, *Downbeat, Jazz, Jazz Review.* Tchr. (poetry), New Sch. for Soc. Res.; (drama), Columbia U.; (lit.), U. of Buffalo. Visiting Prof., San Francisco State U. Leader, Black Community Development & Defense, Newark, 1968. Founder (theaters): Spirit House (Newark); Black Arts Repertory Theatre (Harlem). Pub.: Jihad Publ. Polit. organizer: United Brothers, Newark, 1967; Com. for Unified Newark; Chairman, Congress of African People; Co-Convener, Natl. Black Polit. Convention; Secy.-Gen., Natl. Black Assembly, Natl. Polit. Council of Black Polit. Convention; Polit. Prisoners Fund; All African Games; African Liberation Day Com.; African Liberation Day Support Com.; Pan African Federation Groups; 2nd Intnl. Festival of Black Arts. Tchr., Yale U. (1977-78) & George Wash. U. (1978-79). Asst. Prof., African Studies, SUNY, Stony Brook (present). *Honors:* (Fellow) John Hay Whitney Found. Opportunity, 1961; Guggenheim Found., 1965; Yoruba Acad., 1965; Doctorate of Humane Letters, Malcolm X Coll., Chicago, 1972. *The Slave* won 2nd prize, Intnl. Art Festival, Dakar, 1966. Rockefeller Found. for drama, 1981. *Mailing address:* c/o Sterling Lord Agency, 75 E. 55th St., N.Y., N.Y. 10022.

Writings:
Fiction

Preface to a Twenty-Volume Suicide Note, poems (Millerton, N.Y., Corinth, 1961)

The Moderns: New Fiction in America (Corinth, paper, 1963)

The Dead Lecturer, poems (N.Y., Grove, 1964, 1976)

Dutchman and *The Slave*, plays (N.Y., Morrow, 1964)

Experimental Death Unit #1, play (1965)

J-E-L-L-O, play (Newark, Jihad, 1965)

The System of Dante's Hell, novel (Grove, 1965)

Madheart, play (in Jones and Neal, *Black Fire*)

A Black Mass, play (in *Liberator 6*, June 1966)

Black Art, poems (Jihad, 1966)

The Baptism and *The Toilet*, plays (Grove, 1967)

Arm Yourself or Harm Yourself; A One-Act Play: A Message of Self-Defense to Black Men, (Jihad, 1967)

Tales (Grove, 1967)

Police, play (in *The Drama Review*, Summer 1968)

Black Fire: An Anthology of Afro-American Writing, ed. with Larry Neal (Morrow, 1968, 1971)

Black Magic: Sabotage, Target Study, Black Art; Collected Poetry, 1961-1967 (Indianapolis, Bobbs-Merrill, 1969)

Four Black Revolutionary Plays (Bobbs-Merrill, paper also, 1969)

Slave Ship, play (Jihad, 1969)

It's Nation Time, poems (Chicago, Third World, 1970)

In Our Terribleness, poems (Bobbs-Merrill, 1970)

Spirit Reach, poems (Jihad, 1972)

Afrikan Congress (Morrow, 1972)

Columbia the Gem of the Ocean, play (1972)

Afrikan Revolution, poems (Jihad, 1973)

S-1, play (1976)

The Sidnee Poet Heroical, in 29 Scenes, play (N.Y., Reed & Cannon, 1979)

Selected Poetry and Prose (Morrow, 1979)

Confirmation: An Anthology of African American Women, ed. with Amini Baraka (Morrow, paper also, 1983)

Nonfiction

Blues People; Negro Music in White America, sociol. essay (Morrow, 1963)

Home; Social Essays (Morrow, 1966, 1972; Crowell, Apollo, 1967)

Black Music, essay (Morrow, 1967)

The Cricket (in *Black Music Journal*, 1968)

A Black Value System (Jihad, 1970)

Raise Race Rays Raze (N.Y., Random House, 1971)

Strategy and Tactics of a Pan African Nationalist Party (Newark, Natl. Involvement, 1971)

Kawaida Studies (Third World, 1972)

Imamu A. Baraka (LeRoi Jones). A Collection of Critical Essays (Englewood Cliffs, N.J., Prentice-Hall, 1978)

The Autobiography of LeRoi Jones (N.Y., Freundich, 1983)

Sidelights: With his plays in the mid-1960s he drew into vivid perspective the conditions and difficulties of blacks who sought to forge their own identities. (*Dictionary of Literary Biography*)

Imamu Amiri Baraka has been called the "father" of the Black Arts movement in the 1960s. His plays, including *Dutchman* (the Obie Award winner in 1964), and his poetry, especially *Black Magic Poetry, 1961-1967*, have a tremendous impact not only on modern black writing but also on American literature generally. (Conference Brochure, UCLA Center for Afro-American Studies)

Sources: Author information; *Black Drama in America; Black Insights; Black Voices; Cavalcade;* Conference Brochure, UCLA; *Current Biography,* 1970; *Dictionary of Literary Biography; Poetry of Black America; Who's Who in America,* 37th ed., 1972-73.

BARKER, LUCIUS J. Political Science Professor.
Born June 11, 1928. *Education:* B.A., Southern U., Baton Rouge, La.; M.A., Ph.D., U. of Ill., Urbana. *Career:* Edna Gellhorn Prof. of Public Affairs and Prof. of Polit. Sci., Wash. U., St. Louis, Mo. (Chairman, Dept. of Polit. Sci.). *Honors:* Liberal Arts Fellow in Law and Polit. Sci. at Harvard Law Sch., 1964-65; recipient of an outstanding teaching award, Wash. U. Alumni Federation, 1973-74. *Mailing address:* c/o Prentice-Hall, Englewood Cliffs, N.J. 07632.

Writings:
Nonfiction
Teaching Government with Burns' and Peltason's Government by the People (Englewood Cliffs, N.J., Prentice-Hall, 6th ed., 1966)

Freedoms, Courts, Politics; Studies in Civil Liberties, co-author (Prentice-Hall, 1972)

Civil Liberties and the Constitution, Cases and Commentaries, co-author (Prentice-Hall, 1975, 1978)

Black Americans and the Political System, with Jesse J. McCorry, Jr. (Cambridge, Mass., Winthrop, 1976, 1980)

Sources: *Black Americans and the Political System; Books in Print,* 1980-81; Pub. information.

BARKSDALE, RICHARD KENNETH. English Professor.
Born in Winchester, Mass., Oct. 31, 1915. *Education:* A.B., Bowdoin Coll., 1937; A.M., Syracuse U., 1938; Ph.D., Harvard U., 1951. *Family:* Married Mildred White (a university dean), Apr. 15, 1960; children: Adrienne B. Simkins, Richard K., Jr., James Austin, Calvin. *Career:* Instr., Eng., Southern U., Baton Rouge, La., 1938-39; Asst. Prof., Eng., Tougaloo Coll., Miss., 1939-42; Prof., Eng., and Dean, Grad. Sch., N.C. Coll., Durham, 1949-58; Prof., Eng., and Head, Dept., Morehouse Coll., Atlanta U., 1962-71; Prof., Eng., U. of Ill., Urbana, 1971- . *Honors:* L.H.D., Bowdoin Coll., 1972. *Mailing address:* c/o Eng. Dept., U. of Ill., Urbana 61801.

Writings:
Fiction

Black Writers of America: A Comprehensive Anthology, ed. with K. Kinnamon (N.Y., Macmillan, 1972)

Nonfiction

Langston Hughes: The Poet and His Critics (Chicago, ALA, 1974)

Sources: *Books in Print*, 1980-81; *Contemporary Authors*, vols. 49-52, 1975; *Freedomways*, vol. 18, no. 2, 1978.

BARRAX, GERALD WILLIAM. Poet, Teacher.
Born in Attala, Ala., June 21, 1933. *Education:* B.A., Duquesne U., 1963; M.A., U. of Pittsburgh, 1969. *Career:* U.S. Air Force, 1953-57; Clerk and carrier, U.S. Postal Office, 1958-67; Instr., Eng. Dept., N.C. Central U., 1969-70; Spec. Instr., N.C. State U., 1970- . *Honors:* Bishop Carroll Scholarship for Creative Writing; Gold Medal award, Catholic Poetry Soc. of Amer. *Mailing address:* c/o U. of Ga. Press, Terrell Hall, Athens, Ga. 30602.

Writings:
Fiction

Another Kind of Rain, poems (Pittsburgh, U. of Pittsburgh Press, 1970)

An Audience of One, poems (Athens, U. of Ga. Press, Contemporary Poetry Ser., 1980)

Sidelights: "He says that sometimes he speaks as 'a vulnerable mortal and sometimes as a vulnerable Black American' and that Blackness and death 'are implicit in all my responses to people and the world I live in and in everything I write.' " (*New Black Voices*)

Sources: *New Black Voices; Poetry of Black America.*

BASS, CHARLOTTA A. (Spears) Publisher, Editor.
Born in Little Compton, R.I., in 1890. *Education:* Brown U.; Columbia U.; UCLA. *Career:* Ed. and Pub., *California Eagle.* Western Regional Dir. for Republican Presidential candidate Wendell Wilkie in 1940. Ran for Congress in 14th District of Los Angeles (Progressive Party), 1950. Chosen unanimously for U.S. Vice Presidential candidate by the Progressive Party in 1952. Thus became first Negro woman to run for nation's second highest office. Died in 1969.

Writings:
Nonfiction

Forty Years: Memoirs from the Pages of a Newspaper (L.A., Cal., Charlotta Bass, 1960)

Sidelights: Mrs. Bass, a courageous fighter for civil rights, became editor and publisher of the *California Eagle* following the death of her husband, Joseph B. Bass, the second editor. The man who in 1879 founded the oldest Negro newspaper on the West Coast and who became its first editor was John J. Neimore. (*Forty Years*)

Sources: *Books in Print*, 1978-79; *Forty Years; Negro Almanac; L.A. Sentinel*, Apr. 17, 1969; Pub. information.

BAUGH, EDWARD. (Jamaican). English Professor, Literary Critic.
Born in Jamaica, Brit. W. Indies, Jan. 10, 1936. *Education:* B.A. (hon.), London-U. Coll. of W. Indies; M.A., Queen's, Ontario, Can.; Ph.D., Manchester. *Family:* Married Sheila Watson, 1967; 2 ds. *Career:* Eng. tchr., U. W. Indies, Barbados, 1965-78; Prof., Eng., U. W. Indies, Jamaica, 1978- . Dean, Faculty of Arts & Gen. Studies, U. W. Indies, 1980-82. Visiting Prof., Eng./Afro-Amer. Studies, UCLA, 1980. *Honors:* Chairman, W. Indian Assn. for Commonwealth Lit. & Lang. Studies. *Mailing address:* c/o Dept. of Eng., U. of the W. Indies, Kingston, 7 Jamaica.

Writings:
Fiction
West Indian Poetry 1900-1970; A Study in Cultural Decolonisation (Kingston, Jamaica, Savacou, 1971)

Nonfiction
Derek Walcott: Memory as Vision (London, Longman's, 1978)

Critics on Caribbean Literature; Readings in Literary Criticism (N.Y., St. Martin's, 1978; London, Allyn & Unwin, 1978)

Sidelights: Included in *Seven Jamaican Poets* (Kingston, Bolivar, 1971)

Sources: Author information; *Complete Caribbeana, 1900-1975; Critics on Caribbean Literature; West Indian Literature.*

BEASLEY, DELILAH LEONTIUM. Historian.
Born c. 1871. *Career:* The author traveled all over the state of California at her own expense to gather the information for the work *Negro Trail Blazers of California.* Died in 1934.

Writings:
Nonfiction
The Negro Trail Blazers of California: A compilation of records from the California archives in the Bancroft Library at the University of California, in Berkeley, and from the diaries, old papers and conversations of old pioneers in the state of California. It is a true record of facts, as they pertain to the history of the pioneer and present day Negroes of California. (L.A., Times-Mirror Printing & Binding, 1919)

Negro Trail Blazers of California (reprint, Westport, Conn., Negro Universities Press, n.d.)

Sources: *Books in Print,* 1978-79; *Negro Trail Blazers of California.*

BEBEY, FRANCIS. (Cameroonian). Poet, Novelist, Journalist, Radio Producer, Guitarist.
Born in Douala, Cameroon, July 15, 1929. *Education:* Cameroonian schs.; Sorbonne, U. of Paris (French Lit. and Musicology); N.Y.U. *Family:* Married Jacqueline Edinguele, Aug. 14, 1956; children: Eyidi, Christianne, Fanta, Francis, Jr., Patrick. *Career:* Radio Prod. and Journalist, Paris, France, 1957-61; Program Specialist, UNESCO, Paris, 1961-74; Free-lance Writer & Guitarist, 1974- . Also worked for Radio Ghana and Radio Cameroon. *Honors:* Grand Prix, Littéraire de l'Afrique Noire for novel *Agatha Moudio's Son,* 1968. *Mailing address:* c/o Lawrence Hill & Co., 520 Riverside Ave., Westport, Conn. 06880.

Writings:
(Partial Listing—English Only)
Fiction
An Anthology of African and Malagasy Poetry in French, ed. by Clive Wake (Oxford, Eng., Three Crowns Press, 1965)

Agatha Moudio's Son, novel, transl. by Joyce A. Hutchinson (Nairobi, Heinemann, 1971; N.Y., Lawrence Hill, 1975)

The Ashanti Doll, novel, transl. by Joyce A. Hutchinson (Westport, Conn., Lawrence Hill, 1977)

King Albert, novel, transl. by Joyce A. Hutchinson (Lawrence Hill, 1981)

Nonfiction

African Music: A People's Art (Lawrence Hill, 1975)

Sidelights: Francis Bebey had attained an international reputation as a guitarist and composer of considerable talent by 1967. He has performed in Paris, New York, and Africa. That same year *Agatha Moudio's Son* was published, and the following year it won the Grand Prix Littéraire de l'Afrique, which established Bebey as a writer of note. (*A Reader's Guide to African Literature*)

Sources: *Books in Print*, 1979-80, 1981-82; *A Reader's Guide to African Literature; Who's Who in African Literature.*

BECKFORD, RUTH. Dancer, Choreographer.
Born in Oakland, Cal. *Education:* U. of Cal., Berkeley. *Career:* Dancer, Katherine Dunham Dance Co.; Tchr., Dance, U. Cal., Berkeley; Mills Coll.; Ore. State Coll. Founder-Dir., Mod. Dance Dept., Oakland Recreation & Parks. Tchr., Katherine Dunham Sch., N.Y.C.; Dir., dancer, & choreographer, Ruth Beckford African Haitian Dance Co., 1954-61. *Honors:* Consultant (Dance Panel), NEA. *Mailing address:* c/o Marcel Dekker, Inc., 270 Madison Ave., N.Y., N.Y. 10016.

Writings:
Nonfiction

Katherine Dunham, a Biography (N.Y., Marcel Dekker, 1979)

Sidelights: Beckford is Dunham's long-time friend. (*Freedomways*)

Sources: *Books in Print*, 1980-81; *Freedomways*, vol. 19, no. 3, 1979.

BELL, JAMES MADISON. Poet.
Born in Gallipolis, Ohio, Apr. 3, 1826. *Family:* Married at age 22. *Career:* Plasterer; Abolitionist; Delegate, Republican Convention, Ohio, 1868; Delegate, Natl. Convention (nominated Gen. U. S. Grant). Died in 1902.

Writings:
Fiction

A Poem Entitled The Day and the War, Delivered January 1, 1864, at Platt's Hall, at the celebration of the First Anniversary of President Lincoln's Emancipation Proclamation (San Francisco, Agnew & Diffebach, 1864), poems (reprint of 1901 ed., Freeport, N.Y., Bks. for Lib., Black Heritage Lib. Collection Ser.)

The Progress of Liberty, poems (1866; reprint of 1901 ed., Bks. for Lib., Black Heritage Lib. Collection Ser.)

Poetical Works of James Madison Bell (Lansing, Mich., Wynkoop, 1901; reprint, Bks. for Lib., Black Heritage Lib. Collection Ser.).

Sidelights: This personal friend of John Brown was an able speaker and something of an actor. Some of the best poems were "Emancipation," "The Dawn of Freedom," "Lincoln," "The Future of America in the Unity of the Races," "Song for the First of August," "The Blackman's Wrongs," "The Progress of Liberty," and "The Triumph of the Free." (*Historical Negro Biographies*)

Sources: *Early Black American Poets; Early Negro American Writers; Historical Negro Biographies.*

BELL, ROSEANN P. Black Literature Specialist, Teacher.
Education: B.A., Howard U.; M.A., Ph.D., Emory U., Atlanta. *Career:* Tchr., Black Amer. and Black African Lit., Spelman Coll., Ga. State U., Cornell U. *Mailing address:* c/o Doubleday & Co., 501 Franklyn Ave., Garden City, N.Y. 11530.

Writings:
Nonfiction

Sturdy Black Bridges: Visions of Black Women in Literature, with Others (N.Y., Doubleday, Anchor, 1979)

Sidelights: Now lives in St. Croix, Virgin Islands, and produces radio program on Afro-Caribbean literature and culture. (*Sturdy Black Bridges*)

Sources: *Freedomways*, vol. 19, no. 3, 1979; *Sturdy Black Bridges.*

BENNETT, HAL Z. [George Harold]. Novelist, Free-lance Writer.
Born in Buckingham, Va., Apr. 21, 1930. *Education:* Mexico City Coll. *Career:* Writer, Fiction Ed. of *Afro-Amer.* newspaper, 1953-55. Worked as dancer, iguana hunter, and barman. Served as writer for Public Information Div. of newspaper in Korea (in U.S. Army). *Honors:* Fellow of Centro Mexicano de Escritores. *Mailing address:* c/o Doubleday & Co., 245 Park Ave., N.Y., N.Y. 10017.

Writings:
Fiction

House on Hay, a play in verse (n.p., Obsidian, 1961)

A Wilderness of Vines, novel (N.Y., Doubleday, 1966)

The Black Wine, novel (Doubleday, 1968)

Lord of Dark Places, novel (N.Y., Norton, 1970; N.Y., Bantam, 1971)

Wait Until the Evening, novel (Doubleday, 1974)

Insanity Runs in Our Family: Short Stories (Doubleday, 1977)

Nonfiction

The Well-Body Book, with Michael Samuels (N.Y., Random House, 1973)

Spirit Guides: Access to Secret Worlds, with Michael Samuels (Random House, 1974)

Be Well, with Michael Samuels (Random House, 1975)

Seventh Heaven (Doubleday, 1976)

Remembering the Yellow Journal (Kensington, Cal., Hal Z. Bennett, 1978)

Sewing for the Outdoors (N.Y., Potter, 1980)

The Doctor Within (Potter, 1981)

Sources: *Books in Print*, 1978-79, 1981-82; *Contemporary Authors*, vols. 97-100, 1981.

BENNETT, LERONE, JR. Magazine Editor, Historian, History Professor.
Born in Clarksdale, Miss., Oct. 17, 1928. *Education:* B.A., Morehouse Coll., 1949; D. Letters (hon.), 1965; H.H.D. (hon.), Wilberforce U., 1977; Litt. D. (hon.), Marquette U., 1979. *Family:* Married Gloria Sylvester, July 21, 1956; d. Alma Joy, d. Constance, son Courtney, son Lerone III. *Career:* Reporter, *Atlanta Daily World*, 1949-51, City Ed., 1952-53; Assoc. Ed., *Ebony* mag., 1953-58; Senior Ed., 1958- . Visiting Prof., Hist., Northwestern U., 1969-71, Chairman, Dept. of African-Amer. Studies, 1972- . *Honors:* Patron Saints Award; Soc. of Midland Authors, 1965; Bk. of Yr. Award, Capital Press Club, 1963. Lit. Award, Amer. Acad. of Arts & Letters, 1978. *Mailing address:* 820 S. Mich. Ave., Chicago, Ill. 60605.

Writings:

Nonfiction

Before the Mayflower: A History of the Negro in America, 1619-1964 (Chicago, Johnson, 1962, rev. ed., 1964; Baltimore, Penguin, 1966, 4th ed., 1969)

The Negro Mood and Other Essays (Johnson, 1964; N.Y., Ballantine, 1964)

What Manner of Man: A Biography of Martin Luther King, Jr. (Johnson, 1964; N.Y., Pocket Bks., 1965; N.Y., Simon & Schuster, 1968; Johnson, 3rd ed., 1968, 4th ed., 1976)

Confrontation: Black and White (Johnson, 1965; Penguin, 1965)

Black Power U.S.A. (Penguin, 1967; Johnson, 1968)

Pioneers in Protest: The Human Side of Reconstruction, 1867-1877 (Johnson, 1968; Penguin, 1968)

The Black Mood and Other Essays, originally pub. as *Negro Mood* by Johnson Pub. (N.Y., Barnes & Noble, 1970)

Ebony Pictorial History of Black America, ed., 4 vols. (Johnson, 1971)

The Challenge of Blackness (Johnson, 1972)

Shaping of Black America (Johnson, 1975)

Wade in the Water: Great Moments in Black History (Johnson, 1979)

Sidelights: "As a social historian ... [Bennett's] candid views on the present state of race relations and the resulting social change create a great demand for him as a lecturer." (*Confrontation: Black and White*)

"[His] style has the power and force of the historical writings of W. E. B. DuBois, and reveals the same passionate attack on white racism and the same dedication to human dignity and freedom." (*Black Historians*)

Sources: *Black Historians; Books in Print*, 1981-82; *Confrontation: Black and White; Freedomways*, vol. 19, no. 3, 1979; *Negro Almanac*.

BENNETT, LOUISE SIMONE [Mis Lou]. (Jamaican). Poet, Actress, Folklorist, Popular Singer, Entertainer, Radio Personality.
Born in Jamaica, Brit. W. Indies, Sept. 7, 1919. *Education:* Royal Acad. of Dramatic Art, London *Family:* Married Eric Coverley. *Career:* Resident Actress, BBC, W. Indies Section, 1945-46 & 1950-55, & repertory companies in Coventry, Hudders' Field & Amersham; Spec., Jamaica Soc. Welfare Com., 1955-60; Lect., Drama & Jamaican Folklore, Extra-Mural Dept., U. of W. Indies, Kingston, 1959-61. *Honors:* Represented Jamaica at Royal Commonwealth Arts Festival, Brit., 1965; Musgrave Silver Medal, Inst. of Jamaica; an M.B.E.; Order of Jamaica (Jamaican Natl. Award); Brit. Council Scholar. *Mailing address:* Enfield House, Gordon Town, St. Andrew, Jamaica.

Writings:

Fiction

Dialect Verses (Kingston, Jamaica, Herald, 1942)

Verses in Jamaican Dialect, comp. by George Bowen (Herald, 1942)

Jamaican Humour in Dialect (Kingston, Jamaican Press Assn., 1943)

Anancy Stories and Dialect Verse (n.p., 1945; Kingston, Pioneer Press, 1950, 1957)

M's' Lulu Sez: A Collection of Dialect Poems (Kingston, Gleaner, 1949)

Stories and Dialect Verse, with Others (Pioneer Press, 1951)

"Jamaica Folk Songs," record (Folkways, 1954)

"Jamaican Singing Games," record (Folkways, 1954)

Laugh with Louise, a Pot-pourie of Jamaican Folk-lore, Stories, Songs and Verses (Kingston, City Printery, 1961)

Jamaican Labrish (Kingston, Sangster's Bk. Stores, 1966)

Sidelights: Colin Rickards has stated: "Louise Bennett is ... an articulate voice of the people, a political commentator, a satirist, and in many ways a social historian." Ms. Bennett has also recorded "West Indian Festival of Arts" (1958), "Miss Lou's Views" (1967), and "Listen to Louise" (1968).

"No subject has been sacred from her fancy and biting wit ... and no poet in Jamaica has a better understanding of the island and its people." (*Contemporary Poets*)

Sources: *Complete Caribbeana, 1900-1975; Contemporary Poets*, 2nd ed., 1975; *Jamaican National Bibliography; West Indian Literature; West Indian Poetry; Writers Directory*, 1982-84.

BERRY, MARY FRANCES. Historian, Education Secretary, University Chancellor, Law Professor. Born in Nashville, Tenn., Feb. 17, 1938. *Education:* B.A., 1961, M.A., 1962, Howard U.; Ph.D., 1966, J.D., 1970, U. of Mich. *Career:* Asst. Prof., Hist., Central Mich. U., 1966-68; Asst.-Assoc. Prof., Hist., E. Mich. U., Ypsilanti, 1968-70; Assoc. Prof., Hist., U. of Md., Coll. Park, 1969; Adjunct Assoc. Prof., U. of Mich., 1970-71; Chancellor, U. of Colo., Boulder; Provost, U. of Md.; Asst. Secy. for Education, HEW; Prof., Law, Howard U. Law Sch. (present). *Mailing address:* c/o Howard U. Law Sch., 2400 Sixth St., N.W., Wash., D.C. 20001.

Writings:
Nonfiction

Black Resistance, White Law: A History of Constitutional Racism in America (N.Y., Appleton, 1971)

Military Necessity and Civil Rights Policy: Black Citizenship and the Constitution, 1861-1868 (Port Washington, N.Y., Kennikat, 1977)

Stability, Security and Continuity: Mr. Justice Burton and Decision Making in the Supreme Court, 1945-1958 (Westport, Conn., Greenwood, 1978)

Long Memory: The Black Experience in America, with John W. Blassingame (N.Y., Oxford U. Press, 1982)

Sources: *Black Resistance, White Law; Freedomways*, vol. 17, no. 2, 1977.

BETI, MONGO [Biyidi, Alexandre]. (Cameroonian). Novelist, Teacher.
Born in Mbalmayo, near Yaoundé, Cameroon, June 30, 1932. *Education:* B.A. (French), Yaoundé Lycée, 1951; Faculty of Letters, U. of Aix-en-Province; "Licence" or B.A. (Honors), Sorbonne, Paris; Aggregation (or M.A.), U. of Paris, 1966. *Family:* Married Normandie woman; three children. *Career:* Tchr., Lamballe, Bretagne, France; Tchr. (Greek, Latin, French Lit.), Lycée, Rouen, Normandie. Writer; Pub. *Honors: Mission Accomplished* or *Mission to Kala* won Sainte-Beuve Prize, 1958(?). *Mailing address:* c/o Three Continents Press, 1346 Conn. Ave., N.W., Wash., D.C. 20036.

Writings:
(Partial Listing—English Only)
Fiction

Mission to Kala, novel, transl. by Peter Green (London, Frederick Muller, 1958; N.Y., Macmillan, 1958; London, Heinemann, African Writers Ser., 1964; N.Y., Macmillan, African-Amer. Lib., 1971)

Mission Accomplished, transl. by Peter Green (Macmillan, 1958)

King Lazarus, novel, transl. from French (London, Muller, 1968; Heinemann, 1970; Macmillan, 1971; Heinemann, African Writers Ser., 1981)

The Poor Christ of Bomba, transl. by Gerald Moore (Heinemann, Educational, 1971)

Perpetua and the Habit of Unhappiness, novel, transl. from French (Heinemann, Educational, 1978)

I Remember Ruben, novel, transl. from French (Wash., D.C., Three Continents Press, 1980, 1981).

Sidelights: Lives in exile in France. His novels are considered witty and vivacious. Beti considered, along with Camara Laye, the most famous and well-regarded of all Black Africa's francophone writers, "with Beti the professional critic's usual favorite." (*African Authors)*

Sources: *African Authors; Books in Print*, 1979-80, 1981-82; *A Reader's Guide to African Literature.*

BILLINGSLEY, ANDREW. University Administrator, Sociologist, Sociology Professor.
Born in Marion, Ala., Mar. 20, 1926. *Education:* Hampton Inst., Va., 1947-49; B.A., Grinnell Coll., Grinnell, Iowa, 1951; M.S., Boston U., 1956; M.A., U. of Mich., 1960; Ph.D., Brandeis U., Waltham, Mass., 1964; H.H.D. (hon.), Grinnell Coll., 1971; Aspen Inst. for Humanities, Aspen, Colo., 1979; Inst. for Educational Management, Harvard U., 1981. *Family:* Married Amy Loretta Tate; d. Angela Eleanor, d. Bonita Rebecca. *Career:* Dir. of Youth Serv. Project, Amer. Friends Serv. (Quakers), Chicago, Regional Office, 1951-54; Psychiatric Soc. Worker, Wis. Dept. of Public Welfare (Mendota State Hospital), 1956-58; Soc. Worker & Res. Asst., Mass. Soc. for Prevention of Cruelty to Children, 1960-63; Asst. Dean of Students, U. of Cal., Berkeley, 1964-65; Fellow, Metropolitan Applied Res. Center & Program Consultant, Natl. Urban League, N.Y.C. (on leave), 1968; Asst. Chancellor for Acad. Affairs, U. of Cal., Berkeley, 1968-70; V. Pres. for Acad. Affairs, Prof. of Sociol., Howard U., 1970-75; Pres. & Prof. of Sociol., Morgan State U., 1975- . *Honors:* Michael Schwerner Memorial Award, N.Y.C., 1969; Afro-Amer. Family & Children's Soc., 1st Natl. Leadership Award, 1972; Howard U. Sci. Inst., Appreciation Award, 1974; Natl. Council of Black Child Development Appreciation Award, 1974; Fros Award from Howard Inst. for Arts & Humanities Special Award, 1974; PUSH Natl. Convention, Outstanding Contrib. to Excellence in Educ., 1975; India Forum, Award of Excellence for Community Serv. & Promoting Racial Equality, 1978. *Mailing address:* 4209 St. Paul St., Baltimore, Md. 21214.

Writings:
Nonfiction
Studies in Child Protective Services, with Jeanne M. Giovannoni (Wash., D.C., HEW, 1969)

Children of the Storm; Black Children and American Child Welfare, with Jeanne Giovannoni (N.Y., Harcourt, 1972)

Black Families and the Struggle for Survival: Teaching Our Children to Walk Tall (N.Y., Friendship Press, 1974)

Black Families in White America (Englewood Cliffs, N.Y., Prentice-Hall, 1980)

Source: Author information.

BLASSINGAME, JOHN W. History Professor, Editor.
Born in Covington, Ga., Mar. 23, 1940. *Education:* B.A., Fort Valley State Coll., Ga., 1960; M.A., Howard U., 1961; M. Philosophy, 1968, Ph.D., 1971, Yale U. *Career:* Instr., Soc. Sci., Howard U., 1961-65; Assoc., Curriculum Project in Amer. Hist., Carnegie-Mellon U., Pittsburgh, 1965-70; Lect., 1970-71, Asst. Prof., 1971-72, Assoc. Prof., Hist., 1972-73, Acting Chairman, Afro-Amer. Studies, 1971-72, Prof., 1974, Yale U. Asst. Ed., Booker T. Washington Papers, 1968-69; Ed., Frederick Douglass Papers, 1973- ; Contrib. Ed., *Black Scholar*, 1971- . *Honors:* Fellow, NEH, 1972-73. *Mailing address:* c/o Hist. Dept., Yale U., New Haven, Conn. 06520.

Writings:
Nonfiction
New Perspectives on Black Studies, ed. (Urbana, U. of Ill. Press, 1971)

In Search of America, with Others (N.Y., Holt, 1972)

The Autobiographical Writings of Booker T. Washington, ed. with Louis Harlan (U. of Ill. Press, 1972)

The Slave Community: Plantation Life in the Antebellum South (N.Y., Oxford U. Press, 1972, 1979)

Black New Orleans: 1860-1880 (Chicago, U. of Chicago Press, 1973)

Slave Testimony: Two Centuries of Letters, Speeches, Interviews and Autobiographies (Baton Rouge, La. State U. Press, 1977)

The Frederick Douglass Papers, ed. (New Haven, Conn., Yale U. Press, 1979)

Sources: *Encyclopedia of Black America; Who's Who among Black Americans*, 1977-78.

BOGUS, S. DIANE. Poet, Publisher.
Education: B.A., Stillman Coll., Tuscaloosa, Ala.; M.A., Syracuse U., N.Y. *Career:* Tchr., L.A. Southwest Coll.; Tchr., Compton Senior High Sch., Compton, Cal.; Ed./Owner, feminist Woman in Moon Publ., College Corner, Ohio. *Mailing address:* P.O. Box 367, College Corner, Ohio 45003.
Writings:
Fiction
Woman in the Moon, poems (Stanford, Conn., Soap Box Pub. Co., 1977; Inglewood, Cal., W.I.M., paper, 1979)

Her Poems: An Aniversaric Chronology (W.I.M., 1979)

I'm Off to See the Goddamn Wizard, Alright!, poems (W.I.M., 1980)

Sapphire's Sampler (Coll. Corner, Ohio, W.I.M., 1982)

Sources: Author information; *Books in Print*, 1980-81; Pub. information.

BLOCKSON, CHARLES L. Genealogist, Book Collector.
Born in Norristown, Pa. *Education:* Pa. State U. *Career:* Advisory Specialist, Human Relations & Cultural Affairs, Norristown Area Sch. Dist. *Mailing address:* P.O. Box 681, Norristown, Pa. 19401.
Writings:
Nonfiction
Pennsylvania's Black History (Phila., Portfolio Associates, 1975)

Black Genealogy: How to Discover Your Own Family's Roots, with Ron Fry (Englewood Cliffs, N.J., Prentice-Hall, 1977)

The Underground Railroad in Pennsylvania (Jacksonville, N.C., Flame Intnl., 1981)

Sidelights: "Blockson ... is one of the great private collectors of Black historical material." (*Freedomways*)

Sources: *Black Genealogy; Books in Print*, 1980-81; *Freedomways*, vol. 17, no. 2, 1977.

BOBO, BENJAMIN F. Urban Land Economist.
Education: B.A. (Manufacturing Engineering), Cal. State U., Long Beach; M.B.A. (Management), Ph.D. (Urban Land Econ.), UCLA. *Career:* Asst. Prof., Urban Land Econ. and Management, UCLA. *Mailing address:* c/o Dept. of Urban Land Econ. and Management, UCLA, 405 Hilgard, L.A., Cal. 90024.
Writings:
Nonfiction
Black Internal Migration, United States and Ghana: A Comparative Study (L.A., Center for Afro-Amer. Studies, UCLA, 1974)

No Land Is an Island: Individual Rights and Government Control, with Others (San Francisco, Inst. for Contemporary Studies, 1975)

Emerging Issues in Black Economic Development, with Alfred E. Osborne, Jr. (Lexington, Mass., Lexington Bks., 1976)

Sources: *Books in Print*, 1978-79; *Emerging Issues in Black Economic Development.*

BOGGS, JAMES. Automobile Worker, Activist.
Born in Marion Junction, Ala., May 28, 1919. *Education:* Dunbar High Sch., grad. 1937. *Career:* Auto worker, Detroit, 1941-68. *Mailing address:* 3061 Field St., Detroit, Mich. 48214.

Writings:
Nonfiction

The American Revolution: Pages from a Negro Worker's Notebook (N.Y., Monthly Review Press, 1963)

Racism and the Class Struggle: Further Pages from a Black Worker's Notebook (Monthly Review Press, 1970)

Revolution and Evolution in the Twentieth Century, with Grace Lee Boggs (Monthly Review Press, 1974)

Sidelights: *The American Revolution* has been translated in Latin America, France, and Japan, and articles on Black Power have been published in Italy and Argentina.

Sources: *Black Fire; The Black Seventies.*

BOGLE, DONALD. Editor, Essayist.
Born in N.Y.C. *Education:* Lincoln U. (grad. with honors); Ind. U.; Harvard U.; Columbia U. *Career:* Movie Story Ed.; Staff Writer, Asst. Ed., *Ebony* mag. *Honors: Toms, Coons, Mulattoes, Mammies, and Bucks* won the Theatre Lib. Assn. Award as the best film book of the yr. *Mailing address:* c/o Crown Pub., Inc., 1 Park Ave., N.Y., N.Y. 10016.

Writings:
Nonfiction

Toms, Coons, Mulattoes, Mammies, and Bucks (N.Y., Viking, 1973; N.Y., Bantam, 1974)

Brown Sugar, Eighty Years of America's Black Female Superstars (N.Y., Harmony, Crown, 1980)

Sidelights: "As a history of black entertainers in this country, Bogle's [first work] traces the rise of the race to prominence in the world of show business." "When I'm not on tour for the book, I lecture on the history of black film at Lincoln University in Pennsylvania," Bogle reports.

Sources: *Authors in the News; Brown Sugar;* Pub. information.

BOND, HORACE MANN. Educator, Researcher, Social Scientist, Education Professor.
Born in Nashville, Tenn., Nov. 8, 1904. *Education:* B.A., Lincoln U., Pa., 1923; M.A., 1926, Ph.D., 1936, U. of Chicago. *Family.* Married Julia Agnes Washington, 1929; d. Jane, son Horace Julian (politician), son James. *Career:* Prof., Langston U., Langston, Okla., 1924-27; Prof., Ala. State Coll., Montgomery, 1927-28; Prof. & Researcher, Fisk U. & Rosenwald Fund, 1928-33, 1937-39; Dean, Dillard U., New Orleans, 1933-37; Pres., Fort Valley State Coll., Fort Valley, Ga., 1939-45; Pres., Lincoln U., Pa., 1945-57; Dean, Atlanta U., 1957- . *Honors:* LL.D.: Lincoln U., 1941; Temple U., 1955; Amer. Educ. Res. Assn. Award, 1939; Assn. for Study of Negro Hist. Award, 1943. Died in 1972.

Writings:
Nonfiction

Education of the Negro in the American Social Order (N.Y., Prentice-Hall, 1934; N.Y., Octagon Bks., 1966)

Negro Education in Alabama, a Study in Cotton and Steel (Wash., D.C., Assoc. Pub., 1939)

Education for Production (Athens, U. of Ga. Press, 1944)

The Search for Talent (Cambridge, Mass., Harvard U. Press, 1959)

Black American Scholars: A Study of Their Beginnings (Detroit, Balamp Pub., 1972)

Education for Freedom: A History of Lincoln University, Pa. (Lincoln U., Pa., Lincoln U. Press, 1976)

Sidelights: Dr. Bond made at least 14 trips to Africa for educational surveys.

Sources: *Current Biography*, 1954; *Negro Caravan*; Pub. information.

BONTEMPS, ARNA WENDELL. Librarian, Juvenile Writer, Novelist, Critic, Biographer, Anthologist, Playwright, English Professor.
Born in Alexandria, La., Oct. 13, 1902. *Education:* B.A., Pacific Union Coll., 1923; M.A., Sch. of Lib. Sci., U. of Chicago, 1943. *Family:* Married Alberta Johnson, 1926; d. Joan Marie Williams, son Paul Bismark, d. Poppy Alberta Cooke, d. Camille Ruby Graves, d. Constance Rebecca Thomas; son Arna Alex. *Career:* High sch. Tchr. & Prin., 1924-41; Free-lance Writer, 1941-43; Head Librn., Fisk U., Nashville, 1943-65; Prof., Eng., U. of Ill., Chicago Circle Campus, 1966-69; Curator, James Weldon Johnson Collection, Yale U., 1969-73; Writer-in-Residence, Fisk U., 1973. *Honors:* Julius Rosenwald Fund Fellow, 1938-39, 1942-43; Guggenheim Found. Fellow for creative writing, 1949-50; Jane Addams Children's Bk. Award for *Story of the Negro*; James L. Dow Award, Soc. of Midland Authors, for *Anyplace but Here*, 1967; various poetry & short story prizes. In 1926 & 1927 his poems "Golgotha Is a Mountain" & "The Return" won the Alexander Puskin Awards for Poetry (*Opportunity* mag.). Died June 4, 1973.

Writings:
Fiction

God Sends Sunday, novel (N.Y., Harcourt, 1931; N.Y., AMS, 1959)

Popo and Fifina, Children of Haiti (N.Y., Macmillan, 1932)

You Can't Pet a Possum, juvenile (N.Y., Morrow, 1934)

Black Thunder, novel (Macmillan, 1935; Boston, Beacon, 1968)

Sad Faced Boy, juvenile (Boston, Houghton Mifflin, 1937)

Drums at Dusk, novel (Macmillan, 1939)

Golden Slippers, anthology (N.Y., Harper, 1941)

Chariot in the Sky, a Story of the Jubilee Singers, juvenile (N.Y., Holt, 1941; Phila., Winston, 1951-56)

The Fast Sooner Hound, juvenile (Houghton Mifflin, 1942)

Saint Louis Woman, play (1946 — Musical adaptation of *God Sends Sunday*, 1931)

Poetry of the Negro, 1746-1949, anthology, ed. with Langston Hughes (N.Y., Doubleday, 1949)

Lonesome Boy, juvenile (Houghton Mifflin, 1955)

Book of Negro Folklore (N.Y., Dodd, 1958)

Nonfiction

They Seek a City (N.Y., Doubleday, 1945)

Story of the Negro (N.Y., Knopf, 1948, 2nd ed., 1955, 3rd ed., 1958, 4th ed., 1964, 5th ed., 1969)

The Story of George Washington Carver (N.Y., Grosset, 1954)

Frederick Douglass; Slave Fighter, Free Man (Knopf, 1959)

100 Years of Negro Freedom (N.Y., Dodd, 1961; Westport, Conn., Greenwood, 1961)

Famous Negro Athletes (N.Y., Dodd, 1964; paper, N.Y., Apollo Editions, 1970)

Any Place but Here, rev. of *They Seek a City* (N.Y., Hill & Wang, 1966)

Great Slave Narratives (paper, Boston, Beacon, 1969)

Five Black Lives: The Autobiography of Venture Smith, James Mars, William Grimes, the Rev. G. W. Offley and James L. Smith (N.Y., Columbia U. Press, 1971)

Arna Bontemps-Langston Hughes Letters, 1925-1967, ed. by Charles H. Nichols (Dodd, 1980)

Sidelights: "As poet, novelist, author of short stories and juvenile literature, critic, anthologist, playwright, librarian and educator (Harlem Renaissance writer) Arna Bontemps is a central figure in the creation, dissemination and teaching of Negro American Literature." (*Black Voices*)

"Arna Bontemps became the first historical novelist among Negroes. *God Sends Sunday* portrays the glamorous days of horse racing during the 1890's. *Black Thunder* is a historical novel dealing with a Virginia slave insurrection. *Drums at Dusk* is a re-creation of that phase of the San Domingo Revolution that preceded the leadership of Tousaint L'Ouverture." (*Black Insights*)

At the time of his death he was writing his autobiography. (*Library Journal*)

Sources: *Black American Literature: Poetry; Black Insights; Black Voices; Books in Print*, 1979-80, 1980-81; *Cavalcade; Library Journal*, July 1973.

BOOKER, SIMEON SAUNDERS. Journalist.
Born in Baltimore, Md., Aug. 27, 1918. *Education:* B.A., Va. Union U., Richmond, 1942; further study: Cleveland Coll.; Harvard U. (Nieman Fellow), 1950-51. *Family:* Married Thelma Cunningham; d. Theresa, son Simeon, Jr., son James. *Career:* Chief, Wash., D.C. Bureau, Johnson Pub. Co., Inc. *Mailing address:* Johnson Pub. Co., 1750 Pa. Ave., N.W., Wash., D.C. 20006.

Writings:
Nonfiction

Black Man's America (Englewood Cliffs, N.J., Prentice-Hall, 1964)

Susie King Taylor, Civil War Nurse (N.Y., McGraw-Hill, Black Legacy Ser., 1969)

Sources: *Books in Print*, 1979-80; *Contemporary Authors*, vols. 11-12, 1965.

BRADLEY, DAVID HENRY, JR. Novelist, English Professor.
Born in Bedford, Pa., Sept. 7, 1950. *Education:* B.A., U. of Pa., 1972; M.A., U. of London, 1974. *Career:* Dir., Bradley, Burr & Sherman; Visiting Lect., U. of Pa., 1975-76; Visiting Lect., Temple U., 1976-77; Asst. Prof., Eng., Temple U.- ; Asst. Ed., J. B. Lippincott, 1974-76; Book Reviewer, *Quest 77*, N.Y. Arts Journal. *Mailing address:* c/o Harper & Row, 10 E. 53rd St., N.Y., N.Y. 10022.

Writings:
Fiction

South Street, novel (N.Y., Grossman, 1975)

The Chaneysville Incident, novel (N.Y., Harper, 1982)

Sidelights. "I tried to write the story [of *The Chaneysville Incident*] as a straight narrative at first you know, a typically nice commercial plantation tale with interracial sex and scenes with slaves being boiled in oil. I couldn't do it. I tried, but it was too sensational and, despite the violence and tragedy, it was funny. I kept inserting bits of humorous historical detail to compensate for the excessive violence. I wrote four versions before settling on the final manuscript." (*New York Times Book Review*)

Sources: *Books in Print*, 1981-82; *New York Times Book Review*, Apr. 19, 1981; *Who's Who among Black Americans*, 3rd ed., 1980-81.

BRAITHWAITE, (EUSTACE) E(DWARD) R(ICARDO). (British Guianan). Novelist, Teacher, Diplomat.
Born in Georgetown, Brit. Guiana, June 27, 1912. *Education:* Queen's Coll., Brit. Guiana; B.S. (Physics), City Coll. of N.Y., 1940; M.S. (Physics), Gains Coll., Cambridge U., 1949; London U., Inst. of Educ. *Career:* Writer; Schoolmaster, London, 1950-57; Welfare Officer & Consultant, Dept. of Child Welfare, London County Council, 1958-60; Human Rights Officer, World Veterans Found., Paris, 1960-63; Educ. Consultant & Lect., UNESCO, Paris, 1963-66; Permanent Rep. from Guyana, UN, N.Y.C., 1967-68; Ambassador of Guyana to Venezuela, 1968-69. *Honors:* Anisfield-Wolf Award from *Saturday Review*, 1960, for *To Sir with Love* (filmed by Columbia Pictures with Sidney Poitier). *Mailing address:* The Parker 40, Apt. 16, 305 E. 40th St., N.Y., N.Y. 10017.

Writings:
Fiction
A Choice of Straws, novel (London, Bodley Head, 1965; N.Y., Pyramid, 1966, 1972; London, Pan Bks., 1968; Indianapolis, Bobbs-Merrill, 1966)

Nonfiction
To Sir with Love (Bodley Head, 1959; London, Four Square, 1962; Toronto, Signet Bks., 1968; Englewood Cliffs, N.J., Prentice-Hall, 1959, 1962; Pyramid, 1959, 1966, 1973)

Paid Servant (Bodley Head, 1962; N.Y., McGraw-Hill, 1962, 1968; Pyramid, 1962, 1972; Four Square, 1965; London, New Eng. Lib., 1968, 1969)

A Kind of Homecoming (Prentice-Hall, 1962; London, Muller, 1963)

Reluctant Neighbors (Bodley Head, 1972; McGraw-Hill, 1972)

Honorary White: A Visit to South Africa (McGraw-Hill, 1975)

Sources: *Contemporary Authors*, vol. 106, 1982; *Modern Black Writers; West Indian Literature; Writers Directory*, 1982-84.

BRAITHWAITE, WILLIAM STANLEY. Poet, Anthologist, Critic.
Born in Boston, Mass., Dec. 6, 1878. *Education:* Boston Latin Sch.; M.A. (hon.), Atlanta U., 1918; Litt. D. (hon.), Talladega Coll., 1918. *Family:* Married Emma Kelly of Montrose, Va., 1903. *Career:* Literary Ed., *Boston Transcript*, annual *Anthology of Magazine Verse*, 1913-29; Prof. of Creative Lit., Atlanta U., 1944. *Honors:* NAACP Spingarn Medal, 1918. Died in N.Y.C., June 8, 1962.

Writings:
Fiction
The Canadian, novel (Boston, Small, Maynard, 1901)

Lyrics of Life and Love, poems (Boston, Turner, 1904; Small, Maynard, 1907; Miami, Mnemosyne, 1969)

The Book of Elizabethan Verse, ed., anthology (Turner, 1906; 2nd ed., 1907, 1908)

The Book of Georgian Verse, ed., anthology (London, Duckworth, 1908; N.Y., Brentano's, 1909; Freeport, N.Y., Bks. for Lib., 1969)

The House of Falling Leaves, poems (Boston, Luce, 1908; Mnemosyne, 1969)

The Book of Restoration Verse, ed., anthology (Duckworth, 1909; Brentano's, 1910)

Anthology of Magazine Verse for 1913-1929 and Yearbook of American Poetry (N.Y., Schulte, 1913; Sequi Centennial ed., 1926)

Golden Treasury of Magazine Verse (Small, Maynard, 1918)

Book of Modern British Verse, ed., anthology (Small, Maynard, 1919)

Victory: Celebrated by 38 American Poets, ed. (Small, Maynard, 1919)

Going over Tindel, novel (Boston, Brimmer, 1924)

Selected Poems (N.Y., Coward-McCann, 1948)

The William Stanley Braithwaite Reader (Ann Arbor, U. of Mich. Press, 1972)

Nonfiction

The Poetic Year for 1916, criticism (Small, Maynard, 1917)

The Story of the Great War, juv., essays (N.Y., Frederick A. Stokes, 1919)

House under Arcturus: An Autobiography [summarized in Barton, *Witnesses for Freedom; Phylon 2* (1st-3rd quarters, 1941, 1st & 2nd quarters, 1942), Atlanta, Atlanta U.]

The Bewitched Parsonage, biog. of the Brontës (N.Y., Coward-McCann, 1950)

Sidelights: "Refusing to write as a 'Negro poet' or to use racial themes, he elected to fight for equality by competing with white writers on their terms." (*Negro Almanac*)

"Braithwaite was to be best known and most admired for the yearly anthologies of magazine verse which he edited from 1913 to 1929.... The early work of several important American poets, including Carl Sandburg, Edgar Lee Masters, and Vachel Lindsay, was brought to wider attention through these volumes."

A *Boston Transcript* editorial of 1915 said that he had helped readers as well as poets to understand poetry. "One is guilty of no extravagance in saying that the poets we have ... and the gathering of deference we pay them, are created largely out of the stubborn self-effacing enthusiasm of this one man." (*Dictionary of American Negro Biography*)

Sources: *Afro-American Writers; American Literature by Negro Authors; An Anthology of Verse by American Negroes; Black American Literature: Poetry; Book of American Negro Poetry; Cavalcade; Dictionary of American Negro Biography; Negro Almanac.*

BRANCH, WILLIAM BLACKWELL. Actor, Producer, Director, Playwright.
Born in New Haven, Conn., Sept. 11, 1927. *Education:* B.S. (Speech), Northwestern U., 1949; M.F.A. (Dramatic Arts), Columbia U., 1958, postgrad., 1958-59; Resident Fellow, Yale U. Drama Sch., 1965-66. *Family:* Div.; d. Rochelle Ellen. *Career:* Actor: theater, films, radio & TV, 1946-55; Field Rep., *Ebony* mag., 1949-50; Educ. Instr., U.S. Army, 1951-53; Assoc. in Film, Columbia U. Sch. of the Arts, 1968-69; Visiting Playwright: Smith Coll., Northampton, Mass., 1970; N.C. Central U., Durham, 1971; St. Lawrence U., 1973. Pres., William Branch Assoc. (TV & film production), Council on Student Travel, trans-Atlantic sailing, June 1962, Delegate to Intnl. Conf. on the Arts, Lagos, Nigeria, Dec. 1961. Acted in *Anna Lucasta*. *Honors:* Robert E. Sherwood TV Award (NBC TV drama, "Light in the Southern Sky"), 1958; Natl. Council of Christians and Jews Citation for same drama, 1958; Hannah B. Del Vecchio Prize in Playwriting, 1958; Guggenheim Found. Fellow (creative writing in the drama), 1959-60; Yale U. Amer. Broadcasting Co. Fellow (creative writing in TV drama), 1965-66; Amer. Film Festival Blue Ribbon Award for *Still a Brother*, 1969. Natl. Acad. of TV Arts & Scis. Emmy Award Nomination for *Still a Brother*, 1969; Northern Oratorical Prize; Sigmund Livingston Fellow. *Mailing address:* c/o Natl. Broadcasting Co., 30 Rockefeller Plaza, N.Y., N.Y. 10020.

Writings:
Fiction

A Medal for Willie, play, off-Broadway, 1951-52 (in King & Milner, *Black Drama*, anthology)

In Splendid Error, play, Greenwich New Theatre, N.Y.C. (in Patterson, *Black Theatre*)

Light in the Southern Sky, one-act play (1958)

"The Jackie Robinson Show," NBC Radio (1959)

Benefit Performance, movie for Universal Studios and NBC TV

"Afro-American Perspectives" (30-program TV ser. on Black hist.)

"The Alma John Show" (Coca-Cola)

"The Jackie Robinson Column," N.Y., *N.Y. Post* (writer & gen. partner)

A Wreath for Udomo, play (Lyric Hammersmith Theatre, London, 1961)

Still a Brother: Inside the Negro Middle Class, film (NET, 1968)

Together for Days, film (1971)

Special Unit, NBC News, N.Y.C. (1972-73)

Source: Author information.

BRATHWAITE, EDWARD KAMAU [L. Edward]. (Barbadian). Poet, Critic, History Professor. Born in Bridgetown, Barbados, May 11, 1930. *Education:* Harrison Coll.; B.A. (Hist., hon.), Pembroke Coll., 1953, Certificate of Educ., 1954, Cambridge U.; Ph.D. (Development of Creole Soc. in Jamaica, 1770-1820), U. of Sussex, Eng., 1968. *Family:* Married Doris M. Welcome, 1960; son Michael Kwesi. *Career:* Extra Mural Tutor, U. of W. Indies, St. Lucia; Minister of Educ., Ghana, 1955-62; Prof., Hist., U. of W. Indies, Mona, Jamaica (present); Ed., *Savacou*, 1970; Founder, Caribbean Artist Movement, London; Co-Ed., BIM. *Honors:* Barbados scholar, 1949; Poetry Bk. Soc. Recommendation (*Rights of Passage*), 1967; Hampstead Arts Festival Poetry Prize, United Kingdom, 1967; Arts Council of Great Brit. Poetry Bursary, 1967; Cholmondeley Award, 1970; Guggenheim Found. Fellow, 1971; Bussa Award, 1973. *Mailing address:* c/o Hist. Dept., U. of W. Indies, Mona, Kingston 7, Jamaica.

Writings:
Fiction

Iounaloa: Recent Writing from St. Lucia, anthology ed. (Castries, U. of W. Indies Press, 1963)

Four Plays for Primary Schools (London, Longmans, 1964)

Odale's Choice, play (London, Evans Brothers, 1967)

Rights of Passage, pocms (London & N.Y., Oxford U. Press, 1967)

"The Poet Speaks 10," record (Argo, 1968)

Masks, poems (Oxford U. Press, 1968)

"Rights of Passage," record (Argo, 1969)

Islands, poems (Oxford U. Press, 1969)

"Masks," record (Argo, 1972)

The Arrivants; A New World Trilogy (Oxford U. Press, 1973)

"Islands," record (Argo, 1973)

Contradictory Omens: Cultural Diversity and Integration in the Caribbean, anthology (Mona, Jamaica, Savacou, 1974)

Other Exiles, poems (Oxford U. Press, 1975)

Days and Nights, poems (Mona, Kingston, Jamaica, Caldwell, 1975)

Black and Blues, poems (Havana, Cuba, Casa de las Americas, 1976)

Mother Poem (Oxford U. Press, 1977)

Nonfiction

The People Who Came, essays, Bks. I, II & III, ed. & co-author (Baltimore, Md., Mod. Poets, Penguin, 1968, 1969, 1972)

The Folk Culture of the Slaves in Jamaica (London, New Beacon Bks., 1970)

The Development of Creole Society in Jamaica 1770-1820 (Oxford, Clarendon, 1971)

Caribbean Man in Space and Time, essays (Savacou Publ., 1974)

Sidelights: " ... *Sunday Times* said of *Islands* ... 'This book together with its earlier sections is enough to place Mr. Brathwaite among the finest living poets in the Western hemisphere.' " He is a remarkable reader of his own works.

The Arrivants trilogy has been recorded by Argo Recording Company, 1971. He is included in "West Indian Poets Reading Their Own Poetry," Caedmon. (*Caribbean Writers*)

"Brathwaite's trilogy, *Rights of Passage, Masks,* and *Islands* constitutes an epic of sorts on the Black West Indian's history and culture ...

" ... the trilogy does deserve its reputation as the most important piece of West Indian literature on the relationship between the West Indian's Western and African sources." (*West Indian Poetry*)

Sources: Bibliography of the Caribbean; Caribbean Writers; *Caricom Bibliography; Complete Caribbeana, 1900-1975; Contemporary Poets,* 2nd ed., 1975; *Jamaican National Bibliography; Modern Black Writers; Resistance and Caribbean Literature; West Indian Literature; Writers Directory*, 1982-84.

BRAWLEY, BENJAMIN GRIFFITH. Poet, Literary and Social Historian, English Professor. Born in Columbia, S.C. in 1882. *Education:* B.A., Morehouse Coll., 1901; B.A., U. of Chicago, 1906; M.A., Harvard U., 1908. *Family:* Married Hilda Prowd of Kingston, Jamaica, in 1912. *Career:* Prof. of Eng., Morehouse Coll., Shaw U., & Howard U.; Dean, Morehouse Coll., 1912-? Instr., Summer Sch., Hampton Inst. (several yrs.); Pres., Assn. of Coll. Negro Youth; Lect. Died Feb. 1, 1939.

Writings:

Fiction

A Toast to Love and Death, poems (Atlanta, Atlanta Bap. Coll., 1902)

The Problem and Other Poems (Atlanta Bap. Coll., 1905)

The Seven Sleepers of Ephesys, poems (Atlanta, Foote & Davis, 1971)

Nonfiction

The Negro in Literature and Art in the United States (Atlanta ?, 1910; N.Y., Duffield, 1918; 1921, 3rd ed. 1929, 1934, reprint, St. Clair Shores, Mich., Scholarly, 1981)

A Short History of the American Negro (N.Y., Macmillan, 1913, 1919, 1921, 1924, 1927, 1929, 1931; 4th rev. ed., 1939, 1952)

History of Morehouse College (Atlanta, Morehouse Coll., 1917)

Africa and the War (Duffield, 1918)

Women of Achievement (Chicago, Women's Amer. Bap. Home Mission Soc., 1919)

A Short History of English Drama, criticism (N.Y., Harcourt, Brace, 1921)

A Social History of the American Negro in 1921 (Macmillan, 1921, 1927; N.Y., Johnson, Basic Afro-Amer. Reprint Lib., 1969)

New Survey of English Literature; A Textbook for Colleges (N.Y., Knopf, 1925, 1930)

Doctor Dillard of the Jeanes Fund (N.Y., Chicago, Fleming H. Revell, 1930; reprint, Bks. for Lib., Black Heritage Ser., n.d.)

Early Negro American Writers (Chapel Hill, U. of N.C. Press, 1935)

Paul Laurence Dunbar: Poet of His People (U. of N.C. Press, 1936)

The Negro Genius, essays (N.Y., Dodd, 1937, 1942; Apollo Editions, paper, 1970)

Negro Builders and Heroes (U. of N.C. Press, 1937, 1946)

Sidelights: Brawley's principal concerns ... were the intellectual and social development of his people, popularizing the substantive facts of the Negro experience in the United States, and appealing to white America's sense of justice and truth. (*Dictionary of American Negro Biography*)

Sources: *An Anthology of Verse by American Negroes; Book of American Negro Poetry; Books in Print*, 1981-82; *Dictionary of American Negro Biography; Negro Caravan; Poetry of the Negro, 1746-1949*.

BREWER, JOHN MASON. Folklorist.
Born in Goliad, Tex., Mar. 24, 1896. *Education:* B.A., Wiley Coll., Marshall, Tex.; M.A., Ind. U., Bloomington; Litt.D. (hon.), Paul Quinn Coll., Waco, Tex. *Family:* Married Ruth Helen Brewer; son. *Career:* Distinguished Visiting Prof. of Eng., E. Tex. State U.; Distinguished Visiting Prof. of Anthropology, N.C. Agricultural & Technical U., Greensboro, 1967-69; Gen. Ed., Negro Heritage Ser., Pemberton Press, Austin, Tex. *Honors:* Grant-in-aid, Gen. Educ. Bd.; Amer. Philosophical Soc.; Piedmont U. Center (for res. at Lib. of Congress, Natl. Lib. Mexico, & Natl. U. of Mexico). Died in 1975.

Writings:
Fiction
Negrito, Negro Dialect Poems of the Southwest (San Antonio, Tex., Naylor, 1933; Freeport, N.Y., Bks. for Lib., 1972)

The Life of John Wesley Anderson: A Story in Verse (Dallas, C. C. Cockrell, 1938)

Humorous Folktales of the South-Carolina Negro (Orangeburg, S.C., Negro Folklore Guild, vol. 1, 1945; Ann Arbor, Mich., U. Microfilms, 1971)

The Word on the Brazos; Negro Preacher Tales from the Brazos Bottoms of Texas (Austin, U. of Tex. Press, 1953)

Dog Ghosts and Other Texas Negro Folk Tales (U. of Tex. Press, 1958, 1976)

North Carolina Negro Oral Narratives (n.p., N.C. Folklore Soc., 1961)

Worser Days and Better Times; The Folklore of the North Carolina Negro (Chicago, Quadrangle, 1965)

American Negro Folklore, ed. (N.Y., Quadrangle, 1968)

Dog Ghosts and Other Negro Folk Tales, bound with *The Word on the Brazos: Negro Preacher Tales from the Brazos Bottoms of Texas* (U. of Tex. Press, 1976)

Nonfiction
Negro Legislators of Texaas and Their Descendents (Dallas, Mathis, 1935; reprint, Austin, Jenkins, 1970)

An Historical Outline of the Negro in Travis County (Austin, Samuel Houston Coll., 1940)

Sidelights: *The Word on the Brazos* was called by the *New York Times* "the best book of Negro stories that has made its appearance in this country in twenty-seven years."
" ... rated by American Folklore Scholars and literary critics as America's most distinguished Negro folklorist, and one of the four leading folktale authors writing in this country today, regardless of race, creed, or color." (Author)

Source: Author information.

BRIMMER, ANDREW FELTON. Economist, Public Official.
Born in Newellton, La., Sept. 13, 1926. *Education:* Tensas Parish Training Sch., St. Joseph, La.; B.A. (Econ.), M.A., 1951, U. of Wash.; Ph.D., Harvard U., 1957. *Family:* Married Doris Millicent Scott, July 18, 1953 (then grad. student at Radcliffe Coll.); d. Esther Diane. *Career:* Economist, Fed. Reserve Bank, N.Y., 1955-58; Tchr.: Harvard; City Coll. of N.Y.; U. of Cal., Berkeley; Mich. State U.; Res. at Mass. Inst. of Technology, Center for Intnl. Studies & Wharton Sch. of Finance, U. of Pa.; Apptd. Deputy Asst. Secy. for Econ. Affairs, U.S. Dept. of Commerce, 1964; Asst. Secy., 1965; Apptd. to Bd. of Governors, Fed. Reserve Bd., 1966. *Honors:* Fullbright Fellow, Universities of Bombay & Delhi (India), 1951-52; named Government Man of the Year by Natl. Bus. League, 1963; Arthur S. Fleming Award for outstanding contrib. to public serv., 1966; Russwurm Award of Natl. Newspaper Pub. Assn., 1966; Public Serv. Award of Capital Press Club, 1966; Golden Plate Award of Amer. Acad. of Achievement, 1967. *Mailing address:* c/o Business Div., U. of Mich., Ann Arbor 48109.

Writings:

Nonfiction:

Life Insurance Companies in the Capital Market (E. Lansing, Mich., State U. Press, 1962)

The Road Ahead: Outlook for Blacks in Business (Wash., D.C., Board of Governors, Fed. Reserve System, 1972)

When the Marching Stopped, an Analysis of Black Issues in the Seventies (N.Y., Natl. Urban League, 1973?)

The Economic Position of Black Americans, 1976 (Wash., D.C., Natl. Com. for Manpower Policy, 1976)

Sidelights: Assisted in preparation of Department of Commerce testimony on discrimination in interstate commerce. Particularly interested in impact of desegregation on members of Black middle class. (*Current Biography*)

Sources: *Current Biography*, 1968; *Negro Handbook.*

BROOKE, EDWARD WILLIAM. Former U.S. Senator, Lawyer.
Born in Wash., D.C., Oct. 26, 1919. *Education:* B.S., Howard U., 1941; LL.B., 1948, LL.M., 1949, Boston Law Sch. *Family:* Married Remigia Ferrari-Scacco, June 7, 1947 (div. 1977); children: d. Remi Cynthia, d. Edwina Helene; married 2nd Anne Fleming (of St. Martin, French W. Indies). *Career:* Officer, World War II; Attorney, Boston; Attorney Gen. of Mass., 1963-67; U.S. Senator, Mass., 1967-76? *Honors:* Won Bronze Star & Combat Infantryman's Badge in World War II. Jr. Chamber of Commerce named him one of Ten Outstanding Young Men of Greater Boston, 1952; NAACP Spingarn Medal, 1967; Charles Evans Hughes Award for "courageous leadership in governmental service," Natl. Conf. of Christians & Jews, 1967. Formerly: Pres., Boston Opera Co.; Fellow, Amer. Acad. of Arts & Scis.; Trustee, Boston U. *Mailing address:* c/o Little, Brown & Co., 34 Beacon St., Boston, Mass. 02106.

Writings:

Nonfiction

Manual of Massachusetts Eminent Domain Appraisal Law, with John S. Bottomly (Boston?, Eminent Domain Div., Dept. of the Attorney General, Commonwealth of Mass., 1965-)

The Challenge of Change: Crisis in Our Two-Party System (Boston, Little, Brown, 1966)

Sidelights: "Became a Republican when he cross-filed for state representative in both parties and lost Democratic nomination.... Was sworn in as the 35th Attorney General of Massachusetts on January 16, 1963. In January 1967 Brooke became the first Negro to be seated in the United States Senate during the 20th Century." (*Current Biography*)

Sources: *Current Biography*, 1967; *Los Angeles Times*, May 13, 1979.

BROOKS, GWENDOLYN ELIZABETH. Poet, Teacher.
Born in Topeka, Kan. *Education:* Chicago Public schs.; Wilson Jr. Coll., Chicago, 1936; L.H.D. (hon.), Columbia Coll., Chicago, 1964. *Family:* Married Henry L. Blakely, Sept. 17, 1939; son Henry L., d. Nora. *Career:* Tchr., Creative Writing & Poetry, Columbia Coll., Elmhurst Coll., & Northeastern Ill. State Coll. (all in Chicago); City Coll. of N.Y.; U. of Wis.; Columbia U. *Honors:* *Mademoiselle* Merit Award (one of ten Women of the Year), 1945; Amer. Acad. of Arts & Letters (for creative writing), 1946; Guggenheim Found. Fellow, 1946, 1947; *Poetry* mag.'s Eunice Tietjens Memorial Award, 1949; Pulitzer Prize for Poetry, 1950; Anisfield-Wolf Award, 1969; named Poet Laureate of State of Ill.; Kuumba Award, 1969; Black Award, 1971; many hon. doctorates. *Mailing address:* 7428 S. Evans Ave., Chicago, ILL. 60619.

Writings:

Fiction

A Street in Bronzeville, poems (N.Y., Harper, 1945)

Annie Allen, poems (Harper, 1949; Westport, Conn., Greenwood, 1971)

Maud Martha, novel (Harper, 1953; N.Y., AMS, 1974)

The Bean Eaters, poems (Harper, 1960)

Selected Poems (Harper, 1963)

A Portion of That Field: The Centennial of the Burial of Lincoln—Commemorative Selections, with Others (Urbana, U. of Ill. Press, 1967)

In the Mecca, poems (Harper, 1968)

Riot, poems (Detroit, Broadside, 1969; paper also)

Family Pictures, poems (Broadside, 1970)

A Broadside Treasury, 1965-70 ed. (Broadside, 1971; paper also)

Aloneness, poems (Broadside, 1971)

Jump Bad: A New Chicago Anthology, ed. (Broadside, 1971; paper also)

To Gwen with Love: A Tribute to Gwendolyn Brooks (Chicago, Johnson, 1971)

The Black Position, ed., poems (Broadside, 1971)

The World of Gwendolyn Brooks, poems (Harper, 1971)

The Tiger Who Wore White Gloves or What You Are, You Are, poems (Chicago, Third World, 1974)

Beckonings, poems (Broadside, 1975)

Nonfiction
Bronzeville Boys and Girls (Harper, 1956)

Report from Part One: The Autobiography of Gwendolyn Brooks (Broadside, 1972)

A Capsule Course in Black Poetry Writing, with Others (Broadside, 1975)

Sidelights: First Black poet in the United States to win a Pulitzer Prize. Miss Brooks has contributed to Black self-image by conducting writers' workshops for alienated youth, and by supporting the so-called revolutionary poets, as well as the Black Broadside Press.

Sources: *Black American Literature: Poetry; Black Voices; Books in Print*, 1975-76, 1978-79, 1982-83; *Broadside Authors and Artists; Cavalcade; Kaleidoscope; Poetry of Black America; Soon, One Morning; Who's Who in America*, 37th ed., 1972-73.

BROWN, CLAUDE. Activist.
Born in N.Y.C., Feb. 23, 1937. *Education:* B.A., Howard U., 1965; Stanford U. Law Sch.; Rutgers U. Law Sch. *Family:* Married Helen Jones, Sept. 9, 1961. *Career:* Wrote plays performed by Amer. Negro Theater Guild, 1960-61; Mem. of Harlem Improvement Project Group. *Mailing address:* Stein & Day Pub., Scarborough House, Briarcliff Manor, N.Y. 10510.

Writings:
Fiction
The Children of Ham, fiction (Briarcliff Manor, N.Y., Stein & Day, 1976)

Nonfiction
Manchild in the Promised Land, autobiography (N.Y., Macmillan, 1965; London, Cape, 1966)

Sidelights: He attended and graduated from Washington Irving Evening High School (1957), after being incarcerated in several reform schools. He later attended Howard University on a Methodist Community Church grant. (*Current Biography*)

Sources: *Books in Print*, Supplement, 1975-76; *Cavalcade; Current Biography*, 1967; *Who's Who in America*, 37th ed., 1972-73.

BROWN, FRANK LONDON. Novelist, Editor.
Born in Kan. City, Mo., Oct. 17, 1927. *Education:* Wilberforce U.; Kent Coll. of Law, Chicago; B.A., Roosevelt U., 1951; M.A., U. of Chicago. *Family:* Married Evelyn Marie Brown; d. Debra, d. Cheryl, d. Pamela. *Career:* Machinist, union organizer, govt. employee, jazz singer, journalist, & ed.; appeared with Thelonius Monk at "Gate of Horn" in Chicago; in the "Five Spot" in N.Y.; Assoc. Ed., *Ebony. Honors:* John Hay Whitney Found. Award for creative writing; U. of Chicago Fellow. Died Mar. 13, 1962.

Writings:
Fiction
Trumbull Park, novel (Chicago, Regnery, 1959)

The Myth Maker, novel (Chicago, Path Press, 1969)

Sidelights: Contributed short stories and articles to *Downbeat, Chicago Review, Ebony, Negro Digest, Chicago Tribune, Chicago Sun-Times,* and *Southwest Review.*
Was the first to read short stories, rather than poetry, to jazz accompaniment. At the time of his death, at 34, was working on revised draft of second novel; was director of Union Leadership Program at University of Chicago; and was completing doctorate in political science. (*Black Voices*)

Sources: *American Negro Short Stories; Black Voices;* Pub. information.

BROWN, MARGERY W. Juvenile Writer, Illustrator, Teacher.
Born in Durham, N.C. *Education:* B.A., Spelman Coll.; Art Studies, Ohio State U., 1932-34. *Family:* Married Richard E. Brown, Dec. 22, 1936 (dec.); d. Janice (Mrs. Jan E. Carden). *Career:* Art Tchr., Newark, N.J., 1948- . Retired. *Mailing address:* 245 Reynolds Terrace C-1, Orange, N.J. 07050.

Writings:
Fiction
That Ruby, juv., self-illustrated (Chicago, Reilly & Lee, 1969)

Animals Made by Me, juv., self-illustrated (N.Y., Putnam, 1970)

The Second Stone, juv. (Putnam, 1974)

Yesterday I Climbed a Mountain, juv. (Putnam, 1976)

No Jon, No Jon, No!, juv. (Boston, Houghton Mifflin, 1981)

(Illustrator Only)
Old Crackfoot, by G. Allred (N.Y., Obolensky, 1965)

I'm Glad I'm Me, by Elberta Stone (Putnam, 1971)

Sidelights: Two prime interests have dominated my life—art and children. From both I have gained a wide and varied wealth of experiences. (Author)

Sources: Author information; *Something about the Author*, 1973.

BROWN, ROSCOE C., JR. Institute Director, Radio and Television Host.
Born in Wash., D.C., Mar. 9, 1922. *Education:* B.S., Springfield Coll., Mass.; M.A., Ph.D., N.Y.U. *Family:* Married Josephine; d. Doris, d. Diane, son Dennis, son Donald. *Career:* Dir., Inst. of Afro-Amer. Affairs, N.Y.U.; Host, weekly TV ser. "Black Arts," weekly radio ser. "Soul of Reason"; Co-host, Jersey City State Coll. TV program "Black Letters." *Mailing address:* c/o Johnson Pub. Co., 820 S. Mich. Ave., Chicago, Ill. 60605.

Writings:
Nonfiction
Negro Almanac, co-ed. (N.Y., Bellwether, 1967)

Classical Studies in Physical Activity, co-ed. (Englewood Cliffs, N.J., Prentice-Hall, 1968)

New Perspectives of Man in Action, ed. (Prentice-Hall, 1969)

Sources: *1000 Successful Blacks.*

BROWN, STERLING ALLEN. Poet, Critic, English Professor.
Born in Wash., D.C., May 1, 1901. *Education:* Williams Coll., Phi Beta Kappa, 1921; M.A., Harvard U., 1923. *Family:* Married in 1919. *Career:* Lit. Ed., *Opportunity*; Bk. Reviewer; Ed., *Negro Affairs* for Fed. Writers Project, 1936-39; Staff mem., Carnegie-Myrdal Study of the Negro, 1939; Prof. of Eng., Howard U.; Visiting Prof., N.Y.U., Atlanta U., & Vassar Coll. *Honors:* Guggenheim Found. Fellow, 1937-38. *Mailing address:* c/o Broadside Press, 12651 Old Mill Pl., Detroit, Mich. 48238.

Writings:
Fiction

Southern Road, poems (N.Y., Harcourt, 1932; Boston, Beacon, 1952)

The Negro Caravan, anthology, ed. with Arthur P. Davis & Ulysses Lee (N.Y., Dryden, 1941; paper, N.Y., Arno, 1969)

The Last Ride of Wild Bill, poems (Detroit, Broadside, 1975)

Nonfiction

Outline for the Study of the Poetry of American Negroes (Harcourt, 1931)

The Negro in American Fiction (Wash., D.C., Associates in Negro Folk Educ., 1937)

Negro Poetry and Drama (Associates in Negro Folk Educ., 1937)

Sidelights: "Sterling A. Brown has probably done more than any other one person to influence and direct the cause of Negro American writing." (*Cavalcade*)
John H. Clarke described him as "the dean of American Negro poets" in *American Negro Short Stories*. Brown and Langston Hughes were "the most Negro" poets in American literature, to Leopold Senghor, President of Senegal. (*Black Voices*)

Sources: *Black American Literature: Poetry; Black Insights; Black Poets of the United States; Black Voices; Broadside Authors and Artists; Cavalcade.*

BROWN, WILLIAM WELLS. Abolitionist.
Born near Lexington, Ky., in 1816. *Education:* Self-educated; studied medicine in Europe. *Career:* Served under several masters & performed unusual kinds of work. Hired out to Elijah P. Lovejoy's newspaper office in St. Louis; traveled up & down Ohio & Miss. Rivers with riverboat captain master; worked on steamboats on Lake Erie (helped fugitive slaves to freedom). Agent, Western N.Y., Anti-Slavery Soc., 1844-?; Agent, Mass. Anti-Slavery Soc. (replacing Frederick Douglass). Delegate to Paris Peace Conf. (remained in Europe for several yrs. because of harsh fugitive slave law). Practiced medicine; became writer. Died in 1884.

Writings:
Fiction

Anti-Slavery Harp, ed., collection of abolitionist songs and poems, 2nd ed. (Boston, B. Marsh, 1849)

Clotel; or the President's Daughter, novel (London, Partridge, Oakey, 1853; N.Y., Arno, paper also, 1969)

The Escape, or a Leap for Freedom, 1st play by an American Negro (Boston, R. F. Wallcut, 1858)

Nonfiction

Narrative of William W. Brown, a Fugitive Slave (Boston, Anti-Slavery Office, 1847, 2nd ed. enlarged, 1848; N.Y., Johnson Reprint, 1970)

Three Years in Europe, or Places I Have Seen and People I Have Met (London, C. Gilpin, 1852)

Sketches of Places and People Abroad (Boston, 1855; facsimile ed., Freeport, N.Y., Bks. for Lib., Black Heritage Bks., 1970)

Black Man, His Antecedants, His Genius, and His Achievements, 2nd ed. (N.Y., Hamilton, 1863; R. F. Wallcut, 1863; Arno, Black Heritage Reprint of 1865, 1969)

The Negro in the American Rebellion, His Heroism and His Fidelity (Boston, Lee & Shepard, 1867; Boston, A. G. Brown, 1880, 1885; reprint of 1880 ed., n.p., Basic Afro-Amer. Reprint, 1969)

The Rising Son, or The Antecedents and Advancement of the Colored Race (Boston, A. G. Brown, 1874, 1876; Plainview, N.J., Bks. for Lib., reprint 1970)

My Southern Home, or The South and Its People (Boston, A. G. Brown, 1880; 3rd ed., 1882)

Sidelights: Son of a white father and a mulatto mother. On his second attempt to escape slavery, he was successful. He was helped by his later namesake, Wells Brown, on his way north. He was "the first American Negro to write a novel, the first to write a play, the first to write a book of travels and among the first to write history." (*Cavalcade*)

Sources: *Black American Literature: Essays; Blackamerican Literature; Cavalcade; Early Negro American Writers.*

BRUTUS, DENNIS VINCENT. (Zimbabwean/South African). Poet, Teacher.
Born in Salisbury, S. Rhodesia, Nov. 28, 1924 (son of African "Coloureds" who were both tchrs.). *Education:* B.A. (Eng.), Fort Hare U. Coll., 1946; (Law), U. of Witwatersrand, 1962-63. *Career:* Taught Eng. & Afrikaans in several S. African high schs., 1948-62; worked in London 1966-70 at variety of teaching & journalistic assignments; Tchr., U. of Denver & Northwestern U.; worked on developing Ph.D. program in African Lit. at Northwestern U.; Dir. of World Campaign for Release of S. African Polit. Prisoners; Pres. of S. African Non-Racial Olympic Com.; Rep. in U.S. for Intnl. Defense Aid Fund for S. Africans; in 1972 helped launch, in N.Y.C., Intnl. Campaign against Racism in Sport. *Honors: Sirens, Knuckles, Boots* won Mbari Prize (U. of Ibadan, Nigeria) for poetry in 1962. Nominated "poet laureate of S. Africa" in Horizon Press, *A History of Africa*. *Mailing address:* 18 Hilton Ave., London N12, Eng.

Writings:
Fiction

Sirens, Knuckles, Boots, poems (Ibadan, Nigeria, Mbari Press, 1963)

Letters to Martha and Other Poems from a South African Prison (London, Heinemann, 1968)

Poems from Algiers, no. 2, Occasional Publ. of African & Afro-Amer. Res. Inst. (Austin, Tex., U. of Tex. Press, 1970)

A Simple Lust: Selected Poems Including Sirens, Knuckles, Boots, Letters to Martha, Poems from Algiers, Thoughts Abroad (N.Y., Hill & Wang, 1973)

Strains, poems, ed. with Others (Austin, Tex., Troubador Press, 1975)

Thoughts Abroad, poems (Troubador Press, 1975)

Stubborn Hope; Poems (Wash., D.C., Three Continents, 1978)

Sidelights: With poems, *Letters to Martha*, which delineated his experience as a political prisoner on Robben Island, Brutus made his greatest impact.

Sources: *Books in Print*, 1979-80, 1980-81; *Protest and Conflict in African Literature; A Reader's Guide to African Literature.*

BRYAN, ASHLEY F. Art Professor, Folklorist, Juvenile Writer.
Born in N.Y.C., July 13, 1923. *Education:* Cooper Union; Columbia U. *Career:* Art Prof.,
Dartmouth Coll., Hanover, N.H. *Honors:* Honorable Mention, from Coretta Scott King Award
Com., for *I'm Going to Sing*, 1983. *Mailing address:* Dept. of Art, Dartmouth Coll., Hanover, N.H.
03755.

Writings:
Fiction (Illustrated by Author)
The Ox of the Wonderful Horns and Other African Folktales, juv. (N.Y., Atheneum, 1971)

The Adventures of Aku, juv. (Atheneum, 1976)

The Dancing Granny, juv. (Atheneum, 1977)

I Greet the Dawn: Poems of Paul Laurence Dunbar, ed., juv. (Atheneum, 1978)

Beat the Story-Drum, Pum-Pum, juv. (Atheneum, 1980)

(Illustrator Only)
Moon, for What Do You Wait?, juv., by Rabindranath Tagore (Atheneum, 1967)

Jathro and Jumbie, juv., by Susan Cooper (Atheneum, 1979)

Jim Flying High, juv., by Mari Evans (N.Y., Doubleday, 1979)

Nonfiction
Walk Together Children: Black American Spirituals, juv. (Atheneum, 1974)

I'm Going to Sing, juv., collection of spirituals (Atheneum, 1983)

Sidelights: Ashley Bryan is a preserver of African traditions and folklore in America.

Sources: *American Libraries*, Apr. 1983; *Books in Print*, 1979-80, 1980-81; *Contemporary Authors*,
vol. 107, 1983; *Freedomways*, vol. 17, 1977.

BRYANT, HENRY A., JR. Ethnic Studies Professor.
Born in Shongaloo, La., Mar. 14, 1943. *Education:* A.B. (Polit. Sci. & Hist.), San Jose State U.,
Cal., 1966; M.A. (Polit. Sci. & Hist.), San Jose State U., 1969; Ph.D. candidate, U. Cal., Berkeley.
Family: Married Peggy Knox, Dec. 16, 1967; children: Rehema Kamaria, Moturi Roy. *Career:* Gen.
Medical & Surgical Asst., Cal. Veterans Admin., 1962-63; Psychiatric Nursing Asst., Veterans
Admin., 1963-68; Lect. & Asst. Prof., Polit. Sci., San Jose State U., 1969-70; Chairman, Ethnic
Studies Dept., Laney Coll., Oakland, Cal. (Black, Chicano, & Asian Studies), 1970-present. *Honors:*
Bishop A. D. Bradley Memorial Scholarship; Gold Pen Award (students at Laney Coll.); Notable
American of the Bicentennial Era ("Outstanding Educator"); "Outstanding Instructor" by students at
Laney Coll., 1976, 1978, 1979; "Truth in Education" Award. *Mailing address:* Laney College, 900
Fallon St., Oakland, Cal. 94804.

Writings:
Nonfiction
The Streets of Oakland (n.p., Leseing Press, 1973)

Racism and Black Politics, a Contemporary Reader in Racism and Black Politics (Lanhem, Md.,
U. Press of America, 1977)

Source: Author information; *Contemporary Authors*, vols. 53-56, 1975.

BULLINS, ED. Playwright, Editor, Teacher, Activist.
Born in Phila., Pa., July 2, 1935. *Career:* Formerly Minister of Culture, Black Panther Party;
Playwright-in-Residence, New Lafayette Theatre, N.Y.C.; Assoc. Ed., *The Drama Review*; Co-
founder & Dir., Black Arts/West (community experiment in theater); Ed., *The Drama Review*

(Summer 1968); Ed., *Black Theater Magazine*; Tchr. of Writing & Eng., Fordham U., Columbia U., U. of Mass. (Boston), Bronx Community Coll., Manhattan Community Coll., etc. *Honors:* Drama Desk-Vernon Rice Award; Obie Award for Distinguished Playwright; Guggenheim Found. Fellow; Rockefeller Found. Playwriting Grant; Creative Artists Program Serv. (CAPS) Grant for Playwriting; NEA Grant for Playwriting. *Mailing address:* 932 E. 212th St., Bronx, N.Y. 10469.

Writings:
Fiction

Five Plays: Goin' a Buffalo; In the Wine Time; A Son, Come Home; The Electronic Nigger; Clara's Ole Man (Indianapolis, Bobbs-Merrill, 1968)

New Plays from the Black Theatre (N.Y., Bantam, 1969)

Black Quartet, play, with Others (N.Y., New Amer. Lib., 1970)

The Duplex: A Black Love Fable in Four Movements, play (N.Y., Morrow, 1971)

The Hungered One: Early Writings, short stories (Morrow, 1971)

Four Dynamite Plays (Morrow, 1972)

The Theme Is Blackness: The Corner and Other Plays (Morrow, 1972)

The Reluctant Rapist, novel (N.Y., Harper, 1973)

The New Lafayette Theatre Presents: Plays with Aesthetic Comments by Six Black Playwrights, ed. (N.Y., Anchor, 1974)

Sidelights: "Has written more than thirty plays—some have been seen at the New Lafayette Theatre, LaMama, New Federal Theatre, the Public Theatre, etc." (Author)
"Has the unique distinction of working full time in the Black community as a playwright." " ... Bullins is a leader in the Black Experience School of Afro-Amer. writing, and does not concern himself with whites, their stereotypes, nor their values." (*New Black Playwrights*)

Sources: *Afro-American Literature and Culture since World War II;* Author information; *Black Scenes; Books in Print*, 1978-79; *Forgotten Pages of American Literature; New Black Playwrights; New Black Poetry.*

BUNCHE, RALPH JOHNSON. Diplomat, Political Science Professor (Nobel Peace Prize Laureate). Born in Detroit, Mich., Aug. 7, 1904. *Education:* D.A., UCLA (Polit. Sci., summa cum laude, valedictorian, Phi Beta Kappa), 1927; M.A., 1928, Ph.D. (Govt. & Intnl. Relations), Harvard U., 1934; Northwestern U., 1936; London Sch. of Econ., 1937; Capetown U., S. Africa (2 yr. postdoctoral fellow, Anthropology & Colonial Policy), 1937. *Family:* Married Ruth Harris, June 23, 1930; son Ralph, Jr., d. Joan, d. Jane (Mrs. Burton Pierce). *Career:* Head, Dept. of Polit. Sci., Howard U.; Professor at Harvard U.; Investigator, Imperialism, Africa (Soc. Sci. Res. Council, Fellow); Staff mem., Carnegie-Myrdal Study of the Negro (led to Gunnar Myrdal's *An American Dilemma*); during World War II, Spec. Africa, OSS; Assoc., Chief of Dependent Areas, State Dept.; UN Trusteeship Div., selected to represent UN's Secy.-Gen. in Arab-Israeli crisis; became Acting Mediator when Count Folke Bernardotte assassinated in 1948; apptd. UN Under-Secy. for Spec. Polit. Affairs, 1955 (America's highest-ranking mem. of UN Secretariat); Spec. Peace Envoy, Revolution in Congo, 1960. *Honors:* Some 50 hon. degrees; Tappan Prize, Harvard U., for best doctoral dissertation in soc. sci., 1934; Nobel Peace Prize; One World Award; Spingarn Medal; Four Freedoms Award; Pres. Freedom Medal; Ralph Bunche Hall (Soc. Sci. Bldg., UCLA). Died Dec. 9, 1971.

Writings:
Nonfiction

A World View of Race (Wash., D.C., Associates in Negro Folk Educ., 1936)

A Brief and Tentative Analysis of Negro Leadership, microfilm (Millwood, N.Y., Kraus-Thomson, Carnegie-Myrdal Study of the Negro in America, 1940, 1973 ?)

The Political Status of the Negro in the Age of FDR, ed. by Dewey W. Grantham (Chicago, U. of Chicago Press, 1973)

Sidelights: "First American Negro to win the Nobel Peace Prize, Ralph Bunche is ... among the most significant American diplomats of the 20th Century. Bunche received the coveted award in 1950." (*Negro Almanac*)

"U Thant (United Nations Secretary General) appraised Dr. Bunche as 'an international institution in his own right, transcending both nationality and race in a way that is achieved by very few.' " (*Los Angeles Times*)

Bunche has said, "One must believe that man can be saved — or salvaged — from his inevitable follies, that all problems of human relations are solvable ... that conflict situations, however deep-seated, bitter and prolonged, can be resolved; that a world at peace is, in fact, attainable.

"Otherwise one's work, all diplomacy, the United Nations itself, become a fateful travesty and all mankind would be doomed." (*Los Angeles Times*)

Sources: *Books in Print*, Supplement, 1975-76; *Historical Negro Biographies*; *Los Angeles Herald Examiner*, Dec. 10, 1971; *Los Angeles Sentinel*, Dec. 16, 1971; *Los Angeles Times*, Dec. 10, 1971; *Negro Almanac; Negro Caravan; Negroes in Public Affairs and Government*.

BURRELL, EVELYN (Patterson). Poet, English Teacher.
Born in Baltimore, Md., 1920. *Education:* B.A. (Eng., magna cum laude), Morgan State Coll., Baltimore, 1959; M.A. (Eng.), Howard U., 1966, further study, Afro-Amer. Studies, 1970-73. *Career:* Asst. Prof., Eng., Coppin State Coll., Baltimore; Asst. Prof., Eng., Bowie State Coll., Bowie, Md.; Lect., Afro-Amer. Lit., Hood Coll., Frederick, Md.; Poet-in-Residence, Baltimore Public Schs. (Md. Arts Council); Conductor, Poetry Workshop, Richmond, Va.; Intercultural Center for the Humanities (Poet-in-Residence ser.). *Honors:* Alpha Kappa Mu Honor Soc.; Lambda Iota Tau Honor Soc.; Theta Xi chap.; Kappa Delta Pi Honor Soc.; Grad. fellow, Howard U.; Ford Found. Travel & Study grant. *Mailing address:* c/o Richmond Intercultural Center for Humanities, Richmond, Va. 23225.

Writings:
Fiction
Weep No More, poems (n.p., Burton-Johns, 1973; enlarged ed., 1975)

Son to Mother, poems (Richmond, Va., Richmond Intercultural Center for Humanities, Individual Reading Ser., 1974)

Sources: Pub. information; *Weep No More*.

BURROUGHS, MARGARET G. Artist, Teacher, Museum Director, Juvenile Writer.
Born in St. Rose, La., Nov. 1, 1917. *Education:* Chicago Normal Coll., 1935-37 (Elementary Tchrs. Certificate), 1939 (Upper Grade Art Certificate); Bachelor of Art Education, Art Inst. of Chicago, 1946, Master of Art Education, 1948; Esmerelda Art Sch., Mexico City, 1953; Columbia U., Tchrs. Coll. (postgrad., summers, 1958-60). *Family:* Married 1st Bernard Goss, 1939 (div. 1947); d. Gayle Goss Toller; married 2nd Charles G. Burroughs (mus. curator), 1949; son Paul Burroughs. *Career:* Tchr., Chicago, 1940-46; Art Tchr., 1946- ; Founder, Dir., Mus. of African-Amer. Hist., 1961- ; Asst. Prof., African & African-Amer. Art Hist., Chicago Art Inst., 1968; Asst. Prof., Humanities, Kennedy-King Coll., Chicago. *Honors:* Print, Hon. Mention, Atlanta U., 1947; 1st Watercolor Purchase Award, Atlanta U., 1955; Best in Show Hallmark Award, Lincoln U., Mo., 1962; NEH Fellow, Intern in Mus. Practices, Field Mus., Chicago, 1967-68; Ph.D. (Dr. of Honoris Causis), Lewis Coll., Lockport, Ill., 1972; YWCA Leadership Award for Excellence in Art, 1973; Citation by Pres. Jimmy Carter, 1980; Excellence in Art award, Natl. Assn. of Negro Musicians, 1982. *Mailing address:* 3806 S. Mich. Ave., Chicago, Ill. 60653.

Writings:
Fiction
Jasper the Drummin' Boy, juv., self-illustrated (N.Y., Viking, 1947; rev., Chicago, Follett, 1970)

Did You Feed My Cow? Rhymes and Games from City Streets and Country Lanes, juv., self-illustrated (N.Y., Crowell, 1956; rev., Follett, 1969)

Whip Me Whop Me Pudding, juv. (Chicago, Praga Press, 1966)

For Malcolm; Poems on the Life and Death of Malcolm X, anthology, with Dudley Randall (Detroit, Braodside, paper, 1967; 2nd ed., 1969)

Nonfiction

What Shall I Tell My Children Who Are Black (Chicago, DuSable Museum, 1968)

Africa, My Africa, juv. (DuSable Museum, 1970)

Why Have the Youth of Today Not Heard about This Man — Paul Robeson, juv. (DuSable Museum, 1981)

Sidelights: (Travel) Mexico, Russia, Poland, Czechoslovakia, Ghana, Togo, Dahomey, Nigeria, Ivory Coast, Ethiopia, Kenya, Tanzania, Egypt, Tunisia, Algeria, Morocco, Jamaica, Haiti, Trinidad.

Sources: Author information; *Ebony*, Mar. 1974; *For Malcolm.*

BUTCHER, MARGARET JUST. English Professor.
Born in Wash., D.C., Apr. 28, 1913. *Education:* Ph.D., Boston U., 1947. *Family:* Married James W. Butcher; d. Sheryl Everett. *Career:* Tchr., Va. Union U., 1935-36; Tchr., public schs., Wash., D.C.; Prof., Eng., Howard U., 1942- ; Fulbright Visiting Prof. in Amer. Lit., Universities of Grenoble, Lyon, & Dijon, in France, 1949-50. *Mailing address:* c/o Alfred A. Knopf, Inc., 201 E. 50th St., N.Y., N.Y. 10022.

Writings:
Nonfiction

The Negro in American Culture, essay (N.Y., Knopf, 1956; N.Y., New Amer. Lib., 1957, 1971; 2nd ed., Knopf, 1971)

Sidelights: Daughter of the eminent biologist Ernest Everett Just. "The late Alain Leroy Locke was working on [*The Negro in American Culture*] at the time of his death, and Dr. Butcher has completed it brilliantly along the lines he had laid down." (Book jacket)

Sources: Books in Print, 1980-81; *The Negro in American Culture.*

BUTCHER, PHILIP. English Professor, Educator.
Born in Wash., D.C., Sept. 28, 1918. *Education:* B.A., 1942, M.A., 1947, Howard U.; Ph.D., Columbia U., 1956. *Family:* Married Ruth, d. Wendy, d. Mrs. Laurel B. Miles. *Career:* Tchr., Eng., Morgan State Coll., Baltimore, 1947- . Dean, Grad. Sch., & Prof., Eng., Morgan State Coll. *Mailing address:* c/o Morgan State Coll., Baltimore, Md. 21239.

Writings:
Nonfiction

George W. Cable: The Northampton Years, criticism (N.Y., Columbia U. Press, 1959)

The Minority Presence in American Literature, 1600-1900, 2 vols. (Wash., D.C., Howard U. Press, 1977)

The Ethnic Image of Modern American Literature: 1900-1950, 2 vols. (Howard U. Press, 1983)

Sidelights: "He is a nationally recognized authority on the life of the writer, social critic and humanitarian, George Washington Cable, and is the author of more than 85 books, articles and reviews." (*1000 Successful Blacks*)

Sources: *Books in Print*, 1983-84; *1000 Successful Blacks.*

BUTLER, OCTAVIA E[stelle]. Science Fiction Writer.
Born in Pasadena, Cal., June 22, 1947. *Education:* A.A., Hist., Pasadena City Coll.; further study, Cal. State, L.A. (Anthropology). *Career:* Sci. Fiction Writer. *Mailing address:* P.O. Box 6604, Los Angeles, Cal. 90055.

Writings:
Fiction

Kindred, sci. fiction (N.Y., Doubleday, 1970; N.Y., Pocket Bks., 1980)

Patternmaster, sci. fiction (Doubleday, 1976; N.Y., Avon, 1979)

Mind of My Mind, sci. fiction (Doubleday, 1977; Avon, 1978)

Survivor, sci. fiction (Doubleday, 1978; N.Y., New Amer. Lib., 1979)

Wild Seed, sci. fiction (Doubleday, 1980; n.p., Archway, 1981)

Sidelights: *Publishers Weekly* considers *Mind of My Mind* "Vivid ... Explosive." (Book jacket) "Centuries of genetic mutation gave her the telepathic web—and with it she became the bold and magnetic mistress of human destiny." (*Mind of My Mind*)

Sources: Author information; *Books in Print*, 1979-80; *Mind of My Mind*.

BYRD, HAROLD EUGENE. Telecommunications Engineer.
Born in Monticello, Fla. *Education:* B.S. (Electronic Technology), Fla. A&M U.; M.B.A., Pepperdine U., L.A. *Family:* Married Ellen Marie; children: Harold Eugene, Jr., Michael Julian. *Career:* Video-technician, WCTV-TV, Tallahassee, 1968-69; Transmission Design Engineer, Installation Supervisor, Senior Engineer, Pacific Telephone, L.A. *Mailing address:* 8801 S. Western Ave., L.A., Cal. 90047.

Writings:
Nonfiction

The Black Experience in Big Business (Hicksville, N.Y., Exposition Press, 1977)

Cannot Plead Black Anymore (L.A., Byrd, 1978)

Sources: Author information; *Books in Print*, 1979-80.

CAIN, GEORGE. Novelist.
Born in N.Y.C. in 1943. *Education:* N.Y.C. schs.; Iona Coll. *Family:* Married Jo Lynne, 1968; d. Nataya. *Career:* Traveled to Cal., Mexico, & Tex.; spent some time in prisons; began writing in 1966. Lives in Bedford-Stuyvesant, Brooklyn, N.Y. *Mailing Address:* c/o Dell Pub. Co., One Dag Hammarskjold Plaza, N.Y., N.Y. 10017.

Writings:
Fiction
Blueschild Baby, novel (N.Y., Dell, 1970)

Sidelights: "The most important work of fiction by an Afro-American since *Native Son*." (*New York Times Book Review*)

"It will be inevitably compared to *Manchild in the Promised Land*, perhaps to *Soul on Ice*. It can stand on its own, infused with pride and compassion and revolutionary fervor." (*Publishers Weekly*)

" ... in one sense, *Blueschild Baby* represents a synthesis of a number of black artistic and social concerns. As a fictional autobiography, it stands at the far end of a tradition that begins with the narrative of Briton Hammon, matures in the work of Frederick Douglass, expands with James Weldon Johnson's *Autobiography of an Ex-Coloured Man*, and receives acknowledgement during the early sixties in the works of Claude Brown and Malcolm X." (*Singers of Daybreak*)

Sources: *Blueschild Baby; Singers of Daybreak*.

CARMICHAEL, STOKELY. Civil Rights Leader, Activist.
Born in Port-of-Spain, Trinidad, Brit. W. Indies, June 29, 1941. *Education:* Bronx High Sch. of Sci., N.Y.C.; B.A. (Philosophy), Howard U., 1964. *Family:* Married Miriam Makeba (S. African-born singer), Apr. 1968. *Career:* Organizer, SNCC; Field Organizer, Voter Registration, Lowndes

County, Miss.; organized All-Black Lowndes County Freedom Org.; Dir., Civil Rights activities, Miss. Summer Project, 1964; Prime Minister, Black Panthers. *Mailing address:* Conakry, Guinea, W. Africa.

Writings:
Nonfiction

Black Power; The Politics of Liberation in America, with Charles V. Hamilton (N.Y., Random House, 1967)

Stokely Speaks: Black Power Back to Pan-Africanism (Random House, 1971)

Sidelights: "The slogan 'Black Power,' most popular rallying cry of black liberation groups in the United States in the late 1960's, was coined ... by Stokely Carmichael when he was Chairman of the Student Nonviolent Coordinating Committee.... Since late 1968, Carmichael, a Pan-Africanist, has spent most of his time in self-imposed exile in Guinea, West Africa." (*Current Biography*)

Sources: *Black Power; Current Biography*, 1970.

CARTER, HAROLD A. Clergyman, Theologian.
Born in Selma, Ala., Dec. 24, 1936. *Education:* B.A., Ala. State Coll., Montgomery; Grad., Crozer Theol. Sem.; Dr. of Ministry, Colgate U., Rochester, N.Y., 1974; Ph.D. (Theol.), St. Mary's Sem. & U., Baltimore, 1974. *Family:* Married Weptanomah Washington; children: Harold, Jr., d. Weptanomah. *Career:* Pastor, Court St. Bap. Church, Lynchburg, Va., 1959-64; Pastor, New Shiloh Bap. Church, present. *Honors:* D.D., Va. Sem. & Coll., Lynchburg; magna cum laude (Ph.D. in Theol.); Honor Citizen, Baltimore; Natl. Relig. Soc. Concern, Phi Beta Sigma Fraternity, 1978 Annual Award. *Mailing address:* 3501 Sequoia Ave., Baltimore, Md. 21215.

Writings:
Nonfiction

The Black Church Looks at the Bicentennial (Elgin, Ill., Progressive Natl. Bap. Pub. House, 1976)

The Prayer Tradition of Black People (Valley Forge, Pa., Judson Press, 1976)

Myths That Mire the Ministry (Judson Press, 1980)

Sidelights: NAACP leader; instituted Saturday Church School Program; church provides $200 scholarship to every high school graduate; has served as Denominational Officer in progressive Baptist circles, state and national.

Sources: Author information; *Books in Print*, 1980-81.

CARTER, RUBIN [Hurricane]. Boxer.
Family: Married Mae Thelma; d. Theodora. *Career:* Boxer. *Mailing address:* c/o Viking Press, 625 Madison Ave., N.Y., N.Y. 10016.

Writings:
Nonfiction

The Sixteenth Round: From Number 1 Contender to #45472, autobiography (N.Y., Viking, 1974)

Sidelights: "On May 26, 1967, the spiraling career of Rubin 'Hurricane' Carter, then the top contender for the middleweight boxing title of the world, came to a ... halt: he was convicted of the murder of three white people in a Paterson, New Jersey, bar.... Though he maintained his innocence throughout his ... trial ... he was sentenced to triple life imprisonment. In *The Sixteenth Round*, the Rube pulls no punches. Writing in a language and style all his own, he supplies electrifying descriptions of his fights both in and out of the ring; his stories of the hell that is life in prison are unmatched in contemporary literature. His book is a scathing indictment of the prison system he grew up in and out of, a tingling, soul-stirring, and slyly humorous account of his remarkable life." (Publisher)

Source: Pub. information.

CARTER, WILMOTH ANNETTE. Sociology Professor, Educator.
Born in Reidsville, N.C. *Education:* B.A. (Eng.), Shaw U., Raleigh, N.C.; M.A. (Sociol.), Atlanta U., 1942; Ph.D. (Sociol.), U. of Chicago, 1959. *Family:* Single. *Career:* Assoc. Prof., Sociol., 1950-57, Prof. Sociol., 1959-63, Chairman, Dept. of Sociol., Southern U., New Orleans, 1963-64; Res. Assoc., Race Relations, U. of Mich. & Tuskegee Inst., 1964-66; Prof. of Sociol. & Dir., Div. of Soc. Sci., Shaw U., 1966-69; Distinguished Prof. of Urban Sci. & Dir. of Inst. Res., 1969- ; Educ. Development Officer & Prof. of Urban Sci., 1971-73; V. Pres. of Instruction, 1973-74; Senior V. Pres. & V. Pres. of Res. & Evaluation, 1974- . *Honors:* Alpha Omicron Honor Soc., Alpha Kappa Delta; Rosenwald Fund Fellow, 1947-48; Danforth Found. Fellow, 1957-59; Delta Kappa Gamma, 1972. *Mailing address:* 1400 E. Davie St., Raleigh, N.C. 27610.

Writings:
Nonfiction

The Urban Negro in the South (N.Y., Vantage, 1962)

The New Negro of the South: A Portrait of Movements and Leadership (Hicksville, N.Y., Exposition Press, 1967)

Shaw's Universe (Phila., National Pub., 1973)

Source: Author information.

CARTEY, WILFRED. (Trinidadian). Critic, Professor of Comparative Literature & Culture, Poet.
Born in Port-of-Spain, Trinidad, in 1931. *Education:* U. of W. Indies; Columbia U., N.Y.C. *Career:* Prof., Comparative Lit. & Culture, City Coll. of N.Y. & Columbia U.; Lect., Peace Corps, on Africa & Caribbean Culture; Tchr., Spanish Lang. & Lit.; Visiting Prof., U. of W. Indies & U. of Ghana; Dir., Black & Puerto Rican Studies, City Coll. of N.Y., 1969. *Honors:* Fulbright Travel Grant, Columbia U.; elected to Black Acad. of Arts & Letters; 1st Martin L. King, Jr. Distinguished Prof. at Brooklyn Coll., City of N.Y. *Mailing address:* c/o Random House, Inc., 201 E. 50th St., N.Y., N.Y. 10022.

Writings:
Fiction

Whispers from a Continent: The Literature of Contemporary Black Africa (N.Y., Random House, 1969)

Palaver: Modern African Writings, ed. (N.Y., Elsevier-Nelson, 1970)

Africa Reader, 2 vols. Vol. 1, *Colonial Africa*; Vol. 2, *Independent Africa* (Random House, 1970)

The House of Blue Lightning, poems (N.Y., Emerson Hall, 1973)

Nonfiction

West Indies: Islands in the Sun (Camden, N.J., Nelson, 1967)

Black Images (N.Y., Tchrs. Coll., 1970)

Sources: *Books in Print*, 1979-80; *Caribbean Writers; Complete Caribbeana, 1900-1975; Palaver: Modern African Writings.*

CARWELL, HATTIE. Health Physicist.
Born in Brooklyn, N.Y. *Education:* B.S. (Chemistry & Biology), Bennett Coll., N.C.; M.S. (Health Physics), Rutgers U. *Career:* Health Physicist, Energy Res. & Development Admin., San Francisco. *Mailing address:* c/o Exposition Press, 900 S. Oyster Bay Road, Hicksville, N.Y. 11801.

Writings:
Nonfiction

Blacks in Science: Astrophysicist to Zoologist (Hicksville, N.Y., Exposition Press, 1977)

Sources: *Blacks in Science; Books in Print*, 1981-82.

CAYTON, HORACE R. Sociologist, Researcher, Journalist.
Born in Seattle, Wash., Apr. 12, 1903. *Education:* B.A. (Sociol.), U. of Wash., 1931; grad. study: U. of Chicago, 1931-34; N.Y.U., 1956; Inst. for Psychoanalysis. *Family:* Div. *Career:* Instr., Econ., Fisk U., 1935-36; Res. Asst. & Instr., Dept. of Anthropology, U. of Chicago, 1936-37; Dir., Parkway Community House, Chicago, 1939-49; Study of the Jewish Family, Amer. Jewish Com., N.Y., 1950-51; Correspondent to UN, *Pittsburgh Courier*, 1952-54; Res. Assoc., Natl. Council of Churches, N.Y., 1954-58; Lect. in Sociol., City Coll. of N.Y., 1957-58; Spec. Asst. for Study in Geriatric Mental Illness, Langley Porter Clinic, San Francisco, 1959-60; Inst. for Study of Crime & Delinquency, Intnl. Survey of Correction, Berkeley, Cal., 1960-61. *Honors:* Anisfield-Wolf Award (shared with St. Clair Drake) for *Black Metropolis*, as best scholarly book on race relations (N.Y. Public Lib. named this book Outstanding Book on Race Relations for 1945); Julius Rosenwald Fund Fellow, 1937-39. Died in 1970.

Writings:
Nonfiction

Black Workers and the New Unions, with George S. Mitchell (Chapel Hill, U. of N.C. Press, 1939)

Black Metropolis; A Study of Negro Life in a Northern City, with St. Clair Drake (N.Y., Harcourt, 1945)

The Changing Scene; Current Trends and Issues, with Setsuko M. Nishi (N.Y., National Council of Churches of Christ in U.S.A., 1955)

Social Work and the Church, with S. M. Nishi (N.Y., Natl. Council of Churches, 1956)

Sidelights: "Mr. Cayton's essays on mental illness, race relations, and religion have been included in several important studies...." (*Soon, One Morning*)

Sources: *Anger and Beyond; Current Biography*, 1946; *Soon, One Morning.*

CÉSAIRE, AIMÉ FERNAND. (Martiniquean). Caribbean Poet-Philosopher, Dramatist, Critic, Essayist, Politician.
Born in Basse-Pointe, Martinique, June 25, 1913. *Education:* Ecole Normale Superieure, Paris; Licencie es lettres, Sorbonne, U. of Paris. *Family:* Married Suzanne Roussi (tchr.), July 10, 1937; children: Jacques, Jean-Paul, Francis, Ina, Marc, Michelle. *Career:* Tchr., Lycée, Fort-de-France, Martinique, 1940-45; Mem., two French constituent assemblies, 1940-45; Deputy for Martinique in French Natl. Assembly, 1946-?; Mem., Communist bloc in Assembly, 1946-56; affiliated to Parti du Regroupement Africain et des Federalistes, 1958-59, independent since 1959, Mayor of Port-de-France, Martinique; Conseiller General for 4th canton of Port-de-France; Pres., Parti-Progressiste Martiniquais; Ed., *L'Afrique. Mailing address:* Mairie de Port-de-France, Martinique, W. Indies.

Writings:
(Partial Listing—English Only)
Fiction

Memorandum on My Martinique (N.Y., Macmillan, 1966)

A Season in the Congo, play, transl. by Ralph Manheim (N.Y., Grove, 1968)

Return to My Native Land, poems, transl. by John Berger & Anna Bostock (Baltimore, Penguin, 1969)

The Tragedy of King Christophe, play, transl. by Ralph Manheim (Grove, 1969)

Cadastre, poems, transl. by Emile Snyder & Sanford Upson (N.Y., Third Press, 1973)

The Tempest, play adapted from Shakespeare & transl. (Third Press, 1974)

The Collected Poetry, transl. by Clayton Eshelman & Annette Smith (Berkeley, Cal., U. of Cal. Press, 1983)

Nonfiction

Toussaint Louverture, transl. from French (Havana, Instituto del Libro, 1967)

Letter to Maurice Thorez, transl. from French (Paris, Présence Africaine, 1957; n.p., Panther House, 1971)

Discourse on Colonialism, transl. by Joan Pinkham (N.Y., Monthly Review Press, 1972)

Sidelights: "Negritude, a term Césaire himself coined, symbolizes the rational and emotional renaissance of African culture and commitment to it." He has had an important influence on modern Black poetry and on late surrealist French poetry. Among the intellectual elite of French West Africa his political essays have been most influential in its struggle for independence. His play, *Et les chiens se taissient (And the Dogs Were Silent, A Tragedy)*, is a passionate attack on colonialism. (*Encyclopedia of World Literature in the 20th Century*)

"Kofi Awoonor wrote, 'Césaire's meeting with Leopold Sedar Senghor ... produced not only a large crop of creative work, but, more important, the theoretical formulations that launched negritude as a literary movement and an important twentieth century phenomenon.' " (*Contemporary Authors*)

Sources: *Books in Print*, 1978-79; *Collected Poetry*; *Complete Caribbeana, 1900-1975*; *Contemporary Authors*, vols. 65-68, 1977; *Encyclopedia of World Literature in the 20th Century*.

CHALK, OCANIA. Sports Writer.
Born in Wash., D.C., Mar. 27, 1927. *Education:* Johnson C. Smith U. *Family:* Married Barbara Ann Maxfiele, Oct. 1964; children: Darryl, Lotus. *Career:* Public Assistance Caseworker, York, Pa., 1960-69; Bookstore owner, York, Pa., 1969-70; Reporter, *Washington Star*, 1970-71; Writer & Ed., U.S. Dept. of Labor, Wash., D.C., 1971- . *Mailing address:* c/o Dodd, Mead & Co., 79 Madison Ave., N.Y., N.Y. 10016.

Writings:
Nonfiction

Pioneers of Black Sports; The Early Days of the Black Professional Athlete in Baseball, Basketball, Boxing and Football (N.Y., Dodd, 1975)

Black College Sport (Dodd, 1976)

Sources: *Books in Print*, 1980-81; *Contemporary Authors*, vols. 45-48, 1974.

CHAPMAN, DOROTHY HILTON. Librarian, Compiler.
Born in Victoria, Tex., Sept. 4, 1934. *Education:* B.S., Tuskegee Inst., 1958; M.L.S., Carnegie Inst. of Technology, 1960. *Family:* Married Warren A. Chapman, June 18, 1960 (div. Nov. 10, 1971); children: Dessalyn Renee, Karen Adele. *Career:* Lib. Cataloger, Richard B. Harrison Public Lib., Raleigh, N.C., 1960-61; Cataloger, St. Augustine's Coll., Raleigh, 1961-69; Curator, Spec. Collections, Tex. S. U., 1969- . *Mailing address:* 6913 Burgess St., Houston, Tex. 77021.

Writings:
Fiction
Index to Black Poetry, comp. (Boston, G. K. Hall, 1974)

Sidelights: *Index to Black Poetry* "is a useful reference work sensibly arranged. It is, in fact, the first such volume of its kind and magnitude, and the indexes are admirably complete for black American poets." (*Library Journal*)

Sources: Author information; *Books in Print*, 1981-82; *Contemporary Authors*, vols. 57-60, 1976.

CHASE-RIBOUD, BARBARA. Sculptor.
Born in Phila., Pa. *Education:* B.F.A., Temple U., 1956; M.F.A., Yale U., 1960. *Family:* Married Marc Riboud, 1961; children: David, Alexis. *Career:* One-man museum shows: Mass. Inst. of Technology, Apr. 1970; Berkeley U. Mus., Cal., Jan. 1973; Detroit Art Inst., May 1973; Indianapolis Art Mus., Aug. 1973; Mus. of Mod. Art, Paris, Apr.-June 1974; Kunstmuseum, Dusseldorf, W. Germany, Sept. 1974; Kunsthalle, Baden-Baden, W. Germany, Oct. 1974; Kunstmuseum, Freiburg, W. Germany, Jan. 1976; Musee Reattu, Arles, France, July-Sept. 1976.

Honors: NEA Fellow, 1973; Outstanding Alumni Award, Temple U., 1975; Who's Who in Amer. Art; Intnl. Who's Who of Art; (Architectural Projects) N.Y.C. Subway Competition, 1st Prize, 1973; Janet Heidinger Kafka Prize for Excellence in Fiction by an American Woman. *Mailing address:* c/o Avon Bks., 959 Eighth Ave., N.Y., N.Y. 10019.

Writings:
Fiction

From Memphis and Peking, poems (N.Y., Random House, 1974)

Love Perfecting, poems (N.Y., Viking, 1979)

Sally Hemings, novel (N.Y., Viking, 1979; Avon, 1980)

Sidelights: Has lived in both Canada and Paris. (Travel) USSR, 1963; 1st American woman to visit mainland China, May 1965; State Department tour and lectures: Senegal, Mali, Ghana, Tunisia, Sierra Leone, 1975. Films: "Twentieth Century American Art," documentary, Sunrise Semester, WCBS-TV, 1972; "Five," film documentary (with Others), Seagram Company, Premiere at Museum of Modern Art, N.Y.C., 1971; "Conversations with Chase-Riboud" (in French), video tape, U.S. Information Service Center, Tunis.

Sources: Author information; *Books in Print*, 1980-81; *Ms.* Magazine, Oct. 1980.

CHEEK, DONALD K. Psychologist, Social Psychology Professor, Educator.
Born Mar. 24, 1930. *Education:* B.S. (Sociol.), Seton Hall U., 1953; M.S.W., Fordham Sch. of Soc. Serv., 1955; Ph.D. (Soc. Psychology), Temple U., 1971. *Family:* Wife; five children. *Career:* Deputy Probation Officer, L.A. County, 1956-61; Senior Psychiatric Soc. Worker, Atascadero State Hospital, 1961-65; Sch. system consultant, York, Pa., 1965-67; V. Pres., Student Affairs, Lincoln U., 1967-69; V. Pres., Dir. of Black Studies, Claremont Colleges, 1969-73; Counselor & Prof. of Soc. Psychology, Cal. Polytechnic, San Luis Obispo, Cal., 1973-present. *Honors:* Natl. Inst. of Mental Health Grad. Fellow; Founding Chairman, Minority Task Force of U. Counselors; Consultant & Trainer for Pa. Governor's Conf. on Race Relations. *Mailing address:* P.O. Box 1476, Atascadero, Cal. 93422.

Writings:
Nonfiction

Assertive Black ... Puzzled White (San Luis Obispo, Cal., Impact Pub., 1976)

Sources: Author information; *Books in Print*, 1980-81.

CHESNUTT, CHARLES WADDELL. Novelist, Short Story Writer.
Born in Cleveland, Ohio, in 1858. *Education:* Largely self-educated; studied law & passed Ohio State Bar (with unusually high score), never practiced. *Career:* Stenographer, Dow Jones, N.Y.; Commercial & Legal Stenographer. *Honors:* Spingarn Gold Medal from NAACP in 1928 for "pioneer work as a literary artist depicting the life & struggle of Americans of African descent." Died in 1932.

Writings:
Fiction

"The Goophered Grapevine," short story (Boston, *Atlantic Monthly*, 1887)

The Wife of His Youth, and Other Stories of the Color Line (Boston, Houghton, 1899; 1901)

The Conjure Woman, folk tales (Houghton, 1899, 1927)

The House behind the Cedars, novel (Houghton, 1900)

The Marrow of Tradition, novel (Houghton, 1901; Ann Arbor, Mich., U. Microfilms, 1967)

The Colonel's Dream, novel (N.Y., Doubleday, 1905)

Conjure Tales, retold by Ray Shepard (N.Y., Dutton, 1973)

Nonfiction

Frederick Douglass (Boston, Small, Maynard, 1899; 2nd ed., 1904; reprint, N.Y., Johnson, 1971)

The Short Fiction of Charles W. Chesnutt, ed. by Sylvia L. Rendor (Wash., D.C., Howard U. Press, 1974)

Sidelights: Charles Waddell Chesnutt was a brilliant, abundantly gifted man endowed with an inordinate capacity for hard work and self-discipline. Because of his physical appearance he could have chosen to pass for a white man, but because he did not deny his race, he made to American literature, through his fiction and occasional essays, a lasting contribution which helps to define abiding truths about the Afro-American experience.

"His most significant contribution to American literature may be the tales of *The Conjure Woman*, based on folklore which he heard in North Carolina." (*Black American Literature: Fiction*)

Sources: *Black American Literature: Fiction; Black Voices; Cavalcade; Forgotten Pages of American Literature.*

CHILDRESS, ALICE. Playwright, Actress, Director.
Born in Charleston, S.C., in 1920. *Education:* Studied acting at Amer. Negro Theatre; Radcliffe Inst. *Family:* Married Nathan Woodard; d. Jean Lee. *Career:* While acting and writing, worked as apprentice machinist, photo-negative retoucher, governess, saleslady, & insurance agent. Received Harvard U. appointment to Radcliffe Inst., 1966-68. *Honors:* Obie Award for best original off-Broadway play, 1955-56 season; was produced twice by BBC in London. *Mailing address:* c/o Flora Roberts, Inc., 116 E. 59th St., N.Y., N.Y. 10022.

Writings:
Fiction

Gold through the Trees, play (N.Y., Club Baron Theatre, 1952)

Just a Little Simple, play, 1953 — adaptation of Langston Hughes's *Simple Speaks His Mind* (N.Y., Club Baron Theatre, Sept. 1950)

Like One of the Family, short story (Brooklyn, N.Y., Independence, 1956)

Trouble in Mind, play (in Patterson's *Black Theater*)

Black Scenes: Collection of Scenes from Plays Written by Black People about Black Experience, ed. (Garden City, N.Y., Zenith, 1971)

Wedding Band, play (N.Y., Samuel French, 1973)

A Hero Ain't Nothin' But a Sandwich, juv. (N.Y., Coward, 1973)

When the Rattlesnake Sounds: A Play about Harriet Tubman, rev. ed. (Coward, 1975)

Let's Hear It for the Queen, juv. play (Coward, 1976)

A Short Walk, juv. (Coward, 1981)

Rainbow Jordan, juv. (N.Y., Putnam, 1981; Coward, 1981)

Sidelights: Notable off-Broadway productions: *Gold through the Trees, Just a Little Simple*, and *Trouble in Mind. Wedding Band* presented as Professional Theatre Production of 1966 at University of Michigan. (Ruby Dee, Abbey Lincoln, and Jack Harkins were in the cast.) (Author)

Childress, a feminist and black liberation playwright, focuses primarily on the rights of black women in her plays. She has supplied American theater with an impressive gallery of courageous female protagonists. All of Childress's plays portray survivors searching for joy and dignity in the midst of a hostile world. (*Dictionary of Literary Biography*)

Sources: Author information; *Best Short Stories by Negro Writers; Black Drama; Black Joy; Black Scenes; Books in Print*, 1981-82; *Who's Who in America*, 37th ed., 1972-73.

CHISHOLM, SHIRLEY ANITA. U.S. Congresswoman.
Born in Brooklyn, N.Y., Nov. 30, 1924. *Education:* B.A. (cum laude, Sociol.), Brooklyn Coll.;
M.A. (Childhood Educ.), Columbia U., 1952. *Family:* Married Conrad Q. Chisholm. *Career:* Dir.,
Friends Day Nursery, N.Y.C.; Dir., Hamilton-Madison Day Care Center, Manhattan (largest in
N.Y.C.); Educ. Consultant, Day Care Div., Bureau of Child Welfare, N.Y. State, 1959-64;
Assemblywoman, N.Y. State Legis., 1964-68; Congresswoman, N.Y., 12th Congressional Dist.,
1969-83. *Mailing address:* c/o Harper & Row, Pubs., Inc., 10 E. 53rd St., N.Y., N.Y. 10022.

Writings:
Nonfiction
Unbought and Unbossed, semi-autobiog. (Boston, Houghton Mifflin, 1970)

The Good Fight (N.Y., Harper, 1973)

Sidelights: "In 1968 she defeated James Farmer, former director of CORE, to win election to Congress from New York's 12th Congressional District ... becoming the first black woman in the United
States Congress." (Publisher)

Sources: *Black Politicians*; Pub. information.

CHRISMAN, ROBERT. Publisher, Poet, Essayist.
Career: Pub., *Black Scholar* mag.; Pres., Black World Found. *Mailing address:* c/o Black Scholar
Press, P.O. Box 7106, San Francisco, Cal. 94120.

Writings:
Fiction
Children of Empire: Poems (San Francisco, Black Scholar Press, 1980)

Nonfiction
Contemporary Black Thought. The Best from the Black Scholar, ed. with Nathan Hare (Indianapolis, Bobbs-Merrill, 1973)

Pan-Africanism, co-ed. (Bobbs-Merrill, 1974)

Sources: *Black Scholar*, July-Aug. 1980; *Books in Print*, 1978-79; Pub. information.

CHRISTIAN, BARBARA. Essayist, Afro-American Studies Professor.
Career: Assoc. Prof. & Chairperson, Afro-Amer. Studies, U. of Cal., Berkeley. *Mailing address:* c/o
Afro-Amer. Studies, U. of Cal., Berkeley, Berkeley, Cal. 94720.

Writings:
Nonfiction
Black Women Novelists: The Development of a Tradition, 1892-1976, essays (Contrib. in Afro-
Amer. Studies, no. 52, Westport, Conn., Greenwood Press, 1980)

Creative Escapes; Adventures in Writing for Grades 7-12 (Belmont, Cal., Fearson Teacher's Aides,
1980)

Sidelights: [In *Black Women Novelists*] the works of Paule Marshall, Toni Morrison and Alice Walker
are examined in detail. (*Freedomways*)

Sources: *Black Women Novelists; Books in Print*, 1980-81; *Freedomways*, vol. 20, no. 4, 1980.

CHURCHWELL, CHARLES DARRETT. Librarian, Academic Provost, Library Administrator,
Library School Dean.
Born in Dunnellon, Fla., Nov. 7, 1926. *Education:* B.S. (Math), Morehouse Coll., 1952; M.S. (Lib.
Sci.), Atlanta U., 1953; Ph.D. (Lib. Sci.), U. of Ill., 1966; N.Y.C. Coll.; Hunter Coll.; N.Y.U.

Family: Married Yvonne; d. Linda, d. Cynthia. *Career:* Lib. Sci. Instr., Prairie View A&M Coll., 1953-58; Ref. Librn., Circulation Dept., N.Y. Public Lib., 1959-61; Asst. Circulation Librn., U. of Ill., 1965-67; Asst. Dir., Lib., U. of Houston, 1967-69; Dir., Lib., Miami U., 1969-72; Assoc. Provost for Academic Serv., Miami U.; U. Librn., Brown U., Providence, R.I.; U. Librn., Wash. U., St. Louis, 1978- . *Mailing address:* Wash. U., Skinker & Lindell Blvds., St. Louis, Mo. 63130.

Writings:
Nonfiction

A History of Education for Librarianship, 1919-1939 (n.p., 1974)

Shaping of American Library Education (Chicago, ACRL Publ. in Librarianship, no. 36, ALA, 1975)

Sidelights: "He is responsible for all academic support services, interdisciplinary studies and international programs." (*1000 Successful Blacks*)

Sources: *Books in Print*, 1979-80; *1000 Successful Blacks; Wilson Library Bulletin*, June 1980.

CLARK, JOHN PEPPER. (Nigerian). Playwright, Poet, Teacher, Journalist.
Born in Kiagbodo, Ijaw country, Niger Delta, Western Nigeria, Apr. 6, 1935. *Education:* B.A. (Eng. with honors), U. of Ibadan, 1960; Princeton U. (1 yr.). *Career:* Founded poetry mag. while still in coll., *The Horn*; Nigerian Govt. Information Officer, 1960-61; Head of Features & Editorial Writer, *Daily Express*, Lagos, Nigeria, 1961-62; Lect. in Eng., U. of Lagos, 1964- . *Honors:* Recipient of Parvin Fellowship (Princeton U.). *Mailing address:* Dept. of Eng., U. of Lagos, Lagos, Nigeria.

Writings:
Fiction

Song of a Goat, play (Ibadan, Nigeria, Mbari Press, 1961)

Poems (Mbari Press, 1962)

Three Plays (London, Oxford U. Press, 1964)

America, Their America (London, Deutsch, 1964; N.Y., Africana, 1964; London, Heinemann, 1968; N.Y., Holmes & Meier, 1969)

A Reed in the Tide, poems (London, Longman's, 1965, 1967, 1970; Atlantic Highlands, N.J., Humanities, 1970)

Ozidi, play (Ibadan, Oxford U. Press, 1966)

Casualties: Poems 1966-68 (Africana, 1970; Longman's, 1970)

The Ozidi Saga, ed. (Oxford U. Press, 1979)

Nonfiction

The Example of Shakespeare, essays (N.Y., Harlow, Longman, 1970; Evanston, Ill., Northwestern U. Press, 1970)

Sidelights: John Pepper Clark did some research on Ijaw epic at the Institute of African Studies at the University of Ibadan. (*African Authors*)
Two of his films are: *The Ozidi of Atazi* and *The Ghost Town*.

Sources: *African Authors; Books in Print*, 1980-81; *Writers Directory*, 1980-82.

CLARK, KENNETH BANCROFT. Psychologist, Civil Rights Leader.
Born in Panama Canal Zone, July 24, 1914. *Education:* N.Y. public schs.; B.S., Howard U., 1935, M.S., 1936; Ph.D., Columbia U., 1940. *Family:* Married Mamie Phipps, Apr. 14, 1938; d. Kate Miriam, son Hilton Bancroft. *Career:* Staff, Psychology Dept., City Coll. of N.Y., 1942- , Prof., 1960- ; Pres., Metropolitan Applied Res. Center; Res. Dir., Northside Center; Res. Dir., Northside Center for Child Development (which he & wife founded), 1946- ; Soc. Sci. Consultant, Legal &

Educ. Div., NAACP, 1950- ; Advisory Com. on Foreign Affairs Personnel, 1961-62; Founder, Chairman of Bd., Harlem Youth Opportunity Unlimited (HARYOU), war-on-poverty program; Visiting Prof.: Columbia U., U. of Cal., Berkeley, Harvard U. *Honors:* Spingarn Medal, NAACP, 1961; Kirt Lewin Memorial Award, 1966; 1st recipient, Distinguished Scholar Award, Center for Safety, N.Y., 1968; elected N.Y. Bd. of Regents, 1966; Pres., Amer. Psychological Assn., 1970; Coll. Bd., Medal for Distinguished Serv. to Educ., 1980. *Mailing address:* MARC, 60 E. 86th St., N.Y., N.Y. 10028.

Writings:
Nonfiction

Prejudice and Your Child (Boston, Beacon, 1955; 2nd ed., 1963)

The Negro Protest: James Baldwin, Malcolm X, Martin Luther King, Jr. Talk with Kenneth B. Clark (Beacon, 1963)

Dark Ghetto: Dilemmas of Social Power (N.Y., Harper, 1965)

Negro American, with Talcott Parsons (Boston, Houghton Mifflin, 1966)

A Relevant War against Poverty, with Jeannette Hopkins (Harper, 1969)

Racism and American Education, with Harold Howe (Harper, 1970)

A Possible Reality: A Design for the Attainment of High Academic Achievement for Inner City Students (N.Y., Emerson Hall, 1972)

Pathos of Power (Harper, 1974)

The Nineteen Eighties: Prologue and Prospect, with John H. Franklin (Wash., D.C., Joint Center Polit. Studies, 1981)

Sidelights: Was research psychologist on staff of Gunnar Myrdal study which resulted in *An American Dilemma*. The 1954 Supreme Court decision against separate but equal schools is based largely on his studies showing that segregation causes psychological damage in children. Indeed, it is impossible to record the efforts of the many individuals who have labored to advance racial and human equality without listing the work of Kenneth Bancroft Clark. (*Who's Who in America*)

Sources: *Current Biography*, 1964; *Negro Handbook; Who's Who in America*, 37th ed., 1976-77.

CLARKE, AUSTIN CHESTERFIELD, (Barbadian), Novelist, Short Story Writer, Free lance Writer. Born in Barbados, July 16, 1934. *Education:* Harrison Coll., Barbados; Oxford & Cambridge Higher Certificate, 1950; further study, Trinity Coll., U. of Toronto. *Family:* Married Betty Joyce (registered nurse), Sept. 14, 1958; d. Janice, d. Loretta, son Mphahlele. *Career:* Producer & Free-lance Writer, Canadian Broadcasting Corp., 1963- ; Visiting Prof., Afro-Amer. Lit. & Creative Writing, Yale U., & Jacob Ziskind Visiting Lect. Brandeis U., Waltham, Mass. *Honors:* Can. Council Senior Arts Fellow; U. of W. Ontario President's Medal for best story, 1965; Belmont Short Story Award for "Stations in His Circle." *Mailing address:* c/o Harold Ober Associates, 40 E. 49th St., N.Y., N.Y. 10017.

Writings:
Fiction

The Eye of the Storm, short story (Boston, Little, Brown, 1958)

The Land of the Living, short story (London, Faber, 1961)

The Survivors of the Crossing, novel (Toronto, McClelland & Stewart, 1964)

Amongst Thistles and Thorns, novel (McClelland, 1965)

The Meeting Point, novel (Toronto, Macmillan, 1967)

Storm of Fortune, novel (Little, Brown, 1973)

When He Was Free and Young and He Used to Wear Silks, short stories (Little, Brown, 1973)

The Impuritans, novel (Atlantic Highlands, N.J., Humanities, 1974)

The Bigger Light, a Novel (Little, Brown, 1975)

The Third Kiss, novel (Humanities, 1976)

The Prime Minister, a Novel (Don Mills, Ontario, Gen. Pub., 1977)

The Singing Men of Cashel, novel (Humanities, 1980)

Nonfiction

Growing Up Stupid under the Union Jack: A Memoir (McClelland, 1980)

Sidelights: It is felt that Clarke's achievement is substantial, that he has made a valuable contribution to Black literature.

Sources: *Books in Print*, Supplement, 1975-76; *Contemporary Novelists*, 2nd ed., 1976; *Writers Directory*, 1982-84.

CLARKE, JOHN HENRIK. Editor, Essayist, Biographer.
Born in Union Springs, Ala., Jan. 1, 1915. *Education:* (High sch.), Columbus, Ga. & N.Y.C.; N.Y.U., 1948-52; New Sch. for Soc. Res., 1956-58; U. of Ibadan, Nigeria; U. of Ghana, Accra. *Family:* Married Eugenia Evans; d. Nzingha, son Sonni Kojo. *Career:* Co-founder & Assoc. Ed., *Harlem Quarterly*; Book Review Ed., *Negro Hist. Bull.*; Feature Writer, *Pittsburgh Courier & Ghana Evening News*; Dir., 1st U.S. African Heritage Exposition; Ed., *African Heritage*, 1959; Assoc. Ed., *Freedomways*, 1962- ; (column) "African World Bookshelf," distributed in U.S. & abroad by Assoc. Negro Press & World Mutual Exchange, Intnl. Feature; Tchr., African & Afro-Amer. Hist., Malverne High Sch., Long Island, N.Y.; Dir., Heritage Teaching Program, HARYOU-ACT, 1964-69; Tchr., African & Afro-Amer. Hist., Headstart Training Program, N.Y.U.; Spec. Consultant & Coordinator, CBS-TV Ser., "Black Heritage: The History of the Afro-Americans"; Prof., Dept. of Black & Puerto Rican Studies, Hunter Coll., 1969. *Honors:* Carter G. Woodson Award for Creative Contrib. in Editing, 1968; Natra Citation for Meritorious Achievement in Educ. TV, 1969; Carter G. Woodson Award for Distinguished & Outstanding Work in Teaching of Hist., 1971; L.H.D., U. of Denver, 1970. *Mailing address:* 223 W. 137th St., N.Y., N.Y. 10030.

Writings:
Fiction

Rebellion in Rhyme (Prairie City, Ill., Decker, 1948)

American Negro Short Stories, anthology (N.Y., Hill & Wang, 1966)

Nonfiction

The Lives of Great African Chiefs (Pittsburgh, Pittsburgh Courier Pub., 1958)

Harlem, a Community in Transition (N.Y., Citadel, 1964, 1969; paper also)

Harlem, U.S.A.; The Story of a City within a City (Berlin, Seven Seas, 1964; N.Y., Collier, 1971)

William Styron's Nat Turner: Ten Black Writers Respond, ed. essays (Boston, Beacon, 1968; paper also)

Malcolm X, the Man and His Times (N.Y., Macmillan, 1969)

Slave Trade and Slavery, ed. with Vincent Harding (N.Y., Holt, 1970)

Black Titan; W. E. B. DuBois (Beacon, 1970)

Marcus Garvey and the Vision of Africa, ed. with Amy Jacques Garvey (N.Y., Random House, 1974)

Black Families in the American Economy, ed. (Wash., D.C., Community Council, 1974)

The Prescriber (N.Y., Brit. Bk. Centre, 1975)

Sidelights: Clarke helped develop African Study Center, New School for Social Research. He traveled through 11 countries in West Africa and lectured extensively on African history, 1958-59. (Author)

Sources: *American Negro Short Stories*; Author information; *Best Short Stories; Black Joy; Black Voices; Books in Print*, Supplement, 1975-76; *Freedomways*, vol. 19, 1979, vol. 20, 1980; *Poetry of Black America; Who's Who in America*, 37th ed., 1972-73.

CLEAVER, (LEROY) ELDRIDGE. Activist, Essayist.
Born in Wabbaseka, Ark., in 1935. *Education:* Self-educated. *Family:* Married Kathleen Neal, Dec. 17, 1967; son Antonio, daughter. *Career:* Asst. Ed., *Ramparts*; spokesman for Black Panthers, Minister of Information; Lect. *Mailing address:* c/o Random House, Inc., 201 E. 50th St., N.Y., N.Y. 10022.

Writings:
Nonfiction
Eldridge Cleaver (N.Y., Random, 1967)

Soul on Ice, essays (N.Y., McGraw-Hill, 1968; Dell, 1968; paper also)

Eldridge Cleaver; Post Prison Writings and Speeches, essays, ed. by Robert Scher (Random, 1969)

War Within: Violence or Nonviolence in the Black Revolution, with Others (N.Y., Sheed & Ward, 1971)

Soul on Fire, essays (Waco, Tex., Word Bks., 1978)

Sidelights: Obtained high school diploma, read omnivorously, converted to Black Muslim faith and became ardent follower of Malcolm X while in prison. *Soul on Ice* was written in Folsom Prison (1957-66). Became candidate of Peace and Freedom Party after Governor Reagan tried to stop his lectures on racism at University of California, Berkeley (1968). Lectureship became a major issue in California U.S. Senatorial election. When ordered to return to jail after having been paroled, went underground and fled the country. (*Current Biography*)
Subsequently lived in several countries, including Cuba, Algeria, and France. Returned to United States in fall of 1976.

Sources: *Books in Print*, 1979-80; *Cavalcade; Current Biography*, 1970; *Negro Almanac; Who's Who in America*, 37th ed., 1972-73.

CLIFT, VIRGIL ALFRED. Education Professor, Editor.
Born in Princeton, Ind., May 1, 1912. *Education:* B.A., Ind. U., 1934; M.A., Ind. State Coll., 1939; Ph.D., Ohio State U., 1944. *Family:* Married Nasrine Adibe (tchr.); d. Najiva Adra. *Career:* Prof., Educ., Rust Coll., Holly Springs, Miss., 1938-39; Prof., N.C. A&T Coll., Greensboro, 1939-48; Prof., Educ., Morgan State Coll., Baltimore, 1948-63; Prof., Educ., N.Y.U., 1963-76; Fulbright Lect., Pakistan, 1954-55; Dir., Tchr. Educ., Kingdom of Libya, 1956-58; Distinguished Visiting Prof., Educ., U. of Neb., Omaha. *Honors:* Senior Ed., 16th Yearbook, John Dewey Soc.; Distinguished Alumni Award, Ind. State U., Terre Haute, 1976. *Mailing address:* c/o McGraw-Hill Bk. Co., 1221 Ave. of the Americas, N.Y., N.Y. 10020.

Writings:
Nonfiction
Negro Education in America: Its Adequacy, Problems and Needs (N.Y., Harper, 1962)

Encyclopedia of Black America, ed. with W. Augustus Low (N.Y., McGraw-Hill, 1981)

Sources: *Books in Print*, 1981-82; *Encyclopedia of Black America*.

CLIFTON, LUCILLE T. Poet, Juvenile Writer.
Born in Depew, N.Y., June 27, 1936. *Education:* Howard U.; Fredonia State Tchrs. Coll. *Family:*

Married Fred J. Clifton (Author & Educator); son Sidney, d. Fredrica, son Channing, d. Gillian, son Graham, d. Alexia. *Career:* Poetry readings at colleges & children's bk. fairs; Poet-in-Residence, Coppin State Coll., Baltimore, 1971- . *Honors:* Discovery Award, YMHA, 1969; NEA Awards, 1970, 1972. *Mailing address:* 2605 Talbot Rd., Baltimore, Md. 21216.

Writings:
Fiction

Good Times, poems (N.Y., Random House, 1969)

Some of the Days of Everett Anderson, juv. (N.Y., Holt, 1970)

The Black B.C.'s, juv. (N.Y., Dutton, 1970)

Everett Anderson's Christmas Coming, juv. (Holt, 1971; paper also)

Good News about the Earth; New Poems (Random House, 1972)

All Us Come Cross the Water, juv. (Holt, 1973)

The Boy Who Didn't Believe in Spring, juv. (Dutton, 1973, 1978)

Good, Says Jerome, juv. (Dutton, 1973)

Don't You Remember?, juv. (Dutton, 1973)

An Ordinary Woman, poems (Random House, 1974)

The Times They Used to Be, juv. (Holt, 1974; N.Y., Dell, 1976)

Everett Anderson's Year, juv. (Holt, 1974)

My Brother Fine with Me, juv. (Holt, 1975)

Three Wishes, juv. (N.Y., Viking, 1976)

El Niño Que No Creia En la Primavera. Spanish edition of *The Boy Who Didn't Believe in Spring*, juv., transl. by Alma F. Ada (Dutton, 1976)

Everett Anderson's Friend, juv. (Holt, 1976)

Generations, A Memoir, juv. (Random, 1976)

Amifika, juv. (Dutton, 1977)

Everett Anderson's 1-2-3, juv. (Holt, 1977)

Everett Anderson's Nine Month Long (Holt, 1978)

The Lucky Stone, juv. (N.Y., Delacorte, 1979)

Two-Headed Woman, juv. (Amherst, Mass., U. of Mass. Press, 1980)

Sonora Beautiful, juv. (Dutton, 1981)

Sources: Author information; *Black Books Bulletin; Books in Print*, 1978-79; *Poetry of Black America.*

COBBS, PRICE M. Psychiatrist.

Education: M.D., Meharry Medical Coll., Nashville, Tenn.; Langley Porter Neuropsychiatric Inst., San Francisco. *Career:* Private practice, Psychiatry, San Francisco; Asst. Prof., Psychiatry, San Francisco Medical Center, U. of Cal. *Mailing address:* c/o Basic Bks., Inc., 10 E. 53rd St., N.Y., N.Y. 10022.

Writings:
Nonfiction

Black Rage, with William H. Grier (N.Y., Basic Bks., 1968, 1980; N.Y., Bantam, 1969)

The Jesus Bag, psychology, with William H. Grier (N.Y., McGraw-Hill, 1971)

Source: Pub. information.

COLEMAN, WANDA. Poet.
Career: Medical file clerk; typist; scriptwriter; editor. *Mailing address:* c/o Black Sparrow Press, P.O. Box 3993, Santa Barbara, Cal. 93105.

Writings:
Fiction
Mad Dog Black Lady, poems (Santa Barbara, Cal., Black Sparrow Press, 1979)

Images, poems (Black Sparrow, 1983)

Sidelights: Has been active in writing, producing, and acting of plays in cooperation with Pasadena Museum of Art, University of California at Los Angeles, Stanford University, and University of Southern California. Wanda Coleman has participated in State of California Poets-in-the-Schools. She has also published fiction. (*Mad Dog Black Lady*)

Sources: *Books in Print*, 1983-84; *Los Angeles Times*, Calendar, Jan. 31, 1982; *Mad Dog Black Lady; Obras* (1980).

COLLIER, EUGENIA. English Professor, Essayist.
Born in Baltimore, Md., Apr. 6, 1928. *Education:* B.A. (magna cum laude, Eng.), Howard U., 1948; M.A. (Amer. Lit.), Columbia U., 1950; Doctoral Studies (Amer. Studies), U. of Md. *Family:* Div.; son Charles Maceo, son Robert Nelson, son Phillip Gilles. *Career:* Case Worker, Baltimore Dept. of Public Welfare, 1950-55; Tchr., Eng., Morgan State Coll., 1955-66; Prof., Eng., Community Coll. of Baltimore, 1966- ; Visiting Prof., Eng., S. Ill. U., Carbondale, summer 1970; Afro-Amer. Studies, Atlanta U., summer 1973; Consultant, Workshop, Center for African & Afro-Amer. Studies, 1969; Consultant, Call & Response Workshop, Karamu House, 1970; Mem., Middle States Evaluation Team for Lehigh Community Coll., Schnechtsville, Pa., 1970; Consultant: Bond Humanities Fair, Atlanta, 1973-74; Black Studies Com., Coll. Lang. Assn.; Pine Manor Jr. Coll., Mass., since 1970; elected to Community Coll. of Baltimore Senate Executive Com., 1970. *Honors:* Story "Marigolds" won Gwendolyn Brooks Award for fiction, 1969; selected for *Outstanding Educators of America*, 1972-74. *Mailing address:* 2608 Chelsea Terrace, Baltimore, Md. 21216.

Writings:
Fiction
Afro-American Writing: An Anthology of Prose and Poetry, with Richard A. Long (N.Y., N.Y.U. Press, 1972)

Nonfiction
Impressions in Asphalt: Images of Urban America, essays with Ruthe T. Sheffey (N.Y., Scribner's, 1969)

A Bridge to Saying It Well, with Edward I. Meyers & Others (Springfield, Va., Norvec Co., 1970)

Source: Author information.

COLTER, CYRUS. State Commissioner of Commerce, Novelist, Short Story Writer.
Born in Noblesville, Ind., Jan. 8, 1910. *Education:* Youngstown U., Ohio; Ohio State U.; LL.B., Kent Coll. of Law, Chicago, 1940. *Family:* Married Imogene. *Career:* YMCA, Youngstown, Ohio, 1932-34; YMCA, Chicago, 1934-40; Deputy Collector of Internal Revenue, 1940-42; Captain, U.S. Army, 1942-46; Attorney, Chicago, 1946- ; Asst. Commissioner, Ill. Commerce Com. (Public Utilities), 1950, Commissioner, 1951- ; Chairman, Ill. Emergency Transport Bd. *Honors:* U. of Iowa Sch. of Letters Award for Short Fiction, 1970; Friends of Lit. Prize, 1971; Patron Saints Award of Soc. of Midland Authors, 1971; Prof., Emeritus, Chester D. Tripp Distinguished Chair, Humanities, Northwestern U. *Mailing address:* Popular Library, 600 3rd Ave., N.Y., N.Y. 10016.

Writings:
Fiction
Beach Umbrella, short stories (Iowa City, U. of Iowa, 1970; Chicago, Swallow, 1970, 1971)

The Rivers of Eros, novel (Swallow, 1972; N.Y., Popular Lib., 1979)

The Hippodrome, novel (Swallow, 1973; Popular Lib., 1976)

Night Studies, a Novel (Swallow, 1979)

Sidelights: His stories and novels have been translated into German, Italian, Hungarian, Japanese, and others. His most popular work is "The Beach Umbrella." Novelist Vance Bourjaily, one of the judges for the Iowa School of Letters Award, described Colter as "what a writer is and always has been—a man with stories to tell, a milieu to reveal and people he cares about." (*New Black Voices*)

Sources: *Afro-American Literature: Fiction; Best Short Stories by Negro Writers; Books in Print, 1978-79; New Black Voices; Night Studies; Soon, One Morning.*

CONE, JAMES H. Theologian, Theology Professor.
Born Aug. 5, 1938. *Education:* Shorter Coll., Ark.; B.A., Philander Smith Coll., Little Rock, Ark., 1958; B.D., Garrett Theol. Sem., 1961; M.A., Northwestern U., 1963; Ph.D., 1965. *Family:* Married Rose Hampton; son Michael Lawrence, son Charles Pierson. *Career:* Asst. Prof., Philander Smith Coll., 1964-66; Asst. Prof., Adrian Coll., Mich., 1966-69; Visiting Assoc. Prof. of Relig., Barnard Coll., 1969-71; Visiting Prof. of Theol., Drew U., N.J., 1973; Lect., Systematic Theol., Woodstock Coll., 1971-73; Union Theol. Sem., N.Y.C.: Asst. Prof., 1969-70, Assoc. Prof., 1970-73, Prof., 1973- . *Honors:* Rockefeller Found. res. grant, 1973-74; Contrib. Ed., *Christianity and Crisis*; Ed. Advisory Bd., *Renewal*; Consultant, *Scholastic's Black Culture Program. Mailing address:* c/o Union Theol. Sem., 3041 Broadway, N.Y., N.Y. 10027.

Writings:
Nonfiction
Black Theology and Black Power (N.Y., Seabury, 1969)

A Black Theology of Liberation (Phila., Lippincott, 1970)

The Spirituals and the Blues (Seabury, 1972; reprint, Westport, Conn., Greenwood, 1980)

God of the Oppressed (Seabury, 1975; Cincinnati, Ohio, Crossroad Bks., 1978)

The Social Context of Theology (Seabury, 1975)

Black Theology: A Documentary History, 1966-1979, ed. with Gayraud S. Wilmore (Maryknoll, N.Y., Orbis, 1979)

Sidelights: Has lectured at many colleges and theological seminaries all over the United States. Has lectured abroad at Dar es Salaam and Chateau De Bossey, Tanzania; Geneva, Switzerland; Turin and Milan, Italy; Mainz and Tubingen, Germany. (Author)

Sources: Author information; *Black Theology and Black Power.*

CONYERS, JAMES E. Sociologist, Sociology Professor.
Born in Sumter, S.C., Mar. 6, 1932. *Education:* A.B., Morehouse Coll., 1954; M.A., Atlanta U., 1956; Ph.D., Wash. State U., 1962. *Family:* Married Jean Farris, June 4, 1956 (div.); children: Judith Yolande, James E., Jr., Jennifer June. *Career:* Tchr., LeMoyne Coll., Memphis, 1955-56; Teaching Asst., Ind. State U., 1962-64; Assoc. Prof., Atlanta U., 1964-68; Prof., Indiana State U., 1968- . *Honors:* Pres., Assn. of Soc. & Behavioral Sci., 1970-71; Natl. Chairman, Caucus of Black Sociol. in Amer., 1973-74; Planning Grant, Russell Sage Found., to study Black elected officials—granted and financed for $64,643, 1971-74. On Ed. Bds. of *Phylon, Journal of Afro-Amer. Issues, Journal of Soc. & Behavioral Sci.*; Field Reader, Bureau of Res., U.S. Office of Educ., 1966-69. Prepared questions for Grad. Record Examination in Sociol., Educ. Testing Serv., Princeton, N.J., 1972. *Mailing address:* c/o Dept. of Sociol., Indiana State U., Terre Haute, Ind. 47809.

Writings:
Nonfiction

Sociology for the Seventies, ed. with Morris Medley (N.Y., Wiley, 1972)

Black Elected Officials, with Walter L. Wallace (N.Y., Russell Sage Found., 1976)

Sidelights: " 'Roster of Black Doctorates in Sociology', kept up to date since 1963 and widely requested." (Author)

Source: Author information.

COOK, MERCER. Language Professor, U.S. Ambassador.
Born in Wash., D.C., Mar. 30, 1903. *Education:* B.A., Amherst Coll., 1925, LL.D., 1965; Tchrs. Diploma, U. of Paris, 1926; M.A., Brown U., 1931, Ph.D., 1936, LL.D., 1970. *Family:* Married Vashti Smith, Aug. 31, 1929; son Mercer, son Jacques. *Career:* Asst. prof., Romance Lang., Howard U., 1927-36, Prof., 1945-60; Prof., French, Atlanta U., 1936-43; Prof., Eng., U. of Haiti, 1943-45; Foreign Rep. Amer. Soc. of African Culture, 1958-60; Dir., African program, Congress Cultural Freedom, 1960-61; U.S. Ambassador to Niger, 1961-64, to Senegal & Gambia, 1965-66; Prof., Head of Romance Lang., Howard U., 1970. *Honors:* Phi Beta Kappa; decoration from Haitian Govt., 1945, from Nigerian Govt., 1964, from Senegal, 1966; Palmer Académiques (France). *Mailing address:* 4811 Blagden Ave., N.W., Wash., D.C. 20001.

Writings:
Nonfiction

Le Noir, Morceaux Chaisis de Vingt-neuf Français Cèlèbres (N.Y., Amer. Bk., 1934)

Portraits Americains (Lexington, Mass., Heath, 1939)

Five French Negro Authors, criticism (Wash., D.C., Assoc. Pub., 1943)

Haitian American Anthology; Haitian Readings from American Authors, ed. (Port-au-Prince, Haiti, Imprimerie de l'Etat, 1944)

Education in Haiti (Wash., D.C., Fed. Security Agency, 1948; 1952)

Introduction to Haiti, Selections and Commentaries, ed. (Wash., D.C., Pan Amer. Union, 1951)

African Socialism, transl. of Senghor's work (n.p., 1959)

African Nations and World Solidarity, transl. of Mamadou Dia's work (N.Y., Praeger, 1961)

Militant Black Writer in Africa and the United States, criticism, with Stephen E. Henderson (Madison, U. of Wis. Press, 1969)

The African Origin of Civilization: Myth or Reality, ed. & transl. of Cheikh A. Diop's work (Westport, Conn., Lawrence Hill, 1974)

Sources: *Books in Print*, Supplement, 1975-76; *Negro Handbook; Negroes in Public Affairs and Government*.

COOMBS, ORDE. Essayist, Editor.
Born in St. Vincent, W. Indies. *Education:* B.A., Yale U., 1965; grad. study, Clare Coll., Cambridge, 1965-66; M.A., N.Y.U., 1971. *Career:* Producer of documentaries on W. Indian culture, 1958-61; Assoc. Ed., Doubleday, N.Y.C., 1966-68; Senior Public Relations Spec., 1968-69; Senior Ed., McCall Pub. Co., N.Y.C., 1969. *Mailing address:* c/o Doubleday & Co., Inc., 501 Franklin Ave., Garden City, N.Y. 11530.

Writings:
Fiction

We Speak as Liberators: Young Black Poets, an Anthology, ed. (N.Y., Dodd, 1970)

What We Must See: Young Black Storytellers, an Anthology, ed. (Dodd, 1971)

Nonfiction

Eastern Religions in the Electric Age, essays with John H. Garabedian (N.Y., Grosset & Dunlap, 1969)

Do You See My Love for You Growing?, essays (Dodd, 1972)

Is Massa Day Dead? Black Moods in the Caribbean, ed. (Garden City, N.Y., Anchor, 1974)

Drums of Life (Anchor, 1974)

Sleep Late with Your Dreams (Dodd, 1974)

Sources: *Books in Print*, 1982-83; *Contemporary Authors*, vols. 73-76, 1978.

CORNISH, SAMUEL E. Abolitionist, Editor, Publisher.
Born free in Del. in 1790. *Education:* Migrated to Phila., attended the Free African Sch. Settled in N.Y. in 1822. *Career:* Organized 1st Black Presby. congregation, N.Y.; with John B. Russwurm founded 1st Negro newspaper, *Freedom's Journal*, 1827; also associated with the *Weekly Advocate* (later *Colored American*). Died in 1859.

Writings:
Nonfiction

Freedom's Journal, newspaper (N.Y., 1827-)

The Colonization Scheme Considered, in its rejection by the Colored People—in its Tendency to Uphold Caste—in its Unfitness for Christianizing and Civilizing the Aborigines of Africa, and for Putting a Stop to the African Slave Trade, with Theodore S. Wright (Newark, N.J., A. Guest, 1840)

Sidelights: "*Freedom's Journal* played a major role in shaping a social and economic philosophy for the Negro. ... James McCune Smith, Alexander Crummell, Martin R. Delany and David Ruggles used it to express their opinions. Cornish, as the editor, fought relentlessly for full rights of citizenship and equality for the Negro. Cornish, a trustee of the free schools for Negroes in New York, energetically promoted higher education for Negroes. ... he was an active member of the American Anti-Slavery Society." (*Historical Negro Biographies*)

"Cornish was responsible, in part, for the Negro press becoming identified with the role of protest.... 'Let there be no compromise,' he said, 'but as though born free and equal, let us contend for all the rights guaranteed by the Constitution of our native country.' " (*Negro Handbook*)

Sources: *Historical Negro Biographies; Negro Handbook*.

CORNISH, SAM(UEL) JAMES. Poet, Creative Writing Teacher, Juvenile Writer.
Born in Baltimore, Md., Dec. 22, 1938. *Education:* Northwestern U. *Family:* Married Jean Faxon, Sept. 1967. *Career:* Writing spec., Enoch Pratt Free Lib., Baltimore, 1965-66; Ed., Hist., Assoc. Press; Tchr., Creative Writing, Highland schs., Roxbury, Mass., 1969- ; Ed., *Mimeo* (poetry mag.); Staff Advisor & Consultant, children's writing, Educ. Development Center, Open Educ. Follow Through Project, Newton, Mass., 1973-78; Consultant to Central Atlantic Regional Educ. Laboratories. *Honors:* Poetry Prize, Humanities Inst., Coppin State Coll., 1968; grant, NEA, 1968. *Mailing address:* 50 Monastery Rd., Brighton, Mass. 02135.

Writings:
Fiction

In This Corner: Sam Cornish and Verses (n.p., Fleming McCallister Press, 1964)

People beneath the Window, poems (Baltimore, Sacco Pub., 1965?)

Winters, poems (Cambridge, Mass., Sans Souci Press, 1967)

The Living Underground: An Anthology of Contemporary American Poetry, ed. with Hugh Fox (E. Lansing, Mich., Ghost Dance, 1969)

Chicory: Young Voices from the Black Ghetto, poetry & prose collection, ed. with Lucian Dixon (N.Y., Assoc. Press, 1969)

Generations, poems (Boston, Beacon, 1971)

Streets, poems (Chicago, Third World, 1973)

Sometimes; Ten Poems (Cambridge, Mass., Pym-Randall Press, 1973)

Sam's World, poems (Wash., D.C., Decatur House, 1978)

Nonfiction
Your Hand in Mine, juv. (N.Y., Harcourt, 1970)

Grandmother's Pictures, juv. (Lenox, Mass., Bookstore Press, 1974)

Harriet Tubman, juv. (Third World, n.d.)

Walking the Streets with Mississippi John Hurt, juv. (Scarsdale, N.Y., Bradbury Press, 1978)

Sidelights: Cornish has been influenced by Robert Lowell, T. S. Eliot, and LeRoi Jones.

Sources: *Black Fire; Books in Print*, 1978-79; *New Black Poetry; Poetry of Black America.*

CORTEZ, JAYNE. Poet, Lecturer.
Born in Ariz., May 10, 1936. Reared in Watts. *Family:* Son, Denardo Coleman. *Career:* Guest lect.: Queens Coll., N.Y.; Wesleyan U., Conn.; Claremont Colleges, Cal.; Ohio U., Athens; U. of Conn., Storrs; Creighton U., Omaha, Neb.; Tex. S. U., Houston; Rutgers U., New Brunswick, N.J.; Richmond Coll., Staten Island, N.Y.; Antioch Coll., Yellow Springs, Ohio; Sacramento State Coll., Cal.; Hunter Coll., N.Y.C.; Cape Coast U., Ghana; U. of Ibadan, Nigeria; Chicago Art Inst.; Brooklyn Coll., N.Y.; Princeton U., N.J.; Howard U., Wash., D.C.; Amherst Coll., Mass.; Sarah Lawrence Coll., Bronxville, N.Y.; & Others. *Honors:* Rockefeller Found. Grant for res. & travel, 1970; Community Action Program's N.Y. State Council on the Arts for Poetry, 1973. *Mailing address:* c/o Bola Press, P.O. Box 96, Village Station, N.Y. 10014.

Writings:
Fiction
Pisstained Stairs and the Monkey Man's Wares, poems (N.Y., Phrasetext, 1969)

Festivals and Funerals, poems (N.Y., Cortez, 1971)

Scarifications, poems (Cortez, 1973; N.Y., Bola Press, 1978)

Mouth on Paper, poems (Bola Press, 1977)

Sources: Author information; *Books in Print*, 1978-79; *New Black Voices; Poetry of Black America.*

COTTER, JOSEPH SEAMON, SR. Poet.
Born in Bardstown, Ky., in 1861. *Education:* Self-educated. *Career:* Sch. tchr., Louisville, Ky.; prize fighter. *Honors:* Won *Opportunity* prize contest for "Tragedy of Pete." Deceased.

Writings.
Fiction
A Rhyming (Louisville, Ky., New South, 1895)

Links of Friendship, poems (Louisville, Bradley & Gilbert, 1898)

A White Song and a Black One, poems (Bradley & Gilbert, 1909)

Negro Tales, poems (N.Y., Cosmopolitan, 1912)

Collected Poems of Joseph S. Cotter, Sr. (N.Y., Harrison, 1938)

Sequel to the "Pied Piper of Hamelin," and Other Poems (Harrison, 1939)

Caleb, the Degenerate; A Play in Four Acts (Harrison, 1940)

Sources: *Afro-American Writers; Anthology of American Negro Literature; Caroling Dusk; Negro Caravan.*

COUNTER, S. ALLEN. Neurobiologist, Biological Science Professor.
Career: Biological Sci. Prof., Harvard U.; Res. Fellow & Guest Scientist, Karolinska-Novel Inst., Stockholm. *Mailing address:* c/o Mass. Inst. of Technology, 28 Carleton St., Cambridge, Mass. 02142.

Writings:
Nonfiction

I Sought My Brother: An Afro-American Reunion, with David L. Evans (Cambridge, M.I.T. Press, 1981)

Sidelights: A unique photo-essay on an Afro-American people who have established their own indigenous African society, deep in the jungles of Suriname, South America. (*I Sought My Brother*)

Sources: *Books in Print*, 1981-82; *I Sought My Brother; In Black and White*, 3rd ed., 1980.

COX, OLIVER CROMWELL. Sociology Professor, Sociologist.
Born in Trinidad, Brit. W. Indies, Aug. 25, 1901. *Education:* Bachelor of Library Science, Northwestern U., 1928; M.A., 1932, Ph.D., 1938, U. of Chicago. *Career:* Prof., Econ., Wiley Coll., 1938-44; Prof., Sociol., Tuskegee Inst., 1944-49; Prof., Sociol., Lincoln U., Mo., 1949- . *Honors:* LL.D., Wiley Coll., 1945; George Washington Carver Award for *Caste, Class and Race*, 1948. Died in 1974.

Writings:
Nonfiction

Caste, Class and Race (Garden City, N.Y., Doubleday, 1948; N.Y., Monthly Review Press, 1959, 1970)

Foundations of Capitalism (N.Y., Philosophical Lib., 1959)

Capitalism and American Leadership (Philosophical Lib., 1962)

Capitalism as a System (Monthly Review Press, 1964)

Race Relations: Elements and Social Dynamics (Detroit, Wayne State U. Press, 1976)

Sources: *Authors and Writers Who's Who*, 6th ed., 1971; *Books in Print*, 1980-81.

CRUMMELL, ALEXANDER. Minister, Missionary.
Born in N.Y.C., Mar. 3, 1819. *Education:* Oneida Inst. (sem.), Boston; Queens Coll., Cambridge (grad. 1853). *Career:* Ordained 1844; solicited funds in Eng.; lived in Liberia for 20 yrs.; Rector, St. Luke's Protestant Episcopal Church, Wash., D.C., 1873-94; leader in founding Amer. Negro Acad., 1897. Died in 1898.

Writings:
Nonfiction

The Man: The Hero: The Christian: A Eulogy on the Life and Character of Thomas Clarkson: Delivered in the City of New York, December, 1846 (N.Y., Egbert, Hovey & King, 1847)

The Relations and Duties of Free Colored Men in America to Africa (Hartford, Lockwood, 1861)

The Future of Africa: Being Addresses, Sermons, etc., etc., Delivered in the Republic of Liberia (N.Y., Scribner, 1862)

The Greatness of Christ and Other Sermons (N.Y., Whittaker, 1882)

Africa and America: Addresses and Discourses (Springfield, Mass., Wiley, 1891)

Sidelights: An outstanding spokesman and missionary with a global vision, he went to England to solicit funds and stayed to attend Cambridge. Crummell went to Liberia because of ill health. When he returned to America to stay, he was placed in charge of St. Mary's Mission, Washington, D.C. (*Negro Author in America*)

Sources: *Early Negro American Writers; Great Negroes Past and Present; Men of Mark; Negro Author in America; Negro Genius.*

CRUSE, HAROLD. Researcher, Free-lance Writer, Teacher.
Born in Petersburg, Va.; reared in N.Y.C. *Education:* Brooklyn Film Inst. *Career:* Free-lance Writer, 1940- ; Tchr. of Black Hist. in free schs., researcher, writer, & polit. activist in N.Y.C., 1946-67; assisted LeRoi Jones in establishing Jones' Black Arts Theatre & Sch., N.Y.C., 1965-66; film & drama critic, N.Y. Labor Press; Visiting Prof., Hist., Afro-Amer. Studies, U. of Mich., Ann Arbor, 1968- ; Lect. at universities including U. of London, Harvard U., U. of Wales, & Yale U. *Mailing address:* c/o William Morrow & Co., Inc., 105 Madison Ave., N.Y., N.Y. 10016.

Writings:
Nonfiction

The Crisis of the Negro Intellectual (N.Y., Morrow, 1967)

Rebellion or Revolution? (Morrow, 1968)

Marxism and the Negro Struggle; Articles, with Others (N.Y., Merit, 1968)

Sidelights: "Christopher Lasch called *The Crisis of the Negro Intellectual* a 'most penetrating study' and one that will 'survive as a monument of historical analysis' when 'all the manifestoes and polemics of the Sixties are forgotten.' " (*Contemporary Authors*)

Sources: *Black American Writer; Black Fire; Contemporary Authors*, vols. 77-80, 1979.

CULLEN, COUNTEE PORTER. Poet, Editor, Teacher.
Born in N.Y.C., May 30, 1903. *Education:* B.A., N.Y.U. (Phi Beta Kappa), 1925; M.A., Harvard U., 1926. *Family:* Married 1st Yolande DuBois (d. of W. E. B. DuBois), Apr. 1928; div. 1929; married 2nd Ida M. Cullen. *Career.* Asst. Ed., *Opportunity*, Lit. Ed., *Crisis*; French Tchr., N.Y.C., 1934-45. *Honors: Color* received Harmon Gold Award; N.Y.U. awarded the Witter Bynner Prize for Poetry; Guggenheim Found. Fellow, France (where he edited *Caroling Dusk* and wrote *The Black Christ*). Died Jan. 9, 1946.

Writings:
Fiction
Color, poems (N.Y., Harper, 1925)

Caroling Dusk, anthology (Harper, 1927)

Copper Sun, poems (Harper, 1927; Ann Arbor, Mich., U. Microfilms, 1967)

The Ballad of the Brown Girl; An Old Ballad Retold, poems (Harper, 1927)

The Black Christ; And Other Poems (Harper, 1929)

One Way to Heaven, novel (Harper, 1932)

The Medea and Other Poems (Harper, 1935)

The Lost Zoo, juv. (Harper, 1940)

My Lives and How I Lost Them; A Rhyme for the Young, but Not Too Young, by Christopher Cat, fiction (autobiog.) (Harper, 1942)

St. Louis Woman, musical, with Arna Bontemps, based on Bontemps' novel *God Sends Sunday*— became popular Broadway musical (Martin Beck Theatre, 1946)

On These I Stand; An Anthology of the Best Poems (Harper, 1947)

Sidelights: "Countee Cullen began writing ... much under the influence of Keats and Tennyson, and showing his partiality towards Millay, Housman and E. A. Robinson as well. He has said, 'Most things I write I do for the sheer love of the music in them. Somehow I find my poetry of itself treating of the Negro, of his joys and sorrows—mostly of the latter—and of the heights and depths of emotion I feel as a Negro.' " (*Twentieth Century Authors*)

"A classicist ... and inherently a romantic ... acknowledging Keats as a central influence, Countee Cullen was a central figure of the Negro Renaissance." (*Black Voices*)

Sources: *Black Poets of the United States; Black Voices; Book of American Negro Poetry; Cavalcade; Negro Almanac; Twentieth Century Authors.*

CUNNINGHAM, WILLIAM D. Librarian, Library Science Professor.
Born in Kansas City, Mo., Aug. 9, 1937. *Education:* B.A., U. of Kan., 1959; M.L.S., Ph.D., U. of Tex., 1962. *Family:* Married Mary Carson; d. Crystal. *Career:* Chief, Library Services, Fed. Aviation Agency, Kan. City, Mo., 1965-67; Dir., Adult Services, Topeka, Kan. Public Lib., 1967-68; Regional Program Officer, U.S. Office of Educ., 1968-71; Dir. of U. Libraries, Howard U., 1971-73; Asst. Prof., Coll. of Lib. & Information Services, U. of Md., Coll. Park, 1973- . V. Pres., Soul Journey Enterprises, Inc., Wash., D.C. *Honors:* Citation, Fed. Aviation Agency, 1966; U.S. Office of Educ., 1970. *Mailing address:* c/o Coll. of Lib. & Information Services, U. of Md., Coll. Park, Md. 20742.

Writings:
Nonfiction

Black Guide to Washington, with Ron Powell (Wash., D.C., Black Guide, 1975)

Affirmative Action and Libraries; Problems in Library Services and the Disadvantaged (Black Guide, 1976)

Blacks in the Performing Arts, with Marilyn Mahanand (Hamden, Conn., Shoe String, 1981)

Sources: *Books in Print*, 1980-81; Pub. information; *Who's Who among Black Americans*, 3rd ed., 1980-81.

DABNEY, WENDELL PHILLIPS. Editor.
Born in Richmond, Va., Nov. 4, 1865. *Education:* Oberlin Coll. *Career:* Asst. City Paymaster, Cincinnati, Ohio, 1897-1923; Ed., *Union* (for nearly 50 yrs.). Died in 1952.

Writings:
Nonfiction

Cincinnati's Colored Citizens: Historical, Sociological and Biographical (Cincinnati, Dabney Pub. Co., 1926; reprint, Westport, Conn., Greenwood, 1967; reprint, Westport, Conn., Negro Universities Press, 1967; reprint, N.Y., Basic Afro-Amer. Lib., Johnson Reprint, 1970)

Maggie L. Walker and the I.O. of Saint Luke; The Woman and Her Work (Dabney, 1927)

Sources: *Books in Print*, 1980-81; *Ohio Authors and Their Books.*

DADIÉ, BERNARD. (Ivorian). Novelist, Playwright, Poet.
Born in Assinie, Ivory Coast, in 1916. A Brafe of the Ashanti Clan. *Education:* Catholic Sch., Grand Bassam; L'Ecole Primaire; Supérieure, Bingerville, Ecole Normale, William Ponty, Gorée, Senegal (Diplôme de Commis d'Administration), 1939. *Career:* IFAN (Institut Francais d'Afrique Noir), Dakar; Officer, Ivory Coast Information Serv., 1947-60; Dir., Fine Arts & Res., Ivorian Govt.; Dir. of Cultural Affairs, Ivory Coast; Writer; Tchr.; Founder, Natl. Drama Studio—all Ivory Coast. *Mailing address:* c/o Africana Pub. Co., 101 Fifth Ave., N.Y., N.Y. 10003.

Writings:
(Partial Listing—English Only)
Fiction

(Included in) *The African Assertion*, poems, ed. by Austin J. Shelton (N.Y., Odyssey Press, 1968)

Climbié, novel, transl. by Karen C. Chapman (N.Y., Africana, 1971; London, Heinemann, 1971)

Sidelights: The Brafe people were a group of the Agni Ashante who had emigrated to the Ivory Coast from the Old Gold Coast between 1620 and 1730. (*African Authors*)

Speaking of his stories, proverbs and legends, Dadié states, "these ... are our museums, monuments and street names—our only books, in fact. This is why they have such an important place in our daily lives." (*A Reader's Guide to African Literature*)

He is quoted in *Afrique*, no. 43, 1964, as saying, "Poets must not allow themselves the luxury of ever praising the joys of life when there are genuine problems of making a living which must be solved." (*African Authors*)

Sources: *African Authors; Books in Print*, 1978-79, 1980-81; *A Reader's Guide to African Literature.*

DAMAS, LÉON GONTRAN. [Pseud.: **Lionel George Andre Cabassou**]. (French Guianan). Poet, Editor, Researcher, UNESCO Consultant, Literature Professor.
Born in Cayenne (French Guiana), Mar. 28, 1912. *Education:* Lycée Schoelcher, Fort-de-France, Martinique; Law & Oriental Lang., Paris. *Career:* Ed., Overseas Dept., Editions Fasquelles; Researcher, African Culture, Caribbean & Brazil; Rep., Sociétié Africanine de Culture (SAC), UNESCO; Prof., Lit., Fed. City Coll., Wash., D.C.; Visiting Lect., African Lit. & Negritude, Inst. of African Studies, Howard U. (7 yrs.). *Honors:* Officer of Natl. Order, Honneur et Mérite of Republic of Haiti. Died in Wash., D.C., Jan. 22, 1978.

Writings:
(Partial Listing—English Only)
Fiction

African Songs of Love, War, Grief and Abuse, transl. by Miriam Koskhand & Ulli Beier (Ibadan, Nigeria, Mbari, 1961)

Sidelights: "Damas was introduced to Leopold Sedar Senghor from Africa by Césaire and the trio launched L'Etudiant Noir (1934), and with it the cultural movement internationally known as NEGRITUDE." (*Caribbean Writers*)

Damas represented Ouyana for a brief period in the French National Assembly in the 1950s.
Damas's verse employs the repetitive, circular pattern of much African dance and song.

Sources: *Black Writers in French; Caribbean Writers; Modern Black Writers; Resistance and Caribbean Literature.*

DANCE, DARYL CUMBER. English Professor, Folklorist.
Born in Richmond, Va., Jan. 17, 1938. *Education:* A.B., M.A., Va. State Coll.; Ph.D., U. of Va. *Family:* Married, three children. *Career:* Assoc. Prof., Eng., Va. Commonwealth U. *Honors:* Danforth Found. Fellow; Ford Found. Fellow; NEH Fellow; Fulbright Fellow *Mailing address:* 1701 Littleton Blvd., Richmond, Va. 23228.

Writings:
Fiction

Shuckin' and Jivin': Folklore from Contemporary Black Americans (Bloomington, Ind. U. Press, 1978; Midland Bks., no. 265, Ind. U. Press, 1981)

Sources: Author information; *Books in Print*, 1981-82.

DANIELS, DOUGLAS HENRY. Historian.
Born Oct. 12, 1943. *Education:* B.A., U. of Chicago; M.A., Ph.D., U. of Cal., Berkeley. *Family:* Married Doris Daniels; two children. *Career:* Asst. Prof., Hist. & Ethnic Studies, U. of Tex., Austin; Asst. Prof., Hist. & Black Studies, U. of Cal., Santa Barbara (present). *Honors:* NEH Fellow; Danforth Found. Fellow; Ford Found. Fellow; John Hay Whitney Found. Fellow; Natl. Defense Educ. Act Fellow. *Mailing address:* 7377A Davenport Road, Goleta, Cal. 93017.

Writings:
Nonfiction

Umoja (Phila., Temple U. Press, 1976)

Pioneer Urbanites: A Social and Cultural History of Black San Francisco (Temple U. Press, 1980)

Images of Our Roots: Photographic, Oral, and Written Documents of the San Francisco Bay Area's Black Pioneers, 1850-1930 (Austin, Tex., Stevenson Press, Natl. Hist. Ser., 1981)

Sources: Author information; *Books in Print*, 1980-81.

DANNER, MARGARET ESSE. Poet.
Born in Chicago, Ill., Jan. 12, 1915. *Education:* YMCA Coll. & Roosevelt U., Chicago; Loyola U., Chicago. *Family:* Married 1st Cordell Strickland; married 2nd Otto Cunningham; d. Naomi (Mrs. Sterling M. Washington). *Career:* Asst. Ed., *Poetry* mag. (Chicago), 1951-55; Poet-in-Residence: Wayne State U.; Va. Union U. (1968-69); LeMoyne-Owen Coll., Memphis, Tenn. Founder, Boone House (Center for the Arts), Detroit; Founder, Nologonyu's, Chicago. *Honors:* John Hay Whitney Found. Fellow (poetry)—Senegal, Paris, 1966; Poetry Workshop, Midwestern Writers Conf., 1945; Women's Auxiliary, Afro-Amer. Interest grant, 1950; African Studies Assn., 1950; Amer. Soc. of African Culture, 1960; African Studies Assn., 1961; Poets in Concert. *Mailing address:* 626 E. 102nd Pl., Chicago, Ill. 60628.

Writings:
Fiction

Impressions of African Art Forms, poems (Detroit, Broadside, 1960, 1962)

To Flower, poems (n.p., Hemphill, 1963)

Poem: Counterpoem, with Dudley Randall (Broadside, 1966)

Brass Horses, poems ed. (Richmond, Va. Union U. Press, 1968)

The Iron Lace, poems (Millbrook, N.Y., Kriya Press, 1968)

Regroup, poems (Va. Union U. Press, 1969)

The Down of a Thistle, poems (Waukesha, Wis., Country Beautiful, 1976)

Sidelights: In 1959 came to Detroit, and later founded Boone House, where a group of poets including Gloria Davis, Oliver LaGrone, Edward Simpkins, Alma Parks, Harold Lawrence, Naomi Madgett, Dudley Randall, Betty Ford and Joyce Whitsett met together and gave poetry readings. (*For Malcolm*)

Sources: *Afro-American Writing; Books in Print*, 1978-79; *Ebony*, Mar. 1974; *For Malcolm; Poetry of Black America.*

DATHORNE, OSCAR RONALD. (Guyanan). Novelist, Essayist, Anthologist, English Professor.
Born in Georgetown, Guyana, Nov. 19, 1934. *Education:* B.A., 1958, M.A., 1960, Ph.D., 1966, Sheffield U., Yorkshire, Eng.; Certificate Diploma, Educ., London U. *Family:* Married Hildegard Ostermaier, 1959; two children. *Career:* Assoc. Prof., Ahmadu Bello U., Zaria, Nigeria, 1959-63, & U. of Ibadan, 1963-66; UNESCO Consultant to Govt. of Sierra Leone, 1967-68; Prof., Eng., Njala U. Coll., U. of Sierra Leone, 1968-69; Prof. of African Lit., Howard U., 1970; Prof., Afro-Amer. Lit., U. of Wis., Madison, 1970-71; Prof., Eng. & Black Lit., Ohio State U., 1971-74; Prof., Eng.,

Fla. Intnl. U., 1974-75; Prof., Eng. & Black Lit., Ohio State U., 1975-77; Dir., Afro-Amer. Studies & Prof., Eng., U. of Miami, Coral Gables, Fla., since 1977; Co-ed., *Black Orpheus* mag., Ibadan, Nigeria. *Mailing address:* 8904 Friedberg bei Augsburg, Lullerstrasse 2, Germany.

Writings:
Fiction

Dumplings in the Soup, novel (London, Cassell, 1963)

The Scholar Man, novel (Cassell, 1964)

One Iota of Difference, novel (Cassell, n.d.)

Young Commonwealth Poets '65, anthology, ed. with Others (London, Heinemann, 1965)

Caribbean Narrative, anthology, ed. (Heinemann, 1966)

Caribbean Verse, ed. with W. Feuser (Heinemann, 1967)

Africa in Prose, ed. with Willfried Feuser (Baltimore, Penguin, 1969)

African Poetry for Schools and Colleges (London, Macmillan, 1969)

Nonfiction

The Black Mind: A History of African Literature (Minneapolis, U. of Minn. Press, 1974; London, Oxford U. Press, 1975)

An A to Z of African Writers (Heinemann, 1974)

African Literature in the Twentieth Century (U. of Minn. Press, 1975)

Dark Ancestor, essays (Baton Rouge, La. State U. Press, 1979)

Sources: *Complete Caribbeana, 1900-1975; Contemporary Novelists*, 2nd ed., 1976; *West Indian Literature; Writers Directory*, 1982-84.

DAVIS, ALLISON. Anthropologist, Psychologist, Education Professor.
Born in Wash., D.C., in 1902. *Education:* B.A., 1924; M.A., Harvard U., 1925; London Sch. of Econ.; U. of Chicago, Ph.D., 1942. *Career:* Prof., Educ., U. of Chicago, 1939-? *Honors:* 1st John Dewey Distinguished Serv. Prof., U. of Chicago; Fellow, Amer. Acad. of Arts & Scis. (1st elected from field of Educ.); Fellow, Center for Advanced Study in Behavioral Scis. *Mailing address:* c/o U. of Chicago, Grad. Sch. of Educ., 5835 Kimbark Ave., Chicago, Ill. 60637.

Writings:
Nonfiction

Children of Bondage, with John Dollard (Wash., D.C., Amer. Council on Educ., 1940)

Deep South, with Elizabeth Davis & Burleigh & Mary Gardener (Chicago, U. of Chicago Press, 1941, 1947)

Father of the Man, with Robert J. Havighurst (Boston, Houghton Mifflin, 1947)

Social-Class Influences upon Learning (Cambridge, Harvard U. Press, 1948, 1955)

Intelligence and Cultural Differences, with Kenneth Eells & Others (U. of Chicago Press, 1951)

Davis-Eells Test of General Intelligence, with Kenneth Eells (Yonkers on Hudson, N.Y., World Book Co., 1953)

Psychology of the Child in the Middle Class (Pittsburgh, U. of Pittsburgh Press, 1960)

Relationships between Achievement in High School, College, and Occupation: A Followup Study (Wash., D.C., U.S. Office of Educ., 1963)

Sources: *Negro Caravan; Living Black American Authors.*

DAVIS, ANGELA YVONNE. Political Activist.
Born in Birmingham, Ala., Jan. 26, 1944. *Education:* B.A. (French Lit., magna cum laude), Brandeis U., 1965; Johann Wolfgang von Goethe U., Frankfurt, Germany (Philosophy); M.A. (Philosophy), U. of Cal., San Diego, 1968; further study. *Family:* Married. *Career:* Organizer, Black Student Council, U. of Cal., San Diego; San Diego Black Conf.; SNCC, L.A.; Che-Lumumba Club, Black Panthers; Communist Party (all L.A.); Instr., Philosophy Dept., UCLA; Soledad Brothers Defense Com.; Lect. *Mailing address:* c/o Communist Party, U.S.A., 23 West 26th St., N.Y., N.Y. 10001.

Writings:
Nonfiction

If They Come in the Morning, essays (N.Y., Okpaku, 1971; N.Y., NAL, 1971)

Angela Davis, an Autobiography (N.Y., Random House, 1974)

Women, Race and Class (Random House, 1981)

Sidelights: "In June 1972 ... Miss Davis was aquitted of charges of kidnapping, murder, and conspiracy in connection with a 1970 shoot-out at the Marin County [California] Courthouse....
"On the intellectual level [her radicalization] moved forward under the tutelage of aging political philosopher Herbert Marcuse at Brandeis in 1964-65, Marcuse's last year on the faculty before his mandatory retirement.
" ... after intense soul-searching, she formally joined the Communist Party on June 22, 1968.
"To effect social and economic change, Miss Davis favors a black-white coalition, rather than black separatism, and a strategy that would 'take over, not destroy, the production apparatus.' " (*Current Biography*)

Sources: *Angela Davis, an Autobiography; Current Biography*, 1972.

DAVIS, ARTHUR P. Journalist, Critic, Editor, English Professor.
Born in Hampton, Va., in 1904. *Education:* Howard U.; Columbia Coll., N.Y. (Phi Beta Kappa), 1927; Columbia U., M.A., 1929, Ph.D., 1942. *Career:* Prof., Eng., N.C. Coll., Durham, 1927-28; Prof., Eng., Va. Union U., Richmond, 1929-44; Prof., Howard U., 1944-69; Columnist, "With a Grain of Salt," *Journal and Guide* newspaper (Norfolk, Va.), 1933-50. *Mailing address:* c/o Howard U. Press, 2900 Van Ness St., N.W., Wash., D.C. 20008.

Writings:
Nonfiction

The Negro Caravan, criticism, ed. with Sterling Brown & Ulysses Lee (N.Y., Dryden, 1941)

Isaac Watts: His Life and Works (Dryden, 1943)

Cavalcade: Negro American Writers from 1760 to the Present, ed. with Saunders Redding (Boston, Houghton, 1971)

From the Dark Tower, Afro-American Writers, 1900-1960 (Cambridge, Mass., Harvard U. Press, 1974; Wash., D.C., Howard U. Press, 1981)

The New Negro Renaissance, an Anthology (N.Y., Holt, 1975)

Sidelights: His *Isaac Watts* was hailed by the *Times Literary Supplement* (London) for its "careful scholarship and style." (*Black Voices*)

Sources: *Black Voices; Books in Print*, 1982-83; *Cavalcade*.

DAVIS, CHARLES T. English Professor, Critic.
Born at Hampton Inst., Va., in 1918. *Education:* B.A. (Phi Beta Kappa), Dartmouth Coll., 1939; M.A., U. of Chicago, 1942; Ph.D., N.Y.U. *Career:* Visiting Prof.: Harvard, Rutgers, Bryn Mawr; Tchr.: N.Y.U. & Princeton; Prof., Eng., Pa. State U.; Chairman, Afro-Amer. Studies, Yale U., 1972-81; Ser. Ed., G. K. Hall Ref. Bks. Died in 1981.

Writings:
Nonfiction

Black Is the Color of the Cosmos: Essays on Afro-American Literature and Culture, 1942-1981, ed. by Henry L. Gates, Jr. (N.Y., Garland, 1982)

Richard Wright, a Primary Bibliography, with Michel Fabre (Boston, G. K. Hall, 1982)

The Slave's Narrative, ed. with Henry L. Gates, Jr. (N.Y., Oxford U. Press, 1983)

Sources: *On Being Black*; Pub. information.

DAVIS, FRANK MARSHALL. Poet, Editor.
Born in Ark. City, Kan., in 1905. *Education:* Kan. State Coll. (Journalism), 3 yrs. *Career:* Helped start *Atlanta Daily World*, 1931; Executive Ed., Assoc. Negro Press, Chicago, 1935-40; Executive Ed., *Chicago Star*, 1946-48. *Honors:* Awarded 1st Sigma Chi Perpetual Scholarship ever granted at Kan. State Coll.; Julius Rosenwald Fund Fellow in Poetry, 1937. *Mailing address:* c/o Dorrance & Co., Cricket Terrace Center, Ardmore, Pa. 19003.

Writings:
Fiction

Black Man's Verse (Chicago, Black Cat, 1935; Ann Arbor, Mich., U. Microfilms, 1976)

I Am the American Negro, poems (Black Cat, 1937; facsimile, N.Y., Arno, Black Heritage Lib. Collection, n.d.)

47th Street, poems (Prairie City, Ill., Decker, 1948; U. Microfilms, 1976)

Precision Bridge—A Bid for Every Occasion: From Alpha to Omega, poems (Ardmore, Pa., Dorrance, 1976)

Sources: *Books in Print*, 1978-79; *Encyclopedia of Black America; Negro Caravan*.

DAVIS, GEORGE B. Businessman, Novelist, Journalist, Educator.
Born in Shepherdstown, W. Va., Nov. 29, 1939. *Education:* B.A., Colgate U., 1961; M.F.A., Columbia U., 1971. *Family:* Married Mary Cornelius (secy.), Aug. 31, 1965; children: Pamela, George. *Career:* Captain, U.S. Air Force, 1961-60; Staff Writer/Editor, *Washington Post*, 1960-69; Deskman/Editor, *New York Times*, 1969-70; Tchr., Writing Workshops, Columbia U. & Greenhaven Prison; Co-founder & Pres., Black Swan Communications; Asst. Prof., Bronx Community Coll. of City of N.Y., 1974- . *Honors:* (Military) Air Medal. (Other) Awards from N.Y. State Council on the Arts; America the Beautiful Fund; & NEH. *Mailing address:* c/o Doubleday & Co., Inc., 501 Franklin Ave., Garden City, N.Y. 11530.

Writings:
Fiction

Coming Home, novel (N.Y., Dell, 1971; N.Y., Random House, 1972)

Love, Black Love, novel (Garden City, N.Y., Anchor, 1978)

Nonfiction

Black Life in Corporate America: Swimming in the Mainstream, with Glegg Watson (N.Y., Doubleday, 1982)

Sidelights: Black Swan Communications is a design and marketing firm for books, art objects, and creative leisure products.

Sources: *Black Life in Corporate America; Who's Who among Black Americans*, 1975-76.

DAVIS, LENWOOD G. Bibliographer, Teacher.
Born in Beaufort, N.C., Feb. 22, 1939. *Education:* B.A., 1961, M.A., 1968 (both Hist.), N.C. Central U., Durham; Inst. for African Studies, U. of Ghana, summer 1969; Program on African Studies, Northwestern U., summer 1970; Ph.D. (Hist.), Carnegie-Mellon U., 1979. *Family:* Married 1st Glenda F. Manning, 1967; married 2nd Phyliss Bell, 1974; d. Tatia Mia. *Career:* Instr., Hist., Livingston Coll., Salisbury, N.C., 1968-70; Acting Dir., Black Studies Center & Instr., Hist., Portland State U., Ore., 1971-74; Founder and Pres., Oregon Afro-Amer. Historical Society, Portland, 1972; Associated Ed., *Northwest Journal of African and Black American Studies*, 1973-74; Asst. Prof., African Hist., Black Studies Dept., Ohio State U., 1974-77; Asst. Prof., Black Amer. Studies, U. of Del., Newark, 1977-78; Asst. Prof., Hist., Winston Salem State U., 1978- . *Honors:* Piedmont U. Center Scholars Fellow, U. of Ghana; HEW Fellow for Coll. Tchrs., Northwestern U.; Certificate of Merit from Dictionary of Intnl. Biography for Distinguished Serv. in Educ., 1972. *Mailing address:* c/o Greenwood Press, 88 Post Rd. W., P.O. Box 5007, Westport, Conn. 06881.

Writings:
  Nonfiction
  I Have a Dream: The Life and Times of Martin Luther King, Jr. (Westport, Conn., Negro Universities Press, 1969)

  The Black Woman in American Society: A Selected Annotated Bibliography (Boston, G. K. Hall, 1975)

  A History of Tuberculosis in the Black Community: A Working Bibliography (Monticello, Ill., Council of Planning Libraries, 1975)

  The Black Family in the United States: A Selected Annotated Bibliography (Westport, Conn., Greenwood, 1978)

  Sickle Cell Anemia: A Selected Annotated Bibliography (Newark, Del., Natl. Black Bibliographic & Res. Center, 1978)

  Black Artists in the United States: An Annotated Bibliography of Books, Articles and Dissertations on Black Artists, Seventeen Seventy-Nine to Nineteen Seventy-Nine (Greenwood, 1980)

  Marcus Garvey: An Annotated Bibliography (Greenwood, 1980)

  The Black Aged in the United States: An Annotated Bibliography (Greenwood, 1980)

  Black Athletes in the United States: A Bibliography of Books, Articles, Autobiographies and Biographies on Black Professional Athletes in the United States, 1880 to 1981 (Greenwood, 1981)

Sources: Author information; *Books in Print*, 1980-81, 1982-83.

DAVIS, NOLAN. Novelist, Screenwriter, Composer.
Born in Kan. City, Mo., July 23, 1942. *Education:* Bishop Lillie High Sch.; U.S. Navy Journalist Sch., 1960; San Diego Evening Coll., 1964-65; Stanford U., 1968. *Family:* Married Carol Christian (artist); son Arian, d. Pelia. *Career:* Biochemist; undertaker's apprentice; sailor; janitor; Staff Writer, San Diego *Evening Tribune*, *Newsweek*; Writer & Prod., NBC, ABC, CBS. *Honors:* Attended Stanford U. on communications fellowship. *Mailing address:* 3532 6th Ave., L.A., Cal. 90018.

Writings:
  Fiction
  Six Black Horses, novel (N.Y., Putnam, 1971)

  "Storyline," television script (ABC, 1971)

  "Further Than the Pulpit," television script (NBC, 1972)

  "The Jazz Show with Billy Eckstine," television script (NBC, 1972)

  "Ironside," television script (Universal, 1974)

"Six Black Horses," screenplay (1975)

"The Fighting 99th," screenplay (1975)

"Sanford and Son," television script (NBC, 1975)

Nonfiction
O'Grady, biog. (L.A., Tarcher/Hawthorn, 1974)

Sidelights: Made "The Good News Blues," recording (Crossover Records, 1975). Traveled throughout United States and Mexico in relation to his writing. Co-founder, SHARC International (comprises several subsidiaries dealing with film, records, music publishing and finance). (Author)

Sources: Author information; *Six Black Horses.*

DAVIS, OSSIE. Actor, Playwright, Director.
Born in Cogdell, Ga., Dec. 18, 1917. *Education:* Central High Sch., Waycross, Ga.; Howard U., 1935-38; Columbia U. *Family:* Married Ruby Dee (actress), 1948; d. Nora, son Guy, d. La Verne. *Career:* Began stage career as mem. of Rose McClendon Players, 1941. Broadway debut in title role of *Jeb* (1946). Other roles on Broadway include Gabriel in *Green Pastures*, Walter Lee Younger in *A Raisin in the Sun*, and the title role in his own *Purlie Victorious*. Film debut in *No Way Out* (1950). Directed film *Black Girl*. Acted in: *Anna Lucasta* (1948); *The Wisteria Trees* (1950); *No Time for Sergeants* (1956); Movies: *The Joe Louis Story* (1953); *The Cardinal* (1963). *Mailing address:* P.O. Box 1318, New Rochelle, N.Y. 10802.

Writings:
Fiction
Goldbrickers of 1944, play

Alice in Wonder, one-act play (1953)

Purlie Victorious, play (N.Y., French, 1961)

Curtain Call, Mr. Aldridge, Sir, play (1963) (in Reardon & Pauley, *The Black Teacher and the Dramatic Arts*)

"School Teacher," of *East Side, West Side*, television ser. (1963)

Cotton Comes to Harlem, co-authored film play (n p , United Artists, 1969)

Last Dance for Sybil, play

Purlie, musical (French, 1971)

Escape to Freedom: A Play about Young Frederick Douglass, juv. (N.Y., Viking, 1976)

Sidelights: "In 1961 he wrote and played the title role in *Purlie Victorious* which opened at the Court Theatre on September 28, 1961, and ran for 261 performances. Appearing opposite him was his wife, Ruby Dee, in the role of Lutiebelle....
"*Purlie Victorious* is a deft comic 'put-down' and 'put-on' of both black and white.... Davis has constructed a brilliant comedy containing the most inventive humor of any modern American play." (*Black Drama*)
Davis has performed feature roles on television in *The Defenders, The Nurses*, and *Emperor Jones*. (*Current Biography*)

Sources: *Afro-American Literature: Drama; Black Drama; Black Scenes; Cavalcade; Current Biography*, 1969; *Books in Print*, 1979-80.

DELANY, MARTIN R. Physician, Soldier, Author, Publisher.
Born in Charleston, W. Va., May 6, 1812 (son of free Blacks). *Education:* Attended sch. in Chambersburgh, Pa. (and received training & inspiration in the Thelan Lit. Soc. in Pittsburgh). Began study of medicine at Harvard U. Medical Sch. in 1849. *Family:* Married Katherine A. Richards

in 1843. *Career:* Began publ. of *The Mystery* (newspaper) in 1843; assoc. with Frederick Douglass on *The North Star*, 1847-49; serv. with cholera epidemic in Pittsburgh, 1854; became interested in colonization of Amer. slaves (visiting Africa & Eng.); assisted in recruiting Negro soldiers for Civil War & served as examining physician in Chicago; received commission as Major, Feb. 8, 1865; served in Freedman's Bureau as Custom-House Inspector & as Trial Justice; nominated for Lieutenant Governor of S.C. (defeated). Died in Xenia, Ohio, in 1885.

Writings:
Fiction

Blake; or the Huts of America, novel in seven installments (N.Y., Anglo-African Magazine, Jan.-Aug., 1859; Boston, Beacon, 1970)

Nonfiction

The Condition, Elevation, Emigration, and Destiny of the Colored People of the United States, Politically Considered (Phila., Author, 1852; Ann Arbor, Mich., U. Microfilms, 1969)

Official Report of the Niger Valley Exploring Party (N.Y., T. Hamilton, 1861)

Principia of Ethnology: The Origin of Races and Color (Phila., Harper, 1879)

Sidelights: Writer, doctor, self-taught scholar in an era when most Negroes were barred from learned professions, Delany's vigorous personality and inquiring mind often led him to diverge from the mainstream of his contemporaries. It is precisely these qualities, together with his early awareness of his family history, that contributed to his stature as a pioneering black nationalist and Africanist. (*Dictionary of American Negro Biography*)

Sources: *Early Negro American Writers; Historical Negro Biographies; History of the Negro in Medicine; Men of Mark; Negro Builders and Heroes; Negro Caravan; Negro Genius.*

DELANY, SAMUEL RAY, JR. Science Fiction Writer.
Born in N.Y.C., Apr. 1, 1942. *Education:* City Coll. of City of N.Y., 1960, 1962-63. *Family:* Married Marilyn Hacker (poet), Aug. 24, 1961 (separated 1974); d. Iva Alyxander. *Career:* Writer; Butler Prof. of Eng., SUNY at Buffalo, 1975; Senior Fellow, Center for Twentieth Century Studies, U. of Wis., Milwaukee, 1977. *Honors:* Nebula Award, Science Fiction Writers of America, 1966, 1967, 1969; Hugo Award, World Science Conventions. *Mailing address:* 184 W. 82nd St., N.Y., N.Y. 10024.

Writings:
Fiction

Captives of the Flame, sci. fiction, 1st of trilogy (N.Y., Ace, 1963; N.Y., Avon, 1963)

The Towers of Toron, sci. fiction, 2nd of trilogy (Avon, 1964; Ace, 1977)

The Ballad of Beta 2, sci. fiction (Boston, Gregg, 1965, 1977; Ace, 1965)

The City of a Thousand Suns, sci. fiction, 3rd in trilogy (Ace, 1965, 1977)

Babel-17, sci. fiction (Ace, 1966; Gregg, 1966, 1976)

Empire Star, sci. fiction (Gregg, 1966; Ace, 1966, 1977)

The Fall of the Towers, sci. fiction, trilogy (Ace, 1966, 1972, 1977)

The Einstein Intersection, sci. fiction, ed., Lester Del Rey (Ace, 1967, 1976; N.Y., Garland, 1975)

The Jewels of Aptor, sci. fiction (Gregg, 1967, 1976; Ace, 1972, 1978)

Nova, sci. fiction (Gregg, 1968, 1977; N.Y., Doubleday, 1968; N.Y., Bantam, 1968, 1975)

Quark, no. 1, anthology, ed. (N.Y., Popular Lib., 1970)

Quark, no. 2, anthology, ed. with Marilyn Hacker (Popular Lib., 1971)

Quark, no. 3, & no. 4, anthology, ed. (Popular Lib., 1971)

Driftglass, sci. fiction (Garden City, N.Y., Doubleday, 1971; Gregg, 1971, 1977)

Ten Tales of Speculative Fiction (N.Y., New Amer. Lib., 1971)

The Tides of Lust, sci. fiction (N.Y., Lancer Bks., 1973)

Dhalgren, sci. fiction (Bantam, 1974; Gregg, 1977)

Seventeen, sci. fiction (Ace, 1975)

Triton, sci. fiction (Bantam, 1976; Gregg, 1977)

Out of the Dead City, sci. fiction (Ace, 1977)

The American Shore, sci. fiction (Dragon, 1978)

The Jewel-Hinged Jaw, sci. fiction (Berkley, 1978)

Heavenly Breakfast: An Essay on the Winter of Love (Bantam, 1979)

Tales of Neveryon, sci. fiction (Bantam, 1979)

Fundamental Disch, sci. fiction, with Others (Bantam, 1980)

Nebula Winners Thirteen (Harper, 1980; Bantam, 1981)

Distant Stars, sci. fiction, ed. Byron Preiss (Bantam, 1981)

Nonfiction

The Jewel-Hinged Jaw: Notes on the Language of Science Fiction (N.Y., Berkley, 1977; Elizabethtown, N.Y., Dragon, 1977)

The Science Fiction of Samuel R. Delany (Gregg, 1977)

The Technological Imagination: Theories and Fictions, with Others (N.Y., Coda Press, 1980)

Sidelights: "Perhaps more than any other science-fiction writer, Delany has produced critical articles concerned with theoretical analyses of science fiction as a genre, using the methods of structuralist criticism to examine science fiction.... All of Delany's work to date has been concerned consciously with the nature of language and art, the role of the artist, and the creative process." (*Dictionary of Literary Biography*)

Sources: *Afro-American Writers;* Author information; *Black American Writers: Past and Present; Books in Print*, 1978-79; *Contemporary Authors*, vols. 81-84, 1979; *Dictionary of Literary Biography*, vol. 8, 1981.

DEMBY, WILLIAM. Novelist, Artist, Screenwriter.
Born in Pittsburgh, Pa., Dec. 25, 1922. *Education:* W. Va. State Coll.; B.A., Fisk U., 1947; U. of Rome, Italy. *Family:* Married Lucia Drudi (novelist); son James. *Career:* Wrote for *Stars and Stripes* in Italy (Army); contrib. art & stories to *Fisk U. Herald;* Jazz musician (Rome); wrote screen plays for Roberto Rossellini (Rome); advertising agent, N.Y.; Assoc. Prof., Staten Island Community Coll., N.Y. *Mailing address:* c/o Avon Bks., 959 Eighth Ave., N.Y., N.Y. 10019.

Writings:
Fiction

Beetlecreek, novel (N.Y., Rinehart, 1950; N.Y., Pantheon, 1965; N.Y., Avon, 1967; reprint of 1950 ed., Chatham, N.J., Chatham Bookseller, 1972)

The Catacombs, novel (Pantheon, 1965)

Love Story Black, novel (N.Y., Reed, 1978)

Blueboy, novel (Pantheon, 1979)

Sidelights: Studied art at University of Rome, where he has lived; traveled in Europe, Ethiopia, Japan, and Thailand. (*Black American Literature*)

Sources: *Black American Literature; Books in Print*, 1978-79; *Cavalcade; Dark Symphony; Negro Novel in America; Soon, One Morning.*

DETT, ROBERT NATHANIEL. Composer, Educator.
Born in Drummondsville, Ontario, Can., Oct. 11, 1882. *Education:* Oliver Willis Halsted Conservatory, Lockport, N.Y.; B. Music, Oberlin Coll., 1908; Columbia U.; U. of Pa.; Amer. Conservatory; Harvard U.; Howard U.; Eastman Sch. of Music. *Career:* Church pianist, Niagara Falls, 1898-1903; Dir. of Music: Lane Coll., 1908-11; Lincoln Inst., 1911-13; Hampton Inst., 1913-31; Bennett Coll., 1937. *Honors:* Dr. of Music, Harvard U., 1924; Dr. of Music, Oberlin Coll., 1926; Bowdoin essay prize; Frances Boott prize, composition; Harmon Found.; Palm & Ribbon, Royal Belgian Band. Died, Battle Creek, Mich., Oct. 2, 1943.

Writings:
Fiction

The Album of a Heart, poems (Jackson, Tenn., Mocowat-Mercer, 1911)

Nonfiction

Religious Folk Songs of the Negro (N.Y., Schirmer, 1927; reprint, N.Y., AMS; rev., Hampton, Va., Hampton Inst. Press, 1927, 1981)

The Dett Collection of Negro Spirituals, 4 vols., ed. (Chicago, Hall & McCready, 1938)

Collected Piano Works of R. Nathaniel Dett (Evanston, Ill., Summy-Birchard, 1973)

Sidelights: (Works) "Don't Be Weary Traveler," motet; "Ordering of Moses," oratorio; "Listen to the Lambs," chorus; "The Chariot Jubilee," "Juba Dance," piano suites; "Magnolia Suite," "In the Bottoms," "Enchantment Suite," "Cinnamon Grove," "Tropic Winter Suite."

Sources: *American Authors and Books*, 3rd rev. ed., 1978; *The ASCAP Biographical Dictionary of Composers, Authors and Publishers; Books in Print*, 1980-81; *Crisis*, Feb. 1983.

DIOP, BIRAGO ISMAÏL. (Senegalese). Short Story Writer, Poet, Veterinarian, Diplomat.
Born in Ouakam, near Dakar, Senegal, Dec. 11, 1906. *Education:* Lycée Faidherbe, Saint-Louis, Senegal (French Baccalaureate in Philosophy); Doctorate, Toulouse Sch. of Veterinary Medicine, 1933. *Family:* Married a Frenchwoman. *Career:* Head, Zoological Technical Serv., Haute-Volta, 1945, & Mauritania, 1950-55; Ambassador to Tunis. *Honors:* Awarded Brevet de Capacité, 1925; *Tales of Amoudou Koumba* awarded Grand Prix Littéraire de l'Afrique Occidentale Francaise. *Mailing address:* c/o Northwestern U. Press, Evanston, Ill. 60201.

Writings:
(Partial Listing—English Only)
Fiction

(Included in) *An Anthology of African and Malagasy Poetry in French*, ed. by Clive Wake (Oxford, Eng., Three Crowns Press, 1965)

Tales of Amoudou Koumba, transl. by Dorothy S. Blair (London, Oxford U. Press, 1966)

Sidelights: Diop became a close friend of and collaborated with Leopold Senghor, in editing and publication of the pioneering *L'Edudiant Noir*, forerunner of several negritude journals. (*African Authors*)
His real fame rests on his short stories. "While posing modestly as a mere interpreter of the naive tales of his village griot ..., he cleverly evokes the poetic inspiration of his native land." (*African Writers on African Writing*)
A. C. Brench states that Diop's achievements were: overcoming the stresses which Islam, colonial regimentation and participation in the anticolonial struggle created for Africans; and that by fusing the written and oral traditions he created a feeling of immediacy and dramatic movement. (*African Authors*)

Sources: *African Authors; African Writers on African Writing; Books in Print*, 1979-80; *A Reader's Guide to African Literature.*

DIOP, CHEIKH ANTA. (Senegalese). Historian, Physicist, Philosopher.
Born in Senegal in 1923. *Education:* M.A., Ph.D., U. of Paris. *Career:* Dir., Radiocarbon Lab.,

Institut Fondamental d'Afrique Noire, U. of Dakar, Senegal. *Mailing address:* c/o Freedomways, 799 Broadway, Suite 542, N.Y., N.Y. 10003.

Writings:
(Partial Listing—English Only)
Nonfiction

Black Africa: The Economic and Cultural Basis for a Federated State, transl. by Harold J. Salemson (Westport, Conn., Lawrence Hill, 1960, 1973, 1978)

The African Origin of Civilization: Myth or Reality, transl. from French by Mercer Cook (Lawrence Hill, 1974)

The Cultural Unity of Black Africa, transl. from French (Chicago, Third World, 1978)

Sources: *African Origin of Civilization; Books in Print*, 1979-80, 1980-81; *Freedomways*, vol. 19, 1979; *Who's Who in African Literature.*

DODSON, OWEN VINCENT. Drama Professor, Playwright, Novelist, Poet.
Born in Brooklyn, N.Y., Nov. 28, 1914. *Education:* B.A., Bates Coll., 1936; M.F.A., Yale U., 1939. *Career:* Instr., Atlanta U., summer 1938, full-time, 1939-43; Instr., Hampton Inst. & Spelman Coll.; Lect.: Iowa U., Vassar, Kenyon, Cornell; Conductor of seminars in theater & playwriting; Dir., summer theater, the Theatre Lobby (Wash., D.C.), Lincoln U. (Mo.), Howard U.; Prof., Drama, Howard U., 1936-69; Poet-in-Residence, Ruth Stephan Poetry Center, U. of Ariz., spring 1969. *Honors:* Rosenwald Found. Fellow; Gen. Educ. Bd. Fellow; Guggenheim Found. Fellow, 1953; Paris Review Prize for short story "The Summer Fire"; named Poet Laureate by Her Majesty the Queen of Eng., 1968; Maxwell Anderson verse award; D. Litt., Bates Coll., 1967; Rockefeller Found. Fellow, 1968. *Mailing address:* c/o Farrar, Straus, 19 Union Square W., N.Y., N.Y. 10003.

Writings:
Fiction

Divine Comedy, play (N.Y., Harper, 1938 & in Hatch, James V., *Black Theater*)

Garden of Time, play (produced by American Negro Theatre, 1939)

Powerful Long Ladder, poems (N.Y., Farrar, 1946, 1970)

Boy at the Window, novel (Farrar, 1951, 1977; N.Y., Chatham Bookseller, 1951; paper ed. pub. as *When Trees Were Green* (N.Y., Popular Lib., 1951))

Bayou Legend, play (in Turner, Darwin T., *Black Drama in America*)

Nonfiction

The Confession Stone: Song Cycles, essays (London, Breman, 1970, 1971)

Come Home Early, Child, essays (Popular Lib., 1977)

The Harlem Book of the Dead, essays, with Camille Billope (Dobbs Ferry, N.Y., Morgan, 1978)

Sidelights: "While on a Guggenheim Fellowship to Italy he completed a second novel, *A Bent House*, and a second book of poems, *Cages*." (*Soon, One Morning*)
"Owen Dodson has contributed significantly in Negro college theatre.... His best known play is *Divine Comedy* first produced at Yale University in 1938. Based on the story of Father Divine, it is probably the best verse drama by a black playwright." (*Black American Literature: Poetry*)

Sources: *Black American Literature: Poetry; Black Voices; Books in Print*, 1978-79; *Cavalcade; Interviews with Black Writers; Kaleidoscope; Soon, One Morning.*

DOUGLASS, FREDERICK. Abolitionist, Journalist, Diplomat, Lecturer.
Born in Tuckahoe, Md., c. 1817. (Son of unknown white father & Harriet Bailey.) *Education:* Learned reading & writing from his master's wife; thereafter, self-educated. Escaped slavery in 1838. *Family:* Married 1st Anna Murray, Sept. 1838; married 2nd Helen Pitts, 1884. *Career:* Employed as

Agent, Mass. Anti-Slavery Soc., 1841; became central figure in "One Hundred Conventions" of New Eng. Anti-Slavery Soc.; visited Great Brit. & Ireland to avoid possible re-enslavement as result of his biography, *Narrative of the Life of Frederick Douglass*, 1845-47. Returned to America with money to buy his freedom, established newspaper *North Star*, 1847; it became known as *Frederick Douglass's Paper*, lasted until 1860. From 1858 to 1863 he brought out *Douglass's Monthly*, & from 1869 to 1872 he produced the weekly *New National Era*. Died Feb. 20, 1895, in Wash., D.C.

Writings:

Nonfiction

Narrative of the Life of Frederick Douglass, an American Slave, Written by Himself (Boston, Anti-Slavery Office, 1845, 1847, 1849; Cambridge, Mass., Harvard U. Press, Belknap Press, John Harvard Lib. Ser., 1960; N.Y., New Amer. Lib., 1968)

My Bondage and My Freedom (N.Y., Miller, Orton, 1855; N.Y., Dover, Black Rediscovery Ser., 1969)

Life and Times of Frederick Douglass: The Complete Autobiography (Hartford, Park, 1881; N.Y., Macmillan, 1962; ed. by Barbara Ritchie, juv., N.Y., Crowell, 1966; N.Y., Grosset, 1970)

Frederick Douglass, Selections from His Writings, ed. by Philip S. Foner (N.Y., Intnl., 1945)

The Life and Writings of Frederick Douglass, 4 vols., ed. by Philip S. Foner. Vol. 1, *Early Years*; vol. 2, *Pre-Civil War Decade*; vol. 3, *The Civil War*; vol. 4, *Reconstruction and After* (Intnl., 1950-1975)

Mind and Heart of Frederick Douglass: Excerpt from Speeches of the Great Negro Orator, ed. by Barbara Ritchie, juv. (Crowell, 1968)

From Slave to Statesman, abridged ed. (N.Y., Noble, 1972)

The Life and Writings of Frederick Douglass; Supplementary Volume, 1844-1860, vol. 5, ed. by Philip S. Foner (Intnl., 1975)

A Black Diplomat in Haiti: The Diplomatic Correspondence of United States Minister Frederick Douglass from Haiti, 1889-1891, 2 vols., ed. by Norma Brown (Salisbury, N.C., Documentary Publ., 1977)

The Frederick Douglass Papers: Series One: Speeches, Debates and Interviews. Vol. I: 1841-46, ed. by John W. Blassingame (New Haven, Conn., Yale U. Press, 1979)

The Frederick Douglass Papers: Series One: Speeches, Debates and Interviews. Vol. II: 1847-54, ed. by John W. Blassingame (Yale U. Press, 1982)

Sidelights: Frederick Douglass, significant contributor to the Blackman's freedom struggle, viewed freedom as "the foundation of all manly virtue." In his opinion the Bill of Rights was, for Black people, a "bill of wrongs." Thus efforts of a lifetime were devoted to achieving equality of opportunity for his race.

Served as Lincoln's advisor on the Blackman during the Civil War. Served as President of Freedman's Bank; Chargé d'Affaires to Santo Domingo, 1871; Marshall and Recorder of Deeds, 1877-86; U.S. Minister to Haiti, 1889-91; vigorous supporter of woman's suffrage. (*Afro-American Literature: Non-Fiction*)

Sources: *Afro-American Literature: Non-Fiction; Black American Literature: Essays; Black Voices; Books in Print*, 1980-81, 1981-82, 1982-83; *Cavalcade; Freedomways*, vol. 20, 1980; *Who Was Who in America, Historical Volume, 1607-1896*.

DRAKE, (JOHN GIBBS) ST. CLAIR. Sociologist, Sociology Professor, Anthropologist.
Born in Suffolk, Va., Jan. 2, 1911. *Education:* B.S., Hampton Inst., Va. (with hon.), 1931; Ph.D., U. of Chicago, 1948. *Family:* Married Elizabeth Dewey Johns, June 1942; d. Sandra, d. Kail. *Career:* Res. Assoc., Carnegie-Myrdal Study of the Negro in America, Sept. 1940-June 1942; Instr., Dillard U., New Orleans, Sept. 1935-June 1936, Asst. Prof., Sept. 1941-June 1942; Warrant Officer, U.S. Maritime Serv., Sept. 1943-Dec. 1945; Asst. Prof., Roosevelt U., Chicago, Sept. 1946-Jan. 1954; Visiting Prof., U. of Liberia, Jan.-June 1954; Prof., Roosevelt U., Sept. 1955-Oct. 1958; Head, Dept. of Sociol., U. of Ghana, W. Africa, Oct. 1958-Feb. 1961; Prof., Roosevelt U., Feb. 1961-Oct. 1969; Prof., Sociol. & Anthropology, & Chairman, African & Afro-Amer. Studies Program,

Stanford U., Oct. 1969-?; Training Staff, Peace Corps Tchrs., Ghana, 1961, 1962, 1964. *Honors:* Calliope Medal (Hampton Inst.) for highest average over 4 yrs.; Ford Found. Fellow for study of mass media in W. Africa, 1954-55; for *Black Metropolis*: shared Anisfield-Wolf award, 1946; "One of five best on race relations" (*Negro Digest*). *Mailing address:* c/o Third World Press, 7524 S. Cottage Grove, Chicago, Ill. 60619.

Writings:
  Nonfiction

Black Metropolis; A Story of Negro Life in a Northern City, with Horace Cayton (N.Y., Harcourt, 1945, rev. & enlarged, 1962, 1970)

The American Dream and the Negro. 100 Years of Freedom? (Chicago, Roosevelt U., 1963)

Social Work in West Africa, with Dr. Peter Omari (Accra, Ghana, Dept. of Soc. Welfare & Community Development, 1963)

Race Relations in a Time of Rapid Social Change (N.Y., Natl. Federation of Settlements & Neighborhood Centers, 1966)

The Redemption of Africa and Black Religion (Chicago, Third World, 1970)

Teaching Black; An Evaluation of Methods and Resources (Stanford, Cal., Stanford U. Multi-Ethnic Educ. Resources Center, 1971)

Redemption of Black Religion (Third World, 1980)

Sidelights: *Black Metropolis* was "generally compared to such works as *Middletown* by Robert and Helen Lynd, and *An American Dilemma* by Gunnar Myrdal, it was called 'a landmark not only in race studies but in the broader field of social anthropology.' " (*Current Biography*)

Sources: *Books in Print*, 1981-82; *Current Biography*, 1946; *Soon, One Morning*.

DuBOIS, DAVID GRAHAM. Activist, Editor, Lecturer, Novelist.
Born in Seattle, Wash., in 1925. (Stepfather, W. E. B. DuBois; mother, Shirley Graham). *Education:* Oberlin Conservatory of Music; B.A., (Sociol.), Hunter Coll., 1950; N.Y. Sch. of Soc. Work, Columbia U.; M.A., N.Y.U., 1972; Peking U., China. *Family:* Div. *Career:* Lect., Cairo U., Egypt; Ed. & Reporter, *Arab Observer*, Cairo, 1960-72; News Ed., *The Egyptian Gazette*; Reporter & Ed., Middle East News & Features Agency; Announcer, Program Writer, Radio Cairo; Public Relations, Ghanaian Govt., Cairo, 1965-66 (under Kwame Nkrumah); Lect., Sch. of Criminology, U. of Cal., Berkeley; Ed.-in-Chief, Black Panther Intercommunal News Serv., 1973. *Mailing address:* c/o Ramparts Press, P.O. Box 50128, Palo Alto, Cal. 94303.

Writings:
  Fiction

And Bid Him Sing, novel (Palo Alto, Cal., Ramparts, 1975)

Sidelights: Returned to United States from Cairo and settled in the San Francisco Bay area. He became spokesman for the Black Panthers. His new book links the emergence of Black rule in southern Africa with the struggle for Black equality in the United States. (*And Bid Him Sing*)

Sources: *And Bid Him Sing; Contemporary Authors*, vols. 65-68, 1977.

DuBOIS, WILLIAM EDWARD BURGHARDT. Editor, Professor of History & Sociology, Historian, Scholar, Sociologist, Civil Rights Leader.
Born in Great Barrington, Mass., Feb. 23, 1868, of African, French Huguenot, & Dutch ancestry. *Education:* B.A., Fisk U., 1888, Harvard U., 1890; M.A., 1891, Ph.D., 1895, Harvard U.; U. of Berlin; Hon. LL.D., Howard U., 1930, Atlanta U., 1938; Litt.D., Fisk U., 1938; L.H.D., Wilberforce U., 1940, U. of Sofia, 1958; D.Sci.Hist., Charles U., Prague, 1950, Lomonovska U., Moscow, 1959; Econ.D., Humboldt U., Berlin, 1958. *Family:* Married 1st Nina Gomer, May 12, 1896 (dec. 1950); son Burghardt Gomer (dec.), d. Nina Yolande; married 2nd Shirley Graham, 1951;

son David Graham. *Career:* Prof., Greek & Latin, Wilberforce U., 1894-96; Asst. Instr., Sociol., U. of Pa., 1896-97; Prof., Econ. & Hist., Atlanta U., 1897-1910; Dir., Publ., NAACP, & Ed., *Crisis*, 1910-32; Head, Dept. of Sociol., Atlanta U., 1943-44; V. Chairman, Council on African Affairs, 1949-54; Founder-Ed., *Phylon* (Atlanta U. Review of Race & Culture), 1940-44; Ed.-in-Chief, *Encyclopedia of the Negro*, 1933-45; Dir., Dept. of Spec. Res., NAACP, 1944-48; Head, Preliminary Planning, *Encyclopedia Africana*, 1961-? *Honors:* Recipient, Intnl. Peace Prize, 1952; Lenin Intnl. Peace Prize, 1958; Fellow, Amer. Assn. for Advancement of Science. Died Aug. 29, 1963.

Writings:

Fiction

Quest of the Silver Fleece, novel (Chicago, A. C. McClurg, 1911; N.Y., AMS, N.Y., Arno, 1970; Millwood, N.Y., Kraus Reprint, 1975)

Dark Princess, a Romance (N.Y., Harcourt, 1928; Kraus Reprint, 1975)

The Black Flame, novels (trilogy): Vol. 1, *The Ordeal of Mansart*; vol. 2, *Mansart Builds a School*; vol. 3, *Worlds of Color* (N.Y., Mainstream, 1957-61; Kraus Reprint, 1975)

Nonfiction

The Suppression of the African Slave Trade to the United States of America, 1638-1870, Ph.D. dissertation (Cambridge, Mass., Harvard U., Hist. Studies Ser., 1896; N.Y., Russell, 1965; N.Y., Schocken, paper, 1969; N.Y., Dover, 1970; Baton Rouge, La. State U. Press, 1970; Kraus Reprint, 1973)

Atlanta University Studies, ed. (Atlanta, Atlanta U. Press, 1897-1911; N.Y., Octagon, 1968)

The Negro in Business (Atlanta U. Press, 1899; AMS, 1971)

The Philadelphia Negro: A Social Study (Phila., U. of Pa. Press; Schocken, paper also, 1967; Kraus Reprint, 1973)

The College-Bred Negro American (Atlanta U. Press, 1900, 1902, 1910; Kraus Reprint, n.d.)

Black North in 1901: A Social Study (1901; reprint, Arno, 1970)

The Negro Artisan (Atlanta U. Press, 1902; Kraus Reprint, n.d.)

The Souls of Black Folk (A. C. McClurg, 1903; Kraus Reprint, 1953; N.Y., paper also, NAL, 1969; N.Y., Fawcett, 1977; N.Y., Dodd, 1979; n.p., Peter Smith, n.d.)

The Negro Church (Atlanta U. Press, 1903; reprint, St. Clair Shores, Mich., Scholarly, 1977)

Some Notes on Negro Crime, Particularly in Georgia (Atlanta U. Press, 1904; Kraus Reprint, n.d.)

A Select Bibliography of the Negro American (Atlanta U. Press, 1905; Kraus Reprint, n.d.; Scholarly, 1977)

Economic Co-Operation among Negro Americans (Atlanta U. Press, 1907; Kraus Reprint, n.d.; Scholarly, 1977)

The Negro American Family (Atlanta U. Press, 1908; Westport, Conn., Negro Universities Press, 1908)

John Brown (Phila., G. W. Jacobs, 1909; N.Y., Intnl., 1962; Kraus Reprint Metro Bks., 1972)

Efforts for Social Betterment among Negro Americans (Atlanta U. Press, 1909)

The Common School and the Negro American (Atlanta U. Press, 1911; Kraus Reprint, n.d.)

The Negro American Artisan (Atlanta U. Press, 1912; Kraus Reprint, n.d.)

Morals and Manners among Negro Americans (Atlanta U. Press, 1914; Kraus Reprint, n.d.)

The Negro (N.Y., Holt, 1915; N.Y., Oxford U. Press, paper, 1970; Kraus Reprint, 1975)

Darkwater: Voices from within the Veil, autobiog. (N.Y., Harcourt, 1920; AMS, 1969; Schocken, paper, 1969; Kraus Reprint, 1975)

The Gift of Black Folk, essays (Boston, Stratford, 1924; AMS, 1972)

Black Reconstruction in America, 1860-1880 (Harcourt, 1935; N.Y., Russell, 1956; N.Y., Atheneum, 1969)

Black Folk: Then and Now (Holt, 1939; Kraus Reprint, 1975)

Dusk of Dawn: An Essay toward an Autobiography of a Race Concept (Harcourt, 1940, 1942; Kraus Reprint, 1975)

Color and Democracy: Colonies and Peace (Harcourt, 1945; Kraus Reprint, 1975)

The World and Africa: An Inquiry into the Part Which Africa Has Played in World History (N.Y., Viking, 1947; N.Y., Intnl., paper, 1965)

In Battle for Peace: The Story of My 83rd Birthday (N.Y., Masses & Mainstream, 1952; Kraus Reprint, 1976)

The Book Reviews of W. E. B. DuBois (Millwood, N.Y., Kraus-Thomson Org., n.d.)

A B C of Color: Selections from over a Half-Century of the Writings of W. E. B. DuBois (Berlin, E. Germany, 1963; reprint, Intnl., 1969)

The Autobiography of W. E. B. DuBois: A Soliloquy on Viewing My Life from the Last Decade of Its First Century (Intnl., 1968; Kraus Reprint, paper also, 1970)

W. E. B. DuBois Speaks: Speeches and Addresses, 1890]-1919, ed. by Philip S. Foner (N.Y., Path Press, 1970, 1977)

The Seventh Son: The Thought and Writings of W. E. B. DuBois, 2 vols., ed. with Julius Lester (N.Y., Random, paper also, 1971)

The Correspondence of W. E. B. DuBois:, Vol. I, *Selections, 1877-1934*, ed. by Herbert Aptheker (Amherst, U. of Mass. Press, 1973)

The Education of Black People: Ten Critiques, 1906-1960, ed. by Herbert Aptheker (N.Y., Monthly Review Press, 1975; U. of Mass. Press, 1973)

Writings of W. E. B. DuBois, ed. by Virginia Hamilton (Crowell, 1975)

The Correspondence of W. E. B. DuBois, Vol. II, *Selections, 1934-1944*, ed. by Herbert Aptheker (U. of Mass. Press, 1976)

The Correspondence of W. E. B. DuBois, Vol. III, *Selections, 1944-1963*, ed. by Herbert Aptheker (U. of Mass. Press, 1978)

Prayers for Dark People, ed. by Herbert Aptheker (U. of Mass. Press, 1980)

W. E. B. DuBois on Sociology and the Black Community, ed. by Dan S. Green & Edwin D. Driver (Chicago, U. of Chicago Press, 1980)

Sidelights: This giant of a man was praised for his prophetic foresight. "The problem of the twentieth century is the problem of the color line," he write in *Souls of Black Folk*, in 1903. (*Who Was Who in America*)

The historian John Henrik Clarke called him "truly the father of the modern Black liberation movement, the twentieth-century leader of the struggle against racial oppression and discrimination." (*W. E. B. DuBois*)

Herbert Aptheker, one of his chief biographers, states: "An editor, author, lecturer, scholar, organizer, inspirer, and fighter, he was among the most consequential figures of the century." (*Autobiography of W. E. B. DuBois*)

Sources: *American Negro Reference Book; Annotated Bibliography of the Published Writings of W. E. B. DuBois; The Autobiography of W. E. B. DuBois, Black Voices; Books in Print*, 1978-79, 1980-81; *Cavalcade; Current Biography*, 1940; *Freedomways*, vol. 18, 1978; *Negro Almanac; Novels of the Harlem Renaissance; The Seventh Son; W. E. B. DuBois; Who Was Who in America*, vol. 4, 1961-68.

DUMAS, HENRY. Poet, Short Story Writer.
Born in Ark. in 1935. *Education:* Rutgers U. *Family:* Married Loretta Dumas; two sons. *Career:* Tchr., Hiram Coll., Hiram, Ohio; Dir., Lang. Workshops & Tchr.-Counselor, S. Ill. U. Died May 23, 1968.

Writings:
Fiction

Ark of Bones and Other Stories, ed. by Hale Chatfield & Eugene Redmond (Carbondale, S. Ill. U. Press, 1970; N.Y., Random House, 1974)

Poetry for My People, ed. by Hale Chatfield & Eugene Redmond (S. Ill. U. Press, 1970)

Play Ebony Play Ivory, poems, ed. by Eugene Redmond (Random House, 1974)

Jonoah and the Green Stone, poems (Random House, 1976)

Rope of Wind, poems, ed. by Eugene Redmond (Random House, 1979)

Sidelights: "Was shot and killed by a white policeman on the Harlem Station platform of the New York Central Railroad. Little else is known about the circumstances surrounding his death." (*Poetry of Black America*)

Sources: *Books in Print*, 1978-79; *Poetry of Black America.*

DUNBAR, ERNEST. Editor.
Born in Phila., Pa., Feb. 14, 1927. *Education:* B.S., Temple U., 1954; grad. student in African Studies, Northwestern U., 1957-58. *Family:* Married Dorothy Marie Grabusic, Dec. 18, 1965; d. Adrienne, d. Gail, son Dean Eliot. *Career:* Ed. staff, *Look*, N.Y.C., 1954-?, Asst. Ed., 1958-59, Senior Ed., 1959- ; Moderator of "World at Ten," WDNT, N.Y.: Lect. on African Affairs. *Honors:* Fund for Adult Educ. Mass Media Fellow, 1957-58. *Mailing address:* 33-04 93rd St., Jackson Heights, N.Y. 11372.

Writings:
Nonfiction

The Black Expatriates, collection of interviews (N.Y., Dutton, 1968)

Nigeria (N.Y., Watts, 1974)

Sidelights: Dunbar interviewed American Negroes living in Africa and Europe for his book on sixteen expatriates. (*Contemporary Authors*)

Source: *Contemporary Authors*, vols. 25-28, 1971.

DUNBAR, PAUL LAURENCE. Poet, Novelist.
Born in Dayton, Ohio, June 27, 1872. *Education:* Dayton Public Schs.; Grad. from high sch., 1891. *Family:* Married Alice Moore (writer), Mar. 6, 1898. *Career:* Elevator operator; employee, Lib. of Congress; writer. Died Feb. 9, 1906.

Writings:
Fiction

Oak and Ivey, poems (Dayton, Ohio, United Brethren, 1893; Miami, Mnemosyne, 1969)

Majors and Minors, poems (Toledo, Ohio, Hadley, 1895, 1908)

Lyrics of Lowly Life, poems (N.Y., Dodd, 1896; Toronto, Nusson; N.Y., Arno, 1969)

Poems of Cabin and Field (Dodd, 1896-1899; N.Y., AMS, 1969)

Folks from Dixie, poems (Dodd, 1898; N.Y., Negro Universities Press, 1969)

The Uncalled, novel (Dodd, 1898; AMS, 1972)

Lyrics of the Hearthside, poems (Dodd, 1899; AMS, 1972)

The Love of Landry, novel (Dodd, 1900; Mnemosyne, 1969)

Strength of Gideon and Other Stories (Dodd, 1900; Arno, 1969)

The Fanatics, novel (Dodd, 1901; Negro Universities Press, 1969)

Candle-Lightin' Time, poems (Dodd, 1901; Mnemosyne, 1969)

The Sport of the Gods, novel (Dodd, 1902; Arno, 1969)

Lyrics of Love and Laughter, poems (Dodd, 1903)

When Malindy Sings, poems (Dodd, 1903; AMS, 1972)

In Old Plantation Days, short stories (Dodd, 1903; Negro Universities Press, 1969)

Li'l Gal, poems (Dodd, 1904; AMS, 1972)

The Heart of Happy Hollow (Dodd, 1904; N.Y., Log Cabin, 1921)

Lyrics of Sunshine and Shadow, poems (Dodd, 1905; AMS, 1972)

Howdy Honey Howdy, poems (Toronto, Musson, 1905; Dodd, 1905)

Joggin' erlong, poems (Dodd, 1906; Mnemosyne, 1969)

Complete Poems (Dodd, 1913, 1968)

The Paul Laurence Dunbar Reader; A Selection of the Best of Paul Laurence Dunbar Poetry and Prose... , ed. by Jay Martin & Gossie Hudson (Dodd, 1975)

Nonfiction
The Life and Works of Paul Laurence Dunbar; Containing His Complete Poetical Works, His Best Short Stories and Numerous Anecdotes and a Complete Biography of the Famous Poet, by Lida Keck-Wiggins (Naperville, Ill., J. L. Nichols, 1907; N.Y., Kraus Reprint, 1971)

Sidelights: "First American Negro poet of real literary distinction." (*Book of American Negro Poetry*) " ... his chief talents—rhythm, narrative skill, and satirical characterization—are best revealed in his dialect poems, his major contribution to American literature." (*Black American Literature: Poetry*) Brought to national attention by William Dean Howells. Would like to have been considered for poems in standard English. (*Black Insights*)

Sources: *Afro-American Writers; Black American Literature: Poetry; Black Insights; Black Poets of the United States; Black Voices; Book of American Negro Poetry; Cavalcade; Kaleidoscope; Negro Almanac.*

DUNHAM, KATHERINE. Dancer, Choreographer, Anthropologist.
Born in Glen Ellyn, Ill., in 1910. *Education:* M.A., U. of Chicago; Northwestern U. *Career:* Formed Negro Sch. of the Dance; 1st public appearance, Negro Rhapsody, Chicago Beaux Arts Ball, 1931; 1st major dance performance, Chicago World's Fair, 1934; Chicago Opera Co., 1935-36; Dance Dir., Labor Stage, N.Y.C., 1939-40; movies include: *Cabin in the Sky*, 1940-41; *Carnival of Rhythm*, 1941; *Stormy Weather*, 1943. Choreographer, *Pardon My Sarong*, 1942. Formed Katherine Dunham Sch. Cultural Arts, Inc., N.Y.C., 1945; Prod.-Dir., Katherine Dunham Dance Co.; starred in own production, *Bal Negro*, 1946-47, which toured country, Jan.-Apr. 1948. *Honors:* Julius Rosenwald Fund Travel Fellow to W. Indies, 1936-37. *Mailing address:* c/o Third World Press, 7524 S. Cottage Grove, Chicago, Ill. 60619.

Writings:
Fiction
Kasamance: A Fantasy (N.Y., Odarkai Bks., 1974; Chicago, Third World, 1974)

Nonfiction
Katherine Dunham's Journey to Accompong (N.Y., Holt, 1946; Westport, Conn., Negro Universities Press, 1971)

Dances of Haiti (L.A., UCLA, Center for Afro-Amer. Studies, 1946, 1948, 1983)

A Touch of Innocence, autobiog. (N.Y., Harcourt, 1959)

Island Possessed, Haiti (N.Y., Doubleday, 1969)

Sidelights: *Dances of Haiti* published as *Les Danses d' Haiti*, Paris, Fasquelle, 1950, and *Las Danzas de Haiti*, version Espanola de Javier Romero, Mexico, 1947.

Sources: *Biographical History of Blacks in America since 1528; Dictionary Catalog of the Schomburg Collection of Negro Literature and History; Soon, One Morning*; UCLA, CAAS Newsletter, vol. 8, no. 1, 1984.

DYMALLY, MERVYN MALCOLM. California Congressman.
Born in Trinidad, Brit. W. Indies, May 12, 1926. *Education:* M.A., Cal. State U., Sacramento, 1970; LL.D. (hon.), U. of W. L.A.; further study, Intnl. U., San Diego. *Family:* Married Alice M. Gueno, 1969; son Mark, d. Lynn. *Career:* Elementary sch. tchr., L.A., Cal., 1954-60; Assemblyman, Cal. State Assembly, 1962-66; Chairman, Com. on Industrial Relations, 1965-66; Senator, Cal. State Senate (representing L.A. & Watts), Sacramento, 1967-75; Chairman: Com. on Soc. Welfare, 1968-69, Military & Veterans Affairs, 1969-70, Election & Reapportionment, 1971, Subcom. on Medical Educ. & Health Needs, 1972-?; Child Development & Child Care Program, 1972; Chair of Majority Caucus, 1970; Lect. in Govt. at Claremont Colleges, U. of Cal. (Davis & Irvine), & Whittier Coll.; Visiting Fellow, Metropolitan Applied Res. Center, N.Y.C.; Elected Lt. Governor, Cal., 1975-79; U.S. Congressman, 1980- . *Mailing address:* 4455 W. 126th St., Hawthorne, Cal. 90250.

Writings:
Nonfiction
The Black Politician: His Struggle for Power (Belmont, Cal., Duxbury, 1971)

Sidelights: U.S. Department of State, Goodwill Ambassador to East and Central Africa, 1964, and Guyana and the Caribbean, 1965. Dymally visited Israel as guest of the government, 1967. (*Contemporary Authors*)

Source: *Contemporary Authors*, vols. 41-44, 1974.

EDET, EDNA SMITH. Juvenile Writer.
Career: Compiler; Prof., Medgar Evers Coll., N.Y. *Mailing address:* c/o City U. of N.Y., Medgar Evers Coll., 1150 Carroll St., Brooklyn, N.Y. 11225.

Writings:
Nonfiction
The Griot Sings: Songs from the Black World, juv. (N.Y., Medgar Evers Coll. Press, 1978)

Sidelights: *The Griot Sings* is a collection of 115 children's songs, games and fables from Africa, the West Indies and Black America.

Sources: *Books in Print*, 1980-81; *Freedomways*, vol. 19, 1979.

EDMONDS, RANDOLPH. Drama Professor, Playwright.
Born in Lawrenceville, Va., in 1900. *Education:* St. Paul Normal & Industrial Sch., Lawrenceville; B.A., Oberlin Coll., 1926; M.A., Columbia U., 1932; further study: Dept. of Drama, Yale U.; Dublin U.; London Sch. of Speech Training & Dramatic Art; Hon. Litt.D., Bethune-Cookman Coll., 1947. *Career:* Tchr. of Drama, Dir. & Organizer of dramatic assns. in predominately Negro colleges, for over 40 yrs. While at Morgan Coll., he organized Negro Inter-Collegiate Drama Assn., which included colleges of Pa., Md., Va., N.C., & D.C. At Dillard U. in New Orleans, established nation's 1st drama dept. at a predominately Black coll. (1935) & founded S. Assn. of Drama & Speech Arts. At Fla. A&M U. he chaired Theatre Arts Dept. for 23 yrs. & took the players on two govt.-sponsored foreign tours. (*Black Drama in America*). *Mailing address:* c/o Fawcett Pub. Inc., 1515 Broadway, N.Y., N.Y. 10036.

Writings:
__Fiction__

Shades and Shadows, Six Plays for a Negro Theater (Boston, Meador, 1930)

Six Plays for a Negro Theatre (Boston, Baker, 1934)

The Land of Cotton and Other Plays (Wash., D.C., Associated Pub., 1942)

Earth and Stars, play (1946; rev. 1961 in Darwin T. Turner, *Black Drama in America*)

Sidelights: "In 1970 the National Association of Dramatic and Speech Arts honored Randolph Edmonds as 'the Dean of Black Academic Theatre.' ... [no other] individual has contributed more to the development of dramatic interest and organization in the Afro-American colleges.

"In the original version of *Earth and Stars*, produced in 1946, Edmonds explored problems of Southern leadership during the reconversion following World War II. The revised version brought the problem up to date by emphasizing the civil rights struggle of the 1960's. ...*Earth and Stars* has been staged more widely in Afro-American educational and community theaters than any other play by an Afro-American." (*Black Drama in America*)

Sources: *Afro-American Writers; American Literature by Negro Authors; Black Drama in America; Directory of American Scholars*, vol. II: *English, Speech and Drama*, 5th ed., 1969.

EDWARDS, HARRY. Sociology Teacher, Activist.
Born in 1942. *Career:* Lect. & grad. fellow in Dept. of Sociol., Cornell U.; Tchr., San Jose State Coll., Cal. *Mailing address:* c/o San Jose State U., Wash. Square, San Jose, Cal. 95192.

Writings:
__Nonfiction__

Revolt of the Black Athlete (N.Y., Free Press, 1969, 1970)

Black Students (Free Press, 1970)

Healing Intelligence (N.Y., Taplinger, 1971)

Sociology of Sport (Homewood, Ill., Dorsey, 1973)

The Struggle That Must Be: An Autobiography (N.Y., Macmillan, 1980)

Sidelights: Was instrumental in organizing the United States Black Students for Action. (*Revolt of the Black Athlete*)

Sources: *Books in Print*, 1978-79; *Publishers Weekly*, Oct. 17, 1980; *Revolt of the Black Athlete*.

EKWENSI, CYPRIAN ODIATU DUAKA. (Nigerian). Novelist, Short Story Writer, Pharmacist, Folklorist, Juvenile Writer.
Born in Minna, N. Nigeria, Sept. 26, 1921; an Igbo. *Education:* Govt. Coll., Ibadan; Technical Inst., Lagos; Achimota Coll., Gold Coast; Sch. of Forestry, Ibadan; Pharmacy, London U. *Career:* Dir. of Information Serv., Federal Ministry of Information, since 1966 (Dir. of Information, Lagos, 1961-66); Lect. in Pharmacognosy & Pharmaceutics, Sch. of Pharmacy, Lagos, 1949-56; Pharmacist, Nigerian Medical Serv., & Head of Features, Nigerian Broadcasting Corp., 1956-61; Chairman, E. Central State Lib. Bd., Enugu. *Mailing address:* 50 Ogbete St., P.O. Box 317, Enugu, Nigeria.

Writings:
__Fiction__

Ikolo the Wrestler and Other Ibo Tales (London, Nelson, 1947, 1960?)

The Leopard's Claw, novelette (London, Longman's, 1947)

When Love Whispers, novelette (Onitsha, Nigeria, Tabansi Press, 1948)

People of the City, novel (London, Andrew Dakers, 1954; Evanston, Ill., Northwestern U. Press, 1967; rev. ed., Greenwich, Conn., Fawcett, 1969)

The Drummer Boy, juv. (Cambridge, Eng., Cambridge U. Press, 1960)

Passport of Mallam Illia, juv. (Cambridge U. Press, 1960)

Jagua Nana, novel (London, Hutchinson, 1961; London, Panther, 1963; N.Y., Fawcett, 1969; London, Heinemann, African Writers Ser., 1975)

Burning Grass, novel (Heinemann, 1962)

Yaba Roundabout Murder, novelette (Lagos, Tortoise Ser. Bks., 1962)

An African Night's Entertainment; A Tale of Vengence, juv. (Lagos, African Universities Press, 1962)

Beautiful Feathers, novel (Hutchinson, 1963; Heinemann, African Writers Ser., 1971)

The Rainmaker and Other Stories, juv. (Lagos, African Universities Press, 1965)

The Great Elephant Bird, juv. (Nelson, 1965)

Trouble in Form Six, juv. (Cambridge U. Press, 1966)

Juju Rock, juv. (African Universities Press, 1966)

The Boa Suitor, juv. (Nelson, 1966)

Lokotown and Other Stories (London, Heinemann Educ. Bks., 1966)

Iska, novel (Panther, 1968)

Restless City and Christmas Gold, with Other Stories (Heinemann, 1975)

Samankwe and the Highway Robbers, short stories (London, Evans, 1975)

Survive the Peace, short stories (Heinemann, 1976)

Sidelights: Ekwensi is possibly the most skillful writer in Africa in depicting the vicissitudes of the rural African who has escaped to the city only to find that the excitements and terrors of the urban way of life are almost overwhelming. "His novels, *People of the City* (1954) and *Jagua Nana* (1961), were the first good treatments of the varied peoples of modern Lagos." The most popular and critically acclaimed of his works is *Jagua Nana*. (*African Authors*)

Sources: *African Authors; Books in Print*, 1979-80, 1980-81; *Cyprian Ekwensi; Introduction to West African Literature; Writers Directory*, 1980-82.

ELDER, LONNE, III. Playwright, Filmwriter.
Education: Yale U., Sch. of Drama. *Career:* Worked after-hours clubs; wrote poems, short stories; Dir., Playwright's Div., Negro Ensemble Co., N.Y. *Honors:* Stanley Drama Award; John Hay Whitney Found. Fellow in play-writing; alternate winner, ABC-TV; Writing Fellow Award, Yale Sch. of Drama, 1965-66; "Playwright in Residence" for *Fiddler on the Roof; Charades* commissioned by Cultural Arts Dept., N.Y. Mobilization for Youth, Inc. *Mailing address:* c/o Avon Bks., 959 Eighth Ave., N.Y., N.Y. 10019.

Writings:
Fiction
The Terrible Veil, play for NBS Kaleidoscope (1965)

Charades on East Fourth St., play performed at Expo '67, Montreal (in *Black Drama Anthology*, 1971)

Ceremonies in Dark Old Men, play (N.Y., Farrar, 1969)

Ceremonies in Dark Old Men, a Play in Two Acts (N.Y., S. French, 1969)

Camera 3, documentary teleplay, CBS (n.d.)

Sounder, screenplay (n.d.)

Deadly Circle of Violence, television play (n.d.)

Part Two, Sounder, screenplay

Sidelights: Influenced by Douglas Turner Ward. Negro Ensemble Company produced play *Ceremonies*, which won Stanley Drama Award. Hailed by Richard Watts of the *New York Post* as "best American play of the season." (*Black American Writer*)

Sources: *Black American Writer*, vol. II: *Poetry and Drama; New Black Playwrights*.

ELIJAH MUHAMMAD. *See* MUHAMMAD, ELIJAH

ELLINGTON, EDWARD KENNEDY (Duke). Composer, Band Leader, Pianist.

Born in Wash., D.C., Apr. 29, 1899. *Education:* Public schs., Wash.; studied music with Henry Grant. *Family:* Married Edna Thompson, 1918; son Mercer. *Career:* Toured Europe, 1933, 1950; toured Eng. & France, 1948; annual Carnegie Hall concerts, 1943-50; Metropolitan Opera House, 1951. Motion pictures: *Check and Double Check*, 1930; *She Got Her Man*, 1935; *Murder at the Vanities*, 1935; *The Hit Parade*, 1937; *Cabin in the Sky*, 1943, etc. Records: "Mood Indigo," "Solitude," "Sophisticated Lady," "Take the A Train," etc. *Honors:* "Far East Suite" played by Ellington's orchestra at White House Festival of the Arts, June 1965; "The Golden Broom and the Golden Apple" suite performed at Lincoln Center, where he conducted the N.Y. Philharmonic, July 1965; "In the Beginning, God," 1st sacred concert, at Grace Episcopal Cathedral, San Francisco, Sept. 1965 (repeated at Fifth Ave. Presby. Church, N.Y.C., Christmas 1965; taped by CBS-TV & telecast Jan. 1966). A Billy Strayhorn memorial album, "And His Mother Called Him Bill," was chosen the "best performance by a large group" by the Natl. Acad. of Recording Arts & Scis., 1968. "Ellington has won first place or top rank repeatedly in polls or selections made by the magazines *Esquire, Down Beat,* and *Playboy*." (*Current Biography*) Other medals: Bronze Medal of City of N.Y.; NAACP Spingarn Medal; Pres. Medal of Honor (on his 70th birthday); elected to Natl. Inst. of Arts & Letters, 1970. ASCAP-Deems Taylor Award for *Music Is My Mistress*, 1974. Died Apr. 1974.

Writings:
Nonfiction
Music Is My Mistress (N.Y., Doubleday, 1973; N.Y., DaCapo Press, 1973)

The Great Music of Duke Ellington (Melville, N.Y., Belwin Mills, 1973)

Sidelights: "The single most impressive body of composition in American jazz is the lush, complexly harmonic repertoire that band leader-pianist-composer Duke Ellington has produced over the past half century.... Jazz critic Ralph Gleason has called Ellington 'the greatest single talent ... in the history of jazz.' ...Composer Gunther Schuller, president of the New England Conservatory of Music, described him as 'certainly the greatest American composer.' " (*Current Biography*)

Sources: Current Biography, 1970; *Negro Handbook*.

ELLISON, RALPH WALDO. Novelist, Essayist, Lecturer.

Born in Okla. City, Okla., Mar. 1, 1914. *Education:* Tuskegee Inst., Ala., 1933-36; Hon. Ph.D. in Humane Letters, Tuskegee Inst.; Hon. degrees: Litt.D., Rutgers U., 1966; U. of Mich., 1967; Williams Coll., 1970. L.H.D.: Grinnell Coll., 1967; Adelphi U., 1971. *Family:* Married Fanny McConnell, July 1946. *Career:* Participated in N.Y.C. Writer's Project; Lect., Amer. Negro culture, folklore, creative writing, N.Y.U., Columbia, Fisk, Antioch, Princeton, Bennington, others; Lect., Salzburg Seminar in Amer. Studies, Austria, 1954; USIA, Dept. of State, tour of Italian cities, 1956; Tchr., Russian & Amer. Lit., Bard Coll., 1958-61; Alexander White Visiting Prof., U. of Chicago, 1961; Visiting Prof., Writing, Rutgers U., 1962-64; Albert Schweitzer Prof. of Humanities, N.Y.U., 1970-80. *Honors:* All for *Invisible Man*: Natl. Bk. Award for Fiction, 1953; Russwurm Award, 1953; Natl. Newspaper Pub. Award, 1954; Arts & Letters Award Fellow, Rome, 1955; *N.Y. Herald Tribune*'s Bk. Review Poll, 1965 (for most distinguished novel written between 1945 & 1965). Consultant in Amer. Letters, Lib. of Congress, 1966- ; Julius Rosenwald Fund Fellow, 1945;

Medal of Freedom, 1969; decorated Chevalier Ordre des Artes et Lettres (France); Visiting Fellow, Amer. Studies, Yale, 1966; Amer. Acad. of Arts & Scis.; Rockefeller Found. Award, 1954. *Mailing address:* 730 Riverside Drive, N.Y., N.Y. 10031.

Writings:
Fiction

Invisible Man, novel (N.Y., Random House, 1952, 1972; N.Y., NAL, 1952; N.Y., Mod. Lib., 1952, 1963)

Nonfiction

Shadow and Act, essays (Random House, 1964)

Sidelights: Ellison was recognized as a significant literary talent as soon as *Invisible Man* appeared in 1952. Saul Bellow was not alone when he called the novel "superb." Characteristic of the majority of reviews, an early appraisal in the *Saturday Review* saw *Invisible Man* as not only "a great Negro novel" but "a work of art any contemporary writer could point to with pride." (*Dictionary of Literary Biography*)

John M. Reilly states, "From the fact that he has published a single novel and that nearly twenty years ago, Ralph Ellison's reputation as a major American novelist seems phenomenal, but then his novel is a remarkable work." (*Contemporary Novelists*)

Sources: *Cavalcade; Contemporary Novelists*, 1972; *Current Biography*, 1968; *Dictionary of Literary Biography; Negro Almanac; Negro Novel in America; Who's Who in America*, 37th ed., 1972-73.

EMANUEL, JAMES ANDREW. Poet, Critic, Teacher, Editor.
Born in Alliance, Neb., June 15, 1921. *Education:* B.A., Howard U., 1950; M.A., Northwestern U., 1953; Ph.D., Columbia U., 1962. *Family:* Married Mattie Etha Johnson (div.), son James Andrew, Jr. *Career:* Confidential Secy. to Gen. B. O. Davis, 1942-44; Sgt., 93rd Infantry Div., 1945-46; Supvr., section, Main Army & Air Force Induction Station, Chicago, 1950-52; Tchr., Harlem YWCA, Bus. & Secretarial Sch., N.Y., 1954-56; Prof., Lit., City Coll., CUNY, 1957- ; Gen. Ed., Broadside Critics Ser. Fulbright Prof., U. of Warsaw, Poland, 1975-76. *Honors:* Summa cum laude, 4 yrs., Howard U.; John Hay Whitney Found. Opportunity Fellow, 1952-54; Eugene F. Saxton Memorial Trust Fellow, 1965; Fulbright Visiting Prof. Amer. Lit., U. of Grenoble, France, 1968-69, U. of Toulouse, France, 1971-73, 1979-81; sole representative of U.S. at invitational Sarajevo "Days of Poetry" Festival, 1982. *Mailing address:* 340 E. 90th St., 3B, N.Y., N.Y. 10028.

Writings:
Fiction

The Tree House and Other Poems (Detroit, Broadside, 1968)

Panther Man, poems (Broadside, 1970)

Dynamite Voices 1: Black Poets of the 1960's, anthology, Don L. Lee, Gen. Ed. (Broadside, 1971)

Black Man Abroad: The Toulouse Poems (Detroit, Lotus, 1978)

A Chisel in the Dark, poems (Lotus, 1980)

The Broken Bowl: New and Uncollected Poems (Lotus, 1983)

Nonfiction

Langston Hughes, essays (N.Y., Twayne, 1967; transl. to French, Paris, Noveaux Horizons, 1970)

Dark Symphony, Negro Literature in America, criticism, with Theodore L. Gross (N.Y., Free Press, 1968)

How I Write/2, essays, with Others (N.Y., Harcourt, 1972)

Claude McKay: The Black Poet at War, Addison Gayle, Gen. Ed. (Broadside, 1972)

The Folk Roots of Contemporary Afro-American Poetry, Bernard W. Bell, Gen. Ed. (Broadside, 1973)

A Many-Colored Coat of Dreams: The Poetry of Countee Cullen, Gen. Ed. (Broadside, 1974)

Phillis Wheatley in the Black American Beginnings, by William H. Robinson, Gen. Ed. (Broadside, 1975)

A Poet's Mind (N.Y., Regents, 1983)

Sidelights: "Both my volumes *The Treehouse and Other Poems* and *Panther Man*, read by me, are available in the *Broadside Voices* series, Broadside Press, Detroit, Michigan." (Author)

Sources: Author information; *Books in Print*, 1978-79; *Broadside Authors and Artists; Dark Symphony; Library Journal*, Dec. 15, 1980; *New Black Voices; Poetry of Black America.*

EMECHETA, BUCHI [Florence Onye]. (Nigerian). Novelist, Sociologist.
Born near Lagos, Nigeria, in 1944. *Education:* B.A. (Sociol.), London U. *Family:* Five children. *Career:* Youth Worker & Sociologist, Inner London Educ. Authority, since 1969; Lib. Officer, Brit. Museum, London, 1965-69; Faculty, U. of Calabar (Nigeria). *Mailing address:* 154 Albany St., London NWI, Eng.

Writings:
Fiction
Second Class Citizen, novel (N.Y., Braziller, 1974)

Bride Price, novel (Braziller, 1976)

Slave Girl, novel (Braziller, 1977)

The Joys of Motherhood, novel (Braziller, 1979)

Nonfiction
In the Ditch (London, Barrie & Jenkins, 1972; N.Y., Schocken, 1980)

Nowhere to Play (Schocken, 1980)

Sources: *Books in Print*, 1980-81, 1981-82; *Slave Girl; Writers Directory*, 1980-82.

ESPIRITO SANTO, ALDA DE. (São Toméan). Poet, Journalist, Teacher.
Born in São Tomé, Apr. 30, 1926. *Career:* Arrested in 1965 for taking part in nationalist politics, in opposition to the Portuguese; released in 1966; returned to teaching. *Mailing address:* c/o Penguin Bks., Ltd., Harmondsworth, Middlesex, Eng.

Writings:
(Partial Listing—English Only)
Fiction
Poems in *New Sum of Poetry from the Negro World* (Paris, Présence Africaine, vol. 57, 1966)

Poems in *Modern Poetry from Africa*, ed. by G. Moore & U. Beier (London, Penguin, rev. ed., 1968)

Sources: *African Authors; Sturdy Black Bridges.*

EVANS, MARI. Poet, Teacher, Juvenile Writer.
Born in Toledo, Ohio, 1923. *Education:* U. of Toledo. *Family:* Div. *Career:* Writer-in-Residence & Instr., Black Lit., Ind. U.-Purdue U., Indianapolis; Visiting Asst. Prof., Northwestern U., Evanston, Ill.; Prod.-Dir.-Writer (1968-73) for weekly half-hour TV presentation, "The Black Experience" (Bobbs-Merrill); Consultant in Ethnic Studies (1970-73) for Bobbs-Merrill; Writer-in-Residence & Asst. Prof., Ind. U., Bloomington; Tchr., African Studies & Res. Center, Cornell U. *Honors:* "Her book *I Am a Black Woman* ... received the Indiana U. Writers' Conference Award for

the most distinguished work of poetry published by an Indiana author in 1970, and received the Black Academy of Arts and Letters first annual Poetry Award in September 1971." John Hay Whitney Found. Fellow, 1965-66; received a Woodrow Wilson Found. Grant in 1968; served as Consultant in the 1969-70 Discovery Grant Program of the NEA. *Mailing address:* c/o Doubleday & Co., Inc., 501 Franklyn Ave., Garden City, N.Y. 11530.

Writings:
Fiction

Where Is All the Music?, poems (London, Breman, 1968)

I Am a Black Woman, poems (N.Y., Morrow, 1970)

J.D., juv. (Garden City, N.Y., Doubleday, 1973; N.Y., Avon, 1975)

I Look at Me, preschool reader (Chicago, Third World, 1974)

Rap Stories, juv. (Third World, 1974)

Singing Black, juv. (Indianapolis, Reed Visuals, 1976)

Jim Flying High, juv. (Doubleday, 1979)

Nightstar, 1973-1978, ed. by Romey T. Keys (L.A., UCLA Center for Afro-Amer. Studies, Special Publ. Ser., 1981)

Sidelights: "Her poetry has been used on record albums, several television specials, two off-Broadway productions, and in nearly 150 textbooks and anthologies." (Author)

Sources: Author information; *Afro-American Writing; Black Voices; Books in Print,* 1981-82; *Broadside Authors and Artists; Ebony,* Mar. 1974; *For Malcolm; Kaleidoscope; New Black Voices; Poetry of Black America.*

FABIO, SARAH WEBSTER. Poet, Teacher, Afro-American Literature Professor.
Born in Nashville, Tenn., Jan. 20, 1928. *Education:* B.A., Fisk U., 1946; M.A., San Francisco State U. *Family:* Married Cyril Fabio (div.); children: Cyril Leslie III, Thomas, Cheryl Elisa, Renee Angela, Ronald Eric. *Career:* Tchr., Merritt Jr. Coll., Oakland, Cal.; Afro-Amer. Studies Dept., U. Cal., Berkeley; Assoc. Prof., African & African-Amer. Lit., Oberlin Coll.; Ed., *Phase II*, Journal of Black Arts Renaissance. Died Nov. 7, 1979.

Writings:
Fiction

Saga of the Black Man (Oakland, Cal., Turn Over Bk. Store, 1968)

A Mirror: A Soul, poems (San Francisco, J. Richardson, 1969)

Black Is a Panther Caged, poems (1972)

Soul Ain't: Soul Is ... The Hurt of It All (n.p., 1973)

Together/To the Tune of Coltrane's Equinox (n.p., 1973)

Black Back: Back Black (n.p., 1973)

Boss Soul (n.p., 1973)

My Own Thing (n.p., 1973)

Jujus/Alchemy of the Blues (n.p., 1973)

Jujus and Jubilees, Critical Essays in Rhyme about Poets/Musicians/Black Heroes with Introductory Notes (Oberlin, Ohio, n.p., 1973)

Sidelights: Ms. Fabio participated in the First World Festival of Negro Art, Dakar, Senegal, 1966. She published two LP albums in 1973 and has read her poems with jazz and rock bands. She also participated in the Third Annual Writers Conference, Fisk University, 1968. (*Poetry of Black America*)

Her records are: "Boss Soul" and "Soul Ain't: Soul Is," both Folkways, 1972. (*Black Scholar*)

Sources: Author brochure; *Black Scholar*, Nov./Dec. 1979; *Ebony*, Mar. 1974; *Poetry of Black America.*

FAIR, RONALD. Novelist, Short Story Writer.
Born in Chicago, Ill., Oct. 27, 1932. *Education:* Chicago public sch.; Stenotype Sch. of Chicago; U.S. Navy. *Family:* Div.; son Rodney, son Glen, d. Nile. *Career:* Court Reporter, 1955-56; Tchr., Columbia Coll., Chicago, 1967; Visiting Tchr., Northwestern U.; Visiting Prof., Eng. Dept., Wesleyan U., 1970-71. *Honors:* Arts & Letters Award, 1971; Best Bks. of the Yr., 1972 (ALA for *We Can't Breathe*); NEA Fellow, 1974; Guggenheim Found. Fellow. *Mailing address:* c/o Lotus Press, P.O. Box 21607, Detroit, Mich. 48221.

Writings:
Fiction

Many Thousand Gone; An American Fable (N.Y., Harcourt, 1965; reprint, Chatham, N.J., Chatham Bookseller, 1973)

Hog Butcher, novel (Harcourt, 1966; reprinted as *Cornbread, Earl and Me*, N.Y., Bantam, 1975)

World of Nothing: Two Novellas (N.Y., Harper, 1970; Chatham Bookseller, 1970)

We Can't Breathe, short story (Harper, 1972)

Excerpts (London, Breman, 1975)

Rufus, novel (Stuttgart, Germany, Peter Schlock Verlag, 1976; 2nd ed., Detroit, Lotus, 1980)

Sidelights: Began writing somewhere between the ages of twelve and sixteen because of "my anger with the life I knew and inability of anyone I knew to explain why things were the way they were." (*New Black Voices*)
Fair left the United States in 1971 and has recently been living in Finland.

Sources: Author information; *Best Short Stories by Negro Writers; Books in Print*, 1979-80; *New Black Voices;* Pub. information; *Rufus.*

FANON, FRANTZ. (Martiniquean). Psychiatrist, Revolutionary.
Born in Martinique, French W. Indies, July 20, 1925. *Education:* Martinique; Medicine & Psychiatry, Lyons, France, 1951. *Family:* Married French woman, 1953. *Career:* Dir., Psychiatric Dept., Blida-Joinville Hospital, Algeria. As mem. of Algerian liberation movement (FLN), became ed. writer for party's underground newspaper *El Moudjahid*, Tunis. Attended First Congress of Black Writers & Artists, called by *Présence Africaine*, Paris, 1956; attended All African People's Conf., Accra, Ghana, 1958. Apptd. Ambassador to Ghana by Algerian Provisional Govt. Died Dec. 6, 1961.

Writings
(Partial Listing—English Only)
Nonfiction

The Damned, trans. by Constance Farrington (Paris, Présence Africaine, 1963)

The Wretched of the Earth, transl. by Constance Farrington (N.Y., Grove, 1965)

Studies in a Dying Colonialism, transl. by Haakon Chevalier (N.Y., Monthly Review Press, 1965)

Toward the African Revolution, transl. by Haakon Chevalier (Grove, 1967)

Black Skin, White Masks, transl. by Charles L. Markmann (Grove, 1967)

Sidelights: "*The Wretched of the Earth* ... established Fanon's reputation as a major contributor to the revolutionary philosophy of the Third World ... the colonial victim could free himself of oppression [but] only socialist revolution ... achieved by violence ... the instrument of revolution would ... be ... the poor peasants, the wretched of the earth." (*World Authors*)

Sources: *Black Writers in French; Resistance and Caribbean Literature; World Authors.*

FAUSET, ARTHUR HUFF. Anthropologist, Folklorist, Teacher.
Born in Flemington, N.J., Jan. 20, 1899. *Education:* B.A., 1921, M.A., 1924, Ph.D., 1942, U. of Pa. *Career:* Writer; Tchr., Prin., Phila. public schs., 1918-46; volunteer, Army of the United States, World War II. *Honors:* Fellow, Amer. Anthropological Assn.; Amer. Folklore Soc., studied folklore extant among Blacks in Phila., Brit. W. Indies, Nova Scotia, & the South, 1931; prize, story "Symphonesque," reprinted in various publ., including O'Brien, *Best Short Stories*, & O. Henry, *Best Short Stories. Mailing address:* c/o U. of Pa. Press, 3933 Walnut St., Phila., Pa. 19174.

Writings:
Fiction
Folklore from Nova Scotia (N.Y., Amer. Folklore Society, 1931; Millwood, N.Y., Kraus Reprint, 1931)

Nonfiction
For Freedom: A Biographical Story of the American Negro (Phila., Franklin Pub., 1927)

Sojourner Truth: God's Faithful Pilgrim (Chapel Hill, U. of N.C. Press, 1938; reprint, N.Y., Russell, 1971)

Black Gods of the Metropolis: Negro Religious Cults of the Urban North (N.Y., Octagon, 1944, 1970; Phila., U. of Pa. Press, 1971)

America, Red, White, Black and Yellow, with Nella B. Bright (Franklin Pub., 1969)

Sources: Author information; *Contemporary Authors*, vols. 25-28, 1st rev., 1977.

FAUSET, JESSIE REDMOND. Novelist, Editor, Translator.
Born in Snow Hill, N.J., Apr. 26, 1882. *Education:* Phila. public schs.; B.A., Cornell U. (Phi Beta Kappa); M.A., U. of Pa.; Sorbonne, Paris. *Family:* Married Herbert Harris, 1929. *Career:* Tchr., Dunbar High Sch., Wash., D.C.; Lit. Ed., *The Crisis*; Tchr., French, N.Y. public schs. Died Apr. 30, 1961.

Writings:
Fiction
There Is Confusion, novel (N.Y., Boni & Liveright, 1924; reprint, N.Y., AMS, 1974)

Plum Bun, novel (N.Y., Stokes, 1929)

The Chinaberry Tree: A Novel of American Life (Stokes, 1931; reprint, AMS, n.d.; Westport, Conn., Negro Universities Press, n.d.)

Comedy, American Style, novel (Stokes, 1933; reprint, AMS, n.d.; n.p., Negro Universities Press, n.d.)

Sidelights: Born into upper-class family. Studied French at Sorbonne and lived in Paris for several years. Skillful translator of some of the Black poets of French W. Indies. Taught at Dunbar High School, which was exclusively geared to training college-bound Negroes. Some of her poetry, written in French, attracted attention of W. E. B. DuBois, who invited her to join *The Crisis*. The most prolific of the Renaissance writers of the genteel school. (*Cavalcade*)

Sources: *An Anthology of Verse by American Negroes; Book of American Negro Poetry; Books in Print*, 1980-81; *Cavalcade; Crisis*, June-July 1983.

FAUST, NAOMI F. English Professor, Poet.
Born in Salisbury, N.C. *Education:* B.A., Bennett Coll., 1938; M.A., U. of Mich., 1945; Ph.D., N.Y.U., 1963. *Family:* Married Roy Malcolm Faust (tchr.), Aug. 16, 1948. *Career:* Elementary & high sch. tchr. in Gaffney, S.C., & Winston Salem, N.C., 1938-43; Instr., Eng., 1944-45; Instr., Eng., Southern U., Scotlandville, La., 1945-46; Asst. Prof., Eng., Morgan State Coll., Baltimore, 1946-48; Tchr., Eng., Dudley High Sch., Greensboro, N.C., & Prof., Eng. Educ., Queens Coll., CUNY, 1964- . *Honors:* Alpha Epsilon Honor Soc.; Alpha Kappa Mu Honor Soc.; Certificate of Merit for poems in *Poems by Blacks* (1970). *Mailing address:* 12001 175th St., Jamaica, N.Y. 11433.

Writings:

Fiction

Speaking in Verse (A Book of Poems) (Boston, Branden, 1974)

Nonfiction

Discipline and the Classroom Teacher (Port Wash., N.Y., Kennikat, 1977)

Sidelights: "Dr. Faust is a poet committed to the idea of writing poems with worthwhile content and themes that her readers may read, comprehend, and enjoy." (Publisher)

Sources: Author information; Pub. information.

FAX, ELTON CLAY. Artist-Illustrator, Essayist.
Born in Baltimore, Md., Oct. 9, 1909. *Education:* B.F.A., Syracuse U., 1931. *Family:* (wife deceased); d. Betty L. Evans, son Leon. *Career:* Artist-Illustrator; exhibits: Natl. Gallery of Art & Corcoran Gallery of Art (both Wash., D.C.); Syracuse, N.Y.; Baltimore, Md.; N.Y.C.; Nashville, Tenn.; Huntsville Mus., Ala.; Taskkent, Uzbekistan, USSR. U.S. Dept. of State, spec. in S. Amer. & Caribbean, 1955, & in E. Africa, 1964. *Honors:* Louis E. Seely gold award for painting ordered for U.S. Navy Combat Collection, 1972; Coretta Scott King Award for book *Seventeen Black Artists* (1972). *Mailing address:* Box 2188, Long Island City, N.Y. 11102.

Writings:

Nonfiction

West Africa Vignettes, self-illustrated (N.Y., Amer. Soc. of African Culture, 1960; enlarged ed., 1963)

Contemporary Black Leaders (N.Y., Dodd, 1970)

Seventeen Black Artists (Dodd, 1971)

Garvey: The Story of a Pioneer Black Nationalist (Dodd, 1972)

Through Black Eyes, Journeys of a Black Artist to East Africa and Russia (Dodd, 1974)

Black Artists of the New Generation (Dodd, 1977)

Source: Author information.

FEELINGS, MURIEL (Grey). Juvenile Writer, Teacher.
Born in Phila., Pa., July 31, 1938. *Education:* Phila. Mus. Sch. of Art, 1957-60; B.A., Cal. State U., L.A. *Family:* Married Tom Feelings (div.); children: Zamani, Kamili. *Career:* Tchr., U.S. & E. Africa, 1964-70. *Honors: Moja Means One* was Caldecott runner-up (ALA); *Jambo Means Hello* was Caldecott Honor Book; both *Moja Means One* & *Jambo Means Hello* were ALA Notable Books. *Mailing address:* c/o Dial Press, One Dag Hammarskjold Plaza, 247 E. 47th St., N.Y., N.Y. 10017.

Writings:

Fiction

Zamani Goes to Market, juv., illustrated by Tom Feelings (N.Y., Seabury, 1970)

Moja Means One: The Swahili Counting Book, juv., illustrated by Tom Feelings (N.Y., Dial, 1971, 1976)

Jambo Means Hello: Swahili Alphabet Book, juv., illustrated by Tom Feelings (Dial, 1974, 1981)

Sidelights: "*Zamani Goes to Market*, her first book for children, was inspired by a stay with a family in a small village of Western Kenya.

"Her artist husband, Tom Feelings, traveled to East Africa just before completing the drawings for *Zamani*." (*Zamani Goes to Market*)

Sources: *Books in Print*, 1980-81; *Something about the Author*, vol. 14, 1979; *Zamani Goes to Market*.

FEELINGS, TOM. Artist, Juvenile Writer.
Born in Brooklyn, N.Y. *Education:* Sch. for Visual Arts. *Family:* Married Muriel Grey (div.); children: Zamani, Kamili. *Career:* Illustrator, Ghana Govt. Pub. House, 1964-66; Guyana. *Honors: Jambo Means Hello* was selected Caldecott Honor Book by the ALA; *Moja Means One* was a Caldecott runner-up. *Mailing address:* c/o Dial Press, One Dag Hammarskjold Plaza, 247 E. 47th St., N.Y., N.Y. 10017.

Writings:
Fiction

Black Pilgrimage, juv. (N.Y., Lothrop, 1972)

(Illustrated Books)
Zamani Goes to Market, juv., by Muriel Feelings (N.Y., Seabury, 1970)

Moja Means One: A Swahili Counting Book, juv., by Muriel Feelings (N.Y., Dial, 1971)

Jambo Means Hello: Swahili Alphabet Book, juv., by Muriel Feelings (Dial, 1974)

Sidelights: In Mr. Feelings's words, "My heart is with the Black people of America, but my soul is in Africa." (*Black Pilgrimage*)

"Highly respected for his sensitive portrayal of Black people, ... [Feelings] has illustrated many books of distinction, including *To Be a Slave* and *A Quiet Place*." (*Zamani Goes to Market*)

Sources: *Black Pilgrimage; Black World*, June 1975.

FERGUSON, LLOYD N. Chemist, Chemistry Professor.
Born in Oakland, Cal., Feb. 9, 1918. *Education:* B.A., 1940, Ph.D., 1943, U. of Cal., Berkeley. *Family:* Married Charlotte W. Ferguson; son Lloyd, Jr., son Steve, d. Lisa. *Career:* Res. Asst., Natl. Defense Project, U. of Cal., 1941-44; Asst. Prof., Agricultural & Technical Coll., Greensboro, N.C., 1944-45; Faculty mem., Howard U., 1945-65, Head, Dept. of Chemistry, 1958-65; Prof., Cal. State U., L.A., 1965- ; Chairman, Chemistry Dept., Cal State, 1968-71; Visiting Prof., U. of Nairobi, Kenya, 1971-72; Apptd. mem., Ed. Bd., *Journal of Coll. Sci. Teaching*; Natl. Sci. Tchrs. Assn. Fellowship Fund, Atlanta, Ga., for screening applicants for Ford Found. fellowships from Black predoctoral candidates. *Honors:* Manufacturing Chemists Teaching Award, 1974; Hon. D. Sci., Howard U., 1970; Guggenheim Found. Fellow, Cytochemistry Dept., Carlberg Laboratorium, Copenhagen, 1953-54; Natl. Sci. Found. Fellow, Swiss Fed. Inst. of Technology, Zurich, 1961-62; Oakland Mus. Assn. "in recognition of contributions to science and technology for humanity," 1973; Cal. State Outstanding Prof. Award, 1974. *Mailing address:* c/o Cal. State U., L.A., Cal. 90032.

Writings
Nonfiction

Electron Structures of Organic Molecules (N.Y., Prentice-Hall, 1952)

Textbook of Organic Chemistry (Princeton, N.J., Van Nostrand, 1958; 2nd ed., 1965; Far East ed., New Delhi, Affiliate East West Press, 1966)

The Modern Structural Theory of Organic Chemistry (Prentice-Hall, 1963; Japanese transl., Tokyo, Kagaku Dojin Sha, 1965; Far East ed., New Delhi, Prentice-Hall of India, 1969)

Organic Chemistry: A Science and an Art (Boston, Willard Grant, 1972)

Highlights of Alicyclic Chemistry (Phila., Franklin Pub., vol. 1, 1973, 1977)

Organic Molecular Structures: A Gateway to Advanced Organic Chemistry (Willard Grant, 1975)

Sidelights: Dr. Ferguson gave three talks at international conference on teaching of university chemistry, University of Nairobi, 1971.

"As a member of the National Cancer Institute (NCI) Chemotherapy Advisory Committee, was one of two members to accompany two NCI administrators on a one-month tour of Russian Laboratories in 1973 (Moscow, Riga, Leningrad, Kiev, and Yerevan) to discuss the cancer chemotherapy programs of the two countries and to initiate an exchange of information and drugs under the U.S.-USSR Joint Committee on Research on Oncologic Diseases."

Program Director of 5-yr. $1.1 million grant to California State University, Los Angeles, from U.S. Public Health Service to support biomedical research for minority students. (Author)

Source: Author information.

FIGUEROA, JOHN (Joseph Maria). (Jamaican). Poet, Critic, Anthologist, University Teacher, Editor, Broadcaster, Consultant in Education.
Born in Kingston, Jamaica, Aug. 4, 1920. *Education:* St. George's Coll., Jamaica; Holy Cross Coll., Worchester, Mass.; London U. (Degrees: A.B., M.A., L.H.D.). *Family:* Married Dorothy M. Alexander; four sons, three daughters. *Career:* Sports Reporter, 1946-60; Broadcaster, BBC, London; Lect. in Eng. & Philosophy, U. of London; Tchr., Eng., 1948-53; Prof., Educ. (former Dean), U. Coll., W. Indies, Mona; Tchr., Indiana U.; U. of Puerto Rico; Centro Caribeño de Estudios Postgraduados; 1st Gen. Ed., Heinemann's Caribbean Writers Ser. *Honors:* Awards from British Council; Carnegie Fellow; Guggenheim Fellow. *Mailing address:* Dept. of Educ., U. of W. Indies, Mona, Kingston 7, Jamaica.

Writings:
Fiction

Blue Mountain Peak, poetry & prose anthology (Kingston, Jamaica, n.p., 1944)

Love Leaps Here, poems (London, Evans, 1962)

Caribbean Voices: Anthology of West Indian Poetry, vol. I (Evans, 1966; 6th impression, 1974)

Caribbean Voices, anthology, vol. II — *The Blue Horizons* (Evans, 1970, 2nd ed., 1973)

Caribbean Voices, anthology, combined ed. of vols. I & II (Evans, 1971; Wash., D.C., Luce, 1973)

Ignoring Hurts, Poems (Wash., D.C., Three Continents, 1976)

Nonfiction

Staffing and Examinations in British Caribbean Secondary Schools (Evans, 1964)

Society, Schools and Progress in the West Indies (N.Y., Oxford, N.Y., Pergamon, 1971)

The Poetry of Derek Walcott, criticism (Three Continents, 1980)

Sidelights: Figueroa was one of the main readers on the British Broadcasting Company's Caribbean Voices. He is the editor and producer of "West Indian Poets Reading Their Own Work." His most recent collection, put out in 1976, was *Ignoring Hurts*.
His greatest strength lies in his reflective and philosophical poetry. (*Contemporary Poets*)

Sources: *Bibliography of the Caribbean; Contemporary Poets*, 2nd ed., 1975; *Jamaican National Bibliography; West Indian Literature; Writers Directory*, 1982-84.

FISHER, MILES MARK. Minister, Church History Professor.
Born in Atlanta, Ga., Oct. 29, 1899. *Education:* B.A., Morehouse Coll., 1918; B.D., N. Bap. Theol. Sem., 1922; A.M., 1922, Ph.D., 1948, U. of Chicago Divinity Sch. *Family:* Married Ada Virginia Foster; d. Mrs. Florida Parker, son Miles Mark IV, son Alfred Foster, son Elijah John III, son Christopher Tennant, d. Ada Markita Fisher. *Career:* Minister, White Rock Bap. Church, Durham, N.C., 1933-65, Minister-Emeritus, 1965-70; Prof., Hist., Va. Union U.; Prof., Church Hist., Shaw U., Raleigh, N.C., 1933-65. *Honors: Negro Slave Songs in the United States* won Amer. Historical Assn.'s prize for outstanding hist. vol. of 1953; selected as one of nation's top ten ministers of 1954; recipient of Golden Anniversary Award, Natl. Recreation Assn.; Hon. D.D., Shaw U.; Hon. member, Intnl. Mark Twain Society. Died Dec. 14, 1970, in Richmond, Va.

Writings:
Nonfiction

The Master's Slave — Elijah John Fisher; A Biography by His Son (Phila., Judson, 1922)

Virginia Union University and Some of Her Achievements (Richmond, Brown Print Shop, 1924)

A Short History of the Baptist Denomination (Nashville, Sunday Sch. Pub. Bd., 1933)

Negro Slave Songs in the United States (Ithaca, N.Y., Cornell U. Press, 1953; n.p., Fuller, 1968; Secaucus, N.J., Citadel, 1963, 1978; reprint, N.Y., Russell, 1968)

Sources: Author's widow's information; *Encyclopedia of Black America*; Pub. information.

FISHER, RUDOLPH. Physician, Novelist.
Born in Wash., D.C., in 1897. *Education:* B.A. (honors), 1919, M.A., 1920, Brown U.; Howard U. Medical Sch.; Columbia U. Medical Sch. *Career:* Tchr., Biology; Physician; Affiliate, X-Ray Div., Dept. of Health, N.Y.C.; Writer. *Honors:* Excelled in Eng. Lit. & Biology at Brown U.; member of Phi Beta Kappa, Sigma Psi, & Delta Sigma Rho. Died in 1934.

Writings:
Fiction

The Walls of Jericho, novel (N.Y., Knopf, 1928)

The Conjure Man Dies, a Mystery Tale of Dark Harlem, novel (N.Y., Covici-Friede, 1932)

Sidelights: "Prominently associated with the 'Negro Renaissance' ... [Fisher was] unembittered, and one of the wittiest of the Renaissance group.... He was among the first to light up the dark realities of Negro life with humor." (*Cavalcade*)

"Beneath the comedy and caricature of Fisher, there is a revelation of the truth of Harlem as it was in the late twenties." (*Negro Caravan*)

Sources: *Cavalcade; Dark Symphony; Historical Negro Biographies; Negro Caravan; Negro Genius; Negro Voices in American Fiction.*

FORD, NICK AARON. English Professor, Literary Critic, Consultant.
Born in Ridgeway, S.C., Aug. 4, 1904. *Education:* B.A., Benedict Coll., Columbia, S.C.; M.A., 1934, Ph.D., 1945, U. of Iowa. *Family:* Married Ola M.; son Leonard Aaron. *Career:* Tchr., Coll. & U. in Fla., Tex., Okla., Mass., Md.; Chairman, Dept. of Eng., Morgan State Coll., Baltimore, 1947-70; Alain Locke Prof. of Black Studies, Morgan State, 1970-73; Consultant, Black Studies, U.S. Office of Educ.; Ford Found.; NEH; Dir. & Prof., Union Grad. Sch.-Center for Minority Studies, Brookings Institution, Wash., D.C., 1976-79. *Honors:* U.S. Office of Educ. 3-yr. grant for res. on improvement of reading & writing skills of disadvantaged coll. freshmen, 1964 (resulted in *Extending Horizons*); NEH Grant, evaluative study of Black Studies in Amer. colleges & universities, 1970 (visited more than 100 campuses & wrote *Black Studies: Threat or Challenge?*); Outstanding Serv. Award, Md. Council of Tchrs. of Eng., for "significant efforts toward improving the instruction in the Language Arts for the students in the schools of Maryland and toward raising the professional standards of teachers of English," 1971; Community Serv. Award, African Assn. of Black Studies, 1974; Alumni Award, Distinguished Serv., Benedict Coll., 1975; Paul L. Dunbar Memorial Award, 1978; Award, Natl. Assn. for Equal Opportunity in Higher Educ., 1981; High Individual Contrib. Annual Giving Campaign Award, Benedict Coll., 1982; Distinguished Literary Critics Award, Middle Atlantic Writers Assn., 1982. Died July 1982.

Writings:
Fiction

Songs from the Dark: Original Poems (Boston, Meador, 1940)

Baltimore Afro-American: Best Short Stories by Afro-American Writers, 1925-1950; A Study in Race Relations (Meador, 1950; Millwood, N.Y., Kraus Reprint, 1969)

Nonfiction

The Contemporary Negro Novel (Meador, 1936)

Basic Skills for Better Writing, co-ed. with Waters Turpin (N.Y., Putnam, 1959)

American Culture in Literature (Chicago, Rand McNally, 1967)

Language in Uniform, a Reader on Propaganda (Indianapolis, Odyssey, 1967)

Extending Horizons: Selected Readings for Cultural Enrichment, co-ed. with Waters Turpin (N.Y., Ramdon House, 1969)

Black Insights: Significant Literature by Black Americans—1760 to the Present (Waltham, Mass., Ginn, 1971)

Black Studies: Threat or Challenge? (Port Wash., N.Y., Kennikat, 1973)

Sidelights: "In constant demand as consultant in the use of resources for integrating the study of Afro-American life and culture into courses in American literature and Freshman English and guidance in the organization and effective teaching of courses in Black (Afro-American) literature." (Author)

Sources: Author information; *Contemporary Authors*, vols. 25-28, 1971.

FORTEN, CHARLOTTE L. Abolitionist, Teacher.
Born in Phila., Pa., in 1838. *Education:* Salem, Mass. Normal Sch., grad., 1856. *Family:* Married Francis J. Grimke (Minister, became spokesman for Negro people), 1878. *Career:* Volunteer tchr. during Civil War, St. Helena Island (off coast of S.C.);Tchr., 2 yrs., Salem, Mass. & Phila. Died in 1914.
Writings:
Nonfiction
Charlotte Forten's *Journal*, sporadic, 1854-64 (considered unusual record & important historic document; see *Journal of Charlotte Forten*)

Erckmann-Chartrians's *Madame Therese; or, the Volunteers of '92*, transl. (N.Y., Scribner, 1869)

The Journal of Charlotte Forten, ed. by Ray Allen Billington (N.Y., Dryden, 1953; N.Y., Collier, 1967)

Sidelights: "The Forten family had been actively involved in the black man's cause for two generations, and their Philadelphia home was described as a 'mecca for abolitionists.' Eventually Charlotte herself counted John Greenleaf Whittier, William Lloyd Garrison, and Wendell Phillips among her friends.... Her *Journal* frequently alludes to racial prejudice, discrimination, and injustice; her tone is often one of bitter irony, occasionally hinting at despair. She read widely and insatiably, wrote 'occasional' poems, and taught enthusiastically." (*Cavalcade*)

Sources: *Cavalcade; Historical Negro Biographies; Negro Poets and Their Poems; Profiles of Negro Womanhood.*

FORTUNE, TIMOTHY THOMAS. Journalist, Editor.
Born in Fla. in 1856. *Education:* Stanton Sch., Jacksonville, Fla.; Howard U. *Career:* Tchr., Fla.; compositor, a N.Y. newspaper; collaborator in founding & Ed., *New York Globe*, 1881; Founder, *New York Age* (1880s-1890s); Ed., *The Negro World* (publ. of Marcus Garvey's Universal Negro Improvement Assn.); Co-organizer (with Booker T. Washington) of Natl. Negro Bus. League, 1900; Ed. staff, *New York Evening Sun* (white newspaper). Died in 1928.
Writings:
Fiction
Dreams of Life: Miscellaneous Poems (N.Y., Fortune, 1905; reprint, Plainview, N.Y., Bks. for Libs., n.d.; N.Y., AMS, 1975; reprint, N.Y., Arno, Black Heritage Lib. Collection Ser., n.d.)

Nonfiction
Black and White: Land, Labor, and Politics in the South (N.Y., Fords, 1884; reprint, Arno, 1968; N.Y., Johnson Reprint, Ebony Classics Ser., 1970)

The Negro in Politics (N.Y., Ogilvie & Rowntree, 1885)

Sidelights: "Skilled stylist, and one of the most celebrated journalists of his time." (*Negro Author in America*)

"During the period that he had worked as editor of *The Globe*, Fortune had formulated a policy position for effective journalism; to be a power for good among the people a paper must be fearless in tone, its editor should not fail to speak his just convictions, he should hold himself aloof from parties and maintain his position untrammelled by parties and party bosses." (*Negro Handbook*)

Sources: *Afro-American Writing; Historical Negro Biographies; Men of Mark; Negro Author in America; Negro Caravan; Negro Handbook; Negro Vanguard; 100 Years of Negro Freedom.*

FRANKLIN, J(ENNIE) E(LIZABETH). Playwright.

Born in Houston, Tex., Aug. 19, 1937. *Education:* B.A., U. of Tex., 1964. *Family:* Married Lawrence Siegel, Nov. 12, 1964 (dec.); children: Malika N'zinga. *Career:* Writer; Youth Dir., Neighborhood House Assn., Buffalo, N.Y., 1964-65; U.S. Office of Econ. Opportunity (Analyst in N.Y.), 1967-68; Lect. in Educ., Herbert H. Lehman Coll. of City of N.Y., Bronx, 1969-75. *Honors:* N.Y. Drama Desk Most Promising Playwright Award, 1971, for *Black Girl*; Inst. for the Arts & Humanities Dramatic Arts Award, 1974. *Mailing address:* c/o Howard U. Press, 2900 Van Ness St., N.W., Wash., D.C. 20008.

Writings:
Fiction

A First Step to Freedom, one-act play (produced in Harmony, Miss., 1964)

The Mau Mau Room, three-act play (produced in N.Y. at Negro Ensemble Co., 1969)

Black Girl, two-act play (produced off-Broadway at Theatre de Lys, 1971) (N.Y., Dramatists Play Serv., 1972)

The Prodigal Sister, two-act play (produced off-Broadway at Theatre de Lys, 1976)

Nonfiction

Black Girl: From Genesis to Revelations, includes playscript (Wash., D.C., Howard U. Press, 1977)

Sources: *Books in Print*, 1980-81; *Contemporary Authors*, vols. 61-64, 1976; *Freedomways*, vol. 19, 1979.

FRANKLIN, JOHN HOPE. History Professor, Historian.

Born in Rentiesville, Okla., Jan. 2, 1915. *Education:* B.A. (magna cum laude), Fisk U., 1935; M.A., 1936, Ph.D., 1941, Harvard U. *Family:* Married Aurelia Whittington (librn.), 1940; son John Whittington. *Career:* Mem. Hist. Faculty: Fisk U., 1936-37; St. Augustine's Coll., Raleigh, N.C., 1939-43; N.C. Coll. at Durham, 1943-47; Howard U., 1947-56; Chairman, Dept. of Hist., Brooklyn Coll., 1956-65; William Pitt Prof. Amer. Hist. & Institutions, Cambridge U., 1962-63; Prof. Amer. Hist., U. of Chicago, 1964-82 (Chairman, Dept. Hist., 1967-70; John Manly Distinguished Serv. Prof., 1969-?); James B. Duke Prof., Hist., Duke U., 1982- ; Visiting Prof.: Harvard U., U. of Wis., Cornell U., Salzburg Seminar, U. of Cal., Cambridge U. (Chairman, Bd. of Foreign Scholarships, 1966-69). *Honors:* Edward Austin Fellow, Harvard; Julius Rosenwald Found. Fellow; (postdoctoral) President's Fund, Brown U.; Soc. Sci. Res. Council; John Simon Guggenheim Memorial Found.; Rep., Amer. Council of Learned Soc., U. of Calcutta, Madras, & Bombay, 1957; Fulbright Prof., several Australian universities, 1960; Lincoln Lect., Bd. of Foreign Scholarships in S. Amer., the Pacific, & E. Asia, 1973; hon. degrees from 35 institutions; Ed. Bd., *Journal of Negro Hist.* (20 yrs.); Jefferson Lect. in Humanities, NEH, 1976; cited for Significant Contrib. to Soc. by *Who's Who in America*, 1978; Okla. Hall of Fame, 1978. *Mailing address:* c/o U. of Chicago Press, 5801 Ellis Ave., Chicago, Ill. 60637.

Writings:
Nonfiction

The Free Negro in North Carolina, 1790-1860 (Chapel Hill, U. of N.C. Press, 1943; reprint, N.Y., Norton, 1971)

From Slavery to Freedom: A History of American Negroes (N.Y., Knopf, 1947; 2nd ed., 1956, 3rd ed., 1967, 4th ed., 1974, 5th ed., 1978, paper, 1980)

The Diary of James T. Ayers, Civil War Recruiter, ed. (Springfield, Ill. State Hist. Soc., 1947)

The Militant South, 1800-1861 (Cambridge, Mass., Harvard U. Press, 1956; Boston, Beacon, 1964)

Reconstruction: After the Civil War (Chicago, U. of Chicago Press, 1961; paper, 1963)

Albion Tourgee's *A Fool's Errand*, ed. (Harvard U. Press, 1961; paper, 1965)

T. W. Higginson's *Army Life in a Black Regiment*, ed. (Beacon, 1962)

The Emancipation Proclamation (N.Y., Doubleday, 1963, paper, 1965)

Land of the Free, with John W. Caughey & Ernest R. May (Phila., Franklin, 1965, rev., 1973)

Three Negro Classics, ed. (N.Y., Avon, 1965)

The Negro in Twentieth Century America; A Reader on the Struggle for Civil Rights, ed. with Isadore Starr (N.Y., Vantage, 1967)

American History Series, 17 vols., gen. ed. with A. S. Eisenstadt (Arlington Heights, Ill., Harlan Davidson, 1968)

Color and Race, ed. (Boston, Houghton Mifflin, 1968; Japanese ed., Tokyo, Eihosha, 1969; paper, Beacon, 1969)

Reminiscences of an Active Life: The Autobiography of John R. Lynch, ed. (Baton Rouge, La. State U. Press, 1969)

W. E. B. DuBois, *The Suppression of the African Slave Trade*, ed. (La. State U. Press, 1969)

University of Chicago Press Series on Negro American Biographies and Autobiographies, 7 vols., gen. ed. (U. of Chicago Press, 1969-)

Illustrated History of Black Americans, with eds. of Time-Life Bks. (N.Y., Time-Life, 1970, 1973)

A Southern Odyssey: Travelers in the Antebellum North (La. State U. Press, 1976)

Racial Equality in America (U. of Chicago Press, 1976)

Black Leaders of the 20th Century, gen. ed. with August Meier (Urbana, U. of Ill. Press, 1981)

Sources. Author information, *Black Historians, Books in Print*, 1979-80, 1980-81, *Current Biography*, 1963; *From Slavery to Freedom; Negro Almanac; Who's Who in America*, 37th ed., 1972-73.

FRAZIER, EDWARD FRANKLIN. Sociologist, Sociology Professor.
Born in Eastern Shore, Md., Sept. 24, 1894. *Education:* Baltimore public schs.; B.A. (cum laude), Howard U., 1916; M.A., Clark U., 1920; Ph.D., U. of Chicago, 1931. *Family:* Married Marie E. Brown, Sept. 14, 1922. *Career:* Res. Fellow, N.Y. Sch. of Soc. Work, 1920-21; Fellow, Amer.-Scandinavian Found. to Denmark, 1921-22; Dir. Atlanta U. Sch. of Soc. Work, 1922-27; Prof. of Sociol., Fisk U., 1929-34; Prof. & Head, Dept. of Sociol., Howard U., 1934-59 (25 yrs.); Lect., N.Y. Sch. of Soc. Work, Columbia U.; Chairman, Com. of Experts on Race, UNESCO, 1949; Chief, Div. Applied Soc. Sci., Paris, 1951-53. *Honors:* Anisfield-Wolf Award for *The Negro Family in the United States*, 1939; Fellow, Guggenheim Found. to Brazil & W. Indies, 1940-41; MacIver Lectureship Award, Amer. Sociol. Soc., 1956. Died May 17, 1962.

Writings:
Nonfiction

The Free Negro Family: A Study of Family Origins before the Civil War (Nashville, Fisk U. Press, 1932; reprint, N.Y., Arno; Amer. Negro Hist. & Lit. Ser., no. 1, 1968)

The Negro Family in the United States (Chicago, U. of Chicago Press, 1939; rev. N.Y., Doubleday, 1948, 1966)

The Negro in the United States (N.Y., Macmillan, 1949, 1957)

Black Bourgeoisie (Glencoe, Ill., Free Press, 1957; N.Y., Collier, 1962; N.Y., Free Press, 1965; N.Y., Macmillan)

Race and Culture Contacts in the Modern World (N.Y., Knopf, 1957; Boston, Beacon, 1965)

The Negro Church in America [N.Y., Schocken, 1963; new ed. with C. Eric Lincoln, bound with *The Black Church since Frazier* (N.Y., Schocken, Sourcebooks in Negro Hist. Ser., 1973)]

E. Franklin Frazier on Race Relations, ed. (U. of Chicago Press, Heritage of Sociol. Ser., 1968)

Sidelights: " ... best remembered for his controversial book *Black Bourgeoisie* in which he expounded the theory that the Negro middle class was isolating itself from the problems of marginal or poverty-stricken Negroes.... The MacIver Lectureship for 1956 has been awarded to E. Franklin Frazier for *Black Bourgeoisie* ... by the American Sociological Society ... to the student of society 'who in the opinion of the Selection Committee has contributed to the progress of sociology by his published or unpublished work during the past two years, and is qualified to inform the academic community or the educated public concerning the current achievements and work in progress in sociology.' " (*Black Bourgeoisie*)

Sources: *Black Bourgeoisie; Books in Print*, 1978-79, 1980-81; *Current Biography*, 1940; *Negro Almanac; Negro Church in America; Who Was Who in America*, vol. IV, 1961-68.

FULLER, CHARLES H., JR. Playwright, Television Script Writer.
Born in Phila., Pa., Mar. 5, 1939. *Education:* Villanova U.; La Salle Coll. *Career:* Co-Founder & Co-Dir., Afro-Amer. Arts Theatre, Phila., 1967-71; Lect. in Black Lit., seven-U. tour, 1970-71; Writer-Dir. for "The Black Experience," WIP Radio, Phila., 1970-71; Consultant & format designer, "Speak Out," 90-minute talk show, WKYW-TV (Channel 3), Phila., 1971; Story Ed., "J.T.," WABC-TV pilot, N.Y.C., 1972; writer, additional dialogue for play *The Selling of the President*, Franklin Robert Productions, 1972. *Honors:* Rockefeller Found. Grant for Playwriting; *Zooman and the Sign* won two Obie Awards, 1980; Pulitzer Prize for Drama for *A Soldier's Play*, 1982. *Mailing address:* c/o Ebony, 820 S. Mich. Ave., Chicago, Ill. 60605.

Writings:
Fiction
"Roots, Resistance and Renaissance," 12-week ser. for WHYY-TV (Channel 12) (Phila., 1967)

Love Song for Robert Lee, play (1967)

Mitchell, teleplay, WCAU-TV (Channel 10) (Phila., 1968)

Ain't Nobody, Sarah, But Me, play (1969)

Cabin, play (1969)

Indian Givers, play (1969)

J. J.'s Game, play (1969)

The Perfect Party, or The Village, A Party, play (1969)

"Black America," one-half hour show, WKYW-TV (Channel 3) (Phila., 1970-71)

In the Deepest Part of Sleep, play (N.Y., Negro Ensemble Co., 1974)

The Brownsville Raid, play (Negro Ensemble Co., 1976)

A Soldier's Play (N.Y., Hill & Wang, 1981)

Zooman and the Sign, play (N.Y., French, 1982)

Sidelights: Fuller recently completed the screenplay for *A Soldier's Play* for Warner Brothers. (*Ebony*)

Sources: Black American Writers Past and Present; Books in Print, 1983-84; *Ebony*, Aug. 1983; *National Playwrights Directory*.

FULLER, HOYT W. Editor, Teacher.
Born in Atlanta, Ga., Sept. 10, 1927. *Education:* B.A., Wayne State U., Detroit; advanced study. *Family:* Single. *Career:* Executive Ed., *Black World*; Asst. Ed., *Collier's Encyclopedia*; W. African Correspondent, *Haagse Post* (Amsterdam, Holland); Assoc. Ed., *Ebony*; Feature Ed., *Michigan Chronicle*; Reporter, *Detroit Tribune*; Executive Ed., *First World: An International Journal of Black Thought*; Tchr.: Fiction Writing Seminar, Columbia Coll., Chicago; Afro-Amer. Lit., Northwestern U.; Afro-Amer. Lit., Ind. U., Bloomington; Afro-Amer. Lit., Wayne State U. *Honors:* John Hay Whitney Found. Opportunity Fellow, 1965-66 (travel, study in Africa). Died in 1981.

Writings:
Nonfiction
Journey to Africa (Chicago, Third World, 1971)

Sidelights: "Responding to the challenge of reviving the Johnson Publishing Company's *Negro Digest*, he turned that magazine into a major forum of original black world opinion, an achievement duly commemorated by the change of the name of the magazine to *Black World* in 1970." He has also conducted the weekly OBAC writers workshop in Chicago. (*Afro-American Writing*)

Sources: *Afro-American Writing*; Author information; *Black Collegian*, Oct./Nov. 1979.

GAINES, ERNEST J. Novelist, Short Story Writer.
Born near Oscar, La., Jan. 15, 1933. *Education:* 2 yrs., San Francisco State Coll. (drafted into Army, 1953-55); returned to San Francisco State, B.A., 1957; postgrad., Stanford U., 1958-59. *Career:* Writer; Military Service. *Honors:* Wallace Stegner Fellow in creative writing, Stanford U.; Joseph Henry Jackson Lit. Award for creative writing, 1959. *Mailing address:* 998 Divisadero St., San Francisco, Cal. 94115.

Writings:
Fiction
Catherine Carmier, novel (N.Y., Atheneum, 1964; reprint, Chatham, N.J., Chatham, 1972; Berkeley, Cal., N. Point Press, 1981)

Of Love and Dust, novel (N.Y., Dial, 1967; N.Y., Norton, 1979)

Bloodline, individual stories collected into one (Dial, 1968)

Autobiography of Miss Jane Pittman, novel (Dial, 1971; Boston, G. K. Hall, Adult Ser. reprints, large print, 1971; N.Y., Bantam, 1972)

Long Day in November, short stories (Dial, 1971; N.Y., Dell, 1973)

In My Father's House, novel (N.Y., Random House, 1978)

A Gathering of Old Men (N.Y., Knopf, 1983)

Sidelights: *Autobiography of Miss Jane Pittman* was produced for CBS TV, 1974, with Cicely Tyson in in title role.
"He ... seems intent upon exhuming from his native Louisiana soil ... what Henry James might call the 'stuff of consciousness' for a novel of magnitude. Gaines, who thinks that the artist is the only free man left in the world, has so far been concerned in his fiction ... with individuals determined often heroically, either to maintain their codes of conduct among debasing or confusing forces, or to ride out the storm of consequences attending their decisions to change with the times." (*Dark Symphony*)

Sources: *Best Short Stories by Negro Writers; Books in Print*, 1978-79, 1982-83; *Cavalcade; Dark Symphony; New Black Voices.*

GARDNER, CARL. Free-lance Writer, Beekeeper.
Born in Wash., D.C., July 27, 1931. *Education:* B.A. (Phi Beta Kappa, Eng. Lit.), Howard U., 1960. *Family:* Married Esther McGhee, Sept. 11, 1965; son Coltrane. *Career:* Air Force, 1952-56;

Specifications Writer, Coast Guard, 1960-63; Tech. Ed., Vitro Corp., 1965-69; Free-lance Writer; Beekeeper, Amherst, Va. (present). *Mailing address:* Route 3, Box 321, Amherst, Va. 24521.

Writings:
Nonfiction

The Star Spangled Hustle, autobiog. with Lee Grant (N.Y., Lippincott, 1972)

Andrew Young, a Biography (N.Y., Drake, 1978; N.Y., Sterling, 1978)

Media, Politics and Culture: A Socialist View (Atlantic Highlands, N.J., Humanities, Communication & Culture, 1979)

Sidelights: "Attended Howard University from 1949 to 1951 with Andrew Young; interests include modern day homesteading and counterculture ecology." (*Andrew Young*)

Sources: *Andrew Young, a Biography; Books in Print*, 1980-81; *Contemporary Authors*, vol. 107, 1983.

GARNET, HENRY HIGHLAND. Educator, Lecturer/Abolitionist, Minister.
Born on Eastern Shore, Md., in 1815 (in slavery); escaped with parents & taken to N.Y. *Education:* Oneida Inst., Whitesboro, N.Y., graduated 1840. *Career:* Agent, Amer. Anti-Slavery Soc.; Pastor, Liberty St. Presby. Church, Troy, N.Y.; Missionary, Jamaica (for United Presby. Church of Scotland); Pastor, Shiloh Church, N.Y.; Pres., Avery Coll., Pittsburgh; Minister, Liberia (died in 1882, 2 months after arriving).

Writings:
Nonfiction

An Address to the Slaves of the United States of America (N.Y., J. H. Tobitt, 1848)

Past and Present Condition, and the Destiny of the Colored Race (Troy, N.Y., Kneeland, 1848)

The Memorial Discourse, 1st time a Black spoke to U.S. House of Rep. (Phila., J. M. Wilson, 1865)

Sidelights: "The spiritual successor to David Walker and one of the foremost advocates of full enfranchisement for the Negro, was Henry Highland Garnet, whose militant addresses caused him to be regarded as one of the most extreme of radicals." (*Negro Genius*)
John Brown had *An Address to the Slaves* published at his own expense. It was felt that "*Address to the Slaves* tended to promote insurrection. Among other remarks, Garnet said: 'Brethren, arise, arise, arise! Strike for your lives and liberties. Now is the day and the hour. Let every slave throughout the land do this and the days of slavery are numbered. You can not be more oppressed than you have been; you can not suffer greater cruelties than you have already. Rather die freemen than live to be slaves.' " (*Negro Genius*)

Sources: *Afro-American Writing; Historical Negro Biographies; Negro Genius; Negroes in Public Affairs and Government.*

GARVEY, MARCUS. Black Nationalist; Founder, Universal Negro Improvement Association.
Born in St. Ann's Bay, Jamaica, Aug. 17, 1887. *Education:* Common sch. & Pupil-Teachers' Course, Jamaica; U. of London, Eng. *Family:* Married Amy Jacques Garvey. *Career:* Ed., *Garvey's Watchman*, Kingston, Jamaica; Timekeeper (banana plantation), United Fruit Co., Costa Rica; Founder, United Negro Improvement Assn. (UNIA), Jamaica & U.S.; established *Negro World*, organ of UNIA, N.Y.C. (weekly), 1918-34. Died in 1940.

Writings:
Nonfiction

Philosophy and Opinions of Marcus Garvey, or Africa for the Africans, ed. by Amy Jacques Garvey, 2 vols. (N.Y., Universal, 1923-25; 2nd ed., London, Cass, 1967)

The Tragedy of White Injustice, poems (N.Y., Amy J. Garvey, 1927; N.Y., Haskell House, 1972)

Garvey and Garveyism, ed. by Amy Jacques Garvey (Kingston, Jamaica, n.p., 1963)

Marcus Garvey and the Vision of Africa, ed. by John H. Clarke & Amy Jacques Garvey (N.Y., Random House, 1974)

Collected Papers and Documents, ed. by E. U. Essien-Udom (Atlantic Highlands, N.J., Humanities, Africana Mod. Lib. Ser., 1974)

The Marcus Garvey and Universal Negro Improvement Association Papers, 2 vols., ed. by Robert A. Hill (L.A., UCLA, U. of Cal. Press, 1983)

Sidelights: " ... permanently important for: Black pride, the unity of African people in and out of Africa, the beauty of Blackness, cooperative Black economic activity, the rejection of white religion, the understanding of white racism as a historical constant, distrust of white radicalism — all of these concepts and attitudes so prevalent today were pioneered by Marcus Garvey." (*Black Writers of America*)

Sources: *Black Moses: The Story of Marcus Garvey; Black Writers of America; Harlem: Negro Metropolis; World's Great Men of Color*, vol. 2, 1972; *L.A. Times Book Review*, Mar. 25, 1984.

GARY, LAWRENCE E. University Administrator, Mental Health Director.
Born in Ala. *Education:* B.S., Tuskegee Inst.; M.P.A., M.S.W., Ph.D., U. of Mich. *Family:* Married; three children. *Career:* (Howard U.) Asst. to V. Pres. for Academic Affairs; Res. Dir. of Mental Health Res. & Development Center. *Mailing address:* c/o Dorrance & Co., 828 Lancaster Pike, Bryn Mawr, Pa. 19010.

Writings:
Nonfiction

Crime and Its Impact on the Black Community, ed. with Lee P. Brown (Wash., D.C., Inst. for Urban Affairs & Res., Howard U., 1975)

Restructuring the Educational Process; A Black Perspective, ed. with Aaron Favors (Inst. for Urban Affairs & Res., Howard U., 1975)

Mental Health: A Challenge to the Black Community, ed. (Phila., Pa., Dorrance, 1978)

Sources: *Books in Print*, 1980-81; *Mental Health.*

GATES, HENRY LOUIS, JR. English Professor, Critic.
Born in W. Va., Sept. 16, 1950. *Education:* B.A. (summa cum laude, Phi Beta Kappa), Yale U., 1973; M.A., Ph.D. (Eng. Lang. & Lit.), Cambridge U., 1979. *Career:* Lect., Eng. & Afro-Amer. Studies, 1976-79; Asst. Prof.; Dir., Undergrad. Students, Afro-Amer. Studies, 1978-81; Co-Dir., "Black Periodical Fiction Project," Yale U. *Honors:* Rockefeller Fellow, 1980-81; Mellon Fellow, Aspen Inst., 1983; MacArthur Prize Fellow, 1981-86. *Mailing address:* 3388 Yale Station, New Haven, Conn. 06520.

Writings:
Nonfiction

Black Is the Color of the Cosmos: Essays on Afro-American Literature and Culture, 1942-1981, with Charles T. Davis, ed. (N.Y., Garland, 1982)

In the House of Osugbo: Essays on Wole Soyinka, ed. (N.Y., Oxford U. Press, 1983)

Our Nig, by Harriet E. Wilson, ed. by Henry L. Gates (N.Y., Random House, 1983)

The Slave's Narrative, ed. (Oxford U. Press, 1983)

Sidelights: Gates, panelist in "Of Our Spiritual Strivings," Recent Developments in Black Literature and Criticism (UCLA Center for Afro-Amer. Studies, Apr. 22-23, 1983), states: "The mixed blessing of African-American literary criticism is that the critic must often resurrect his or her texts even before the true work of explication can commence. I derive energy from this very challenge."

Sources: Author information; *Conference Notes (Recent Developments in Black Literature and Criticism)*, Apr. 1983.

GAYLE, ADDISON, JR. Editor, Teacher, Critic, Essayist.
Born in Newport News, Va., June 2, 1932. *Education:* B.A., City Coll. of N.Y.; M.A., U. of Cal., 1966. *Family:* Separated from Rosalie Gayle. *Career:* Prof., Lit., Bernard M. Baruch Coll. of CUNY, 1969; Asst. Prof., Creative Writing, Dept. of Eng., Livingston Coll., Rutgers U., 1971-72; Lect., including "Black Heritage," Channel 2 TV, Oberlin Coll., U. of Va., Yale U., Dunbar Centenary, U. of Cal., Irvine; Consultant, Minority Writers, Doubleday & Random House; Ed. staffs, *Amistad* mag., Third World Press, *Black Lines* mag.; sponsor of Richard Wright Award for SEEK student with highest average for semester; lectures extensively, including Atlanta U., Clark Coll., U. of Paris. *Mailing address:* c/o Doubleday & Co., 501 Franklyn Ave., Garden City, N.Y. 11530.

Writings:
Nonfiction

Black Expression, Essays; By and about Black Americans in the Creative Arts (N.Y., Weybright & Talley, 1969)

The Black Situation, essays, ed. (N.Y., Horizon, 1970)

The Black Aesthetic, essays, ed. (Garden City, N.Y., Doubleday, 1971)

Bondage, Freedom and Beyond; The Prose of Black Americans, essays (Doubleday, Zenith, 1971)

Oak and Ivy: A Biography of Paul Laurence Dunbar (Doubleday, 1971)

Claude McKay: The Black Poet at War (Detroit, Broadside, 1972)

The Way of the New World: The Black Novel in America (Garden City, N.Y., Anchor, 1975, 1976)

Wayward Child: A Personal Odyssey, essays (Anchor, 1977)

Richard Wright: Ordeal of a Native Son (Anchor, 1980)

Sidelights: In his introduction to *The Black Aesthetic*, he writes: "The black artist in the American society who creates without interjecting a note of anger is creating not as a black man, but as an American.... The serious black artist of today is at war with the American society as few have been throughout American history.... The problem of the de-Americanization of black people lies at the heart of the Black Aesthetic." (*New Black Voices*)

Sources: Author information; *Black Expression; Black World*, Dec. 1974; *Books in Print*, 1978-79, 1980-81; *Kirkus Review Service*, Apr. 15, 1980; *New Black Voices*.

GIBSON, D. PARKE. Marketing Specialist, Newsletter Publisher.
Born in Seattle, Wash. *Career:* Head (natl. marketing & public relations firm); publishes newsletters: *Gibson Report; Race Relations and Industry*. *Mailing address:* c/o Macmillan Pub. Co., 866 Third Ave., N.Y., N.Y. 10022.

Writings:
Nonfiction

The $30 Billion Negro (N.Y., Macmillan, 1969)

$70 Billion in the Black; America's Black Consumers (Macmillan, 1978)

Sidelights: Gibson has been providing marketing and public affairs counsel to domestic and international clients for over twenty years. (*$70 Billion in the Black*)

Sources: *Freedomways*, vol. 19, 1979; *Negro Almanac; $70 Billion in the Black*.

GIBSON, DONALD B. English Professor, Essayist, Critic.

Born in Kansas City, Mo., July 2, 1933. *Education:* B.A., 1955, M.A., 1957, U. of Kan. City; Ph.D., Brown U., 1962. *Family:* Married Jo Anne Ivory, Dec. 14, 1963; children: David, Douglas. *Career:* Eng. Instr., Brown U., 1960-61; Asst. Prof., Eng., Wayne State U., Detroit, 1961-67; Assoc. Prof., U. of Conn., Storrs, 1967-69, Prof., Eng., 1969-74; Prof., Eng., Rutgers U., 1974- ; Mem. of faculty, Jagiellonian U., Cracow, Poland, 1964-66. *Honors:* NEH Award, 1970-71; Amer. Philosophical Soc. Award, 1970. *Mailing address:* c/o Dept. of Eng., Rutgers U., New Brunswick, N.J. 08903.

Writings:

Fiction

Black and White: Stories of American Life, anthology, ed. with Carol Anselment (N.Y., Wash. Square Press, 1971)

Nonfiction

The Fiction of Stephen Crane (Carbondale, S. Ill. U. Press, 1968)

Five Black Writers: Essays on Wright, Ellison, Baldwin, Hughes and LeRoi Jones, ed. (N.Y., N.Y.U. Press, Gotham Lib., 1970)

Modern Black Poets: A Collection of Critical Essays (N.Y., Prentice-Hall, 1973)

The Politics of Literary Expression: A Study of Major Black Writers (Westport, Conn., Greenwood, Contrib. in Afro-Amer. & African Studies, no. 63, 1981)

Sources: *Books in Print*, 1981-82; *Dictionary Catalog of the Schomburg Collection of Negro Literature and History*, Supplement, 1974; *Encyclopedia of Black America*.

GILLESPIE, MARCIA ANN. Magazine Editor.

Born in Rockville Centre, N.Y., July 10, 1944. *Education:* Southside High Sch., Rockville Centre; B.A. (Amer. Studies, honors), Lake Forest Coll., Ill., 1966. *Family:* Single. *Career:* Res. reporter, Time, Inc., Time-Life Bks., 1966-70; Managing Ed., 1970-71; Ed.-in-Chief, *Essence*, 1971- . *Honors:* Distinguished Alumni Award, Lake Forest Coll.; Bus. Achievement Awards, Natl. Assn. Black Bus. & Professional Women's Clubs, Nassau Chap., N.Y. *Mailing address: Essence* Mag., 300 E. 42nd St., N.Y., N.Y. 10017.

Writings:

Nonfiction

Assisted with *Illustrated History of Black Americans*, ed. by John Hope Franklin (N.Y., Time-Life Bks., 1970)

Columnist, "Getting Down," *Essence* mag. (1971-)

Sidelights: Made repeated trips to more than 25 states as lecturer, speaker, panel member. (Author)

Source: Author information.

GILMORE, AL-TONY. History Professor.

Born in S.C., June 29, 1946. *Education:* B.A. (Amer. Hist.); M.A. (Amer. Hist.); Ph.D. (Amer. Hist.-Afro-Amer. & Progressive Era). *Career:* Hist. Prof.; has read papers before numerous scholarly organizations & colleges all over U.S. *Honors:* Outstanding Young Man in America, 1974; listed in *Directory of American Scholars*; Gussie Hudson's *Directory of Black Historians*; Rayford Logan's & Michael Winston's *Directory of American Negro Biography*. *Mailing address:* c/o Garland Pub. Inc., 136 Madison Ave., N.Y., N.Y. 10016.

Writings:

Nonfiction

Bad Nigger!: The National Impact of Jack Johnson (Port Wash., N.Y., Kennikat, 1975)

The Afro-American in Sport: An Annotated Bibliography (N.Y., Garland, Critical Studies on Black Life & Culture, 1981)

Sources: Author information; *Books in Print*, 1981-82.

GIOVANNI, NIKKI [Yolande Cornelis Giovanni, Jr.]. Poet, Activist, Lecturer, Recording Artist.

Born in Knoxville, Tenn., June 7, 1943. *Education:* B.A. (Hist., honors), Fisk U., 1967; U. of Pa.; Columbia U. *Family:* Single; son Thomas Watson Giovanni. *Career:* Arranged Black Arts Festival, Cincinnati, 1967; helped in growth of Black Theatre; Dir., Black Hist. Workshop; Founded pub. coop., TomNik Ltd., 1970; taught creative writing, Livingston Coll., Rutgers U.; Lect., Coll. campuses; Ed. consultant, *Encore* Mag. *Honors:* Hon. Doctorate of Humanities, Wilberforce U., 1972; Hon. Doctorate of Lit.: U. of Md., Princess Anne, 1974; Smith Coll.; Ripon Coll., Wis.; Plaque, Cook County Jail, 1971; Life Membership & Scroll, Natl. Council of Negro Women, 1972; *Mademoiselle* mag. award for outstanding achievement, 1971; Sun Shower Award, Prince Matchiabelli, 1972; Omega Psi Phi Fraternity award, outstanding contrib. to Arts & Letters, 1971; Proclamation, Mayor of Lincoln Heights, Ohio, Nikki Giovanni Day; Black Heroines for People United to Save Humanity, 1972; Woman of the Yr., *Ladies Home Journal*, 1973. Grants: Ford Found.; Natl. Found. on the Arts & Humanities; Harlem Council on the Arts. *Mailing address:* c/o Wm. Morrow Co., 105 Madison Ave., N.Y., N.Y. 10016.

Writings:

Fiction

Black Feeling; Black Talk, anthology (Detroit, Broadside, 1968; 2nd ed., N.Y., Afro-Arts, 1968; 3rd rev. ed., Broadside, 1970)

Black Judgment, poems (Broadside, 1968)

Re: Creation, poems (Broadside, 1970)

Black Feeling Black Talk/Black Judgment, poems (N.Y., Morrow, 1970)

Night Comes Softly, ed., poetry anthology (Newark, N.J., Medic, 1970)

Poem of Angela Yvonne Davis (Afro-Arts, 1970)

Spin a Soft Black Song; Poems for Children (N.Y., Hill & Wang, 1971)

My House, poems (Morrow, 1972)

Ego Tripping and Other Poems for Young People (N.Y., Lawrence Hill, 1973)

The Women and the Men, poems (Morrow, 1975, 1979)

Cotton Candy on a Rainy Day, juv. poems (Morrow, 1978)

Vacation Time: Poems for Children (Morrow, 1980, 1981)

Those Who Ride the Night Wind, poems (Morrow, 1983)

Nonfiction

Gemini: An Extended Autobiographical Statement on My First Twenty-five Years of Being a Black Poet (Indianapolis, Bobbs-Merrill, 1971)

A Dialogue: James Baldwin and Nikki Giovanni (Phila., Lippincott, 1973)

A Poetic Equation: Conversations between Nikki Giovanni and Margaret Walker (Wash., D.C., Howard U. Press, 1974)

Sidelights: This young Black revolutionary writer has been hailed by a reviewer for *Variety* as "Probably the most prominent Black poetess in America." She became a political activist at age 16 when she entered Fisk. After expulsion and return to Fisk, was instrumental in having SNCC reinstated on campus.

Records: "Truth Is on Its Way" (Right On Records, 1971); "Like a Ripple on a Pond" (NikTom, Ltd., Atlantic, 1973); "The Way I Feel" (NikTom, Atlantic); "Legacies" (Folkways Records); "The

Reason I Like Chocolate" (Folkways); "Cotton Candy on a Rainy Day" (Folkways).

Sources: *Black American Literature; Books in Print*, 1978-79, 1980-81; *Current Biography*, 1973; Pub. information; *Soulscript; Today's Negro Voices.*

GLISSANT, EDOUARD. (Martiniquean). Poet, Novelist, Playwright, Activist.
Born in Sainte-Marie, Martinique, Sept. 21, 1928. *Education:* Lycée Schoelcher, Fort-de-France, Martinique; License (Philosophy), Sorbonne; Ethnology, Musée de l'Homme. *Career:* Staff, Centre National de la Recherche Scientifique, Paris; Founder, Institut Martiniquais d'Etudes; Ed., *Acoma* review, 1970-73. *Mailing address:* c/o George Braziller, One Park Ave., N.Y., N.Y. 10016.

Writings:
(Partial Listing—English Only)
Fiction
The Ripening, novel, transl. into Eng. by Frances Frenaye (N.Y., Braziller, 1959)

Sidelights: Glissant was active in the Societé Africaine de Culture and other leftist West Indian Political groups in Paris. With Paul Niger of Guadaloupe, was one of the directors of "Front antillo-guyanais pour l'independence." Was prevented from returning to Martinique between 1959 and 1965; and even from going to Algeria from France.
"Glissant argues for a diversified Caribbean ... heritage that includes the vast spectrum of people that go to make up the Caribbean." (*Resistance and Caribbean Literature*)

Sources: *Black Writers in French; Caribbean Writers; Resistance and Caribbean Literature.*

GLOSTER, HUGH MORRIS. College President, English Professor.
Born in Brownsville, Tenn., in 1911. *Education:* B.A., Morehouse Coll., Atlanta, 1931; M.A., Atlanta U., 1933; Ph.D., N.Y.U., 1943. *Career:* Tchr., Eng., Le Moyne Coll., Memphis, Tenn., 1933-41; Prof., Eng., & Chairman, Dept. of Lang. & Lit., Hampton Inst., Va., 1946-67; Pres., Morehouse Coll., 1967- ; Founder of Coll. Lang. Assn. & its Pres. 1937-38 & 1948-50; Contrib. Ed., *Phylon*, 1948-53. *Mailing address:* c/o Morehouse Coll., Atlanta, Ga. 30314.

Writings:
Fiction
The Brown Thrush: Anthology of Verse by Negro Students, co-ed. (Bryn Athyn, Pa., Lawson-Roberts, 1932; Memphis, Tenn., Malcolm Roberts, 1935)

Nonfiction
Negro Voices in American Fiction (Chapel Hill, U. of N.C. Press, 1948, 1965)

My Life, My Country, My World: College Readings for Modern Living, ed. (N.Y., Prentice-Hall, 1952)

Sources: *Encyclopedia of Black America; The Negro Novel in America*; Pub. information.

GLOSTER, JESSE E. Business Writer, Economics Professor.
Born in Mulbury, Fla., Apr. 15, 1915. *Education:* A.B., Lincoln U., 1941; M. Litt., U. of Pa., 1947. *Career:* Combination Agent, N.C. Mutual Life Insurance Co., Pittsburgh; Instr., Econ., Tex. S. U.; Assoc. Prof. of Econ., Tex. S. U., 1948- . *Mailing address:* c/o University Press, Wolfe City, Tex. 75496.

Writings:
Nonfiction
North Carolina Mutual Insurance Company: Its Historical Development and Current Operations (Pittsburgh, U. of Pittsburgh, 1955; reprint, N.Y., Arno, Companies & Men: Business Enterprises in America, 1976)

Minority Economic, Political and Social Development (Wash., D.C., U. Press of America, 1978)

Sources: *Books in Print*, 1979-80, 1980-81; *North Carolina Mutual Life Insurance Company.*

GOODE, KENNETH GREGORY. Historian, Legal Editor, University Administrator.
Born in New Orleans, Aug. 11, 1932. *Education:* B.A., 1957; LL.B., 1960, U. of Ariz., Tucson; Ph.D. candidate, U. of Cal., Berkeley. *Family:* Married Etsuko Yoneda; children: Georgia, Gregory. *Career:* Instr., Polit. Sci. & Afro-Amer. Hist., Laney Coll., Oakland, Cal., 1964-67; Contract Admin., U.S. Atomic Energy Com., Berkeley, 1963-67; Asst. V. Chancellor, Admin. Services, U. of Cal., Berkeley, since 1973; Instr., Afro-Amer. Hist. Extension Div., 1967-68; Asst. to Executive V. Chancellor, 1968-69; Asst. Chancellor, Special Serv., 1969-70; Asst. V. Chancellor, 1970-73. *Honors:* Senior Honors, U. of Ariz., 1957; Citation, Inst. of Educ. Management, Harvard U., 1973. *Mailing address:* 200 California Hall, Office of the Chancellor, U. of Cal., Berkeley, Cal. 94720.

Writings:
Nonfiction

Federal Civil Practice, legal ed. with Others (Berkeley, Cal., U. of Cal. Press, Continuing Educ. of the Bar, 1961)

Handling Federal Tax Litigation, legal ed. with Others (U. of Cal. Press, Continuing Educ. of the Bar, 1961)

The California Family Lawyer, 2 vols., legal ed. with Others (U. of Cal. Press, Continuing Educ. of the Bar, 1962-63)

California Law Office Practice Handbook, legal ed. with Others (U. of Cal. Press, Continuing Educ. of the Bar, 1962)

California's Workmen's Compensation Practice, legal ed. with Others (U. of Cal. Press, Continuing Educ. of the Bar, 1962)

Government's Contracts Practice, legal ed. with Others (U. of Cal. Press, Continuing Educ. of the Bar, 1964)

From Africa to the United States and Then, syllabus (Glenview, Ill., Scott, Foresman, 1969)

From Africa to the United States and Then; A Concise Afro-American History (Scott, Foresman, 1969; 2nd ed., 1976)

California's Black Pioneers; A Brief Historical Survey (Santa Barbara, Cal., McNally & Loftin, 1973)

Sources: *Contemporary Authors*, vols. 49-52, 1975; Pub. information; *Writers Directory*, 1976-78.

GOODWIN, RUBY B. Free-lance Writer, Columnist.
Born in Duquoin, Ill., Oct. 17, 1903. *Education:* A.B., San Gabriel Coll., 1949. *Career:* Columnist, "Hollywood in Bronze"; Publicist & Secy. for Hattie McDaniel, 1936-52. *Honors:* Gold Medal, Commonwealth Award for Best Non Fiction Book by California Author, 1953. *Mailing address:* c/o S. Ill. U. Press, P.O. Box 3697, Carbondale, Ill. 62901.

Writings:
Fiction

From My Kitchen Window, poems (N.Y., Malliet, 1942, 2nd ed., 1946)

Nonfiction

Twelve Negro Spirituals, by William Grant Still (N.Y., Handy Brothers, 1937)

It's Good to Be Black (Garden City, N.Y., Doubleday, 1953; paper, Carbondale, S. Ill. U. Press, Arcturus Bks., 1976)

Sidelights: Ms. Goodwin also contributed "Stories of Negro Life" to *Twelve Negro Spirituals*, by William Grant Still (Handy Brothers Music Co., 1937).

Sources: *Black American Writers Past and Present; Books in Print*, 1980-81.

GORDON/E, CHARLES EDWARD. Playwright, Director, Actor.
Born in Cleveland, Ohio, Oct. 12, 1927. *Education:* B.A., L.A. State Coll.; N.Y.U.; Columbia U. *Family:* Div.; nine children. *Career:* Playwright, Dir., Actor; Assoc. Prod. of play *Nothing But a Man. Honors:* Drama Desk, N.Y.; Critics Circle Award, N.Y. & L.A.; Pulitzer Prize, 1970. *Mailing address:* c/o Bobbs-Merrill Co., 4300 W. 62nd St., Indianapolis, Ind. 46268.

Writings:
Fiction

A Little More Light around the Place, play (Sheridan Square Playhouse, N.Y.C., 1964)

No Place to Be Somebody; A Black Comedy in Three Acts (Indianapolis, Bobbs-Merrill, 1969)

Gordone Is a Muthah, miscellany (Radnor, Pa., Chilton, 1973)

Baba Chops, play (Wilshire Ebell, L.A., Cal., 1974)

The Lost Chord, play (Billie Holiday Theatre, N.Y.C., 1976)

Anabiosis, play (City Players, St. Louis, Mo., 1979)

Sidelights: Won award as Best Actor of the Year Off-Broadway in Luther James' all-black production of *Of Mice and Men.* His first successful play, *No Place to Be Somebody ...* won acclaim for performances at the New York Shakespeare Festival's Public Theater and a two-week engagement at the NTA Theater on Broadway.
"Gordone is the only black playwright that critics have favorably compared with Eugene O'Neill, William Saroyan, and Arthur Miller." (*Black Insights*)

Sources: Author information; *Black Insights; Contemporary Dramatists; National Playwrights Directory; Writers Directory*, 1980-82.

GRAHAM, LORENZ BELL. Juvenile Writer, Lecturer, Probation Officer, Teacher.
Born in New Orleans, Jan. 27, 1902. *Education:* (Undergrad.) UCLA, Columbia U., U. of Paris; B.A., Va. Union U., Richmond, 1936; (Grad.) N.Y.U.; Columbia U.; UCLA. *Family:* Married Ruth Morris, Aug. 20, 1929; son Lorenz, Jr., d. Mrs. Joyce G. Johnson, d. Mrs. Ruth G. May, son Charles M. Graham. *Career:* Tchr. & Missionary, Monrovia Coll., Liberia, W. Africa, 1924-28; Lect. & Fundraiser in U.S. for Foreign Mission Bd., Natl. Bap. Convention, 1929-32; Tchr., Richmond, 1933-35; Camp Educ. Advisor, Civilian Conservation Corps, Va. & Pa., 1936-42; Mgr., Public Housing, Newport News, Va., 1943-45; free-lance writer, real estate salesman, & bldg. contractor, Long Island, N.Y., 1946-49; Soc. Worker, Queens Federation of Churches, N.Y., 1950-57; Probation Officer, L.A., Cal., 1958-66; Instr., Cal. State U., Pomona, 1970- . *Honors:* Thomas A. Edison Citation, 1956; Queens Federation of Churches Citation, 1957; Charles W. Follett Award, 1958; Child Study Assn. of America Award, 1958; ASNLH Citation, 1959; Cal. Assn. of Tchrs. of Eng. Citation, 1973; L.H.D., Va. Union U., 1983. *Mailing address:* 1400 Niagara Ave., Claremont, Cal. 91711.

Writings:
Fiction
How God Fix Jonah, juv. (N.Y., Reynal, 1946)

Every Man Heart Lay Down, juv. (N.Y., Crowell, 1946, 1970)

God Wash the World and Start Again, juv. (Crowell, 1946, 1971)

Tales of Momolu, juv. (Reynal, 1946, 1974)

The Story of Jesus, juv. (N.Y., Gilbertson, 1955)

The Ten Commandments, juv. (Gilberton, 1956)

South Town, juv. (Chicago, Follett, 1958; N.Y., New Amer. Lib., 1966)

North Town, juv. (Crowell, 1965; New Amer. Lib., 1977)

Whose Town?, juv. (Crowell, 1969)

A Road down in the Sea, juv. (Crowell, 1970)

David He No Fear, juv. (Crowell, 1971)

Novelettes: *John Brown's Raid* (N.Y., Scholastic, 1971); *Runaway* (Boston, Houghton Mifflin, 1972); *Carolina Cracker* (Houghton Mifflin, 1972)—all juv., Firebird Ser.

Return to South Town, juv. (Crowell, 1976)

Nonfiction
John Brown: A Cry for Freedom, a Biography for Young Readers—Authentic but Lively (Crowell, 1980)

Sources: Author information; *Books in Print*, 1980-81; *Something about the Author*.

GRAHAM, SHIRLEY LOLA. Biographer, Musician, Editor, Juvenile Writer.
Born in Indianapolis, Ind., Nov. 11, 1906. *Education:* Advanced musical training, Paris; B.A., Oberlin Coll., 1934; M.A., 1935; Yale U. Drama Sch., 1938-40; L.H.D. (hon.), U. of Mass., 1973. *Family:* Married 1st Shadrach T. McCanns, son Robert Graham McCanns; married 2nd W. E. B. DuBois, son David Graham. *Career:* Head, Fine Arts Dept., Tenn. State Coll., 1935-36; Dir., Negro Unit, Chicago Fed. Theater, 1936-38; United Serv. Org. Dir.; YWCA Dir., 1940-42; Field Secy., NAACP, 1942-44; Organizing Dir., Ghana TV, 1964-66; Founding Ed., *Freedomways*, 1960-63; Eng. Ed., Afro-Asian Writers Bureau, Peking, China, 1968. *Honors:* Julius Rosenwald Fund Fellow, Yale U. Drama Sch., 1938-40; Guggenheim Found. Fellow for hist. res., 1945-47; Julian Messner award, *There Was Once a Slave*, 1950; Anisfield-Wolf Award, *Your Most Humble Servant*, 1950; Natl. Inst. of Arts & Letters grant for "Contributions to American Literature," 1950. Died in 1977.
Writings:
Fiction
Tom Tom, music drama (Cleveland, n.p., 1932)

The Zulu Heart; A Novel (N.Y., Third Press, 1974)

Nonfiction
Dr. George Washington Carver, Scientist, with George Lipscomb (N.Y., Messner, 1944; N.Y., Archway, 1967)

Paul Robeson, Citizen of the World (Messner, 1946, 1971)

There Was Once a Slave, biog. of Frederick Douglass (Messner, 1947, 1968)

The Story of Phillis Wheatley (Messner, 1949; N.Y., Wash. Square, 1969)

Your Most Humble Servant, biog. of Benjamin Banneker (Messner, 1949, 1965)

Jean Baptiste Pointe de Sable, Founder of Chicago (Messner, 1953, 1968)

The Story of Pocahontas (Westport, Conn., Grosset & Dunlap, 1953)

Booker T. Washington: Educator of Hand, Head and Heart (Messner, 1953, 1955)

His Day Is Marching On: A Memoir of W. E. B. DuBois (Phila., Lippincott, 1971)

Gamal Abdel Nasser: Son of the Nile (Third Press, 1972)

Julius K. Nyerere: Teacher of Africa (Messner, 1975)

Pictorial History of W. E. B. DuBois (Chicago, Johnson, 1976)

Sidelights: Shirley Graham stated that her father was a devout Methodist minister who traveled from place to place to "mend broken fences." This father instilled in his daughter a keen appreciation for the background of the Negro in Africa and of his contribution to American life. (*Twentieth Century Authors*)

The author and Dr. DuBois became citizens of Ghana, where he spent his final days. Mrs. DuBois subsequently moved to Cairo, Egypt. She died in Peking, China.

Sources: *Books in Print*, 1980-81; *DeBois: A Pictorial Biography; Negro Almanac; Paul Robeson, Citizen of the World; Twentieth Century Authors*, 1st Supplement, 1955.

GREEN, ROBERT L. Urban Specialist, Educator, Educational Psychology Professor.
Born in Detroit, Mich., Nov. 23, 1933. *Education:* B.A., San Francisco State Coll., 1958, M.A., 1960; Ph.D., Mich. State U., 1963. *Career:* Res. Asst., Langley Porter Res. Inst., U. Cal., San Francisco, 1959-60; Psychological Intern, public schs., Oakland, Cal., 1959-60; Group Counselor, Juvenile Court, San Francisco, 1960; Instr., Mich. State U., E. Lansing, 1960-62, Asst. Prof. of Educ., 1963-65; SCLC, Educ. Dir., Atlanta, 1965-66, Dir. of Adult Educ. Project, 1967; Prof., Educ. Psychology, Mich. State U., 1968- , Asst. Provost, 1968-72, Dir. of Center for Urban Affairs, 1968-74, Acting Dean, Coll. of Urban Development, 1972-73, Dean, 1973- . *Mailing address:* c/o Coward McCann, 200 Madison Ave., N.Y., N.Y. 10016.

Writings:
Nonfiction

The Educational Status of Children in a District without Public Schools, with Louis J. Hoffmann et al. (E. Lansing, Mich. State U., 1964)

The Educational Status of Children during the First School Year following Four Years of Little or No Schooling, with Others (Coll. of Educ., Mich. State U., 1966)

Racial Crisis in American Education, ed. (Chicago, Follett, 1969)

American Negro Musicians, ed. with Nicholas Peter Georgiady (Milwaukee, Wis., Franklin, 1969)

Robert L. Green's Live with Style (N.Y., Coward, 1978)

Sources: *Books in Print*, 1979-80; *Freedomways*, vol. 19, 1979.

GREENE, J. LEE. English Professor, Literary Critic.
Career: Prof., Eng., U. of N.C., Chapel Hill. *Mailing address:* U. of N.C., Chapel Hill, N.C. 27514.

Writings:
Nonfiction

Time's Unfading Garden: Ann Spencer's Life and Poetry (Baton Rouge, La. State U. Press, 1977)

Sources: *Books in Print*, 1980-81; *Freedomways*, vol. 18, 1978; *Time's Unfading Garden*.

GREENE, LORENZO JOHNSTON. History Professor, Historian.
Born in Ansonia, Conn., Nov. 16, 1899. *Education:* B.A., Howard U., 1924; M.A., Columbia U., 1926, Ph.D. (Hist.), 1942; L.H.D. (Hon.), U. of Mo., 1971. *Family:* Married Thomasina T. Greene, son Lorenzo Thomas Greene. *Career:* Res. Asst. (to Carter G. Woodson, Dir., ASNLH), 1928-32; Mem., Contrib. Staff, *Social Science Abstracts*, Columbia U., 1932; Asst. Prof. & Prof. of Hist., Lincoln U., Mo., 1933- ; Visiting Prof., Hist.: Tenn. Agricultural & Industrial U., summer 1945, S. Ill. U., U. of Kan., spring 1969, 1970; former ed., *Midwest Journal*, 1947-56; Lect.: Yale; Dartmouth; City Coll., Brooklyn Coll., & Hunter Coll. (N.Y.C.); U. of Mo.; Baker U.; Central Mo. State Coll., etc. Dir., Consortium, Lincoln U., Westminster Coll., & William Woods Coll. on Inst. for Coll. Tchrs. in Afro-Amer. Hist. & Culture, summer 1970. Consultant on introducing courses in Negro history in public schs. and/or colls. Black Studies Paperback Bk. Project Study of Negroes on Western Frontier, Taft TV & Radio Corp., 1971. *Honors:* Grants: ASNLH, 1931-32; Julius

Rosenwald Fund Fellow, 1934, 1940-41; Gen. Educ. Bd., 1935, 1945, 1947. *Mailing address:* c/o Hist. Dept., Lincoln U., Jefferson City, Mo. 65101.

Writings:
Nonfiction

The Negro Wage Earner, with Carter G. Woodson (Wash., D.C., ASNLH, 1930; N.Y., Russell, 1969)

The Employment of Negroes in the District of Columbia, with Myra Colson Callis (ASNLH, 1931)

The Negro in Colonial New England, 1620-1776 (N.Y., Columbia U. Press, 1942; N.Y., Atheneum, 1968)

Sidelights: "For more than thirty years, as member of the Missouri Association for Social Welfare he worked to improve the health and welfare of all Missouri citizens." (Author)

Source: Author information.

GREENFIELD, ELOISE. Juvenile Writer.
Born in Parmele, N.C., May 17, 1929. *Education:* Miners Teachers Coll., 1946-49. *Family:* Married Robert J. Greenfield (procurement specialist), Apr. 29, 1950; children: Steven, Monica. *Career:* U.S. Patent Office, Wash., D.C., Clerk-Typist, 1949-56, Supervisory Patent Asst., 1956-60; Secy., Case-Control Technician, & Admin. Asst., Wash., D.C., 1964-68; Co-Dir., Adult Fiction, D.C. Black Writers' Workshop, 1971-73; Dir., Children's Lit., 1973-74; Writer-in-Residence with D.C. Commission on the Arts, 1973. *Honors:* Coretta Scott King Award for *Africa Dream*; Jane Addams Award for *Paul Robeson*. *Mailing address:* c/o Curtis Brown, Ltd., 595 Madison Ave., N.Y., N.Y. 10022.

Writings:
Fiction

Bubbles, picture bk. (paper, Wash., D.C., Drum & Spear Press, 1972; later issued as *Good News*, 1977)

Sister, juv. (N.Y., Crowell, 1974)

She Come Bringing Me That Little Baby Girl, picture bk. (Phila., Lippincott, 1974)

Me and Nessie, juv. (Crowell, 1975)

First Pink Light, juv. (Crowell, 1976)

Africa Dream, juv. with L. J. Little (N.Y., John Day, 1977)

Honey, I Love and Other Poems, juv. (Crowell, 1978)

Talk about a Family, juv. novel (Lippincott, 1978)

I Can Do It by Myself, juv. (Crowell, 1978)

Childtimes: A Three-Generation Memoir, juv. with Lessie J. Little (Crowell, 1979)

Darlene, juv. (Agincourt, Ontario, Methuen, 1980)

Grandmama's Joy, juv. (N.Y., Philomel, 1980)

Nonfiction

Rosa Parks, juv. (Crowell, 1973)

Paul Robeson, juv. (Crowell, Biographical Ser., 1975)

Mary McCleod Bethune, juv. (Crowell, 1977)

Alesia, with Alesia Revis (Philomel, 1981)

Sources: *Books in Print*, 1979-80; *Freedomways*, vol. 17, 1977; *Writers Directory*, 1980-82.

GREGORY, RICHARD CLAXTON (Dick). Social Satirist, Civil Rights Leader, Pacifist, Athlete. Born in St. Louis, Mo., Oct. 12, 1932. *Education:* S. Ill. U., Carbondale, Ill. *Family:* Married Lillian Gregory, 1959; d. Michele, d. Lynn, ds. Pamela & Paula (twins), d. Stephanie, son Gregory, d. Miss, son Christian, d. Ayanna, son Yohance. *Career:* Won Mo. State Mile Championship, 1951, 1952, while in high sch.; named outstanding athlete, S. Ill. U., 1953; U.S. Army, Spec. Serv.; night club performer; civil rights protester; Lect., coll. campuses. *Honors:* Doctor of Humane Letters, Malcolm X U., Chicago; Doctor of Laws, Lincoln U., Pa. *Mailing address:* 1451 E. 55th St., Chicago, Ill. 60603.

Writings:
Nonfiction

From the Back of the Bus (N.Y., Avon, 1962; N.Y., Dutton, 1964)

Nigger, autobiog., ed. by Robert Lipsyte (Dutton, 1965; N.Y., McGraw-Hill, 1970)

What's Happening (Dutton, 1965)

The Shadow That Scares Me (Garden City, N.Y., Doubleday, 1968; N.Y., Pocket Bks., 1968, 1971)

Write Me In! (N.Y., Bantam, 1968)

No More Lies: The Myth and Reality of American History, ed. by James R. McGraw (N.Y., Harper, 1971)

Dick Gregory's Political Primer (Harper, 1972)

Dick Gregory's Natural Diet for Folks Who Eat: Cookin' with Mother Nature, ed. by James R. McGraw & Alvemia M. Fulton (Harper, 1973, 1974)

Dick Gregory's Bible Tales, with Commentary, ed. by James R. McGraw (N.Y., Stein & Day, 1974; N.Y., Har-Row, 1978)

Up from Nigger (Stein & Day, 1976; N.Y., Fawcett, 1978)

Code Name "Zorro": The Murder of Martin Luther King, Jr., with Mark Lane (Englewood Cliffs, N.J., Prentice-Hall, 1977)

Sidelights: Candidate for President of the United States in 1968; candidate for Mayor of Chicago in 1967. As a pacifist, has staged fasts to protest the war in Vietnam. Over 300 lectures annually on college campuses; concert, stage, television performances as a social satirist; numerous appearances on behalf of human rights causes. (Author)

Sources: *Afro-American Literature: Non-Fiction;* Author information; *Black Joy; Books in Print*, 1978-79, 1980-81; *Code Name "Zorro"; Current Biography*, 1962; *Negro Handbook; Writers Directory*, 1980-82.

GRIER, WILLIAM H. Psychiatrist.
Education: M.D., U. of Mich. Medical Sch.; Psychiatric residence, Menninger Clinic. *Career:* Psychiatrist; Asst. Prof. of Psychiatry, San Francisco Medical Center, U. of Cal. *Mailing address:* c/o Basic Bks., 10 E. 53rd St., N.Y., N.Y. 10022.

Writings:
Nonfiction

Black Rage, with Price Cobbs (N.Y., Bantam, 1969, 1980)

The Jesus Bag, with Price Cobbs (N.Y., McGraw-Hill, 1971)

Sources: *Books in Print*, 1980-81; Pub. information.

GRIGGS, SUTTON E. Minister, Religious Administrator, Novelist.
Born in Chatfield, Tex., in 1872. *Education:* Bishop Coll., Dallas, Tex.; Richmond Theological Sem., grad. 1893. *Career:* Minister, Bap. Church, Berkeley, Va., 2 yrs.; Corresponding Secy., Educ.

Dept., Natl. Bap. Convention, Nashville, Tenn., 20 yrs.; Founder, Natl. Relig. & Civic Inst., Houston, Tex. Died in 1930.

Writings:
Fiction

Imperio in Imperio, novel (Cincinnati, Editor, 1899; Miami, Mnemosyne, 1969)

Overshadowed, novel (Nashville, Tenn., Orion, 1901; Freeport, N.Y., Bks. for Lib., 1971)

Unfettered, novel with *Dorland's Plan* (Orion, 1902; N.Y., AMS, 1971)

The Hindered Hand; or The Reign of the Repressionist, novel (Orion, 1902; AMS, 1969)

Pointing the Way, novel (Orion, 1908)

Wisdom's Call, novel (Orion, 1911; Mnemosyne, 1969)

Sidelights: These novels are among thirty works altogether.

Sources: *Cavalcade; Negro Novel in America; Negro Voices in American Fiction.*

GRIMKÉ, ANGELINA WELD. Playwright, Poet.
Born in Boston, Mass. in 1880. *Education:* Girls' Latin Sch.; Boston Latin Sch.; Boston Normal Sch. of Gymnastics. *Career:* Tchr., Eng., Dunbar High Sch.; Tchr., Armstrong Manual Training Sch. (both Wash., D.C.). Died in 1958.

Writings:
Fiction

Rachel, a Play in Three Acts (produced 1916; Boston, Cornhill, 1920; College Park, Md., McGrath, 1969)

Nonfiction

Letters to Catherine E. Beecher (reprint of 1938 ed., Freeport, N.Y., Black Heritage Bks. for Libs., n.d.)

Sources: *Negro Caravan; Negro Vanguard; Poetry of Black America.*

GRIMKÉ, ARCHIBALD H. Abolitionist, Attorney, Educator, Editor, Biographer.
Born in Charleston, S.C., Aug. 17, 1849. *Education:* B.A., 1870, M.A., 1872, Lincoln U., Pa. (then a white sch.); LL.B., Harvard U., 1874. *Family:* Married Sarah E. Stanley in 1879. *Career:* Lawyer, Boston; Assoc. of Abolitionists: Sumner & Garrison; U.S. Consul, Santo Domingo, 1894-98; Pres., Amer. Negro Acad., Wash., D.C., 1903-16; NAACP: Pres., Boston Branch, V. Pres., Natl.; Ed., *Hub* newspaper; Free-lance Writer, *Boston Traveler, Boston Herald, Atlantic Monthly. Honors:* NAACP Spingarn Medal, 1919. Died in 1930.

Writings:
Nonfiction

William Lloyd Garrison, the Abolitionist (N.Y., Funk & Wagnalls, Amer. Reformers Ser., 1891; N.Y., Negro Universities Press, 1969)

The Life of Charles Sumner, the Scholar in Politics (Funk & Wagnalls, Amer. Reformers Ser., 1892)

Charles Sumner Centenary; Historical Address (N.Y., Arno, 1969)

The Shame of America: or The Negro's Case against the Republic (Arno, 1969)

Sidelights: "Son of Henry Grimké (white) and Nancy Weston (a slave), Archibald H. Grimké was one of two brothers well known for their public spirit, the other being the Rev. Francis J. Grimké.... He with his brother was encouraged even while in college by two sisters of his father who found the South uncongenial." (*Negro Genius*)

Sources: *Historical Negro Biographies; Negro Author in America; Negro Genius; Negroes in Public Affairs and Government; They Showed the Way.*

GUILLEN, NICOLÁS. (Cuban). Journalist, Poet, Folklorist, Politician.
Born in Camagüey, Cuba, July 10, 1902. *Education:* Bachiller en Letras y Ciencias, Inst. of Camagüey, 1920. *Career:* Journalist; Politician (Cuba); Ed., *Mediodia* journal; Founder, Sociedad des Estudios Afro-cubanos. *Honors:* Awarded Stalin Prize, 1953, after becoming Communist; "Poeta Nacional," 1961; Pres., Union of Cuban Writers, 1961. *Mailing address:* c/o Broadside Press, 74 Glendale Ave., Highland Park, Mich. 48203.

Writings:
(Partial Listing — English Only)
Fiction
Cuba Libre, poems, transl. from Spanish by Langston Hughes & Ben Carruthers (L.A., Anderson & Ritchie, 1948)

Man-Making Words: Selected Poems of Nicolás Guillen, transl. from Spanish by Robert Marquez & David A. McMurray (Amherst, U. of Mass. Press, 1972)

Patria o Muerte: The Great Zoo and Other Poems by Nicolás Guillen, 1928-1970 (N.Y., Monthly Review Press, 1972)

Tengo, poems, transl. by Richard Carr (Detroit, Broadside, 1974)

Sidelights: "Guillen's pioneering interest in Afro-Cuban culture led him to create works in the *son*, a particular Cuban popular song form derived from African folklore and music." (*Caribbean Writers*)
Cuban representative to First International Congress of Writers for the Defense of Culture, in Spain, in 1936. Also visited Venezuela, Colombia, Peru, Chile, Argentina and Brazil. Attended Congress of League of Revolutionary Writers and Artists in Mexico, 1937.

Sources: *Books in Print*, 1980-81; *Caribbean Writers; Cuba Libre, Poems; Freedomways,* vol. 19, 1979; *Resistance and Caribbean Literature.*

GUTHRIE, ROBERT VAL. Psychologist.
Born in Chicago, Ill., Feb. 14, 1930. *Education:* B.S., Fla. U., 1955; M.A., U. of Ky., 1960; Ph.D., U.S. Intnl. U., 1970. *Family:* Married Elodia S. Guthrie, Sept. 15, 1952; children: Robert, Paul, Michael, Ricardo, Sheila, Mario. *Career:* Instr., Psychology, San Diego Mesa Coll., 1963-70; Asst. Prof., U. of Pittsburgh, 1970-71; Assoc. Prof., Psychology, 1971-73; Senior Res. Psychologist, Natl. Inst. of Educ., Wash., D.C., 1973-74; Res. Psychologist & Assoc. Dir., Psychological Sci., Office of Naval Res., Arlington, Va., 1975- *Mailing address:* Harper & Row, 10 E. 53rd St., N.Y., N.Y. 10022.

Writings:
Nonfiction
Psychology in the World Today: An Interdisciplinary Approach (Reading, Mass., Addison-Wesley, 1968, 1971)

Encounter: Issues on Human Concerns (Menlo Park, Cal., Cummings, 1970)

Being Black: Psychological-Sociological Dilemmas (San Francisco, Canfield, 1970)

Man and Society: Focus on Reality, with Edward Barnes (Palo Alto, Cal., J. E. Freel, 1972)

Even the Rat Was White: Historical Views in Psychology (N.Y., Harper, 1976)

Sources: *Contemporary Authors*, vols. 53-56, 1975; Pub. information.

GUY, ROSA GUTHBERT. Novelist, Juvenile Writer.
Born in Trinidad, Brit. W. Indies, Sept. 1, 1925. *Education:* N.Y.U. (Writing). *Family:* Married Warner Guy (dec.); son Warner. *Career:* Amer. Negro Theatre; garment piece worker; helped found Harlem Writers Guild. *Mailing address:* Agent, Bill Berber Assoc., 538 E. 72nd St., N.Y., N.Y. 10021.

Writings:
Fiction

Venetian Blinds, one-act play (1954)

Bird at My Window, novel (Phila., Lippincott, 1965)

Birago Diop's Mother Crocodile: An Uncle Amadu Tale from Senegal, transl. and adapted (N.Y., Delacorte, 1971)

The Friends, juv. novel (N.Y., Holt, 1973)

Ruby; A Novel, juv. (N.Y., Viking, 1976; N.Y., Bantam, 1979)

Edith Jackson, juv. novel (Viking, 1978; Bantam, 1981)

The Disappearance, juv. novel (Delacorte, 1979)

Mirror of Her Own, juv. novel (Delacorte, 1981)

Measure of Time, novel (Holt, 1983)

Nonfiction

Children of Longing, ed. (Bantam, 1970)

Sidelights: " ... interested in the historical and cultural aspects of all peoples of African descent. Have been to Haiti and back to Trinidad to study the ways, customs, and language retained over the years from Africa." (*Something about the Author*)

Sources: *Bird at My Window; Books in Print*, 1978-79, 1981-82; *Something about the Author*, vol. 14, 1978.

GWALTNEY, JOHN LANGSTON. Anthropologist, Ethnographer.
Born in Orange, N.J., Sept. 15, 1928. *Education:* B.A., Upsala Coll., E. Orange, N.J., 1952; M.A., New Sch. for Soc. Res., 1957; Ph.D. (Anthropology), Columbia U., 1967. *Career:* Past Faculty Advisor to Uhuru Assn. of Black Students, Cortland Coll.; Past Chairman, Presidential Advisory Com. on the Caste Disadvantaged, Cortland Coll.; Ethnographer, Allopsychic Res. Project, 1961; Ethnographer among the highland Chinantec of Oaxaca, Mexico, 1963-64; Asst. & Assoc. Prof., SUNY at Cortland, Dept. of Sociol. & Anthropology, 1967-71; Consultant to Presidential Com. on Black Studies, Harpur Coll., SUNY at Binghamton, Nov. 1969; Ethnographer among the Shinnecook & Poospatuck Indians of Suffolk Co., Long Island, N.Y., summer 1969; Ethnographer among highland Maroons of St. Elizabeth Parish, Jamaica, summer 1972; Ethnographer among Northeastern urban Afro-Americans, July 1973-present; Assoc. Prof., Syracuse U., Dept. of Anthropology, 1971-present. *Honors:* Ruth Benedict Memorial Award; John Hay Whitney Found. Fellow; Natl. Inst. of Health Fellow; Ansley Dissertation Award; Faculty Grant, N.Y. State Educ. Dept.; Faculty Res. Fellow & Grant-in-Aid, SUNY; Grant-in-Aid to Minority Scholars, Soc. Sci. Res. Council; Grant-in-Aid, Amer. Philosophical Soc.; NEH Senior Fellow. *Mailing address:* Anthropology Dept., 500 University Pl., Syracuse U., Syracuse, N.Y. 13210.

Writings:
Nonfiction

The Thrice Shy: Cultural Accommodation to Blindness and Other Disasters in a Mexican Community (N.Y., Columbia U. Press, 1970)

Drylongso: A Self-Portrait of Black America, ed. (N.Y., Random, 1980, 1981)

Sidelights: "John Langston Gwaltney, a distinguished anthropologist who is black and blind, set out to record representative voices of black America." (*Drylongso*)

Sources: Author information; *Black Scholar*, Sept./Oct. 1980; *Drylongso*.

HALEY, ALEX. Biographer, Genealogist.
Born in Ithaca, N.Y., Aug. 11, 1921. *Education:* Alcorn Coll.; Elizabeth City State Tchrs. Coll.; Litt.D. (hon.), Simpson Coll., Indianola, Iowa. *Career:* Chief Journalist, U.S. Coast Guard, 1939-59; Free-lance Writer. *Honors:* Anisfield-Wolf Award for *Autobiography of Malcolm X*, 1965. *Mailing address:* Kinte Found., P.O. Box 3338, Beverly Hills, Cal. 90212.

Writings:
Nonfiction
The Autobiography of Malcolm X, collaborator (N.Y., Grove, 1965, 1968)

Roots (Garden City, N.Y., Doubleday, 1976; N.Y., Dell, 1977; 3 vols. large print, Boston, G. K. Hall, 1979)

Sidelights: *Roots* is the extraordinary result of Haley's twelve-year search for authentication of the story of his ancestor, "the African," told to him during his childhood. (*Roots*)

Sources: *Books in Print*, 1978-79, 1980-81; *Roots.*

HALLIBURTON, WARREN J. Teacher, Editor, Novelist, Juvenile Writer.
Born in N.Y.C., Aug. 2, 1924. *Education:* Euander Childs High Sch., Bronx, N.Y.; B.S., M.A., N.Y.U.; Educ. Doctorate, Tchrs. Coll., Columbia U. *Family:* Married Frances Halliburton; d. Cheryl, d. Stephanie, son Warren, Jr. *Career:* Assoc., Inst. for Intnl. Educ.; Assoc., N.Y. State Dept. of Educ.; Tchr.; Ed., McGraw-Hill; Visiting Prof., Eng., Hamilton Coll.; Dir., Center for Ethnic Studies, Tchrs. Coll., Columbia U.; Consultant & Lect.: Dade County, Fla.; U. of Cal., Santa Cruz; Princeton U.; Columbia U.; N.Y.C. Bd. of Educ. *Mailing address:* c/o McGraw-Hill Bk. Co., 1221 Ave. of the Americas, N.Y., N.Y. 10020.

Writings:
Fiction
New Worlds of Literature, anthology (N.Y., Harcourt, 1966)

The Heist, novella (N.Y., McGraw-Hill, 1968)

Cry Baby!, novel (McGraw-Hill, 1968)

Negro Doctor, juv. adaptation (McGraw-Hill, 1968)

Marty, juv. adaptation (McGraw-Hill, 1968)

Printer's Measure, juv. adaptation (McGraw-Hill, 1968)

Call of the Wild, juv. adaptation (McGraw-Hill, 1968)

Some Things That Glitter, novel (McGraw-Hill, 1970)

Short Story Scene, ed. (N.Y., Globe, 1973)

Nonfiction
The Year the Yankees Lost the Pennant, juv. adaptation for Douglas Wallop (McGraw-Hill, 1968)

American Majorities and Minorities; A Syllabus of United States History for Secondary Schools, with William L. Katz (N.Y., Arno, 1970)

The Picture Life of Jesse Jackson, juv. (N.Y., Watts, Picture Life Bks., 1972)

Harlem: A History of Broken Dreams, with Ernest Kaiser (Garden City, N.Y., Zenith, Macmillan Reading Ser., 1974)

Composing with Sentences, with Agnes A. Postva, Sr. (N.Y., Cambridge Bks., Cambridge Writers Program Ser., 1974)

Sidelights: In addition to the listed works, "approximately 100 short stories and plays." (Author)

Sources: Author information; *Books in Print*, Supplement, 1975-76.

HAMILTON, CHARLES VERNON. Political Science Professor, Lawyer.
Born in Muskogee, Okla., Oct. 19, 1929. *Education:* B.A., Roosevelt U., Chicago, 1951; J.D., Loyola U., Sch. of Law, Chicago, 1954; M.A., 1957, Ph.D., 1963, U. of Chicago. *Family:* Married Dona Louise Hamilton; d. Valli, d. Carol. *Career:* Tchr.: Tuskegee Inst.; Albany State Coll., Ga.; Rutgers U., Newark; Lincoln U.; Chairman, Dept. of Polit. Sci., Roosevelt U.; Prof., Dept. of Polit. Sci., Columbia U. (present). *Honors:* John Hay Whitney Found. Fellow; U. of Chicago Professional Alumni Award; Roosevelt Alumni Award; Phi Beta Kappa Visiting Lect. Scholar, 1972-73. *Mailing address:* c/o Dept. of Polit. Sci., Columbia U., N.Y., N.Y. 10027.

Writings:
Nonfiction

Black Power: The Politics of Liberation in America, with Stokely Carmichael (N.Y., Vintage, 1967)

The Black Preacher in America (N.Y., Morrow, 1972)

The Black Experience in American Politics (N.Y., Putnam, 1973)

The Bench and the Ballot, Southern Federal Judges and Black Voters (N.Y., Oxford U. Press, 1973)

American Government (Glenview, Ill., Scott, Foresman, 1982)

Sources: Author information; *Black Power; Books in Print*, 1983-84.

HAMILTON, VIRGINIA ESTHER. Juvenile Writer, Lecturer.
Born in Yellow Springs, Ohio, Mar. 12, 1937. *Education:* Antioch Coll., 1953-56; Ohio State U., 1956-58; New Sch. for Soc. Res., 1958-59. *Family:* Married Arnold Adoff (anthologist & writer); d. Leigh Hamilton, son Jaime Levi. *Career:* "Every source of occupation imaginable, from singer to bookkeeper" (*Something about the Author*); Symposium on Children's Lit., Marymount Coll., N.Y.; Symposium, U. of Cal., Berkeley; lectures all over the country. *Honors:* For *Zeely* (ALA Notable Bk. List; Nancy Block Memorial Award); for *The House of Dies Drear* (ALA Notable Bk. List; Edgar Allan Poe award for best juv. mystery; Ohioana Lit. Award for 1968); for *Time-Ago Tales of Jahdu* (ALA Notable Bk. List); for *Planet of Junior Brown* (ALA Notable Bk. List; Newbery Honor Bk. Award, 1972); for *M. C. Higgins, the Great* (Newbery Award, 1975). Lewis Carroll, Shelf Award, Natl. Bk. Award nominee. Natl. Bk. Awards, Children's Lit., for *M. C. Higgins, the Great*, 1975; Newbery Honor Bk. for *Sweet Whispers, Brother Rush*, 1983, also Coretta Scott King Award for same. Listed in *Thirty Mid-Century Children's Books Every Adult Should Know*, issued by *Horn Bk.; More Books by More People* (interviews with 65 authors of bks. for children by Lee Hopkins). *Mailing address:* Box 293, Yellow Springs, Ohio 45387.

Writings:
Fiction

Zeely, juv. novel (N.Y., Macmillan, 1967, 1971; N.Y., Dell, 1978)

The House of Dies Drear, juv. novel (Macmillan, 1968, 1970; Dell, 1978)

Time-Ago Tales of Jahdu, juv. novel (Macmillan, 1969)

The Planet of Junior Brown, juv. novel (Macmillan, 1971, 1974; Dell, 1978; N.Y., Philomel, 1982)

Time-Ago Lost: More Tales of Jahdu, juv. novel (Macmillan, 1973; N.Y., Greenwillow, Read Alone Bks., 1980)

M. C. Higgins, the Great, juv. novel (Macmillan, 1974; Dell, 1976; large print, Boston, G. K. Hall, 1976)

Arilla Sun Down, juv. novel (Greenwillow, 1976)

Justice and Her Brothers, juv. novel (Greenwillow, 1978)

Jahdu, juv. novel (Greenwillow, 1980)

The Gathering, juv. novel (Justice Cycle Ser., vol. 3, Greenwillow, 1980; N.Y., Avon, 1981)

The Magical Adventures of Pretty Pearl, juv. novel (N.Y., Harper, 1982)

Sweet Whispers, Brother Rush, juv. novel (Philomel, 1983)

Nonfiction
W. E. B. DuBois: A Biography (N.Y., Crowell, 1972)

Paul Robeson: The Life and Times of a Free Black Man (Harper, 1974)

Sidelights: Virginia Hamilton has the following to say of her work: "Time, place and family are at the heart of the fictions I create. My commitment to family in my books has its foundation in my background and the intimate and shared places of the hometown and the hometown's parade of life. Time, place, the hometown, become almost mythical for me." (Publisher)

Sources: Author information; *Books in Print*, 1981-82; Pub. information; *Something about the Author*, vol. 4, 1973.

HAMMON, JUPITER. Poet.
Born on Long Island, N.Y., about 1720. Slave of Henry Lloyd and descendants; esteemed by family, who assisted him in placing verses before the public; won his freedom. Died c. 1800.

Writings:
Fiction
"An Evening Thought. Salvation by Christ, with Penitential Cries: Composed by Jupiter Hammon, a Negro belonging to Mr. Lloyd of Queens Village on Long Island, the 25th of December, 1760" (1st poetical composition by a Black published in this country)

"An Address to Miss Phyllis Wheatly (sic), etc.," broadside (Hartford, n.p., 1778)

"An Essay on Ten Virgins," broadside (1779)

"A Winter Piece," broadside (Hartford, Hudson & Goodwin, 1782)

"A Poem for Children, with Thoughts on Death," broadside (1782)

"An Evening's Improvement ...," broadside (of autobiog. interest, Hartford, n.p., 1790)

Nonfiction
"An Address to the Negroes in the State of New York," Sept. 24, 1786, broadside presented to African Soc. of City of N.Y. (N.Y., Carroll & Patterson, 1787, went into 3rd ed.)

Jupiter Hammon, American Negro Poet; Selections ..., ed. by Oscar Wegelin (N.Y., C. F. Heartman, 1915)

America's First Negro Poet; The Complete Works ..., ed. by Stanley A. Ransom, Jr. (Port Wash., N.Y., Kennikat, 1970)

Sidelights: "Revealing as much about the White world in which he moved as anything else, Hammon's broadside verses have historical, sociological and some literary interest." (*Early Black American Poets*)

"His 'Address ...' shows the writer as feeling it his personal duty to bear slavery with patience, but strongly opposed to the system and as urging that young Negroes be manumitted." (*Early Negro American Writers*)

Sources: *Early Black American Poets; Early Negro American Writers; Famous American Negro Poets; Historical Negro Biographies; Negro Almanac; Negro Poets and Their Poems; Negro Vanguard.*

HANDY, WILLIAM CHRISTOPHER. Composer, Publisher.
Born in Florence, Ala., Nov. 16, 1873. *Career:* Composer, Publisher (own works). Died Mar. 28, 1958.

Writings:
Nonfiction

Negro Authors and Composers of the United States (N.Y., Handy Brothers, 1938; N.Y., AMS, 1976)

Collection of Negro Spirituals ... (Handy Brothers, 1938)

Father of the Blues, autobiog. (N.Y., Macmillan, 1941, 1970; reissued as *A Treasury of the Blues*, 1949)

Unsung Americans Sung, 2nd ed. (N.Y., 1944; Handy Brothers, 1946)

Blues: An Anthology, ed. by Jerry Silverman (Macmillan, 1972)

Sidelights: (Compositions of Note) "Memphis Blues" (1909); "St. Louis Blues" (1914); "Joe Turner Blues" (1915); "Beale Street Blues" (1917); "Loveless Love" (1921); "Got No Mo' Home Dan a Dog" (1926).

Sources: *American Authors and Books; Books in Print*, 1980-81; *Reader's Encyclopedia of American Literature.*

HANSBERRY, LORRAINE. Playwright.
Born in Chicago, Ill., May 19, 1930. *Education:* Art Inst. of Chicago; U. of Wis.; Guadalajara, Mexico. *Family:* Married Robert Nemiroff (music pub. & song writer), June 20, 1953. *Career:* Playwright. *Honors:* Youngest American, fifth woman, and only black dramatist to win New York Drama Critics Circle Award for Best Play of the Year, 1959 (*Raisin in the Sun*). Film adaptation of *Raisin* received numerous awards. Produced and published in 30 countries. Recipient special award, Cannes Film Festival, 1961. Died of cancer, Jan. 2, 1965.

Writings:
Fiction

Raisin in the Sun, a Drama in Three Acts (N.Y., Random, 1959; N.Y., NAL, 1961; Random, 1969)

The Sign in Sidney Brustein's Window, a Drama in Three Acts (Random, 1965; N.Y., Samuel French, paper, 1965)

To Be Young, Gifted and Black, play adapted from her writings, by her husband, after her death (NAL, 1965, 1970; Englewood Cliffs, N.J., Prentice-Hall, 1969)

Les Blancs, the Drinking Gourd, What Use Are Flowers, plays, all pub. by former husband, Robert Nemiroff, who produced her musical *Raisin* (Random, 1972, paper also)

Les Blancs: The Collected Last Plays of Lorraine Hansberry, ed. by Robert Nemiroff (Random, 1972)

Nonfiction

The Movement; Documentary of a Struggle for Equality, essays (N.Y., Simon & Schuster, Touchstone Bks., 1964, paper also)

Sidelights: Coming of age during what might be described as the "great thaw" in contemporary race relations, Miss Hansberry's artistic and social vision was far-reaching and optimistic. Not only American Negroes, but colored peoples throughout the world were on the move, and she doubtless had this in mind when she proclaimed herself part of a "world majority, and a very assertive one." The chief characters in her plays share this feeling. They are insistent, committed, and enduring because they wish to impose a purpose, a raison d'être, on life. (*Dictionary of American Negro Biography*)

Sources: *Afro-American Literature: Drama; Authors in the News; Black American Writers*, vol. II: *Poetry and Drama; Black Insights; Black Scenes; Books in Print*, 1980-81, 1981-82; *Dictionary of American Negro Biography; Negro Almanac; Who Was Who in America*, vol. IV, 1961-68.

HANSBERRY, WILLIAM LEO. African Historian, History Professor.

Born in Gloster, Miss., in 1894. *Education:* B.A., 1921, M.A., 1932 (African Anthropology & Archaeology), both Harvard U.; Oxford U., 1937-38. *Family:* Married Myrtle Kelso in 1937. *Career:* Prof., Hist., Howard U., 1922-59; Distinguished Visiting Prof., U. of Nigeria, Nsukka, 1963. *Honors:* Received highest civilian award (1st African Res. Award, Haile Selassie I Prize Trust of $28,000) from Ethiopian govt., 1964; Hansberry Inst. of African Studies, U. of Nigeria, Nsukka, established in his name, 1963; hon. degrees: LL.D., Va. State Coll.; LL.D., Morgan State Coll.; Litt.D., U. of Nigeria, Nsukka; Fulbright Res. Scholar, Egypt, 1953; Award of Honor, African Student Assn. of U.S. & Canada, 1951, 1959, 1963; Bronze citation for "Forty Years of Service in the Cause of African Freedom," United Friends of Africa, 1961; Achievement Award, Omega Psi Phi Fraternity, 1961. Died in Chicago, Nov. 3, 1965.

Writings:

Nonfiction

Pillars in Ethiopian History: The William Leo Hansberry African History Notebook, vol. I, ed. by Joseph E. Harris (Wash., D.C., Howard U. Press, 1974, 1981)

Africa and Africans as Seen by Classical Writers. The William Leo Hansberry African History Notebook, vol. II, ed. by Joseph E. Harris (Howard U. Press, 1977, 1981)

Sidelights: Professor Hansberry was unable to take the Ph.D. degree because no institution had developed an adequate program for the study of Africa. (*Africa and Africans*)

"He was one of the early exponents of the idea of African genesis." (*Negro Handbook*)

"... the African-American Institute, founded originally by Dr. W. Leo Hansberry of Howard University, but destined to become a large-scale, foundation-supported effort with a scholarship and teacher placement program and a publication, *Africa Report*." (*American Negro Reference Book*)

Sources: *Africa and Africans as Seen by Classical Writers; American Negro Reference Book; Negro Almanac; Negro Handbook; Pillars in Ethiopian History.*

HARDING, VINCENT. Historian, History Professor, Civil Rights Leader, Television Program Coordinator.

Born in N.Y.C., July 25, 1931. *Education:* B.A., City Coll. of N.Y., 1952; M.S. (Journalism), Columbia U., 1953; M.A. (Hist.), 1956, Ph.D., 1965, U. of Chicago. *Family:* Married Rosemarie Feeney; d. Rachel Sojourner, son Jonathan DuBois. *Career:* U.S. Army, 1953-55; Lay Pastor (part time), Seventh Day Adventist Mission Church, Chicago, 1955-57; Lay Pastor (part time), Woodlawn Mennonite Church, Chicago, 1957-61; S. Rep., Mennonite Serv. Com., Atlanta, Ga.; Acting, Civil Rights Negotiator, various "Movement" orgs., 1961-65; Chairman, Dept. of Hist. & Sociol., Spelman Coll., 1965-69; Dir., Martin Luther King Lib. Project, 1968-70; Dir., Inst. of the Black World, 1969- ; Chairman, Advisory Coordinator Com. for "Black Heritage" (108 TV programs on Afro-Amer. Hist, CBS TV), 1968-69. *Honors:* Res. grants: Amer. Council of Learned Socs.; Atlanta U. Center Res. Com.; Atlanta U. Center Non-Western Studies Com.; Kent Fellow, Sociol. of Relig. in Higher Educ. *Mailing address:* 87 Chestnut St., Atlanta, Ga. 30314.

Writings:

Nonfiction

Must Walls Divide?, hist. (N.Y., Friendship Press, 1965)

Black Heritage Books, 22 vols., ser. ed. with John H. Clarke (N.Y., Holt, 1971)

The Other American Revolution: A Brief History of the Struggle for Black Freedom (Center for Afro-Amer. Studies, Atlanta U., & Inst. of Black World, Atlanta, 1980)

There Is a River: The Black Struggle for Freedom in America (N.Y., HarBraceJ, 1981)

Sources: *Books in Print*, 1981-82; *Freedomways*, vol. 20, 1980; *Who's Who in America*, 37th ed., 1972-73.

HARPER, FRANCES ELLEN WATKINS. Poet, Abolitionist.

Born in Baltimore, Md., in 1825. *Education:* Baltimore. *Family:* Married Fenton Harper. *Career:* Tchr., Union Sem., Columbus, Ohio; "underground railroad" worker, Little York, Pa.; Lect., Anti-Slavery Soc. of Maine (lectured in Boston, Phila., & New Bedford, Mass., and in every S. state but Tex. & Ark.). After the Civil War she traveled extensively as Women's Christian Temperance Union rep. Died in 1911.

Writings:

Fiction

Poems on Miscellaneous Subjects (Boston, Yerrinton, 1854; Wilmington, Del., Scholarly Resources, 1970?; Ann Arbor, Mich., U. Microfilms, 1972)

Moses, a Story of the Nile, poems (Phila., Merrihew, 1869, 2nd ed., 1889)

Sketches of Southern Life, poems (Merrihew, 1873)

Iola Leroy, or the Shadows Uplifted, best known prose work (Phila., Garrigues Brothers, 1892)

Poems (Phila., George S. Ferguson, 1895; N.Y., AMS, 1975)

Atlanta Offering, poems (Phila., George S. Ferguson, 1895)

Idylls of the Bible (Phila., Author, 1901; reprint, AMS, 1975)

Sources: *Afro-American Writers; American Negro Reference Book; Anthology of Verse by American Negroes; Books in Print*, Supplement, 1975-76; *Early Black American Poets; Poetry of the Negro*, 1749-1949.

HARPER, MICHAEL STEVEN. Poet, Teacher.

Born in Brooklyn, N.Y., Mar. 18, 1938. *Education:* B.A., 1961, M.A. (Eng.), 1963, UCLA; M.A. (M.F.A.), Writer's Workshop, U. of Iowa. *Family:* Married Shirley Harper; son Roland, son Patrice, d. Rachel. *Career:* Prof., Dir. Writing Program, Brown U.; Center for Advanced Study, U. of Ill., Urbana; Cal. State U., Hayward; Lewis & Clark Coll. (Poet-in-Residence); Reed Coll., Ore.; Contra Costa Coll., Cal.; L.A. City Coll.; Tchr., Lit., & Dir., Writing Program, Brown U. *Honors:* Postdoctoral fellow, U. of Ill., Center for Advanced Study, 1970-71; award for creative writing, Amer. Acad./Natl. Inst. of Arts & Letters, 1972; Best Poetry Bk., Black Acad. of Arts & Letters, 1972 (for *History Is Your Own Heartbeat*). *Mailing address:* 26 First St., Barrington, R.I. 02806.

Writings:

Fiction

Dear John, Dear Coltrane, poems (Pittsburgh, U. of Pittsburgh Press, 1970)

History Is Your Own Heartbeat, poems (Urbana, U. of Ill. Press, 1971)

Song: I Want a Witness, poems (U. of Pittsburgh Press, 1972)

Photographs, Negatives: History as Apple Tree, poems (San Francisco, Scarab Press, 1972)

Debridgement, poems (N.Y., Doubleday, 1973)

Heartblow: Black Veils, poems (U. of Ill. Press, 1974)

Nightmare Begins Responsibility, poems (U. of Ill. Press, 1975)

Images of Kin: New and Selected Poems (U. of Ill. Press, 1977)

Healing Songs for the Inner Ear, poems (Doubleday, 1979)

Nonfiction

A Chant of Saints: A Gathering of Afro-American Literature, Art, and Scholarship, with Robert B. Stepto (U. of Ill. Press, 1979)

Sources: Author information; *Books in Print*, 1981-82; *Chant of Saints; New Black Voices; Poetry of Black America*; Pub. information.

HARRIS, ABRAM LINCOLN. Economist, Economics Professor.
Born in Richmond, Va., in 1899. *Education:* Armstrong High Sch., Richmond; Va. Union U., Richmond, grad., 1922; M.A., U. of Pittsburgh; Ph.D. (Econ.), Columbia U., 1931. *Career:* Instr., Econ., W. Va. State Coll., 1924; Executive Secy., Minneapolis Urban League, 1925; Researcher, Columbia U. Dept. of Banking, 1926; Asst. Prof., 1927, Head, Dept. of Econ., 1930, Prof., 1936, Howard U.; Visiting Prof., Econ., U. of Chicago, 1946-63; Visiting Prof., summer: City Coll. of N.Y., 1942; U. of Puerto Rico, 1957. *Honors:* Soc. Sci. Res. Council Fellow, 1928-30; Simon Nelson Patten Res. Fellow, 1932-33; Guggenheim Found. Fellow, 1935-36, 1943-44, 1953-54. Died in 1963.

Writings:
Nonfiction
The Black Worker; The Negro and the Labor Movement, with Sterling Spero (N.Y., Columbia U. Press, 1931)

The Negro as Capitalist; A Study of Banking and Business among American Negroes (Phila., Amer. Acad. of Polit. & Social Sci., 1936)

Economics and Social Reform (N.Y., Harper, 1958)

Sidelights: "The most outstanding academic economist among American blacks was Abram Lincoln Harris ... he divided his teaching career between a black school, Howard University (1927-1945), and a white school, the University of Chicago (1946-63). His best known work was *The Negro as Capitalist* (1936), a definitive study of the black man in banking, insurance, and other enterprises." (*Biographical History of Blacks in America since 1528*)

Sources: *Biographical History of Blacks in America since 1528.*

HARRIS, JOSEPH E. Historian, History Professor, Africa Specialist.
Education: B.A., M.A. (Hist.), Howard U.; Ph.D. (African Hist.,), Northwestern U., 1965. *Family:* Married Rosemarie Harris; d. Joanne; son Joseph Earl. *Career:* Instr., Hist., Howard U., 1958-59; Instr., Hist., Morgan State Coll., 1959-60; Contract Tchr., Agency for Intnl. Development, Guinea, W. Africa, 1960-62; Asst. Prof., Hist., Loch Haven State Coll., Pa., 1963-65; Assoc. Prof., Hist., SUNY, New Paltz, 1965-69; Prof., Hist., Williams Coll., 1969-75; Visiting Prof., Hist., U. of Nairobi, Kenya, 1972-74; Prof., Hist., & Chairman of Dept., Howard U., 1975- ; Consultant: Dartmouth Coll., Peace Corps Program—African Studies; N.Y. State Dept. of Educ., Coll. Proficiency Examination, African & Afro-Amer. Hist.; Educ. Testing Serv.; "Meeting of Experts," African Slave Trade, UNESCO, Haiti; Chairman, Planning Com., Cultural Program, Exhibition Contemporary Senegalese Art & Visit of Pres. Leopold S. Senghor, Corcoran Gallery of Art, Wash., D.C. (TV) Black Heritage, African Hist., CBS, 1969; Black Educational Enterprises (video), E. African Slave Trade, 1977. *Honors:* African Studies Scholarship, Northwestern U., 1956-58; N.Y. State Dept. of Educ. Grant, 1967; SUNY, Faculty Fellow, 1967; SUNY, New Paltz Grant, 1967; Rockefeller Found. Fellow, Kenya, June 1972-Jan. 1974. *Mailing address:* 10726 Hintock Rd., Silver Spring, Md. 20603.

Writings:
Nonfiction
The African Presence in Asia: Consequences of the East African Slave Trade (Evanston, Ill., Northwestern U. Press, 1971)

Africans and Their History (N.Y., New Amer. Lib., 1972)

Pillars in Ethiopian History: The William Leo Hanberry African History Notebook, vol. I, ed. (Wash., D.C., Howard U. Press, 1974, 1981)

Africa and Africans as Seen by Classical Writers, the William Leo Hansberry African History Notebook, vol. II, ed. (Howard U. Press, 1977, 1981)

Recollections of James Juma Mbotela (Nairobi, Kenya, E. African Pub. House, 1977)

Sources: Author information; *Books in Print,* 1981-82; *Freedomways,* vol. 19, 1979.

HARRIS, (THEODORE) WILSON. (Guyanan). Novelist, Critic, Poet.
Born in New Amsterdam, Brit. Guiana, Mar. 24, 1921. *Education:* Queen's Coll., Georgetown, Guyana. *Family:* Married Margaret Whitaker. *Career:* Govt. Surveyor, Senior Surveyor, 1955-58; Writer; Visiting Lect.: SUNY, Buffalo, 1970; U. of W. Indies, Mona, Jamaica; Writer-in-Residence, Scarborough Coll., U. of Toronto, 1970; Commonwealth Fellow in Caribbean Lit., Leeds U., Yorkshire, 1971; delegate to UNESCO Symposium on Caribbean Lit., Cuba, 1968; Visiting Prof., Ethnic Studies & Eng., U. of Tex., Austin, 1972. *Honors:* Arts Council Grant, 1968. *Mailing address:* c/o Faber & Faber, Ltd., 3 Queen Square, London, WC I 3AU, Eng.

Writings:
Fiction

Fetish, poems (Brit. Guiana, Miniature Poets Ser., 1951)

Eternity to Season, poems (Brit. Guiana, Magnet Printery, 1952; reprint, London, Kraus, Nendelon, 1970)

The Well and the Land, poems (Brit. Guiana, Studies in Time, 1952)

Palace of the Peacock, novel (London, Faber, 1960, 1968)

The Far Journey of Oudin, novel (Faber, 1961)

The Whole Armour, novel (Faber, 1962), combined with *The Secret Ladder* (Faber, 1963, 1973)

The Secret Ladder, novel (Faber, 1963), combined with *The Whole Armour* (Faber, 1962, 1973)

Heartland, novel (Faber, 1964)

The Waiting Room, novel (Faber, 1967)

Tumatumari, novel (Faber, 1968)

Ascent to Omai, novel (Faber, 1970)

The Sleepers of Roraima; A Carib Trilogy, short stories (Faber, 1970)

The Age of the Rainmakers, short stories (Faber, 1971)

Black Marsden; A Tabula Rasa Comedy, novel (Faber, 1972)

The Eye of the Scarecrow, novel (Faber, 1974)

Companions of the Day and Night, novel (Faber, 1975)

Genesis of the Clowns, novel (Faber, 1975), repub. with *Da Silva, Da Silva's Cultivated Wilderness* (Faber, 1977)

Nonfiction

Tradition and the West Indian Novel (London, W. Indian Students Union, 1965; London & Port of Spain, Trinidad, New Beacon Bks., 1965)

Tradition, the Writer and Society: Critical Essays (New Beacon Bks., 1967; N.Y., Panther, 1971)

History, Fable and Myth in the Caribbean and Guianas (Georgetown, Guyana, Natl. Hist. & Arts Council, 1970)

Sidelights: Wilson Harris exploits excellently and draws upon a large scale of community consisting of ancestral Indians, Caribs, Arawaks, African slaves and European immigrants. (*Resistance and Caribbean Literature*)
   "The landscape always acts as a prime mover to consciousness in Wilson Harris' novels, stirring man's imagination and helping him to define himself." (Hena Maes-Jelinek, from *Contemporary Novelists*)

Sources: *Complete Caribbeana; Contemporary Novelists*, 2nd ed., 1976; *Modern Black Writers; Resistance and Caribbean Literature; West Indian Literature; Writers Directory*, 1982-84.

HARRIS, WILLIAM M., SR. Urban Planner, Physicist, Educator.
Born in Richmond, Va., Oct. 29, 1941. *Education:* B.S., Howard U., 1964; Master of Urban Planning; Ph.D., U. of Wash., 1974. *Family:* Married Catherine Branch; children: Rolisa, Dana D., William M., Jr. *Career:* Res. Physicist, U.S. Atomic Energy Com., 1966-68; Experimental Physicist, Battelle Northwest, 1969-71; Visiting Student, Battelle Res. Center, 1971-73; Dir., Center for Urban Studies, W. Wash. State Coll., 1973-79; Coordinator, Black Studies Center, Asst. Prof., Urban Studies, Portland State U., 1974-76; Dean, Office of Afro-Amer. Affairs, Asst. Provost, Assoc. Prof. of City Planning, U. of Va., 1976-present. *Honors:* NDEA Fellow, U. of Wash., 1971-74; Regional Ed., *Western Journal of Black Studies. Mailing address:* Div. of Urban & Environmental Planning, Sch. of Architecture, U. of Va., Charlottesville, Va. 22903.

Writings:
Nonfiction

Black Community Development (San Francisco, R & E Res. Assoc., 1976)

Ethics of Social Intervention (Wash., D.C., Hemisphere, 1977)

Perspectives of Black Studies, joint reader with Darrell Millner (Wash., D.C., U. Press of America, 1977)

The Harder We Run: Black Workers since the Civil War (N.Y., Oxford U. Press, 1982)

Sidelights: " 'Freedom Frontier,' award-winning television documentary of Black experience in Oregon, Oregon Educational and Public Broadcasting service; produced by Pat Wheeler, narrated by William Harris, 60 minutes, 1976." (Author)

Sources: Author information; *Books in Print*, 1982-83.

HASKETT, EDYTHE RANCE. Teacher, Juvenile Writer.
Born in Suffolk, Va., Dec. 28, 1915. *Education:* St. Paul's High Sch., Lawrenceville, Va.; B.A., Shaw U., Raleigh, N.C.; M.A., N.Y.U.; Postgrad: Rutgers U., New Brunswick, N.J.; Columbia U. *Family:* Div.; son John O. Haskett. *Career:* Tchr., Norfolk, Va.; Tchr., Episcopal High Sch., Robertsport, Liberia, W. Africa. *Honors:* "Outstanding Citizen," Radio Station WRAP, Norfolk, 1962; "Distinguished Community Service," Alpha Kappa Alpha Sorority, 1967; Citation for "Building Bridges of Understanding," Com. for Improvement of Educ., 1968; Certificate of Hon., St. Paul's Coll., Lawrenceville, Va., 1972. *Mailing address:* 2741 Woodland Ave., Norfolk, Va. 23504.

Writings.
Fiction

Grains of Pepper; Folktales from Liberia, juv. (London, Abelard-Schuman, 1970)

Some Gold, a Little Ivory: Country Tales from Ghana and the Ivory Coast, juv. (N.Y., John Day, 1971)

Sidelights: Spent two years teaching in Liberia, where she collected the stories told in her two books. Three subsequent trips to Liberia, Ghana, Ivory Coast, Nigeria, Dahomey. Two trips to Europe. (Author)

Source: Author information.

HASKINS, JAMES. Juvenile Writer, Biographer.
Born in Ala., Sept. 19, 1941. *Education:* B.A., Georgetown U., 1960; Ala. State U., 1962; M.A., U. of N. Mex., 1963; further study: New Sch. for Soc. Res., N.Y.C.; Queens Coll., Flushing, N.Y. *Career:* Stock trader, Smith, Barney & Co., 1963-65; Tchr., N.Y.C. Bd. of Educ., 1966-68; Instr. in Urban Educ., New Sch. for Soc. Res., 1970- ; Instr. in Psychology of Black Lang., 1971; Assoc. Prof., Staten Island Community Coll., 1970-76; Mem., Bd. of Dir. Psi Systems. *Honors:* Coretta S. King Award for *The Story of Stevie Wonder*, 1977. *Mailing address:* 325 West End Ave., Apt. 70, N.Y., N.Y. 10023.

Writings:
  <u>Nonfiction</u> (Juvenile)
  Resistance: Profiles in Nonviolence (N.Y., Doubleday, 1970)

  The War and Protest: Vietnam (Doubleday, 1971)

  Revolutionaries: Agents of Change (Phila., Lippincott, 1971)

  A Piece of the Power: Four Black Mayors (N.Y., Dial, 1972)

  Profiles in Black Power (Doubleday, 1972)

  From Lew Alcindor to Kareem Abdul Jabbar (N.Y., Lothrop, 1972, 1978)

  Religions (Lippincott, 1973)

  Jobs in Business and Office (N.Y., Lothrop, 1974)

  Babe Ruth and Hank Aaron: The Home-run Kings (Lothrop, 1974)

  Witchcraft, Mysticism and Magic in the Black World (Doubleday, 1974)

  Snow Sculpture and Ice Carving (N.Y., Macmillan, 1974)

  Adam Clayton Powell; Portrait of a Marching Black (Dial, 1974)

  Creoles of Color of New Orleans (N.Y., Crowell, 1975)

  Fighting Shirley Chisholm (Dial, 1975)

  Doctor J: A Biography of Julius Erving (Doubleday, 1975)

  A Time to Win: The Story of the Kennedy Foundation's Special Olympics for the Mentally Retarded (Doubleday, 1976)

  New Kind of Joy: The Story of the Special Olympics (Doubleday, 1976)

  Aging in America: The Great Denial (N.Y., Hastings, 1976)

  The Story of Stevie Wonder (Lothrop, 1976; Dell, 1979)

  The Life and Death of Martin Luther King, Jr. (Lothrop, 1977)

  Barbara Jordan (Dial, 1977)

  The Cotton Club (N.Y., Random House, 1977)

  Bob McAdoo, Superstar (Lothrop, 1978)

  Who Are the Handicapped? (Doubleday, 1978)

  George McGinnis: Basketball Superstar (Hastings, 1978)

  Andrew Young: Man with a Mission (Lothrop, 1979)

  James Van Der Zee: The Picture-Takin' Man (N.Y., Dodd, 1979)

  The Quiet Revolution: The Struggle for the Rights of Disabled Americans (Crowell, 1979)

  Scott Joplin: The Man Who Made Ragtime (N.Y., Stein & Day, 1980; Mexico, Editores Asociados, 1980).

  I'm Gonna Make You Love Me; The Story of Diana Ross (Dial, 1980)

  The Magic Johnson Story (Short Hills, N.J., Enslow, 1980)

  New Americans: Vietnamese Boat People (Enslow, 1980)

  Werewolves (N.Y., Watts, 1981)

  The New Americans: Cuban Boat People (Enslow, 1982)

  Magic: A Biography of Earvin Johnson (Enslow, 1982)

  Katherine Dunham (N.Y., Coward, 1982)

Sugar Ray Leonard (Lothrop, 1982)

Nonfiction (Adult — "Jim Haskins")

Diary of a Harlem School Teacher (N.Y., Grove, 1969; Stein & Day, 1979)

The Psychology of Black Language, with Hugh Butts (N.Y., Barnes & Noble, 1973)

Black Manifesto for Education (N.Y., Morrow, 1973)

Pinckney Benton Steward Pinchback: A Biography (N.Y., Macmillan, 1973)

Street Gangs: Yesterday and Today (Hastings, 1974)

The Consumer Movement (Watts, 1975)

Children Have Rights, Too (N.Y., Hawthorn, 1975)

Your Rights, Past and Present (Hawthorn, 1975)

Pele: A Biography (Doubleday, 1976)

Teen-Age Alcoholism (Hawthorn, 1976)

The Long Struggle: The Story of American Labor (Phila., Westminster, 1976)

Real Estate Careers (Watts, 1978)

Voodoo and Hoodoo; Their Tradition and Craft As Revealed by Actual Practitioners (Stein & Day, 1978)

Gambling — Who Really Wins? (Watts, 1979)

The Child Abuse Help Book, with Patt Connolly (Reading, Mass., Addison-Wesley, 1982)

Black Theater in America (Crowell, 1982)

Donna Summer (Boston, Little, Brown, 1983)

Sources: *Books in Print*, 1979-80, 1981-82; *Contemporary Authors*, vols. 33-36, 1973; *Forthcoming Books*, Sept. 1975; *14th Annual Booklist*, 1979.

HAYDEN, ROBERT C. Science Teacher, Science News Writer.
Education: M.S., Boston U.; Harvard U. (grad. study). *Career:* Sci. Tchr.; Sci. News Writer; Sci. Ed.; Executive Dir., Metropolitan Council for Educational Opportunity (METCO), Boston, Mass. *Honors:* Julius Rosenwald Fund Fellow. *Mailing address:* c/o Addison-Wesley Pub. Co., Jacob Way, Reading, Mass. 01867.

Writings:
Nonfiction

Seven Black American Scientists (Reading, Mass., Addison-Wesley, 1970)

Eight Black American Inventors (Addison-Wesley, 1972)

Nine Black American Doctors (Addison-Wesley, 1976)

Sidelights: "In his research ... Mr. Hayden often had thrilling experiences. In 1967, he flew in an Air Force plane to experience the sensation of weightlessness for an article he was preparing on the subject of zero-gravity. The feature article he developed afterward won an award from the Educational Press Association of America." (*Seven Black American Scientists*)

Sources: *Books in Print*, 1978-79; *Seven Black American Scientists*.

HAYDEN, ROBERT E. Poet, English Professor.
Born in Detroit, Mich., Aug. 4, 1913. *Education:* B.A., Wayne State U.; M.A., U. of Mich. *Family:* Married; one d. *Career:* Tchr., Eng., U. of Mich., 1944-46; Prof., Eng., Fisk U., Nashville, 1946-69;

Writer-in-Residence & Prof. of Eng., U. of Mich., 1969- . Has ed. & pub. the Counterpoise Ser.; Ed., Ba-ha'i mag., *World Order. Honors:* Grand Prize for Poetry, 1st World Festival of Negro Arts, Dakar, Senegal, for *A Ballad of Remembrance*, 1965; Hopwood Award from U. of Mich., 1938, 1942; Rosenwald Fellow, 1947; Ford Found. grant for travel & writing in Mexico, 1954; *Words in the Mourning Time* nominated for Natl. Bk. Award, 1972; 1st Black to hold position of Consultant in Poetry to Lib. of Congress; Mem. of Acad. of Amer. Poets. Died Feb. 25, 1980.

Writings:
Fiction

Heart-Shape in the Dust, poems (Detroit, Falcon, 1940, 1973)

The Lion and the Archer, poems, with Myron O'Higgins (Nashville, Hemphill, 1948)

Figure of Time; Poems (Hemphill, 1955)

A Ballad of Remembrance, poems (London, Bremen, 1962)

Selected Poems (N.Y., October House, 1966)

Kaleidoscope; Poems by American Negro Poets, anthology ed. (N.Y., Harcourt, 1967)

Words in the Mourning Time, poems (October House, 1970)

Afro-American Literature, an Introduction, ed. with Others (Harcourt, 1971)

Night Blooming Cereus, poems (Bremen, 1972)

The United States in Literature, comp. with Others (Glenview, Ill., Scott, Foresman, 1973)

Angle of Ascent: New and Selected Poems (N.Y., Liveright, 1975)

American Journal, poems (Liveright, 1982)

Nonfiction

Mastering American English: A Handbook-Workbook of Essentials, with Others (Englewood Cliffs, N.J., Prentice-Hall, 1956)

Sidelights: "Very much in demand as lecturer, reader-of-his-own-works and visiting professor." (*Cavalcade*)

Sources: *Black Voices; Books in Print*, 1980-81; *Cavalcade; Dark Symphony; For Malcolm; Interviews with Black Writers; Jet* mag., Mar. 20, 1980; *Kaleidoscope: Poetry of Black America.*

HEAD, BESSIE. (South African). Novelist, Short Story Writer, Teacher.
Born in Pietermaritzburg, S. Africa, July 6, 1937. *Education:* Primary tchr. education. *Family:* Married Harold Head (separated); son Howard. *Career:* Has been in exile since the sixties in Botswanna, where she is now a citizen; Tchr., elementary sch., 6 yrs. *Mailing address:* P.O. Box 15, Serowe, Botswanna, Africa.

Writings:
Fiction

When Rain Clouds Gather, novel (N.Y., Simon & Schuster, 1968)

Maru, novel (N.Y., McCall, 1971; London, Heinemann, African Writers Ser., 1972)

A Question of Power, novel (N.Y., Pantheon, 1973; Heinemann, African Writers Ser., 1974)

The Collector of Treasures, and Other Botswanna Village Tales, short stories (London, Heinemann Educ., 1977)

Serowe: Village of the Rain-Wind, short stories (Heinemann, African Writers Ser., 1981)

Sidelights: Bessie Head comments: "I call myself The New African. It is an extremely painful title full of sudden and disastrous changes of fortune and a sort of mental tight-rope walk with an abyss underneath...."

"These themes are the basis of my preoccupations, the equality of man, the equality of God and the devil in Africa." (*Contemporary Novelists*)

Sources: *Books in Print*, 1981-82; *Contemporary Authors*, vols. 29-32, 1978; *Contemporary Novelists*, 1972.

HEARD, NATHAN CLIFF. Novelist, Teacher.
Born in Newark, N.J., Nov. 7, 1936. *Education:* Elementary sch. *Family:* Son Melvin, son Cliff, d. Natalie. *Career:* Laborer; factory worker; musician; Lect., Fresno State Coll.; Asst. Prof., Eng., Livingston Coll., Rutgers U. *Honors:* Author Award, N.J. Assn. of Tchrs. of Eng.; award, Newark Coll. of Engineering. *Mailing address:* c/o Macmillan Pub. Co., 866 Third Ave., N.Y., N.Y. 10022.

Writings:
Fiction
Howard Street, novel (N.Y., Dial, 1968; N.Y., NAL, 1973)

To Reach a Dream, novel (Dial, 1971; NAL, 1973)

A Cold Fire Burning, novel (N.Y., Simon & Schuster, 1974)

When Shadows Fall, novel (Chicago, Playboy, 1976)

The House of Slammers, a Novel (N.Y., Macmillan, 2nd ed., 1982)

Sidelights: "The *Chicago Sun-Times Book Week* called [*Howard Street*] 'The stunningly rich story of the very bottom of the black ghetto, of the men whose idea of success is persuading their sweethearts to turn prostitute, of the women who give in because they need a strong pimp.... *Howard Street* tells everything ... tells it like it is'; and *To Reach a Dream*, hailed by the *New York Times* as a 'raw, brutal portrayal of street life in a Newark ghetto. The setting is vividly drawn, the bars, after hours joints and predawn haunts of living predators ... overwhelming.' "
"Nathan Heard's checkered past includes 12 years in Trenton Prison for armed robbery and several movie roles, including one in ... *Gordon's War*" (*A Cold Fire Burning*)

Sources: Author information; *Books in Print*, 1978-79; *A Cold Fire Burning*.

HEARNE, JOHN [John Morris]. (Jamaican). Novelist, Public Official, Teacher.
Born in Montreal, Can. (of Jamaican parents), Feb. 4, 1926. *Education:* Jamaica Coll.; M.A., Edinburgh U., 1949; Teacher's Diploma, London U., 1950. *Family:* Married Joyce Veitch, 1947; Leeta Hopkinson, 1955; two children. *Career:* Air Gunner, Royal Air Force, 1943-46; Tchr., London & Jamaica, 1950-59, 1962; Information Officer, Govt. of Jamaica; Resident Tutor, Dept. of Extra Mural Studies, U. W. Indies, 1962-67; Head, Creative Arts Center, U. W. Indies, Mona, since 1968; Asst. to Prime Minister of Jamaica. *Honors:* Visiting Fellow in Commonwealth Lit., U. of Leeds, 1967; O'Connor Prof. in Lit., Colgate U., Hamilton, N.Y., 1969-70; Rhys Memorial Prize, 1956; Inst. of Jamaica Silver Musgrave Medal, 1964. *Mailing address:* c/o Creative Arts Centre, U. of W. Indies, Kingston 7, Jamaica.

Writings:
Fiction
Voices under the Window, novel (London, Faber, 1955, 1973)

A Stranger at the Gate, novel (Faber, 1956)

The Faces of Love, novel (Faber, 1957, entitled *The Eye of the Storm*; Boston, Little, Brown, 1958)

Autumn Equinox, novel (Faber, 1959; N.Y., Vanguard, 1961)

The Land of the Living, novel (Faber, 1961; N.Y., Harper, 1962)

(As John Morris, Pseudonym):

Fever Grass, novel, with Morris Cargill (London, William Collins, 1969; Huntington, N.Y., Fontana Bks., 1970)

The Candywine Development, novel, with Morris Cargill (William Collins, 1970; Fontana Bks., 1971)

Sidelights: John Hearne has had two plays produced on television in England: *Freedom Man*, produced in Jamaica, and *The Golden Savage*, produced in London, 1968.

Sources: *Contemporary Novelists*, 2nd ed., 1976; *Jamaican National Bibliography*; *Resistance and Caribbean Literature*; *West Indian Literature*; *Writers Directory*, 1982-84.

HEDGEMAN, ANNA ARNOLD. Social Worker, Federal Official, Civil Rights Leader.
Born in Marshalltown, Iowa. *Education:* B.A., L.H.D. (hon.), 1948, Hamline U., St. Paul, Minn.; further study: N.Y. Sch. of Soc. Work; U. of Minn. *Family:* Married Merritt A. Hedgeman (concert artist & Dir., consulting serv.), 1933. *Career:* Consultant on Urban Affairs & African Amer. Studies; Tchr., Rust Coll., Holly Springs, Miss., 1922-24; Executive Secy., YWCA: Springfield, Ohio, Jersey City, N.J., N.Y.C., 1924-34, Brooklyn, 1938-41; Executive Dir., Natl. Council for a Permanent Fair Employment Practices Commission, 1943-45; Asst., Oscar R. Ewing, Administrator, Fed. Security Agency, 1949-53; Asst., Mayor Wagner, N.Y.C., 1954-58; Ed. & Columnist, *New York Age*, 1958-61; Consultant, Div. of Higher Educ., United Church Bd. for Homeland Ministries, 1961- ; served variously as Assoc. Dir., Dept. of Soc. Justice, & Dir., Ecumenical Action, Natl. Council of Churches, 1963-68; a major architect of 1963 March on Washington; keynote speaker, 1st Conf. of Women of Africa & African descent, Accra, Ghana, 1960; N.Y.C. official rep. 10th Anniversary Observation, UN, San Francisco, 1955. *Honors:* United Church Women's Award for Christian Citizenship; Natl. Human Relations Award—State Fair Bd. of Tex.; Guardians Assn. of the Police Dept., N.Y.C.; Leadership for Freedom Award, Women's Scholarship Assn., Roosevelt U., Chicago, 1965; LL.D. (hon.), Upsala Coll., E. Orange, N.J., 1970; Urban League's Frederick Douglass Award for "Distinguished Leadership toward Equal Opportunity," 1974; Spec. Achievement Award, Natl. Conf. of Christians & Jews. *Mailing address:* 10 W. 135th St., Suite 15P, N.Y., N.Y. 10037.

Writings:
Nonfiction

The Trumpet Sounds; A Memoir of Negro Leadership, autobiog. (N.Y., Holt, 1964)

The Gift of Chaos: Decades of American Discontent (N.Y., Oxford U. Press, 1977)

Sources: Author information; *Kirkus Reviews*, Mar. 1, 1977; *Negro Almanac*; *Negro Handbook*.

HENDERSON, DAVID. Poet, Teacher.
Born in Harlem, N.Y., in 1942. *Education:* Bronx Community Coll.; Hunter Coll.; New Sch. for Soc. Res.; E.-W. Inst., Cambridge, Mass. *Career:* Tchr., Columbia U.; Tchr., City Coll., N.Y.; with Free Theatre, New Orleans; active in org. of *Umbra* mag. & *East Village Other*; Poet-in-Residence, City Coll. of N.Y., 1969-70; Tchr., Berkeley, Cal., & Ed. *Umbra/Black Works*. As mem. of "Umbra Poets" group, participated in more than 100 poetry readings: Vassar, Princeton, Carnegie Hall, San Francisco State Coll. Poetry has been transl. into French, Italian, Spanish, & Chinese. *Mailing address:* c/o Bantam Bks., 666 Fifth Ave., N.Y., N.Y. 10019.

Writings:
Fiction

Felix of the Silent Forest (N.Y., Poets Press, 1967)

De-Mayor of Harlem (N.Y., Dutton, 1971)

Nonfiction

Jimi Hendrix: Voodoo Child of the Aquarian Age (N.Y., Doubleday, 1978)

Scuse Me While I Kiss the Sky: Life of Jim Hendrix (N.Y., Bantam, 1981)

Sources: *Black Fire*; *Books in Print*, 1981-82; *For Malcolm*; *Jimi Hendrix*; *Poetry of Black America*.

HENDERSON, STEPHEN E. English Professor, Critic.
Born in Key West, Fla., Oct. 13, 1925. *Education:* A.B., Morehouse Coll., 1949; M.A., 1950, Ph.D., 1959, U. of Wis. *Family:* Married Jeanne Holman, June 14, 1958; children: Stephen E., Jr., Timothy A., Philip L., Alvin Malcolm. *Career:* Tchr., Va. Union U., Richmond, 1950-62; Prof., Eng., & Chairman of Dept., Morehouse, 1962-71; Prof., Afro-Amer. Studies, & Dir., Inst. for the Arts & Humanities, Howard U., 1971 to present. *Honors:* Phi Beta Kappa; Danforth res. grant; Amer. Council of Learned Societies, Gen. Educ. grant. *Mailing address:* c/o Dir., Inst. for Arts & Humanities, Howard U., 2400 Sixth St., N.W., Wash., D.C. 20001.

Writings:
Nonfiction

The Militant Black Writer in Africa and the United States, with Mercer Cook (Madison, U. of Wis. Press, 1969)

Understanding the New Black Poetry; Black Speech and Black Music As Poetic References (N.Y., Morrow, 1973; paper also)

Sidelights: Gwendolyn Brooks gives Professor Henderson credit for spawning much of the contemporary black-consciousness literature. (*Drumvoices*)

Sources: *Conference Notes (Recent Developments in Black Literature and Criticism)*, Apr. 1983; *Contemporary Authors*, vols. 29-32, 1978; *Drumvoices*.

HENRIES, A. DORIS BANKS. (Liberian). Educator, Biographer.
Born in Live Oak, Fla., c. 1913. *Family:* Married Richard A. Henries (Speaker, Liberian House of Rep.). *Career:* Asst. Minister of Educ., Liberia. Died Feb. 16, 1981, in Middleton, Conn.

Writings:
Fiction

Poems of Liberia, 1836-1961 (London, Macmillan, 1963)

Liberian Folklore; A Compilation of Ninety-Nine Folktales (Macmillan, 1966)

Nonfiction

Liberia, the West African Republic, with Richard A. Henries (N.Y., F. R. Bruns, 1950)

Heroes and Heroines of Liberia (Macmillan, 1962)

More about Heroes and Heroines of Liberia, Book II (Monrovia, Liberian Information Serv., 1962)

The Life of Joseph Jenkins Roberts, 1809-1876, and His Inaugural Address (Macmillan, 1964)

The Liberian Nation: A Short History (N.Y., Collier-Macmillan, 1966)

A Biography of President William V. S. Tubman (Macmillan, 1967)

Africa: Our History (Collier-Macmillan, 1969)

Liberia's Fulfillment: Achievements of the Republic of Liberia during Twenty-Five Years under the Administration of President William V. S. Tubman, 1944-1969, comp. & ed. (Monrovia, Banks, 1969)

Curriculum Development in Liberia (Monrovia, Ministry of Educ., 1974)

Development of Textbooks and Instructional Materials in Liberia, 1964-1974 (Ministry of Educ., 1974)

The Educational System of Liberia (Ministry of Educ., 1974)

Higher Education in Liberia: Retrospect-Present-Prospect (Ministry of Educ., 1974)

Sidelights: One of the most active Liberian writers. Lived in Liberia for 41 years. Left when her husband was executed following overthrow of government of William R. Talbot, Jr., by the revolutionary forces of Samuel K. Doe. (*Contemporary Authors*)

Sources: *African Authors*; *Contemporary Authors*, vol. 103, 1983; *Sturdy Black Bridges*.

HERCULES, FRANK. Novelist, Essayist.
Born in Port-of-Spain, Trinidad, Brit. W. Indies, Feb. 12, 1917. *Education:* U. Tutorial Coll., London, 1934-35; Hon. Soc. of the Middle Temple, Inns of Court, London (for the Eng. Bar), 1934-35. (Came to U.S.) *Family:* Married Dellora C. Howard (an Amer.; became an Amer. citizen); son Eric. *Career:* Lect.; Tchr.; Essayist. *Honors:* Fletcher Pratt Memorial Fellowship in Prose, Bread Loaf Writers Conf., Middlebury Coll., Vt.; Rockefeller Fellowship of the Aspen Inst. for Humanistic Studies, Aspen, Colo. *Mailing address:* Rivercross, 531 Main St., Roosevelt Island, N.Y., N.Y. 10044.

Writings:
Fiction
Where the Hummingbird Flies, novel (N.Y., Harcourt, 1961)

I Want a Black Doll, novel (N.Y., Simon & Schuster, 1967)

On Leaving Paradise, novel (Harcourt, 1980)

Nonfiction
American Society and Black Revolution (Harcourt, 1972)

Sidelights: His article "To Live in Harlem," published by *National Geographic Magazine*, was read into the Congressional Record by Senator Javits of New York.... This article also appeared in *Reader's Digest*. (Author)

Sources: Author information; Pub. information.

HERNTON, CALVIN C. Social Worker, Teacher.
Born in Chattanooga, Tenn., Apr. 28, 1932. *Education:* B.A., Talladega Coll., Ala., 1954; M.A. (Sociol.), Fisk U., 1956; Columbia U., 1961. *Family:* Married; son Anton. *Career:* Soc. Worker, Leake & Watts Home for Children, Yonkers, N.Y., summer 1954; Youth House for Boys, Welfare Island, N.Y., 1956-57; Soc. Investigator, N.Y., Dept. of Welfare, 1961-62; Instr., Sociol. & Hist., S. U., Baton Rouge, La.; Edward Waters Coll., Jacksonville, Fla.; Ala. A&M Coll., Normal, Ala., 1957-61; Tech. Typist, Chemical Bank, N.Y. Trust Co.; Coding & Res. Technician, Richard Manville Market Res., N.Y.; Writer-in-Residence, Central State U., Wilberforce, Ohio, 1970; Assoc. Prof., Afro-Amer. Studies, Oberlin Coll.; Lect.: W. Indian Writers' Conf. of Kent, Eng., 1967; Columbia U., 1964; Clarte Soc., Stockholm, 1967; New Sch. for Soc. Res., 1964; & Others; Co-founder, *Umbra* mag. *Honors:* Fellow, Inst. of Phenomenological Studies, London, 1965, 1968-69. *Mailing address:* c/o Humanities Press, Inc., Atlantic Highlands, N.J. 07716.

Writings:
Fiction
The Coming of Chronos to the House of Nightsong; An Epical Narrative of the South, poems (N.Y., Interim Bks., 1964)

Scarecrow, poems (Garden City, N.Y., Doubleday, 1974)

Nonfiction
Sex and Racism in America (N.Y., Doubleday, 1965)

White Papers for White Americans (Doubleday, 1966)

Coming Together; Black Power, White Hate and Sexual Hang-ups, ed. (N.Y., Random House, 1971)

The Cannabis Experience: An Interpretive Study of the Effects of Marijuana and Hashish, with Joseph Berke (London, P. Owen, 1974)

Sources: *Amistad* 1; *Black Fire*; *New Black Poetry*; *Poetry of Black America*.

HICKS, H. BEECHER, JR. Minister, Counselor.
Education: B.A., U. of Ark., 1964; M. Divinity, 1967, D. Ministry, 1975, Colgate Rochester Divinity Sch.; (further study): U. of Nigeria, Lagos; U. of Ife, Nigeria; Inst. of Church & Soc., Ibadan, Nigeria; U. of Ghana, Legon; Inst. of Sci. & Technology, Kumasi, Ghana. *Career:* Counselor, Urban League, Rochester, N.Y., 1967-68; Coordinator, Rochester Training Seminars, Natl. Urban League, N.Y.C., 1967-68; Minister, Mt. Ararat Bap. Church, 1968-73; Marriage & Family Counselor, Planned Parenthood Center, Pittsburgh, Pa., 1971-72; Minister, Antioch Missionary Bap. Church, Houston, Tex., 1973-77; Minister, Metropolitan Bap. Church, Wash., D.C. (present). *Honors:* Outstanding Personalities of the South Award, 1977; Community Leaders & Noteworthy Americans Award, 1977 (both Amer. Biographical Inst.); Rockefeller Protestant Fellow, 1964-65; M. L. King Fellow in Black Church Studies, 1972-75. *Mailing address:* Metropolitan Bap. Church, 1225 R St., N.W., Wash., D.C. 20009.

Writings:
Nonfiction

Give Me This Mountain, compiled sermons (limited ed., Houston, Tex., Antioch Missionary Bap. Church, 1976)

Images of the Black Preacher: The Man Nobody Knows (Valley Forge, Pa., Judson Press, 1977)

Source: Author information.

HIGGINBOTHAM, A. LEON, JR. Circuit Judge (U.S. Court of Appeals), Federal Trade Commissioner, Law School Professor.
Born Feb. 25, 1929. *Education:* B.A., Antioch Coll., 1949; LL.B., Yale Law Sch., 1952. *Family:* Married Jeanne Foster; children: Stephen, Karen, Kenneth. *Career:* Asst. Dist. Attorney, Phila., 1953-54; Spec. Deputy Attorney, 1956-62; Spec. Hearing Officer, U.S. Dept. of Justice, 1961-62; Partner, Norris, Green, Harris & Higginbotham, 1954-62; Commissioner, Fed. Trade Com., 1962-63; Judge, U.S. Dist. Court, 1964- ; Lect., Adjunct Visiting Prof., U. Pa. Grad. Sch., 1970- ; U. of Hawaii, 1973-74; Circuit Judge, U.S. Court of Appeals, 3rd Circuit, 19-?. *Honors:* Trustee: Yale U.; Thomas Jefferson U.; U. of Pa., Citizen Regent; Smithsonian Institution, one of ten Outstanding Men in Amer.; Outstanding Young Man in Govt., 1964; Outstanding Young Man of the Year, Phila. Jr. Chamber of Commerce, 1964; Natl. Arthur S. Fleming Award, 1964; Natl. Human Relations Award, Natl. Conf. of Christians & Jews, 1968; William C. Menninger Mem. Medallion, 1969; Samuel S. Fels Award, Sch. Dist., Phila., 1969; Russwurm Award, Natl. Newspaper Pub. Assn., 1969; Annual Brotherhood Award, Congressman Rodeph Sholam, 1970; Outstanding Layman of the Yr. Award, YMCA, 1970; Citation of Merit Award, Yale Law Sch., 1975; Martin L. King Award for Outstanding Serv. in Civil Rights, Educator's Roundtable, Phila. *Mailing address:* c/o Oxford U. Press, 200 Madison Ave., N.Y., N.Y. 10016.

Writings:
Nonfiction

In the Matter of Color: Race and the American Legal Process: The Colonial Period, vol. I (N.Y., Oxford U. Press, 1978; paper ed., 1980)

In the Matter of Color: Race and the American Legal Process: 1776-1865, vol. II (Oxford U. Press, 1980)

Sources: *Books in Print*, 1981-82; *Freedomways*, vol. 18, 1978; *Publishers Weekly*, Nov. 12, 1979; *Who's Who among Black Americans*, 2nd ed., 1977-78.

HIGGINS, CHESTER ARCHER, JR. Photographer, Artist.
Born in Lexington, Ky., Nov. 6, 1946. *Education:* B.S., Tuskegee Inst., 1970. *Family:* Married Renelda Meeks (painter), Apr. 22, 1971; children: Nataki Olamina, Chester Damani III. *Career:* Instr., Fine Arts, N.Y.U., 1975-77; Staff Photographer, *N.Y. Times*, 1975- . *Honors:* Ford Found. Fellow, 1972-74; NEA, Fellow, 1973; Rockefeller Found. Fellow, 1974; *Graphis & Print* mag. awards, 1974 & 1975. *Mailing address:* c/o Doubleday & Co., 501 Franklyn Ave., Garden City, N.Y. 11530.

Writings:
Nonfiction

Student Unrest at Tuskegee Institute (Tuskegee, Ala., Behavioral Sci. Res. Inst., Tuskegee [Ala.] Inst., 1968)

Black Woman, photo-essay with Harold McDougall (N.Y., McCalls, 1970)

Drums of Life, photo-essay with Orde Coombs (Garden City, N.Y., Anchor, 1974)

My Name Is Black, photo-essay with Amanda Ambrose (N.Y., Scholastic Bk. Serv., 1974)

The Day We Won, photo-essay with Kathryn Parker (Doubleday, 1977)

Some Time Ago: A Historical Portrait of Black Americans, photo-essay with Orde Coombs (Doubleday, 1978, 1980)

Sources: *Books in Print*, 1981-82, 1982-83; Pub. Information.

HILL, LESLIE PINCKNEY. College President, Poet.
Born in Lynchburg, Va., May 14, 1880. *Education:* B.A., 1903, M.A., 1904, Harvard U.; Hon. degrees: Lincoln U., Morgan State Coll., Haverford Coll., & R.I. Coll. of Educ. *Career:* Tchr., Eng. Educ., Tuskegee Inst.; Prin., Manassas (Va.) Industrial Sch.; Pres., Cheyney State Tchrs. Coll. (Pa.); Founder & Pres., Bd. of W. Chester Community Center; Founder & Past Pres., Pa. State Negro Council. Died Feb. 16, 1960, in Phila., Pa.

Writings:
Fiction

The Wings of Oppression, poems (Boston, Stratford, 1921)

Toussaint L'Ouverture—A Dramatic History, blank-verse drama in five acts (Boston, Christopher, 1928; Ann Arbor, Mich., U. Microfilms, 1970)

Sources: *Amsterdam News*, Jan. 15, 1928; *Book of American Negro Poetry*; *Negro Caravan*; *Negro Poets and Their Poems*; *New York Times*, Feb. 16, 1960.

HIMES, CHESTER BOMAR. Detective Story Writer.
Born in Jefferson City, Mo., July 29, 1909. *Education:* Ohio State U., 1926-29. *Family:* Married Jean Lucinda Johnson; married 2nd Lesley Himes. *Career:* Bellhop, Cleveland, Ohio; sentenced at 19 to 20 yrs. for armed robbery, served 7 yrs. in Ohio State Penitentiary, where he began to write & contribute stories to mags.; released 1935; employed in various capacities as writer, WPA; worked on Louis Bromfield's farm, Malabar; shipyard & aircraft employee, World War II, L.A. & San Francisco; traveled abroad, 1953. *Honors:* Grand Prix Policier for mystery writing, 1958; Julius Rosenwald Fund Fellow, Creative Writing, 1944-45. Died Nov. 12, 1984, in Morara, Spain.

Writings:
Fiction

If He Hollers Let Him Go, novel (Garden City, N.Y., Doubleday; N.Y., New Amer. Lib., 1945; reprint, Chatham, N.J., Chatham Bookseller, 1975)

Lonely Crusade U.S.A., novel (N.Y., Knopf, 1947, 1954; reprint, Chatham, 1973)

Cast the First Stone, a Novel (N.Y., Coward-McCann, 1952; NAL, 1953, 1973; reprint, Chatham, 1973)

The Third Generation, novel (Cleveland, World, 1954; reprint, Chatham, 1973)

The Primitive, novel (NAL, 1955)

For Love of Imabelle, novel (N.Y., Fawcett, 1957, 1965; Chatham, 1973; NAL, Chester Himes Ser., 1974)

Real Cool Killers, novel (N.Y., Berkeley, 1959; N.Y., Avon, 1959; reprint, Chatham, 1973; NAL, 1975)

Crazy Kill, novel (Berkeley, 1959; Avon, 1959; reprint, Chatham, 1973; NAL, 1975)

All Shot Up, novel (Berkeley, 1960; reprint, Chatham, 1973; NAL, 1975)

The Big Gold Dream, novel (Berkeley, 1960; reprint, Chatham, 1973; NAL, 1975)

Pinktoes, novel (N.Y., Paris, Olympia, 1961; N.Y., Putnam, 1965; N.Y., Dell, 1965; reprint, Chatham, 1975)

Cotton Comes to Harlem, novel, since made into a film (Putnam, 1965; Dell, 1968; Chatham, 1975)

The Heat's On, novel (Putnam, 1965, 1968; Chatham, 1975)

Run Man Run, novel (Putnam, 1966, 1968; reprint, Chatham, 1975)

Blind Man with a Pistol, novel (N.Y., Morrow, 1969)

Black on Black; Baby Sister and Selected Writings (Doubleday, 1973)

Nonfiction
Quality of Hurt; The Autobiography of Chester Himes, vol. I (Doubleday, 1972)

My Life of Absurdity: The Autobiography of Chester Himes, vol. II (Doubleday, 1976)

Sidelights: John M. Reilly summarizes, "Recently critics have begun to acknowledge the presence in Afro-American writing of an intuitive existentialism. Chester Himes' work might well serve as an illustration." (*Contemporary Novelists*)

Sources: *Afro-American Writers*; *Blackamerican Literature*; *Books in Print*, Supplement, 1975-76; *Cavalcade*; *Contemporary Novelists*, 1972; *Facts on File*, 1984; *Soon, One Morning*; *Who's Who in America*, 37th ed., 1972-73.

HINTON, WILLIAM AUGUSTUS. Physician, Serologist, Bacteriologist.
Born in Chicago, Ill., Dec. 15, 1883. *Education:* B.A., 1905, M.D. (honors), 1912, Harvard U. *Career:* Dir., Lab. Dept., Boston Dispensary, 1915; Chief, Wasserman Lab., Mass. Dept. of Public Health; Harvard U.: Instr., Preventive Medicine & Hygiene; Instr., Bacteriology & Immunology, 1921-46; Clinical Prof., 1946-50; Prof. Emeritus, 1950-59; Spec. Consultant, U.S. Public Health Serv., Mass. Sch. for Crippled Children; Lect., Simmons Coll., Boston. *Honors:* 1st Black granted a professorship at Harvard (1949). Died Aug. 8, 1959.

Writings:
Nonfiction
Syphilis and Its Treatment, universally used professional ref. (N.Y., Macmillan, 1936)

The Hinton and Davies-Hinton Tests for Syphilis, with John A. V. Davies (n.p., 1938?)

Sidelights: "William A. Hinton [was a] bacteriologist in the area of diseases of the blood.... As a serologist he originated the Hinton test, an authoritative test for syphilis, and the serum used to fight the disease." (*Historical Negro Biographies*)
"Long one of the world's authorities on venereal disease ... he collaborated with Dr. J. A. V. Davies in what is now called the 'Davies-Hinton test' for the detection of syphilis." (*Negro Almanac*)

Sources: *Historical Negro Biographies*; *Negro Almanac*.

HODGE, MERLE. (Trinidadian). Novelist, Translator, Teacher.
Born in Trinidad in 1944. *Education:* B.A. (French), U. Coll., London, 1965, M. Philosophy, 1967. *Career:* Governess; Typist, Transl., Leon Damas' poetry (unpub.); Lect., French, U. of W. Indies. *Honors:* Trinidad & Tobago Girls' Island Scholarship, 1962. *Mailing address:* c/o G. K. Hall & Co., 70 Lincoln St., Boston, Mass. 02111.

Writings:
Fiction
Crick Crack Monkey, novel (London, Deutsch, 1970)

Sources: *Caribbean Writers*; *Complete Caribbeana, 1900-1975*; *West Indian Literature*.

HOLLAND, JEROME HEARTWELL. College President, U.S. Ambassador to Sweden, Corporation Board Member.
Born in 1916. *Education:* B.A., Cornell U.; Ph.D., U. of Pa. *Career:* Pres., Del. State Coll.; Pres., Hampton Inst., Va.; Ambassador to Sweden; Corp. directorships: Amer. Telephone & Telegraph, Chrysler Corp., Continental Corp., Federated Dept. Stores, Gen. Cigars, Gen. Foods, Manufacturers Hanover Trust, N.Y. Stock Exchange, Union Carbide; Chairman: Planned Parenthood; World Population Council. *Honors:* Received many hon. degrees & numerous awards from religious, civic, & fraternal orgs. Died Jan. 16, 1985.

Writings:
Nonfiction
Black Opportunity (N.Y., Weybright & Talley, 1969)

Sidelights: At Cornell "was All-American football player — the famous 'Brud' Holland of the sports pages and the campus." (*Black Opportunity*)

Sources: *Black Enterprise*, Sept. 1973; *Black Opportunity*; *In Black and White*; *Los Angeles Times*, Jan. 17, 1985.

HOLMES, OAKLEY N., JR. Art Professor, Art Historian.
Born in Richmond, Va., in 1941. *Education:* B.S., Va. State U., 1965; Master of Education, Va. Commonwealth U., 1969; Doctor of Education, Tchrs. Coll., Columbia U., 1973. *Family:* Married Gloria Tancil; d. Sekila Mali. *Career:* Art Tchr., public schs., Richmond, 1965-67; Art Spec., Title III Government Program, Powhatan, Va., 1969; Asst. Prof., Art Educ., Va. State Coll., 1969-70; Art Tchr., Hatch-Billops Collection, Spring Valley, N.Y., 1972-78; Assoc. Prof. of Art, Jacksonville State U., Ala., 1978- . *Honors:* Arts Award, Westchester African-Amer. Inst., 1979. *Mailing address:* 305 Adelaide Dr., Jacksonville, Ala. 36265.

Writings:
Nonfiction
The Complete Annotated Resource Guide to Black American Art (Spring Valley, N.Y., Black Artists in Amer., 1978)

Missing Pages: Black Images — World Art (Jacksonville, Ala., Author, 1982)

Sidelights: Holmes includes in *The Complete Annotated Resource Guide* ... books, dissertations, exhibitions, catalogs, art show brochures and periodicals. There are also photos in books and audiovisual resources. (*Freedomways*)
He also has the following: "Black Artists: 12,000 B.C. to Present," lecture, slide, and tape; "Motion Pictures," Parts 1-4 (Black Artists in America), 1970-75.

Sources: Author information; *Books in Print*, 1980-81; *Freedomways*, vol. 20, 1980.

HOPKINS, PAULINE ELIZABETH. Stenographer, Playwright.
Born in Portland, Maine, in 1859. *Education:* Grad. Girls High Sch., Boston. *Career:* Stenographer; on staff of *Colored American Magazine* (Boston), 1900-04, Literary Ed., 1903-04; one of founders, Colored Amer. League. Died (in a fire), Aug. 13, 1930.

Writings:
Fiction

Slaves' Escape: Or the Underground Railroad (1879; revised as *Peculiar Sam, or the Underground Railroad*, musical drama)

Contending Forces, a Romance Illustrative of Negro Life North and South (Boston, Colored Co-operative, 1900; N.Y., AMS Press, 1971; N.Y., Popular Lib., 1980; Carbondale, S. Ill. U. Press, Black Heritage Lib. Collection Ser., ed. by Matthew J. Bruccoli, Lost Amer. Fiction reprint, 1978)

Nonfiction

Pauline E. Hopkins Papers (Nashville, Fisk U. Lib., n.d.)

A Primer of Facts Pertaining to the Early Greatness of the African Race and the Possibility of Restoration by Its Descendents (Cambridge, Mass., P. E. Hopkins, 1905)

Sidelights: With her father and mother, "toured with Hopkins' Colored Troubadors, presenting plays, recitals, and concerts in the early 1880's." Contributed both fiction and nonfiction to periodicals, wrote plays some of which were: *One Scene from the Drama of Early Days, Of One Blood, or the Hidden Self,* and *Winona: A Tale of Negro-Life in the South and Southwest* (all serialized in *Colored Magazine*). *Colored American Magazine* was devoted to Afro-American art and literature. This "most important Black Magazine of the time" ceased publication in 1909. (*Contending Forces*)

Sources: *Books in Print,* 1981-82; *Contending Forces; Freedomways,* vol. 19, 1979; *Negro Author; Negro Novel in America; Negro Voices in American Fiction.*

HORNE, FRANK S. Ophthalmologist, College President, Agency Administrator.
Born in N.Y.C. in 1899. *Education:* City Coll. of N.Y.; Columbia U.; U. of S. Cal.; N. Ill. Coll. of Ophthalmology (grad.). *Career:* Ophthalmologist; Pres., Fort Valley State Coll., Ga.; Dir. of Negro Affairs, Natl. Youth Admin.; Office of Race Relations, U.S. Housing Authority, Housing & Home Finance Agency; Dir., N.Y.C. Com. on Intergroup Relations; N.Y.C. Housing Redevelopment Bd. *Honors:* Won *Crisis* mag. award for *Letters Found Near a Suicide,* 1925. Died in N.Y.C., Sept. 7, 1974.

Writings:
Fiction

Letters Found Near a Suicide, poems, one of a ser. (*Crisis,* 1925?)

Haverstraw, poems, one of a ser. (London, Bremen, 1963)

Sources: *Black World,* Nov. 1974; *Poetry of Black America.*

HORNSBY, ALTON, JR. History Professor, Historian.
Born in Atlanta, Ga., Sept. 3, 1940. *Education:* B.A., Morehouse Coll., 1961; M.A., 1962, Ph.D., 1969, U. of Tex., Austin. *Family:* Married Anne R. Lockhart, June 5, 1965; children: Alton III, Angela. *Career:* Instr., Hist., Tuskegee Inst., 1962-65; Asst. Prof., Morehouse, 1968-71, Assoc. Prof., 1971-74, Prof., Hist., 1974, Chairman, Dept., 1971- ; Ed., *Journal of Negro History,* 1976- ; Chairman, State Com. on Life & Hist. of Black Georgians. *Honors:* Woodrow Wilson Found. Fellow, 1961-62; Phi Alpha Theta (Intnl. Honor Soc. in Hist.) *Mailing address:* Dept. of Hist., Morehouse Coll., 223 Chestnut St., S.W., Atlanta, Ga. 30314.

Writings:

Nonfiction

In the Cage: Eyewitness Accounts of the Freed Negro in Southern Society, 1877-1929 (Chicago, Quadrangle, 1971)

The Black Almanac, 4 eds. (Woodbury, N.Y., Barron's, 1972-77)

Sources: Author information; *Contemporary Authors*, vols. 37-40, 1979.

HORTON, GEORGE MOSES. Poet.
Born in Northampton County, N.C., in 1797. Horton had an alert mind, and was almost entirely self-taught. He married a slave belonging to Franklin Snipes; became father of two children. *Career:* Janitor, U. of N.C., Chapel Hill; Poet to students. Died in 1883.

Writings:

Fiction

The Hope of Liberty, poems (Raleigh, N.C., J. Gales, 1829; reprinted as *Poems by a Slave*, Phila., 1837)

The Poetical Works of George M. Horton, the Colored Bard of North Carolina (N.Y., Knapp, 1838, 1854)

Poetical Works (Hillsborough, N.C., Heartt, 1845; at Harvard U., 1865)

Naked Genius, poems (Raleigh, N.C., n.p., 1865; at Athenaeum in Boston, 1865)

Sidelights: Permitted to go to Chapel Hill and hire himself out. In 1829 a booklet, *The Hope of Liberty*, was published. However, Horton's hope of obtaining his freedom from the sale of this did not materialize. He settled down at the University of North Carolina at Chapel Hill for the next 30 years, working as a janitor and executing little commissions in verse from the students. (*Early Negro American Writers*)

Sources: *Cavalcade*; *Early Black American Poets*; *Early Negro American Writers*; *Negro Caravan*.

HOWARD, JOHN ROBERT. Sociology Professor.
Born in Boston, Mass., Jan. 24, 1933. *Education:* B.A., Brandeis U., 1955; M.A., N.Y.U., 1961; Ph.D., Stanford U., 1965. *Family:* Married Mary Doris Adams (a prof.), June 22, 1968. *Career:* Asst. Prof., Sociol., U. of Ore., Eugene, 1964-68; Asst. Prof., Sociol., City Coll. of CUNY, 1968-69; Asst. Prof., Sociol., Rutgers U., Div. of Soc. Sci., Black Studies, Livingston Coll., 1969-70; Prof. of Sociol. & Dean of Div. of Soc. Sci., SUNY, Purchase, 1971- . *Honors:* Woodrow Wilson Found. Fellow, 1955-56. *Mailing address:* c/o Amer. Acad. of Polit. & Soc. Sci., 3937 Chestnut St., Phila., Pa. 19104.

Writings:

Nonfiction

Life Styles in the Black Ghetto, with Others (N.Y., Norton, 1969)

Where It's At: Radical Perspectives in Sociology, ed. with Steven E. Deutsch (N.Y., Harper, 1970)

The Awakening Minorities: American Indians, Mexican Americans, Puerto Ricans, ed. (Chicago, Aldine, 1970)

An Overview of International Studies, ed. (N.Y., MSS Information Corp., 1972)

The Cutting Edge: Social Movements and Social Change in America (Phila., Lippincott, 1974)

Urban Black Politics, ed. with Robert C. Smith (N.Y., Amer. Acad. of Polit. & Soc. Sci., annal no. 439, 1978)

Source: *Urban Black Politics*.

HUGGINS, NATHAN IRVIN. Historian, History Professor.
Born in Chicago, Ill., Jan. 14, 1927. *Education:* B.A., 1954, M.A., 1955, U. Cal., Berkeley; A.M., 1957, Ph.D., 1962, Harvard U. *Family:* Married Brenda Carlita Huggins. *Career:* Asst. Prof., Cal. State U., Long Beach, 1962-64; Asst. Prof., Lake Forest Coll., Ill., 1964-66; Asst./Assoc. Prof., U. of Mass., Boston, 1966-75; Visiting Prof., U. of Cal., Berkeley, 1969-70; Prof., Hist., Columbia U., 1970-80; W. E. B. DuBois Prof. of Hist. & Afro-Amer. Studies, Dir. of DuBois Inst., Harvard U., 1980- ; Guest Prof., Heidelberg U., summer 1979. *Honors:* John Hay Whitney Found. Fellow, 1955-56; 1958-59; Guggenheim Found. Fellow, 1971-72; Ford Found. Travel Fellow, Fulbright-Hayes Senior Lect., France, 1974-75; Fellow of Center for Advance Studies in Behavioral Sciences, 1974; NEH Fellow, 1979; Natl. Bk. Award Nominee (for *Harlem Renaissance*), 1971; U.S. State Dept. Amer. Spec. Award, 1976; Andrew W. Mellon Award, 1979-80; Ford Found. Res. Grant, 1979-80. *Mailing address:* W. E. B. DuBois Inst., Canaday Hall, B., Harvard U., Cambridge, Mass. 02138.

Writings:
  Nonfiction
  Protestants against Poverty: Boston's Charities, 1870-1900 (Westport, Conn., Greenwood, 1971)

  Key Issues in the Afro-American Experience, ed., 2 vols. (N.Y., Harcourt, 1971)

  Harlem Renaissance (N.Y., Oxford U. Press, 1971, 1973)

  Voices from the Harlem Renaissance, ed. (Oxford U. Press, 1976)

  Black Odyssey: The Afro-American Ordeal in Slavery (N.Y., Pantheon, 1977; N.Y., Random House, 1979)

  Slave and Citizen: The Life of Frederick Douglass (Boston, Little, Brown, 1980)

Sources: Author information; *Books in Print*, 1981-82.

HUGHES, (JAMES) LANGSTON. Poet, Novelist, Short Story Writer, Biographer, Playwright, Lecturer, Editor.
Born in Joplin, Mo., Feb. 1, 1902. *Education:* Columbia U., 1921-22; (Grad.), Lincoln U., Pa., 1929, Litt.D. (hon.), 1943. *Family:* Single. *Career:* Seaman; poetry reading, cross country, 1946-48; Poet-in-Residence, U. of Chicago, Lib. Sch., 1949; Lyricist & radio writer; Columnist: *Chicago Defender, New York Post*; Madrid correspondent for *Baltimore Afro-American* (Spanish Civil War, 1937). *Honors:* Winner, 1st prize, poetry, *Opportunity* mag. (offered to Negro writers), 1925; 1st prize, Witter Bynner Undergrad. Poetry Contest, 1926; Harmon Gold Award for Lit., 1930; Guggenheim Found. Fellow, 1941; $1,000 grant from Natl. Inst. of Arts & Letters, 1946; Anisfield-Wolf Award, Best Bk. on Race Relations, for *Simple Takes a Wife*, 1954; Spingarn Medal, NAACP, 1960. Died May 22, 1967.

Writings:
  Fiction
  Weary Blues, poems (N.Y., Knopf, 1926; Ann Arbor, Mich., University Microfilms, 1972)

  Fine Clothes to the Jew, poems (Knopf, 1927)

  Not without Laughter, novel (Knopf, 1930; N.Y., Collier, 1969)

  The Negro Mother and Other Dramatic Recitations (N.Y., Golden Stair, 1931; Freeport, N.Y., Bks. for Libraries, 1971)

  Popo and Fifina; Children of Haiti, juv. novel with Arna Bontemps (N.Y., Macmillan, 1932)

  The Dream Keeper and Other Poems, collection (Knopf, 1932, 1963)

  Scottsboro Limited, Four Poems and a Play in Verse (Golden Stair, 1932)

  The Ways of White Folks, short stories (Knopf, 1934, 1963)

  A New Song, poems (N.Y., Intnl. Workers Order, 1938)

  Shakespeare in Harlem, poems (Knopf, 1942)

Freedom's Plow, poems (N.Y., Musette, 1943)

Jim Crow's Last Stand, poems (N.Y., Negro Pub. Soc. of Amer., 1943)

Fields of Wonder, poems (Knopf, 1947)

Street Scene, lyricist of Elmer Rice-Kurt Musical (N.Y., Chappell, 1948)

Cuba Libre, transl. of Nicolas Guillen poems (L.A., Anderson & Ritchie, 1948)

One Way Ticket, poems (Knopf, 1948)

Poetry of the Negro, 1746-1949, anthology with Arna Bontemps (N.Y., Doubleday, 1949; rev. ed., 1970)

Troubled Island, libretto of William Grant Still work (n.p., Leeds, Music Corp., 1949)

The Barrier, libretto of opera (Milano, Italy, Sonsogno, 1950)

Simple Speaks His Mind, novel (N.Y., Simon & Schuster, 1950; Ann Arbor, Mich., U. Microfilms, 1975)

Montage of a Dream Deferred, poems (N.Y., Holt, 1951)

Laughing to Keep from Crying, short stories (Holt, 1952)

Simple Takes a Wife, humor (Simon & Schuster, 1953)

Simple Stakes a Claim, humor (N.Y., Rinehart, 1957)

The Langston Hughes Reader, anthology (N.Y., Braziller, 1958)

Book of Negro Folklore, with Arna Bontemps (N.Y., Dodd, 1958)

Tambourines to Glory, a Novel (N.Y., Day, 1958; N.Y., Hill & Wang, 1970)

Selected Poems (Knopf, 1959; N.Y., Vintage, 1974)

African Treasury: Articles, Essays, Stories, Poems by Black Africans, ed. (N.Y., Crown, 1960)

Ask Your Mama: 12 Moods for Jazz (Knopf, 1961, 1969)

The Best of Simple, humor (Hill & Wang, 1961, 1968; paper also)

Poems from Black Africa (Bloomington, Ind. U. Press, 1963)

Five Plays by Langston Hughes (Ind. U. Press, paper, 1963)

Simple's Uncle Sam, humor (Hill & Wang, 1965)

Book of Negro Humor, ed. (Dodd, 1966; paper also)

The Panther and the Lash; Poems of Our Times, posthumous (Knopf, paper, 1967)

The Best Short Stories by Negro Writers; An Anthology from 1899 to the Present, ed. (Boston, Little, Brown, 1967)

Nonfiction

The Big Sea, autobiog. (Knopf, 1940; Hill & Wang, 1963)

The First Book of Negroes, juv. (N.Y., Watts, 1952)

Famous American Negroes, juv. (Dodd, 1954, 1966; paper; N.Y., Apollo Editions, 1969)

First Book of Rhythms, juv. (Watts, 1954)

First Book of Jazz, juv. (Watts, 1955, 1976; 3rd ed., 1982)

Famous Negro Music Makers, juv. (Dodd, 1955)

I Wonder As I Wander, autobiog. (Holt, 1956; Hill & Wang, 1964; N.Y., Octagon, 1974)

First Book of the West Indies, juv. (Watts, 1956; London, Ward, 1965)

Famous Negro Heroes of America, juv. (Dodd, 1958)

First Book of Africa, juv. (Watts, 1960)

Black Magic: A Pictorial History of the Negro in American Entertainment (Englewood Cliffs, N.J., Prentice-Hall, 1967)

Don't You Turn Back, essays, ed. by Lee B. Hopkins (Knopf, 1969)

Good Morning Revolution: Uncollected Social Protest Writings, ed. by Faith Berry (Westport, Conn., Lawrence Hill, 1973)

Arna Bontemps-Langston Hughes Letters, 1925-1967 (Dodd, 1980)

Sidelights: Poet, fiction writer, playwright, journalist, biographer, historian, anthologist, translator, and critic, Langston Hughes was one of the best known and most versatile black American writers of the twentieth century. While a poet first and foremost, from his professional beginnings as part of the Harlem Renaissance of the 1920s to his death in the late 1960s, Hughes experimented with varying degrees of success in almost every literary genre. (*Dictionary of Literary Biography*)

Sources: *Black American Literature: Poetry*; *Black Drama in America*; *Black Insights*; *Black Poets of the United States*; *Black Voices*; *Books in Print*, Supplement, 1975-76; *Cavalcade*; *Dictionary of Literary Biography*; *Kaleidoscope*; *Poetry of the Negro, 1746-1949*; *Twentieth Century Authors*; *Who Was Who in America*, vol. IV, 1961-68.

HUNKINS, LEE (CYNTH). Playwright, Civil Service Administrator.
Born in N.Y.C., Jan. 8, 1930. *Education:* N.Y.U. *Career:* Executive, Soc. Security Admin. (30 yrs.), Flushing, N.Y.; Playwright: CBS Playhouse; Negro Ensemble Co.; Community Theater (Harlem). *Honors:* ABC $10,000 prize for new writing; Eugene O'Neill Memorial Theater Center TV Workshop. *Mailing address:* c/o Negro Ensemble Co., 133 Second Ave., N.Y., N.Y. 10003.

Writings:
Fiction
The Dolls, play, with Steve Chambers (Old Reliable Theatre, N.Y.C., 1971)

Hollow Image, Off-Broadway TV play (N.Y., ABC Theater, Herb Brodkin's Titus Productions, 1979)

Sidelights: Stars in *Hollow Image*: Saundra Sharp and Robert Hooks. Lee Hunkins has "written three full-length plays and more than a dozen one-acts. Several have been produced in Harlem's Community Theater, and one of her one-acts had an experimental production by the prestigious Negro Ensemble Theater." (*Los Angeles Times*)
　　Others of her plays are: *The Square Peg*; *The Cage*; and *Another Side of Tomorrow* (all produced at American Community Theatre, New York City). Finally, *Maggie* was performed at the Negro Ensemble Summer Festival, New York City.

Sources: *Black American Writers Past and Present*; *Los Angeles Times*, June 22, 1979; *National Playwrights Directory*, 2nd ed., 1981.

HUNTER, KRISTIN EGGLESTON. Novelist, Juvenile Writer.
Born in Phila., Pa., Sept. 12, 1931. *Education:* B.A., U. of Pa., 1951. *Family:* Married John I. Lattany; son Andrew Lattany. *Career:* Columnist & Feature Writer, *Pittsburgh Courier*, Phila., Ed., 1946-52; Copywriter, Lavenson Bureau of Advertising, Phila., 1952-59; Wermen & Schoor, Inc., Phila., 1962-63; Information Officer, City of Phila., 1963-64; Free-lance Writer, 1964- ; Lect., Creative Writing, U. of Pa., 1972; Keynote Speaker, ALA, Atlantic City, N.J., 1970; Delegate, Conf. to Assess State of Black Arts & Letters, U. of Chicago, 1972 (Black Acad. of Arts & Letters). *Honors:* Fund for the Republic Prize, best TV documentary script, 1955; John Hay Whitney Found. Fellow, 1959-60; Phila. Athenaeum Literary Award, for *God Bless the Child*, 1964; Bread Loaf Writers' Conf., Fellow, 1965. For *The Soul Brothers and Sister Lou*, 1968: Natl. Conf. of Christians & Jews Mass Media Award; Council on Interracial Bks. for Children Award; Lewis Carroll Shelf Award; Red Fist Award (Holland); Silver Slate-Pencil Award (Holland). Sigma Delta Chi Best Mag. Reporting of the Yr. Award, 1968 (for an article on unwed mothers in *Philadelphia Magazine*). For *Guests in the Promised Land*, 1973: *Chicago Tribune* Bk. World Award for the best bk. for older

children, 1973; Christopher Award; nomination for Natl. Bk. Award. *Mailing address:* P.O. Box 8371, Phila., Pa. 19101.

Writings:
Fiction

"Minority of One," drama (CBS TV documentary, 1955)

God Bless the Child, novel (N.Y., Scribner's, 1964; paper, N.Y., Bantam, 1970)

The Landlord, novel (Scribner's, 1966; paper, N.Y., Avon, 1970)

The Soul Brothers and Sister Lou, teenage novel (Scribner's, 1968; paper, Avon, 1968)

Boss Cat, juv. (Scribner's, 1971)

Guests in the Promised Land, short stories for older children (Scribner's, 1973)

The Survivors, juv. (Scribner's, 1975)

Sources: Author information; *Best Short Stories by Negro Writers*; *Black American Literature: Fiction*; *Boss Cat*.

HURSTON, ZORA NEALE. Novelist, Folklorist.
Born in Eatonville, Fla., in 1903. *Education:* Morgan Coll., grad. 1921; Howard U., 1921-24; B.A., Barnard Coll., 1928; Litt.D. (hon.), Morgan Coll., 1939. *Career:* Res. (with Dr. Franz Boas) & writing folklore, Columbia U. (private grant from Mrs. R. Osgood Mason & Fellow, Rosenwald Found.), 1928-32; Haiti & Brit. W. Indies (Guggenheim Fellow), 1936-38; Scriptwriter, Paramount Pictures; Head, Drama Dept., N.C. Coll. for Negroes (Durham). *Honors:* Received $1,000 Anisfield-Wolf Award for *Dust Tracks on a Road*, 1943; Howard U. Alumni Award, Distinguished Postgrad. Work in Lit., 1943. Died Jan. 28, 1960.

Writings:
Fiction

Jonah's Gourd Vine, novel (Phila., Lippincott, 1934, 1971)

Mules and Men, folklore (Lippincott, 1935; Bloomington, Ind. U. Press, Midland Bks., no. 208, 1978)

Their Eyes Were Watching God, novel (Lippincott, 1937; reprint, Westport, Conn., Negro Universities Press, n.d.; Urbana, U. of Ill. Press, 1978)

Moses, Man of the Mountain, satirical novel (Lippincott, 1939; Old Greenwich, Conn., Chatham reprint, 1975)

Tell My Horse, folklore (London, J. M. Dent, 1939, as *Voodoo Gods*, 1938; Berkeley, Cal., Turtle Island Found., New World Writing Ser., 1981)

Seraph on the Suwanee, novel (N.Y., Scribner's, 1948)

Nonfiction

Dust Tracks on a Road, autobiog. (Lippincott, 1942, paper also; reprint, N.Y., Arno, Amer. Negro, His Hist. & Lit. Ser., no. 3, 1970)

I Love Myself When I Am Laughing ... and Then Again When I Am Looking Mean and Impressive: A Zora Neale Hurston Reader, ed. by Alice Walker (Old Westbury, N.Y., Feminist Press, 1979)

Sidelights: Miss Hurston has been placed "in the front rank, not only of Negro writers, but all American writers." (*Black Joy*)

She "became the first black writer since Charles Chesnutt to concentrate on the literary and cultural importance of folk material." (*Black American Literature: Fiction*)

"During the Renaissance ... she ... joined such writers as Langston Hughes and Wallace Thurman on the editorial staff of the avant-garde magazine *Fire*." (*Cavalcade*)

Sources: *American Negro Short Stories*; *Black American Literature: Fiction*; *Black Joy*; *Books in Print*, 1979-80, 1980-81, 1981-82; *Cavalcade*; *Who Was Who in America*, vol. III, 1951-60.

INNIS, DORIS FUNNYE. Editor, Teacher.
Born in Georgetown, S.C. *Education:* B.A. (Eng., Hist.), M.A. (Amer. Civilization, Journalism), N.Y.U.; M.A., Grad. Inst. of Bk. Pub., N.Y.U. *Career:* Editor, Writer, Teacher. *Honors:* Alpha Kappa Delta, Natl. Honor Soc. in Sociol. *Mailing address:* 800 Riverside Dr., N.Y., N.Y. 10032.

Writings:
  Nonfiction

  Profiles in Black, Biographical Sketches of 100 Living Black Unsung Heroes (N.Y., CORE, 1976)

  Achievement Sketches of 100 Living Black Americans, ed. with Others (CORE, 1976)

Source: Author information.

JACKSON, BLYDEN. English Professor.
Born in Paducah, Ky., Oct. 12, 1910. *Education:* B.A., Wilberforce U., 1930; M.A., 1938, Ph.D., 1952, U. of Mich. *Family:* Married Roberta Bowles Hodges (U. tchr.), Aug. 2, 1958. *Career:* High Sch. Eng. Tchr., Louisville, Ky., 1934-45; Asst. Prof., Fisk U., 1945-53; Southern U.: Assoc. Prof. of Eng., 1953-54; Prof. of Eng., 1954-64; Dept. Head, 1954-63; Dean, Grad. Sch., 1963-69. U. of N.C.: Prof. of Eng., 1969- ; Assoc. Dean, Grad. Sch., 1973- . Assoc. Ed., *College Language Association Journal. Honors:* Julius Rosenwald Fund Fellow, 1947-49; U. of Mich., Fellow, 1947-49; Honors Convocation, Mich., 1948. *Mailing address:* c/o Dept. of Eng., 216 Greenlow Hall, U. of N.C., Chapel Hill, N.C. 27514.

Writings:
  Fiction

  Operation Burning Candle; A Novel (N.Y., Third Press, 1973)

  Totem, a Novel (Third Press, 1975)

  Nonfiction

  Black Poetry in America; Two Essays in Historical Interpretation, with Louis Rubin (Baton Rouge, La. State U. Press, 1974)

  The Waiting Years: Essays on American Negro Literature (La. State U. Press, 1976)

Sources: *Books in Print*, 1979-80, 1980-81; *Contemporary Authors*, vols. 57-60, 1976.

JACKSON, CLYDE OWEN. Editor, Composer.
Born in Galveston, Tex., Apr. 7, 1928. *Education:* Central High Sch., Galveston, 1945; B.S., Tuskegee Inst., 1949; Music Educ., Tex. S. U., 1960, M. Music Educ., 1964. *Family:* Single. *Career:* Ed., Informer Group of Newspapers, Tex., 1969-72; Gen. News Ed. & Information Officer, Tex. S. U., 1968-71; Music Dept., Tex. S. U. (organizer, conductor, Men's Glee Club), U.S. Army, Infantry. Holds lectures & workshops on Negro spirituals. *Honors:* Natl. Newspaper Pub. Assn. Merit Award for study on sch. desegregation, 1955; Natl. Council of Negro Women (Houston Chap.), award for community serv., 1974; U.S. Army Commendation Award for news writing, 1954. *Mailing address:* 10863 Fairland Dr., Houston, Tex. 77051.

Writings:
  Nonfiction

  The Songs of Our Years, a Study of Negro Folk Music (Hicksville, N.Y., Exposition Press, 1968)

  Before the Darkness Covers Us, essays, speeches, ed. (Exposition Press, 1969)

  In This Evening Light, biography (Exposition Press, 1980)

Come Like the Benediction: A Tribute to Tuskegee Institute and Other Essays (Exposition Press, 1981)

Sidelights: "Commenting on 'The Songs of Our Years,' internationally acclaimed composer William Grant Still called the book, 'thoughtful and carefully researched.' Popular folk singer, Leon Bibb, declared: 'historians and collectors of Negro music will welcome this book,' and *Freedomways* magazine (Spring 1969) declared: 'The Songs of Our Years' ... is a useful companion to music history texts in the schools which may have omitted so much of the contributions of Black Americans.' " (Program Notes; Workshop on Negro Spirituals, Houston, Tex.)

Sources: Author information and brochure.

JACKSON, GEORGE. Revolutionary.
Born in Chicago, Ill., Sept. 23, 1941. *Education:* Self-educated. *Career:* "Arrested at the age of eighteen for allegedly taking part in the robbery of a gas station netting $70, George Jackson was sentenced to one year to life in prison. At the time of his death he had served eleven years behind prison walls, seven of those years in solitary confinement. Long before the world had heard of him, George Jackson had already become a legendary figure inside the California prison system. When *Soledad Brother* ... was published, he was hailed at home and abroad." (Pub. brochure) Died Aug. 21, 1971.

Writings:
Nonfiction
Soledad Brother: The Prison Letters of George Jackson (N.Y., Coward-McCann, 1970; N.Y., Bantam, 1970)

Blood in My Eye (N.Y., Random House, Bantam, 1972)

Sidelights: *Soledad Brother* is "the most important single book from a black since *The Autobiography of Malcolm X*" (Julius Lester, *New York Times Book Review*); *New York Times* described *Blood in My Eye*, as 'the last will and testament of George Jackson.' " *Library Journal* described it as "a powerful and disturbing manifesto ... both simplistic and complex." *The Louisville Times* viewed *Blood in My Eye* as "an important and significant contribution." (Publisher)

Sources: Pub. information; *Soledad Brother*.

JACKSON, JESSE. Juvenile Writer, Free-lance Writer.
Born in Columbus, Ohio, Jan. 1, 1908. *Education:* Ohio State U., 1927-29; Breadloaf Writers Conf., Breadloaf, Vt. *Family:* Married Ann Newman (soc. worker), Sept. 19, 1938; d. Judith Ann. *Career:* Sewer Inspector; Laborer; Postal Worker; Journalist; Ed. Dept., Natl. Bureau of Econ. Res.; Lect., Elementary Educ., Appalachian State U., 1974 to present; Free-lance Author. *Honors:* Carter G. Woodson Award, 1975; Hon. LL.D., Appalachian State U., N.C. *Mailing address:* c/o Duncan Hall, Appalachian State U., Boone, N.C. 28608.

Writings:
Fiction
Call Me Charley, juv. (N.Y., Harper, 1945; N.Y., Dell, 1967)

Anchor Man, juv. (Harper, 1947; Dell, 1968)

Room for Randy, juv. (N.Y., Friendship Press, 1957)

Charley Starts from Scratch, juv. (Harper, 1958; Dell, 1968)

Tessie, juv. (Harper, 1968; Dell, 1969)

Tessie Keeps Her Cool, juv. (Harper, 1970)

The Sickest Don't Always Die the Quickest, juv. (Garden City, N.Y., Doubleday, 1971)

The Fourteenth Cadillac, juv. (Doubleday, 1972)

Nonfiction

I Sing Because I'm Happy, juv. biog. of Mahalia Jackson (N.Y., Rutledge Bks., 1970)

Black in America: A Fight for Freedom, juv. with Elaine Landau (N.Y., Messner, 1973)

Make a Joyful Noise to the Lord: The Life of Mahalia Jackson; Queen of Gospel Singers (Dell, Women of Amer. Ser., 1974; N.Y., Crowell, 1974)

Sidelights: "As a boy, Jackson lived much the same as his hero, Charles Moss in *Call Me Charley*, and *Charley Starts from Scratch.... Call Me Charley* was written with the hope that it would be 'a small tribute to the good people who somehow or other succeed in making bad things better.' " (*Something about the Author*)

Sources: *Books in Print*, Supplement, 1975-76; *Something about the Author*, 1973.

JACKSON, MILES MERRILL, JR. Librarian, Library Science Professor.
Born in Richmond, Va., Apr. 28, 1928. *Education:* U. of N. Mex., 1949-?; B.A., Va. Union U., 1955; M.S.L.S., Drexel U., 1956; Ind. U., 1961, 1964. *Family:* Married Bernice O. Roane, Jan. 7, 1954; children: Miles III, Marsha, Muriel, Melia. *Career:* Librarian, Free Lib., Phila., 1956-58; Hampton Inst., Hampton, Va., 1958-62; Territorial Librn., Govt. of Amer. Samoa, Pago Pago, 1962-64; Lib. Dir., Atlanta U., 1965-69; Assoc. Prof. of Lib. Sci., SUNY, Geneseo, 1969- ; Columnist, "Libraries Abroad," *Journal of Library History*, 1965-69. *Honors:* Senior Fulbright Lect., U. of Tehran, 1968-69; Grant, Amer. Philosophical Soc., 1966; Area Study Award, travel in Africa, summer 1969; Fellow, Council of Library Resources, 1970. *Mailing address:* c/o Greenwood Press, 88 Post Rd., W., P.O. Box 5007, Westport, Conn. 06881.

Writings:
Nonfiction

Bibliography of Negro History and Culture for Young Readers, ed. (Pittsburgh, U. of Pittsburgh Press, 1968)

Comparative and International Librarianship: Essays on Themes and Problems, ed. (Westport, Conn., Greenwood, 1970)

International Handbook of Contemporary Developments in Librarianship, ed. (Greenwood, 1981)

Sources: *Books in Print*, 1981-82; *Living Black American Authors*.

JACKSON, RICHARD L. Latin-American Literature Professor.
Education: B.A., Knoxville Coll.; M.A., Ph.D., Ohio State U. *Career:* Prof., Latin-Amer. Lit.; Chairman, Dept. of Spanish & Italian, Carleton U., Ottawa, Ontario, Can. *Honors:* Woodrow Wilson Found. Can. Council Fellow; Andrew Mellon Postdoctoral Fellow. *Mailing address:* Garland Pub., Inc., 136 Madison Ave., N.Y., N.Y. 10016.

Writings:
Nonfiction

The Black Image in Latin American Literature (Albuquerque, U. of N. Mex. Press, 1979)

Black Writers in Latin America (U. of N. Mex. Press, 1979)

The Afro-Spanish American Author, an Annotated Bibliography of Criticism (N.Y., Garland Res. Lib. of the Humanities, Garland, 1980)

Sources: *Black Image in Latin American Literature*; *Books in Print*, 1980-81.

JAMES, CHARLES LYMAN. English Professor.
Born in Poughkeepsie, N.Y., Apr. 12, 1934. *Education:* B.S., State U. Coll., New Paltz, N.Y.; M.S., SUNY, Albany; Yale U. (1 yr. fellowship). *Family:* Married Jane Fisher; d. Sheila Ellen, d. Terri

Lynn. *Career:* Assoc. Prof., Eng., Swarthmore Coll., Swarthmore, Pa. *Honors:* Danforth Found. Fellow, Yale U., 1972.

Writings:
Fiction
From the Roots: Short Stories by Black Americans, ed. (N.Y., Dodd, 1970)

Nonfiction
The Black Writer in America, ed. (Albany, SUNY, 1969)

Source: Author information.

JAMES, C(YRIL) L(IONEL) R(OBERT). (Trinidadian). Journalist, Historian, Novelist, Essayist, Lecturer.
Born in Trinidad, Jan. 4, 1901. *Education:* Queens' Royal Coll., Port-of-Spain, Trinidad, 1911-18. *Family:* Married Selma Jones, 1955; child by previous marriage. *Career:* Journalist & Tchr., W. Indies; Press Correspondent, Eng., 1932-38; Lect. (Politics & Lit.), U.S., 1938-53; Secy., W. Indian Fed. Labour Party, 1958-60. *Mailing address:* c/o Allison & Busby Ltd., 6a Noel St., London WIV 3RB, England.

Writings:
Fiction
Minty Alley, a Novel (London, Secker, 1936; London, New Beacon, 1971)

Nonfiction
Cricket and I, essays, with L. R. Constantine (London, Allan, 1933)

The Case for West Indian Self-Government (London, Hogarth, 1933)

World Revolution. 1917-1936. The Rise and Fall of the Communist International (Secker, 1937; Westport, Conn., Hyperion, 1973)

The Black Jacobins: Toussaint L'Ouverture and the San Domingo Revolution (Secker & N.Y., Dial, 1938; rev. ed., N.Y., Random House, 1963; London, Allison & Busby, 1980)

A History of Negro Revolt (London, Fact, 1938; reprint, Brooklyn, N.Y., Haskell, Studies in Black Hist. & Culture, no. 54, n.d.)

Mariners, Renegades and Castaways, the Story of Herman Melville and the World We Live In (N.Y., n.p., 1953; 2nd ed., Detroit, Bewick Ed., 1978)

Beyond a Boundary, essays (London, Hutchinson, 1963)

Spheres of Existence, Selected Writings, essays (Allison & Busby, 1980; Westport, Conn., Lawrence Hill, Selected Writings Ser., vol. 2, 1981)

Modern Politics, 2nd ed. (Detroit, Bewick Ed., 1973)

Selected Writings of C. L. James (Bowling Green Station, N.Y., Gordon, 1977)

Nkrumah and the Ghana Revolution (Lawrence Hill, 1977)

The Future in the Present: Selected Writings of C. L. R. James (Lawrence Hill, 1977)

Notes on Dialectics, Hegel and Marxism, essays (Lawrence Hill, 1981)

Sidelights: James resided in England after 1953. He had *Toussaint L'Ouverture*, a play, produced in in London, 1935. Has recently been on the faculty of Federal City College, Washington, D.C.

Sources: *Books in Print*, 1981-82; *Contemporary Novelists*, 2nd ed., 1976; *Freedomways*, vol. 17, 1977; *The Future in the Present*; *International Authors and Writers Who's Who*, 7th ed., 1976; *Nkrumah and the Ghana Revolution*; *Resistance and Caribbean Literature.*

JAY, JAMES MONROE. Bacteriology and Microbial Ecology Professor.
Born in Ben Hill County, Ga., Sept. 17, 1927. *Education:* A.B., Paine Coll., Ga., 1950; M.S., 1953, Ph.D. (Bacteriology), Ohio State U., 1956. *Career:* Asst. (Ohio State U.), 1953-55; Agricultural Experiment Station, 1955-56; Res. Assoc., 1956-57; from Asst. Prof. to Prof., Bacteriology, S. U., 1957-61; from Asst. Prof. to Assoc. Prof., 1961-69; Prof., Bacteriology, Wayne State U., 1969- . *Mailing address:* c/o Dept. of Biology, Wayne State U., Detroit, Mich. 48202.

Writings:
Nonfiction

Modern Food Microbiology (N.Y., Van Nostrand, 1970)

Negroes in Science: Natural Science Doctorates, 1876-1969 (Detroit, Balamp Pub., 1971)

Sidelights: "Presents a profile of 587 of the then estimated total of 650 American-born Negroes to earn doctorates in the natural sciences." (Publisher)

Sources: *American Men and Women of Science: Physical and Biological Science*, 15th ed., 1982; *Encyclopedia of Black America.*

JEFFERS, LANCE. Poet, English Professor.
Born in Fremont, Neb., Nov. 28, 1919. *Education:* B.A. (cum laude), 1951, M.A., Columbia U.; U. of Toronto, Can. *Family:* Married Trellie Lee James (tchr.); son Lance, d. Valjeanne, d. Sidonie Colette, d. Honoree. *Career:* Prof., Eng., Fla. A&M, 1964-65; Tchr. Fellow, Eng., U. of Toronto, 1965-66; Lect., Eng., Ind. U., 1966-68; Prof., Creative Writing & Black Lit., Cal. State Coll., Long Beach, 1968-71; Chairman, Dept. of Eng., Bowie State Coll., Bowie, Md. *Honors:* Franklin T. Baker Citation, Tchrs. Coll., Columbia U. *Mailing address:* c/o Lotus Press, P.O. Box 21607, Detroit, Mich. 48221.

Writings:
Fiction

My Blackness Is the Beauty of This Land, poems (paper, Detroit, Broadside, 1970)

When I Know the Power of My Black Hand, poems (Broadside, 1974)

O Africa, Where I Baked My Bread, poems (Detroit, Lotus, 1977)

Grandsire, poems (Lotus, 1979)

Sources: *Black Voices; Cavalcade; Freedomways*, vol. 19, 1979; *New Black Poetry; New Black Voices; Nine Black Poets; Poetry of Black America.*

JEFFERSON, ROLAND S. Psychiatrist, Novelist, Film Writer.
Born in Wash., D.C., May 16, 1939. *Education:* B.S., U. S. Cal., 1961; M.D., Howard U. Medical Coll., 1965; Psychiatry, Ill. State Psychiatric Inst.; Camarillo State Hosp., 1967-69. *Career:* Captain, U.S. Air Force, 1969-71; Psychiatrist; Film Producer, "Disco 9000"; "Do They Ever Cry in America" (both 1977); "The Wack Attack" (ABC TV), 1979. *Honors:* Golden Quill Award for Lit., by Abfriham Found., 1977; Entertainer of Year Award, Sons of Watts, 1977. *Mailing address:* 3870 Crenshaw Blvd., No. 215, L.A., Cal. 90008.

Writings:
Fiction
School on 103rd Street, novel (N.Y., Vantage Press, 1976)

A Card for the Players, a Novel (L.A., New Bedford Press, 1978)

The School on One Hundred Third Street, 2nd ed., Saul Burnstein, ed. (New Bedford Press, 1980)

Sources: Author information; *Books in Print*, 1980-81.

JEFFERSON, XAVIER THOMAS [Omar Xavier Jefferson]. Novelist, Playwright.
Born in Phila., Pa., Jan. 4, 1952. *Education:* Coll. of St. Thomas, 1969-71; U. of Minn. *Family:* Married Lynne Elaine Smith (mgr., bk. distributor); children: Toby Bryant, Omar Xavier. *Career:* Dir., New Art Workshop, Phila., 1969-70; Dir., Communications Dept., Inner City Youth League, St. Paul, Minn., 1976- ; Alderman, Methuslah Bradley, Minn.; Consultant, Manchild World Corp. *Mailing address:* c/o Ashley Bks., Box 768, Port Wash., N.Y., 11050.

Writings:
Fiction
Blessed Are the Sleepy Ones, novel (Port Wash., N.Y., Ashley Bks., 1977)

The Killing Force, novel (Ashley Bks., 1978)

No Great Heroes, No Great Villains, novel (Ashley Bks., 1978)

Nonfiction
Winterkill, ed. by Billie Young (Ashley Bks., 1979)

Sidelights: His plays were written under the name Omar Xavier Jefferson. They are *Gravity* and *Feelings*, both two-act plays.

Sources: *Books in Print*, 1980-81; *Freedomways*, vol. 19, 1979.

JOANS, TED. Poet, Jazz Musician, Surrealist Painter.
Born in Cairo, Ill., July 4, 1928. *Education:* B.A. (Fine Arts-Painting), Ind. U., 1950. *Family:* Married a Norwegian; son Patrice Lumumba. *Career:* Trumpeter; Jazz Poet; Surrealistic Painter. *Mailing address:* c/o Merrimack Bk. Serv., 5 S. Union St., Lawrence, Mass. 01843.

Writings:
Fiction
All of Ted Joans, and No More: Poems and Collages (N.Y., Excelsior, 1961)

Black Pow-Wow, jazz (N.Y., Hill & Wang, paper also, 1969)

Afrodisia, novel (Hill & Wang, paper also, 1970, 1971)

Black Manifesto in Jazz Poetry and Prose (London, Caldar & Boyars, 1971; Topsfield, Mass., Merrimack Bk. Serv., 1979)

Sidelights: Was for a while one of the "Beats" of Greenwich Village. In an autobiographical note for *Beyond the Blues* he wrote: "Jazz is my religion.... I have traveled to twenty-eight countries and dug the foreign scene and that's for me.... I want to be free now ... free as the white American that is involved in the arts." Joans lived in Morocco, where he wrote and painted. (*Kaleidoscope*)

Sources: *Books in Print*, 1979-80; *For Malcolm*; *Kaleidoscope*; *New Negro Poets, U.S.A.*

JOHNSON, CHARLES RICHARD. Editorial Cartoonist, Novelist, Teacher.
Born in Evanston, Ill., Apr. 23, 1948. *Education:* B.S. (Journalism), M.A. (Philosophy), S. Ill. U., 1973; further study (Philosophy), SUNY, Stony Brook. *Family:* Married Joan New. *Career:* Creator, Host, & Co-prod., educational TV ser. "Charlie's Pad," distributed nationally, prod. by WSIU TV; S. Ill. U., 1969; Teaching Asst., Dept. of Black Amer. Studies, 1969-70; Tutor, Marxist & Oriental Philosophy, SUNY, Stony Brook, 1973-74, Instr., Philosophy, 1974-75; Ed. & Comic strip artist, *Daily Egyptian*, S. Ill. U., 1966-71; Ed. Cartoonist, *Southern Illinoisan*, Cartoonist reporter, *Chicago Tribune*, 1969-70; Art Staff, St. Louis *Proud* mag., 1971-72. *Mailing address:* c/o Ind. U. Press, Tenth & Morton Sts., Bloomington, Ind. 47405.

Writings:
Fiction
Faith and the Good Thing, novel (N.Y., Viking, 1974)

The Oxherding Tale, novel (Bloomington, Ind. U. Press, 1982)

Nonfiction

Black Humor, drawings (Chicago, Johnson, 1970)

Half-Past Nation Time (Westlake Village, Cal., Aware Press, 1972)

Sources: Author information; *Kirkus Reviews*, 1982; *New York Times Book Review*, Jan. 9, 1983; Pub. information.

JOHNSON, CHARLES SPURGEON. Sociologist, Social Science Professor, Editor, College President.
Born in Bristol, Va., in 1893. *Education:* B.A. (hon.), Va. Union U.; Ph.D., U. of Chicago; (hon. doctorates): Howard U.; Columbia U.; Harvard U.; U. of Glasgow, Scotland; Va. Union U. *Career:* Assoc. Executive Secy., Chicago Race Relations Com.; Dir., Res. & Publ., Natl. Urban League; Ed., *Opportunity* mag.; Head, Dept. of Soc. Sci, Fisk U., 1928-46; Pres., Fisk U., Nashville, 1946-? *Honors:* On President's commissions under Hoover, Roosevelt, Truman, & Eisenhower; 2nd Distinguished Amer. named to *Ebony* Hall of Fame; *The Negro College Graduate* won Anisfield-Wolf Award. Died in Oct. 1956.

Writings:
Nonfiction

Ebony and Topaz, ed. (N.Y., N.Y. Urban League, *Opportunity*, 1927; Freeport, N.Y., Bks. for Libraries, 1971)

The Negro in American Civilization: A Study of Negro Life and Race Relations in the Light of Social Research (N.Y., Holt, 1930; reprint, Chicago, Johnson, Basic Afro-Amer. Reprint Ser., 1970)

The Shadow of the Plantation (Chicago, U. of Chicago Press, 1934; Midway Reprint Ser., 1979)

The Collapse of the Cotton Tenancy, with Edwin R. Embree & W. W. Alexander (Chapel Hill, U. of N.C. Press, 1935; N.Y., Arno, Select Bibliog. Reprint Ser., 1972)

A Preface to Racial Understanding (N.Y., Friendship Press, 1936)

The Negro College Graduate (U. of N.C. Press, 1938; reprint, Westport, Conn., Negro Universities Press, 1969)

Growing Up in the Black Belt; Negro Youth in the Rural South (Wash. D.C., Amer. Council on Educ., 1941; Ann Arbor, Mich., University Microfilms, 1967)

Education and the Cultural Process: Papers Presented at Symposium Commemorating the Seventy-Fifth Anniversary of the Founding of Fisk University, April 29-May 4, 1941 (U. of Chicago Press, 1943; reprint, Negro Universities Press, n.d.)

Patterns of Negro Segregation (N.Y., Harper, 1943)

To Stem This Tide, a Survey of Racial Tension Areas in the States (Chicago, Pilgrim, 1943; reprint, N.Y., AMS, 1969)

Sidelights: He contributed to Chicago Race Relations Commission's report *The Negro in Chicago* "The observations he made about mankind and its institutions and problems now fill 18 books. One of them, *The Negro in Chicago*, is considered to be a 'landmark' in social research."
In 1923, while serving as director of research and investigation for the Chicago and National Urban Leagues, Dr. Johnson founded the magazine *Opportunity: Journal of Negro Life* ... which provided an avenue of expression for Negroes in literature, art and music." (*Ebony*)

Sources: *Anthology of American Negro Literature*; *Books in Print*, 1978-79, 1980-81; *Current Biography*, 1946; *Ebony*, Feb. 1957; *Great Negroes Past and Present*; *Historical Negro Biographies*; *Negro Caravan*; *100 Years of Negro Freedom*; *13 Against the Odds*.

JOHNSON, FENTON. Poet, Editor.
Born in Chicago, Ill., in 1888. *Education:* Chicago public schs.; U. of Chicago. *Career:* Magazine Ed.; Writer. Died in 1958.

Writings:
Fiction

A Little Dreaming, poems (Chicago, Peterson, 1913)

Visions of the Dusk, poems (N.Y., Author, 1915; Freeport, N.Y., Books for Libraries, 1971; reprint, N.Y., Arno, Black Heritage Lib. Collection, n.d.)

Songs of the Soil, poems (N.Y., Author, 1916; reprint, N.Y., AMS, 1975)

Tales of Darkest America, short stories (Chicago, Favorite Magazine, 1920; reprint, facsimile ed., Arno, Black Heritage Lib. Collection, 1971)

Nonfiction

For the Highest Good, essays (Favorite Magazine, 1920)

Sidelights: Johnson "was one of the first black revolutionary poets." (*Book of American Negro Poetry*)
"In 1918 and 1919 he published poems in *Poetry* magazine and Alfred Kreymborg's *Others*, where he appeared along with William Carlos Williams, Wallace Stevens, and Marianne Moore. He never became a major figure, but he cultivated his own distinctive voice and a fatalistic, nihilistic vision of life which was very rare in Negro American Literature." (*Black Voices*)

Sources: *Black Voices*; *Book of American Negro Poetry*; *Books in Print*, 1978-79; *Caroling Dusk*; *Kaleidoscope*; *Negro Almanac*; *Negro Caravan*; *Negro Poets and Their Poems*; *Negro Voices in American Fiction*.

JOHNSON, GEORGIA DOUGLAS. Poet.
Born in Atlanta, Ga., in 1886. *Education:* Atlanta U.; Oberlin Coll., Conservatory of Music. *Family:* Married Henry L. Johnson (Recorder of Deeds under William Howard Taft). *Career:* Commissioner of Conciliation, Dept. of Labor; with other govt. agencies; Writer. Died in 1966.

Writings:
Fiction

The Heart of a Woman, and Other Poems (Boston, Cornhill, 1918; reprint, N.Y., AMS Press, 1975)

Bronze, a Book of Verse (Boston, Brimmer, 1922; reprint, AMS, 1975)

An Autumn Love Cycle, poems (N.Y., Neal, 1938)

Share My World, poems (Wash., D.C., Author, 1952)

Sidelights: Had two poems published in *Crisis* by W. E. B. DuBois. "She was helped to gather material for *Heart of a Woman* by Jessie Fauset. W. S. Braithwaite, a person she had admired since a little girl, wrote the introduction. *Bronze* had an introduction by DuBois, *An Autumn Love Cycle* had an introduction by Alain Locke." (*Caroling Dusk*)

Sources: *American Negro Poetry*; *Book of American Negro Poetry*; *Caroling Dusk*; *Kaleidoscope*; *Negro Caravan*; *Negro Genius*; *Negro Poets and Their Poems*.

JOHNSON, JAMES WELDON. Poet, Essayist, Critic, Civil Rights Executive, Teacher, Lawyer, Consul.
Born in Jacksonville, Fla., June 17, 1871. *Education:* B.A., 1894, M.A., 1904, Atlanta U.; Columbia U. (postgrad., 3 yrs.); Hon. degrees: Litt.D., Talledega Coll., Ala., 1917; Litt.D., Howard U., 1923. *Family:* Married Grace Nail, Feb. 3, 1910. *Career:* Prin., high sch., Jacksonville, Fla. (several yrs.); admitted to Fla. bar, 1897, practiced law, Jacksonville; moved to N.Y.C., 1901, to collaborate with

brother, J. Rosamond Johnson (Musician), in writing for light opera stage; Apptd. U.S. Consul to Puerto Cabello, Venezuela, 1906; Consul at Corinto, Nicaragua, 1909-12 (served during revolution which overthrew Zelaya & through abortive revolution against Diaz); Secy., NAACP, 1916-30; Prof., Creative Lit., Fisk U., 1930-38; Visiting Prof., Creative Lit., N.Y.U., 1934-38; Dir., Amer. Fund for Public Serv. *Honors:* Trustee, Atlanta U.; Spingarn Medal, NAACP, 1925; *God's Trombones* won Harmon Gold Award for Lit.; Julius Rosenwald Fund Grant, 1929. Killed in automobile accident, June 26, 1938.

Writings:
Fiction

The Autobiography of an Ex-Coloured Man, novel (Boston, Sherman, French, 1912; N.Y., Hill & Wang, 1912, 1927; paper also, 1960)

The Book of American Negro Poetry, ed. (N.Y., Harcourt, 1913, 1922, 1931, 1959)

Fifty Years and Other Poems (Boston, Cornhill, 1917; N.Y., AMS, reprint, 1975)

God's Trombones: Seven Negro Sermons in Verse (N.Y., Viking, 1927, 1935, 1948, 1955, 1969, 1976, paper also)

St. Peter Relates an Incident of the Resurrection Day, satirical narrative poem (Viking, 1930, 1935; AMS, 1974)

Utopian Literature: A Selection (N.Y., Random House, 1968)

Nonfiction

Self Determining Haiti (N.Y., The Nation, 1920)

The Book of American Negro Spirituals, with J. Rosamond Johnson (Viking, 1925, 1933, 1951)

Second Book of Negro Spirituals, with J. Rosamond Johnson (Viking, 1926, 1933)

Black Manhattan (N.Y., Knopf, 1930; N.Y., Arno, 1968)

Along This Way; The Autobiography (Viking, 1933; paper also, 1968)

Negro Americans, What Now? (Viking, 1934; AMS, 1961)

Sidelights: "A major figure in the creation and development of Negro American Literature and culture. He contributed in many ways: as a poet and songwriter, novelist, essayist and critic, collector of spirituals, pioneer anthologist and interpreter of black poetry, pioneer student of the history of the Negro in the drama, educator and active participant in the early development of the civil rights movement." (*Black Voices*)

Sources: *An Anthology of Verse by American Negroes*; *Black American Literature: Poetry*; *Black Insights*; *Black Voices*; *Book of American Negro Poetry*; *Books in Print*, Suppl., 1975-76; *Cavalcade*; *Who Was Who in America*, vol. 1, 1897-1942.

JOHNSON, JESSE J. Lieutenant Colonel (U.S. Army), Military Historian.
Born in Hattiesburg, Miss., May 15, 1914. *Education:* B.A., Tougaloo Coll., Miss. 1939; LL.B., Amer. Extension Sch. of Law, Chicago, 1950; M.A., Hampton Inst., 1964. *Family:* Married. *Career:* U.S. Army, 1942-62 (retired as Lt. Colonel); Military Historian. *Mailing address:* P.O. Box 6002, Hampton Inst., Hampton, Va. 23668.

Writings:
Nonfiction

Ebony Brass, an Autobiography of Negro Frustration and Aspiration (N.Y., William Frederick, 1967)

The Black Soldier Documented 1619-1815; Missing Pages in United States History (Hampton, Va., Author, 1969)

A Pictorial History of the Black Soldiers in the United States (1619-1969) in Peace and War (Author, 1970, 1976)

A Pictorial History of Black Servicemen (Air Force, Army, Navy, Marines) (Author, 1970)

Black Armed Forces Officers, 1736-1971: A Documented Pictorial History (Author, 1971)

Roots of Two Black Marine Sergeants Major: Sergeant Major Edgar R. Huff and Gilbert H. "Hashmark" Johnson (Author, 1978)

Sources: Author information; *Books in Print*, 1980-81; *Writers Directory*, 1976-78.

JOHNSON, JOHN HAROLD. Publisher, Editor.
Born in Ark. City, Ark., Jan. 19, 1918. *Education:* DuSable High Sch., Chicago, Ill.; U. of Chicago (2 yrs.); Northwestern U., Sch. of Commerce; Hon. LL.D.: Central State Coll.; Shaw U. *Family:* Married Eunice Walker, 1941; son John, d. Linda. *Career:* Asst. to Ed., Supreme Life Insurance Co., house organ, 1936, later Managing Ed.; Pub., Johnson Publications, all dealing with Black topics & aimed at the Black market. *Honors:* Selected one of ten outstanding men of the yr. by U.S. Jr. Chamber of Commerce, 1951; accompanied V. Pres. Richard Nixon on goodwill trips to nine African countries, 1957, to Russia & Poland, 1959; Spec. Ambassador, rep. U.S. at Independence Ceremonies, Ivory Coast, 1961, & Kenya, 1963; NAACP 1958 Freedom Fund Award (shared with Rudolph Bing); 1966 Horatio Alger Award; 1966 Lincoln Acad. of Ill. Order of Lincoln Award; Russwurm Award. *Mailing address:* Johnson Pub. Co., 820 S. Mich. Ave., Chicago, Ill. 60605.

Writings:
Nonfiction

Negro Digest/Black World, mag., 1st issue, 1942 (monthly)

Ebony, mag., 1st issue, 1945 (monthly)

Tan, mag., 1st issue, 1950 (monthly)

Jet, mag., 1st issue, 1951 (newsweekly)

Sidelights: The most prosperous and influential publisher in American Negro history. Has published several magazines in addition to books; most popular is *Ebony*, founded in 1945, which passed 1 million mark in circulation in 1967.
   "In civil rights (*Ebony*) has geared its pace to that of the Negro community as a whole, so that it has now reached a point of restrained militancy, particularly in its editorials.
   "Dr. Kenneth B. Clark, the noted Negro psychologist, has said of *Ebony*: 'It is almost impossible to measure the morale-lifting value of such a magazine. The mere fact of its existence and success has been an inspiration to the Negro masses.' " (*Current Biography*)

Sources: *Current Biography*, 1968; *Historical Negro Biographies*; *Negro Handbook*.

JOHNSTON, PERCY EDWARD. Humanities Professor, Poet, Playwright, Editor.
Born in N.Y.C., May 18, 1930. *Education:* A.B., Howard U.; M.A., Montclair State Coll., Upper Montclair, N.J., 1968; Claire Heywood's Studio (painting & drawing); David Allentuck's Studio (serigraph); Arnold Eagle's Studio (filmmaking); St. Peter's Coll.; Long Island U.; New Sch. for Soc. Res. *Career:* Ed. & Founder, Dassein: Aesthetics, Lit. & Philosophy, 1961- ; Adjunct Prof., Essex County Coll., 1968-69; Prof., Humanities, Montclair State Coll., N.J., 1967-82; Ed., *Afro-American Journal of Philosophy*, 1977- ; Adjunct Prof. of Black Studies, St. Peter's Coll. 1982- ; Executive Dir., Afro-Amer. Philosophy Assn., 1978- ; V. Pres., R. C. Richardson Found., 1979- . *Honors:* Aliope Poetry Award, 1977; Phi Sigma Tau (philosophy honor fraternity); Pi Delta Epsilon (journalism honor fraternity). *Mailing address:* G.P.O. Box 2121, N.Y., N.Y. 10116.

Writings:
Fiction

Concerto for Girl and Convertible, Opus No. 5 and Other Poems, (n.p., Murray Brothers, 1960; Wash., D.C., Dasein-Jupiter Hammon Press, 1961)

Sean Pendragon Requiem: In Memoriam J. F. K., poems (N.Y., DJH Press, 1964)

Six Cylinder Olympus, poems (DJH Press, 1964)

'Round 'Bout Midnight, poems (DJH Press, 1964)

John Adams, a Historical Drama, parts I & II (N.Y., Rinjohn, 1972)

Emperor Dessalines, play (Rinjohn, 1973)

Dawitt II, play (Rinjohn, 1973)

Crispus Attucks, play, parts I & II (Rinjohn, 1974)

Boston Common, play (Rinjohn, 1975)

Antigone, play (DJH Press, 1977)

Dessalines, play (DJH Press, 1977)

Brushes, poems (N.Y., New Merry Mount, 1977)

Frankie & Johnnie, play (Annapolis, Md., Drama Jazz House, 1980)

Loft Jazz & Miriny Blues, poems (Annapolis, Md., Drama Jazz House, 1983)

Nonfiction

Afro-American Philosophies: Selected Readings from Jupiter Hammon to Eugene C. Holmes, ed. (Upper Montclair, N.J., Montclair State Coll. Press, 1970)

Phenomenology of Negritude, ed. (New Merry Mount, 1973)

A Dictionary of Elizabethan English: The Anglo Saxon Language as Spoken and Written during the Tudor, Elizabethan and Jacobean Periods, ed. (New Merry Mount, 1973)

Phenomenology of Space and Time: An Examination of Eugene Clay Holmes Studies in the Philosophy of Time and Space, ed. (DJH Press, 1976)

Sidelights: "Johnston as a poet is a landscape painter; his landscape is the city." (James A. Porter)

Sources: Author information; *Black American Writers Past and Present*; *Freedomways*, vol. 20, 1980.

JONES, CLARA STANTON. Library Administrator, National Library Official, Library Science Lecturer.
Born in St. Louis, Mo., May 14, 1913. *Education:* A.B. (Eng. & Hist.), Spelman Coll., Atlanta, 1934; A.B. (Lib. Sci.), U. of Mich., 1938. *Family:* Married Albert D. Jones (soc. worker), June 25, 1938; children: Stanton W., Kenneth A., Vinetta C. Johnson. *Career:* Ref. Librn., Dillard U., New orleans, 1938-40; Detroit Public Lib.: Librn., Jr. & Senior, 1944-49; Chief of Div., 1950-63; Chief of Dept., 1963-68; Lib. Neighborhood Consultant, 1968-70; Dir., 1970-78; Regents Lect., Grad. Sch., Lib. & Information Sci., U. Cal., Berkeley, 1979; Centenary guest, The (Brit.) Lib. Assn., London, 1977; Workshop Lect. (information & referral serv., public lib.), Lib. Assn. of Australia, Melbourne, 1977. *Honors:* Pres., ALA, 1976-77; Award for Distinguished Serv. to Librarianship, Black Caucus, ALA, 1970; Distinguished Alumnus Award for Outstanding Serv. to lib. profession, U. of Mich. Sch. of Lib. Sci., 1971; Athena Award for Humanitarian Serv., U. of Mich., Alumnae, 1975; hon. doctoral degrees: Shaw Coll., Ball State U., N.C. Central U., Grand Valley State Coll., St. John's U., Pratt Inst., N. Mich. U., Wayne State U. *Mailing address:* c/o Shoe String Press, P.O. Box 4327, 995 Sherman Ave., Hamden, Conn. 06514.

Writings:
Nonfiction
"Reflections on Library Service to the Disadvantaged," ALA Annual Conf. lect., pamphlet (Chicago, ALA, 1974)

The Information Society: Issues and Answers, collected lectures, ALA President's Program, 1977 (Phoenix, Ariz., Oryx Press, 1978)

Public Library Information and Referral Service, textbook (Syracuse, N.Y., Gaylord Professional Publ., 1978; Hamden, Conn., Shoe String Press, 1981)

Sources: Author information; *Black Scholar*, July/Aug. 1975; *Books in Print*, 1981-82; *Current Biography*, 1976.

JONES, CLARENCE B. Publisher, Editor, Attorney.
Born in Phila., Pa., Jan. 8, 1931. *Education:* Columbia U.; Boston U. Law Sch. *Family:* Married Charlotte; d. Christine, son Clarence, Jr., son Dana, d. Alexia. *Career:* Attorney, entertainment & copyright law, corporate finance & org., state & fed. civil rights litigation; firm: Lubell, Lubell & Jones; Spec. Council to Dr. Martin L. King, Jr. & S. Christian Leadership Conf.; Ed. & Pub., *Amsterdam News*, N.Y. *Mailing address:* 2340 Eighth Ave., N.Y., N.Y. 10027.

Writings:
Nonfiction
Amsterdam News, newspaper (N.Y., weekly)

Source: *1000 Successful Blacks*.

JONES, FAUSTINE CHILDRESS. Education Professor.
Born in Little Rock, Ark., Dec. 3, 1927. *Education:* A.B. (summa cum laude), Agricultural, Mechanical, & Normal Coll., Ark., 1948; A.M., U. of Ill., Urbana, 1951, Ed.D., 1967. *Family:* Div.; children: Brian Vincent, Yvonne Dianne. *Career:* Tchr., Gary, Ind., 1955-62; Teaching Asst., Coll. of Educ., U. of Ill., Urbana, 1962-64; Tchr., Gary High Sch., 1964-67; Asst. Prof., U. of Ill., Chicago, 1967-69; Asst. Prof., Howard U., 1969-70; Assoc. Prof., Fed. City Coll., Wash., D.C., 1970-71; Prof., Educ., Chairman, Found. Dept., Sch. of Educ., Howard U., 1971- ; Senior Fellow, Inst. for Study of Educ. Policy, Howard U. *Honors:* U. Fellow, U. of Ill., 1950-51; plaque from students for excellence in teaching, 1972; Outstanding Tchr. Award, Howard U., 1974-75; Distinguished Faculty Award, Howard U., 1977; Outstanding Alumnus Award, Dunbar Alumni Assn., 1973; Outstanding Tchr. in Sch. of Educ., Howard U., 1974-75. *Mailing address:* c/o Howard U. Press, 2900 Van Ness St., N.W., Wash., D.C. 20008.

Writings:
Nonfiction
The Changing Mood in America: Eroding Commitment? (Wash., D.C., Howard U. Press, 1977)

A Traditional Model of Educational Excellence: Dunbar High School of Little Rock, Arkansas (Howard U. Press, 1981)

Sources: *Books in Print*, 1981-82; *Freedomways*, vol. 18, 1978; *Who's Who among Black Americans*, 2nd ed., 1977-78.

JONES, GAYL AMANDA. Novelist, Poet, Playwright.
Born in Lexington, Ky., Nov. 23, 1949. *Education:* B.A. (Eng.), Conn. Coll., New London, 1971; M.A. (Creative Writing), 1973; Dr. of Arts (Creative Writing), Brown U., 1975. *Family:* Single. *Career:* Novelist, Poet, Playwright. *Honors:* One of four undergrad. poets to tour Conn. Poetry Circuit, 1970; Conn. Coll. Award, best original poem, 1969, 1970; Frances Steloff Award for Fiction, 1970, for "The Roundhouse," scholarship to Breadloaf Writer's Conf.; Acad. of Amer. Poets Charles & Fanny Fay Wood Poetry Prize (Brown U.), 1973; Shubert Found. Grant for Playwriting, 1973-74; Grant in Writing, R.I. Council of Arts, 1974-75; Fellow, Yaddo Artist's Colony, summer 1974. *Mailing address:* c/o Bantam Bks., 666 Fifth Ave., N.Y., N.Y. 10019.

Writings:
Fiction
Chile Woman, play (Providence, R.I., Hellcoal Press, Brown U., 1974)

Corregidora, novel (N.Y., Random House, 1975)

Eva's Man, novel (Random House, 1976; N.Y., Bantam, 1978)

The White Rat: Collected Stories (Random House, 1977)

Song for Anninho, poems (Detroit, Lotus, 1981)

Sources: Author information; *Books in Print*, 1978-79, 1981-82.

JONES, REGINALD L(ANIER). Psychology Professor.
Born in Clearwater, Fla., Jan. 21, 1931. *Education:* A.B., Morehouse Coll., Atlanta, 1952; M.A., Wayne State U., Detroit, 1954; Ph.D., Ohio State U., 1959. *Family:* Married Johnette Turner (artist), Sept. 8, 1959; children: Juliette Melinda, Angela Michelle, Cynthia Ann. *Career:* Res. & Asst. Prof., Instructional Res. Serv., Miami U., Oxford, Ohio, 1959-63; Assoc. Prof., Psychology, Fisk U., Nashville, 1963-64; Asst. Prof., Educ., UCLA, 1964-66; Prof. of Psychology, Ohio State U., Columbus, 1966-69, V. Chairman, Dept., 1968-69; Prof., Educ., U. Cal., Riverside, 1969-73, Chairman, Dept., 1971-72; Prof., Educ. & Ethnic Studies, U. Cal., Berkeley, 1973- ; Dir., U. Testing Center, Haile Selassie I U., 1972-74; V. Chairman, Sch. Bd., Amer. Community Sch., Addis Ababa, Ethiopia; Consultant, Natl. Inst. of Mental Health & U.S. Office of Educ. *Mailing address:* c/o Harper & Row, 10 E. 53rd St., N.Y., N.Y. 10022.

Writings:
Nonfiction
Management Controls for Professional Firms (N.Y., Amer. Management Assn., 1968)

New Directions in Special Education, ed. (Boston, Allyn & Bacon, 1970)

Problems and Issues in the Education of Exceptional Children, ed. (Boston, Houghton Mifflin, 1971)

Budgeting: Key to Planning and Control, Practical Guidelines for Managers, rev. ed. with George H. Trentin (Amer. Management Assn., 1971)

Student Dissent in the Schools, ed. with I. H. Hendrick (Houghton Mifflin, 1972)

Black Psychology, ed. (N.Y., Harper, 1972; 2nd ed., 1980)

Special Education in Transition, with D. L. Macmillan (Allyn & Bacon, 1974)

Sources: *Books in Print*, 1979-80, 1981-82; *Contemporary Authors*, vols. 45-48, 1974.

JONES, SILAS. Science Fiction Writer, Playwright, Film Writer.
Born in Cynthiana, Ky., Jan. 17, 1942. *Education:* Theater Arts major, L.A. City Coll. (Screenwriting). *Career:* Creative Writer, Performing Arts Soc. of L.A.; Creative Writer, Raymond Ave. Elementary Sch., L.A.; Dramatic Writer, Paradox Playhouse; Creative Writer & Dramatist, Central City Adult Sch. *Honors:* Gwendolyn Brooks Literary Award, best short story, 1972; NEA, Artact Playwriting Competition, 1977. *Mailing address:* c/o Funshunal Features Press, P.O. Box 47725, L.A., Cal. 90047.

Writings:
Fiction
The Afrindi Aspect, play produced off-Broadway (1977)

Children of All, juv. sci. fiction (L.A., Funshunal Features Press, 1978)

Waiting for Mongo, play produced off-Broadway; also radio play

Black Image Syndrome, television play

Denise Douglass, D.D.S., television play

Protest and Beyond, television play

Sweet Billy and the Zooloos, television play

That Girl from Boston, feature film

Witness, radio play

Sidelights: "Silas was the writer/consultant for the special ABC-TV documentary, 'TV's Black Image Syndrome.' He rewrote the feature film, 'That Girl from Boston.' His TV Sitcom, 'Denise Douglass, D.D.S.' was optioned by 20th Century Fox.

"Silas's latest play, 'The Afrindi Aspect' was a 1977 NEA-sponsored ARTACT award winner, and [was] in production at the Negro Ensemble Company in New York." Other plays by Silas Jones are: *Waiting for Mongo* (Produced off-Broadway and also for radio); *Protest and Beyond*, and *Sweet Billy and the Zooloos* (produced for television); and *Witness* (produced for radio. (Author)

Source: Author information; *Black American Writers Past and Present.*

JORDAN, JUNE [June Meyer]. Poet, Juvenile Writer, Lecturer.
Born in Harlem, N.Y., July 9, 1936. *Education:* Barnard Coll., N.Y.; U. of Chicago. *Family:* Married Michael Meyer, 1955 (div., 1965); son Christopher David. *Career:* Visiting Lect., Depts. of Eng. & Afro-Amer. Lit., Writing Faculty, Sarah Lawrence Coll., 1973-74; Eng. Faculty, City Coll., CUNY; Eng. Faculty, Conn. Coll., New London; Eng. Faculty, SEEK Program, City Coll., CUNY; Eng. Faculty, Upward Bound Program, Conn. Coll.; Co-founder & Dir., Voice of the Children, Inc.; Res. Assoc. & Writer in Tech. Housing Dept. Mobilization for Youth; Asst. to the Prod., Frederick Wiseman, for motion picture *The Cool World. Honors:* U.S. Lib. of Congress, 1-hr. recording of her poems, June 14, 1973; Rockefeller Grant in Creative Writing, 1969-70; Prix de Rome in Environmental Design, 1970-71; novel *His Own Where* selected as one of the most outstanding bks. of 1971 by the *New York Times*, as one of ALA Best Bks. in 1972, & nominated in 1972 for the Natl. Bk. Award; Nancy Bloch Award, as co-ed., *The Voice of the Children*, 1971. *Mailing address:* c/o Jean Daves, 505 Madison Ave., N.Y., N.Y. 10022.

Writings:
Fiction
Who Look at Me, juv. (N.Y., Crowell, 1969)

Soulscript, Afro-American Poetry, juv. (N.Y., Doubleday, 1970; paper also)

The Voice of the Children, juv. (N.Y., Holt, 1970; paper, N.Y., Wash. Square, 1974)

Some Changes, juv. (N.Y., Dutton, 1971; paper also)

His Own Where, juv. (Crowell, 1971; N.Y., Dell, 1973)

Dry Victories, juv. (Holt, 1972; N.Y., Avon, 1975)

New Days: Poems of Exile and Return (N.Y., Emerson Hall, 1974)

I Love You (Emerson Hall, 1974)

New Life: New Room (Crowell, 1975)

Okay Now (N.Y., Simon & Schuster, 1975)

Things That I Do in the Dark: Selected Poetry (N.Y., Random House, 1977; Boston, Beacon, 1981)

Passion: New Poems, 1977-1980 (Beacon, 1980)

Civil Wars (Beacon, 1981, 1982)

Kimako's Story (Boston, Houghton Mifflin, 1981)

Nonfiction
Fannie Lou Hamer, biog. (Crowell, 1972, 1975)

Sources: *Author information; Books in Print*, 1978-79, 1982-83; *His Own Where*; *Library Journal*, Dec. 1, 1980; *New York Times Book Review*, Aug. 9, 1981; *Soulscript*.

JOSEY, E(LONNIE) J(UNIUS). State Library Administrator, Social Critic.
Born in Norfolk, Va., Jan. 20, 1924. *Education:* B.A., Howard U., 1949; M.A. (Hist.), Columbia U., 1950; M.S.L.S., SUNY, 1953; L.H.D. (Honoris Causa), Shaw U., Raleigh, N.C., 1973. *Family:* Married Dorothy Johnson, Sept. 11, 1954 (div.); d. Elaine Jacqueline. *Career:* Librn. I, Free Lib. of Phila., 1953-55; Librn. & Asst. Prof., Del. State Coll., 1955-59; Librn. & Asst. Prof., Savannah State Coll., 1959-66; Assoc. in Acad. & Res. Lib., N.Y. State Educ. Dept., 1966-68; Chief, Bureau of Acad. & Res. Lib., Div. of Lib. Development, N.Y. State Educ. Dept., Albany, 1968- ; Founder & 1st Chairman, ALA Black Caucus; V. Pres./Pres. Elect, ALA, 1983-84. *Honors:* ALA John Cotton Dana Award, 1962, 1964; Savannah State Coll. Chap., NAACP Award, 1964; NAACP Natl. Office Award, 1965; Ga. State Conf., NAACP Award, Youth Work, 1966; Savannah Chatham County Merit Award for Work on Econ. Opportunity Task Force, 1966; Savannah State Coll. Lib. Award for Distinguished Serv. to Librarianship, 1967; Journal of Lib. Hist. Award, 1970. *Mailing address:* 120 Old Hickory Dr., Apt. 1A, Albany, N.Y. 12204.

Writings:
Nonfiction

The Black Librarian in America (Metuchen, N.J., Scarecrow, 1970)

What Black Librarians Are Saying (Scarecrow, 1972)

New Dimensions in Academic Library Service (Scarecrow, 1975)

Essays in Honor of Libraries and Librarianship in North America, 1876-1976, co-ed. with Sidney L. Jackson & Eleanor B. Herling, Sch. of Lib. Sci., Kent State U., by ALA for 1976 Centennial (Chicago, ALA, 1976)

A Century of Service: Librarianship in the United States and Canada, with Others (ALA, 1976)

Handbook of Black Librarianship, ed. with Ann A. Shockley (Littleton, Colo., Libraries Unlimited, 1977)

Opportunities for Minorities in Librarianship, ed. with Kenneth E. Peoples, Jr. (Scarecrow, 1977)

Information Society: Issues and Answers (Phoenix, Ariz., Oryx, Neal-Schuman Professional Bks., 1979)

Libraries in the Political Process (Oryx, Neal-Schuman Professional Bks., 1980)

Sources: Author information; *Books in Print*, 1980-81; *Contemporary Authors*, vols. 29-32, 1972.

JOURDAIN, ROSE L. Researcher, Journalist, History Teacher, Editor.
Born in 1925. *Education:* B.A., Lake Forest Coll.; Medill Sch. of Journalism, Northwestern U. *Family:* Div.; one child. *Career:* Journalist, Researcher, Editor, Teacher (Hist.). *Honors:* Distinguished Alumni Award, Lake Forest Coll., 1979; Achievement Award, Intnl. Black Writers, 1979; elected to Intnl. Assn. of Playwrights, Poets, Essayists and Novelists (P.E.N.), 1978. *Mailing address:* c/o Ned Leavitt, William Morris Agency, 1350 Ave. of the Americas, N.Y., N.Y. 10019.

Writings:
Fiction
Those the Sun Has Loved, novel (Garden City, N.Y., Doubleday, 1978; N.Y., Ballantine, 1979)

Nonfiction
Around You, juv. (Glenview, Ill., Scott, Foresman, 1973)

Sidelights: *Around You*, primary social studies book for inner city children; *Those the Sun Has Loved*, a seven-generational historical novel of the free Black tradition in America. [Also has written] television plays, articles, essays, etc. (Author)

Sources: Author information; *Books in Print*, 1980-81.

JUMNINER, BERTÈNE. (French Guianan). Novelist, Playwright, Short Story Writer, Medical Science Professor.
Born in Cayenne, Guyane, Aug. 6, 1927. *Education:* Medical degree, U. of Montpellier, France, 1953. *Career:* (Physician) Saint-Laurent Hospital, Moroni, Guyane, 1956-58, & Institut Pasteur, Tunis, Tunisia, 1958-60; Faculty, Medical Sch., Mesched, Iran, 1966-67, & U. of Dakar, Senegal, 1967-73; Prof., Medical Sch., U. of Picardie, Amiens, France. *Honors:* 1st Prize, French Natl. Radio-TV Org., for play in French, 1970. *Mailing address:* c/o Temple U. Press, Phila., Pa. 19122.

Writings:
(Partial Listing — English Only)
Fiction
Bozambo's Revenge: or Colonialism Inside Out, a Novel, transl. from French by Alexandra B. Warren (Wash., D.C., Three Continents, 1976)

Sources: *Black Writers in French*; *Caribbean Writers*; *Resistance and Caribbean Literature*.

JUST, ERNEST EVERETT. Biologist, Zoologist, Physiology Professor.
Born in Charleston, S.C. in 1883. *Education:* B.A. (magna cum laude, Phi Beta Kappa), Dartmouth Coll.; Ph.D., U. of Chicago, 1916. *Family:* Married; d. Margaret Just Butcher (Eng. Prof., Howard U.). *Career:* Head, Dept. of Zoology, Howard U., 1912-41; Head, Dept. of Physiology, & Prof., Howard U. Medical Sch.; Researcher, Marine Biological Lab., Woods Hole, Cape Cod, Mass. (summers), 1909-30; Assoc. Ed., *Physiological Zoology* (Chicago), the *Biological Bulletin* (Woods Hole, Mass.), & the *Journal of Morphology* (Phila.). *Honors:* 1st recipient of NAACP Spingarn Medal, 1914; V. Pres., Amer. Soc. of Zoologists; name starred in *American Men of Science*, when other distinguished biologists voted him a leader in the field. Died in 1941.

Writings:
Nonfiction
Basic Methods for Experiments in Eggs of Marine Animals (Phila., Blakiston's, 1939)

The Biology of the Cell Surface (Blakiston's, 1939)

Sidelights: "He brought a keen and highly trained mind to bear upon the problem of life, conducting research in fertilization, artificial parthenogenesis, and cell division." (*Negro Builders and Heroes*)
Sources: *Historical Negro Biographies*; *Negro Almanac*; *Negro Builders and Heroes*; *Seven Black American Scientists*.

KAISER, ERNEST DANIEL. Anthologist, Reviewer, Consultant, Editor.
Born in Petersburg, Va., Dec. 5, 1915. *Education:* City Coll. of CUNY; decades of further study. *Family:* Married Mary Orford; son Eric, d. Joan. *Career:* Staff, Schomburg Center for Res. in Black Culture, Harlem (35 yrs.); Advis., Aron Press Ser., "The American Negro: His History and Literature" (wrote introduction for 145 vols.); Reviewer, W. E. B. DuBois papers (3 vols.), U. of Mass. Press, with Herbert Aptheker and Sidney Kaplan (mem., Bd. of Dir., Amer. Inst. for Marxist Studies). *Mailing address:* 3137 95th St., E. Elmhurst, N.Y. 11369.

Writings:
Fiction
A Freedomways Reader, anthology (N.Y., Intnl. Pub., 1978, 1979)

Nonfiction
Black Titan: W. E. B. DuBois, ed. (Boston, Beacon, 1970)

In Defense of the People's Black and White History and Culture, (N.Y., Freedomways, 1970)

The Negro Almanac, co-ed., also pub. as *AFROUSA: A Reference Work on the Black Experience* (N.Y., Bellwether, 1971)

Paul Robeson: The Great Forerunner, ed. (N.Y., Dodd, 1978)

Sidelights: "Has also done some work with L. D. Reddick of Temple University, Philadelphia, on the documentation phase of Alex Haley's Kinte genealogical library project funded by the Carnegie Corporation.... Herbert Aptheker has stated in the American Institute for Marxist Studies *Newsletter* (January-February 1972) that Kaiser 'has the most vast bibliographical knowledge in the area of Black life and history of any person now living.' " (Author)

Sources: Author information; *Books in Print*, 1980-81.

KAUFMAN, BOB GARNELL. Poet.
Born in New Orleans, La., Apr. 18, 1925 (father German, mother from Martinique). *Education:* 6th grade; self-taught. *Family:* Married Eileen Kaufman; son Parker. *Career:* Merchant Marine; Poet; acted in "The Flower Thief," Spoleto, Italy, Film Award for 1960; NET TV "Soul" show (nationwide), "Coming from Bob Kaufman, Poet," 1972-73 (in which Ruby Dee & Ossie Davis acted). *Honors:* Nominated for Guinness Poetry Award for "Bagel Shop Jazz," 1960-61. *Mailing address:* c/o Alfred A. Knopf, 201 E. 50th St., N.Y., N.Y. 10028.

Writings:
Fiction

Solitudes Crowded with Loneliness, poems (N.Y., New Directions, 1965)

The Golden Sardine, poems (San Francisco, City Lights, 1967)

Watch My Tracks, poems (N.Y., Knopf, 1971)

The Ancient Rain: Poems, 1956-1978, co-ed. (New Directions, 1981)

Sidelights: "Was a leading poet during the 1950's ... 'renaissance.' He was influential in the development of white 'beat' poets such as Allen Ginsberg, Gregory Corso, and Lawrence Ferlinghetti. Bob Kaufman had earned great respect for his work in England and France before it became well known in this country." (*Poetry of Black America*)

Sources: Author information; *Books in Print*, Supplement, 1975-76; *New Black Voices*; *Poetry of Black America*.

KAUNDA, KENNETH (DAVID). (Zambian). President of Zambia, Autobiographer.
Born in Lubwa, N. Province, N. Rhodesia (Church of Scotland Mission), Apr. 28, 1924 (son of Presby. minister & tchr.). *Education:* Lubwa Training Sch., 1939-41; Munale Secondary Sch.; (hon.) LL.D., Fordham U., 1963; U. of Sussex, Eng., 1965. *Family:* Married Betty Banda, June 1946; children: two ds. *Career:* Tchr., Lubwa Training Sch., 1944-47 (Headmaster); Boarding Master, Mufulira Upper Sch.; a founder, N. Rhodesia African Natl. Congress, Provincial Organizing Secy., 1953, Secy. Gen. of Party, 1953-58; established Zambia African Natl. Congress & became Pres.; Prime Minister, Zambia; Pres., Zambia, 1964- . *Mailing address:* State House, Lusaka, Zambia.

Writings:
Nonfiction

Black Government?, with Rev. Colin M. Morris (Lusaka, Zambia, United Soc. for Christian Literature, 1960)

Zambia Shall Be Free, autobiog. (London, Heinemann, African Writers Ser., 1962)

Kenneth Kaunda of Zambia; Selections from His Writings, ed. by Patrick Melady (N.Y., Praeger, 1964)

A Humanist in Africa: Letters to Colin M. Morris from Kenneth D. Kaunda (Nashville, Tenn., Abingdon, 1966)

Humanism in Zambia and a Guide to Its Implementation (Lusaka, Zambia Information Services, 1968)

The Riddle of Violence, ed. by Colin M. Morris (N.Y., Harper & Row, 1981)

Sidelights: Kaunda's United National Independence Party scored a victory and he became the youngest Prime Minister in the British Commonwealth—at age 39. When Northern Rhodesia became the Republic of Zambia on October 24, 1964, Kenneth Kaunda became the first president. (*Current Biography*)

Sources: *Books in Print*, 1980-81, 1981-82; *Current Biography*, 1966; *A Humanist in Africa*; *Who's Who in African Literature*; *Zambia Shall Be Free*.

KAYIRA, LEGSON. (Malawian). Novelist, Autobiographer.
Born in Nyasaland (now Malawi). *Education:* Livingstonia Mission Sch., Nyasaland; Skagit Valley Jr. Coll., Wash. State; U. of Wash. (Polit. Sci.); Cambridge U. *Career:* Novelist, Autobiographer. *Honors:* Northwest Non-Fiction Prize for autobiog. *I Will Try*; 2-yr. scholarship, Cambridge U. *Mailing address:* c/o Three Continents Press, 1346 Conn. Ave., Suite 224, Wash., D.C. 20036

Writings:
Fiction

The Looming Shadow, novel (N.Y., Doubleday; London, Longman's, 1968; N.Y., Collier, Macmillan, 1970)

Jingala, novel (Longman's; Doubleday, 1969; Wash., D.C., Three Continents, 1979)

The Civil Servant, novel (Longman's, 1971)

The Detainee, novel (London, Heinemann, African Writers Ser., 1974)

Nonfiction

I Will Try, autobiog. (Garden City, N.Y., Doubleday, 1966; N.Y., Bantam, 1966)

Sidelights: "Lacking funds and passport, but carrying a Bible and a copy of *Pilgrim's Progress*, he set out on foot to journey 2,500 miles across Africa, from Nyasaland to Khartoum." *I Will Try* recounts Kayira's determined struggle to come to and gain an education in America. (*Reader's Guide to African Literature*)

Sources: *Books in Print*, 1979-80, 1980-81; *Reader's Guide to African Literature*; *Who's Who in African Literature*.

KELLEY, WILLIAM MELVIN. Novelist, Short Story Writer.
Born in N.Y.C. in 1937. *Education:* Fieldston Sch.; Harvard Coll. *Family:* Married Karen Gibson; d. Jessica Gibson. *Career:* Has taught at the New Sch.; served as author-in-residence at State U. Coll., Geneseo, N.Y. *Honors:* Dana Reed Prize, 1960, for Harvard writing; Breadloaf Writers Conf. Fellow (Vt.); N.Y. Writers Conf. Fellow; John Hay Whitney Found. grant; for *A Different Drummer*, the Richard & Hinda Rosenthal Found. Award of Natl. Inst. of Arts & Letters. *Mailing address:* c/o Doubleday & Co., 277 Park Ave., N.Y., N.Y. 10017.

Writings:
Fiction

A Different Drummer, novel (N.Y., Doubleday, 1962, 1969)

Dancers on the Shore, short stories (Doubleday, 1964; Chatham, N.J., Chatham Bookseller, 1973)

A Drop of Patience, novel (Doubleday, 1965; Chatham Bookseller, 1973)

dem, novel (Doubleday, 1967; N.Y., Macmillan, 1969)

Dunfords-Travels Every Wheres, novel (Doubleday, 1970; Hastings-on-Hudson, N.Y., Ultramarine, 1970)

Sidelights: Has lived in Jamaica in recent years. (*Dark Symphony*)

Sources: *Black American Literature: Fiction*; *Black Insights*; *Books in Print*, 1978-79, 1980-81; *Cavalcade*; *Dark Symphony*; *Who's Who in America*, 37th ed., 1972-73.

KELSEY, GEORGE DENNIS. Religion Professor.

Born in Columbus, Ga., July 24, 1910. *Education:* B.A., Morehouse Coll., Atlanta, 1934; B.D., Andover Newton Theol. Sch., 1937; Ph.D., Yale U., 1946; Harvard U.; London Sch. of Econ.; Morehouse Coll., D.D., 1970. *Family:* Married Leola Brunnette (Hanks); son George D., Jr., son Everett N. Kelsey (dec.). *Career:* Dir., Sch. of Relig., Morehouse Coll., 1945-48, Prof. of Relig. & Philosophy, 1938-48; Assoc. Dir., Field Dept., Natl. Council of Churches, 1948-52; Guest Lect., 1950-51; Assoc. Prof., 1952-56, Prof. of Christian Ethics, 1956-72; Prof. of Relig. (Amer. Bap.), Drew U., Madison, N.J., Henry Anson Butts Prof. of Christian Ethics, 1972- . *Mailing address:* 5 Cedar St., Madison, N.J. 07940.

Writings:
Nonfiction

Racism and the Christian Understanding of Man (N.Y., Scribner's, 1965)

Social Ethics among Southern Baptists, 1917-1969 (Metuchen, N.J., Scarecrow, 1973)

Sidelights: Addressed World Baptist Alliance in Rio de Janeiro, Brazil, 1960. (Author)

Source: Author information.

KENNEDY, ADRIENNE. Playwright.

Born in Pittsburgh, Pa., in 1931. *Education:* Ohio State U.; Edward Albee's Workshop, 1962. *Family:* Married. *Career:* Instr., Lect., Playwriting, Yale U., 1972-73. *Honors:* Stanley Drama Award, 1963, & Village Voice Obie Distinguished Play Award, 1964, for *Funnyhouse of a Negro*. *Mailing address:* 172 W. 79th St., N.Y., N.Y. 10024.

Writings:
Fiction

The Owl Answers, play (Westport, Conn., White Barn Theater, 1963; N.Y., Shakespeare Festival Pub. Theatre, 1968)

A Lesson in Dead Language, play (1964)

A Rat's Mass, play (1965; Theater Co. of Boston, April 1966)

A Beast's Story, play (1966)

The Lennon Clay: In His Own Write, play, adapted from book by John Lennon (London, Cape, 1968)

Funnyhouse of a Negro, a Play in One Act (N.Y., French, 1969)

Cities in Bezique, Two One-Act Plays: The Owl Answers; A Beast's Story (French, 1969)

Sidelights: Miss Kennedy acknowledges Edward Albee as a major influence; was member of his Playwright Workshop. First production of *The Owl Answers*, at White Barn Theater, Westport, Connecticut, sponsored by Eva Le Gallienne, Ralph Alswang, and Lucille Lortel; directed by Michael Kahn. The Theater Company of Boston performed *A Rat's Mass*, April, 1966. *In His Own Write*, presented by National Theatre in London. New York Shakespeare Festival Public Theatre produced *The Owl Answers*, 1968. (*Black Drama*)

Sources: *Black Drama; New Black Playwrights.*

KENT, GEORGE EDWARD. English Professor, Literary Critic, Literary Consultant.

Born in Columbus, Ga., May 31, 1920. *Education:* B.A. (Eng.), Savannah State Coll., 1941; M.A., 1949, Ph.D., 1953 (both Literary Criticism), Boston U. *Family:* Married Désire Ash; children: Sherald Anne, Edward Austin. *Career:* Prof., Eng., Delaware State Coll., 1949-60; Dean of Coll. & Chairman, Liberal Arts Div., Quinnipiac Coll., Hamden, Conn., 1960-69; Prof. of Eng., U. of Chicago, 1969 to present; Visiting Prof.: Fla. A&M U.; Grambling State Coll., La.; U. of Conn., Storrs; Wesleyan U.; Advisory Ed., Coll. Lang. Assn. Journal; Literary Consultant, U. of Chicago Press, 1970, Macmillan Co., 1971. *Honors:* Fellow, Conf. on African & African-Amer. Studies,

Atlanta U.; Civic Leadership Plaque, State Conf., NAACP, Del.; Distinguished Lect., Natl. Council of Tchrs. of Eng., 1972; Contrib. Ed.: Black Bks. Bull., 1971- ; Negro Lit. Forum, 1971- . *Mailing address:* Dept. of Eng., U. of Chicago, Chicago, Ill. 60637.

Writings:
Nonfiction

Blackness and the Adventure of Western Culture (Chicago, Third World, 1972)

Sidelights: He "has contributed substantial renown as a scholar of Richard Wright." (*Blackness and the Adventure of Western Culture*)

Sources: *Black Voicies*; *Blackness and the Adventure of Western Culture*; *Directory of American Scholars*, vol. II: English, Speech and Drama; *In Black and White*, 3rd ed., vol. 1, 1980; *World Encyclopedia of Black Peoples*, vol. 1, *Conspectus*.

KENYATTA, JOMO [Kamaua Ngengi]. (Kenyan). President of Kenya, Anthropologist, Publisher. Born in Ichaweri, Kenya, c. 1893; a Kikuyu. *Education:* Scottish Presby. mission sch.; (Eng.), Quaker Coll., Woodbrooke, Selly Oak, Eng.; U. of Moscow; London Sch. of Econ. & Polit. Sci., U. of London (grad. diploma, Anthropology). *Family:* Married 1st Edna Clark (Englishwoman), 1943; married 2nd Ngina (d. of Kikuyu chief), four children. *Career:* Pub. newspaper, *Muigwithania*, in Kikuyu, 1920s; helped establish Kikuyu Independent Sch. Assn., 1921; Pres., Kenya African Union (KAU) — Kikuyus, 1947; Pres., Kenya African Natl. Union, 1960; Prime Minister, Kenya, on Dec. 11, 1963; Pres., Kenya, 1964. Died in 1978.

Writings:
Nonfiction

Facing Mount Kenya: The Tribal Life of the Gikuyu, autobiog. & anthropology (London, Secker & Warburg, 1938; N.Y., Vintage, Random House, 1963; reprint, N.Y., AMS, 1976)

My People of Kikuyu and the Life of Chief Wangombe (London, United Society for Christian Lit., 1942; Nairobi, Oxford U. Press, 1966)

Kenya: The Land of Gold (Manchester, Eng., Panal, 1945; n.p., Intnl. African Serv. Bureau, 1971)

Harambee: The Prime Minister of Kenya's Speeches, 1963-1964; From the Attainment of Internal Self-Government to the Threshold of the Kenya Republic (Nairobi & London, Oxford U. Press, 1964)

Suffering without Bitterness: The Founding of the Kenya Nation (Nairobi, E. African Pub. House, 1968)

The Challenge of Uhuru: The Progress of Kenya, 1968-70 (N.Y., Intnl. Publ. Serv., 1971)

Sidelights: Bronislaw Malinowski stated in the introduction to *Facing Mount Kenya*, "The book is one of the first really competent and instructive contributions to African ethnography by a scholar of African parentage." (*Current Biography*)
Kenyatta continued to work for African rights. He was one of the organizers of the Pan-African Federation, along with George Padmore, Kwame Nkrumah and others.
Kenyatta was charged with fomenting the Mau-Mau, which he denied. Despite defense efforts of notable attorneys from England, Nigeria, India and the West Indies, he was convicted on April 8, 1953, and sentenced to seven years imprisonment. (*African Authors*)

Sources: *African Authors*; *Books in Print*, 1979-80; *Current Biography*, 1953; *Who's Who in African Literature*.

KGOSITSILE, KEOROPETSE (WILLIAM). (South African). Poet, Essayist, Critic.
Born in Johannesburg, S. Africa, Sept. 19, 1938. *Education:* Lincoln U.; U. of N.H.; Columbia U.; New Sch. for Soc. Res. *Career:* Visiting Prof.: Sarah Lawrence Coll., Queens Coll., Bennett Coll. (N.C.), N.C. Central U., U. of Denver. *Honors:* Conrad Kent Rivers Memorial Award & Others.

Mailing address: c/o Shakong, 610 W. 115th St., N.Y., N.Y. 10025.

Writings:
Fiction
Spirits Unchained, Paeans (Detroit, Broadside, 1969)

For Melba, poems (Chicago, Third World, 1970)

My Name Is Afrika, poems (N.Y., Doubleday, 1971)

The Word Is Here; Poetry from Modern Africa, ed. (N.Y., Anchor, 1973)

The Present Is a Dangerous Place to Live, poems (Third World, 1974)

Nonfiction
A Capsule Course in Black Poetry Writing (Broadside, 1975)

Sources: *For Malcolm*; *Pittsburgh Courier*, Dec. 7, 1974; *Poetry of Black America.*

KILLENS, JOHN OLIVER. Novelist, Essayist, Biographer, Playwright, Teacher. Born in Macon, Ga., Jan. 14, 1916. *Education:* Edward Waters Coll.; Morris Brown Coll.; Howard U.; Terrell Law Sch.; Columbia U.; N.Y.U. *Family:* Married Grace Killens; son Jon C., d. Barbara E. Wyn. *Career:* Writer-in-Residence, Howard U.; Founder, Chairman, Harlem Writers' Guild Workshop; Writer-in-Residence, Fisk U.; Tchr., Creative Writing, New Sch. for Soc. Res.; Adjunct Prof., Columbia U.; Head, Creative Writer's Workshop, Black Culture Seminar, formerly Natl. Labor Relations Bd. staff; served with armed forces, World War II, Pacific Theater of Operations. *Honors:* Afro-Arts Theatre Cultural Award, 1955; NAACP Literary Arts Award, 1957; Culture, Human Relations Award, Climbers Bus. Club; Citation, Empire State Federation of Women; Cultural Award, N.Y. State Elks; Charles Chesnutt Award, N.Y. Branch, ASNLH; Award, N.Y. Chap. of Links. *Mailing address:* 1392 Union St., Brooklyn, N.Y. 11212.

Writings:
Fiction
Youngblood, novel (N.Y., Dial, 1954, 1966; Athens, U. of Ga., Brown Thrasher Ser., 1982)

And Then We Heard the Thunder, novel (N.Y., Knopf, 1962; N.Y., Pocket Bks., 1971)

Lower Than the Angels, play (staged by Amer. Pl. Theatre, 1965)

'Sippi, novel (N.Y., Trident, 1967)

Slaves, play (produced by Theatre Guild, 1969)

A Man Ain't Nothing but a Man: The Adventures of John Henry, novel (Boston, Little, Brown, 1970, 1975)

The Cotillion, novel (Trident, 1971; Pocket Bks., 1972)

John Henry; or, One Good Bull Is Half the Herd, novel (Little, Brown, 1975)

Nonfiction
Black Man's Burden (Trident, 1965; Pocket Bks., 1969)

Slaves (N.Y., Pyramid, 1969)

Great Gittin' Up Morning; The Story of Denmark Vesey (N.Y., Doubleday, 1972; N.Y., Shamal Bks., 1980)

Sidelights: Blyden Jackson claims, "At the beginning of his career as an author Killens was very clearly an advocate of integration.... Increasingly ... it has been the "black is beautiful" theme, even to the extreme of Black Separatism, which has governed Killens in his affirmation of his art, as well as, indeed, in his conduct as a citizen of the world." (*Contemporary Novelists*)

Sources: *Afro-American Literature: Non-Fiction*; *American Negro Short Stories*; Author information; *Black American Literature: Essays*; *Black Insights*; *Books in Print*, 1978-79, 1981-82, 1982-83; *Contemporary Novelists*, 1972; *To Gwen with Love*; *Who's Who in America*, 37th ed., 1972-73.

KILSON, MARTIN LUTHER. Government Professor.
Born in E. Rutherford, N.J., Feb. 14, 1931. *Education:* B.A. (magna cum laude), Lincoln U. (Pa.), 1953; M.A. (Polit. Sci.), 1958, Ph.D. (Polit. Sci.), 1959, Harvard U.; Postdoctoral, Oxford U., 1959. *Family:* Married Marion Dusser De Barenne, Aug. 8, 1959; children: Peter, Jennie, Hannah. *Career:* Tchg. Fellow, Harvard U., Dept. of Govt., 1957-59; Res. Fellow, Harvard Center for Intnl. Affairs, 1961-72; Lect., Govt., Harvard U., 1962-66; Asst. Prof., Harvard U., 1966-68; Visiting Prof., U. of Ghana, W. Africa, 1964-65; Prof., Govt., Harvard U., 1968- ; Ford Found. Consultant, 1973-74. *Honors:* John Hay Whitney Opportunity Fellow, 1955-56, 1957-58; Ford Found. Foreign Area Grant, 1959-61, W. Africa; Recipient, Harvard Grad. Fellowship, 1953-55; Fellow, Guggenheim Found., 1975-76; Visiting Scholar, U. Chap. of Phi Beta Kappa, 1974-75; Consultant, Fulbright-Hayes Intnl. Exchange Program, 1972- . *Mailing address:* Dept. of Govt., Littauer Center, Harvard U., Cambridge, Mass. 02138.

Writings:
  Nonfiction
  Political Awakening of Africa, co-ed. with Rupert Emerson (Englewood Cliffs, N.J., Prentice-Hall, 1965)

  Political Change in a West African State: A Study of the Modernization Process in Sierra Leone (Cambridge, Harvard U. Press, 1966)

  Apropos of Africa: Sentiments of Negro American Leaders on Africa from the 1800's to the 1950's, with Adelaide C. Hill (Atlantic Highlands, N.J., Humanities, 1969)

  The Africa Reader, co-ed. with Wilfred Cartey (N.Y., Random House, 1970)

  Key Issues in the Afro-American Experience, 2 vols., ed. with Others (N.Y., Harcourt, 1971)

  New States in the Modern World, ed. (Harvard U. Press, 1975)

  The African Diaspora: Interpretive Essays, ed. with Robert I. Rotberg (Harvard U. Press, 1976)

Sidelights: It was said of the *Political Awakening of Africa*, "The excerpts are well chosen from sources not commonly quoted nor easily available, yet they are important not only for the thinking of the authors but also for the groups the latter represent." (*Book Review Digest*)

Sources: *Book Review Digest*, 1966; *Contemporary Authors*, vol. 103, 1982; *Who's Who among Black Americans*, 3rd ed., 1980-81.

KIMENYE, BARBARA. (Ugandan). Short Story Writer, Journalist.
Born in Uganda, c. 1940. *Education:* Locally educated. *Career:* Widely known columnist for a Nairobi newspaper. *Mailing address:* c/o Oxford U. Press, Dover St., London W.I., Eng.

Writings:
  Fiction
  Kalasanda, short stories (London & N.Y., Oxford U. Press, 1965)

  Kalasanda Revisited, short stories (Oxford U. Press, 1966)

  The Smugglers, short stories (London, Nelson, 1966, 1968)

Sources: *African Authors*; *Sturdy Black Bridges*.

KING, CORETTA SCOTT. Lecturer, Civil Rights Leader, Concert Singer.
Born in Marion, Ala., Apr. 27, 1927. *Education:* B.A., Antioch Coll., 1951; Mus. B., New Eng. Conservatory of Music, 1954; L.H.D. (hon.): Boston U., 1969, Marymount Manhattan Coll., 1969, Brandeis U., 1969, Wilberforce U., 1970, Bethune-Cookman Coll., 1970, Morehouse Coll., 1970, Princeton U., 1970, Keuka Coll., 1970; LL.D. (hon.): U. of Bridgeport, 1970, Morgan State Coll., 1970. *Family:* Married Martin Luther King, Jr. (civil rights leader), June 18, 1953; d. Yolanda Denise, son Martin Luther III, son Dexter Scott, d. Bernice Albertine. *Career:* Concert singer debut, Springfield, Ohio, 1948; concerts throughout U.S.; Instr., Voice, Morris Brown Coll., Atlanta, 1962;

Lect., 1st woman to deliver Class Day address, Harvard U., 1968; 1st woman to preach, Statutory Serv., St. Paul's Cathedral, London, 1969; Pres., Martin Luther King, Jr. Memorial Center. *Honors:* Annual Brotherhood Award, Natl. Council of Negro Women, 1957; Louise Waterman Wise Award, Amer. Jewish Congress of Women's Auxiliary, 1963; Woman of Conscience Award, Natl. Council of Women, 1968; Acad. Nazionale Del Lincei, Human Relations Award, Italy; Gallup Poll, Fifth Most Admired Woman in the World, 1968; & others. *Mailing address:* 234 Sunset Ave., N.W., Atlanta, Ga. 30314.

Writings:
Nonfiction
My Life with Martin Luther King, Jr. (N.Y., Holt, 1969; N.Y., Avon, 1969)

Sidelights: "Her particular contribution to the civil rights movement is the freedom concert, inaugurated at Town Hall in New York, November, 1964; since then she has presented ... [many] freedom concerts in which she sings, recites poetry, and lectures, with benefits going to the Southern Christian Leadership Conference, its affiliates, and ... the Martin Luther King, Jr. Memorial Center, Atlanta." (*Contemporary Authors*)

Sources: *Contemporary Authors*, vols. 29-32, 1978.

KING, HELEN H. Teacher, Editor, Juvenile Writer, Free-lance Writer.
Born in Clarksdale, Miss., Oct. 15, 1931. *Education:* DuSable High Sch., Chicago; Wilson Jr. Coll.; DePaul U., Chicago; B.A. (Educ. & Eng. Lit.), U. of Mich., Ann Arbor. *Family:* Div.; son Chad, d. Fenote. *Career:* Tchr.: Pontiac, Mich.; Chicago, Ill.; Roeper City & County Sch. for Gifted, Birmingham, Mich.; Assoc. Ed., *Jet* mag.; Assoc. Ed., *Ebony* mag.; Assoc. Ed. & Free-lance Writer, *The Chicago Courier*, & Ed., "Wee Black World" (children's page); Pres., Let's Save the Children, Inc. (Chicago, textbook pub. co.). *Mailing address:* P.O. 29747, Chicago, Ill. 60620.

Writings:
Fiction
Willy, juv. (N.Y., Doubleday, 1971)

The Soul of Christmas, juv. (Chicago, Johnson, 1972)

Sidelights: Participant (via *Willy*) in Chicago Children's Book Festival, Chicago Public Lib.; Speaker, Jackson, Michigan, Children's Book Festival; Guest Moderator: Merri Dee Show (twice); Speaker, Howard University—all in 1971.

Sources: Author information; *Books in Print*, 1980-81.

KING, MARTIN LUTHER, JR. Clergyman, Civil Rights Leader (Nobel Peace Prize Winner).
Born in Atlanta, Ga., Jan. 15, 1929. *Education:* B.A., 1948, L.H.D., Morehouse Coll., Atlanta; B.D., Crozier Theol. Sem., 1951; Ph.D., Boston U., 1955. *Family:* Married Coretta Scott, June 18, 1953; d. Yolanda Denise, son Martin Luther III, son Dexter Scott, d. Bernice Albertine. *Career:* Began career as Pastor, Dexter Ave. Bap. Church, Montgomery, Ala. Organized & directed boycott of city's buslines, resulting in U.S. Supreme Court's declaring Alabama's bus segregation laws unconstitutional (1956). Organized Southern Christian Leadership Conference (1957), became 1st pres., & remained its leader until his death. *Honors:* Pearl Plafkner for Scholarship, Crozier Theol. Sem., Chester, Pa., 1951; selected one of ten outstanding personalities of 1956, *Time* mag., 1957; Anisfield-Wolf Award for *Stride toward Freedom*, 1958; numerous awards for leadership, Montgomery Movement; Nobel Peace Prize, Oslo, Norway, 1964. Assassinated Apr. 4, 1968, in Memphis, Tenn.

Writings:
Nonfiction
Stride toward Freedom: The Montgomery Story (N.Y., Harper, 1958; N.Y., Ballantine, 1958)

Strength to Love (Harper, 1963; N.Y., Collins, Fount Relig. Paperback Ser., 1977; Phila., Fortress, 1981)

A Martin Luther King Treasury (Yonkers, N.Y., Educational Heritage, 1964)

Why We Can't Wait (Harper, 1964; N.Y., New Amer. Lib., 1964)

Where Do We Go from Here: Chaos or Community (Harper, 1967)

Trumpet of Conscience (Harper, 1968)

Sidelights: "In April and May, 1963, King led a series of massive demonstrations against racial segregation in Birmingham, Alabama.... [His] classic 'Letter from a Birmingham Jail' became a new document in the history of human freedom. Later that year King reached new heights as a national leader with his 'I Have a Dream' speech at the historic March on Washington."

Dr. King won national acclaim for the Black voter registration campaign in Selma, Alabama. "Increasingly in 1966 and 1967 he criticized the American war effort [in Vietnam] and became actively involved in antiwar demonstrations." (*Black Insights*)

He was assassinated in Memphis, Tennessee, April 4, 1968, while leading a garbage collector's strike. A number of books have since been written on Dr. King, his assassination, and his legacy for history. (Compilers)

Sources: *Afro-American Literature: Non-Fiction*; *Afro-American Writing*, vol. 1; *Black Insights*; *Who Was Who in America*, vol. IV, 1961-68.

KING, MARTIN LUTHER, SR. Clergyman.
Born in Stockbridge, Ga., Dec. 19, 1899. *Education:* Morehouse Coll. Sch. of Relig., Atlanta. *Family:* Married Alberta; children: Christine, Martin L., Jr. (dec.), Alfred D. (dec.). *Career:* Pastor, Ebenezer Bap. Church, Atlanta, 1932-?; Past Moderator, Atlanta Missionary Bap. Assn. *Honors:* (Hon. degree) Morris Brown Coll., 1945; Wilberforce U., 1965; Morehouse Coll., 1969; U. of Haiti; named Clergyman of the Year, Ga. Region of Natl. Conf. of Christians and Jews, 1972. Died Nov. 11, 1984.

Writings:
Nonfiction

Daddy King, an Autobiography, with Clayton Riley (N.Y., Morrow, 1980)

Sources: *Daddy King*; *Los Angeles Times*, Nov. 12, 1984; *Who's Who among Black Americans*, 2nd ed., 1977-78, Vol. I, 1978.

KING, WOODIE. Director, Producer, Free-lance Writer, Anthologist.
Born in Ala., July 27, 1937. *Education:* Will-o-way Sch. of Theatre, Bloomfield Hills, Mich. (Theatre Arts), 1958-62; Wayne State U., Detroit (Theatre), 1961. *Family:* Married Willie Mae King; d. Michelle, son W. Geoffry, son Michael. *Career:* Drama Critic, *Detroit Tribune* (Free-lance Writer), 1959-62; Founder-Mgr., Concept-E. Theatre, Detroit, 1960-63; Cultural Arts Dir., Mobilization for Youth, N.Y.C., 1965-70; Consultant, Arts & Humanities, Rockefeller Found., 1968-70; Artistic Dir., Henry St. Settlement, N.Y.C., 1970; Theatrical Prod. *Honors:* John Hay Whitney Fellowship for Dir., 1965-66; Mobilization for Youth film won Venice Festival Award, Oberhausen Award, Intnl. Film Critics Award, A. Philip Randolph Award. *Mailing address:* Woodie King Assoc., 417 Convent Ave., N.Y., N.Y. 10031.

Writings:
Fiction

A Black Quartet; Four One-Act Plays, ed. (N.Y., New Amer. Lib., n.d.)

Black Drama Anthology, ed. with Ron Milner (N.Y., Columbia U. Press, 1972; NAL, paper, 1973)

Black Poets and Prophets, the Theory, Practice, and Esthetics of the Pan-Africanist Revolution, ed. with Earl Anthony (NAL, 1972)

Black Short Story Anthology, ed. (Columbia U. Press, 1972)

Black Spirits: A Festival of New Black Poets in America, ed. (N.Y., Random House, 1972)

The Forerunners, Black Poets in America, ed. (Wash., D.C., Howard U. Press, 1976; paper, 1981)

Sidelights: King produced the following in Black theatre: LeRoi Jones, Ed Bullins, Ronald Milner, and Ben Caldwell in *A Black Quartet*; LeRoi Jones's *Slaveship*; William Mackey's *Behold! Cometh the Vankerkellans*; Ed Bullin's *In New England Winters*; and J. E. Franklin's *Black Girl*.... [Some] motion pictures are: *The Game*; *Ghetto*; *Where We Live*; *You Did It?*; and *Epitaph*. Produced record albums, "The New Black Poets in America" (Motown) and "Nation Time" by LeRoi Jones (Motown). Plays directed at Concept-East Theatre, Detroit: *Study in Color*; *God's Trombones*; *The Toilet & the Slave*; *Who's Got His Own*; *The Connections*; *Zoo Story*; and *Death of Bessie Smith*. (Author)

Source: Author information.

KNIGHT, ETHERIDGE [Imamu Etheridge Knight Soa]. Poet.
Born in Corinth, Miss., Apr. 19, 1931. *Education:* 9th grade; self-educated. *Family:* Married 1st Sonia Sanchez (poet); married 2nd Mary Ellen McAnally; children: 2nd marriage, d. Mary Tandiwe, son Etheridge Bambata. *Career:* Punch Press Operator; Poetry Ed., *Motive* mag., 1969-71; Instr., U. of Pittsburgh, 1969-70; Instr., U. of Hartford, 1970-71; Poet-in-Residence, Lincoln U., Mo., Dec. 1971-72; Contrib. Ed., *Newsletters*, 1973-74; Dir., "Self-Development through the Arts" project in 1973 in Indianapolis on a $2,500 grant from United Presby. Church (community workshops, etc.). *Honors:* $5,000 grant NEA, 1971; Guggenheim Found. Fellow, 1974 ($12,000). *Mailing address:* 3323 W. 33rd Pl., Apt. 4, Indianapolis, Ind. 46222.

Writings:
Fiction
Poems from Prison (Detroit, Broadside, 1968)

Black Voices from Prison, poems (Minneapolis, Pathfinder, 1970)

Belly Songs and Other Poems (Broadside, 1972)

Born of a Woman: Selected and New Poems (Boston, Houghton Mifflin, 1980)

Sidelights: "In 1960 I was given a 20-year prison sentence for robbery. After serving 18 months in jail awaiting trial, I was sent to the Indiana State Prison in Michigan City where I spent over six years, not emerging until 1968. It was during those years in prison that ... I began to write poetry."

Sources: Author information; *Black Voices from Prison*; *Books in Print*, 1978-79, 1980-81; *For Malcolm*; *New Black Voices*; *Poetry of Black America*.

KNOX, GEORGE L. Barber, Realtor, Publisher, Politician.
Born (a slave) in Tenn. in 1841. Migrated to Ind. *Career:* Barber, politician, realtor, all in Greenfield, Ind.; barbershop owner, newspaper publisher, both in Indianapolis; member of Indiana State organization of Republican Party. Died in 1927.

Writings:
Nonfiction
Slave and Freeman: The Autobiography of George L. Knox, ed. by Willard B. Gatewood, Jr. (Lexington, U. Press of Ky., 1979)

Sidelights: *Slave and Freeman* was first published in 1894-95, in the pages of Knox's *Indianapolis Freeman*. (Slave and Freeman)

Sources: *Books in Print*, 1980-81; *Slave and Freeman*.

KUNENE, MAZISI RAYMOND. (South African). Zulu Poet, Professor of African Literature & Language.
Born in Durban, S. Africa, in 1930. *Education:* M.A. (Zulu Poets), Natal U.; Sch. of Oriental & African Studies, U. of London, 1959. *Career:* Head, Dept. of African Studies, U. Coll. at Rome, Lesotho; Dir. of Educ. for S. African United Front; Chief Rep., African Natl. Congress in Europe &

U.S., 1962, Dir. of Finance, 1972; Visiting Prof., African Lit., Stanford U., Palo Alto, Cal.; Assoc. Prof. & Prof., African Lit. & Lang., UCLA. *Honors:* Winner, Bantu Literary Competition, 1956. *Mailing address:* c/o Dept. of African Lit. & Lang., UCLA, 405 Hilgard, L.A., Cal. 90024.

Writings:
Fiction

Zulu Poems, transl. from Zulu by the author (London, Deutsch, 1970; N.Y., Africana, 1970)

Emperor Shaka the Great: A Zulu Epic, transl. from Zulu by the author (London, Heinemann, African Writers Ser., 1979)

Anthem of the Decades: A Zulu Epic (Heinemann, African Writers Ser., 1981)

The Ancestors & the Sacred Mountain: Poems (Heinemann, African Writers Ser., 1982)

Sidelights: Kunene's Master of Arts thesis, "An Analytical Survey of Zulu Poetry both Traditional and Modern," is much quoted and well-regarded. (*Who's Who in African Literature*)

Sources: *Books in Print*, 1979-80, 1981-82; *Emperor Shaka the Great*; *Who's Who in African Literature*.

LACY, LESLIE ALEXANDER. Essayist, Juvenile Writer, Teacher.
Born in Franklin, La., Aug. 8, 1937. *Education:* Private sch.; coll. (New Eng.); M.A., U. of Cal., Berkeley; M.A., U. of Ghana, 1964. *Career:* Tutor, Dept. of Polit. Sci., U. of Ghana, 1964-66; Lect., N.Y.U., 1968-70; Lect., Howard U., 1968-70; Lect., New Sch. for Soc. Res., 1969-70; Tchr., Creative Writing, Fed. City Coll., Wash., D.C.; Operator, Free Sch., Wash., D.C. *Mailing address:* 3200 16th St., Apt. 508, N.W., Wash., D.C. 10010.

Writings:
Nonfiction

Black Africa on the Move, juv. (N.Y., Watts, 1969, 1972)

Cheer the Lonesome Traveler: The Life of W. E. B. DuBois (N.Y., Dial, 1970)

The Rise and Fall of a Proper Negro: An Autobiography (N.Y., Macmillan, 1970)

Contemporary African Literature, with Edris Makward (N.Y., Random House, 1972)

Native Daughter (Macmillan, 1974)

The Soil Soldiers: The Civilian Conservation Corps in the Great Depression (Radnor, Pa., Chilton, 1976)

Sidelights: "Active with political groups embracing 'explicit socialist alternatives to capitalism' while a law student in California ... went to Africa in 1962 and spent four years studying and teaching at University of Ghana, Legon; returned to United States after Ghana's President, Kwame Nkrumah was deposed in 1966." (*Contemporary Authors*)

Sources: *Black Fire*; *Contemporary African Literature*; *Contemporary Authors*; vols. 33-36, 1973; *Native Daughter*.

LADNER, JOYCE A. Sociologist.
Born in Waynesboro, Miss., Oct. 12, 1943. *Education:* B.A., Tougaloo Coll., Miss., 1964; M.A., 1966, Ph.D., 1968, Wash. U., St. Louis, Mo.; postdoctoral res., U. of Dar es Salaam, Tanzania. *Family:* Married William C. Carrington (formerly Ambassador to Senegal). *Career:* Sociologist, Hunter Coll., N.Y.; Assoc. Prof., Sociol., Howard U.; Contrib. & Advisory Ed., *Black Scholar*. *Mailing address:* Sociology Dept., Howard U., Wash., D.C. 20001.

Writings:
Nonfiction

Tomorrow's Tomorrow: The Black Woman (N.Y., Anchor, 1971)

The Death of White Sociology, ed. (N.Y., Random House, 1973)

Mixed Families—Adopting across Racial Boundaries (Anchor, 1977)

Sources: *Books in Print*, 1978-79; *Who's Who among Black Americans*, 3rd ed., 1980-81.

LA GUMA, (JUSTIN) ALEX(ANDER). (South African). Novelist, Free-lance Journalist, Short Story Writer.
Born in Cape Town, S. Africa, Feb. 20, 1925. *Education:* Trafalgar High Sch., Cape Town; Cape Technical Coll., Cape Town; London, Sch. of Journalism. *Family:* Married Blanche Valerie, 1954; 2 children. *Career:* Staff Writer, *New Age Weekly*, 1955-62; City Councillor. Active in polit. movement in S. Africa; arrested for treason 1956, acquitted 1960; proscribed under Suppression of Communism Act, 1962; under house arrest, Cape Town, 1962-66. Free-lance Journalist since exile to Brit. by S. African govt. in 1966. Lived in Cuba. *Honors:* Recipient, Afro-Asian Writers Assoc. Lotus Prize, 1969. *Mailing address:* c/o Hope Leresche & Sayle, 11 Jubilee Pl., London SW3, Eng.

Writings:
Fiction

A Walk in the Night, and Other Stories (Ibadan, Nigeria, Mbari Press, 1962; London, Heinemann Educ. Bks., 1967; Evanston, Ill., Northwestern U. Press, 1967)

Quartet: New Voices from South Africa, short stories (N.Y., Crown, 1963)

And a Threefold Cord, novel (Berlin, Seven Seas Bks., 1964)

The Stone Country, novel (Seven Seas, 1967; Heinemann Educ. Bks., 1974)

In the Fog of the Season's End, novel (Heinemann, 1972; N.Y., Okpaku, 1973)

Time of the Butcherbird, novel (Heinemann, African Writers Ser., 1979)

Nonfiction

Apartheid: A Collection of Writings on South African Racism by South Africans, ed. (N.Y., Intnl. Pub. Co., 1971)

Sidelights: "Bernth Lindfors writes that the most accomplished nonwhite short story writers in South Africa today are Richard Rive and Alex La Guma." (*Reader's Guide to African Literature*)
Lindfors also proclaims, "Alex La Guma is a naturalistic novelist and short story writer who specializes in documenting the misery in which lower-class nonwhites in South Africa are forced to live." (*Contemporary Novelists*)

Sources: *African Writers Talking*; *African Writing Today*; *Books in Print*, 1981-82; *Contemporary Novelists*, 1972; *International Authors and Writers Who's Who*, 7th ed., 1976; *Reader's Guide to African Literature*.

LAMMING, GEORGE ERIC. (Barbadian). Novelist, Critic, Teacher.
Born in Barbados in 1927. *Education:* Combemere High Sch., Barbados. *Career:* Tchr., Venezuelan Coll. for boys, Trinidad; Lect.: U. of W. Indies, Mona, Jamaica (Creative Arts Dept. & Dept. of Educ.); Aarhus, Denmark; Austin, Tex., African & Afro-Amer. Res. Inst., U. of Tex., Tanzania & Australia; Organizer, Barbados Workers' Union, Labour Coll. *Honors:* Guggenheim Found. Fellow, 1954; *Kenyon Review* Fellow, 1954; Maugham Award, 1957. *Mailing address:* c/o Longman Group, Ltd., 74 Grosvenor St., London WIX 0A5, Eng.

Writings:
Fiction

In the Castle of My Skin, novel (London, Joseph, 1953; N.Y., McGraw-Hill, 1953)

The Emigrants, novel (Joseph, 1954; McGraw-Hill, 1954)

Of Age and Innocence, novel (Joseph, 1958)

Season of Adventure, novel (Joseph, 1960)

Water with Berries, novel (London, Longman's, 1971)

Natives of My Person, novel (N.Y., Holt, 1972)

Cannon Shot and Glass Beads; Modern Black Writing, anthology (London, Pan Bks., 1974)

Nonfiction
The Pleasures of Exile (Joseph, 1960)

Sidelights: "Lamming's fiction is rewarding and rich; it struggles with the complexities of the culture of the Caribbean Basin.... His control of language, at a variety of levels and registers and dialects, is powerful and impressive." (*Caribbean Writers*)

Sources: *Caribbean Writers*; *Contemporary Novelists*, 2nd ed., 1976; *Modern Black Writers*; *Resistance and Caribbean Literature*; *Writers Directory*, 1982-1984.

LANE, PINKIE GORDON. English Professor, Poet, Anthologist.
Born in Phila., Pa., Jan. 13, 1923. *Education:* B.A., Spelman Coll., Atlanta, 1949; M.A., Atlanta U., 1956; Ph.D., La. State U., 1967. *Family:* Widow; son Gordon Edward Lane. *Career:* Tchr.; Prof. of Eng., Southern U., Baton Rouge, La.; Poetry Reading: Ill., Okla., Utah, N.Y., La., Miss., Tenn., & Ark. *Honors:* Certificates of Merit: Natl. Writers' Club; The Tulsa Poets; South West, Inc.; Southern U. Lib. Staff; recognized in 1972 as one of "Louisiana Women in the Seventies"; works appear in: the Beineche Rare Bk. & Manuscript Lib., Yale U., James Weldon Johnson Memorial Collection of Negro Arts & Letters. *Mailing address:* 2738 77th Ave., Baton Rouge, La. 70807.

Writings:
Fiction
Discourses on Poetry, ed. (Fort Smith, Ark., South & West, 1972)

Poems by Blacks, ed., anthology (South & West, vols. II & III, 1972)

Wind Thoughts, poems (South & West, 1972)

The Mystic Female, poems (South & West, n.d.)

Sources: Author information; *First World*, vol. 2, no. 4, 1980.

LANGSTON, JOHN MERCER. Lawyer, Public Official, Educator.
Born in Louisa County, Va., Dec. 14, 1829. Son of Ralph Quarles, slave owner, and Lucy Langston, slave. He passed to guardianship of Colonel William D. Gooch of Chillicothe, Ohio (after his parents died). The Colonel left John in care of Richard Long, abolitionist from New Eng. *Education:* Oberlin Coll. (grad. from the coll. & the theol. sch.); studied in law office of Philemon Bliss. *Family:* Married Caroline M. Wall (Oberlin grad.). *Career:* Admitted to Ohio Bar, 1855 (1st Black to practice in West); tried both civil & criminal cases (mostly whites), but some fugitive slave cases; with brother Charles, dominant figure in antebellum Negro conventions; elected several times to township offices, twice to Oberlin council, served 11 yrs. on Oberlin Bd. of Educ.; Supvr., schooling of Negro youth in Ohio; helped recruit black troops in the Civil War; Inspector Gen., freedman's schs.; Dean of Law Dept. & Acting Pres. (of newly established) Howard U.; apptd. Minister-Resident & Consul-Gen. to Haiti, 1877; Pres., Va. Normal & Collegiate Inst.; elected to Congress from Va., 1888. Died in 1897.

Writings:
Nonfiction
Freedom and Citizenship: Selected Lectures and Addresses, ed. by J. E. Rankin (Wash., D.C., Darby, 1983; facsimile ed., N.Y., Arno, Black Heritage Lib. Ser., 1883; Coral Gables, Fla., Mnemosyne, 1969)

The Civil Rights Law, Definition of Citizenship and the Rights Attaching to It (N.Y., Globe, 1884)

From the Virginia Plantation to the National Capitol: Or the First and Only Negro Representative in Congress from the Old Dominion, an Autobiography (Madison, Wis., Amer. Pub. Co., 1894; Humanities reprint, 1969; reprint, Arno, Amer. Negro—His Hist. & Lit. Ser., no. 2, 1969; Millwood, N.Y., Kraus Reprint, 1969)

Sidelights: Langston's father "believed that slaves should be emancipated as rapidly as possible by the voluntary act of owners. Accordingly he manumitted his children. The father was legally estopped from giving his four children by Lucy Langston his name, but he showed solicitude for their welfare, made provision for each of the sons, and was especially interested in John." (*Negro Builders and Heroes*)

Sources: *Books in Print*, 1979-80; *Negro Author in America*; *Negro Builders and Heroes*; *Negro Caravan.*

LANUSSE, ARMAND. Creole Poet.
Born in New Orleans, La., in 1812 of French Creole ancestry. He received an excellent education, and may have studied in France, as did others of his class. *Career:* Served as conscripted Confederate soldier; leader of group of young poets (in New Orleans) writing in French; Prin., Catholic Sch. for Indigent Orphans of Color, 1852-66. Died in 1867.

Writings:
Fiction
Les Cenelles: Choix de Poésies Indigenes (New Orleans, H. Lauve, 1845)

Creole Voices; Poems in French by Free Men of Color, 1st pub. in 1845 (Wash., D.C., Associated Pub., centennial ed., 1945)

Sidelights: Lanusse was one of the most distinguished of a group of free men of color in New Orleans. His *Les Cenelles* was the first anthology of poetry by an American Negro.

Sources: *American Negro Reference Book*; *Early Black American Poets*; *Poetry of the Negro.*

LARSEN, NELLA. Novelist.
Born in the Virgin Islands in 1893. (Her mother was Danish, her father black.) *Education:* Nursing Sch., Lincoln Hospital, N.Y.C. (grad. 1915); N.Y. Public Lib. Training Sch. *Career:* Apptd. Asst. Supt. of Nurses, Tuskegee (Ala.) Hospital (2 yrs.); City Health Dept., N.Y.C., 1918-22; Asst. & Children's Librn., N.Y. Public Lib., until 1926. Date of death unknown.

Writings:
Fiction
Quicksand, novel (N.Y., Knopf, 1928; N.Y., Negro Universities Press, 1969; reprint, Westport, Conn., Greenwood, n.d.)

Passing, novel (Knopf, 1929; Negro Universities Press, 1969; reprint, Salem, N.Y., Ayer, 1970)

Sidelights: "Her novel, *Passing* ... is probably the best treatment of the subject in ... fiction."
"Her first novel, *Quicksand* ... is, perhaps the best of the [Renaissance] period, with the exception of Jean Toomer's *Cane*." (*Negro Novel in America*)

Sources: *Afro-American Writers*; *From the Dark Tower*; *Negro Novel in America.*

LAYE, CAMARA [Kamara]. (Guinean). Novelist, Short Story Writer.
Born in Louroussa, Upper Guinea, Malinké country along Niger River, Jan. 1, 1928. (Son & grandson of goldsmiths.) *Education:* Coll. Poitet, Conakry; Engineering, Automobile Mechanical Sch., Argenteuil, France (Professional Certificate); Conservatoire des Art et Metiers. *Family:* Married Marie Laye; four children. *Career:* Attache, Ministry of Youth, Paris, 1955; Engineer, Guinea; Dir., Study & Res. Center, Ministry of Information, Conakry, Guinea; Institut Francais

d'Afrique Noir (IFAN), collected & ed. folktales of his Malinké people, Dakar, Senegal; Res. Fellow, Islamic Studies, Dakar U. *Honors:* Autobiographical novel (*The Dark Child*) won the famed Prix Charles Veillon, 1954. *Mailing address:* c/o Northwestern U. Press, Evanston, Ill. 60201.

Writings:
(Partial Listing—English Only)
Fiction

The Dark Child, novel, transl. by James Kirkup (N.Y., Noonday Press, 1954; London, Collins, 1955; as *The African Child*, Collins, Fontana Bks., 1959; N.Y., Farrar, 1969)

The Radiance of the King, novel, transl. by James Kirkup (Collins, 1956; Fontana Bks., 1965; N.Y., Collier Bks., Macmillan, 1965, 1971)

A Dream of Africa, novel, transl. by James Kirkup (Collins, 1968; Macmillan, African-Amer. Lib., 1971)

Sidelights: "Considered one of the most important of the francophone novelists from Africa." (*African Authors*)

Thomas Lask of the *New York Times* considered that *The Dark Child* was written for Laye himself, and neither for show nor consumption, and that it was a tender re-creation of African life.

In 1954 Laye's *The Radiance of the King* was published, and considered an ingenious allegory about man's search for God. (*Reader's Guide to African Literature*)

Sources: *African Authors*; *African Writers on African Writing*; *Books in Print*, 1979-80, 1980-81; *Reader's Guide to African Literature*.

LEE, DON LUTHER [Haki R. Madhubuti]. Poet, Black Nationalist, Editor, Publisher, Teacher. Born in Little Rock, Ark., Feb. 23, 1942. *Education:* A.A., Chicago City Coll., Wilson Branch, 1963; DuSable Mus. of African Amer. Hist. Curator Apprenticeship, 1963-67; Roosevelt U., 1966-67. *Family:* Div.; son Don. *Career:* Tchr.: Columbia Coll., Chicago, 1968; Northeastern Ill. State Coll., 1969-70; Tchr., Afro-Amer. Lit., Roosevelt U.; Poet-in-Residence, Cornell U., 1968-69; Instr., Black Lit., U. of Ill., 1969-71; Writer-in-Residence, Howard U., 1971; Morgan State Coll., 1972-73; Founder-Dir., Third World Press, Chicago, 1968; Ed., *Black Books Bulletin*; Founder, Inst. of Positive Educ.; Ed., *Black Pages Series*; Ed., Spec. Pan African Issue, *Journal of Black Poetry. Honors:* Annual Poetry Award, Ellis's Bk. Stores, 1969; Natl. Foundation on the Arts & Humanities (a working & recognition grant), 1970; Black Recognition Award, Howard U. Student Govt., 1973. *Mailing address:* Institute of Positive Educ., 7848 S. Ellis Ave., Chicago, Ill. 60619.

Writings:
Fiction

Think Black, poems (Detroit, Broadside, 1967)

Black Pride, poems (Broadside, 1968)

For Black People, poems (Chicago, Third World, 1968)

Don't Cry, Scream, poems (Broadside, 1969)

We Walk the Way of the New World, poems (Broadside, 1970)

Directionscore: Selected and New Poems (Broadside, 1971)

Dynamite Voices: Black Poets of the 1960's (Broadside, 1971)

To Gwen with Love, ed. with Others (Chicago, Johnson, 1971)

Book of Life (Broadside, 1973)

Minds and Institutions (Broadside, 1973)

Nonfiction

From Plan to Planet: Life Studies: The Need for Afrikan Minds and Institutions, essays (Broadside, 1973)

Sidelights: Lee's new name means: Justice, Awakening, Strong.

"Gwendolyn Brooks has written ... 'Don Lee has no patience with black writers who do not direct their blackness toward black audiences.' He has written, 'The Black writer learns from his people.... Black Artists are culture stabilizers, bring back old values, and introducing new ones.' " (*New Black Voices*)

Sources: *Black American Literature: Poetry*; *Black Insights*; *Black World*, Oct. 1974; *Books in Print*, 1978-79, 1980-81; *Broadside Authors and Artists*; *Cavalcade*; *Jump Bad*; *New Black Voices*; *To Gwen with Love*; *Who's Who in America*, 37th ed., 1972-73.

LEE, ULYSSES. Lecturer, Historian.
Born in Wash., D.C., in 1914. *Education:* Dunbar High Sch., Wash., D.C.; B.A. (summa cum laude), Howard U.; Ph.D. (with honors), U. of Chicago. *Career:* Tchr.: Lincoln U. (Pa.), Virginia Union U., Lincoln U. (Mo.), Morgan State Coll., U. of Pa.; Major, U.S. Army (World War II). *Honors:* Phi Beta Kappa; Rosenwald Fellow; Rockefeller Found. Post-War Fellow. Died in 1969.

Writings:
Fiction
The Negro Caravan; Writings by American Negroes, ed. with Sterling A. Brown & Arthur P. Davis (Hinsdale, Ill., Dryden, 1941)

Nonfiction
The Employment of Negro Troops (Wash., D.C., Office of Chief of Military Hist., U.S. Army, Spec. Studies Ser., 1966)

Sidelights: Lee was in great demand as a lecturer on college campuses. He lectured in Nigeria, in Sierra Leone, and in the Cameroons under the sponsorship of the American Society of African Culture during 1965. (*Cavalcade*)

Source: *Cavalcade.*

LEONARD, WALTER J. Lawyer, University President.
Born in Alma, Ga., Oct. 3, 1929. *Education:* Savannah State Coll., Ga., 1947-50; Morehouse Coll., 1959-60; Grad. Sch. Bus. Admin., Atlanta U., 1961-62; J.D., Howard U. Sch. of Law, 1968. *Family:* Married Betty Leonard; children: Anthony, Angela. *Career:* Asst. Dean & Asst. Dir. of Admissions & Financial Aid, Harvard U. Law Sch., 1969-71; Spec. Asst. to Pres., Harvard U., 1971-?; Pres., Fisk U., Nashville, Tenn. *Honors:* Natl. Bar Assoc. President's Award for Distinguished Serv., 1972. *Mailing address:* c/o Fisk U., 17th Ave. North, Nashville, Tenn. 37203.

Writings:
Nonfiction
Black Lawyers: Training and Results Then and Now (Boston, Mass., Senna & Shih, 1977)

Sidelights: Dr. Leonard conducted a symposium on "The Black Lawyer in America Today" at Harvard University. (*1000 Successful Blacks*)

Sources: *Books in Print*, 1980-81; *Freedomways*, 3rd quarter, 1978; *1000 Successful Blacks.*

LESTER, JULIUS. Activist, Essayist, Juvenile Writer, Folklorist.
Born in St. Louis, Mo., Jan. 27, 1939. *Education:* B.A. (Music & Lit.), Fisk U., 1960. *Family:* Married Joan Steinau; d. Jody Simone, son Malcolm Coltrane. *Career:* Field Secy., SNCC; Columnist, *The Guardian*; conducted weekly radio program, WBAI, N.Y., "The Great Proletarian Revolution," 1968; Photographer, SNCC, 1966-68; Tchr., New Sch. for Soc. Res., "The History of Black Resistance," 1968-70; Co-host, weekly TV program, WNET, N.Y.; Prof., Afro-Amer. Studies, U. of Mass.; traveled in Deep South collecting folk material; Folk Singer; has released two albums. *Honors:* Nancy Block Award, ALA; Runner-up, John Newbery Medal (both awards for *To*

Be a Slave) & *N.Y. Times* Outstanding Book. *Long Journey Home* won: Natl. Bk. Award Finalist (*Sch. Lib. Journal*); Best Books Award, Lib. of Congress, Children's Bks. of Yr.; Child Study Assn., Lewis Carroll Shelf Award. Honorable Mention, Coretta Scott King Award, for *This Strange New Feeling*, 1983. *Mailing address:* c/o W. E. B. DuBois Institute, U. of Mass., Amherst, Mass. 01002.

Writings:
Fiction

To Be a Slave, juv. (N.Y., Dial, 1968; N.Y., Dell, 1971, 1975)

Black Folktales (N.Y., Baron, 1969; N.Y., Grove, 1969)

Two Love Stories (Dial, 1972)

The Knee-High Man and Other Tales (Dial, 1972)

Who I Am, photopoems (Dial, 1974)

Nonfiction

Look Out Whitey! Black Power's Gon' Get Your Mama! (Dial, 1968; Grove, 1969)

Search for the New Land, History as Subjective Experience (Dial, 1969; Dell, 1969)

Revolutionary Notes (Baron, 1969; Grove, 1970)

Young and Black in America, with Rae P. Alexander (N.Y., Random House, 1970)

The Seventh Son; The Thought and Writings of W. E. B. DuBois, ed. (Random House, 1971)

Ain't No Ambulances for No Nigguhs Tonight, by Stanley Crouch, ed. by Julius Lester (Baron, Black Poets Ser., 1972)

Long Journey Home: Stories from Black History (Dial, 1972; Dell, 1975)

All Is Well, autobiog. (N.Y., Morrow, 1976)

This Strange New Feeling, juv. (Dial, 1982)

Sidelights: Lester attended the Bertrand Russell War Crimes Tribunal in Stockholm, and photographed the Vietnam bombing on the scene. (*Afro-American Literature: Non-Fiction*)
His books have been translated into Swedish, Finnish, Japanese, Spanish, and German.

Sources: *Afro-American Literature: Non-Fiction*; *American Libraries*, Apr. 1983; *Books in Print*, 1978-79; *Kaleidoscope*; *Soulscript*.

LEWIS, DAVID LEVERING. Modern French History Professor.
Born in Little Rock, Ark., May 25, 1936. *Education:* B.A., Fisk U., 1956; M.A., Columbia U., 1958; Ph.D., London Sch. of Econ. & Polit. Sci., U. of London, 1962. *Family:* Married Sharon Siskind (bk. clerk) Apr. 15, 1966; son Eric Levering, d. Allison Lillian. *Career:* Lect., Mod. French Hist., U. of Ghana, Accra, 1963-64; Lect., Mod. French Hist., Howard U., 1964-65; Asst. Prof., Mod. French Hist., U. of Notre Dame, 1965-66; Assoc. Prof., Mod. French Hist., Morgan State Coll., 1966-70; Assoc. Prof., Mod. French Hist., Fed. City Coll., Wash., D.C., 1970- . *Honors:* Grants from Amer. Philosophical Soc., 1967, & Soc. Res. Council, 1971; Fellow, Drug Abuse Council of Ford Found., 1972-73. *Mailing address:* c/o Alfred A. Knopf, Inc., 201 E. 50th St., N.Y., N.Y. 10028.

Writings:
Nonfiction

Martin Luther King, a Critical Biography (London, Allen Lane, 1970; 2nd ed., Urbana, U. of Ill. Press, 1978); also pub. as *King; A Critical Biography* (N.Y., Praeger, 1970; Baltimore, Penguin, 1971)

Prisoners of Honor: The Dreyfus Affair (N.Y., Morrow, 1973)

The Public Image of Henry Ford: An American Folk Hero and His Company (Detroit, Wayne State U. Press, 1975)

District of Columbia: A Bicentennial History (N.Y., Norton, States of the Nation Ser., 1976)

The Book of Ford Book (Baltimore, Bookman, 1980)

When Harlem Was in Vogue (N.Y., Knopf, 1981)

Sidelights: Bruce Douglas in *Christian Century*, notes "a young black intellectual has written one of the best biographies of Martin Luther King, Jr., to have appeared.... It is a craftsman's piece of work, carefully researched ... well organized, felicitously written and sober and reflective in its judgments." (*Contemporary Authors*)

Sources: *Contemporary Authors*, vols. 45-48, 1974; *King: A Biography*; *New York Times Book Review*, May 3, 1981; Pub. information; *Washington Post Book Review*, May 24, 1981.

LEWIS, EDWARD. Publisher.
Born in N.Y.C., May 15, 1940. *Education:* B.A. (Polit. Sci.), 1963, M.A. (Intnl. Relations), 1965, U. of N. Mex.; Public Admin.: Georgetown U., 1965-66; N.Y.U., 1967-69. *Family:* Single. *Career:* Admin. Asst., City Mgr., Albuquerque, N. Mex., 1964; Tchr., Intnl. Relations (Peace Corps Volunteers), U. of N. Mex., 1964-65; Financial Analyst, 1st Natl. City Bank of N.Y., 1964-65; Founder, Pub., *Essence* mag., 1970- . *Mailing address:* 300 E. 42nd St., N.Y., N.Y. 10017.

Writings:
Nonfiction
Essence, mag. (N.Y., 1970-)

Source: *1000 Successful Blacks.*

LEWIS, IDA ELIZABETH. Publisher, Editor, Publishing Company Executive.
Born in Malverne, Pa. *Education:* B.S., Sch. of Public Communications, Boston U., 1956. *Career:* Financial & Bus. Writer, *Amsterdam News*, 1956-59; Financial Ed., *New York Age*, 1960-63; Writer, *Life* mag., 1964-65; Writer-Broadcaster, BBC, 1967; Correspondent, *Jeune Afrique* mag., 1968-71; Ed.-in-Chief, *Essence* mag., 1970-71; Pres., Tanner Pub. Co., N.Y.C., 1972- ; Pub.-Ed., *Encore American & Worldwide News* mag.; Pres., Teil House, Inc. *Honors:* Scarlet Key, Boston U., 1956; Journalism Award, Assn. Study of Afro-Amer. Life & Hist., 1974; Citizen of Yr. Award, Omega Psi Phi Fraternity, 1975; Intnl. Benin Award for contrib. to Black people throughout world, 1975; media executive award, Natl. Youth Movement, 1975; Bicentennial Award, *Crisis* mag., 1975. *Mailing address:* (Office) 515 Madison Ave., N.Y., N.Y. 10022.

Writings:
Nonfiction
Encore American & Worldwide News, biweekly (N.Y., Encore Communications, 1975-)

Source: *Who's Who in America*, 39th ed., 1976-77.

LEWIS, SAMELLA SANDERS. Art Historian, Art Professor.
Born in New Orleans, La., Feb. 27, 1924. *Education:* Dillard U., 1941-43; B.S., Hampton Inst., Va., 1945; Pa. State U., 1947; M.A., 1948, Ph.D., 1951, Ohio State U.; Tung-Hai U., Taiwan, 1962; N.Y.U., summer 1965; U. of S. Cal., 1964-66. *Family:* Married Paul G. Lewis; son Alan, son Claude. *Career:* Hampton Inst.; Morgan State Coll., Fla. A&M U.; SUNY; Cal. State U. at Long Beach; Cal. State Coll. at Dominguez Hills; Coordinator of Educ., L.A. County Mus. of Art; Assoc. Prof. of Art, Scripps Coll. (Claremont Colls.), 1970- . *Honors:* Delta Sigma Theta Scholarship, Dillard U.; Hampton Inst. Art Scholarship; Amer. U. Fellow, Ohio State U.; Fulbright—1st Inst. of Chinese Civilization (Taiwan), Travel & Study Grant to Far East—Chinese Art Hist., Lang. & Gen. Civilization; NDEA Post-Doctorate Fellowship for study of Chinese lang. & Chinese civilization; N.Y. State Found. Grant for study of Chinese art hist.; seminars: N.Y.U.; Metropolitan Mus. of Art; Boston Mus. of Art; Harvard U. *Mailing address:* 1237 Masselin Ave., L.A., Cal. 90019.

Writings:
Nonfiction

Black Artists on Art, vol. I, with Ruth Waddy (L.A., Contemporary Crafts, 1969, rev. ed. 1976)

Black Artists on Art, vol. II, with Ruth Waddy (Contemporary Crafts, 1971)

Benny, Bernie, Betye, Noah & John: Five Black Artists (Contemporary Crafts, 1971)

Portfolios on Contemporary American Artists: Raymond Saunders, Floyd Coleman, Elizabeth Catlett (Contemporary Crafts, 1972)

Art: African American (N.Y., Harcourt, 1975, 1977)

Sidelights: Language proficiency: Chinese, French, Spanish; educational specialties: Art History, Asian-African, African-American, and European Humanities, Studio-Painting, Graphics and Sculpture, Art Education. (Author)

Sources: Author information; *Books in Print*, 1978-79.

LEWIS, SIR WILLIAM ARTHUR. (Saint Lucian). Economist, Economics Professor (Nobel Laureate, Economics).
Born in St. Lucia, Brit. W. Indies, Jan. 23, 1915. *Education:* St. Mary's Coll., St. Lucia; B. Commerce, 1937, Ph.D., 1940, U. of London (London Sch. of Econ.). *Family:* Married Gladys Jacobs; d. Elizabeth Anne, d. Barbara Jean. *Career:* Lect., U. of London, 1939-48; Stanley Jevons Prof., Polit. Economy, U. of Manchester, 1948-58; V. Chancellor, U. of W. Indies, Kingston, Jamaica, 1959-63; Deputy Managing Dir., UN Spec. Fund, 1959-60; Spec. Advisor to Prime Minister of W. Indies, 1961-62; Dir., Central Bank, Jamaica, 1961-62; Dir., Industrial Development Corp., Jamaica, 1962-63; James Madison Prof., Econ. & Intnl. Affairs, Princeton U., 1963- . *Honors:* Nobel Prize for Economics, 1979; Consultant, Gold Coast & W. Nigeria (govts.); Econ. Advisor, Prime Minister, Ghana, 1957-58. Hon. degrees: M.A., U. of Manchester; L.H.D., Columbia U.; LL.D., U. of Toronto; Williams Coll.; U. of Wales; U. of Bristol; U. of Dakar; U. of Leicester; Rugers U.; U. of W. Indies. Hon. Fellow: London Sch. of Econ., 1959; Weizman Inst., 1961. Hon. Foreign Mem., Amer. Acad. of Arts & Sci.; Amer. Philosophical Soc. *Mailing address:* c/o Woodrow Wilson Sch., Princeton U., Princeton, N.J. 08540.

Writings:
Nonfiction

Economic Problems of Today (London, Longman's, 1940)

Overhead Costs: Some Essays in Economic Analysis (Winchester, Mass., Allen & Unwin, 1945)

Principles of Economic Planning: A Study Prepared for the Fabian Society (Allen & Unwin, 1949; 2nd ed., London, Dobson, 1965; paper, 1969)

Economic Survey, 1919-1923 (Allen & Unwin, 1949, 1960)

Attitude to Africa (Harmondsworth, Middlesex, Penguin, 1951)

The Theory of Economic Growth (Allen & Unwin, 1955, 1961; also paper, 1955)

Politics in West Africa (Allen & Unwin, 1965)

Development Planning; The Essentials of Economic Policy (Allen & Unwin, 1966)

The Evolution of the International Economic Order (Princeton, N.J., Princeton U. Press, 1978)

Growth and Fluctuations, 1870-1913 (Allen & Unwin, 1978)

Sidelights: Knighted by Queen Elizabeth II, 1963. Widely recognized as eminent authority in interdisciplinary field of economic growth and political and social change in emerging countries. Directs research program in economic development, Woodrow Wilson School, Princeton University.

In 1964, with Sir John Mordecai, Deputy Governor-General, West Indies Federation, undertook study of factors involved in breakup of that Federation in 1962. Installed as Chancellor of Guyana University, Georgetown (honorary), since 1967. Princeton University bestowed McCosh Faculty Fellowship (highest honor University can bestow on members).

"First Black to win a Nobel other than Peace Prize. He was the first president of the Caribbean Development Bank." (*Time*) "Along with Theodore Schultz, 77, an American professor at the University of Chicago, awarded Nobel Prize (for their work on the development of human resources and the struggles of emerging Third World Nations)." (*L.A. Times*)

"Sir Arthur argued that industrial revolution is impossible without an agrarian revolution first," says Mahbub ul Hag, World Bank. (*Newsweek*)

Sources: *Authors and Writers Who's Who*; *Black Heritage*, Mar.-Apr., 1980; *Books in Print*, 1980-81; *Los Angeles Times*, Oct. 10, 1979; *Newsweek*, Oct. 29, 1979; *Time*, Oct. 29, 1979.

LIGHTFOOT, CLAUDE M. Marxist Historian and Analyst.
Born in Lake Village, Ark., in 1910. *Education:* Va. Union U., Richmond. *Career:* In 1930 became active spokesman for the Democratic Party, and was founder of 1st Young Men's Democratic org. in Chicago. Joined Communist Party; headed Chicago-area campaign to free Scottsboro Boys and Angelo Herndon. Became Secy., League of Struggle for Negro Rights. Elected to Communist Natl. Com. Since functioned on both natl. & local levels. *Mailing address:* c/o Intnl. Pub. Co., 381 Park Ave. S., N.Y., N.Y. 10016.

Writings:
Nonfiction

Black Power and Liberation: A Communist View (N.Y., New Outlook, 1967)

Ghetto Rebellion to Black Liberation (N.Y., Intnl., 1968)

Black America and the World Revolution (New Outlook, 1970)

Four Score Years in Freedom's Fight, a Tribute to William L. Patterson on the Occasion of Celebrating His 80th Birthday (New Outlook, 1972)

Racism and Human Survival: Lessons of Nazi Germany (Intnl., 1972)

The Effect of Education on Racism: The Two German States and the USA (New Outlook, 1973)

Human Rights U.S. Style: From Colonial Times through the New Deal (Intnl., 1977)

Sidelights: In Chicago ... "in 1919 he witnessed the race riots.... Banned from the membership in the American Federation of Labor, he was arrested and beaten by police as a result of numerous picket lines and demonstrations. Under the Smith Act, he was sentenced to five years in jail and a $10,000 fine and later reversed by the United States Supreme Court." (*Ghetto Rebellion to Black Liberation*)

Sources: *Books in Print*, Supplement, 1975-76; *Ghetto Rebellion to Black Liberation*; *Human Rights U.S. Style*.

LINCOLN, CHARLES ERIC. Religion Professor, Sociology Professor, Lecturer, Consultant.
Born in Athens, Ala., June 23, 1924. *Education:* B.A., LeMoyne Coll., 1947; M.A., Fisk U., 1954; B.D., U. of Chicago, 1956; M. Educ., 1960, Ph.D., 1960, Boston U.; U. of Chicago Law Sch. (Post Baccalaureate), 1948-49; Brown U. (Post Doctorate), 1964-65. *Family:* Married 1st Lucy Cook, 1961; son Cecil Eric, d. Joyce Elaine; from 2nd marriage: d. Hillary Anne, son Less Charles II. *Career:* LeMoyne Coll., 1950-51; Fisk U., 1953-54; Clark Coll.: Asst. Personnel Dean, Asst. & Assoc. Prof. of Relig. & Philosophy, Admin. Asst. to Pres., Prof. of Soc. Philosophy, Prof. of Soc. Relations, Dir. of Inst. of Soc. Relations, 1954-64; Boston U.: Dir. of Panel of Amer., Human Relations Center, 1963-65; Dartmouth Coll., 1962-63; Brown U., Post-Doctoral Intern, Coll. Admin., 1964-65; Portland State Coll., Prof. of Sociol., 1965-67; Spelman Coll., 1966; San Francisco Theol. Sem., 1966-67; Union Theol. Sem., Prof. of Sociol. & Relig., 1967-73; Vassar Coll., Adjunct Prof. of Sociol., 1969-70; SUNY at Albany, Visiting Prof., 1970-72; Fordham U., Lincoln Center, Dir., African Studies Program U. of Ghana at Fordham, summer 1970; U. of Ghana, Dir. of Africa '70 Program of African Studies, Accra, Ghana, 1968-70; Queens Coll., Visiting Prof., Philosophy & Sociol., 1972; Prof. of Relig. & Sociol., Chairman, Dept. of Relig. & Philosophy Studies, Fisk U.; Adjunct Prof. of Ethics & Sociol., Sch. of Divinity, Vanderbilt U. *Honors:* Carleton Coll., LL.D., 1968; St. Michael's Coll., L.H.D., 1972; John Hay Whitney Fellow, 1957-58; Crusade Fellow,

1958-59; Human Relations Fellow, Boston U., 1958-60; Eli Lilly Fellow, 1959; Res. Grant, Taconic Found., 1960; Postdoctoral, Fund for Advancement of Educ., 1964; Lect., Amer. Spec. Abroad Program (State Dept.), W. Europe, 1965; Art Inst. of Boston, Creative Communications Award for "Distinguished Achievement in Lit.," 1970; Ford Found. Res. Grant, 1970. *Mailing address:* Dept. of Relig., Duke U., Durham, N.C. 27706.

Writings:

Nonfiction

The Black Muslims in America (Boston, Beacon, 1961, 1973)

My Face Is Black (Beacon, 1964)

Sounds of the Struggle: Persons and Perspectives in Civil Rights (N.Y., Morrow, 1967)

The Negro Pilgrimage in America: The Coming of Age of the Blackamericans (N.Y., Bantam, 1967; rev., N.Y., Praeger, 1969)

Is Anybody Listening to Black America? (N.Y., Seabury, 1968)

A Pictorial History of the Negro in America, with Langston Hughes & Milton Meltzer (3rd rev. ed., N.Y., Crown, 1968, 1973)

The Blackamericans (Bantam, 1969)

Martin Luther King, Jr.; A Profile (N.Y., Hill & Wang, 1970)

The Black Church since Frazier (N.Y., Schocken, 1974)

The Black Experience in Religion (N.Y., Anchor, 1974)

Sidelights: Edited C. Eric Lincoln Series in Black Religion (6 titles, 1970-73). Toured Ethiopia as guest of His Holiness Abuna Theophilos, Patriarch of Ethiopian Orthodox Church. (Author)

Sources: Author information; *Contemporary Authors*, vols. 1-4, 1967; *Something about the Author*, 1973.

LITTLE, MALCOLM [Malcolm X]. Black Nationalist.
Born in Omaha, Neb., May 19, 1925. *Education:* 8th grade; self-educated. *Family:* Married Betty Shabazz; six daughters. *Career:* Sentenced to 10 yrs. in Charlestown (Mass.) State Prison for burglary; Black Muslim minister, Detroit; Founder, Black Muslim Temples throughout U.S.; Founder, Org. of Afro-Amer. Unity. *Honors:* Anisfield-Wolf Award for *The Autobiography of Malcolm X*, 1965. Assassinated Feb. 21, 1965.

Writings:

Nonfiction

The Autobiography of Malcolm X, in collaboration with Alex Haley (N.Y., Grove, 1965)

Malcolm X Speaks; Selected Speeches and Statements (N.Y., Merit, 1965)

For Malcolm, ed. by Dudley Randall & Margaret G. Burroughs (Detroit, Broadside, 1967)

Malcolm X on Afro-American History (Merit, 1967)

Malcolm X and the Negro Revolution; The Speeches of Malcolm X, ed. by Archie Epps (London, Owen, 1969)

By Any Means Necessary; Speeches, Interviews and a Letter, ed. by George Breitman (N.Y., Pathfinder, 1970)

Sidelights: "*The Autobiography of Malcolm X* ... is one of the greatest American success stories and most important social documents ever written." (*Black Insights*)

One of Malcolm's comments was: "In the society to which I was exposed as a black youth in America ... for me to wind up in prison was just about inevitable." He also ... remarked: "I believe that it would be almost impossible to find anywhere in America a black man who has lived further down in the mud of human society than I have been; or a black man who has been any more ignorant than I have been; or a black man who has suffered more anguish during his life than I have. But it is only after the deepest darkness that the greatest joy can come; it is only after slavery and prison that the sweetest appreciation of freedom can come." (*Afro-American Literature: Non-Fiction*)

Sources: *Afro-American Literature: Non-Fiction*; *Black Insights*; *Black Voices*; *Forgotten Pages of American Literature.*

LOCKE, ALAIN LEROY. Philosophy & Education Professor, Critic, Essayist (Rhodes Scholar). Born in Phila., Pa., Sept. 13, 1886. *Education:* Phila. Sch. of Pedagogy, grad. 1904; B.A., Harvard U., 1907; Bachelor of Litt. (Rhodes Scholar from Pa.), Oxford U., 1907-10; U. of Berlin, 1910-11; Ph.D., Harvard U., 1918. *Family:* Single. *Career:* Asst. Prof., Philosophy & Educ., Howard U., 1912-16, Prof. & Head of Dept. of Philosophy for 40 yrs.; Exchange Prof., New Sch. for Soc. Res., 1947; Coll. of City of N.Y., 1948; Founder, Assoc. in Negro Folk Educ. *Honors:* Phi Beta Kappa; Corresponding Mem., Academie des Sciences Coloniales (Paris). Died June 1954.

Writings:
Fiction

Four Negro Poets, anthology (N.Y., Simon & Schuster, 1927)

Nonfiction

The New Negro: An Interpretation, ed. (N.Y., A. and C. Boni, 1925; N.Y., Gordon; N.Y., Atheneum, Studies in Amer. Life, 1968; N.Y., Arno, Amer. Negro—His Hist. & Lit. Ser., no. 1, 1968; N.Y., Johnson Reprint, 1968)

Plays of Negro Life; A Source-Book of Native American Drama, with Montgomery Gregory (N.Y., Harper, 1927)

The Negro and His Music (Wash., D.C., Assoc. in Negro Folk Educ., 1936)

Negro Art; Past and Present (Assoc. in Negro Folk Educ., 1936)

Associates in Negro Folk Education, ed. (n.p., Bronze Booklet Ser., 1937)

Critical Temper and Aesthetic Vision: Selected Essays of Alain Locke, ed. with Heffrey C. Stewart (1940; N.Y., Garland, Critical Studies on Black Life & Culture, 1981)

The Negro in Art; A Pictorial Record of the Negro Artist and of the Negro Theme in Art, ed. (Assoc. in Negro Folk Educ., 1940; n.p., Metro Bks., 1969; n.p., Hacker, 1971)

When Peoples Meet; A Study in Race and Culture Contacts, ed. with Bernhard Stern (N.Y., Progressive Educ. Assn., 1942, N.Y., Hinds, 1946; reprint, N.Y., AMS, 1977)

Sidelights: "As a philosopher, writer, critic, scholar in the social sciences, cultural mentor, and editor of *The New Negro*—the Landmark collection of writing which registered the arrival of the 'Negro Renaissance,' Alain Locke was a major force and figure in the development of modern Negro American literature and culture." (*Black Voices*)

"Toward the end of his life, Locke was preparing a study of the Negro's place in American culture, which would have represented his final views.... Margaret Just Butcher completed the study, *The Negro in American Culture* (Knopf, 1956)." (*Dark Symphony*)

Sources: *Blackamerican Literature*; *Black Voices*; *Cavalcade*; *Dark Symphony*; *Who Was Who in America*, vol. III, 1951-60.

LOGAN, RAYFORD WHITTINGHAM. Historian, History Professor. Born in Wash., D.C., Jan. 7, 1897. *Education:* B.A., 1917, M.A., 1929, Williams Coll.; M.A., 1932, Ph.D., 1936, Harvard U. *Family:* Married Ruth Robinson, 1927. *Career:* Head, Dept. of Hist., Va. Union U., Richmond, 1925-30; Head, Dept. of Hist., Atlanta U., 1933-38; Prof., Howard U., 1938- , Head, Hist. Dept., 1942-64. *Honors:* Phi Beta Kappa; Commander, Natl. Order of Honor & Merit, Republic of Haiti; Fulbright Res. Fellow, France, 1950s; NAACP, 65th Spingarn Medal, 1980. Died in 1982.

Writings:

Nonfiction

The Attitude of the Southern White Press toward Negro Suffrage, 1932-1940 (Wash., D.C., Foundation, 1940)

The Diplomatic Relations of the United States with Haiti, 1776-1891 (Chapel Hill, U. of N.C. Press, 1941; Millwood, N.Y., Kraus Reprint, 1969)

What the Negro Wants (U. of N.C. Press, 1944; reprint, N.Y., Agathon Press, 1969)

The Senate and the Versailles Mandate System (Wash., D.C., Minorities Pub., 1945; reprint, Westport, Conn., Greenwood, 1975)

Memoirs of A Monticello Slave (Charlottesville, U. of Va. Press, 1951)

The Negro in American Life and Thought: The Nadir, 1877-1901 (N.Y., Dial, 1954)

The Betrayal of the Negro, from Rutherford B. Hayes to Woodrow Wilson (N.Y., Collier-Macmillan, 1965)

Four Took Freedom: The Lives of Harriet Tubman, Frederick Douglass, Robert Smalls and Blanche K. Bruce (N.Y., Doubleday, 1967)

The American Negro; Old World Background and New World Experience, with Irving S. Cohen (Boston, Houghton Mifflin, 1967, 1970)

Haiti and the Dominican Republic (N.Y., Oxford U. Press, 1968)

Howard University: The First Hundred Years, 1867-1967 (N.Y.U., auspices of Howard U., 1969)

The Negro in the United States, a Brief History (N.Y., Van Nostrand, 1970-71)

W. E. B. DuBois: A Profile, ed. (N.Y., Hill & Wang, 1971)

Dictionary of American Negro Biography (N.Y., Norton, 1983)

Sidelights: Assistant to Carter G. Woodson, Association for the Study of Negro Life and History. (*AFRO USA*)

Developed program for Doctor of Philosophy in History at Howard University. Recently completed *Dictionary of American Negro Biography* with Michael R. Winston. (*Crisis*)

Sources: *AFRO USA*; Author information; *Books in Print*, Supplement, 1975-76; *Crisis*, Nov. 1982; *Negro Caravan.*

LOMAX, LOUIS EMANUEL. Journalist.

Born in Valdosta, Ga., Aug. 16, 1922. *Education:* B.A., Paine Coll., Augusta, Ga., 1942; grad. study: American U.; Yale U. *Family:* 4th marriage, Robinette Kirk, Mar. 1, 1968; stepchildren: William Kirk, Robinette Kirk. *Career:* Asst. Prof. of Philosophjy, Ga. State Coll., Savannah; Newspaperman; Newscaster, WNTA-TV, N.Y., 1958-60; News Writer, "Mike Wallace Show"; Host on TV program, "Louis Lomax," L.A., Cal.; News Analyst, KTTV, L.A.; Syndicated Columnist, N. Amer. Newspaper Alliance. *Honors:* Anisfield-Wolf Award for best book concerned with racial problems, 1960, for *The Reluctant African*; two honorary doctorates. Killed in automobile accident, 1970.

Writings:

Nonfiction

The Reluctant African (N.Y., Harper, 1960)

The Negro Revolt (Harper, 1962)

When the Word Is Given; A Report on Elijah Muhammad, Malcolm X, and the Black Muslim World (Cleveland, World, 1963)

Thailand: The War That Is, the War That Will Be (N.Y., Random House, 1967)

To Kill a Black Man (L.A., Holloway, 1968)

Sidelights: First member of his race to appear on television as a newsman; later became Director of News for WNEW-TV, in New York. (*The Reluctant African*)

Sources: *Negro Handbook*; *The Reluctant African*.

LOMAX, PEARL CLEAGE. Playwright, Poet.
Born in Springfield, Mass., Dec. 7, 1948. *Education:* Howard U., 1966-69; Yale U., 1969; U. of W. Indies, 1971; B.A., Spelman Coll., 1972; Atlanta U. (grad. study), 1972- . *Family:* Married Michael L. Lomax (grad. student & tchr.), Oct. 31, 1969. *Career:* Martin Luther King, Jr., Archival Lib., Atlanta (mem. of field staff), 1969-70; Asst. Dir., S. Educ. Prog., Inc., 1970- ; Writer & Assoc. Prod., WQXI, Atlanta, 1972- ; Hostess/Interviewer, "Black Viewpoints," prod. by Clark Coll., WETV, Atlanta, 1972; Staff Writer, *Ebony Beat Journal*, WQXI, Atlanta, 1972. *Mailing address:* c/o Broadside Press, 12651 Old Mill Pl., Detroit, Mich. 48238.

Writings:
Fiction

Hymn for the Rebels, one-act play (Wash., D.C., Howard U., 1968)

Duet for Three Voices, one-act play (Howard U., n.d.)

The Sale, one-act play (Atlanta, Spelman Coll., 1972)

We Don't Need No Music, poems (Detroit, Broadside, 1972)

Sidelights: Pearl Cleage is quite aware of being a Black Woman. She writes out of her concern and consciousness of that blackness and womanness. (*Contemporary Authors*)

Sources: *Contemporary Authors*, vols. 41-44, 1974; *Poetry of Black America*.

LONG, CHARLES HOUSTON. History of Religions Professor.
Born in Little Rock, Ark., Aug. 23, 1926. *Education:* B.D., 1953, Ph.D., 1961, U. of Chicago. *Family:* Married Alice Freeman; son John, d. Carolyn, son Christopher, son David. *Career:* U. of Chicago: Dean of Students, Divinity Sch., & Instr., Hist. of Relig., 1956-60; Asst. Prof., Hist. of Relig., 1960-62; Assoc. Prof., Hist. of Relig., 1963-71; Prof., Hist. of Relig., 1971-74. William Rand Kenan, Jr., Prof. of Relig., U. of N.C. at Chapel Hill, & Prof., Hist. of Relig., Duke U., Durham, N.C., 1974- . Consultant, *Encyclopaedia Britannica. Honors:* U. Fellow, U. of Chicago, 1955; Guggenheim Found. Fellow, 1971-72; Doctor of Humane Letters, Dickinson Coll., 1971. *Mailing address:* c/o Dept. of Relig., U. of N.C., Chapel Hill, N.C. 27514.

Writings:
Nonfiction

Alpha, the Myths of Creation (N.Y., Braziller, 1963)

The History of Religions: Essays in Understanding, ed. with Joseph Kitagawa (Chicago, Ill., U. of Chicago Press, 1967)

Myths and Symbols: Studies in Honor of Mircea Eliade, ed. with Joseph Kitagawa (U. of Chicago Press, 1969)

Sidelights: Dr. Long was one of the founders, with Mircea Eliade and Joseph Kitagawa, of journal, *History of Religions* and served as one of the editors from 1961 through 1974. (Author)

Source: Author information.

LONG, RICHARD ALEXANDER. Afro-American Studies Professor, Anthologist, Essayist, Critic.
Born in Phila., Pa., Feb. 2, 1927. *Education:* B.A., M.A., Temple U.; Docteur ès Lettres, U. of Poitiers. *Family:* Single. *Career:* Dir., Center for African and African-Amer. Studies, Atlanta U.; Visiting Prof., Afro-Amer. Studies Dept., Harvard U. *Honors:* Fulbright Scholar, France, 1957-58.

Mailing address: c/o Atlanta U., 223 Chestnut St., S.W., Atlanta, Ga. 30314.

Writings:

Fiction

Afro-American Writing: An Anthology of Prose and Poetry, co-ed. with Eugenia Collier (N.Y., N.Y.U. Press, 1972)

Nonfiction

Negritude: Essays and Studies, co-ed. with Albert H. Berrian (Hampton, Va., Hampton Inst. Press, 1967)

Sidelights: As President of the College Language Association, Dr. Long stated, "the contemporary Black Arts and Black Studies movements are devoting attention to the African roots of Black cultures.... Professor Long has made more than ten trips to Europe ... and has traveled extensively in North and West Africa, the West Indies, South America, and Mexico." (*New Black Voices*)

Sources: *Afro-American Writing*; Author information; *New Black Voices*.

LORDE, AUDRE. Poet, Librarian.

Born in N.Y.C., Feb. 18, 1934. *Education:* U. of Mexico, 1954-55; B.A., Hunter Coll., 1959; M.L.S., Columbia U., 1961. *Family:* Married Edwin A. Rollins; d. Elizabeth, son Jonno. *Career:* Lib. Clerk, N.Y. Public Lib., 1955-58; Arts & Crafts Supvr., Police Athletic League, 1958-59; Soc. Investigator, Bureau of Child Welfare, 1959-60; Young Adult Librn., Mt. Vernon Public Lib., 1960-62; self-employed, 1962-65; Head Librn., Town Sch., 1965-68; Poet-in-Residence, Tougaloo Coll., summer 1968; Lect., City Coll., N.Y., 1968-69; Lect., Lehman Coll., City Coll., N.Y., 1968-70; Lect., John Jay Coll., City Coll., N.Y., 1970- . *Honors:* NEA Grant, Poet-in-Residence, Tougaloo Coll., Miss. *Mailing address:* 207 St. Paul's Ave., Staten Island, N.Y. 10304.

Writings:

Fiction

The First Cities, poems (N.Y., Poets Press, 1968)

Cables to Rage, poems (London, Bremen, 1970)

From a Land Where Other People Live, poems (Detroit, Broadside, 1973)

New York Head Shop and Museum, poems (Broadside, 1974)

Coal, poems (N.Y., Norton, 1976)

The Black Unicorn, poems (Norton, 1978)

The Cancer Journal, poems (Argyle, N.Y., Spinsters Inc., 1980)

Chosen Poems Old and New (Norton, 1982)

Sources: *Books in Print*, 1978-79; *Chosen Poems Old and New*; *Ebony*, Mar. 1974; *New Black Voices*; *Poetry of Black America*.

LOW, W. AUGUSTUS. History Professor, Editor.

Education: Lincoln U. (Mo.); Ph.D. (Hist.), State U. of Iowa. *Career:* Prof., Hist., U. of Md., Baltimore County, 1966- ; Ed., *Journal of Negro History*, 1970-74. *Mailing address:* c/o McGraw-Hill, 1221 Ave. of the Americas, N.Y., N.Y. 10020.

Writings:

Nonfiction

Encyclopedia of Black America, ed. with Virgil A. Clift (N.Y., McGraw-Hill, 1981)

Sources: *Books in Print*, 1981-82; *Encyclopedia of Black America*; *Book Review Digest*.

LUCAS, WILMER FRANCIS, JR. Short Story Writer, Playwright-Producer, Editor, Teacher.
Born in Brooklyn, N.Y., Sept. 1, 1927. *Education:* N.Y.U. (Eng. Lit.), 1945-48. *Family:* Married
Cleo Melissa Martin (dec.); son Alain Francis. *Career:* Faculty, New Sch. for Soc. Res., N.Y.C.,
1962-68; Writer-in-Residence, Knoxville Coll., 1968-70; Dir., Black Experience Inst. & Related Spec.
Program, U. of Tenn., 1970-71; Spec. Humanities Consultant & Lect., Educ. Opportunities Plan
Center, U. of Tenn., 1971-72; Instr., Humanities, Div. of Continuing Educ., U. of Tenn., 1971- ;
Founder, Artistic & Executive Dir., Carpetbag Theatre, Inc., Knoxville, 1971- ; Prod.-Dir., "The
Carpetbag Theatre Presents," Radio Station WUOT-FM, Knoxville, 1972- ; Playwright, 1965- ;
Technical Consultant, film "Lord Shango," 1974. *Honors:* Day Found. grant (for Writer-in-
Residency, Knoxville Coll.), 1968-70; NEA Award & Grant (for perpetuation of Carpetbag Theatre,
Inc.), 1973- . *Mailing address:* 1936 Prospect Pl., Knoxville, Tenn. 37015.

Writings:
Fiction

Bottom Fishing: A Novella and Other Stories (Knoxville, Carpetbag Press, 1974)

Patent Leather Sunday: And S'more One Act Plays, collection of 10 one-act plays (Carpetbag
Press, 1975)

The Planet of President Pandora, full-length play produced at U. of Tenn. (1977)

Sidelights: (Other Works) "Afro-American Literature," film strip with companion recording, Educational Dimensions, 1969-70; "Destinations," four contemporary American poets, Essence Recording
label. The following are affiliated with the Carpetbag Theatre, Inc.: Dance Theatre, Writers
Workshop, Artists Workshop, Press, Drum and Bugle Ensemble, Children's Theatre, Film
Associates, Lecture Bureau, and Summer Street Theatre. (Author)

Source: Author information.

LUTHULI [Lutuli], CHIEF ALBERT JOHN MVUMBI. (Zimbabwean/South African). African
Liberation Leader (Nobel Laureate), Autobiographer, Teacher.
Born near Bulawayo, S. Rhodesia, in 1898; grandson of a Zulu chief. *Education:* Groutville Mission
Sch.; Adams Coll.; (Tchr. training) Methodist Inst., Edendale, near Pietermaritzburg, S. Africa.
Family: Married Nokukhanya Bhengu in 1927; seven children. *Career:* Tchr., Adams Mission Station
Coll., 15 yrs.; Chief, Abasemakholweni tribe (5,000 members), 17 yrs.; Delegate, Intnl. Missionary
Council, India, 1938; Rep., Christian Council of S. Africa; Chairman, Congregational Churches of
Amer. Bd.; Pres., Natal Mission Conf., & executive mem., Christian Council of S. Africa; Pres.,
Natal Provincial Div., African Natl. Congress. *Honors:* Nobel Prize for Peace, 1960 (only African to
receive a Nobel Prize). Died on his farm in Natal, S. Africa, in 1964.

Writings:
Nonfiction

Let My People Go; An Autobiography (Johannesburg, Collins, 1962; N.Y., McGraw-Hill, 1962;
N.Y., World Pub. House, 1969; Meridian, N.Y., New Amer. Lib., 1962)

Sidelights: After protesting the Western Areas Removal Scheme, through which Africans lost their
property rights in and around Johannesburg, Luthuli was arrested for high treason (1956). He was
restricted to his home for one year, and banished again in 1959, under the Suppression of
Communism Act and Riotous Assemblies Act. (*Current Biography*)
    The Nobel Peace Committee awarded Lutuli the Nobel Prize, "and surprisingly, he was permitted
to travel to Oslo to accept his award on December 10, 1961!... Lutuli had argued moderately for a
multiracial society with justice for all, but his writings were finally his only way to address the world."
(*African Authors*)

Sources: *African Authors*; *Books in Print*, 1979-80; *Current Biography*, 1962.

McCLUSKEY, JOHN A. Novelist, Teacher.
Born in Middletown, Ohio, in 1944. *Education:* B.A., Harvard U., 1966; M.A. (Eng. & Creative
Writing), Stanford U., 1972. *Family:* Wife & son. *Career:* Tchr. in Ala. & Ind.; Tchr., Afro-Amer.

Lit., Humanities Div., Case-Western Reserve U., Cleveland. *Mailing address:* c/o Random House, 201 E. 50th St., N.Y., N.Y. 10022.

Writings:
Fiction

Look What They Done to My Song: A Novel (N.Y., Random House, 1974)

Stories from Black History: Nine Stories, 5 vols., ed. (Cleveland, New Day Press, 1975)

Source: *Look What They Done to My Song.*

McCORRY, JESSE J., JR. Political Scientist.
Born Dec. 4, 1935. *Education:* B.A., M.A., U. of Mich., Ann Arbor; Ph.D., U. of Cal., Berkeley. *Career:* Asst. Prof., Polit. Sci., Wash. U., St. Louis, Mo. *Mailing address:* c/o U. of Cal. Press, 2223 Fulton St., Berkeley, Cal. 95720.

Writings:
Nonfiction

Black Americans and the Political System, with Lucius J. Barker, 2nd ed. (Cambridge, Mass., Winthrop, 1976, paper, 1980)

Marcus Foster and the Oakland Public Schools: Leadership in Urban Bureaucracy (Berkeley, Cal., U. of Cal. Press, 1978)

Sources: *Books in Print*, 1980-81; Pub. information.

McELROY, COLLEEN J. Anthologist, Poet, English Professor.
Born in St. Louis, Mo., Oct. 30, 1935. *Education:* Ph.D. (Linguistics & Educ./Children's Lit.), U. of Wash., Seattle, 1973. *Family:* Son Kevin, d. Venessa. *Career:* Poet, Artist; Speech Pathologist, Rehabilitation Inst., Kan. City, Mo., 1963-66; Consultant, Projects Upward Bound & New Careers, 1967-69; Asst. Prof., Speech Pathology, Western Wash. U., 1966-72; Prof., Eng., U. of Wash., 1973- . *Honors:* Carnation Tchr. Incentive Award, 1973; Bridgman Scholarship (fiction), Bread Loaf Writers Conf., 1974; Pushcart: Best of Small Presses (poetry), 1975; NEA Creative Writing Fellow (poetry), 1978; Callaloo Creative Writing Award, U. of Ky. (fiction), 1981. *Mailing address:* c/o S. Ill. U. Press, Box 3697, Carbondale, Ill. 62901.

Writings:
Fiction

The Mules Done Long Since Gone, poems (Seattle, Harrison-Madrona Press, 1973)

Music from Home: Selected Poems (Carbondale, S. Ill. U. Press, 1976)

Winters without Snow, poems (N.Y., Reed & Cannon, 1979)

Lie and Say You Love Me, poems (Tacoma, Wash., Circinatum, 1981)

Nonfiction

Speech and Language Development of the Preschool Child (Springfield, Ill., Thomas, 1972)

Sidelights: Colleen McElroy has the following to say: "John Gardner described my poetry as 'a singing instrument, flexible, capable of humor, unwhining pain, and above all, love.' Gwendolyn Brooks has said 'Her language is richly dexterous, yet accessible.' " (Author)

Sources: Author information; *Books in Print*, 1980-81; *Freedomways*, vol. 17, no. 2, 1977; *Music from Home.*

McGAUGH, LAWRENCE WALTER, JR. Art Teacher, Poet.
Born in Newton, Kan., Oct. 11, 1940. *Education:* B.F.A., San Francisco Art Inst., 1971. *Family:* Married Marcy McGaugh; d. Jhana, d. Genesse. *Career:* Art Tchr., Berkeley public schs. *Mailing address:* 2419 Prince St., Berkeley, Cal. 94705.

Writings:
Fiction
A Fifth Sunday and Other Poems (Berkeley, Oyez, 1965)

Vacuum Cantos and Other Poems (Oyez, 1969)

Sidelights: He has had his artwork exhibited in San Francisco, in the Oakland Museum show "New Perspectives in Black Art." (Author)

Sources: Author information; *Poetry of Black America.*

McKAY, CLAUDE. Poet, Novelist.
Born in Sunny Ville, Jamaica, Brit. W. Indies, Sept. 15, 1889. *Education:* Tuskegee Inst., 1912; Kan. State Coll., 1912-14. *Family:* Married & div. *Career:* Apprentice to cabinet maker & wheelwright in Jamaica; Reporter, Workers' Dreadnaught, London; Assoc. Ed., *The Liberator* (under Max Eastman), 1919-22; Researcher, Natl. Catholic Org. *Honors:* 1st Black awarded Medal of Inst. of Arts & Scis. (Jamaica); winner, Harmon Gold Medal Award for Lit. (for *Home to Harlem*). Died in Chicago, Ill., May 22, 1948.

Writings:
Fiction
Songs of Jamaica, poems (Kingston, Jamaica, Gardner, 1912; Miami, Mnemosyne, 1969)

The Dialect Poems of Claude McKay, 2 vols. in 1, facsimile ed., includes vol. 1, *Songs of Jamaica*, and vol. 2, *Constabulary Ballads* (N.Y., Arno, Black Heritage Lib. Collection, reprint of 1912 ed.)

Constabulary Ballads (London, Watts, 1912; N.Y., Gordon, 1977)

Spring in New Hampshire and Other Poems (London, Richards, 1920)

Harlem Shadows: The Poems of Claude McKay (N.Y., Harcourt, 1922)

Home to Harlem, novel (N.Y., Harper, 1928; reprint, Chatham, N.J., Chatham Bookseller, 1973)

Banjo: A Story with a Plot (Harper, 1929; N.Y., HarBraceJ, 1970)

Gingertown, short stories (Harper, 1932; N.Y., reprint, Arno, Short Story Index Reprint Ser.)

Banana Bottom, novel (Harper, 1933; reprint, Chatham, 1971; HarBraceJ, 1974)

Selected Poems, posthumous (N.Y., Bookman, 1953; HarBraceJ, 1969)

Selected Poems of Claude McKay (Harcourt, 1953; Boston, Twayne, 1971)

My Green Hills of Jamaica, poems (Wash., D.C., Howard U. Press, 1975)

Nonfiction
A Long Way from Home, travel autobiog. (N.Y., Furman, 1937; reprint, Arno, The Amer. Negro: His Hist. & Lit., 2nd ser., 1969)

Harlem: Negro Metropolis (N.Y., Dutton, 1940; Harcourt, 1972)

The Negroes in America, ed. by Alan L. McLeod; transl. from Russian by Robert J. Winter (Port Wash., N.Y., Kennikat, Natl. U. Publ. Ser., 1979)

Sidelights: Greatly influenced by an elder brother, a teacher and possessor of a good library, who contributed to his early education. Considered "l'enfant terrible" of Harlem Renaissance. (*Negro Novel in America*)
Led revolt against middle class and identified with the masses. Travelled widely, living in England, France, Russia, and North Africa. (*Broadside Authors and Artists*)

Sources: *Black Insights*; *Black Poets of the United States*; *Black Voices*; *Book of American Negro Poetry*; *Books in Print*, Supplement, 1975-76; *Broadside Authors and Artists*; *Negro Novel in America*; *Who Was Who in America*, vol. 2, 1943-50.

McKISSICK, FLOYD BIXLER. Activist, Lawyer, Organization Executive.
Born in Asheville, N.C., Mar. 9, 1922. *Education:* Morehouse Coll., Atlanta; B.A., N.C. Coll., Durham; LL.B., U. of N.C., Chapel Hill, 1952. *Family:* Married Evelyn Williams, Sept. 1, 1942; d. Jocelyn, d. Andree Y., son Floyd Bixler, d. Stephanie Charmaine. *Career:* Attorney, 1952- ; Counsel, CORE, & Natl. Dir., 1960-68. *Mailing address:* 414 W. 149th St., N.Y., N.Y. 10031.

Writings:
Nonfiction
Three-fifths of a Man (N.Y., Macmillan, 1969)

Black Power and the World Revolution, with W. W. Worthy (N.Y., Harper, 1972)

Sidelights: "McKissick joined Stokely Carmichael in his rallying cry of 'Black Power' during the James Meredith March against Fear in Mississippi.... 'The black masses have not been elevated by the [anti-poverty] program,' McKissick explained. 'As long as the white man has all the power and money, nothing will happen. The only way to achieve meaningful change is to take power.' "
"...'Black power ... means putting power in black people's hands. We don't have any, and we want some. That is simply what it means.' " (*Current Biography*)

Source: *Current Biography*, 1968.

McLLELAN, GEORGE MARION. Poet, Minister, Teacher.
Born in Belfast, Tenn., in 1860. *Education:* B.A., 1885, M.A., 1890, Fisk U.; B.D., Hartford Theol. Sem., 1886. *Family:* Married in 1888. *Career:* Tchr. & Chaplain, State Normal Sch., Normal, Ala.; Pastor, Congregational Church, Memphis, Tenn., 1897-99; Tchr., Eng. & Latin, Central High Sch., Louisville, Ky., 1911-17. Died in 1934.

Writings:
Fiction
Poems (Nashville, n.p., 1895)

Book of Poems and Short Stories (Nashville, n.p., 1895)

Old Greenbottom Inn, poems (1896)

Songs of a Southerner, poems (Boston, n.p., 1896)

Path of Dreams, poems (Louisville, n.p., 1916)

Sidelights: "He is a gentle poet of nature, of the seasons, of birds and flowers and woodland scenes. His work ... possesses a distinct charm. His best poems are collected in *The Path of Dreams*.... He is exceptional in that writing when and where he did, this collection contains no dialect poetry." (*Book of American Negro Poetry*)

Sources: *Book of American Negro Poetry*; *Early Black American Poets*.

McPHERSON, JAMES ALAN. Short Story Writer, Contributing Editor, Teacher.
Born in Savannah, Ga., Sept. 16, 1943. *Education:* Morris Brown Coll., Atlanta, 1961-63, 1964-65 (B.A., 1965); LL.B., Harvard U., 1968; M.F.A., U. of Iowa, 1969. *Family:* Married Sarah C. McPherson. *Career:* Instr., Writing Law Sch., U. of Iowa, Iowa City, 1968-69; U. Instr. in Afro-Amer. Lit., 1969; Tchr., Fiction & Critical Writing, U. of Cal., Santa Cruz, 1969-70; Tchr., Fiction Writing, Harvard U., summer 1972; Contrib. Ed., *Atlantic Monthly*, 1969- . *Honors:* Combined *Reader's Digest*-United Negro Coll. Fund Prize for Lit., 1965; *Atlantic* award for best new story of 1968; award from *Atlantic* to write (what was to become) *Hue and Cry*; Playboy Writing Awards,

1972; Guggenheim Found. Fellow, 1972-73. *Mailing address:* c/o Atlantic Monthly Press, 8 Arlington St., Boston, Mass. 02116.

Writings:
Fiction
Hue and Cry, short stories (Boston, Atlantic-Little, Brown, 1969; N.Y., Fawcett, 1979)

Elbow Room: Stories (Boston, Little, Brown, 1977; Fawcett, 1979)

Nonfiction
Railroad: Trains and Train People, with Miller Williams (N.Y., Random House, 1976)

Sidelights: Ralph Ellison has hailed McPherson as a "writer of insight, sympathy, and humor and one of the most gifted young Americans I've had the privilege to read." (*New Black Voices*)

Sources: Author information; *Black Insights*; *Books in Print*, 1978-79, 1980-81; *New Black Voices*.

MADGETT, NAOMI LONG. Poet, English Professor.
Born in Norfolk, Va., July 5, 1923. *Education:* B.A. (honors), Va. State Coll., 1945; M.A., Wayne State U., 1956; (grad. study): U. of Detroit & Wayne State U. *Family:* Married Leonard P. Andrews, Sr.; d. Jill (Witherspoon) Boyer. *Career:* Tchr., Eng., Northwestern High Sch., Detroit, 1955-68; Assoc. Prof. of Eng., E. Mich. U., 1968-73, Prof., 1973- ; Assoc. Ed., Lotus Press, 1974- ; staff, Writers' Workshop (annual), Oakland U.; participant, Poetry Readings in the Classroom (Mich. Council for the Arts). *Honors:* 1st recipient of $10,000 Mott Fellowship in Eng. at Oakland U., 1965-66; named Distinguished Tchr. of Yr. by Metropolitan Detroit Eng. Club, 1967; one of two Soror of the Yr. Awards, Alpha Kappa Alpha Sorority, 1969; papers being collected at Fisk U.; Spec. collection. *Mailing address:* 16886 Inverness Ave., Detroit, Mich. 48221.

Writings:
Fiction
Songs to a Phantom Nightingale, poems (N.Y., Fortuny's, 1941; Ann Arbor, Mich., U. Microfilms, 1970)

One and the Many, poems (Hicksville, N.Y., Exposition Press, 1956; U. Microfilms, 1970)

Star by Star, poems (Detroit, Harlo, 1965; reprint, Detroit, Lotus, 1970)

Pink Ladies in the Afternoon, poems (Lotus, 1972)

Exits and Entrances: New Poems (Lotus, 1978)

Phantom Nightingale: Juvenile, poems (Lotus, 1981)

Nonfiction
Success in Language and Literature, with Ethel Tincher & Henry B. Maloney (Chicago, Follett, 1967)

A Student's Guide to Creative Writing (Detroit, Penway Bks., 1980)

Sources: Author information; *Black Voices*; *Broadside Authors and Artists*; *Ebony*, Mar. 1974; *Kaleidoscope*; *Poetry of Black America*; *Right On!*.

MAIS, ROGER. (Jamaican). Novelist, Playwright, Short Story Writer.
Born in Jamaica in 1905. *Education:* Calabar High Sch. *Career:* Journalist: *Daily Gleaner & Public Opinion*. Died in 1955.

Writings:
Fiction
And Most of All Man, short stories and verse mixed (Kingston, Jamaica Printery, 1939)

Face and Other Stories (Kingston, Universal Printery, 1942)

The Potter's Field in Public Opinion, play (Jamaica, Dec. 23, 1950)

Atalanta at Calydon, novel (London, Cape, 1950)

The Hills Were Joyful Together; A Novel (Cape, 1953)

Brother Man, novel (Cape, 1954)

Black Lightning, novel (Cape, 1955)

The First Sacrifice in Focus, play, ed. by Edna Manley (Kingston, U. of W. Indies, Extra Mural Dept., 1956)

The Three Novels of Roger Mais (Cape, 1966)

Sidelights: With novelist Mais there is "a split between two competing demands, one social and communal, the other private and artistic." (*West Indian Novel*)

Sources: *Caribbean Writers*; *West Indian Literature*; *West Indian Novel*.

MAJOR, CLARENCE. Novelist, Poet, Short Story Writer, Essayist, Teacher, Editor.
Born in Atlanta, Ga., Dec. 31, 1936. *Education:* Art Inst. of Chicago, 1952-54; Armed Forces Inst., 1955-56; New Sch. for Soc. Res., N.Y.C., 1972. *Career:* Ed., *Coercion Review*, 1961-63; Proof, *Journal of Black Poetry*, 1967-70; *Caw!*, 1967-70; *Dues*, 1972- ; Guest Ed., *Works*, 1972-73; Lect., Creative Writing & Lit., Harlem Educ. Program, 1967; Brooklyn Coll., 1968-72; Cazenovia Coll., 1969; Sarah Lawrence Coll., 1972; Queen's Coll., 1972; Visiting Writer (coll.): Goucher, Skidmore, Bowdoin, Aurora, New Sch., Old Westbury, Orange County Community, Barnard, Marist, Conn.; Visiting Writer (U.): Columbia, Nebraska, Rhode Island, Wesleyan, Wis. State, SUNY (Stony Brook), SUNY (Plattsburgh), 1967-74; Radio: Natl. Public, Pacific; TV: CBS, ABC; Columnist, *The American Poetry Review*, 1973- . *Honors:* James Nelson Raymond Scholarship, Art Inst. of Chicago, 1951; Natl. Council on the Arts Award, 1970; N.Y. Cultural Found. Grant, 1971; recipient of grants from the State Dept. & the Holland Festival in Rotterdam; Major's poetry won the 1976 Pushcart Prize. *Mailing address:* c/o Howard Moorepark, 444 E. 82nd St., N.Y., N.Y. 10028.

Writings:
Fiction

The New Black Poetry, ed. (N.Y., Intnl., 1969)

Swallow the Lake, poems (Middletown, Conn., Wesleyan U. Press, 1970)

Private Line, poems (London, Breman, 1971)

Symptoms and Madness: Poems (Chevy Chase, Md., Corinth, 1971)

The Cotton Club, New Poems (Detroit, Broadside, 1972)

All-Night Visitors, novel (N.Y., Grove, 1969; N.Y., U. Place Bookshop, 1973)

No, novel (N.Y., Emerson Hall, 1973)

The Dark and Feeling: Black American Writers and Their Work (N.Y., Okpaku, 1974)

The Syncopated Cakewalk, poems (N.Y., Barlenmir House, 1974)

Reflex and Bone Structure, short stories (N.Y., Fiction Collective, 1975)

Emergency Exit, short stories (Fiction Collective, 1979)

The Other Side of the Wall, poems (San Francisco, Black Scholar, 1982)

Nonfiction

Dictionary of Afro-American Slang (Intnl., 1970)

Sidelights: Major's works have been translated into German, Italian, French, Spanish, and other languages. (*Emergency Exit*)

Sources: Author information; *Black Voices*; *Books in Print*, 1978-79, 1982-83; *Broadside Authors and Artists*; *Emergency Exit*; *For Malcolm*; *New Black Poetry*; *Soulscript*.

MAJOR, GERALDYN (GERRI) HODGES. Social Commentator, Editor.

Born July 29, 1894. *Education:* Bachelor of Philosophy, U. of Chicago, 1915; Chicago Tchrs. Coll., grad. degree in Educ., 1917; Columbia U.; N.Y.U. *Family:* Married H. Binga Dismond, Dec. 17, 1917 (div. Dec. 22, 1939); married John R. Major, June 6, 1946 (dec.). *Career:* N.Y. Society Ed., *Pittsburgh Courier*, 1924-27; Managing Ed., Interstate Tattler, N.Y.C., 1927-32; Women's Ed., *Daily Citizen*, 1933-34; Administrative Asst., Bureau of Public Health, Educ. & Information, N.Y.C., 1934-46; Women's Ed., *New York Amsterdam News*, N.Y.C., 1948-53; Assoc. Ed., Johnson Pub. Co., N.Y.C., 1953-67, Head of Paris Bureau, 1967-68, Sr. Staff Ed., 1967- ; Dir. of Geraldyn Dismond Bureau of Specialized Publicity, 1924-34. *Office:* Johnson Pub. Co., 1270 Ave. of the Americas, N.Y., N.Y. 10020.

Writings:

Nonfiction

Gerri Major's Black Society, with Doris E. Saunders (Chicago, Johnson Pub. Co., 1976)

Sidelights: Also author of "Gerri Major's Society World," a column in *Jet* magazine.

Sources: *Books in Print*, 1980-81; *Contemporary Authors*, vols. 85-88, 1980; *Gerri Major's Black Society*; Pub. information.

MANDEL, BERNARD. Teacher, Historian.

Born in Cleveland, Ohio, Jan. 4, 1920. *Education:* Ph.D., Case Western Reserve U., Cleveland, 1952. *Family:* Married H. Althea Warner; d. Ann, d. Carla, d. Anita. *Career:* Tchr.; Lect.; Historian. *Mailing address:* 13509 Southview Ave., Cleveland, Ohio 44120.

Writings:

Nonfiction

Labor, Free and Slave: Working Men and the Anti-Slavery Movement in the United States (N.Y., Assoc. Authors, 1955)

Samuel Gompers: A Biography (Yellow Springs, Ohio, Antioch Press, 1963)

Young People's History of the United States (n.p., Rawlings, 1968)

Sidelights: Extensive traveling in Africa. Lectures on the Black experience. (Author)

Source: Author information; *Contemporary Authors*, vols. 1-4, 1969.

MAPP, EDWARD. Library Administrator.

Born in N.Y.C. *Education:* B.A., City Coll. of N.Y., 1953; M.S., Columbia U., 1956; Ph.D., N.Y.U., 1970. *Family:* Son Andrew. *Career:* Lib. Asst., Ref. Dept., N.Y. Public Lib., 1948-55; Asst. Librn., N.Y.C. Community Coll., 1956-57; Tchr. Librn., Bd. of Educ., N.Y.C., 1957-64; Chief Librn., N.Y.C. Community Coll., 1964- ; Reviewer, *Lib. Journal*, served on Middle States Assn. Evaluation Teams; appearance on WPIX-TV, "The Puerto Rican New Yorker," Feb. 1974; Ed. of column "Black Media Beat" in *Movie/TV Marketing*, 1979- . *Honors:* Founders Day Award for Outstanding Scholarship, N.Y.U., 1970. *Mailing address:* Borough of Manhattan Community Coll., 1633 Broadway, N.Y., N.Y. 10019.

Writings:

Nonfiction

Books for Occupational Education Programs: A List for Community Colleges, Technical Institutes, and Vocational Schools (N.Y., Bowker, 1971)

Blacks in American Films, Today and Yesterday (Metuchen, N.J., Scarecrow, 1972)

Puerto Rican Perspectives (Scarecrow, 1974)

Directory of Blacks in the Performing Arts (Scarecrow, 1978)

Source: Author information.

MARAN, RENÉ. (Martiniquean). Novelist, Poet, Biographer, Critic, Government Official.
Born in Fort-de-France, Martinique, Nov. 5, 1887. *Education:* Grad., Lycée de Talance, Bordeaux, France, 1909. *Career:* French Colonial Serv. (Equatorial Africa), 1909-23; Writer. *Honors:* Prix Goncourt, for *Batouala*, 1921; Grand Prix Broguette-Gonin, French Acad., 1942; Grand Prix de la Société des Gens de lettres, 1949; Prix de la Mer et de l'Outre-Mer, 1950; Prix de Poèsie de l'Académie Francaise, 1959. Died May 9, 1960 in Paris.

Writings:
(Partial Listing—English Only)
Fiction
Batouala: A Negro Novel from the French (London, Cape, 1922)

Batouala, novel, transl. by Adele S. Seltzer (N.Y., Thomas Seltzer, 1922)

Batouala, a Novel, transl. by Alvah C. Bessie (N.Y., Limited Editions Club, 1932)

Batouala: A True Black Novel, transl. of definitive 1938 ed. (Wash., D.C., Black Orpheus, 1972)

Batouala, an African Love Story, transl. of definitive 1938 ed. by Barbara Beck & Alexandre Mboukou (Black Orpheus, 1973)

Sidelights: By winning the Prix Goncourt, Maran became the center of world interest, for he is the only author of African blood—even to this time—who ever was so honored. *Batouala* was translated into fifty languages.
In his fiction Maran employs work, hunting, funeral and love songs, as well as lullabies. He also included dances and proverbs, combined with graphic description. "... these 'African' works are among the most documentary and vivid ever written about people from the continent." (*Caribbean Writers*)

Sources: *Caribbean Writers*; *Modern Black Writers*; *Resistance and Caribbean Literature*.

MARGARIDO, MARIA MANUELA. (São Toméan). Poet.
Born in São Tomé in 1926. *Family:* Married Alfredo Margarido (Portuguese poet & novelist). *Career:* Has contrib. to various journals. *Mailing address:* c/o Présence Africaine, Paris, France.

Writings:
(Partial Listing—English Only)
Fiction
Poems in *New Sum of Poetry from the Negro World* (Paris, Présence Africaine, vol. 57, 1966)

Sources: *African Authors*; *Sturdy Black Bridges*.

MARSHALL, PAULE. Novelist, Short Story Writer, Lecturer.
Born in Brooklyn, N.Y., Apr. 9, 1929 (of Barbadian parents). *Education:* B.A. (Phi Beta Kappa), Brooklyn Coll., 1953; Hunter Coll., 1955. *Family:* Son, Evan. *Career:* Staff Writer, *Our World* mag., 1953-56; Lect., Black Lit., numerous colleges & universities, including Cercle Cultural de Royaumont (Paris), Oxford U. (Eng.), Columbia U., Cornell U., Mich. State U., Fisk U., Wesleyan U., Lake Forest Coll.; Lect., Creative Writing, Yale U.; Adjunct Prof. of Writing, Columbia U., & Visiting Scholar to Natl. Humanities Faculty, Concord, Mass. *Honors:* Guggenheim Found. Fellow, 1960; Rosenthal Found. Award, Amer. Acad. of Arts & Sci., 1961; Ford Found. Grant for Poets & Fiction Writers, 1964-65; Natl. Endowment for Arts & Humanities, 1967-68. *Mailing address:* 407 Central Park W., N.Y., N.Y. 10025.

Writings:
Fiction
Brown Girl, Brownstones, novel (N.Y., Random House, 1959; reprint, Old Greenwich, Conn., Chatham Bookseller, 1972; N.Y., Feminist Press, 1981)

Soul Clap Hands and Sing, four novellas (N.Y., Atheneum, 1961; reprint, Chatham Bookseller, 1971)

The Chosen Place, the Timeless People, short stories (N.Y., Harcourt, 1969; N.Y., Avon, 1976)

Praisesong for the Widow, novel (N.Y., Putnam, 1982)

Sidelights: Marshall in *Praisesong for the Widow* "... chose a strong figure for her heroine, a woman in her 60s who had learned to stay her anger and to swallow her grief, making her day of reckoning all the more poignant." (*Los Angeles Times*)

Sources: *Black Insights*; *Books in Print*, 1979-80, 1981-82; *Cavalcade*; *Dark Symphony*; *Kirkus Reviews*, Nov. 15, 1982; *L.A. Times Book Review*, Feb. 27, 1983.

MARTIN, ELMER P. Social Welfare Professor, Social Worker.
Born in Kan. City, Mo., Oct. 31, 1946. *Education:* B.A. (Sociol.), Lincoln U. (Mo.), 1968; M.A. (Sociol.), Atlanta U., 1971; Ph.D. (Soc. Welfare), Case W. Reserve U., Cleveland, 1975. *Family:* Married Joanne Mitchell; two children (previous marriage). *Career:* Soc. Worker, Dept. of Public Welfare, Cleveland; Soc. Worker, St. Louis, Mo.; Prof.: Cleveland State U.; Case W. Reserve U.; Grambling State U.; Morehouse Coll.; Assoc. Prof., Morgan State U. *Mailing address:* Morgan State U., Dept. of Social Work, Baltimore, Md. 21239.

Writings:
Nonfiction

The Black Extended Family: Portrait and Perspective, with Joanne M. Martin (Chicago, U. of Chicago Press, 1978, paperback ed., 1980)

Sources: Author information; *Books in Print*, 1981-82.

MARTIN, HERBERT WOODWARD. Poet, Playwright.
Born in Birmingham, Ala., Oct. 4, 1933. *Education:* B.A., U. of Toledo, 1964; M.A., SUNY, Buffalo, 1967; M. Litt. (Drama), Breadloaf Sch. of Eng., Middlebury Coll., 1972. *Career:* Tchg. Asst., SUNY, Buffalo, 1964-67; Instr., Asst. Prof., & Poet-in-Residence, Aquinas Coll., 1967-70; Asst. Prof. of Eng. & Poet-in-Residence, U. of Dayton, 1970-73; Distinguished Prof., Central Mich. U., 1973- ; poetry reading, coll. & universities, including Breadloaf, Mich. State Apple Blossom Festival, The Enjoyment of Poetry (WEVD radio); Classical & Folk Singer; Spec., 16th & 17th Century lit. & drama (directing, technicalities, acting, & critical readings of plays). *Honors:* Scholarships in poetry: Antioch Coll., U. of Colo., Breadloaf Sch. of Middlebury Coll.; Fellow in Drama, Wagner Coll.; Fellow in Eng.: SUNY, Breadloaf Sch. of Eng. *Mailing address:* c/o Lotus Press, P.O. Box 601, Coll. Park Station, Detroit, Mich. 48221.

Writings:
Fiction

Three Garbage Cans, a Play (1969)

New York the Nine Million and Other Poems (Grand Rapids, Mich., Abracadabra Press, 1969)

The Shit-Storm Poems (Grand Rapids, Pilot Press, 1973)

The Persistence of the Flesh, poems (Detroit, Lotus, 1976)

The Forms of Silence, poems (Lotus, 1980)

Nonfiction

Paul Laurence Dunbar, a Singer of Songs (Columbus, State Lib. of Ohio, 1979)

Sources: *Books in Print*, 1979-80, 1980-81; *Poetry of Black America*.

MARTIN, JOANNE MITCHELL. Teacher.
Born in Yulee, Fla., June 12, 1947. *Education:* B.A. (French), Fla. A&M U., Tallahassee, 1968; M.A. (French), Atlanta U., 1971; M.A. (Reading), Case W. Reserve U., 1976. *Family:* Married

Elmer P. Martin. *Career:* Tchr.: Wash. High Sch., Blakely, Ga.; Fernandina Beach High Sch., Fla.; Grambling Coll., La.; E. Cleveland High Sch., Ohio; Volunteer Reading, Baltimore Urban League. *Mailing address:* 3105A Woodford Pl., Baltimore, Md. 21207.

Writings:

Nonfiction

The Black Extended Family: Portrait and Perspective, with Elmer P. Martin (Chicago, U. of Chicago Press, 1978, paperback ed., 1980)

Sources: Author information; *Books in Print*, 1981-82.

MARTIN, LOUIS E. Publisher, Editor.
Born in Shelbyville, Tenn., Nov. 18, 1912. *Education:* B.A., 1934, M.S., U. of Mich.; D. Litt., Wilberforce U., 1951. *Family:* Married Gertrude Scott, Jan. 2, 1937; d. Gertrude, d. Anita, d. Toni, d. Linda, d. Lisa. *Career:* Ed.-Pub., *Michigan Chronicle*, Detroit, 1936- ; Ed.-in-Chief, *Chicago Defender*, 1947- ; Dir., Fed. Savings Loan Assn. of Chicago, 1950- ; Secy.-Treasurer, *New York Age* Pub. Corp., 1952-60; V. Pres., Defender Pub.; V. Pres., Dir., Guaranty Life Insurance Co., Ga. *Mailing address:* c/o Chicago Defender, 2400 Mich. Ave., Chicago, Ill. 60616.

Writings:

Nonfiction

Michigan Chronicle, newspaper (Detroit, 1936-)

Chicago Defender, newspaper (1947-)

New York Age, newspaper (1952-60)

Sources: *Negro Handbook*; *Who's Who in the American Negro Press*.

MATHIS, SHARON BELL. Teacher, Juvenile Writer, Columnist.
Born in Atlantic City, N.J., Feb. 16, 1937. *Education:* B.A., Morgan State Coll., Baltimore, 1958; M.S.L.S., Catholic U., 1974. *Family:* Married Leroy F. Mathis; d. Sherie, d. Stacy, d. Stephanie. *Career:* Spec. Educ. Tchr., Stuart Jr. High; Writer-in-Residence, Howard U., 1972-74; Columnist, "Ebony Jrs.! Speak," *Ebony Jr.!* mag.; former Head, Children's Div., D.C. Black Writers' Workshop. *Honors:* Council on Interracial Bks. for Children Award for *Sidewalk Story*; Coretta Scott King Award for *Ray Charles*; ALA Notable Bk. of 1972 for *Teacup Full of Roses*. *Mailing address:* 1274 Palmer Rd., Oxon Hill, Md. 20022.

Writings:

Fiction

Brooklyn Story, juv. (N.Y., Hill & Wang, 1970)

Sidewalk Story, juv. (N.Y., Viking, 1971)

Teacup Full of Roses, juv. (Viking, 1972; Boston, G. K. Hall, 1972)

Listen for the Fig Tree, juv. (Viking, 1974; N.Y., Avon, 1974)

The Hundred Penny Box, juv. (Viking, 1975)

Nonfiction

Ray Charles, juv. (N.Y., Crowell, 1973)

Sources: Author information; Pub. information.

MATNEY, WILLIAM C., JR. Editor, Journalist.
Born in Bluefield, W. Va., Sept. 2, 1924. *Education:* B.A., U. of Mich., 1946. *Family:* Widower; children: Alma, Angelique, William III. *Career:* Reporter, Sports Ed., City Ed., Managing Ed., *Mich. Chronicle*, 1946-61; 1st Black executive secy., Mich. State Athletic Assn., 1950-61; Natl.

Mays, Benjamin Elijah / 191

Acad. TV Arts & Scis., 1st Black reporter, *Detroit News*, 1960-63; TV & Radio reporter, WMAQ-NBC, 1963-65; 1st Black network news coordinator, NBC News, 1965-70; 1st Black correspondent permanently assigned to White House to cover Presidential candidate, TV Network News, 1970-72; ABC Network News, 1972-78; Ed., *Who's Who among Black Americans*, 1974- . *Honors:* Natl. Achievement Award, Lincoln U., 1966; Man of Yr., Intnl. Pioneers, 1966; Outstanding Achievement Citation, Natl. TV Arts & Scis., 1967; Hon. Dr. Journalism, Benedict Coll., 1973; Outstanding TV Correspondent, Women in the Media, 1977; Outstanding Natl. Serv. Award, Mich. Minority Bus. Enterprise Assn. *Mailing address:* 1124 Connecticut Ave., N.W., Wash., D.C. 20036.

Writings:
   Nonfiction
   Who's Who among Black Americans, 1st-3rd eds., ed. (Lake Forest, Ill., Who's Who among Black Amer., Inc. 1976-81)

Sources: *Books in Print*, 1980-81; *Who's Who among Black Americans.*

MAYFIELD, JULIAN. Novelist, Essayist, Editor, Actor.
   Born in Greer, S.C., June 6, 1928. *Education:* Dunbar High Sch., Wash., D.C.; Lincoln U. (Pa.). *Family:* Married Ana Livia Cordero (physician); son Rafael Ariel, son Emiliano Kwesi. *Career:* Actor, Broadway play, *Lost in the Stars*; Ed. & Theater Reviewer, *Puerto Rico World Journal*; Ed., *African Review*, Accra, Ghana; Pub., *Living Ghana*, in collaboration with Leslie Lacy (1966); Tchg. Fellow, Cornell U.; worked for Guyana govt. (S. Amer.)—edited newspaper, information arm of country's admin. *Mailing address:* Chaka Farm, R.F.D. 2, Spencer, N.Y. 14883.

Writings:
   Fiction
   The Hit; A Novel (N.Y., Vanguard, 1957; London, M. Joseph, 1959)

   The Long Night, novel (Vanguard, 1958)

   The Grand Parade, novel (Vanguard, 1961)

   Nowhere Street, original title, *The Grand Parade* (N.Y., Paperback Lib., 1961)

   Ten Times Black: Stories from the Black Experience (N.Y., Bantam, 1972)

   Nonfiction
   Selections from the Papers of the Accra Assembly, ed. (Accra, The Secretariat of the Accra Assembly, 1963)

Sidelights: *Uptight*, screenplay with Ruby Dee and Jules Dassin, 1968. Has spent many years in both Africa and Europe. His works have been translated into French, Japanese, Czech, and German. He has reviewed, written, produced, and directed plays, as well as acted in them. (*AFRO USA*)

Sources: *AFRO USA*; *Books in Print*, Supplement, 1975-76; *Dark Symphony*; *From the Dark Tower.*

MAYS, BENJAMIN ELIJAH. College President, Theologian.
   Born in Epworth, S.C., Aug. 1, 1894. *Education:* High Sch. Dept., S.C. State Coll. (valedictorian), 1916; B.A. (with honors), Bates Coll., Lewiston, Maine, 1920; M.A., 1925, Ph.D., 1935, U. of Chicago; 37 hon. doctorates. *Family:* Widower (Sadie G. Mays). *Career:* Tchr., Higher Mathematics, Morehouse Coll.; Pastor, Shiloh Bap., 1921-24; Eng. Instr., State Coll., Orangeburg, S.C., 1925-28; Natl. Student Secy., YMCA, 1928-30; Study Dir., Negro churches, U.S.A. (Inst. of Soc. & Religious Res.), 1930-32; Dean, Sch. of Relig., Howard U., 1934-40; Pres., Morehouse Coll., Atlanta, 1940-67; Pres. Emeritus, 1967- . *Honors:* V. Pres., Fed. Council of Churches of Christ in America, 1944-46; Alumnus of the Yr., Divinity Sch., U. of Chicago, 1949; Pres., United Negro Coll. Fund, 1958-61; Apptd. Advisory Council, Peace Corps, 1961; recipient of Christian Culture Award, Assumption U., Windsor, Ontario, Can., 1961; U.S. Rep., State Funeral, Pope John XXIII, Rome, 1963; Peace Corps Rep., All-African Conf. on Educ., Addis Ababa, Ethiopia, 1961; Man of

the Yr. Award, Soc. for Advancement of Management, Greenville, S.C., 1968; Award of Achievement, Black Educ. Serv., Chicago, 1970; Relig. Leaders Award, Natl. Conf. of Christians & Jews, 1970; and Others. Died Apr. 4, 1984.

Writings:
Nonfiction

The Negro's Church, co-author (N.Y., Inst. of Soc. & Relig. Res., 1933; N.Y., Arno, 1969)

The Negro's God as Reflected in His Literature (Boston, Chapman-Grimes, 1938; N.Y., Atheneum, 1938; N.Y., Russell, 1968)

Seeking to Be Christian in Race Relations (N.Y., Friendship Press, 1946, 1952, 1957)

A Gospel for the Social Awakening (N.Y., Assn. Press, 1950)

Disturbed about Man (Richmond, John Knox Press, 1969)

Born to Rebel, autobiog. (N.Y., SCribner's, 1971)

Sidelights: Elected to Atlanta Board of Education, 1969 (elected President, 1970, reelected President, 1971-74, reelected to Board, 1974-78. (Representative) World Conference of Young Men's Christian Association, Mysore, India, 1937; Young Men's Association of America, Plenary Session World Committee, Stockholm, Sweden, 1938; Oxford Conference on Church, Community and State, Oxford U., England, 1937.

Sources: Author information; *Negro Handbook*; Pub. information.

MAYS, JAMES ARTHUR. Cardiologist, Novelist.
Born in Pine Bluff, Ark., May 1, 1939. *Education:* B.S. (pre-medicine), U. of Ark. at Pine Bluff, 1960; B.S. (Medicine) & M.D., U. of Ark. Medical Center, 1965. *Family:* Married Lovella Geans (Project Headstart Tchr.), July 15, 1962; children: James Arthur, Jr., James Earl, James Ornett. *Carrer:* Intern, Queen of Angels Hospital, L.A., 1965-66; Resident in Internal Medicine, Wadsworth Veterans Admin. Hospital, L.A., 1968-70; Fellow in Cardiology, Long Beach Veterans Admin. Hospital & U. Cal., Irvine, 1970-72; Acting Chief of Cardiology, Martin L. King, Jr., Gen. Hospital, L.A., 1972-78; Asst. Prof. of Medicine, Charles R. Drew Medical Sch., U. S. Cal., 1972- ; Co-Founder & Medical Dir., United High Blood Pressure Found., 1974- ; Executive Secy., West Coast Medical Management, 1970- ; Member, Bd. of Dir., Cherkey Stroke Program, 1974- . *Home:* 19808 Galway Ave., Carson, Cal. 90247.

Writings:
Fiction

Mercy Is King, novel (L.A., Crescent, 1975)

Chameleon, novel (Crescent, 1978)

Sidelights: Dr. Mays is a nationally recognized authority on the subject of high blood pressure. (Cal. Librns. Black Caucus, Brochure)

Sources: *Contemporary Authors*, vols. 57-60, 1976; "Second Annual Authors Autograph Party," 1975.

M'BAYE, ANNETTE. (Senegalese). Poet.
Born in Senegal c. 1940. *Education:* Locally educated. *Mailing address:* c/o Présence Africaine, Paris, France.

Writings:
(Partial Listing—English Only)
Fiction

Poems in *New Sum of Poetry from the Negro World* (Paris, Présence Africaine, vol. 57, 1966)

Sources: *African Authors*; *Sturdy Black Bridges*.

MBITI, JOHN SAMUEL. (Kenyan). Kikamba Poet, Religious Studies Professor, Theologian.
Born in Kitui, Kamba country, Kenya, Nov. 30, 1931. *Education:* Alliance High Sch.; B.A.,
Makerere Coll., Uganda; A.B., Th.B., Barrington Coll., R.I.; Ph.D., Cambridge U. *Family:*
Married; two children. *Career:* Prof., Relig. Studies, & Head, Dept. of Relig. Studies & Philosophy,
Makerere Coll., 1964- . *Honors:* Hon. L.H.D., Barrington Coll., R.I., 1973. *Mailing address:* c/o
Oxford U. Press, 200 Madison Ave., N.Y., N.Y. 10016.

Writings:
  Fiction
  Akamba Stories, folklore, transl. & ed. (Oxford, Clarendon Press, 1966)

  Poems of Nature and Faith (Nairobi, E. African Pub. House, Poets of Africa Ser., 1969)

  Nonfiction
  M. and His Story, biog. (London, Nelson, 1954, 1958)

  English-Kamba Vocabulary (Nairobi, E. Africa Lit. Bureau, 1959)

  African Religions and Philosophy (N.Y., Doubleday-Anchor, 1969, 1970; N.Y., Praeger, 1969)

  Concepts of God in Africa (London, S.P.C.K., 1970; Praeger, 1970)

  New Testament Eschatology in an African Background (London, Oxford U. Press, 1971)

  The Crisis of Mission in Africa (Merkono, Uganda Church Press, 1971)

  Love and Marriage in Africa (London, Longman's, 1973)

  The Voice of the Nine Bible Trees (n.p., 1973)

  Introduction to African Religion (n.p., 1975; London, Heinemann, 1981)

  The Prayers of African Religion (S.P.C.K., 1975; reprint, Maryknoll, N.Y., Orbis Bks., 1976)

Sidelights: Mbiti is a member of the Akamba people, of which every person is expected to tell stories
skillfully. He collected about 1,500 folktales of which 78 appear in his *Akamba Stories*. "He writes
original poetry in both his mother tongue, Kikamba, and in English." (*African Authors*)

Sources: *African Authors*; *Books in Print*, 1980-81, 1981-82; *International Authors and Writers Who's
Who*, 7th ed., 1976; *Reader's Guide to African Literature*.

MEBANE, MARY ELIZABETH. English Professor.
Born in Durham, N.C., June 26, 1933. *Education:* B.A. (summa cum laude), N.C. Coll., Durham,
1955; M.A., 1961, Ph.D., 1973, U. of N.C., Chapel Hill. *Career:* Eng. Tchr. in public schs. in
Durham, 1955-60; Instr. in Eng., N.C. Coll., Durham, 1960-65; Assoc. Prof. of Eng., S.C. State
Coll., Orangeburg, 1967-74; Prof. of Eng., U. of S.C., Columbia, 1974- ; Tchr., U. of Wis.,
Milwaukee. *Mailing address:* c/o Viking Press, 625 Madison Ave., N.Y., N.Y. 10022.

Writings:
  Fiction
  Take a Sad Song, two-act play (1st produced in Columbia, S.C., at Playwrights' Corner, Feb.
  1975)

  Nonfiction
  Mary, autobiog. (N.Y., Viking, 1981)

Sources: *Contemporary Authors*, vols. 73-76, 1978; *Kirkus Reviews*, Jan. 1, 1981; *Mary*.

MERIWETHER, LOUISE. Free-lance Writer, Juvenile Writer.
Born in Haverstraw, N.Y., May 8, 1923. *Education:* B.A., N.Y.U.; UCLA (Journalism). *Family:*
Divorced. *Career:* Reporter, *Los Angeles Sentinel*; Story Analyst, Universal Studios; Staff Mem.,
Watts Writers' Workshop; Legal Secy.; an organizer & mem., Black Concern (against

accommodation with Republic of S. Africa). *Mailing address:* c/o Jenkins, 1691 E. 174th St., Bronx, N.Y. 10472.

Writings:
Fiction

Daddy Was a Number Runner, novel (Englewood Cliffs, N.J., Prentice-Hall, 1970; N.Y., Pyramid, 1976)

Nonfiction

The Freedom Ship of Robert Smalls, juv. (Prentice-Hall, 1971)

The Heart Man; Dr. Daniel Hale Williams, juv. (Prentice-Hall, 1972)

Don't Ride the Bus on Monday: The Rosa Parks Story, juv. (Prentice-Hall, 1973)

Sources: Author information; *Books in Print*, 1979-80; *Daddy Was a Number Runner*; *1000 Successful Blacks.*

METCALF, GEORGE R. State Senator, Teacher.
Education: (Grad.), Princeton U.; Columbia U., Sch. of Journalism. *Career:* State Senator, N.Y.; Tchr., Black Studies, Auburn Community Coll. *Mailing address:* c/o McGraw-Hill Bk. Co., 1221 Ave. of the Americas, N.Y., N.Y. 10020.

Writings:
Nonfiction

Black Profiles (N.Y., McGraw-Hill, 1968, expanded ed., 1970, paper, 1971)

Up from Within: Today's New Black Leaders (N.Y., McGraw-Hill, 1971)

Sidelights: Between 1951 and 1965, as a New York State Senator, Metcalf sponsored an outstanding series of bills in civil rights and public health. He co-sponsored fair housing laws that formed the basis for similar legislation enacted throughout the United States. He also pioneered health insurance legislation and co-sponsored New York State's basic law on narcotics addiction. (*Up from Within*)

Sources: *Books in Print*, 1978-79; *Dictionary Catalog of the Schomburg Collection of Negro Literature and History*, 2nd Supplement, 1972; *Dictionary Catalog of the Vivian G Harsh Collection of Afro-American History and Literature*; *Up from Within.*

MICHEAUX, OSCAR. Novelist, Film Producer.
Born in 1884. *Career:* Founder, Oscar Micheaux Corp. (films). Died in 1951.

Writings:
Fiction

The Conquest; The Story of a Negro Pioneer, by the Pioneer (Lincoln, Neb., Woodruff, 1913; College Park, Md., McGrath, 1969)

The Forged Note; A Romance of the Darker Races (Lincoln, Neb., Western Bk. Supply, 1915)

The Homesteader: A Novel (Sioux City, Iowa, Western Bk. Supply, 1917; McGrath, 1969)

The Wind from Nowhere, novel, 11 editions (N.Y., Bk. Supply, 1941; Freeport, N.Y., Bks. for Libs., 1972)

The Case of Mrs. Wingate, novel, 6 editions (Bk. Supply, 1945; N.Y., reprint, AMS, 1975)

The Story of Dorothy Stanfield, Based on a Great Insurance Swindle, and a Woman! (Bk. Supply, 1946)

The Masquerade: An Historical Novel, 3 editions (Bk. Supply, 1947; reprint, AMS, 1975)

Sidelights: This first Black film producer made 34 films over a period of 30 years.

Sources: *Afro-American Writers*; *Books in Print*, 1980-81; *The Case of Mrs. Wingate*; *Negro Novel in America*; *Negro Voices in American Fiction*.

MILLER, JAKE C. Political Science Professor (Foreign Affairs).
Born in Hobe Sound, Fla., Dec. 28, 1929. *Education:* B.S. (Soc. Sci.), Bethune-Cookman Coll., 1947; M.A. (Polit. Sci.), U. of Ill., Urbana, 1957; Ph.D. (Polit. Sci.), U. of N.C., Chapel Hill, 1967. *Family:* Married Nellie Carroll Miller; sons: Charles, Wayne, Warren. *Career:* Instr., Bethune-Cookman Coll., 1954-59; Asst. Prof., Fisk U., Nashville, 1959-64, Assoc. Prof. & Dir., Intnl. Studies, 1967-76; Prof., Bethune-Cookman Coll., 1976- . *Honors:* S. Educ. Fellow, 1964-67; Taconic Polit. Sci. Career Fellow, 1964-67; Alpha Kappa Mu Honor Soc.; Dansforth Found. Award for Outstanding Achievement as a tchr., 1970- . *Mailing address:* 1103 Lakewood Park Dr., Daytona Beach, Fla. 32010.

Writings:
Nonfiction

The Black Presence in American Foreign Affairs (Wash., D.C., U. Press of Amer., 1978)

The Plight of Haitian Refugees (N.Y., Praeger, 1984)

Sidelights: Dr. Miller has contributed to *World Affairs*, the *Middle East Journal*, and *Horn of Africa*. (Author)

Sources: Author information; *Books in Print*, 1980-81.

MILLER, KELLY. Educator, Mathematics & Sociology Professor.
Born in Winnsboro, S.C., July 23, 1863. *Education:* B.A., Howard U.; M.A., Johns Hopkins U. *Family:* d. May Miller (writer). *Career:* Howard U. for 44 yrs. as: Prof. of Mathematics; Prof. of Sociol.; Dean, Coll. of Arts & Scis.; & Dean, Jr. Coll. Died in 1939.

Writings:
Nonfiction

Race Adjustment; Essays on the Negro in America (N.Y., Neale, 1908; facsimile ed., N.Y., Arno, Black Heritage Lib. Collection Ser., 1968)

Out of the House of Bondage (Neale, 1914; N.Y., Schocken, 1971)

An Appeal to Conscience; America's Code of Caste a Disgrace to Democracy (N.Y., Macmillan, 1918; Arno, 1969)

History of the World War and the Important Part Taken by the Negroes (Wash., D.C., Austin Jenkins, 1919)

Kelly Miller's History of the World War for Human Rights; Being an Intensely Human and Brilliant Account of the World War and Why and for What Purpose America and the Allies Are Fighting and the Important Part Taken by the Negro (Austin Jenkins, 1919; reprint, Westport, Conn., Negro Universities Press, 1969)

The Everlasting Stain (Wash., D.C., Associated Pub., 1924; reprint, Arno, Amer. Negro — His Hist. & Lit. Ser., no. 1, 1968)

Radicals and Conservatives, and Other Essays on the Negro in America (Shocken, 1968)

Sidelights: "Helped W. E. B. DuBois edit *Crisis* magazine....
"Miller was called the father of the Sanhedrin, a 1924 movement which attempted to unite all Negro organizations into one front.
"One of the major spokesman ... of his race in the early 20th Century, Kelly Miller has been referred to as a 'marginal man,' racially separated from the white world, and intellectually distinct from his own group." (*Historical Negro Biographies*)

Sources: *Afro-American Writing*; *Anthology of American Negro Literature*; *Books in Print*, 1980-81; *Historical Negro Biographies*; *Negro Caravan*; *Negro Poets and Their Poems*, 3rd ed. rev.

MILLER, LOREN. Lawyer, Judge, Editor.
Born in Pender, Neb., Jan. 29, 1903. *Education:* U. of Kan., 1920-23; Howard U., 1926-27; LL.B., Washburn Sch. of Law, Topeka, Kan., 1929. *Family:* Married Juanita Ellsworth, 1930; son Loren, Jr., son Edward E. *Career:* Admitted to Kan. bar, 1929, Cal. bar, 1934, Fed. Dist. Court, U.S. Court of Appeals, 9th Circuit, & U.S. Supreme Court, 1947; Ed., *California Eagle, California News, Los Angeles Sentinel,* 1930-34; European correspondent, Assoc. Negro Press, for 6 months, 1931-32; apptd. Judge of Municipal Court of L.A., 1964. Died in 1967.

Writings:
 Nonfiction
  The Petitioners; The Story of the Supreme Court of the United States and the Negro (N.Y., Pantheon, 1966)

Sidelights: Judge Miller practiced law in Los Angeles from 1934, argued many civil rights cases, especially housing discrimination suits. (*Negro Handbook*)

Sources: *Black Writers in Los Angeles, California; Negro Handbook;* Pub. information.

MILLER, MAY. Poet, Playwright.
Born in Wash., D.C. (daughter of Kelly Miller, writer). *Education:* Howard U. grad.; advanced work at Amer. U. & Columbia U. *Family:* Married John Sullivan. *Career:* Tchr., Speech & Dramatics, Frederick Douglass High Sch., Baltimore; Reader, Panelist, Lect. & Poet-in-Residence, Monmouth Coll., Monmouth, Ill.; coordinator for performing poets, Friends of the Arts, D.C. public schs.; Mem., Commission of the Arts, Wash., D.C. *Mailing address:* c/o Lotus Press, P.O. Box 601, Coll. Park Station, Detroit, Mich. 48221.

Writings:
 Fiction
  Negro History in Thirteen Plays, comp., with Willis Richardson (Wash., D.C., Assoc. Pub., 1935)

  Into the Clearing, poems (Wash., D.C., Charioteer, 1959)

  Poems (Thetford, Vt., Cricket Press, 1962)

  Lyrics of Three Women; Poems by Katie Letcher Lyle, Maude Rubin and May Miller (Baltimore, Linden Press, 1964)

  Not That Far, poems (San Luis Obispo, Cal., Solo Press, 1973)

  The Clearing and Beyond, poems (Wash., D.C., Christian Press, 1974)

  Dust of Uncertain Journey, poems (Detroit, Lotus, 1975)

Sources: *Books in Print*, Supplement, 1975-76; *Cavalcade.*

MILNER, RON(ALD). Playwright.
Born in Detroit, Mich., May 29, 1938. *Education:* Attended various colls. in Detroit; Harvey Swado's writing workshop, Columbia U. *Career:* Writer-in-Residence, Lincoln U. (Pa.), 1966-67; Conductor, Cultural Workshop, Mich. State U.; Dir., Spirit of Shango Theater Co., Detroit. *Honors:* Rockefeller Found. Fellow; John Hay Whitney Found. fellow. *Mailing address:* c/o New Amer. Lib., 1301 Sixth Ave., N.Y., N.Y. 10019.

Writings:
 Fiction
  Who's Got His Own, play (1966)

  The Monster, play (1968)

  The Warning: A Theme for Linda, play (1969)

  These Three, play (n.d.)

Black Drama Anthology, ed. with Woodie King (N.Y., New Amer. Lib., 1971; N.Y., Columbia U. Press, 1972; paperback ed., New Amer. Lib., 1973)

What the Wine Sellers Buy; A Three-Act Play (N.Y., S. French, 1974)

Sidelights: "*Who's Got His Own* ... first presented at the American Place Theater in New York City ... toured through New York State colleges under the auspices of the New York State Council of the Arts. It was also the premiere show at Harlem's New Lafayette Theatre. Milner's other New York productions include ... *The Warning: A Theme for Linda*, which was presented as a part of *A Black Quartet*, four one-act plays produced by Woodie King Associates, Incorporated." (*Black Drama Anthology*)

Sources: *Black Drama Anthology*; *Books in Print*, 1978-79.

MITCHELL, HENRY H. Theologian, Minister.
Born in Columbus, Ohio, Sept. 19, 1919. *Education:* B.A. (cum laude), Lincoln U., 1941; M. Divinity, Union Theol. Sem., N.Y., 1944; M.A., Cal. State U., Fresno, 1966; Th.D., Sch. of Theol., Claremont, Cal., 1973. *Family:* Married Ella Parson (tchr.), Aug. 12, 1944; children: Henry H., Jr., Muriel (Mrs. Spurgeon Smith), Elizabeth, Kenneth. *Career:* Executive staff, N. Cal. Bap. Convention, Oakland, 1945-59; Pastor, Fresno, Cal., 1959-66; Pastor, Santa Monica, Cal., 1966-69; Martin Luther King Prof. of Black Church Studies, Colgate Divinity Sch., Rochester, N.Y., 1969-74; Dir., Ecumenical Center for Black Church Studies, L.A., Cal., 1974- ; Adjunct Prof., Fuller Theol. Sem., 1974- ; S. Cal. Sch. of Theol., Claremont, 1974- . *Honors:* Pres., N. Cal. Bap. Convention, 1961-62; Chairman of Bd., 1963-64; Pres., Fresno County Econ. Opportunity Com., 1966. *Mailing address:* c/o Harper & Row, 10 E. 53rd St., N.Y., N.Y. 10022.

Writings:
Nonfiction
Black Preaching (Phila., Lippincott, 1970; N.Y., Harper, 1978)

Black Belief: Folk Beliefs of Blacks in America and West Africa (Harper, 1975)

This Far by Faith: American Black Worship and Its African Roots, with Robert Hovda et al., eds. (Wash., D.C., Liturgical, 1977)

The Recovery of Preaching (Harper, 1977)

Sources: *Books in Print*, 1978-79, 1980-81; *Contemporary Authors*, vols. 57 60, 1976.

MITCHELL, LOFTEN. Playwright, Editor.
Born in N.Y.C. in 1919. *Education:* De Witt Clinton High Sch., the Bronx; City Coll. of N.Y.; B.A. (honors), Talladega Coll., 1943; Columbia U. (playwriting). *Career:* Soc. Investigator; has written stage plays, radio scripts, TV documentaries, & screenplays; Ed., *Freedom Journal* (NAACP). *Honors:* Guggenheim Found. Award for Creative Writing in the Drama, 1958 59; Rockefeller Found. Grant (New Dramatists Com.), 1961. *Mailing address:* 3217 Burrie Rd., Vestal, N.Y. 13850.

Writings:
Fiction
The Cellar, play (1947)

Integration Report, screenplay (1959)

Report One, screenplay (n.d.)

I'm Sorry, screenplay (n.d.)

Tell Pharaoh, play (1963)

Land Beyond the River; A Play in Three Acts (Cody, Wyo., Pioneer Drama Serv., 1963)

Ballad for Bimshire, play, with Irving Burgie (1963)

Ballad of the Winter Soldiers, play, with John O. Killens (1964)

Star of the Morning, play (N.Y., Free Press, 1965)

The Stubborn Old Lady Who Resisted Change, play (N.Y., Emerson Hall, 1973)

Voices of the Black Theater (Clifton, N.J., J. T. White, 1975)

Nonfiction
Black Drama; The Story of the American Negro in the Theatre (N.Y., Hawthorn Bks., 1967)

Sidelights: Mitchell studied playwriting with John Gassner. An interesting late play is *The Final Solution of the Black Problem in the United States of America or the Fall of the American Empire.* (*Black Scenes*)

Sources: *Afro-American Literature: Drama; Black American Writer*, vol. II: *Poetry and Drama; Black Scenes; Books in Print*, 1978-79; *Negro Almanac.*

MITTELHÖLZER, EDGAR AUSTIN. (British Guianan). Novelist, Free-lance Journalist.
Born in New Amsterdam, Guyana, in 1909. *Education:* Berbice High Sch. *Family:* Married 1st Roma Erica Halfhide; married 2nd Jacqueline Pointer; five children. *Career:* Customs Officer; Sales Clerk; Meteorological Observer; Free-lance Journalist; Brit. Council, Book Dept., Eng. Died May 6, 1965, in Eng.

Writings:
Fiction
Corentyne Thunder, novel (London, Eyre & Spottiswoode, 1941)

A Morning at the Office; A Novel (London, Hogarth, 1950; also as *A Morning in Trinidad*, N.Y., Doubleday, 1950)

Shadows Move among Them, novel (Phila., Lippicott, 1951; London, Peter Nevill, 1952)

Children of Kaywanna, novel (London, Secker, 1952, 1956; N.Y., John Day, 1952)

The Weather in Middenshot; A Novel (Secker, 1952; Day, 1953)

The Life and Death of Sylvia, novel (Secker, 1953; Day, 1954)

The Adding Machine, a Fable for Capitalists and Commercialists, novel (Kingston, Jamaica, Pioneer Press, 1954)

The Harrowing of Hubertus, novel (Secker, 1955; as *Hubertus*, Day, 1955)

My Bones and My Flute; A Ghost Story in the Old-Fashioned Manner (Secker, 1955)

Of Trees and the Sea, novel (Secker, 1956)

A Tale of Three Places, novel (Secker, 1957)

Kaywanna Blood, novel (Secker, 1958; as *The Old Blood*, Doubleday, 1958)

The Weather Family, novel (Secker, 1958)

The Mad McMullochs, novel (London, Peter Owen, 1959)

A Tinkling in the Twilight, novel (Secker, 1959)

Latticed Echoes; A Novel in the Leitmotiv Manner (Secker, 1960)

Eltonsbrody; A Novel (Secker, 1960)

The Piling of Clouds, novel (London, Putnam, 1961)

Thunder Returning; A Novel in the Leitmotive (Secker, 1961)

The Wounded and the Worried, novel (Putnam, 1962)

Uncle Paul, novel (London, McDonald, 1963)

The Aloneness of Mrs. Chatham, novel (London, Library 33, 1965)

The Jilkington Drama, novel (London & N.Y., Abelard-Schumann, 1965)

Nonfiction

A Swarthy Boy, autobiog. (Putnam, 1963)

Sidelights: "... one of modern giants of Caribbean writing." (*Caribbean Writers*)
"... it was Mittelhölzer who first raised the question of psychic imbalance and the resultant *angst* of identity which is the most central and urgent theme of West Indian literature." (*West Indian Novel*)

Sources: *Caribbean Writers*; *Modern Black Writers*; *West Indian Literature*; *The West Indian Novel*; *World Authors*.

MOLETTE, BARBARA JEAN. Costumer, Drama Instructor, Playwright.
Born in L.A., Cal., Jan. 31, 1940. *Education:* B.A. (with highest honors), Fla. A&M U., 1966; M.F.A., Fla. State U., 1969. *Family:* Married Carlton W. Molette II (drama prof.), June 15, 1960; d. Carla Evelyn, d. Andrea Rose. *Career:* Drama Coordinator for Upward Bound Program, Fla. A&M U., Tallahassee, summer 1969; Costumer, Morehouse-Spelman Players, Atlanta, 1969- ; Instr. in Fine Arts, Spelman Coll., Atlanta, 1969-72, Instr. in Drama, 1972- ; Costumer for motion picture "Together for Days," 1971; Book review ed., *Encore*, 1970-72. *Honors:* Fla. Upward Bound Program Play Festival, 1st place award, 1969. *Mailing address:* c/o Spelman Coll., 350 Spelman Lane, S.W., Atlanta, Ga. 30314.

Writings:
Fiction

Doctor B. S. Black, play with Carlton Molette & Charles Mann (*Encore*, vol. 13, 1970)

Rosalee Pritchett, play with Carlton Molette (N.Y., Dramatist Play Service, 1972)

Booji Wooji, play with Carlton Molette (1st produced at Atlanta U. Summer Theatre, July 8, 1971)

Sidelights: *Doctor B. S. Black* was first produced in Atlanta by Morehouse-Spelman Players, Nov. 10, 1969. The musical version was produced at Atlanta University Summer Theatre, July 20, 1972. *Rosalee Pritchett* was first produced in Atlanta by Morehouse-Spelman Players, March 20, 1970; produced off-Broadway, St. Marks Playhouse, January 12, 1971. It has been included in *Black Writers of America*, edited by Richard Barksdale and Kenneth Kinnamon. She is also author with husband Carlton Molette of a screenplay of *Booji Wooji*. (*Contemporary Authors*)

Sources: *Black Writers of America*; *Contemporary Authors*, vols. 45/48, 1974.

MOLETTE, CARLTON WOODARD, II. Drama Professor, Playwright, Theatre Consultant.
Born in Pine Bluff, Ark., Aug. 23, 1939. *Education:* B.A., Morehouse Coll., 1959; M.A., U. of Iowa, 1962; Ph.D., Fla. State U., 1968. *Family:* Married Barbara Jean Roseburr (coll. instr. & costumer), June 15, 1960; d. Carla Evelyn, d. Andrea Rose. *Career:* Asst. Prof., 1964-66, Assoc. Prof., Speech & Drama, 1967-69, Fla. A&M U., Tallahassee; Assoc. Prof. of Drama, Spelman Coll., Atlanta, 1969- , Chairman of Dept., 1971 ; Theatre consultant to coll. festivals & org.; Ed., *Encore*, 1965-71; Ed. Consultant, *Southern Speech Journal*, 1966-68; Mem., Advisory Ed., *Journal of Black Studies*, 1970-73. *Honors:* Carnegie Found. Grant, 1966-68; Atlanta U. Center Faculty Res. Grant, 1970-71. *Mailing address:* c/o Spelman Coll., 350 Spelman Lane, S.W., Atlanta, Ga. 30314.

Writings:
Fiction

Doctor B. S. Black, play with Barbara Molette & Charles Mann (*Encore*, vol. 13, 1970)

Rosalee Pritchett, play with Barbara Molette (N.Y., Dramatist Play Service, 1972)

Booji Wooji, play with Barbara Molette (1st produced at Atlanta U. Summer Theatre, July 8, 1971)

Sidelights: "Doctor B. S. Black" was first produced in Atlanta by Morehouse-Spelman Players, Nov. 10, 1969. The musical version was produced at Atlanta University Summer Theatre, July 20, 1972. *Rosalee Pritchett* was first produced in Atlanta by Morehouse-Spelman players, March 20, 1970; produced off-Broadway, St. Marks Playhouse, January 12, 1971. It has been included in *Black Writers of America*, edited by Richard Barksdale and Kenneth Kinnamon. Carlton Molette is also author with wife Barbara Molette of a screenplay of *Booji Wooji*. (*Contemporary Authors*)

Sources: *Black Writers of America*; *Contemporary Authors*, vols. 45/48, 1974.

MOODY, ANNE. Short Story Writer, Civil Rights Advocate.
Born in Wilkerson County, Miss., in 1941. *Education:* Natchez Jr. Coll.; Tougaloo Coll., Miss. *Career:* Civil rights worker for SNCC. *Honors:* Natchez Jr. Coll. scholarship. *Mailing address:* c/o Harper & Row, 10 E. 53rd St., N.Y., N.Y. 10022.

Writings:
Fiction
Mr. Death: Four Stories (N.Y., Harper, 1975)

Nonfiction
Coming of Age in Mississippi, autobiog. (N.Y., Dial, 1968)

Sources: *Afro-American Literature: Nonfiction*; *Mr. Death*.

MORGAN, KATHRYN L. Folklorist, History Professor.
Education: Ph.D. *Career:* Assoc. Prof., Hist., Swarthmore Coll., Swarthmore, Pa. *Mailing address:* c/o Temple U. Press, Broad & Oxford St., Phila., Pa. 19122.

Writings:
Nonfiction
Children of Strangers: The Stories of a Black Family, biog. (Phila. Temple U. Press, 1980, paperback ed., 1981)

Sidelights: Carolyn See of the Book Review staff reviewed *Children of Strangers* as follows: "What an absolutely charming book this is. Amusing, touching, funny ... where what you'd really like to do is meet the characters you've read about and spend more time with them, make them part of your life.
"... I found myself totally captivated.... This family was happy, and they loved each other." (*Los Angeles Times*)

Sources: *Books in Print*, 1980-81; *Freedomways*, vol. 21, no. 1, 1981; *Kirkus Reviews*, Nov. 15, 1980; *Los Angeles Times*, Jan. 1, 1981.

MORRISON, TONI [Chloe Anthony Wofford]. Novelist, Editor, Teacher.
Born in Lorain, Ohio, Feb. 18, 1931. *Education:* B.A., Howard U., 1953; M.A., Cornell U., 1955. *Family:* Son Harold Ford, son Slade Kevin. *Career:* Instr., Eng., Tex. S. U., Houston, 1955-57; Instr., Eng., Howard U., 1957-64; Senior Ed., Random House, N.Y., 1965- ; Assoc. Prof., SUNY at Purchase, 1971-72; Tchr., Bard Coll. *Mailing address:* c/o Random House, Inc., 201 E. 50th St., N.Y., N.Y. 10022.

Writings:
Fiction
The Bluest Eye, novel (N.Y., Holt, 1970)

Sula, a Novel (N.Y., Knopf, 1973; N.Y., Bantam, 1975)

Song of Solomon, novel (Knopf, 1977; N.Y., New Amer. Lib., 1978)

Tar Baby, novel (Knopf, 1981; Franklin Center, Pa., Franklin Lib., 1981; New Amer. Lib., 1982)

Sidelights: Morrison has extraordinary ability to create beautiful language and striking characters; but the insight she brings to problems all humans face gives her universality. (*Dictionary of Literary Biography*)

Sources: *Books in Print*, 1979-80, 1982-83; *Dictionary of Literary Biography, Yearbook: 1981*; *Contemporary Authors*, vols. 29-32, 1978; *Kirkus Reviews*, Jan. 1, 1981; *Publishers Weekly*, Jan. 23, 1981.

MORROW, EVERETT FREDERIC. Administrator, Businessman, Civil Rights Advocate.
Born in Hackensack, N.J., Apr. 20, 1909. *Education:* Bowdoin Coll.; LL.B., LL.D., Dr. Juris, Rutgers U. Sch. of Law. *Family:* Married Catherine Gordon of Chicago. *Career:* Bus. Mgr., *Opportunity* mag. (Natl. Urban League), 1935; Coordinator of Branches, NAACP, 1937-49; Major, U.S. Army Artillery; with CBS, 1949- ; Consultant Advisor, Eisenhower campaign train, 1952; Advisor, Bus. Affairs, Secy. of Commerce; Admin. Asst. to Pres. Eisenhower, 1955; Asst. V. Pres., Bank of Amer., Intnl. *Honors:* Bowdoin Coll., LL.D., 1971. *Mailing address:* 1270 Fifth Ave., N.Y., N.Y. 10029.

Writings:
Nonfiction

Black Man in the White House: A Diary of the Eisenhower Years by the Administrative Officer for Special Projects, the White House, 1955-1961 (N.Y., Coward-McCann, 1963)

Way Down South Up North (Phila., United Church Press, 1973)

Forty Years a Guinea Pig, a Black Man's View from the Top (N.Y., Pilgrim, 1980)

Sidelights: "Has chalked up many firsts. Perhaps most significant was appointment as Administrative Assistant to President Eisenhower in 1955.... Also first in an executive position with Columbia Broadcasting System in 1949. He became Assistant Vice President of Bank of America International." (*Negroes in Public Affairs and Government*)

Sources: Author information; *Los Angeles Times*, Dec. 5, 1980; *Negroes in Public Affairs and Government.*

MOSES, WILSON JEREMIAH. History Professor.
Born Mar. 5, 1942. *Education:* A.B. (Eng.), 1965, M.A. (Eng. Lit.), 1967, Wayne State U.; Ph.D. (Amer. Civilization), Brown U., 1975. *Family:* Married Nov. 1963; two sons born 1964, 1974. *Career:* Tchg. Asst. & Instr., Dept. of Eng., Wayne State U., 1966-70; Teaching Assoc., Brown U., 1970-71; Instr. & Asst. Prof., Dept. of Hist., U. of Iowa, 1971-76; Assoc. Prof., Hist., & Dir., Black Studies, S. Methodist U., 1976- . *Honors:* U. Fellow, Brown U., 1969-70; NEH, 1978; S. Fellowship Fund, 1978-79; Amer. Council of Learned Societies, 1979-80; Amer. Philosophical Soc., 1979-80. *Mailing address:* 3312 Whitehall Dr., Dallas, Tex. 75229.

Writings:
Nonfiction

The Golden Age of Black Nationalism, 1850-1925 (Hamden, Conn., Archon Bks., Shoe String Press, 1978)

Black Messiahs and Uncle Toms: Social and Literary Manipulations of a Religious Myth (U. Park, Pa. State U. Press, 1982)

Sources: Author information; *Books in Print*, 1980-81, 1982-83.

MOTLEY, WILLARD. Novelist.
Born in Chicago, Ill., in 1912. *Career:* Farm worker, waiter, shipping clerk, cook, and "coal hiker." Wrote articles for *Commonweal*; worked for Fed. Writers Project (studying living conditions in Chicago Black community). Died in 1965 in Mexico City, where he had lived for 12 yrs.

Writings:

Fiction

Knock on Any Door, novel (N.Y., Appleton, 1947; paper, N.Y., New Amer. Lib., 1958)

We Fished All Night, novel (Appleton, 1951)

Let No Man Write My Epitaph, novel (N.Y., Random House, 1958)

Tourist Town, novel (N.Y., Putnam, 1965)

Let Noon Be Fair, novel (Putnam, 1966)

Nonfiction

The Diaries of Willard Motley, ed. by Jerome Klinkowitz (Ames, Iowa State U. Press, 1979)

Sidelights: Motley chose to live on Chicago's Skid Row in order to write about its derelicts. *Knock on Any Door* became an immediate best seller, later made into a successful motion picture. This work caused the *New York Times* to comment: "An extraordinary and powerful new naturalistic talent herewith makes its debut in American letters."

"In his second and third novels ... Mr. Motley continued to write in the 'environmentalist' tradition of Richard Wright, although his characters were not Negroes but Italian immigrants living and dying in the slums of Chicago.... [Here we have] protest but without considerations of race and racial conflict." (*Soon, One Morning*)

Sources: *Afro-American Writers*; *Best Short Stories by Negro Writers*; *Negro Almanac*; *Soon, One Morning*.

MOTON, ROBERT RUSSA. Principal, Tuskegee Institute.
Born in Amelia County, Va., Aug. 26, 1867. *Education:* Hampton Inst., Va. *Family:* Married 1st Elizabeth Hunt Harris, 1905 (dec. 1906); married 2nd Jennie D. Booth; five children. *Career:* Commandant, Hampton Inst., 1890-1914; Prin., Tuskegee Inst., 1915-1935. *Honors:* Harmon Award, 1930; Spingarn Medal, 1932; several degrees conferred, including: M.A., Harvard; LL.D., Va. Union U., Oberlin, Williams, & Howard U. Died 1940.

Writings:

Nonfiction

Racial Good Will; Addresses (Hampton, Va., Hampton Inst., 1916)

Finding a Way Out; An Autobiography (Garden City, N.Y., Doubleday, 1920, 1921, 1922)

What the Negro Thinks (Doubleday, 1929; Garden City, N.Y., Garden City Pub., 1942)

Sidelights: "Robert R. Moton was successor to Booker T. Washington as principal of Tuskegee Institute; as such he inherited his predecessor's position as spokesman for industrial education." (*Negro Caravan*)

Dr. Moton became one of the leading spirits in organizing the Commission on Interracial Cooperation in 1918.

"Moton stood his ground against bigotry when a hospital for Negro veterans was proposed at Tuskegee. He persisted until finally all black doctors and staff were appointed." (*Negro Builders and Heroes*)

Sources: *Negro Builders and Heroes*; *Negro Caravan*.

MPHAHLELE, EZEKIEL. (South African). Literary Critic, Autobiographer, Journalist, Dramatist, Novelist, Short Story Writer, Lecturer.
Born in Pretoria, S. Africa, Dec. 17, 1919. *Education:* U. of S. Africa, Pretoria, 1946-49, 1953-54, 1956, B.A. (honors), 1949; M.A. (Eng.), 1956; Ph.D. (Eng.), U. of Denver, Colo., 1968. *Family:* Married Rebecca Mphahlele, 1945; five children. *Career:* Tchr., Eng. & Afrikaans, Orlando High Sch., Johannesburg, 1945-52; Fiction Ed., *Drum* mag., Johannesburg, 1955-57; Lect., Eng. Lit., U. of Ibadan, Nigeria, 1957-61; Dir., African Program, Intnl. Assn. for Cultural Freedom, Paris, 1961-63; Dir., Chemchemi Creative Centre, Nairobi, Kenya, 1963-65; Visiting Lect., U. of Denver,

1966-68; Senior Lect., Eng., U. of Zambia, Lusaka, 1968-70; Assoc. Prof., U. of Denver, 1970-74; Prof., Eng., U. of Pa., Phila., 1974-77; Senior Res. Fellow, U. of Witwatersrand, Johannesburg, 1978- . *Mailing address:* c/o African Studies Inst., U. of Witwatersrand, Johannesburg, 20001, S. Africa.

Writings:

Fiction

The Living and Dead, and Other Stories (Ibadan, Ministry of Educ., 196-?)

Man Must Live, and Other Stories (Cape Town, African Bookman, 1964)

Modern African Stories, ed. with Ellis Komey (London, Faber, 1964; London, Merrimack Bk. Serv., 1966)

African Writing Today, ed. (London, Penguin, 1967)

In Corner B., Short Stories (Nairobi, E. African Pub. House, 1967; Evanston, Ill., Northwestern U. Press, 1967)

The Wanderers; A Novel of Africa (n.p., 1968; N.Y., Macmillan, 1971; Ann Arbor, Mich., U. Microfilms, 1974)

Chirundu Eskia Mphahlele, novel (Johannesburg, S. Africa, Raven Press, 1979)

Nonfiction

Down Second Avenue, autobiog. (Garden City, N.Y., Anchor, 1959; Faber, 1959; N.Y., Doubleday, 1971)

The African Image, criticism (N.Y., Praeger, 1962; Faber, 1962; 2nd ed., Merrimack Bk. Serv., 1972; rev. ed., Faber, 1974; Praeger, 1974)

Voices in the Whirlwind, and Other Essays (N.Y., Hill & Wang, 1972)

Sidelights: "Ezekiel Mphahlele has been one of the most versatile and influential of African authors. As literary critic, autobiographer, journalist, short story writer, novelist, dramatist and poet, he has probably contributed more than any other individual to the growth and development of an African literature in English." (*Contemporary Novelists*)

Sources: *Books in Print*, 1980-81; *Contemporary Novelists*, 2nd ed., 1976; *Who's Who in African Literature*; *Writers Directory*, 1980-82.

EL MUHAJIR [Marvin X]. Poet, Playwright-Director, Editor.
Born in Fowler, Cal., May 29, 1944. *Education:* Edison High Sch.; Fresno, Cal.; Oakland City Coll., 1962-64; B.A. (Eng.), San Francisco State U., 1964-66 (grad. study), 1974. *Family:* Married; five children. *Career:* Founder (with Ed Bullins), Blackarts/W. Theatre/Sch., San Francisco, 1966; Founder, Al Kitab Sudan Pub. Co., San Francisco, 1967; Fiction Ed., *Black Dialogue* mag., 1965- ; Contrib. Ed., *Journal of Black Poetry*, 1965- ; Assoc. Ed., *Black Theatre*, 1968; Foreign Ed., *Muhammad Speaks*, 1970; Founder, Dir., Your Black Educ. Theatre, Inc., San Francisco, 1971; Tchr., Black Studies: Fresno State U., 1969; U. of Cal., Berkeley, 1972, Mills Coll., 1973; lecture/readings at Stanford, Cornell, Loyola of Chicago, U. of Toronto, U. of Cal. (Davis), UCLA, U. of Cal. (San Diego), U. of Okla., Manhattan Community Coll. (N.Y.C.). *Honors:* Life mem., Cal. Scholarship Fed.; Dean's List, San Francisco State U.; writing grants totaling $8,000 from Columbia U., 1969; NEA, 1969. *Mailing address:* c/o Broadside Press, 12651 Old Mill Rd., Detroit, Mich. 48238.

Writings:

Fiction

Flowers for the Trashman, play (first produced in San Francisco, Drama Dept., San Francisco State Coll., 1965)

Come Next Summer, play (produced by Black Arts West, 1966)

Sudan Rajul Samia, poems (Fresno, Cal., Al Kitab Sudan, 1967)

Black Dialectics, proverbs (Al Kitab Sudan, 1967)

Fly to Allah, poems (Al Kitab Sudan, 1969)

Son of Man, proverbs (Al Kitab Sudan, 1969)

Black Man Listen, poems & proverbs (Detroit, Broadside Press, 1970)

The Trial, play (first produced in Harlem, 1970)

Take Care of Business (musical version of *Flowers for the Trashman*, produced in San Francisco by Black Education Theater, 1971)

Resurrection of the Dead, ritual dance drama (first produced in San Francisco by Black Education Theater, 1972)

Black Bird, parable (Al Kitab Sudan, 1972)

Woman — Man's Best Friend, poems, proverbs, parables, songs (Al Kitab Sudan, 1973)

Woman — Man's Best Friend, musical dance drama (first produced in Oakland at Mills Coll., 1973)

Source: Author information.

MUHAMMAD, ELIJAH. Religious Leader.
Born in Sandersville, Ga., Oct. 10, 1897. Self-educated. *Family:* Married Clara Evans, Mar. 7, 1919; six sons, two d's. *Career:* Field hand, railroad laborer; Chevrolet Co., Detroit, 1923-29; on relief, 1929-31. In 1930 met the founder of the Nation of Islam (Black Muslims), Wallace D. Fard, changed his name to Muhammad and took over leadership on disappearance of Fard in 1934. Died Feb. 27, 1975.

Writings:
Nonfiction

Message to the Black Man in America (Chicago, Muhammad Mosque of Islam No. 2, 1965)

How to Eat to Live, (Muhammad Mosque No. 2, 1967)

The Fall of America (Chicago, Muhammad's Temple of Islam No. 2, 1973)

Sidelights: "Like Marcus Garvey ... [his predecessor] Elijah Muhammad preaches that the only salvation for the black man in the United States is withdrawal into his own autonomous nation, away from a white social and economic system that is—in Muhammad's view—rigged against him. Tough-minded Muhammad claims to be the divinely appointed 'Messenger' of Allah, and thousands of poor, alienated blacks have accepted his message, changing their lives to join the Nation of Islam, with its stern morality, strict authoritarianism, pacifism (except in self-defense), racial dignity, and program of economic self-improvement...." (*Current Biography*)

Sources: *Books in Print*, 1978-79; *Current Biography*, 1971; *Negro Almanac*; *Negro Handbook*.

MURPHY, BEATRICE CAMPBELL. Editor, Poet.
Born in Monessen, Pa., June 25, 1908. *Education:* High sch. & spec. courses. *Family:* Div.; son Alvin H. Murphy. *Career:* Secy. to Head, Dept. of Sociol., Catholic U. of Amer., 1935-41; Secy., Correspondence Reviewer, Ed. Clerk, Fed. Govt., 1942-59; Managing Ed.-Dir., Minority Res. Center, Inc.; Dir., Negro Bibliographic & Res. Center, Inc.; Managing Ed., *Bibliographic Survey: The Negro in Print*; Executive Dir., Beatrice M. Murphy Found., 1977- . *Honors:* 1st Prize, "Something to Remember," *Easterner Mag.*; Special Citation, Emery Community Center (for donating lib.). *Mailing address:* 2737 Devonshire Pl., N.W., No. 222, Wash., D.C. 20008.

Writings:
Fiction

Negro Voices, poems, ed. (N.Y., H. Harrison, 1938; Ann Arbor, Mich., U. Microfilms, 1971)

Love Is a Terrible Thing, poems (N.Y., Hobson Bk., 1945)

Ebony Rhythm: An Anthology of Contemporary Negro Verse, ed. (Hicksville, N.Y., Exposition Press, 1948)

The Rocks Cry Out, poems, with Nancy L. Arnez (Detroit, Broadside, 1969)

Today's Negro Voices: An Anthology by Young Negro Poets, ed. (N.Y., Messner, 1970)

Negro Voices, microfilm (U. Microfilms, 1971)

Sidelights: Purposes of Beatrice M. Murphy Foundation: To encourage reading of literature by Blacks; to disseminate information concerning this literature; to promote and encourage this study; to encourage further such works.
"In 1967 she began losing her sight, and is now legally blind." (Author)

Sources: Author information; *Books in Print*, 1980-81; *Today's Negro Voices.*

MURPHY, CARL. Publisher.
Born in Baltimore, Md., Jan. 17, 1889. *Education:* B.A. (cum laude), Howard U., 1911; M.A., Harvard U., 1913; U. of Jena (E. Germany); LL.D., Lincoln U. (Pa.), 1948; L.H.D., Central State Coll., 1960. *Family:* Married 1st Vashti Turley, 1916 (dec. 1960); d. Martha Elizabeth, son Phillips, d. Ida Ann Smith, d. Carlita Jones, d. Vashti Turley Matthews, d. Frances L. Wood; married 2nd Lillian Matthews Prescott, 1961. *Career:* Instr., Asst. Prof., German, Howard U., 1913-18; Ed., *Afro-American* newspaper, 1918-44, Pub. & Chairman, Bd. of Dir., 1922- . *Honors:* Amer. Teamwork Award, Natl. Urban League, 1956; 30th Spingarn Medalist, NAACP, 1955. Died in 1967.

Writings:
Nonfiction

Afro-American, newspaper (Baltimore, 1918-)

Sources: *In Black and White*; *Negro Handbook.*

MURRAY, ALBERT L. Air Force Officer, Teacher, Consultant.
Born in Nokomis, Ala., May 12, 1916. *Education:* B.S., Tuskegee Inst.; M.A., N.Y.U.; U. of Mich.; U. of Chicago; U. of Paris; Northwestern U. *Family:* Married Mozelle Menefee; d. Michele. *Career:* U.S. Air Force Major, retired; Tchr., Lit., Tuskegee Inst.; Consultant (Cultural Hist.), Natl. Educ. TV; USIA. *Honors:* ASCAP-Deems Taylor Award for *Stomping the Blues*, 1977. *Mailing address:* 45 W. 132nd St., N.Y., N.Y. 10037.

Writings:
Nonfiction

The Omni-Americans; New Perspectives on Black Experience and American Culture (N.Y., Outerbridge & Dienstfrey, 1970)

South to a Very Old Place (N.Y., McGraw-Hill, 1971)

The Hero and the Blues (Columbia, U. of Mo. Press, 1973)

Trainwhistle Guitar (McGraw-Hill, 1974)

Stomping the Blues (McGraw-Hill, 1976)

Sidelights: *Book World* says: "Murray has set up an identifying mirror for Negroes, and for all of us, more inviting, more durable and truer to our history than the separatist-nihilist ones now so voguish." (*Omni-Americans*)

Sources: Author information; *Omni-Americans.*

MURRAY, PAULI. Lawyer, Priest.
Born in Baltimore, Md., in 1910. *Education:* B.A., Hunter Coll.; LL.B. (cum laude), Harvard U. Sch. of Law; LL.M., Sch. of Jurisprudence, U. of Cal., 1945; LL.D., Yale U. Sch. of Law, 1965; (studied for priesthood). *Career:* Mem., Cal. & N.Y. State bars; Deputy Attorney Gen., Cal.; Staff, Com. on Law & Soc. Action, Amer. Jewish Congress; Tchr., Ghana Sch. of Law & Brandeis U. (Mass.); Episcopal Priest. *Honors:* Eugene F. Saxton Fellow; Resident Fellow, MacDowell Colony, Peterboro, N.Y.; *Mademoiselle* mag. award for distinguished achievement in practice of law. *Mailing address:* c/o Harper & Row, 10 E. 53rd St., N.Y., N.Y. 10022.

Writings:
Fiction
Dark Testament and Other Poems (Norwalk, Conn., Silvermine, 1970)

Nonfiction
States' Laws on Race and Color, and Appendices Containing International Documents, Federal Laws and Regulations, Local Ordinances and Charts, ed. (Cincinnati, Women's Div. of Christian Serv., Bd. of Missions & Church Extension, Methodist Church, 1950)

Proud Shoes, the Story of an American Family, biog. (N.Y., Harper, 1956; reprint, Spartanburg, S.C., Reprint Co., 1973, 2nd ed., 1978)

The Constitution and Government of Ghana, with Leslie Rubin (London, Sweet & Maxwell, 1961, 2nd ed., 1964)

Human Rights U.S.A.; 1948-1966 (Cincinnati, Serv. Center, Bd. of Missions & Church Extension, Methodist Church, 1967)

Sidelights: of *Proud Shoes* (the story of her own family) it has been said: "This extraordinary memoir is important both as literature and as social history, and is based upon a record of fact." (*Soon, One Morning*)
"She was the first black attorney general of California. The only woman in the New York law firm of Paul, Weiss, Rifkin, Wharton and Garrison, she has taught law at Yale ... in Ghana, and at Boston and Brandeis Universities.... A dedicated feminist, she was one of the founders of the National Organization of Women (NOW)." (Publisher)
Became first Black woman priest in the country.

Sources: *American Negro Poetry*; *Books in Print*, 1980-81; *Poetry of Black America*; Pub. information; *Soon, One Morning.*

MYERS, WALTER DEAN. Juvenile Writer.
Born in Martinsburg, W. Va., Aug. 12, 1937. *Education:* City U. *Family:* Son Michael, d. Karen. *Career:* Juvenile Author. *Honors:* Council on Interracial Bks. for Children Award, 1968. *Mailing address:* 150 W. 225th St., Section 10, Bronx, N.Y. 10463.

Writings
Fiction
Where Does the Day Go?, juv. (N.Y., Parents Mag. Press, 1969)

The Dancers, juv. (Parents Mag., 1972; n.p., Scholarly Bk. Serv., 1972)

The Dragon Takes a Wife (Indianapolis, Bobbs-Merrill, 1972)

Fly, Jimmy, Fly!, juv. (N.Y., Putnam, 1974)

Fast Sam, Cool Clyde and Stuff, juv. (N.Y., Viking, 1975)

Brainstorm, novel (N.Y., Watts, 1977; N.Y., Dell, 1979)

Mojo and the Russians, juv. (Viking, 1977; Avon, 1979)

It Ain't All for Nothing, juv. (Viking, 1978; N.Y., Avon, 1979)

The Young Landlords, juv. (Viking, 1979)

Black Pearl and the Ghost; or, One Mystery after Another, juv. (Viking, 1980)

The Golden Serpent, juv. (Viking, 1980)

Hoops, juv. (N.Y., Delacorte, 1981; paper, N.Y., Dell, 1983)

The Legend of Tarik, juv. (Viking, 1981; paper, N.Y., Scholastic, 1982)

Won't Know till I Get There (Viking, 1982)

The Nicholas Factor, juv. (Viking, 1983)

Nonfiction
The World of Work: A Guide to Choosing a Career (Bobbs-Merrill, 1975)

Sidelights: In *Fast Sam, Cool Clyde, and Stuff*, a funny and energetic book, Walter Dean Myers "brings to life with warmth and good humor an unusual group of boys and girls, who grow to know the meaning of friendship." (Book jacket)

Sources: Author information; *Books in Print*, 1979-80, 1980-81, 1983-84; *Fast Sam, Cool Clyde, and Stuff*.

NEAL, LAWRENCE P. (LARRY) Anthologist, Editor, Critic, Activist.
Born in Atlanta, Ga., Sept. 5, 1937. *Education:* B.A., Lincoln U., 1961; M.A., U. of Pa., 1963. *Family:* Married Evelyn Rodgers of Birmingham, Ala. *Career:* Arts Ed., *The Cricket & Journal of Black Poetry*, 1964-66; Tchr., City Coll. of N.Y., 1968-69; Writer-in-Residence, Wesleyan U., 1969-70; Fellow, Yale U., 1970-75. Died in 1981.

Writings:
Fiction
Black Fire; An Anthology of Afro-American Writings, co-ed. with LeRoi Jones (N.Y., Morrow, 1968)

Nonfiction
Black Boogaloo, Notes on Black Liberation (San Francisco, Journal of Black Poetry Press, 1969)

Bowling, with Lou Bellisimo (Englewood Cliffs, N.J., Prentice-Hall, Sports Ser., 1971)

Hoodoo Hollerin' Behop Ghosts (N.Y., Random House, 1971, Wash., D.C., Howard U. Press, 1974)

Analytical Study of Afro-American Culture (Random House, 1972)

Perspective Concepts in Therapeutic Recreation, with Chris Edginton (n.p., Uniform Officer Record Center Leisure, 1982)

Sidelights: With LeRoi Jones and Black Arts Movement for several years. Educational Director for New York Black Panther Party. "I see my work as the spiritual, cultural, and political voice of my people, and I place it at their service. I feel that Black America is the final arbiter of the works of her artists." (*For Malcolm*)
Suffered fatal heart attack while lecturing at Cornell, Jan. 5, 1981.

Sources: *Blackamerican Literature; Black American Writer, vol II: Poetry and Drama; Black Fire; Black Scholar*, vol. 11, no. 8, Nov.-Dec. 1980; *Books in Print*, 1978-79; *For Malcolm; New Black Voices; Soulscript*.

NELL, WILLIAM COWPER. Historian.
Born in Boston, Mass., in 1816. Self-educated. *Career:* Closely associated with William Lloyd Garrison in publication of the *Liberator* (as copyist, accountant, & collector), & for a time with Frederick Douglass in publ. of the *North Star* in Rochester, N.Y. Died in 1874.

Writings:
Nonfiction

Services of Colored Americans, in the Wars of 1776 and 1812 (Boston, Prentiss & Sawyer, 1851; 2nd ed. Boston, R. F. Walcutt, 1852; reprint, Phila., A.M.E. Pub. House, 1894)

The Colored Patriots of the American Revolution, with Sketches of Several Distinguished Colored Persons: To Which Is Added a Brief Survey of the Condition and Prospects of Colored Americans, with an Introduction by Harriet Beecher Stowe (R. F. Wallcut, 1855)

Sidelights: "Upon the suggestion of Whittier, Nell gathered the facts for a pamphlet, *Services of Colored Americans...*, which he enlarged into *The Colored Patriots of the American Revolution....* Wendell Phillips and Harriet Beecher Stowe prepared introductions to this work, one of the best examples of early historical writing by American Negroes." (*Negro Caravan*)

Sources: *Historical Negro Biographies*; *Negro Author*; *Negro Caravan*.

NELSON, ALICE DUNBAR. Journalist, Poet, Lecturer, Short Story Writer.
Born in New Orleans, La., in 1875. *Education:* Straight Coll., New Orleans; U. of Pa.; Cornell U.; Sch. of Industrial Art. *Family:* Married 1st Paul Laurence Dunbar (poet), 1898; married 2nd Robert J. Nelson, 1916. *Career:* Tchr., New Orleans & Brooklyn, N.Y.; Journalist; Lect.; one of founders of White Rose Industrial Sch. for Colored Girls, Del. Died in 1935.

Writings:
Fiction

Violets and Other Tales (Boston, Monthly Review, 1894)

The Goodness of St. Roque and Other Stories (N.Y., Dodd, 1899; reprint, N.Y., AMS, 1975)

Nonfiction

Masterpieces of Negro Eloquence; The Best Speeches Delivered by the Negro from the Days of Slavery to the Present Time, ed. (N.Y., Bookery, 1914; reprint, N.Y., Johnson Reprint, 1970)

The Dunbar Speaker and Entertainer, Containing the Best Prose and Poetic Selections by and about the Negro Race, with Programs Arranged for Special Entertainment, ed. (Naperville, Ill., J. L. Nichols, 1920)

People and Music, new ed. (Boston, Allyn, 1973)

An Alice Dunbar-Nelson Reader, ed. by Ruby Ora Williams (Wash., D.C., U. Press of Amer., 1979)

Sources: *Books in Print*, Supplement, 1975-76; *Caroling Dusk*; *Negro Poets and Their Poems*; *Poetry of Black America*.

NGUGI, (JAMES) WA THIONG'O. (Kenyan). Novelist, Playwright, Critic (Literary, Cultural, and Political), Literature Professor.
Born in Limuru, Central Province, near Nairobi, Kenya, Jan. 5, 1936; a Gikuyu. *Education:* Makerere Coll., Kampala, Uganda, grad. 1964; U. of Leeds, Eng. *Career:* Spec. Lect., Eng., U. Coll. of Nairobi; Visiting Prof., Northwestern U., Evanston, Ill., 1970- ; Ed., "Penpoint" Journal & "Zuku" Journal, Makerere Coll., 1967-69; Prof., Lit., U. of Nairobi; Writer & Farmer. *Honors:* Received awards from both 1966 Dakar Festival of Negro Arts & the E. African Lit. Bureau. *Mailing address:* c/o William Heinemann Ltd., 15-16 Queen St., London WIX 8BE, Eng.

Writings:
Fiction

Weep Not, Child, novel (London, Heinemann, 1964, 1966, 1967; N.Y., Collier, 1969)

The River Between, novel (Heinemann, 1965, 1966)

A Grain of Wheat, novel (Heinemann, 1967, 1968)

The Black Merit, play (Heinemann, 1968)

This Time Tomorrow [Three Plays] (Nairobi, E. African Lit. Bureau, 1970?)

Secret Lives, and Other Stories (N.Y., Lawrence Hill, 1974)

Petals of Blood, novel (N.Y., Dutton, 1977)

I Will Marry When I Want, play (Heinemann, 1982)

Nonfiction

Homecoming: Essays on African and Caribbean Literature, Culture and Politics (Heinemann, 1972; Lawrence Hill, 1973)

The Trail of Dedan Kimothi, essays (Heinemann, 1977)

Mtawa Mweusi (Heinemann, 1978)

Detained: A Writer's Prison Diary (Heinemann, 1981)

Writers in Politics (Heinemann, 1981)

Sidelights: Ngugi's education was interrupted in 1948-50 by the Mau Mau conflict. *Weep Not, Child* was first English-language novel to be written by an East African writer. (*Who's Who in African Literature*)

His novel *Devil on the Cross* was originally published in Gikuyu. Ngugi has found plays to be the most effective way of politicizing the people. His first play in Gikuyu was translated as *I Will Marry When I Want*.

In commenting on *A Grain of Wheat*, Arthur Ravenscroft states, "A great strength of this finely orchestrated novel is Ngugi's skillful use of disrupted time sequence to indicate the close inter-relatedness between the character's behaviour in the Rebellion and the state of their lives (and of the nation at Independence)." (*Contemporary Novelists*)

Sources: *Books in Print*, 1981-82, 1983-84; *Contemporary Novelists*, 1972; *Who's Who in African Literature*; *Writers Directory*, 1980-82.

NICHOLS, CHARLES HAROLD. English Professor, Folklorist.

Born in Brooklyn, N.Y., July 6, 1919. *Education:* B.A., Brooklyn Coll., 1942; Ph.D., Brown U., 1948. *Family:* Married Mildred Thompson; son David, son Keith, son Brian. *Career:* Prof., Eng., Hampton Inst., 1949-59; Prof. of N. Amer. Lit., Free U. of Berlin, 1959-69; Prof. of Eng. & Chairman, Afro-Amer. Studies Program, Brown U. *Honors:* Rachel Herstein Scholarship, 1938-42; N.Y. State Regents Scholar; Rosenwald Fellow; Fulbright grants; Senior Fellow, NEH, 1973-74; Guest Prof. of Amer. Lit., Aarhus U., 1954-55; Guest Lect.: Oxford, Stockholm, Oslo, Rome, and Others. *Mailing address:* Box 1852, Brown U., Providence, R.I. 02912.

Writings:
Fiction
African Nights: Black Erotic Folk Tales (n.p., Herden, 1971)

Nonfiction
Many Thousand Gone, the Ex-Slaves' Account of Their Bondage and Freedom (Leiden, E. J. Brill, 1963; Bloomington, Ind. U., 1969)

Instructor's Guide to Accompany Cavalcade: Negro American Writing (Boston, Houghton Mifflin, 1970)

Black Men in Chains; Narratives by Escaped Slaves, ed. (N.Y., Lawrence Hill, 1972)

Arna Bontemps-Langston Hughes Letters, 1925-67, ed. (N.Y., Dodd, Mead, 1980)

Sources: Author information; *Books in Print*, 1980-81; *Library Journal*, Apr. 1, 1980.

NKRUMAH, KWAME. (Ghanaian). President of Ghana, Pan-Africanist, Activist.
Born in Nkroful, Ghana, Sept. 21, 1909 (son of a goldsmith). *Education:* Prince of Wales Coll., Achimota, Ghana; B.A., Lincoln U., Pa., 1939; U. of Pa. (B. Theol., M. Sci. in Educ.); Hon. Ph.D., Lincoln U., 1951. *Career:* Instr., Philosophy, Lincoln U.; Founder, African Students Assoc. of U.S. & Can.; Gen. Secy., W. African Natl. Secretariat; Ed., W. African Students' Union publ.; Secy., Pan-African Congress; Gen. Secy., United Gold Coast Convention; Chairman, Convention People's Party; Prime Minister & Pres., Ghana, 1952- . Died in exile in Guinea in 1972.

Writings:
Nonfiction

Ghana: The Autobiography of Kwame Nkrumah (N.Y., Nelson, 1957; N.Y., Intnl., 1971)

Towards Colonial Freedom; Africa in the Struggle against World Imperialism (Accra, Guinea Press, 1957?; London, Heinemann, 1962)

I Speak of Freedom; A Statement of African Ideology (Heinemann, 1961)

Africa Must Unite (Heinemann, 1963, 1970)

Challenge of the Congo (Intnl., 1967; London, Panaf Bks.-State Mutual Bks., 1981)

Axioms of Kwame Nkrumah (Panaf Bks., 1967; Intnl., 1969)

Dark Days in Ghana (Intnl., 1968)

Handbook of Revolutionary Warfare; A Guide to the Armed Phase of the African Revolution (Panaf Bks., 1968; Intnl., 1969)

Neo-Colonialism: The Last Stage of Imperialism (Heinemann, 1968)

Class Struggle in Africa (Intnl., 1970)

Consciencism; Philosophy and Ideology for Decolonisation (N.Y., Monthly Review Press, 1970)

Revolutionary Path (Intnl., 1973; State Mutual Bks., 1981)

Sources: *Books in Print*, 1980-81, 1981-82; *Ghana: The Autobiography of Kwame Nkrumah*; *Emerging African Nations and Their Leaders*, vol. 1, 1963; *Who's Who in African Literature*.

NOBLE, JEANNE L. Human Relations Professor, Guidance Expert.
Born in Albany, Ga., July 18, 1926. *Education:* Howard U., 1946; M.A., Tchrs. Coll., Columbia U. (Guidance & Developmental Psych.), 1948, Ed.D., 1955. *Career:* Tchr., Soc. Sci., Albany State Coll., Ga.; Visiting Prof.: Tuskegee Inst. & U. of Vermont; Prof., Human Relations, N.Y.U. *Honors:* "One of 100 most influential Negroes of the Emancipation Centennial Year," *Ebony* mag., 1964; Bethune-Roosevelt Award, 1965 (Educ.). *Mailing address:* c/o Prentice-Hall, Englewood Cliffs, N.J. 07632.

Writings:
Nonfiction

Beautiful, Also, Are the Souls of My Black Sisters: A History of the Black Woman in America (Englewood Cliffs, N.J., Prentice-Hall, 1978)

Sources: *Books in Print*, 1978-79; *Negro Almanac.*

NOKAN, CHARLES. (Ivorian). Novelist, Poet, Playwright, Sociologist.
Born in Yamoussokra, Ivory Coast, Dec. 28, 1936; a Baoulé. *Education:* At Yamoussokra & Toumodi; Paris lycée; U. of Poitiers; U. of Paris? (two degrees in Sociol.; the "licence" & the doctorate). *Career:* Writer: novels, poetry, plays; Sociologist. *Mailing address:* c/o Three Continents Press, 1346 Conn. Ave., Suite 224, Wash., D.C. 20036.

Writings:
(Partial Listing—English Only)
Fiction

Poems in *New Sum of Poetry from the Negro World* (Paris, Présence Africaine, vol. 57, 1966)

Poems in *Modern Poetry from Africa*, ed. by Moore & Beier, rev. ed. (London, Baltimore, 1968)

Sidelights: Nokan said of his novel (*Wild Blew the Wind*) that his work sought to conform to the esthetics of his own Baoulé people where the dance satisfies at one and the same time the ear and the eye, because of its use of both masks and chants. Therefore, he has mixed poems with prose passages in musical order, so as to recapture the quality of the tom-toms. (*African Authors*)

Sources: *African Authors*; *Books in Print*, 1979-80; *Reader's Guide to African Literature.*

(NWAPA), NWAKUCHE FLORA. (Nigerian). Novelist, Short Story Writer.
Born in Oguta, E. Nigeria, in 1931. *Education:* U. Coll. of Ibadan (Arts degree); diploma in Educ., Edinburgh U. *Family:* Married; one son. *Career:* Woman Educ. Officer, Calabar, Nigeria; Eng. & Geography Tchr., Enugu, Nigeria; Asst. Registrar, Public Relations, U. of Lagos. *Mailing address:* c/o William Heinemann Ltd., 15-16 Queen St., London WIX 8BE, Eng.

Writings:
Fiction

Efuru, novel (London, Heinemann, African Writers Ser., 1966; Heinemann Educ. Bks., 1966)

Idu, novel (Heinemann, African Writers Ser., 1970; Heinemann Educ. Bks., 1970)

This Is Lagos, and Other Stories (Enugu, Nigeria, Nwankwo-Ifejika, 1971)

Sources: *Books in Print*, 1980-81; *Interview with Six Nigerian Writers*; *Reader's Guide to African Literature.*

NYERERE, JULIUS KAMBARAGE. (Tanzanian). President of Tanzania, Essayist, Translator, Socialist and Pan-Africanist.
Born in Butiama, eastern shore of Lake Victoria, Northern Province, Tanganyika, Mar. 1922 (son of Chief Nyerere Burito of Zanski tribe). *Education:* Roman Catholic Mission Sch., Tabora, Central Province; Teaching diploma, Makerere Coll., Kampala, Uganda, 1945; M.A. (Hist. & Econ.), U. of Edinburgh, Scotland. *Family:* Married Maria Magige; five sons, one d. *Career:* Tchr., St. Mary's Mission Sch., Tabora; St. Francis X Sch., near Dar es Salaam; helped to found Tanganyika African Assn., elected Pres., 1953 (became Tanganyika African Natl. Union—TANU); elected to Legislative Council, 1958, & became Chief Minister, 1960; Prime Minister, Tanganyika (now Tanzania), May 1, 1961; Pres., 1962. *Honors:* LL.D., Duquesne U., Pittsburgh, Pa. *Mailing address:* c/o Oxford U. Press, 200 Madison Ave., N.Y., N.Y. 10016.

Writings:
(Partial Listing—English Only)
Nonfiction

Democracy and the Party System (Dar es Salaam, Tanganyika Standard, 1963?; London, Oxford U. Press, 1965)

Education for Self-Reliance (Dar es Salaam, Govt. Printer, 1967?)

Freedom and Unity: Uhuru na Umoja; A Selection from Writings and Speeches 1952-65 (Oxford U. Press, 1967)

Freedom and Development (Dar es Salaam, Govt. Printer, 196?; Oxford U. Press, 1974)

Freedom and Socialism: Uhuru na Ujamaa; A Selection from Writings and Speeches 1965-1967 (Oxford U. Press, 1968)

Ujamaa: Essays on Socialism (Dar es Salaam, Oxford U. Press, 1968; N.Y., Oxford U. Press, 1971)

Nyerere on Socialism (Oxford U. Press, 1969)

Man and Development ... (Oxford U. Press, 1974)

Crusade for Liberation (Oxford U. Press, 1978)

Sidelights: "Once described by an American official at the United Nations as a symbol of African hopes, African dignity, and African successes." Nyerere is among the most respected and influential leaders of the newly emerging African states. (*Current Biography*)
Maria Magige Nyerere became President of Tanganyika Council of Women. Julius Nyerere became first Chancellor of the University of East Africa (three colleges in Uganda, Kenya and Tanganyika), 1963. (*Current Biography*)

Sources: *African Authors*; *Books in Print*, 1979-80, 1981-82; *Current Biography*, 1963.

OBICHERE, BONIFACE IHEWUNWA. (Nigerian). History Professor, Historian.
Born in Awaka, Owerri, Nigeria, Nov. 4, 1932. *Education:* B.A. (Honors) U. of Minn., 1961; M.A., U. Cal., Berkeley, 1963; D. Phil., Oxford U., 1967. *Family:* Married Armer Gean Brown (tchr.), Aug. 22, 1964; child: Chikere. *Career:* Senior Prefect, Mt. Saint Mary's Tchrs. Coll., Azaraegbelu, Owerri, Nigeria, 1956-57, Tutor & Lect., Hist., 1957-59, Procurator, 1958-59; Tutor, Hist., Inst. of Commonwealth Studies, Oxford U., Eng., 1966-67; Prof., Hist., Cal. State U., L.A., 1969-70; Co-Dir., Ethnic Studies Program, U. S. Cal., 1969-70; Asst. Prof., 1967-68, Assoc. Prof., 1969-73, Prof., Hist., 1973- , Dir., African Studies Center, 1972-78 — all UCLA; Assoc. Prof., Hist., UCLA & Irvine (U. of Cal. Extension), 1968-70; Visiting Prof.: U. of Hawaii, summers, 1969 & 1970; U. of Ghana, 1970-71; U. of Ibadan, Nigeria, 1976-77; Ed. & Founder, *Journal of African Studies*, 1974- ; Editorial Advisor, *Journal of Black Studies*. *Honors:* Nigerian Fed. Govt. scholar, 1959-63; Beit Scholar, Oxford U., 1964-67, 1965-66; Cyril Foster Fund res. grant, Oxford U., 1966; Commonwealth Scholarship, Eng., 1966-67; Amer. Council of Learned Societies & Soc. Sci. Res. Council faculty res. grant & fellow in African Studies, 1970-71; Humanities Inst., fellow, U. of Cal., 1972-73. *Mailing address:* c/o Dept. of Hist., UCLA, L.A., Cal. 90024.

Writings:
Nonfiction

West African States and European Expansion: The Dahomy-Niger Hinterland: 1885-1898 (New Haven, Conn., Yale U. Press, 1971)

Studies in Southern Nigerian History (London, Cass, 1978; Totowa, N.J., Bibliographic Distribution Center, 1980-81)

African States and the Military: Past and Present, ed. (Bibliographic Distribution Center, 1980)

Sources: *Books in Print*, 1980-81, 1981-82; *Contemporary Authors*, vols. 41-44, 1979.

O'DANIEL, THERMAN BENJAMIN. Editor, English Professor, Critic.
Born in Wilson, N.C., July 9, 1908. *Education:* B.A., Lincoln U. (Pa.), 1930; M.A., U. of Pa., 1932; Ph.D., U. of Ottawa (Can.), 1956; further study: Harvard U., U. of Chicago, Pa. State U. *Family:* Married Lillian Davis. *Career:* One of founders, *CLA Journal*, & Ed., 1957- ; Eng. Tchr. (41 yrs.): Allen U., Columbia, S.C. (Head, Eng. Dept.; Dean, Liberal Arts Coll.; Acting Pres.); Fort Valley State Coll., Ga. (Head, Eng. Dept.; Acting Registrar; Acting Dean; Registrar; Dir., Summer Sch.); Morgan State Coll., Baltimore (Dir., Summer Sch., 2 yrs.); Dillard U., New Orleans. *Honors:* Gen. Educ. Fellow, U. of Chicago; Ford Found. Fellow, U. of Ottawa; recipient of Spec. Alice E. Johnson Memorial Fund Award (from Black Acad. of Arts & Letters) for *CLA Journal*, 1972. *Mailing address:* c/o CLA Journal, Morgan State Coll., Baltimore, Md. 21212.

Writings:
Nonfiction

Langston Hughes, Black Genius: A Critical Evaluation, ed. (N.Y., Morrow, 1971)

International Dimensions II. African, Afro-American, Caribbean, Japanese, ed. (Baltimore, Coll. Lang. Assn. Journal, 1972)

James Baldwin: A Critical Evaluation (Wash., D.C., Howard U. Press, 1977)

Sources: Author information; *Books in Print*, Supplement, 1975-76.

OGOT, BETHWELL ALAN. (Kenyan). Historian, History Professor.
Family: Married Grace Akinye, 1959; three children. *Career:* Historian; Chairman, Hist. Dept., U. Coll., Nairobi, Kenya. *Mailing address:* c/o Humanities Press, Inc., Atlantic Highlands, N.J. 07716.

Writings:
Nonfiction

A History of the Southern Luo, vol. 1, *Migration and Settlement, 1500-1900* (Nairobi, E. African Pub. House, 1967- ; N.Y., Intnl. Pub. Serv., 1967)

Zamani: A Survey of East African History, ed. with J. A. Kieran (N.Y., Humanities, 1968)

War and Society in Africa, ed. (Totowa, N.J., Bibliographic Distribution Center, 1972, 1975)

Economic and Social History of East Africa, ed. (Nairobi, E. Africa Lit. Bureau, 1976)

Kenya before 1900, ed. (E. African Pub. House, 1976)

A Historical Dictionary of Kenya (Metuchen, N.J., Scarecrow, 1981)

Sources: *Books in Print*, 1980-81, 1981-82; *Journal of African History*, vol. 20, 1979.

OGOT, GRACE AKINYE. (Kenyan). Novelist, Short Story Writer.
Born in Central Nyanza Province, Kenya, in 1930. *Education:* Butere High Sch.; Ng'iya Girls' Sch.; Gen. Nurse & Midwife, Uganda & Brit. *Family:* Married Dr. Bethwell Alan Ogot, 1959; three children. *Career:* Script Writer & Announcer, Brit. Broadcasting Co., London, 1955-58; Community Development Officer, Kisumu; Nursing Sister & Midwifery Tutor, Masemo Hospital, Nyanza; Public Relations Officer for Air India, Nairobi. *Mailing address:* c/o Humanities Press, Inc., Atlantic Highlands, N.J. 07716.

Writings:
Fiction

The Promised Land, novel (Nairobi, E. African Pub. House, 1966)

Land without Thunder; Short Stories (E. African Pub. House, 1968)

The Other Woman: Selected Short Stories (Nairobi, Trans-Africa Pub., 1976)

Sidelights: Grace Ogot's husband is an historian who became Chairman of the History Department at University College, Nairobi. She has contributed to *Pan African Short Stories*, 1965.

Sources: *African Writing Today*; *Reader's Guide to African Literature*; *Who's Who in African Literature*.

OKARA, GABRIEL IMOMOTIMI OBAINGAING. (Nigerian). Novelist, Short Story Writer, Script-writer, Civil Servant.
Born in Mumodi (or Bumdi), Ijaw District, Delta Region, W. Nigeria, Apr. 21, 1921; an Ijaw. *Education:* Govt. Coll., Umuahia, Nigeria; Journalism, Northwestern U., Evanston, Ill. *Career:* Principal Information Officer, Ministry of Information, Eastern Nigerian Govt. Serv.; Information Officer, Biafra, 1967-69; Press Officer, Enugu; Rivers State Ministry of Information, Port Harcourt. Has done film scripts & radio features. *Honors:* Poem "The Call of the River Nun," won Nigerian Festival of Art award, 1953. *Mailing address:* c/o William Heinemann Ltd., 15-16, Queen St., London WIX 8BE, Eng.

Writings:
Fiction

The Voice; A Novel (London, Deutsch, 1964; London, Heinemann, African Writers Ser., 1970; N.Y., Watts, 1964; N.Y., Holmes & Meier, 1970)

The Fisherman's Invocation, short stories (Heinemann, African Writers Ser., 1978)

Sidelights: Okara, considered by many to be the outstanding Nigerian poet, translated the folklore of his Ijaw heritage. He has read his poems in various countries of Africa, in Europe and the United States. They have been published in England, America, Sweden, West Germany, and Italy and have been translated into Hebrew. (*African Writers on African Writing*)

"Okara has attempted with some success to work from Ijaw directly into English, preserving some of the power and style of the original." (*African Authors*)

Sources: *African Authors*; *African Writers on African Writing*; *Books in Print*, 1979-80, 1980-81; *Poems from Black Africa*.

OKIGBO, CHRISTOPHER. (Nigerian). Poet, Teacher.
Born in Ojoto, near Onitsha, E. Nigeria, in 1932. *Education:* Govt. Coll., Umuahia; B.A. (Classics), U. Coll. of Ibadan, 1956. *Family:* Wife; daughter. *Career:* Private Secy. to Fed. Minister of Res. & Information, 1955-56; Mem., Lib. staff, U. of Nigeria at Nsukka, 1956-58; Tchr., Didity, near Ibadan; W. African Rep. for Cambridge U. Press (1960s). One of eds. of *Transition* mag. (Kampala, Uganda) & of Mbari Press at Ibadan. Widely anthologized & critiqued. Refused 1st Prize at Dakar Festival of African Arts in 1966. Died Aug. 1967.

Writings:
Fiction

Heavensgate, poems (Ibadan, Nigeria, Mbari Pub., 1962)

Limits, poems (Mbari Pub., 1964)

Labyrinths, with Path of Thunder, poems, posthumous (London, Heinemann; N.Y., African Pub., 1971; also paper, N.Y., Holmes & Meier)

Sidelights: Christopher Okigbo was also included in Heinemann's African Writers Series, number 62 (with six poems). He founded a small publishing company with Chinua Achebe in Enugu in 1967, but was killed in action near Nsukka, the provisional capital of Biafra. "... considered finest and most complex of all the Nigerian poets." (*African Authors*)

Sources: *African Authors*; *Books in Print*, 1979-80, 1980-81; *Reader's Guide to African Literature*.

OKPAKU, JOSEPH OHIOMOGBEN. (Nigerian). Playwright, Critic, Engineer, Publisher.
Born in Lokoja, Nigeria, Mar. 24, 1943. *Education:* B.A. (Civil Engineering), Northwestern U.; M.S. (Structural Engineering), Stanford U., Cal.; doctoral work (Theatre Hist.), Stanford. *Career:* Pres. & Pub., Third Press, N.Y.C.—now Okpaku Communications (1st major Black-owned trade book pub. firm in U.S.); Assoc. Prof. of Lit., Sarah Lawrence Coll.; Ed., *Journal of the New African Lit. & the Arts* (UCLA). *Mailing address:* c/o Okpaku Communications, 444 Central Park W., N.Y., N.Y. 10025.

Writings:
Fiction

The Two Faces of Anirejuortse; A Social Drama (Minneapolis, n.p., 1965?)

The Virtues of Adultery Play (Palo Alto, Cal., Stanford U. Press, 1966)

The King's Son; or, After the Victory Was Lost; An African Play in Three Acts (N.Y., n.p., 1966)

The Presidents: The Frogs on Capitol Hill; A Ritual in 3 Acts (Stanford U. Press, 1967)

The Silhouette of God, play (performed in Berkeley, Cal., May 17, 1969)

New African Literature and the Arts, ed., vols. 1-3 (N.Y., Crowell, 1969-72; vol. 3, N.Y., Okpaku Communications, 1973)

Nonfiction

Four Months and Fifteen Days—the Chicago Trial, with Verna Sadock (N.Y., Third Press, 1970)

Verdict: The Exclusive Picture Story of the Trial of the Chicago Eight (Third Press, 1970)

Nigeria, Dilemma of Nationhood: An African Analysis of the Biafran Conflict, ed. (Westport, Conn. Greenwood, Contrib. in Afro-Amer. Studies, no. 12, 1971; Third Press, 1970; Okpaku Communications, 1974)

Superfight No. 11: The Story behind the Fights between Muhammad Ali and Joe Frazier (Okpaku, 1974)

Sidelights: Another play is *Born Astride the Grave*. An unpublished novel is *Under the Iroko Tree*.

Sources: *Books in Print*; *Contemporary Authors*, 1978; *Who's Who in African Literature*.

OTTLEY, ROI VINCENT. Social Historian, Journalist.
Born in N.Y.C., Aug. 2, 1906. *Education:* St. Bonaventure Coll., 1926-27; U. of Mich. (2 yrs.); Columbia U., 1934-35; N.Y.U., 1935-36; St. John's U. Sch. of Law. *Family:* Married Gladys Tarr, Apr. 1941. *Career:* Reporter, Columnist, Ed., *Amsterdam News*, N.Y., 1930-37; Publicity Dir., Natl. CIO War Relief Com., 1943; War Correspondent, *Liberty* mag. Died in 1960.

Writings:
Fiction
White Marble Lady, novel (N.Y., Farrar, Straus, 1965)

Nonfiction
New World A-Coming: Inside Black America (Boston, Houghton Mifflin, 1943; reprint, N.Y., Arno, 1968)

Black Odyssey; The Story of the Negro in America (N.Y., Scribner's, 1948; London, Murray, 1949)

No Green Pastures (Scribner's, 1951; Murray, 1951)

Lonely Warrior. Life and Times of Robert S. Abbott (Chicago, Regnery, 1955)

The Negro in New York: An Informal Social History, with William J. Weatherby, eds. (N.Y., Public Lib., 1967)

Sidelights: *New World A-Coming* is described by John Chamberlain in the *New York Times*: "He writes a vigorous prose, mingling history, humor, irony, drama, and sober reflection in a work that explains the current status and the wholly reasonable demands of the Negroes as no other does." Lewis Gannett describes it as "a shrewd, lively, and often surprising interpretation of the present state of mind of Negro America." Sam Halper of the New York *Post* wrote, "The way to start in to learn about the Negroes is to read Ottley's fine book." (*Current Biography*)

Sources: *Afro-American Writers*; *Books in Print*, Supplement, 1975-76; *Current Biography*, 1943; *Lonesome Road; Negro Almanac.*

OUSMANE, SEMBÈNE. (Senegalese). Filmmaker, Novelist.
Born in Zinguinchor-Casamance, Senegal, in 1923. *Education:* l'Ecole de Céramique at Marsassoum. *Career:* Plumber; bricklayer; fisherman; apprentice mechanic; French Colonial Army; docker; trade union leader; filmmaker. *Honors: White Genesis & The Money Order* won francophone prize, Dakar Festival. *Mailing address:* c/o Inscape Corp., 1629 K St., N.W., Wash., D.C. 20006.

Writings:
(Partial Listing—English Only)
Fiction

God's Bits of Wood, novel, transl. by Francis Price (N.Y., Doubleday, 1970; N.Y., Anchor, 1970)

The Money-Order; With, White Genesis, novel, transl. by Clive Wake (London, Heinemann, 1972)

Tribal Scars and Other Stories, transl. from French by Len Ortzen (Wash., D.C., Inscape, 1974; Heinemann, African Writers Ser., 1974)

Xala, novel, transl. by Clive Wake (Westport, Conn., Lawrence Hill, 1976)

The Last of the Empire (Heinemann, 1983)

Sidelights: Sembène made films from *The Money Order* and *Xala* himself.

Sources: *Books in Print*, 1980-81, 1983-84; *The Money-Order*; *Who's Who in African Literature*.

OWENS, CHARLES EDWARD. Psychology Professor, Psychologist, Criminologist.
Born Mar. 7, 1938. *Education:* B.A. (Elementary Educ.), W. Va. State Coll., 1961; M.A. (Guidance & Counseling), W. Va. U., 1965; D. Ed. (Pupil Personnel Serv.), U. of N. Mex., 1971. *Family:* Married Otis Owens; children: three sons. *Career:* Counselor/Coordinator of Testing & Referrals: Job Corps Centers for Women; Packard Bell Electronics Corp., 1966-68; Counselor/Assoc. Dir., Tutorial & Financial Assistance, U. of Wis., Madison, 1969-71; Counselor, Asst. Prof. of Educ., Va. Commonwealth U., Richmond, 1971-73; Assoc. Prof., Dept. of Psychology, U. of Ala., 1973- . *Honors:* Fellowship recipient, U.S. Office of Educ., 1968-69. *Mailing address:* 33 Parkside, Tuscaloosa, Ala. 35401.

Writings:
Nonfiction

Blacks and Criminal Justice, with Jimmy Bell, eds. (Lexington, Mass., Lexington Bks., 1977)

Mental Health and the Black Offender (Lexington Bks., D. C. Heath, 1980)

Sources: Author information; *Books in Print*, 1980-81.

OWENS, JESSE. Track and Field Star.
Born in Danville, Ala., Sept. 12, 1913. *Education:* E. Tech. High Sch., Cleveland, Ohio; B.A., Ohio State U., 1937. *Family:* Married Ruth Solomon, 1935; d. Gloria Hemphill, d. Beverly Prather, d. Marlene Runkin. *Career:* Athlete; Org. official; Sales Executive; Public Speaker; Consultant. *Honors:* Black Hall of Fame; E. Tech. Hall of Fame; U.S. Track & Field Hall of Fame; State of Ala. Hall of Fame; Ambassador of "Good Will" to Far East (Eisenhower Admin.); hon. doctorates: Otterbein Coll. (Public Serv.); Nev. U. (Law); Ohio State U. (Athletic Arts). Died in Tucson, Ariz., Mar. 31, 1980.

Writings:
Nonfiction

Blackthink; My Life as Black Man and White Man (N.Y., Morrow, 1970)

The Jesse Owens Story (N.Y., Putnam, 1970)

I Have Changed, with Paul G. Neimark (Morrow, 1972)

Track and Field, juv., with Dick O'Connor (N.Y., Atheneum, 1976)

Jesse: A Spiritual Autobiography (Plainfield, N.J., Logos Intnl., 1978)

Jesse: The Man Who Outran Hitler, with Paul Neimark & Benjamin Mercado, eds., Rhode Flores, transl. from Eng. (Spanish), paper ed. (n.p., Vida Publ., 1979; N.Y., Fawcett, 1979)

Sidelights: "In 1936, at the Berlin Olympics, Owens won four gold medals, at that time the most universally acclaimed feat in the history of the games. When Adolf Hitler refused to present him medals he had won in the various competitions, Owen's fame became even more widespread as a result of the publicity." (*Negro Almanac*)

Sources: Author information; *Current Biography*, 1956; *Famous Negro Athletes*; *Negro Almanac*.

OYONO, FERDINAND LÉOPOLD. (Cameroonian). Novelist, Short Story Writer, Lawyer, Diplomat.
Born in N'goulemakong, near Ebolowa, Cameroon, Sept. 14, 1929 (son of a Béti chief & a Catholic mother). *Education:* Lycée de Provins; Faculté de Droit; Ecole Nationale d'Admin.; (Dr. of Law), Paris. *Career:* Dir., Bureau d'Etudes, Yaoundé, Cameroon; Permanent Delegate, UN; Consul Gen., Brussels; Ambassador to Liberia; Minister Plenipotentiary to Common Market. *Mailing address:* c/o Africana Pub. Co., 101 Fifth Ave., N.Y., N.Y. 10003.

Writings:
(Partial Listing—English Only)
Fiction

Houseboy, novel, transl. by John Reed (London, Heinemann, 1966; as *Boy!*, N.Y., Collier, Macmillan, 1970)

The Old Man and the Medal, novel, transl. by John Reed (Heinemann, 1967; N.Y., Humanities, 1967; N.Y., Collier, 1971)

Sidelights: "[*Houseboy*] denounced openly the excesses of colonial society.... Ferdinand Oyono's novels celebrate the disillusionment of the African with the white man's world." He is considered probably the greatest master of construction among African novelists. (*A Reader's Guide to African Literature*)

Sources: *African Writing Today*; *Books in Print*, 1979-80, 1980-81; *Reader's Guide to African Literature*.

PAGE, JAMES ALLEN. Librarian, Adult Educator.
Born in Lexington, Ky., Jan. 31, 1918. *Education:* B.A. (Psychology), Roosevelt U., Chicago, 1950; M.S.L.S., U. S. Cal., 1957; M.A. (Adult Educ.), Ind. U., Bloomington, 1967. *Family:* Married Ethel S. Ross, Jan. 29, 1949; children: Ramona Jean Page, Anita Maria Assemian. *Career:* Elementary Sch. Tchr., 1951-56; Adult Sch. Tchr., 1954-59, 1974-77; Branch & Regional Ref. Librn., L.A. County Public Lib., 1961-64; Coll. Librn., Hampton Inst., Va., 1964-65; Coordinator of Adult Educ., Gary (Ind.) Public Lib., 1966-68; Adult Services Consultant, Mid-Hudson Lib., Poughkeepsie, N.Y., 1968-71; Senior Librn., L.A. Public Lib., 1971-83; Ref. Librn., L.A. Southwest Community Coll., 1974- . *Honors:* 1st Prize, Annual Essay Contest, Negro Hist. Week, L.A., 1954; Fellowship, Adult Educ. Dept., Ind. U., 1966; Resolutions or Certificates of Appreciation or Commendation: L.A. Mayor Tom Bradley; L.A. City Council; Cal. State Senate; Bd. of Lib. Commissioners, L.A.; Grant, Amer. Forum for Intnl. Study, 1977; 2nd Pl. Award, Congregational Christian Hist. Soc., 1980. *Mailing address:* 1205 S. Spaulding Ave., L.A., Cal. 90019.

Writings:
Nonfiction

Selected Black American Authors: An Illustrated Bio-Bibliography, comp. (Boston, G. K. Hall, 1977)

History of Congregational Church of Christian Fellowship (L.A., Church of Christian Fellowship, 1980)

Sources: Author information; *Books in Print*, 1980-81; *Contemporary Authors*, vol. 107, 1983.

PAINTER, NELL IRVIN. History Professor, Historian.
Born in Houston, Tex., Aug. 2, 1942. *Education:* B.A., U. Cal., Berkeley, 1964; M.A., UCLA, 1967; Ph.D., Harvard U., 1974; U. of Bordeaux, 1962-63; U. of Ghana, 1965-66. *Career:* Asst. Prof. of Amer. & Afro-Amer. Hist., 1974- , Assoc. Prof. of Hist., U. of Pa., Phila. *Honors:* Coretta Scott King Award, Amer. Assn. of U. Women, 1969; Amer. Council of Learned Societies Fellow, 1976-77; Fellow, Charles Warren Center for Studies in Amer. Hist., Harvard U., 1976-77; Radcliffe Inst. Fellow, 1976-77. *Mailing address:* Dept. of Hist., U. of Pa., Phila. 19174.

Writings:
Nonfiction

Exodusters: Black Migration to Kansas after Reconstruction (N.Y., Knopf, 1976; N.Y., Norton, 1979)

The Narrative of Hosea Hudson: His Life as a Negro Communist in the South (Cambridge, Harvard U. Press, 1979)

The Progressive Era (Knopf, 1984)

Sidelights: William E. Leuchtenburg explains that *The Narrative of Hosea Hudson* is unique. He felt that in fashioning this book, Nell Painter had gone well beyond the role of interviewer and editor and had become a skillful, resourceful collaborator who had created a vivid record of what it meant to be both red and black in the Deep South during the Great Depression. Hudson himself had had published *Black Worker in the Deep South: A Personal Record* (N.Y., Intnl. Pub., 1972). (*Narrative of Hosea Hudson*)

Sources: *Books in Print*, 1980-81, 1983-84; *Contemporary Authors*, vols. 65-68, 1977; *Exodusters*; *Narrative of Hosea Hudson*.

PALMER, C(YRIL) EVERARD. (Jamaican). Juvenile Writer, Teacher.
Born in Kendal, Jamaica, in 1930. *Education:* Mico Coll., Kingston, Jamaica. *Career:* Tchr., public sch., 1956-57 & 1965-70; Tchr., high sch., 1958-62; Tchr., Red Rock, Ontario, Can., 1971- . *Honors:* Certificate of Merit, Jamaica Reading Assn., for Contributions to Jamaican Children's Lit. *Mailing address:* Box 31, Nipigon, Ontario POT 2J0, Can.

Writings:
Fiction

A Broken Vessel, juv. (Kingston, Jamica, Pioneer Press, 1960)

The Adventures of Jimmy Maxwell, juv. (Jamaica Publ. Branch, Ministry of Educ., 1962)

A Taste of Danger, juv. (Kingston Publ. Branch, 1963)

The Cloud with the Silver Lining, juv. (London, Deutsch, 1966; N.Y., Pantheon, 1967)

Big Doc Bitteroot, juv. (Deutsch, 1968; Indianapolis, Ind., Bobbs-Merrill, 1971)

The Sun Salutes You, juv. (Deutsch, 1970; Bobbs-Merrill, 1971)

Hummingbird People, juv. (Deutsch, 1971)

The Wooing of Beppo Tate, juv. (Deutsch, 1972)

Baba and Mr. Big, juv. (Bobbs-Merrill, 1972)

A Cow Called Boy, juv. (Bobbs-Merrill, 1972)

My Father, Sun-Sun Johnson, juv. (Deutsch, 1974)

Dog Called Houdini, juv. (Deutsch, 1979)

Sources: *Authors and Writers Who's Who*; *Jamaican National Bibliography*; *West Indian Literature*.

PARKS, GORDON ALEXANDER. Photographer, Editorial Director, Film Producer, Director, Poet. Born in Fort Scott, Kan., Nov. 30, 1912. *Education:* High Sch., St. Paul, Minn.; self-educated. *Family:* Married 1st Sally Alvis, 1933 (div. 1961); son Gordon, Jr., d. Toni (Mrs. Jean-Luc Brouillard), son David; married 2nd Elizabeth Campbell (high fashion model & d. of E. Sims Campbell, cartoonist), Dec. 1962 (div. 1973); d. Leslie. *Career:* Wartime serv.: Office of War Information; Photographer & Correspondent, 1942-45; Photographer, *Life* mag., 1948-72; Ed. Dir., *Essence*, 1970- ; Prod. & Dir., Warner Brothers, 1968; Dir., Metro-Goldwyn-Mayer, 1970-72; Pres., Winger Corp. *Honors:* Hon. degrees from educ. institutions; Photographer of Yr., Assn. of Mag. Photographers; Mass Media Award, Natl. Conf. of Christians & Jews, for outstanding contrib. to better human relations; Carr Ban Adna Award, 1970; Spingarn Medal, NAACP, 1972. *Mailing address:* 860 United Nations Plaza, N.Y., N.Y.

Writings:
Fiction

A Poet and His Camera, poems with own photographs (N.Y., Viking, 1968)

In Love, poems (Phila., Lippincott, 1971)

Gordon Parks: Whispers of Intimate Things, poems with own photographs (Viking, 1971)

Moments without Proper Names, poems (Viking, 1975)

To Smile in Autumn, poems (N.Y., Norton, 1979)

Shannon, novel (Boston, Little, Brown, 1981)

Nonfiction

The Learning Tree, autobiog. (N.Y., Harper, 1963; paper, N.Y., Fawcett, 1970)

A Choice of Weapons, autobiog. (Harper, 1966; paper, N.Y., Noble & Noble, 1968; N.Y., Berkley Pub., 1969; Har-Row, 1973)

Born Black with Photos (Lippincott, 1971)

Flavio (Norton, 1978)

Sidelights: In 1960s filmed three documentaries on Black ghetto life for National Educational Television, and "The Weapons of Gordon Parks," a television adaptation of his autobiography, narrated by Parks, was presented over Columbia Broadcasting System network in April 1968. *The Learning Tree* was filmed by Warner Brothers-Seven Arts — for which Parks wrote the score. Musical compositions include a piano concerto and three piano sonatas. (*Current Biography*)

Sources: *Books in Print*, 1978-79, 1981-82; *Current Biography*, 1968; Pub. information.

PATTERSON, HORACE ORLANDO. (Jamaican). Sociologist, Sociology Professor, Novelist. Born in Jamaica, June 5, 1940. *Education:* B. Sci. (Econ.), 1962, Ph.D. (Sociol.), 1965, London U.; U. of W. Indies; London Sch. of Econ. *Family:* Married Merys Wyn Thomas, Sept. 5, 1965; children: Rhiannon, Barbara. *Career:* Asst. Lect., Sociol., London Sch. of Econ., 1965-67; Lect., Sociol., U. of W. Indies, 1967-70; Visiting Lect., Harvard U., 1970-71, Prof., Sociol., 1971- ; Allston Burr Sr. tutor, 1971-73; Mem. Tech. Advisory Com. to Prime Minister & Govt. of Jamaica, 1972- . *Honors:* Jamaica Govt. Exhibition Scholar, 1959-62; Commonwealth scholar, Great Brit., 1962-65; 1st Prize for *Children of Sisyphus*, Dakar Festival of Negro Arts. *Mailing address:* Leverett House, F 112 De Wolf St., Cambridge, Mass. 02138.

Writings:
Fiction

The Children of Sisyphus, novel (London, Hutchinson, 1964; Boston, Houghton Mifflin, 1965; pub. as *Dinah*, Elmhurst, N.Y., Pyramid Bks., 1968)

An Absence of Ruins, novel (Hutchinson, 1967)

Die the Long Day, novel (N.Y., Morrow, 1972; Phila., Curtis, 1973)

Nonfiction

The Sociology of Slavery; An Analysis of the Origins, Development and Structure of Negro Slave Society in Jamaica (London, MacGibbon & Kee, 1967; Cranbury, N.J., Fairleigh Dickinson U. Press, 1969)

An Analysis of the Origins, Development and Structure of Negro Slave Society in Jamaica (Rutherford, N.J., Fairleigh Dickinson U. Press, 1968)

Ethnic Chauvinism: The Reactionary Impulse (Briarcliff Manor, N.Y., Stein & Day, 1977)

Slavery and Social Death: A Comparative Study (Cambridge, Mass., Harvard U. Press, 1982)

Sidelights: "Orlando Patterson's interpretation of Ras Tafarians in *The Children of Sisyphus ... [is]* handled realistically and with compassion." *(West Indian Novel and Its Background)*

Sources: *Bibliography of the Caribbean*; *Black American Writers Past and Present*; *Books in Print*, 1982-83; *Complete Caribbeana, 1900-1975*; *Jamaican National Bibliography*; *West Indian Novel and Its Background.*

PATTERSON, LINDSAY. Editor, Anthologist, Literary Critic.
Born in Bastrop, La. *Education:* B.A. (Eng.), Va. State Coll., Petersburg. *Family:* Single. *Career:* (U.S. Army): Information Spec., Correspondent for *Stars and Stripes* in Europe; Feature Writer & Managing Ed., the *Patton Post*, Army Headquarters, Heidelberg, Germany. Account Executive, Harrison Advertising Agency; Feature Writer & Columnist, Associated Negro Press; Ed. Asst. to Langston Hughes; Adjunct Prof., Hunter Coll.; Co-host, "Celebrity Hour," WRVR-FM, N.Y.C., 3 yrs.; Co-host, "Black Conversations," Channel 11, N.Y.C. (2½ yrs.) *Honors:* Natl. Found. on the Arts & Humanities; MacDowell Colony, three fellowships; Edward Albee Found., two fellowships. *Mailing address:* 42 Perry St., N.Y., N.Y. 10014.

Writings:
Fiction

Anthology of the American Negro in the Theatre; A Critical Approach, ed. (N.Y., Publishers Co., Intnl. Lib. of Negro Life & Hist., 1967, 2nd rev. ed., 1969)

Black Theater: A 20th Century Collection of the Work of Its Best Playwrights, ed. (N.Y., Dodd, 1971)

A Rock against the Wind: Black Love Poems; An Anthology, ed. (Dodd, 1973)

Nonfiction

The Negro in Music and Art, ed. (Publishers Co., 1967, 2nd ed., 1968, 1969)

An Introduction to Black Literature in America, from 1746 to the Present (Publishers Co., 1968)

The Afro-American in Music and Art (Wash., D.C., Assn. for Study of Afro-Amer. Life & Hist., 1970)

Black Films and Film-Makers (Dodd, 1973)

Sources: Author information; *Books in Print*, 1979-80.

PAYNE, DANIEL A. Minister, Bishop, Educator.
Born in Charleston, S.C., Feb. 24, 1811 (son of free parents). *Education:* "Learned shoemaking and carpentry and tailoring as a youth. At eighteen ... converted and received great inspiration from the *Self-Interpreting Bible of John Brown of Scotland....* Went North and entered Lutheran Seminary at Gettysburg, Pa." *(Early Black American Poets)*. *Career:* "Ordained as Lutheran clergyman in 1839.... Joined AME church. Was appointed a bishop in 1852. He ... organized historical and literary societies.He led in the purchase by his church of Wilberforce University. He later served as president for 16 years." (First Negro college president.) *(Early Black American Poets)*. Died Nov. 20, 1893.

Writings:
Fiction

Pleasures and Other Miscellaneous Poems (Baltimore, Sherwood, 1850)

Nonfiction

The Semi-Centenary and the Retrospection of the African Methodist Episcopal Church (Sherwood, 1866; Freeport, N.Y., Bks. for Libraries, 1972)

A Treatise on Domestic Education (Cincinnati, Cranston & Stowe, 1885)

Recollections of Seventy Years (Nashville, Tenn., AME Sunday Sch. Union, 1888; N.Y., Arno, 1968)

History of the African Methodist Episcopal Church (AME Sunday Sch. Union, 1891; N.Y., Johnson Reprint, 1968; Arno, 1969)

Sidelights: "His life was one ceaseless round of activity.... He was an advocate of a trained ministry.... Payne also introduced choral singing into worship.... He traveled (widely) from New Orleans to Canada, consulting as to welfare of congregations, visiting homes of fugitive Negroes.... He and Carl Schurz urged upon President Lincoln the signing of the emancipation in the District of Columbia." (*Early Negro American Writers*)

Sources: *Early Black American Poets*; *Early Negro American Writers*; *Negro Caravan.*

p'BITEK, J. P. OKOT [Okot, p'Bitek]. (Ugandan). Novelist, Poet, Anthropologist, Essayist, Song Collector.
Born in Gulu, Acoli District, N. Uganda, in 1931. *Education:* King's Coll., Budo, Uganda; Certificate in Educ., Bristow U., Eng.; LL.B., U. of Wales; B. Litt. (Anthropology), Oxford U.— traditional songs of Acoli & Lango peoples, 1963. *Career:* Dir., Uganda Natl. Theatre & Ugnada Cultural Center, Kampala, 1964-68; Prof., Makerere U., Uganda, & Lect., Sociol.; organized Art Festival of 1968 in Kisuma, Kenya; Writer-in-Residence, U. of Iowa, 1971- ; Prof., U. of Nairobi, Kenya. Died July 19, 1982.

Writings:
Fiction

Song of Lawino, a Lament, poetic novel (Nairobi, London, E. African Pub. House, 1966; Cleveland, Ohio, World-Meridian Bks., 1969)

Song of Ocol, poetic novel (E. African Pub. House, 1970)

The Song of the Prisoner, poetic novel (E. African Pub. House, 1970; N.Y., Third Press, 1971)

The Revelations of a Prostitute, poetic novel (E. African Pub. House, 1971)

Two Songs; The Song of the Prisoner and the Song of Malaya, poetic novels (E. African Pub. House, 1971)

Song of Lawino and Song of Ocol, poetic novels (E. African Pub. House, 1972)

Horn of My Love, novel (London, Heinemann, 1974)

The Hare and the Hornbill, novel (Heinemann, 1978)

Nonfiction

African Religion in Western Scholarship (Nairobi, E. African Lit. Bureau, 1970)

Religion of Central Luo (E. African Lit. Bureau, 1971)

Africa's Cultural Revolution (Nairobi, Macmillan, 1973)

Sidelights: James T. Ngugi and p'Bitek are considered the leading East African writers. *The Song of Malaya* is a poetic farce attacking the new politicians of Africa. *The Song of Lawino* transforms into written literature a ballad which addresses a fictive audience, thus creating the illusion of a singer confronting a crowd. (*African Authors*)

Sources: *African Authors; Books in Print*, 1979-80, 1980-81; *Contemporary Poets*, 3rd ed., 1980; *Reader's Guide to African Literature.*

PERRY, MARGARET. Librarian, Bibliographer, Juvenile Writer.
Born in Cincinnati, Ohio, Nov. 15, 1933. *Education:* A.B., Western Mich. U., 1954; Certificate, U. of Paris, 1956; further grad. study, City Coll. of CUNY, 1957-58; M.S.L.S., Catholic U. of America, 1959. *Career:* Young Adult & Ref. Librn., N.Y. Public Lib., 1954-55, 1957-58; Civilian Librn., U.S. Army, in Metz, Nancy, Toul, & Verdun, France, 1959-63, Orleans, France, 1964-65, & Hanau, Germany, 1965-67; Ref. Librn., U.S. Military Acad., W. Point, N.Y., 1967-68, Chief of Circulation, 1968-70; Head of Educ. Lib., 1970-75, Asst. Prof., 1973-75, Assoc. Prof. of Eng., 1975- , Asst. Prof. of Educ., 1974- , Head of Library's Reader Serv., 1978, Acting Dir. of Libs., 1976-77, Head, Reader Services Div. — all River Campus, U. of Rochester, Rochester, N.Y. *Mailing address:* c/o Dr. R. Perry, 1725 T St., N.W., Wash., D.C. 20009.

Writings:
Nonfiction

Rainy Day Magic: The Art of Making Sunshine on a Stormy Day, juv. (N.Y., M. Evans, 1970)

A Bio-Bibliography of Countee P. Cullen, 1903-1946 (Westport, Conn., Greenwood, 1971)

Silence to the Drums: A Survey of the Literature of the Harlem Renaissance (Greenwood, 1976)

The Harlem Renaissance: An Annotated Bibliography (N.Y., Garland, 1981)

Sources: *Books in Print*, 1978-79, 1980-81; *Contemporary Authors*, vols. 89-92, 1980; *Freedomways*, vol. 17, no. 1, 1977; *Writers Directory*, 1982-84.

PETRY, ANN LANE. Novelist, Short Story Writer, Juvenile Writer.
Born in Old Saybrook, Conn., Oct. 12, 1911. *Education:* U. of Conn., Coll. of Pharmacy, grad. 1931; Columbia U. (Creative Writing). *Family:* Married George D. Petry, Feb. 22, 1938; d. Elizabeth Ann. *Career:* Pharmacist, 1934-48; Newspaperwoman, *Amsterdam News & The People's Voice* (Women's Ed.); with soc. agencies; Visiting Prof. of Eng., U. of Hawaii, 1974-75. *Honors:* Completed *The Street* on a Houghton Mifflin Literary Fellowship. Martha Foley dedicated annual volume *The Best American Short Stories in 1946* to Miss Petry. *Mailing address:* c/o Russell & Volkening, Inc., 551 Fifth Ave., N.Y., N.Y. 10017.

Writings:
Fiction

The Street, novel (Boston, Houghton Mifflin, 1946; N.Y., Pyramid, 1961, 1969)

Country Place, novel (Houghton Mifflin, 1947; Old Greenwich, Conn., Chatham, 1971)

The Drug Store Cat, juv. (N.Y., Crowell, 1949)

The Narrows, novel (Houghton Mifflin, 1953; Pyramid, 1971; Chatham, 1973)

Harriet Tubman: Conductor on the Underground Railroad, juv. (Crowell, 1955; n.p., Archway, 1971)

Tituba of Salem Village, juv. (Crowell, 1964)

Legends of the Saints, short stories (Crowell, 1970)

Miss Muriel and Other Stories (Houghton Mifflin, 1971)

Sidelights: Ms. Petry is absolutely convinced that the most dramatic material which a writer can obtain in this country is that which deals with the Negro, and his history in the United States. (*Afro-American Literature: Fiction*)

Sources: *Afro-American Literature: Fiction*; Author information; *Black Voices; Books in Print*, 1979-80; *Cavalcade; Negro Almanac; Something about the Author; Soon, One Morning.*

PHARR, ROBERT DEANE. Novelist.

Born in Richmond, Va., July 5, 1916. *Education:* New Haven High Sch.; B.A., Virginia Union U., Richmond. *Career:* Novelist. *Mailing address:* c/o Doubleday & Co., 245 Park Ave., N.Y., N.Y. 10017.

Writings:
Fiction

Book of Numbers, novel (N.Y., Doubleday, 1969; N.Y., Avon, 1970)

S.R.O., novel (Doubleday, 1971)

The Soul Murder Case: A Confession of the Victim, novel (Avon, 1972, 1975)

The Welfare Bitch, novel (Doubleday, 1973)

Giveadam Brown, novel (Doubleday, 1978)

Sidelights: Robert Deane Pharr exemplifies the frequent difficulties Black Americans have in attaining publication and in having the conditions to devote time to writing at all. He was in his fifties when his first novel was published. (*New Black Voices*)

Sources: *Books in Print,* 1979-80; *New Black Voices.*

PHINAZEE, ANNETTE ALETHIA (LEWIS). Librarian, Educator.

Born in Orangeburg, S.C., July 25, 1920. *Education:* B.A., Fisk U., 1939; B.L.S., 1941, M.S.L.S., 1948, U. of Ill.; D.L.S., Columbia U., 1961; U. of Ill., 1968. *Family:* Married Joseph Phinazee. *Career:* Tchr.-Librn., Caswell County Training Sch., 1939-40; Cataloger, Talladega Coll., 1941-42; Journalism Librn., Lincoln U., 1942-44; Tchr., Atlanta U., 1946-57; Asst. Cataloger, S. Ill. U., 1957-62; Head, Spec. Serv., Atlanta U., 1963-69; Assoc. Dir., Co-op. Lib. Center, 1969-70; Dean, N.C. Central U., 1970- . *Honors:* Gen. Educ. Fellow, 1947-48, 1953-54; Southern Fellow, Fund Grant, 1956; U. of Chicago Inst. on Bibliographic Org., 1950; Phi Beta Sigma Certificate of Recognition for Contrib. to Educ.; Woman of the year, Eno Bus. & Professional Women's Club, 1976; Distinguished Lib. Serv. Award, Durham County Lib. Assn. Died in 1983.

Writings:
Nonfiction

The Black Librarian in the South, ed. (Syracuse, N.Y., Gaylord Professional Publ., 1979)

The Black Librarian in the Southeast: Reminiscences, Activities, Challenges (Durham, N.C., Central U. Sch. of Lib. Sci., 1980)

Sources: *American Libraries,* Apr. 1983; *Books in Print,* 1978-79; *Who's Who among Black Americans,* 2nd ed., vol. 1, 1977-78.

PICKENS, WILLIAM. Biographer, Professor of Latin, Greek, & German, Educator, NAACP Field Secretary.

Born in Anderson County, S.C., Jan. 15, 1881 (son of former slaves). *Education:* B.A., Talladega Coll., 1902; B.A. (Phi Beta Kappa), Yale U., 1904; M.A., Fisk U.; Diploma, Brit. Esperanto Assn., 1906. *Career:* Prof. of Latin, Greek, & German, Talladega Coll., Ala., 1904-14; Prof., Greek & Sociol., Wiley Coll., Marshall, Tex., 1914-15; Dean, Morgan State Coll., Baltimore, 1915-20; Field Secy., NAACP, 1920-41; Official, Treasury Dept. *Honors:* Hon. degrees from: Fisk U., Selma U., Wiley Coll. Died in 1954.

Writings:
Fiction

The Vengeance of the Gods, and Three Other Stories of Real American Color Line Life (Phila., AME Bk. Concern, 1922; reprint, N.Y., Arno, Black Heritage Lib. Collection Ser., N.Y., AMS, 1975)

American Aesop: Negro and Other Humor (Boston, Jordan & More, 1926; reprint, AMS, 1969)

Nonfiction

Abraham Lincoln, Man and Statesman (Talladega?, Ala., n.p., 1910; N.Y., n.p., 1930)

The Heir of Slaves; An Autobiography (N.Y., Pilgrim Press, 1911; rev. as *Bursting Bonds*, Jordan & More, 1923)

Frederick Douglass and the Spirit of Freedom (Boston, Arakelynn, 1912; N.Y., n.p., 1931)

The New Negro, His Political, Civil and Mental Status and Related Essays (N.Y., Neale, 1916; reprint, Westport, Conn., Negro Universities Press, 1969)

Sources: *Afro-American Writing; Books in Print*, 1978-79, 1980-81; *Historical Negro Biographies; Negro Caravan; Negroes in Public Affairs and Government.*

PLATO, ANN. Poet.
(The only fact) "... known of Miss Plato [is] that she was a Negro member of the Colored Congregational Church in Hartford, Connecticut in 1841, so identified in the preface by her pastor, the Reverend J. W. C. Pennington, about whom much is known. Certainly Hartford of the 1840's was one of New England's busiest centers for anti-slavery agitation and sentiment. Frederick Douglass spoke there during this time." (*Early Black American Poets*)

Writings:
Fiction

Essays;/Including/Biographies and Miscellaneous Pieces in/Prose and Poetry (Hartford, Author, 1841)

Sidelights: "Important historically as the author of the second volume of poetry by an American Negro woman published in the United States." (*Early Black American Poets*)

Source: *Early Black American Poets.*

PLUMPP, STERLING DOMINIC. Editor, Poet, Teacher.
Born in Clinton, Miss., Jan. 30, 1940. *Education:* St. Benedict's Coll., 1960-62; B.A., Roosevelt U., 1968, grad. study, 1968-71. *Family:* Married Falvia Delgrazia Jackson (registered nurse), Dec. 21, 1968. *Career:* Clerk, U.S. Post Office, 1962-69; Counselor, N. Park Coll., 1969-71; Instr., Black Studies, U. of Ill., Chicago Circle, 1970- ; Managing Ed., *Black Books Bulletin* (Inst. of Positive Educ.); Dir., Young Writer's Workshop for Urban Gateways; Ed., Third World Press. *Mailing address:* 1401 E. 55th, Apt. 816-N, Chicago, Ill. 60615.

Writings:
Fiction

Portable Soul, poems (Chicago, Third World, 1969)

Half Black, Half Blacker, poems (Third World, 1970)

Black Rituals, poems (Third World, 1972)

Muslim Men, poems (Detroit, Broadside, 1972)

Steps to Break the Circle, poems (Third World, 1974)

Somehow We Survive, ed. (N.Y., Thunder's Mouth, 1981)

The Mojo Hands Call, I Must Go (Thunder's Mouth, 1982)

Sources: *Books in Print*, 1983-84; *Contemporary Authors*, vols. 45-48, 1974; *Poetry of Black America.*

POINDEXTER, HILDRUS A. Medical Director (Public Health), Medical Professor, Biographer.
Born in Memphis, Tenn., May 10, 1901. *Education:* A.B., Lincoln U. (Pa.), 1924; M.D., Dartmouth
Coll., Harvard U., 1929; A.M., Columbia U., U. of Puerto Rico. *Family:* Married Ruth V. Grier;
d. Patchechole Barbara. *Career:* Prof., Microbiology, Community Health, Howard U., 1931-43;
Senior Surgeon, Medical Dir., U.S. Public Health Serv., 1947-65; Prof., Community Health,
Howard U., Coll. of Medicine- ; Chief, Health & Sanitation Div., U.S. Foreign Aid Mission:
Liberia, French Indochina, Surinam, Iraq, Jamaica, Sierra Leone, Nigeria. *Honors:* Bronze Star;
two commendation medals; four Battle Stars; Knight Commander, Liberia. *Mailing address:* c/o
Howard U., Coll. of Medicine, Wash., D.C. 20059.

Writings:
  Nonfiction
   My World of Reality; An Autobiography (Detroit, Balamp Pub., 1973)

Sources: Pub. information; *Who's Who among Black Americans*, 3rd ed., 1980-81.

POINSETT, ALEX. Editor.
Born in Chicago, Ill., Jan. 27, 1926. *Education:* B.S. (Journalism), 1952, M.A. (Philosophy), U. of
Ill., 1953; further study (Lib. Sci.) U. of Chicago. *Family:* Married Norma R. Poinsett, Aug. 1951;
d. Pierrette, son Pierre. *Career:* Yeoman 3/c, U.S. Navy, 1944-47; Asst. Ed., Senior Ed., *Ebony*
mag. *Honors:* J. C. Penney, U. of Mo. Journalism Award, 1968, ($1,000) for Aug, 1967 *Ebony*
story, "Ghetto Schools: An Educational Wasteland." Author of four *Ebony* mag. articles reprinted
in the *Congressional Record. Mailing address:* 53 Rustic Gate Lane, Dix Hills, N.Y. 11746.

Writings:
  Nonfiction
   Black Power: Gary Style; The Making of Mayor Richard Gordon Hatcher, political biog. (Chi-
    cago, Johnson, 1970)

   Common Folk in an Uncommon Cause, church hist. (Liberty Bap. Church, 1972)

Sidelights: "Lectured at ... universities on black politics, the black press, etc. under contract to Ameri-
can Program Bureau in Boston, Massachusetts; traveled to the Soviet Union, Kenya, Haiti, Jamaica,
Canada, Mexico ... traveled more than one million miles as Johnson Publishing Company editor.
Former speech writer for Mayor Richard Hatcher and John H. Johnson (Publisher)." (Author)

Source: Author Information.

POITIER, SIDNEY. Actor, Producer, Director.
Born in Miami, Fla., Feb. 20, 1927. *Education:* High sch., Nassau. *Family:* Married Juanita Hardy,
1950 (div.); 4 ds.: Beverly, Pamela, Sherry, Gina; married 2nd, Joanna Shimkus; 2 ds.: Sydney,
Anika. *Career:* Film actor; Director; Producer. *Honors:* Silver Bear Award for acting in *The Defiant
Ones*, 1958; Academy Award for Best Actor in *Lilies of the Field*, 1963. *Mailing address:* c/o Alfred
A. Knopf, Inc., 201 E. 50th St., N.Y., N.Y. 10028.

Writings:
  Nonfiction
   This Life (N.Y., Knopf, 1979; paper, N.Y., Ballantine, 1981)

Sidelights: Brooks Atkinson of the *New York Times* said, "Mr. Poitier is a remarkable actor with
enormous power that is always under control." Poitier produced, directed, and acted in *Buck and the
Preacher, Uptown Saturday Night, Let's Do It Again*, and *A Piece of the Action.*

Sources: *Books in Print*, 1981-82; *Current Biography*, 1959; *Jet* mag., May 22, 1980; *Kirkus Reviews*,
Mar. 1, 1980.

POLITE, CARLENE HATCHER. Novelist, English Professor, Dancer, Elected Official.
Born in Detroit, Mich., Aug. 28, 1932. *Education:* Detroit public schs.; Martha Graham Sch. of Contemporary Dance. *Family:* Div. from Allen Polite; d. Glynda Bennett, d. Lila Polite. *Career:* Dancer, Concert Dance Theatre, N.Y.C., 1956-59; Actress & Dancer, Equity Theatre, Detroit, 1960-62; Guest Instr., YWCA, 1960-62; Organizer, Girl Friday, Mich. Democratic Party, 1962; elected Mich. Democratic State Central Com., 1962-63; Co-ordinator, Detroit Council for Human Rights, 1963; participated in "Walk for Freedom" with Martin L. King, Jr., June 23, 1963; Assoc. Prof., Dept. of Eng., SUNY, Buffalo, 1971- . *Honors:* Natl. Found. of Arts & Humanities, 1965; nominated for Pulitzer Prize, 1967. *Mailing address:* c/o Farrar, Straus & Giroux, 19 Union Sq., W., N.Y., N.Y. 10003.

Writings:
  Fiction
  The Flagellants, novel (N.Y., Farrar, 1967; N.Y., Dell, 1968)

  Sister X and the Victim of Foul Play, novel (Farrar, 1975)

Sidelights: *The Flagellants* has been published in five languages and six countries. A film option was made August 1974. (Author)

Source: Author information.

PORTER, DOROTHY BURNETT. Librarian, Bibliographer.
Born in Warrenton, Va., May 25, 1905. *Education:* B.A., Howard U., 1928; B.S., Columbia U., 1931; M.S. (Lib. Sci.), Columbia U., 1932; Amer. U., Certificate, Preservation & Admin. of Archives, 1957; D. Litt. (hon.), Susquehanna U., 1971. *Family:* Married 1st James A. Porter (dec.); d. Constance Uzelac.; married 2nd Charles H. Wesley, Nov. 30, 1979. *Career:* Librn., Moorland-Spingarn Collection, Howard U., 1930-73; Consultant: Ford Found., Natl. Libs., Lagos, Nigeria; Kraus Pub.; Arno Press Negro Hist. Project. Advisory Ed., Black Studies, G. K. Hall; Bd. of Advisors, Booker T. Washington Papers. *Honors:* Julius Rosenwald Scholar, 1931-32; Julius Rosenwald Fellow, 1944-45; Distinguished Achievement Award, Natl. Barristers Wives, Inc., for outstanding serv., human relations, 1968; Distinguished Serv. to Howard U., 1970; Inst. of Arts & Humanities Award, Howard U., 1973. *Mailing address:* 7632 17th St., N.W., Wash., D.C. 20012.

Writings:
  Nonfiction
  Catalogue of Books in the Moorland Foundation Collection, ed. (Wash., D.C., Howard U. Lib., 1939)

  North American Negro Poets, a Bibliographical Checklist of Their Writings, 1760-1944 (Hattiesburg, Miss., Book Farm, 1945)

  Catalogue of the African Collection at Howard University (Howard U. Press, 1958)

  Index to the Journal of Negro Education, 1932-1962 (Howard U. Press, 1963)

  The Negro in American Cities: A Selected and Annotated Bibliography (Howard U. Press, 1967; Wash., D.C., U.S. Govt. Printing Office, 1970)

  A Working Bibliography on the Negro in the United States (Ann Arbor, Mich., U. Microfilms, 1968, 1969)

  Negro Protest Pamphlets (N.Y., Arno, 1969)

  The Negro in the United States, a Selected Bibliography (Wash., D.C., Lib. of Congress, 1970)

  Early Negro Writing, 1760-1837 (Boston, Beacon, 1971)

  Afro-Braziliana: A Working Bibliography (Boston, G. K. Hall, 1978)

Sources: Author information; Pub. information.

PORTER, JAMES AMOS. Art Professor, Painter.
Born in Baltimore, Md., Dec. 22, 1905. *Education:* B.S. (Art), Howard U., 1927; M.A. (Art Hist.), Fine Arts Grad. Center, N.Y.U., 1936; studied in Paris, W. Africa, Egypt, Cuba, Haiti. *Family:* Married Dorothy Burnett; d. Constance. *Career:* Prof. & Head, Dept. of Art, Howard U. (40 yrs.); Curator, Gallery of Art, Howard U. *Honors:* Summer fellow, Belgium-Amer. Art Seminar (stud. of 16th, 17th, & 18th century Dutch & Flemish art). Died in 1970.

Writings:
Nonfiction

Modern Negro Art (N.Y., Dryden, 1943; reprint, N.Y., Arno, Amer. Negro—His Hist. & Lit. Ser., no. 2, 1969)

Robert S. Duncanson, Midwestern Romantic-Realist (Springfield, Mass., n.p., 1951)

Sidelights: Mr. Porter was illustrator for *Playsongs of the Deep South* and *Talking Animals*. He was a delegate to the International Congress on African Art and Culture, which was held in Salisbury, Rhodesia, sponsored by the Rhodes National Gallery.

Sources: *Afro-American Encyclopedia*, vol. 7; *Books in Print*, 1980-81; *Negro Almanac*; *Negro Handbook*; *Who's Who in American Art*.

POUSSAINT, ALVIN FRANCIS. Psychiatrist, Psychiatry Professor.
Born in East Harlem, N.Y., May 15, 1934. *Education:* B.A., Columbia U., 1956; M.D., Cornell U., 1960; M.S., UCLA, 1964. *Family:* Married Ann Ashmore (Soc. Worker), Nov. 4, 1973. *Career:* UCLA, Intern, Center for Health Sci., 1960-61, Psychiatric Resident, Neuropsychiatric Inst., 1961-64, Chief Resident, 1964-65; Tufts U. Medical Sch., Boston, Senior Clinical Instr., Psychiatry, 1965-66, Asst. Prof., Psychiatry & Preventive Medicine, 1967-69; Harvard U. of Medicine, Assoc. Prof., Psychiatry, 1969- , Assoc. Dean for Student Affairs, 1969- , Assoc. Psychiatrist, Mass. Mental Health Center, 1969- . *Mailing address:* c/o Sch. of Medicine, Harvard U., 25 Shattuck St., Boston, Mass. 02115.

Writings:
Nonfiction

Why Blacks Kill Blacks (N.Y., Emerson Hall, 1972)

Black Child Care, with James P. Comer (N.Y., Simon & Schuster, 1975)

The Black Family, ed. (n.p., ECCA Publ., no. 2, 1976)

Sources: *The Black Family*, no. 2; *Contemporary Authors*, vols. 53-56, 1975.

POWELL, ADAM CLAYTON, JR. Congressman, Clergyman.
Born in New Haven, Conn., Nov. 29, 1908 (son of Rev. Adam C. Powell, Senior). *Education:* B.A., Colgate U., 1930; M.A., Columbia U., 1932; D.D., Shaw U., 1935; LL.D., Va. Union U., 1947. *Family:* Married 1st Isabel G. Washington, Mar. 8, 1933 (separated Nov. 1944); married 2nd Hazel Scott (Aug. 1955 div.); son Adam Clayton III; married 3rd Yvette Diago; son Adam Diago. *Career:* Minister, Abyssinian Bap. Church, 1937- ; elected to N.Y.C. Council, 1941; Founder, *People's Voice*, Ed. in Chief, co-pub., 1942; elected to Congress, Nov. 1945, Mem. 79th to 87th Congresses from N.Y.'s 16th Dist., Chairman, Com. on Educ. & Labor; Mem. 88th to 89th Congresses, N.Y., 18th Dist.; Delegate, Parliamentary World Govt., Conf., London, 1951-52; ILO Conf., Geneva, 1961. *Honors:* Decorated Knight of the Golden Cross, Ethiopia, 1954. Died Apr. 1972.

Writings:
Nonfiction

Marching Blacks, an Interpretative History of the Rise of the Black Common Man (N.Y., Dial, 1945)

Keep the Faith, Baby! (N.Y., Trident, 1967)

Adam by Adam; The Autobiography of Adam Clayton Powell, Jr. (Dial, 1971)

Sidelights: "He went from the street corners of Harlem (where he preached black nationalism and passive resistance in the thirties) to the New York City Council ... and to Congress (where he was the first Negro member from the East in 1945). In the process he acquired three wives (in lawful succession) ... a string of winter and summer homes stretching from Westhampton, Long Island, to Cerro Gordo, Puerto Rico, a block of real estate, a directorship of an international insurance company, a Jaguar, a Nash-Healy and a host of passionate enemies.... [In the sixties he became] chairman of the House Education and Labor committee ... one of the most powerful men in Congress." (*Ebony*)

Sources: *Ebony*, June 1963; *Los Angeles Times*, Apr. 5, 1972; *Negro Handbook*.

POWELL, ADAM CLAYTON, SR. Clergyman.
Born in Franklin County, Va., May 5, 1865. *Education:* Grad., Wayland Academy (Va. Union U.), 1892; D.D., Va. Union U., 1904; D.D., Va. Sem. & Coll., 1904; D.D., Howard U., 1924; attended Yale U. Divinity Sch. *Family:* (Father of Adam C., Jr.). *Career:* Pastor, Emanuel Bap. Church, New Haven, Conn., 1893-1908; Pastor, Abyssinian Bap. Church, N.Y.C., 1908-37; Dir., NAACP. *Honors:* Harmon Award as leader of best-organized church among Negroes in America, 1928. Died in 1953.

Writings:
Fiction
Picketing Hell: A Fictitious Narrative (N.Y., Malliet, 1942)

Nonfiction
Patriotism and the Negro (N.Y., Beehive, 1918)

Against the Tide, an Autobiography (N.Y., R. R. Smith, 1938; reprinted by Edwin S. Gaustad, N.Y., Arno, Bap. Tradition Ser., 1980)

Palestine, and Saints in Caesar's Household (R. R. Smith, 1939)

Riots and Ruins (R. R. Smith, 1945)

Upon This Rock: The History of the Abyssinian Baptist Church (N.Y., Abyssinian Bap. Church, 1949)

Sidelights: The Reverend Powell was the builder of America's largest Negro congregation (14,000). Abyssinian had assets of $400,000 when he retired. It had departments in social service, recreation, crime prevention, adult education, a day nursery, and an employment agency.

Sources: *American Authors and Books, 1640 to the Present Day*, 3rd rev. ed.; *Books in Print*, 1981-82; *Historical Afro-American Biographies*.

PRATHER, JEFFREY LYNN. Psychotherapist.
Born in N.Y.C., May 14, 1941. *Education:* B.A. (Biology, Chemistry, & Psychology), Queens Coll., CUNY, 1965; M.S. equivalent (Psychology & Chemistry), Cal. State U., Northridge, 1967. *Family:* Single. *Career:* Escort/Interpreter, U.S. Dept. of State; Instr., Psychology, Malcolm-King Coll., N.Y.C.; Consultant, Operation Head Start, N.Y.C.; Cal. Project Dir., Literacy Volunteers of Amer.; Coordinator, Attica Correctional Facility. *Mailing address:* 1201 P St., #3, Sacramento, Cal. 95814.

Writings:
Nonfiction
A Mere Reflection: The Psychodynamics of Black and Hispanic Psychology (Phila., Dorrance, 1977)

Four Hundred Days at Attica (Dorrance, 1982)

Sidelights: Recently chaired session, International Association for Cross-Cultural Psychology, Second Regional Pan-African Conference, University of Nairobi, Kenya.

Sources: Author information; *Books in Print*, 1983-84; Pub. information.

PRICE, ROBERT E. [Bashiri]. Poet, Journalist, Screenwriter, Filmmaker.
Born in Va. *Family:* Married; three children. *Career:* Screenwriter; Filmmaker. *Honors:* Broadside Press Award for Poetry, 1975; William Wyler (Amer. Film Inst.) Fellowship for screenwriting & filmmaking, 1976. *Mailing address:* P.O. Box 75796, Sanford Station, L.A., Cal. 90075.

Writings:
Fiction
Blood Lines, short stories and poems (N.Y., Togetherness Productions, Poets Pay Rent Too, n.d.)

Sidelights: "*Polished Ebony* was written, produced and directed by Bashiri. Served as dialog consultant to director Jan Kadir and wrote additional dialog for Television mini-series *Freedom Road*." (Publisher)

Sources: *Freedomways*, vol. 19, no. 2, 1979; Pub. information.

QUARLES, BENJAMIN ARTHUR. History Professor, Historian, Biographer.
Born in Boston, Mass., Jan. 23, 1904. *Education:* B.A. (Hist.), Shaw U., Raleigh, N.C., 1931; M.A., 1937, Ph.D., 1940, U. of Wis. *Family:* Married 1st Vera Bullock (dec.); married 2nd Ruth Brett; d. Mrs. Roberta Allain Knowles, d. Pamela Anne Quarles. *Career:* Instr., Hist., Shaw U., 1934-36; Assoc. Prof., Dillard U., 1939-42, Prof., 1942-53 (Dean of Instr., 1945-53); Prof. of Hist. & Head of Dept., Morgan State Coll., 1953-?; Emeritus Prof. of Hist., Morgan State U. *Honors:* Advisory Bd., Amer. Hist. & Life, Amer. Bibliographical Center; Com. of Advisers, Natl. Humanities Center; Fellowship Selection Com. for 1976-77 & 1977-78, Amer. Council of Learned Societies; Dept. of the Army Hist. Advisory Com., 1977-80; V. Pres. Emeritus, Assn. for Study of Afro-Amer. Life & Hist.; Hon. Consultant in U.S. Hist., Lib. of Congress, 1970-71; Hon. Chairman, Md. State Com. on Afro-Amer. Hist. & Culture; Hon. Fellow, Center for African & African-Amer. Stud.; Hon. Doctorates, 14: Shaw U., Towson State Coll., Kenyon Coll., U. of Md., Howard U., Morgan State Coll., Colby Coll., Kent State U., Lincoln U. (Pa.), Salisbury State Coll., Seton Hall U., Rutgers U., Kean Coll. of N.J., U. of Wis. at Madison. *Mailing address:* 2205 Southern Ave., Baltimore, Md. 21214.

Writings:
Nonfiction
Frederick Douglass (Wash., D.C., Assoc. Pub., 1948; Englewood Cliffs, N.J., Prentice-Hall, 1968; N.Y., Antheneum, 1968)

The Negro in the Civil War (Boston, Little, Brown, 1953; N.Y., Russell, 1968; Little, Brown, 1969)

The Negro in the American Revolution (Chapel Hill, N.C., U. of N.C. Press, 1961; N.Y., Norton, 1973)

Lincoln and the Negro (N.Y., Oxford U. Press, 1962)

The Negro in the Making of America (N.Y., Collier, 1964, 2nd ed., 1965; N.Y., Macmillan, 1965; rev. ed., Collier, 1969)

Lift Every Voice, collaborator with Dorothy Sterling (N.Y., Doubleday, 1965)

The Negro American: A Documentary History, with Leslie H. Fishel, Jr. (Glenview, Ill., Scott, Foresman, 1967)

Black Abolitionist (Oxford U. Press, 1969)

The Black American: A Documentary History, with Leslie H. Fishel, Jr. (Scott, Foresman, 1970)

Blacks on John Brown, comp. (Urbana, U. of Ill. Press, 1972)

Allies for Freedom: Blacks and John Brown (Oxford U. Press, 1974)

Black History's Antebellum Origins (n.p., Amer. Antiquarian, 1979)

Sidelights: August Meier states: "... in *Black Abolitionists* (Quarles) wrote: 'Freedom is and has always been America's root concern, a concern that found dramatic expression in ... the most important and revolutionary movement in our country's past,' the abolitionist movement."

"Like (John Hope) Franklin he has served as a model to a whole generation of scholars in Afro-American history, white and black alike. His syntheses of Civil War and abolition, his authoritative book on the Revolution, his sensitive analysis of Lincoln and the blacks are all volumes that remain unequalled or unsurpassed." (Essay: "Benjamin Quarles and the Historiography of Black America")

Sources: *Allies for Freedom*; Author information; "Benjamin Quarles and the Historiography of Black America"; *Black Historians*; *Books in Print*, 1980-81; *Directory of American Scholars*, vol. I: *History*, 5th ed.; *Negro Almanac*; Pub. information; *Who's Who in America*, 37th ed., vol. 2, 1972-73.

RAMPERSAD, ARNOLD. English Professor, Literary Critic.
Career: Prof., Amer. Lit., Eng. Dept., Stanford U. *Mailing address:* c/o Eng. Dept., Stanford U., Stanford, Cal. 94305.

Writings:
Nonfiction

Melville's Israel Potter, a Pilgrimage and Progress (Bowling Green, Ohio, Bowling Green U. Popular Press, 1969)

The Art and Imagination of W. E. B. DuBois (Cambridge, Mass., Harvard U. Press, 1976)

Sidelights: In the Preface to *The Art and Imagination of W. E. B. DuBois*, Rampersad states: "I write of DuBois' 'art and imagination' because it is clear to me that his greatest gift was poetic in nature and that his scholarship, propaganda, and political activism drew their ultimate power from his essentially poetic vision of human experience and from his equally poetic reverence for the word."

Sources: *The Art and Imagination of W. E. B. DuBois*; *Book Review Digest*, 1977; *Books in Print*, 1981-82.

RANDALL, DUDLEY FELKER. Publisher, Poet, Librarian, Anthologist.
Born in Wash., D.C., Jan. 14, 1914. *Education:* B.A. (Eng.), Wayne State U., 1949; M.A.L.S., U. of Mich., 1951;; Postgrad.: Wayne State (Humanities); U. of Ghana (African Arts). *Family:* Married Vivian Barnett Spencer, 1957; d. Mrs. Phillis Ada Sherron III (from previous marriage). *Career:* Ford Motor Co., Dearborn, Mich., 1932-37; U.S. Post Office, Detroit, 1937-51; Librn., Lincoln U., Jefferson City, Mo., 1951-54; Librn., Morgan State Coll., Baltimore, 1954-56; Librn., Wayne County Federated Lib. System, Detroit, 1956-69; Poet-in-Residence & Librn., U. of Detroit, 1969- ; Pub., Broadside Press, 1965- . *Honors:* Wayne State U.'s Tompkins Award (Poetry & Fiction), 1962; Tompkins Award (Poetry), 1966; Kuumba Liberation Award, 1973; Detroit Metropolitan Eng. Club, Citation, 1972. *Mailing address:* 12651 Old Mill Place, Detroit, Mich. 48348.

Writings:
Fiction

Poem Counterpoem, with Margaret Danner (Detroit, Broadside, 1966)

Cities Burning (Broadside, 1968)

Black Poetry; A Supplement to Anthologies Which Exclude Black Poets, ed. (Broadside, 1969)

Love You (London, P. Breman, 1970, 2nd ed., 1971)

More to Remember; Poems of Four Decades (Chicago, Third World, 1971; Broadside, 1971)

After the Killing, poems (Third World, 1973)

Broadsides, no. 1, 1965; no. 3, 1965; no. 8, 1966; no. 62, 1972 (Broadside)

A Litany of Friends: Poems Selected and New (Detroit, Lotus, 1981)

Nonfiction

For Malcolm; Poems on the Life and Death of Malcolm X, ed. with Margaret G. Burroughs (Broadside, paper, 1967, 2nd ed., 1969)

The Black Poets, ed. (N.Y., Bantam, 1971)

Broadside Memories: Poets I Have Known (Broadside, 1975)

A Capsule Course in Black Poetry Writing, with Gwendolyn Brooks & Keorapetse W. Kgositsile (Broadside, 1975)

Sidelights: "Perhaps [Randall's] greatest contribution to the black revolution in poetry is his establishment and active directorship of the Broadside Press, which was started in 1965 ... at first it reprinted favorite poems of well-known black poets, but the Broadside Series widened its scope to publish previously unpublished poems by new writers." (*Black Insights*)

Sources: Author information; *Black Insights*; *Black Voices*; *Books in Print*, 1981-82; *Broadside Authors and Artists*; *Dark Symphony*; *Kaleidoscope*.

RANDOLPH, ASA PHILIP. Labor Leader.
Born in Crescent City, Fla., Apr. 15, 1889. *Education:* Cookman Inst., Jacksonville, Fla.; City Coll. of N.Y.; LL.D., Howard U. *Family:* Married Lucille E. Campbell, 1914. *Career:* Organized Brotherhood of Sleeping Car Porters, 1925; *The Messenger* became official organ of union; Amer. Federation of Labor granted union a charter (1st granted an all-Negro union in Amer.); Randolph was 1st Pres.; organized protest demonstration, March-on-Washington Movement, 1941, to get Blacks into defense industry & unions generally; Pres. Roosevelt issued Executive Order 8802 against discrimination in employment by firms holding defense contracts (brought about with *threats* of march). Regarded as "elder statesman" among civil rights leaders. Pres. of Negro Amer. Labor Council. *Honors:* 1st Black V. Pres. of AFL-CIO. Died in 1979.

Writings:
Nonfiction
The Messenger, mag. (N.Y., Brotherhood of Sleeping Car Porters, 1925-)

The Negro Freedom Movement (Lincoln U., Pa., Lincoln U., Amer. Studies Inst., 1968?)

Sidelights: "In 1917 he helped launch a magazine in New York, *The Messenger,* to crusade for full democratic rights of Negroes. Subtitle was, 'The only radical Negro magazine in America.' Editorials were bitterly critical of the *status quo.* Randolph ... was called 'the most dangerous Negro in America' (1918). He contended that he was simply agitating for fulfillment of Constitutional guarantees for *all* citizens and protection of law for everybody." (*Famous American Negroes*)

Sources: *Famous American Negroes*; *The Lonesome Road*; *Negro Almanac.*

RAY, HENRIETTA CORDELIA. Poet, Teacher.
Born in Falmouth, Mass. in 1850, "... one of two daughters born to the distinguished minister and eloquent abolitionist, Rev. Charles B. Ray ... reared in New York, receiving an excellent traditional education which helped her to graduate from both New York University in Pedagogy and from the Sauveveur School of Languages, where she became proficient in Greek, Latin, French and German in addition to developing into an English Scholar." (*Early Black American Poets*) *Career:* Tchr., Grammar Sch. No. 80 (while poet Charles L. Reason was prin.); Writer. Died in 1916.

Writings:
Fiction
Commemoration Ode on Lincoln/Written for the Occasion of the/Unveiling of the Freedman's Momument (in Memory of Abraham Lincoln) Apr. 14, 1876 (N.Y., J. J. Little, 1893)

Sonnets (J. J. Little, 1893)

Poems (N.Y., Grafton, 1910)

Nonfiction
Sketch of the Life of the Rev. Charles B. Ray, with her sister (N.Y., n.p., 1887)

Source: *Early Black American Poets.*

REDDING, JAY SAUNDERS. English Professor, Essayist, Critic.
Born in Wilmington, Del., Oct. 13, 1906. *Education:* Lincoln U. (Pa.) 1923-24; B. Phil. (Eng.), 1928; M.A. (Eng. & Amer. Lit.), 1933, Brown U.; L.H.D. (hon.): Hobart Coll., 1964, Dickenson Coll., U. of Del., U. of Portland, 1970. *Family:* Married Esther Elizabeth James, July 19, 1929; son Conway Holmes, son Lewis Alfred. *Career:* Instr., Morehouse Coll., 1928-31; Instr., Louisville Municipal Coll., 1933-35; Eng. Prof. & Chairman, Southern U., 1936-38; Eng. Prof. & Chairman, Tchrs. Coll., Elizabeth City, N.C.; Prof., Eng., Hampton Inst., 1943-66 (Johnson Prof. of Creative Lit.); Dir., Div. of Res. & Publ., NEH, Wash., D.C., 1966-70; Ernest L. White Prof., of Amer. Studies & Humane Letters, Cornell U., 1970- . Visiting Prof., Eng., Brown U., 1949-50; Fellow in Humanities, Duke U., 1964-65. *Honors:* Phi Beta Kappa; Rockefeller Found. Fellow, 1940-41; Guggenheim Found. Fellow, 1944-45; Mayflower Award, N.C. Hist. Soc. (1st Black), 1944; cited by N.Y. *Amsterdam News* "for distinction," 1944; by N.Y. Public Lib. "for outstanding contribution to interracial understanding," 1945, 1946; by Natl. Urban League "for outstanding achievement," 1949. *Mailing address:* c/o Cornell U., Dept. of Eng., Ithaca, N.Y. 14853.

Writings:
Fiction

Stranger and Alone, a Novel (N.Y., Harcourt, 1950)

Cavalcade; Negro American Writing from 1760 to the Present, anthology with Arthur P. Davis (Boston, Houghton Mifflin, 1971)

Nonfiction

To Make a Poet Black, essays (Chapel Hill, U. of N.C. Press, 1939; College Park, Md., McGrath, 1968; Essay Index reprint, Ser. Core Collection, 1978)

No Day of Triumph, autobiog. (Harcourt, 1942; N.Y., Har-Row, 1968)

They Came in Chains: Americans from Africa (Phila., Lippincott, 1950, 1968, 1973)

On Being Negro in America (Indianapolis, Bobbs-Merrill, 1951, 1962; N.Y., Bantam, 1964; Har-Row, 1969)

The Lonesome Road; The Story of the Negro's Part in America (N.Y., Doubleday, Mainstream of Amer. Ser., 1958)

The Negro (Wash., D.C., Potomac, 1967)

Sidelights: Redding "established a national reputation with his essays, literary criticism, fiction and educational activities as Professor of English at Hampton Institute." (*Black Voices*)
"Redding has earned a reputation as a perceptive and knowledgeable historian of literature by Afro-Americans." (*Black American Literature: Essays*)

Sources: *Black American Literature: Essays*; *Black Insights*; *Black Voices*; *Books in Print*, 1979-80; *Cavalcade*; *Current Biography*, 1969; *Negro Almanac*; *Who's Who in America*, 37th ed., 1972-73.

REDMOND, EUGENE BENJAMIN. Poet, Editor, Teacher, Anthologist.
Born in St. Louis, Mo., Dec. 1, 1937. *Education:* B.A. (Eng. Lit.), S. Ill. U., 1964; M.A. (Eng. Lit.), Wash. U., St. Louis, 1966. *Family:* Single. *Career:* Senior Consultant, Katherine Dunham's Performing Arts Training Center, S. Ill. U.; Dir., Lang. Workshops, and Poet-in-Residence, S. Ill. U. (Experiment in Higher Educ.); Writer-in-Residence (Ethnic Studies), Cal. State U., Sacramento; Ed. Dir., Black Anthology Project (campus-prison-residential co-op.); Co-Founder & Pub., Black River Writers Press; Literary Executor for estate of the late Henry Dumas. *Honors:* 1st Prize, Annual Festival of the Arts Poetry Contest, Wash. U., 1965; 1st Prize, Annual Free-lance Poetry Contest, 1966; Hon. Mention, Annual Wednesday Club, Senior Original Verse Contest, 1968; Award for Community Development & Creative Excellence, Community Sch. of E. St. Louis, Ill., 1972; resolutions citing "Community Work & Literary Excellence" from Governor of Cal. & Cal. State Assembly, 1974; award for Literary Achievement, Sacramento Regional Arts Council, 1974. *Mailing address:* 3700 Kings Way 2, Sacramento, Cal. 95821.

Writings:
Fiction

A Tale of Two-Toms; or, Tom-Tom (E. St. Louis, Ill., Black River Writers, 1968)

A Tale of Time and Toilet Tissues, poems (Black River Writers, 1968)

Sides of the River: A Mini-Anthology of Black Writings (Black River Writers, 1969)

'Ark of Bones' and Other Stories, ed. with Hale Chatfield (Carbondale, S. Ill. U. Press, 1970, 1974)

Poetry for My People, with Hale Chatfield (S. Ill. U. Press, 1970)

Sentry of the Four Golden Pillars (Sacramento?, 1970; Black River Writers, 1972)

River of Bones and Flesh of Blood: Poems (Black River Writers, 1971)

Songs from an Afro/Phone; New Poems (Black River Writers, 1972)

In a Time of Rain and Desire: New Love Poems (Black River Writers, 1973)

Consider Loneliness as These Things (Italy, Centro Studie e Scambi Internazionale, 1973, by the late Henry Dumas)

Play Ebony Play Ivory, ed. (N.Y., Random House, 1974)

Grief of Joy: Selected Contemporary Afro-American Poetry for Students (Black River Writers, 1976)

Nonfiction

Drumvoices: The Mission of Afro-American Poetry: A Critical History (Garden City, N.Y., Anchor, 1976)

Sidelights: Some of Redmond's adaptations and scenarios are: *9 Poets with the Blues* (1971, 1972); *Face of the Deep: A Black Ritual* (1971); *River of Bones: A Poetic Ritual* (1971); *The Night John Henry Was Born* (1972, 1974); *Will I Still Be Here Tomorrow?* (1972, 1973); *There's a Wiretap in My Soup; or Quit Bugging Me!* (1974)

Sources: Author information; *Books in Print*, 1979-80; *Drumvoices*; *New Black Voices*; *Poetry of Black America*; Pub. information.

REED, ISHMAEL S. Novelist, Poet, Editor, Teacher.
Born in Chattanooga, Tenn., Feb. 22, 1938. *Education:* U. of Buffalo. *Career:* Co-founder: the *East Village Other*, 1965; *Advance*, Newark Community newspaper, 1965; Yardbird Pub. Co., Ed. Dir., 1971; Reed, Cannon & Johnson Communications Co., Dir., 1973; Tchr.: Saint Mark's in the Bowrie Prose Workshop, 1966; Amer. Fiction, Dept. of Eng., U. of Cal., Berkeley, 1968-69; Amer. Fiction, Dept. of Eng., U. of Wash., Seattle, 1969-70; U. of Cal., Berkeley, at present. *Honors:* Nominated for 1973 Natl. Bk. Awards in fiction & poetry, & in 1973 for Pulitzer Prize in poetry; awarded the 1972 Cal. Assn. of Eng. Tchrs. Certificate of Merit for *19 Necromancers from Now*; R. & H. Rosenthal Found. Award, 1975. *Mailing address:* 8646 Terrace Dr., El Cerrito, Cal. 94530.

Writings:
Fiction

The Free-Lance Pallbearers, novel (N.Y., Doubleday & Bantam, 1967; N.Y., Avon, 1972; Old Greenwich, Conn., Chatham, 1975)

Yellow Back Radio Broke-Down, novel (Doubleday & Bantam, 1969; Chatham, 1975; Avon, 1977)

19 Necromancers from Now, anthology (Doubleday, 1970)

Catechism of a Neoamerican Hoodoo Church, poems (London, Breman, 1970, 3rd ed. 1971)

Conjure; Selected Poems (Amherst, U. of Mass. Press, 1972)

Mumbo Jumbo, novel (Doubleday & Bantam, 1972; Avon, 1978)

Yardbird Reader, vol. I (Berkeley, Cal., Yardbird Pub. Co., 1972)

Chattanooga; Poems (N.Y., Random House, 1973)

Yardbird Reader, vol. II (Yardbird Pub. Co., 1974)

The Last Days of Louisiana Red, novel (Random House, 1974; Avon, 1976)

Flight to Canada, novel (Random House, 1976; Avon, 1977)

Yardbird, vol. I, no. 1, paper (Yardbird Pub. Co., 1977)

Calafia: The California Poetry (Berkeley, Reed & Young Quilt, 1977)

A Secretary to the Spirits, poems (N.Y., NOK, NOK Poets Ser., 1978)

Yardbird Lives!, anthology with Al Young (N.Y., Grove, 1978)

Shrovetide in Old New Orleans, novel (Doubleday, 1978, Avon, 1979)

Quilt One, anthology with Al Young (Reed & Young Quilt, Quilt Ser., 1981)

Quilt Two (Reed & Young Quilt, Quilt Ser., 1981)

Quilt Three (Reed & Young Quilt, Quilt Ser., 1982)

God Made Alaska for the Indians (N.Y., Garland, 1982)

The Terrible Twos (N.Y., St. Martin's, 1982; Avon, 1983)

Sidelights: Addison Gayle states, "Reed is our most important Black satirist.... A warrior against rationalism, science and technology, he also inveighs against politics, religion and schism in the ranks of Blacks." (*Contemporary Novelists*)
Gerald Duff feels that Ishmael Reed has done a dazzling job in his writings, and that what he has accomplished in his first five novels predicts a brilliant future. (*Dictionary of Literary Biography*)

Sources: Author information; *Books in Print*, 1979-80, 1982-83, 1983-84; *Dictionary of Literary Biography* (American Novelists since World War II), 2nd Ser.; *Flight to Canada*; *New Black Poetry*; *New Black Voices*; *Poetry of Black America*; *Soulscript*.

REID, IRA DE AUGUSTINE. Sociologist, Educator.
Born in Clifton Forge, Va., July 2, 1901. *Education:* B.A., Morehouse Coll., 1922; M.A., U. of Pittsburgh, 1925; Ph.D., Columbia U., 1939; London Sch. of Econ. *Family:* Married Gladys Russell Scott in Oct. 1925. *Career:* Instr., Soc. Sci., Tex. Coll., Tyler, 1922-23; Instr., Douglass High Sch., Huntington, W. Va., 1923-24; Industrial & Res. Secy., N.Y. Urban League, 1925-28; Dir. of Res., Natl. Urban league, 1928-41; Dir., People's Coll., Atlanta U., & Chairman, Sociol. Dept., 1942- ; Lect., Negro Culture & Educ., N.Y.U. Sch. of Educ., 1946-47; Visiting Prof. of Sociol., Haverford Coll., 1946- ; Ed., *Phylon. Honors:* Fellow, Julius Rosenwald Fund; 1st Black to be named to full-time professorship at N.Y.U. Died in 1968.

Writings:
Nonfiction

The Negro Population of Denver, Colorado (Denver, Lincoln Press, 1929)

Social Conditions of the Negro in the Hill District of Pittsburgh, Pennsylvania (Pittsburgh, Gen. Com. on the Hill Survey, 1930)

The Urban Negro Worker in the United States: 1925-1936 (Wash., D.C., Govt. Printing Office, 1938)

The Negro Immigrant, His Background, Characteristics and Social Adjustment, 1899-1937 (N.Y., Columbia U., 1939; reprint, N.Y., AMS, n.d.)

In a Minor Key; Negro Youth in Story and Fact (Wash., D.C., Amer. Council on Educ., 1940; reprint, Westport, Conn., Greenwood, n.d.)

The Negro in the American Economic System, 3 vols. (Madison, N.J., Carnegie, Myrdal Study, 1940)

Sharecroppers All, with Arthur F. Raper (Chapel Hill, U. of N.C. Press, 1941)

Changes in Values and Attitudes (Tuskegee, Ala., Tuskegee Inst., 1954)

Sidelights: "... highly regarded by sociologists ... at least two of [Professor Reid's books], *Sharecroppers All*, which he wrote with A. F. Raper, and *In a Minor Key*, have been considered by reviewers to be worth the attention of everyone concerned with the future of our civilization." (*Current Biography*)

Sources: *Current Biography*, 1946; *Dictionary Catalog of the Schomburg Collection of Negro Literature and History*; *Jet* mag., July 9, 1970; *Negro Caravan*.

REID, V(ICTOR) S(TAFFORD). (Jamaican). Novelist, Short Story Writer, Reporter, Editor, Businessman.
Born in Kingston, Jamaica, May 1, 1913. *Education:* Jamaica. *Career:* Foreign Correspondent; Journalist, *Daily Gleaner*; Ed., *Public Opinion*; sponsored *Spotlight* (newsmag. akin to *Time*); Managing Dir. & Chairman, printing & pub. co., Kingston. *Honors:* Musgrave Silver Medal for Lit., 1950; Guggenheim Found. Fellow, 1959; Can. Council Fellow; Mexican Writers Fellow. *Mailing address:* Valley Hill Farm, Rock Hall, Jamaica.

Writings:
Fiction
New Day, novel (N.Y., Knopf, 1949; Chatham, N.J., Chatham Bookseller, 1972)

Fourteen Jamaican Short Stories, with Others (Kingston, Pioneer Press, 1950)

The Leopard, novel (N.Y., Viking, 1958; N.Y., Collier, 1971; Chatham Bookseller, 1972)

Sixty Five, juv. novelette (London, Longman's, 1960, 1968)

The Young Warriors, juv. novelette (Longman's, 1967)

Peter of Mount Ephraim, juv. novelette (Kingston, Jamaica Pub. House, 1971)

Sidelights: "*New Day* manages in large measure to convey this rooted sense of identity within a lived landscape. And it is Reid's major achievement." (*West Indian Novel*)

Sources: *Contemporary Novelists*, 2nd ed., 1976; *West Indian Literature*; *Writers Directory*, 1982-84.

REYNOLDS, BARBARA A. Journalist, Journalism Teacher, Editorial Director.
Born in Columbus, Ohio, Aug. 17, 1942. *Education:* B.A., Ohio State U., 1966; attended Harvard U., 1976-77, & Boston U. *Career:* Police Reporter, Cleveland, Ohio; Public Relations Dir., Columbus, Ohio; Asst. Ed., *Ebony*; Urban Affairs Writer, *Chicago Today*; Gen. Assignment Reporter, *Chicago Tribune*; Commentator, WBBM radio; regular panelist, WGN TV, "Issues Unlimited"; Ed. Dir., *Dollars and Cents* & the *Black Book Minority Business and Reference Guide*; Correspondent, *National Observer*; Instr., Journalism, Columbia Coll., Chicago. *Honors:* Journalist of the Year Award, Black Business Awards Dinner, Chicago, 1974 (annual affair which honors achievements of outstanding Black professionals); Nieman Fellow at Harvard U., 1976-77; Natl. Headliner Award, 1977, for outstanding contribution to journalism. *Mailing address:* c/o Nelson Hall Pub., 111 N. Canal St., Chicago, Ill. 60606.

Writings:
Nonfiction
Jesse Jackson: The Man, the Movement, the Myth (Chicago, Nelson-Hall, 1975)

Sidelights: Barbara Reynolds is the author of the following screenplays: "The Murder of Fred Hampton" and "Vengeance Is Mine." (*Contemporary Authors*)

Sources: *Contemporary Authors*, vols. 73-76; *Jesse Jackson: The Man, the Movement, the Myth*.

RICHARDSON, NOLA M. Poet.
Born in L.A., Cal., Nov. 12, 1936. *Education:* Certificate in Management; Compton Jr. Coll. (Bus. & Eng.); Sawyer Bus. Coll. *Family:* Div.; son Nolan, son Virgil, son Anthony, d. Julie, d. Dawn. *Career:* Watts Writers Workshop. Has appeared at colleges, libraries, conventions, etc., reciting poetry. Lectured at coll. & bk. clubs. Completed program "Poetry in the Schools," Instr., creative writing students, Wash. High Sch., L.A. *Mailing address:* 10426 Crenshaw Blvd., No. 1, Inglewood, Cal. 90303.

Writings:
Fiction
When One Loves; The Black Experience in America, poems (Milbrae, Cal., Celestial Arts, 1974)

Even in a Maze, poems (L.A., Crescent, 1975)

Sidelights: Nola Richardson has written some interesting medical poems, such as: "Hypertension/ Apprehension" and "Lead Poisoning." She has also written *Just a Teardrop*, a skit for a "One Woman Show" (a narrative love story in poetry).

Sources: Author information; *Books in Print*, 1979-80.

RIVE, RICHARD. (South African). Novelist, Short Story Writer, Teacher.
Born in Cape Town, S. Africa, in 1931. *Education:* (Tchr. Training), Hewat Training Coll.; Grad., U. of Cape Town; M.A. (Eng. Lit.), Columbia U.; Oxford U. *Career:* Tchr., Eng. & Latin, S. Peninsula High Sch., Diep River, near Cape Town; Writer. *Honors:* On a Farfield Scholarship, traveled through East, Central, & W. Africa; recipient of Fulbright Grant; *Make Like Slaves* won BBC African Theatre Competition Prize, May 1972. *Mailing address:* c/o Heinemann Educ. Bks., 4 Front St., Exeter, N.H. 03833.

Writings:
Fiction
Quartet; New Voices from South Africa, short story (N.Y., Crown, 1963; London, Heinemann, 1965)

African Songs, short stories (Berlin, Seven Seas, 1963)

Modern African Prose, an Anthology (Heinemann, African Writers Ser., 1964)

Emergency, a Novel (London, Faber, 1964)

Make Like Slaves, play (n.p., 1972?)

Sources: *African Writers Talking*; *Books in Print*, 1980-81, 1981-82; *Who's Who in African Literature*.

RIVERS, CONRAD KENT. Poet, Teacher.
Born in Atlantic City, N.J., Oct. 15, 1933. *Education:* B.A., Wilberforce U.; Chicago Tchrs. Coll.; Ind. U. *Career:* Served in U.S. Army; taught high sch. Eng., Gary, Ind.; one of founders, with Ronald Fair and others, of OBAC. *Honors:* Savannah State Poetry Prize for 1951 (while still in high sch.); three times included in "America Sings," coll. verse annuals. Died (suddenly) in 1968.

Writings:
Fiction
To Make a Poet Black, play

Perchance to Dream, Othello, poems (Wilberforce, Ohio, Wilberforce U., 1959)

These Black Bodies and This Sunburnt Face, poems (Cleveland, Free Lance, 1962)

The Still Voice of Harlem, poems (London, Breman, 1968)

The Wright Poems (Breman, 1973)

Sidelights: Since his death *Negro Digest/Black World* has established an annual Conrad Kent Rivers Poetry Award for the best poem published in that magazine during the year. (*Poetry of Black America*)

Sources: *For Malcolm*; *Kaleidoscope*; *New Black Poetry*; *Poetry of Black America*.

ROACH, HILDRED ELIZABETH. Music Professor, Pianist.
Born in Charlotte, N.C., Mar. 14, 1937. *Education:* B.A. (Applied Piano), Fisk U., 1957; Master of Music (Performance), Yale U., 1962; Juilliard Sch., 1958-59; Oakland U., Rochester, Mich., 1966; U. of Ghana, 1969. *Career:* Instr., Piano, Tuskegee Inst., 1957-58 & 1959-60; Instr., Piano, Fayetteville State Coll., 1962-66; Asst. Prof., Piano, Howard U., 1966-67; Asst. Prof., Piano, Va. State Coll., 1967-68; Prof., Dept. of Music, Fed. City Coll., Wash., D.C., 1968- . *Honors:* Sarah McKim Maloney Award, 1954; Theodore Presser Award, 1954; John Hay Whitney Found. Scholar, 1960; State of Ala. Scholar, 1960-62; Lockwood Competition & Concerto Performance Prize, Yale U., 1961; Phi Beta Kappa, Fisk U., 1957. *Mailing address:* 10700 Cavalier Dr., Silver Spring, Md. 20901.

Writings:
Nonfiction

Black American Music: Past and Present (Boston, Crescendo, 1973, rev. ed., 1976)

The Black Music Resource Book, ed. with Marva Cooper (N.Y., Taplinger, 1981)

Sidelights: Two half-hour television shows on Black Music; narrated original scripts, performed (Knowledge Series—shown in New York, Boston, Washington, D.C., Los Angeles, California, and Chicago—WRC-TV, Channel 4). (Author)

Sources: Author information; *Books in Print*, 1980-81.

ROBERTS, JAMES DEOTIS, SR. Clergyman, Religion Professor, Educator, Theologian.
Born in Spindale, N.C., July 12, 1927. *Education:* B.A. (magna cum laude), Johnson C. Smith U., Charlotte, N.C., 1947; B.S., Shaw U., Raleigh, N.C., 1950; S.T.M., Hartford Sem., 1952; Ph.D., U. of Edinburgh, 1957; further study: Cambridge U., Duke U., U. of Wis., U. of Chicago, U. of Cal. (Berkeley), Harvard Divinity Sch. & World Relig. Center, U. of Mich., Mich. State U. *Family:* Married Elizabeth Caldwell; d. Edin Charmaine, son James Deotis, Jr., d. Carlita Rose, d. Kristina LaFerne. *Career:* Pastor, Union Bap. Church, Tarbora, N.C., 1948-50; Asst. Pastor, Union Bap. Church, Hartford, Conn., 1950-52; Dean of Relig., Ga. Bap. Coll., Macon, 1952-53; Asst. & Assoc. Prof. of Philosophy & Relig. & Dir. of Relig. Life & Activities, Shaw U., 1953-55, 1957-58; Pastor-ad-interim, Radnor Park Congregational Church, Clyde Bank, Glasgow, Scotland, 1956-57; from Instr. to Prof. of Hist. & Philosophy of Relig. & Christian Theol., Sch. of Relig., Howard U., 1958-73; Dean, Sch. of Theol., Virginia Union U., 1973- . *Honors:* Study-Travel Fellow (Japan, Korea, Formosa, Hong Kong, Thailand, Burma, India, Pakistan, Lebanon, Jordan, Egypt, Greece, Turkey, Italy, Switzerland, France, & United Kingdom). *Mailing address:* 1205 Palmyra Ave., Richmond, Va. 23227

Writings:
Nonfiction

Faith and Reason; A Comparative Study of Pascal, Bergson, and James (Boston, Christopher, 1962)

From Puritanism to Platonism in Seventeenth Century England (The Hague, Martinus Nijhoff, 1968, 1969)

Liberation and Reconciliation: A Black Theology (Phila., Westminster, 1971)

Quest for a Black Theology, with Father James Gardiner (Phila., Pilgrim, 1971)

Extending Redemption and Reconciliation (St. Louis, Mo., Christian Bd. of Publ., 1973)

A Black Political Theology (Westminster, 1974)

Roots of a Black Future: Family and Church (Westminster, 1980)

Sources: Author information; *Library Journal*, Oct. 15, 1980.

ROBESON, ESLANDA (GOODE). Anthropologist, Journalist, Lecturer.
Born in Wash., D.C., Dec. 15, 1896. *Education:* U. of Chicago; B.S. (Chemistry), Columbia U., 1923; London U. & London Sch. of Econ. (Anthropology), 1935-37; Ph.D., Hartford Sem. Found. (African Studies), 1945. *Family:* Married Paul Robeson (internationally known concert singer & actor), Aug. 17, 1921; son Paul Robeson, Jr. *Career:* Surgical Technician & Chemist, Presby. Hospital, N.Y. (in charge of Surgical Pathological Lab.), 1918-24; Bus. Mgr. (for husband); Council on African Affairs; UN Correspondent for *New World Review*; Lect.: Africa & Race Relations. Died Dec. 13, 1965.

Writings:
Nonfiction

Paul Robeson, Negro (N.Y., London, Harper, 1930)

African Journey (N.Y., John Day, 1945; London, Gollancz, 1946)

What Do the People of Africa Want? (N.Y., Council on African Affairs, 1945)

American Argument, with Pearl S. Buck (N.Y., John Day, 1949; London, Methuen, 1950)

Sidelights: "Mrs. Robeson ... attended, and covered as a correspondent, the founding of the United Nations in San Francisco, in May 1945, the Federation celebrations of the West Indies in Trinidad in April 1958, the All-African Peoples Conference in Accra, in December 1958, and the first All-Asian Women's Conference in Peking, China, in December 1949, as well as the Anti-Fascist Women's Conference in November 1949 in Moscow, USSR." (*The Worker*)
African Journey was called "an excellent tourist account as well as a treatise on the color line." (Ernestine Evan)

Sources: *Current Biography*, 1945; *National Guardian*, Dec. 18, 1965; *Negro Caravan*; *Negro Digest*, Oct. 1945; *New York Herald Tribune*, Dec. 14, 1965; *New York Times*, Dec. 14, 1965; *The Worker*, Dec. 19, 1965.

ROBESON, PAUL. Singer, Actor, Civil Rights Activist.
Born in Princeton, N.J., Apr. 9, 1898. *Education:* B.A. (honors, Phi Beta Kappa), Rutgers U., 1919; grad., Columbia U. Law Sch., 1923. *Family:* Married Eslanda Cardozo Goode, 1921; son Paul. *Career:* Actor, Singer; Civil Rights Activist. *Honors:* Won 12 letters in track, football, baseball, and basketball, at Rutgers; All-American, 1917 & 1918; Stalin Peace Prize; Spingarn Medal, NAACP; Whitney Young, Jr. Memorial Award, N.Y. Urban League; Donaldson Award for Best Acting Performance of 1944 (in *Othello*). Died in 1976.

Writings:
Nonfiction

Here I Stand, autobiog. (Boston, Beacon, 1958, 1971)

Paul Robeson, Tributes, Selected Writings (N.Y., The Archives, 1976)

Sidelights: Walter Camp called Robeson "the greatest defensive end that ever tred (sic) the gridiron." Some stage successes were *Showboat*, *Porgy* and *Othello*. When he did *Othello* in New York in 1943, his ovation was called "one of the most prolonged and wildest ... in the history of the New York Theatre." (*Negro Almanac*)

Sources: *Current Biography*, 1975; *Negro Almanac*; *Paul Robeson: The Life and Times of a Free Black Man*.

ROBESON, SUSAN. Filmmaker, Television Producer.
   Born in N.Y.C., Feb. 27, 1953. *Education:* Hunter Coll., High Sch., N.Y.C.; Antioch Coll., Yellow Springs, Ohio; N.Y.U. *Career:* Filmmaker, 1972- ; Documentary Camerawoman; Assoc. Producer, WABC-TV's *Like It Is. Mailing address:* c/o Citadel Press, 120 Enterprise Ave., Secaucus, N.J. 07094.

Writings:
   Nonfiction

   The Whole World in His Hands: A Pictorial Biography of Paul Robeson (Secaucus, N.J., Citadel, 1981)

Sidelights: Ms. Robeson's grandfather, the greatly renowned and revered artist and staunch civil rights fighter, Paul Robeson, made a profound and unshakable impact on the young woman. As a result, she has studied communications and the history and culture of the African Diaspora, and has written and produced this remarkable record of achievement of one of our greatest Americans. (Compilers)

Sources: *Books in Print,* 1981-82; *The Whole World in His Hands.*

ROBINSON, JAMES HERMAN. Clergyman, Executive Director (Operation Crossroads).
   Born in Knoxville, Tenn., Jan. 24, 1907. *Education:* U. of Pa., grad. 1935; Union Theol. Sem., N.Y.C., 1938. *Career:* Ordained 1938, Presby. Church; Founder & Dir., Church of the Master & Morningside Community Center, Harlem, 1938-61; 1st Operation Crossroads Project, 1958; apptd. Consultant on African Affairs for United Presby. Church, 1961; Consultant to Africa Desk, State Dept., 1962; also served as Advisory Chairman to Peace Corps; apptd. Chairman, Youth Activities Com. of Intnl. Cooperation Year, 1965. Died in 1972.

Writings:
   Nonfiction

   Road without Turning, the Story of Reverend James H. Robinson; An Autobiography (N.Y., Farrar, 1950)

   Tomorrow Is Today (Phila., Christian Educ. Press, 1954)

   Adventurous Preaching (Great Neck, N.Y., Channel Press, 1956)

   Love of This Land; Progress of the Negro in the United States, ed. (Christian Educ. Press, 1956)

   Africa at the Crossroads (Phila., Westminster, 1962?)

Sidelights: Reverend Robinson made several missions to Africa and Europe; fostered many international student programs; took student seminars and work camp projects to five West African countries. (*Negro Handbook*)

Source: *Negro Handbook.*

ROBINSON, WILHELMENA SIMPSON. Historian, History Professor.
   Born in Pensacola, Fla., Nov. 12, 1912. *Education:* B.S. (cum laude), Tenn. State U., 1933; M.A., Columbia U., 1934; grad. study: Boston U., 1943, & Ohio State U., 1953-56. *Family:* Married Collins H. Robinson (electrical engineer), Dec. 28, 1939; son Antoine LaRue. *Career:* Instr., Hist. & Eng., Edward Waters Coll., Jacksonville, Fla., 1934-36; Head, Tchr. Training, Fla. Normal Coll., St. Augustine, 1936-37; Ala. State U., Montgomery, Supervisor, rural tchr. training program, 1937-40; Asst. Prof. of Hist., Central State U., Wilberforce, Ohio, 1947-53, Head of Dept., 1950-53; Instr., Amer. Hist., Ohio State U., 1954-56; Assoc. Prof. & Prof. of Hist., Central State U., 1956-74. *Honors:* Ford Found. Grant for Faculty Inst. on Near East & North Africa, U. of Mich., 1965; Bd. of Dir., U. Regional Broadcasting, Dayton, Ohio. *Mailing address:* c/o Dept. of Hist., Central State U., Wilberforce, Ohio 45384.

Writings:
   Nonfiction

   Historical Negro Biographies (N.Y., Publishers, Inc., 1967)

Man in America, with Others (Morristown, N.J., Silver Burdett, 1974)

Afro-Americans in Ohio: The Quest for First Class Citizenship (Cincinnati, Ohio Historical Soc., 1976)

Sources: *Contemporary Authors*, vols. 25-28, rev. ed.; *Historical Negro Biographies*.

ROBINSON, WILLIAM HENRY, JR. English Professor, Literary Critic, Anthologist.
Born in Newport, R.I., Oct. 29, 1922. *Education:* B.A., N.Y.U., 1951; M.A., Boston U., 1957; Ph.D., Harvard U., 1964. *Family:* Married Doris Carol Johnson, June 8, 1948. *Career:* Instr., Eng., Prairie View A&M Coll., Tex., 1951-53; Eng. Faculty, N.C. A&T State U., Greensboro, 1956-61, 1964-66; Assoc. Prof., Eng. & Humanities, Boston U., 1966-68; Prof., Eng., Howard U., 1968-70; Prof. of Eng. & Black Studies, R.I. Coll., Providence, 1970- . *Mailing address:* R.I. Coll., 600 Mount Pleasant Ave., Providence, R.I. 02908.

Writings:
Fiction

Early Black American Poets; Selections with Biographical and Critical Introductions (Dubuque, Iowa, William C. Brown, 1969, 1971)

Early Black American Prose; Selections with Biographical Introductions, 1734-1930 (William C. Brown, 1971)

Nomo: A Modern Anthology of Black African and Black American Literature, ed. (N.Y., Macmillan, 1972)

Nonfiction

Phillis Wheatley in the Black American Beginnings, biog. (Detroit, Broadside, 1975)

The Proceedings of the Free African Union Society and the African Benevolent Society, Rhode Island, 1780-1824 (R.I. Urban League, 1976)

New England Black Letters (Boston, Boston Pub. Lib., 1978)

Phillis Wheatley: A Bio-Bibliography (Boston, G. K. Hall, 1981)

Phillis Wheatley and Her Writings, ed. (N.Y., Garland, 1982)

Sources: *Early Black American Poets*; Publisher's brochure.

RODGERS, CAROLYN MARIE. Poet, Teacher, Columnist.
Born in Chicago, Ill. *Education:* U. of Ill.; B.A., Roosevelt U., 1965. *Career:* YMCA Soc. Worker, 1963-66; Columbia Coll., Writer & Lect., 1968-69; U. of Wash., Writer-in-Residence, summer 1970; Poet-in-Residence, Malcolm X Community Coll., 1972; Visiting Writer-in-Residence, Natl. Found. of Humanities & Arts, Albany State Coll., 1972; Ind. U., summer 1973; Columnist, *Milwaukee Courier*; bk. reviewer, *Chicago Daily News*. *Honors:* 1st Conrad Kent Rivers Writing Award, 1969; NEA Award, 1970; Soc. of Midland Authors, Poet Laureate Award, 1970. *Mailing address:* 5954 S. Bishop, Chicago, Ill. 60636.

Writings:
Fiction

Paper Soul, poems (Chicago, Third World, 1968)

2 Love Raps, poems (Third World, 1969, 1973)

Songs of a Blackbird, poems (Third World, 1969)

How I Got Ovah: New and Selected Poems (Garden City, N.Y., Anchor, 1975)

The Heart as Ever Green, poems (Anchor, 1978)

Sidelights: Carolyn Rodgers, Johari Amini and Don L. Lee founded Third World Press in 1968. (*Broadside Authors and Artists*)

Sources: *Books in Print*, 1979-80; *Broadside Authors and Artists.*

ROGERS, JOEL AUGUSTUS. Historian, Journalist, Newspaper Columnist.
Born in Jamaica, Brit. W. Indies, in 1883. Came to U.S. in 1906; naturalized in 1917. Self-educated. *Career:* Originally a journalist traveling in Europe, Asia, and Africa in search of material on the Black Man. Served with Brit. Army for 4 yrs.; covered Haile Selassie's coronation, Addis Ababa, Ethiopia, 1930; War Correspondent on Italo-Ethiopian conflict, 1935-36, for *Pittsburgh Courier* (thus became 1st Negro war correspondent in U.S. hist.); wrote an illustrated feature, "Your History," for *Pittsburgh Courier.* Died Jan. 1966 in N.Y.C.

Writings:
Fiction
She Walks in Beauty, novel (L.A., Western, 1963)

Nonfiction
From Superman to Man (N.Y., M. A. Donohue, 1917; N.Y., Author, 1941, 5th ed., 1957)

As Nature Leads; An Informal Discussion of the Reason Why Negro and Caucasian Are Mixing in Spite of Opposition (Donohue, 1919)

The Maroons of the West Indies and South America (N.Y., Author, 1921)

The Ku Klux Klan Spirit (N.Y., Messenger, 1923)

World's Greatest Men of African Descent (Author, 1931, 1935, 1946)

100 Amazing Facts about the Negro, with Complete Proof; Short Cut to the World History of the Negro (N.Y., Hubner, 1934, 23rd ed., 1957; Author, 1963)

The Real Facts about Ethiopia (Author, 1936)

Sex and Race; Negro-Caucasian Mixing in All Ages and All Lands, 3 vols. (Author, 1940-44; N.Y., J. A. Rogers, 1957-61, 9th ed., 1967)

World's Great Men of Color, 2 vols. (Author, 1946-47; N.Y., Macmillan, 1972)

Nature Knows No Color Line, Research into the Negro Ancestry in the White Race (N.Y., Helga M. Rogers, 1952)

Africa's Gift to America; The Afro-American in the Making and Saving of the United States (N.Y., n.p., 1959; New Rochelle, N.Y., Sportshelf, 1961)

Facts about the Negro (Pittsburgh, Lincoln Park Studios, 1960)

Sidelights: "For more than 50 years, Joel A. Rogers was one of the foremost Negro historians in the United States.
"... the work of Joel Rogers ... is ... impressive when one considers that Rogers was conducting much of his research at a time when Negro historians were virtually non-existent in the United States." (*Negro Almanac*)

Sources: *Negro Almanac*; *Negro Caravan*; *Who's Who in Colored America*, 7th ed., 1950.

ROLLINS, BRYANT. Editor, Journalist, Civil Rights Activist.
Born in Boston, Mass., Dec. 13, 1937. *Education:* B.A., Northwestern U., 1961; grad. study, U. of Mass. *Family:* Married Judith Rollins (separated); children: Malikkah Kenyatta, Kari Camara. *Career:* Reporter, *Boston Globe*, 1961-65; Founder/Ed., *Bay State Banner* (Black newspaper), Boston, 1965-66; coordinator, Afro-Amer. Hist. curriculum working party, Educ. Development, Urban League of Greater Boston, 1967-69; Dir., Boston Coll.-Urban League Joint Center for Inner-City Change, 1968-69; Dir., Small Bus. Development Center; V. Pres., H. Carl McCall & Assoc.

(urban affairs consultants), N.Y., 1969-71; Executive Dir., N.Y. *Amsterdam News*, 1971-72; Admin., Michele Clark fellowship program, Grad. Sch. of Journalism, Columbia U., 1973-74; Ed. & Writer, "Week in Review," *N.Y. Times*, 1974. *Honors:* Obie Award for *RIOT*, 1969; Annual Poet of the Year Award, Northeastern U., 1959. *Mailing address:* c/o Thomas Y. Crowell, 10 E. 53rd St., N.Y., N.Y. 10022.

Writings:
   Fiction
Danger Song, novel (N.Y., Doubleday, 1967; N.Y., Collier, African-Amer. Lib., 1971)

RIOT, play, with Julie Portman (1969?)

Greens and Blues and All the Rhythms in Between, poems (Harlem, N.Y., Collins, 1973)

Sources: *Books in Print*, 1980-81; Pub. information.

ROLLINS, CHARLEMAE HILL. Librarian, Juvenile Writer, Teacher, Library Administrative (Official).
   Born in Yazoo City, Miss., June 20, 1897. *Education:* Columbia U.; Grad. Lib. Sch., U. of Chicago. *Family:* Married Joseph W. Rollins, Apr. 8, 1918; son Joseph W. Rollins, Jr. *Career:* Chicago Public Lib., 1927-63, Children's Librn., George C. Hall Branch, 1932-63; Instr., Children's Lit., Roosevelt U., Chicago, 1949-?; Morgan State Coll., 1953-54; Human Relations Workshop, San Francisco State Coll.; Dept. of Lib. Sci., Rosary Coll., River Forest, Ill.; Pres., Children's Div., ALA, 1957-58; Chairman, Children's Div., Ill. Lib. Assn., 1954-55; Newbery Caldecott Awards Com. ALA, 1956-57; Elementary Section, Ill. Unit, Catholic Lib. Assn. *Honors:* Amer. Brotherhood Award, Natl. Council of Christians & Jews, 1952; Lib. Letter Award, ALA, 1953; Grolier Soc. Award, ALA, 1955; Good Amer. Award of Chicago, Com. of One Hundred, 1962; Negro Centennial Awards (in three areas), 1963; Children's Reading Round Table Award, 1963; Hon. Dr. of Humane Letters, Columbia Coll., Chicago; Mem., Ed. Bd., *World Book Encyclopedia & American Educator*; Constance Lindsay Skinner Award, Women's Natl. Bk. Assn., 1970; Coretta Scott King Award, 1971; room dedicated in her name at Carter G. Woodson Regional Lib., Chicago, Nov. 1977. Died Feb. 3, 1979.

Writings:
   Fiction
Christmas Gif': An Anthology of Christmas Poems, Songs and Stories, juv. (Chicago, Follett, 1963)

   Nonfiction
We Build Together; A Reader's Guide to Negro Life and Literature for Elementary and High School Use, ed. (Chicago, Natl. Council of Tchrs. of Eng., 1941, rev. ed., 1948, 1967)

The Magic World of Books (Chicago, Science Res. Assoc., 1954)

They Showed the Way: Forty American Negro Leaders, juv. (N.Y., Crowell, 1964)

Famous American Negro Poets, juv. (N.Y., Dodd, 1965)

Great Negro Poets for Children (Dodd, 1965)

Famous Negro Entertainers of Stage, Screen and TV, juv. (Dodd, 1967)

Black Troubadour: Langston Hughes, juv. (Chicago, Rand McNally, 1970)

Sidelights: One of the most noteworthy facets of the professional career of the *grand dame* of children's librarianship was the publication of *We Build Together*. "This was an annotated list of 18 books which were least offensive in their stories and illustrations. Publishers were roundly criticized, in the book's introduction, for the caricatures, plantation themes, and homemade dialects directed toward impressionable young minds. This ... became the conscience and guidebook for the industry and professionals around the country." (*Ebony*)

Sources: *Authors of Books for Young People*; *Chicago Daily Defender*, Feb. 7, 1979; *Chicago Tribune*, Feb. 7, 1979; *Famous American Negro Poets*; "Goodbye Black Sambo" (1972); *School Library Journal*, Mar. 1979; *Something about the Author*, vol. 3, 1965; Pub. information.

ROSSER, JAMES MILTON. Bacteriologist, Health Educator, University President.
Born in E. St. Louis, Ill., Apr. 16, 1939. *Education:* B.A., 1962, M.A., 1963 (both in Microbiology), Ph.D. (Health Educ.), 1969 – all S. Ill. U., Carbondale. *Family:* Married Carmen Rosita Colby, Dec. 27, 1962; son Terrence. *Career:* Diagnostic Bacteriologist, Holden Hospital, Carbondale, 1961-63; Res. Bacteriologist, Eli Lilly & Co., Indianapolis, 1963-66. S. Ill. U., Carbondale: Coordinator, Black Amer. Studies, & Instr., Health Educ., 1968-69; Asst. Prof. & Dir., Black Amer. Studies, 1969-70; Asst. to Chancellor, 1970. U. of Kan., Lawrence: Assoc. V. Chancellor for Acad. Affairs, 1970-74; Assoc. Prof., Educ., Pharmacology & Toxicology, 1971-74. Dept. of Higher Educ., State of N.J., Trenton: V. Chancellor, 1974-79 (Acting Chancellor, 1977). Cal. State U., L.A., Pres., 1979- ; Prof., Health Care Management, 1979- . *Honors:* Most Valuable Varsity Basketball Player, Langston U., 1957-58; Coll. Stud. of Yr., E. St. Louis, 1957-58; Natl. Sci. Found. Fellow, 1961; NDEA Fellow, 1967-68; Kappa Delta Pi (Educ.); Phi Kappa Phi (scholastic). *Mailing address:* 225 El Cielo Lane, Bradbury, Cal. 91010.

Writings:
Nonfiction
Black Studies Debate, with Jacob U. Gordon, eds. (Lawrence, U. of Kan. Press, 1974)

An Analysis of Health Care Delivery, with Howard E. Mossberg (N.Y., Wiley, 1977; reprint, Huntington, N.Y., Krieger, 1980)

Sources: Author information; *Books in Print*, 1981-82; *Los Angeles Times*, May 22, 1979; *Who's Who among Black Americans*, vol. I, 2nd ed., 1977-78; *Who's Who in America*, vol. 2, 41st ed., 1980-81.

ROUMAIN, JACQUES (JEAN BAPTISTE). (Haitian). Poet, Novelist, Short Story Writer, Journalist, Anthropologist.
Born in Port-au-Prince, Haiti, June 4, 1907 (grandson of General Tancrède Auguste, former President). *Education:* Saint Louis de Gonzague, Port au Prince, Institut Gruneau, Switzerland; Zurich (German Poetry); Spain (Agriculture); Musée de l'Homme, Paris. *Career:* Founder, *La Revue Indigène*, with Others, & *La Trouée 559*; Chief, Dept. of Interior, Haiti; Founder, Communist Party, Haiti; Founder, Bureau d'Ethnologie. Died Aug. 18, 1944, in Port-au-Prince.

Writings:
(Partial Listing – English Only)
Fiction
Masters of the Dew, novel, transl. from French by Mercer Cook & Langston Hughes (N.Y., Reynal & Hitchcock, 1947; N.Y., Macmillan, Collier, 1971)

Ebony Wood, poems, transl. by Sidney Shapiro (N.Y., Interworld Press, 1972)

Sidelights: Roumain has been considered possibly Haiti's most important writer. He was so interested in exploring the African origins of the Haitian people that he founded the Bureau d'Ethnologie, with Jean Price-Mars and other anthropologists.
  "Roumain said the poet is 'un être qui vit' in a special way and that his work should express an excitement of thought, a veritable fever of feeling of his deepest emotions on important themes." (*Caribbean Writers*)

Sources: *Caribbean Writers*; *Modern Black Writers*; *Resistance and Caribbean Literature*.

ROWAN, CARL THOMAS. Former USIA Director, Syndicated Columnist, Journalist, Civil Rights Advocate.

Born in Ravenscroft, Tenn., Aug. 11, 1925. *Education:* B.A., Oberlin Coll., 1947; M.A. (Journalism), U. of Minn., 1948; Litt. D. (hon.), Simpson Coll., 1957, Hamline U., 1958; L.H.D. (hon.) Washburn U., 1964, Talladega Coll., 1965, St. Olaf Coll., 1966, Knoxville Coll., 1966; LL.D. (hon.), Howard U., 1964; Alfred U., 1964; Temple U., 1964, Atlanta U., 1965, Allegheny Coll., 1966; D. Public Admin., Morgan State Coll., 1964. *Family:* Married Vivien L. Murphy (public health nurse), Aug. 2, 1950; d. Barbara, son Carl, Jr., son Geoffrey. *Career:* U.S. Navy, 1943, Ensign, Naval Reserve; Copywriter, 1948-50, Staff Writer, 1950-61, *Minneapolis Tribune*; Deputy Asst. to Secy. of State for Public Affairs, Dept. of State, 1961-63; U.S. Ambassador to Finland, 1963-64; Dir., USIA, Wash., D.C., 1964-65; Columnist, *Chicago Daily News*, 1965- ; Syndicated Columnist. *Honors:* Sidney Hillman Award, best newspaper reporting, 1952; ALA annual list of best books, *South of Freedom*, 1953; Amer. Teamwork Award, Natl. Urban League, 1955; Foreign Correspondence Medallion for article on India, 1955, & on S. E. Asia coverage of Bandung Conf., 1956; ALA annual list of best bks., *The Pitiful and the Proud*, 1956; Phila. Fellowship Com., 1961; Communications Award, Human Relations, Anti-Defamation League, B'nai Brith, 1964; Distinguished Serv. Award, Capital Press Club, 1964; Natl. Brotherhood Award, Natl. Conf. of Christians & Jews, 1964; Amer. S. Region Press Inst. Award, 1965. *Mailing address:* c/o Random House, Inc., 201 E. 50th St., N.Y., N.Y. 10022.

Writings:

Nonfiction

South of Freedom (N.Y., Knopf, 1952)

The Pitiful and the Proud (N.Y., Random House, 1956)

Go South to Sorrow (Random House, 1957)

Wait till Next Year; The Life Story of Jackie Robinson (Random House, 1960)

Just between Us Blacks (Random, 1974)

Sidelights: "As Director of USIA, Carl Rowan supervised 12,000 employees in 106 countries, was the highest ranking Negro in the federal government, and the first to sit in on meetings of the national Security Council." (*Negroes in Public Affairs and Government*)

Sources: *Current Biography*, 1958; *Negro Handbook*; *South of Freedom*; *Negroes in Public Affairs and Government*; Pub. information.

RUSSWURM, JOHN B. Editor, Politician, Statesman.

Born in Jamaica, Brit. W. Indies, Oct. 1, 1799 (son of a White Amer. father & a Jamaican mother). *Education:* Sent by father to Canada, where he received early training; grad., Bowdoin Coll., Maine, 1826, Master's degree, 1829, *Career:* Established *Freedom's Journal*, 1827 (with Samuel E. Cornish); Ed., *The Rights of All* (newspaper), 1828. (Anti-slavery societies used *The Rights of All* as a forum, and the editor became a staunch advocate of immediate emancipation.) In Liberia: Supt. of Schs.; Governor of Md. Province (at Cape Palms) before it became part of Liberia; founded *Liberia Herald*. Died June 17, 1851.

Writings:

Nonfiction

Freedom's Journal, newspaper, with Samuel E. Cornish (N.Y., 1827-)

The Rights of All, newspaper (N.Y., 1828-)

Liberia Herald, newspaper (after 1830)

Sidelights: "John B. Russwurm, the founder of the first Negro newspaper, *Freedom's Journal*, was also the first Negro to receive a degree from a college in the United States....

"For four years, Russwurm directed his paper toward a program of abolition, of equal rights for the Negro in America and of opposition to the colonizationists. In 1830, *The Rights of All* published an article that praised the work of Paul Cuffee, the colonizationist who had taken 30 Negroes to Sierra Leone.... Subsequently joining the colonizationists, he went to Liberia, where he served creditably as superintendent of schools and as governor of the Maryland Province." (*Historical Negro Biographies*)

Sources: *Historical Negro Biographies*; *Negro Handbook*.

RUSTIN, BAYARD. Civil Rights Leader.
Born in West Chester, Pa., Mar. 17, 1910. *Education:* Wilberforce U., 1930-31; Cheyney State Coll., 1931-33; City Coll. of CUNY, 1933-35. *Career:* Race Relations Dir., Fellowship of Reconciliation, 1941-53; Executive Secy., War Resisters' League, 1953-55; Special Asst. to Martin L. King, Jr., 1955-60; Dir., A. Philip Randolph Inst., N.Y., 1966- ; Field Secy., CORE, 1941; Organizer, March on Washington for Jobs and Freedom, 1963. *Honors:* Eleanor Roosevelt Award from Trade Union Leadership Council, 1966; Liberty Bell Award, Howard U. Law Sch., 1967; LL.D., New Sch. for Soc. Res., 1968, & Brown U., 1972; Litt. D., Montclair State Coll., 1968; John Dewey Award, United Fed. of Tchrs., 1968; Family of Man Award, Natl. Council of Churches, 1969; John F. Kennedy Award, Natl. Council of Jewish Women, 1971; Lyndon Johnson Award, Urban League, 1974. *Mailing address:* A. Philip Randolph Inst., 260 Park Ave., S., N.Y., N.Y. 10010.

Writings:
Nonfiction
Down the Line; The Collected Writings of Bayard Rustin (Chicago, Quadrangle, 1971)

Strategies for Freedom: The Changing Patterns of Black Protest (N.Y., Columbia U. Press, 1976)

Sidelights: In 1957, Mr. Rustin coordinated the Prayer Pilgrimage to Washington for civil rights. The Youth Marches for Integrated Schools, which he also directed, followed in 1958 and 1959.
He aided the striking Memphis sanitation workers in raising $100,000 and organized the massive march following Dr. King's assassination in 1968. During his career, Mr. Rustin was arrested 24 times in the struggle for Civil Rights. (Author)

Sources: Author information; *Books in Print*, 1978-79.

SALKEY, (FELIX) ANDREW (ALEXANDER). (Panamanian). Poet, Novelist, Anthologist, Juvenile Writer, Critic, Journalist.
Born in Colon, Panama, Jan. 30, 1928. *Education:* St. George's Coll., Kingston, Jamaica; Munro Coll., St. Elizabeth, Jamaica; B.A. (Eng.), U. of London. *Family:* Married Patricia Verden in 1957; two sons. *Career:* Lect.; Prof., Writing, Sch. of Arts & Humanities, Hampshire Coll., Amherst, Mass.; Eng. Tchr., London Comprehensive Sch., 1957-59; regular outside contrib. as interpreter & scriptwriter, BBC External Serv. (radio), London, since 1952. *Honors:* Casa de Las Americas Poetry Prize (Cuban), awarded for *In the Hills Where Her Dreams Live*; Guggenheim Found. Fellow, 1960; Deutschen Kinderbuchpreis, 1967; Thomas Helmore Prize, U. of London, 1955. *Mailing address:* Flat 8, Windsor Ct., Moscow Rd., Queensway, London W2, Eng.

Writings:
Fiction
A Quality of Violence, novel (London, Hutchinson, 1959)

West Indian Stories, anthology (London, Faber, 1960, 1968)

Escape to an Autumn Pavement, novel (Hutchinson, 1960)

Stories from the Caribbean; An Anthology, ed. (London, Elek, 1965; as *Island Voices: Stories from the West Indies*, N.Y., Liveright, 1970)

Caribbean Prose; An Anthology for Secondary School, ed. (London, Evans, 1967)

The Late Emancipation of Jerry Stover, novel (Hutchinson, 1968)

The Adventures of Catullus Kelly, novel (Hutchinson, 1969)

One Love, anthology (London, Bogle-L'Ouverture, 1971)

Breaklight, an Anthology of Caribbean Poetry, ed. (London, Hamilton, 1971)

Breaklight: The Poetry of the Caribbean, ed. (N.Y., Doubleday, 1972)

Jamaica, poems (Hutchinson, 1973)

Caribbean Essays, ed., anthology (Evans, 1973)

Anancy's Score, short stories (Bogle-L'Ouverture, 1973)

Caribea, poems (Hutchinson, 1975)

Come Home, Malcolm Heartland, novel (Hutchinson, 1975)

Caribbean Folk Tales and Legends, ed. (Evans, 1975)

Writing in Cuba since the Revolution, anthology (Bogle-L'Ouverture, 1975)

In the Hills Where Her Dreams Live: Poems for Chile (Habana, Cuba, Casa de Las Americas, 1979; Sausalito, Cal., Black Scholar Press, 1980)

Away: Poems (N.Y., Allison & Busby, 1980)

Nonfiction
Hurricane, juv. (London, Oxford U. Press, 1964; n.p., New Oxford Lib. Ser., 1979)

Earthquake, juv. (Oxford U. Press, 1965; N.Y., Roy, 1969)

The Shark Hunters, reader (London, Nelson, 1966)

Drought, juv. (Oxford U. Press, 1966)

Riot, juv. (Oxford U. Press, 1967)

Jonah Simpson, juv. (Oxford U. Press, 1969; Roy, 1970)

Havana Journal (Harmondsworth, Penguin, 1971)

Georgetown Journal: A Caribbean Writer's Journey from London via Port of Spain to Georgetown, Guyana, 1970 (London, New Beacon Bks., 1972)

Joey Tyson, juv. (Bogle-L'Ouverture, 1974)

Sidelights: "... one of the best interviewers in the radio business and does regular work for the BBC." (*Caribbean Writers*)

Editor, with others, of *Savacore*, journal of the Caribbean Artists Movement, quarterly (4th issue each year).

Sources: *Books in Print*, 1980-81; *Caribbean Writers*; *Complete Caribbeana, 1900-1975*; *Contemporary Novelists*, 2nd ed., 1976; *Freedomways*, vol. 21, 1981; *Jamaican National Bibliography*.

SAMPSON, HENRY T., JR. Nuclear Engineer, Theater Enthusiast.
Born in Jackson, Miss., Apr. 22, 1934. *Education:* B.S. (Chemical Engineering), Purdue U., W. Lafayette, Ind., 1956: M.S. (Engineering), UCLA, 1961; Ph.D. (Nuclear Engineering), U. of Ill., 1967. *Family:* Div.; children: Henry T. III, Martin. *Career:* Res. Chemical Engineer, U.S. Naval Ordnance Test Station, China Lake, Cal., 1956-61; Dir., Planning & Operations Space Test Program, Aerospace Corp., El Segundo, Cal., 1967- ; holds three scientific patents. *Honors:* Navy Educational Fellow, 1962; Atomic Energy Com. Fellow, 1963. *Mailing address:* 1501 Espinosa Circle, Palos Verdes Estates, Cal. 90274.

Writings:
Nonfiction
Blacks in Black and White: A Source Book on Black Films (Metuchen, N.J., Scarecrow, 1977)

Blacks in Blackface: A Source Book on Early Black Musical Shows (Scarecrow, 1980)

Sources: Author information; *Books in Print*, 1981-82; *Freedomways*, vol. 21, no. 1, 1981.

SAMUELS, WILFRED D. (Costa Rican). English Professor, Literary Critic, Editor.

Born in Costa Rica in 1947. *Education:* B.A. (Eng./Black Studies), U. of Cal., Riverside; M.A. (Amer. Studies/Afro-Amer. Studies), Ph.D. (Amer. Studies/Afro-Amer. Studies)—both U. of Iowa. *Family:* Married Barbara Fikes; son Michael Alain, son Detavio Ricardo. *Career:* Instr., Iowa Wesleyan Coll., Mt. Pleasant, Iowa; Asst. Prof., U. of N. Iowa, Cedar Falls; Asst. Prof., Eng. & Black Studies, U. of Colo., Boulder. Assoc. Ed., *UMOJA: Scholarly Journal of Black Studies,* 1978- . *Honors:* Elks Leadership Award; NEH Fellow; Postdoctoral Fellow, Center for Afro-Amer. Studies, UCLA, 1982-83. *Mailing address:* c/o Dept. of Eng., U. of Colo., Boulder, Colo. 80310.

Writings:

Nonfiction

Five Afro-Caribbean Voices in American Culture, 1917-1929, socio-literary criticism (n.p., Belmont Bks. 1979)

Sources: Author information; Conference Notes (Recent Developments in Black Literature and Criticism), 1983.

SANCHEZ, SONIA. Poet, Activist, Playwright.

Born in Birmingham, Ala., Sept. 9, 1934. *Education:* B.A., Hunter Coll., 1955; N.Y.U., 1958. *Family:* sons, Morani, Mungu (twins). *Career:* Instr., San Francisco State Coll., 1966-67; Instr., U. of Pittsburgh, 1968-69; Asst. Prof., Rutgers U., 1969-70; Asst. Prof. of Black Lit., Creative Writing, Manhattan Community Coll., 1971-73; Tchr. of Writing, City Coll. of CUNY, 1972; Assoc. Prof., Amherst Coll., 1972-73; Poet/Prof., Temple U., present. *Honors:* P.E.N. Writing Award, 1969; Amer. Acad. of Arts & Letters $1,000 award to continue writing; Hon. Ph.D. in Fine Arts, Wilberforce U., 1973; NEA Award, 1977-78; Honorary Citizen of Atlanta, 1982; "Tribute to Black Womanhood Award," Black Students of Smith Coll., 1982. *Mailing address:* 407 W. Chelton Ave., Phila., Pa. 19144.

Writings:

Fiction

Homecoming; Poems (Detroit, Broadside, 1969)

We a BaddDDD People, poems (Broadside, 1970)

The Bronx Is Next, play (produced at Theater Black,d N.Y.C., Oct. 3, 1970)

It's a New Day: Poems for Young Brothas and Sistuhs, juv. (Broadside, 1971)

Three Hundred and Sixty Degrees of Blackness Comin' at You, poems, ed. (N.Y., 5X Publ. Co., 1971)

Sister Son/ji, play (first produced as *Black Visions,* N.Y., Shakespeare Festival Public Theater, 1972)

Dirty Hearts, play (n.d.)

The Adventures of Fathead, Smallhead, and Squarehead, juv. (N.Y., Third Press, 1973)

We Be Word Sorcerers, novel (N.Y., Bantam, 1973)

Love Poems (Third Press, 1973)

A Blues Book for Blue Black Magical Women, poems (Broadside, Pets Scr., 1974)

Sound Investment, poems (Chicago, Third World, 1980)

Sidelights: The author states that critics/writers have written the following about her books: (George Kent) "*A Blues Book for Blue Black Magical Women* possesses an extraordinary culmination of spiritual and poetic powers...." (Gwendolyn Brooks) "Her canvas accommodates her various brushes, big and little, and accommodates both her grand point and her whimsey. She likes involving herself with the 'small' details. But there are mountains in her mites." (Ezekiel Mphahlele) "The poetry reflects a tough intellect, a hardnosed attitude toward Black life and the context of the American reality. At the same time it ... breathes warmth and love for the lovable."

Sources: Author information; *Black Books Bulletin*, vol. 7, no. 1; *Black Fire*; *Books in Print*, 1979-80; *Broadside Authors and Artists*; *Ebony*, Mar. 1974; *For Malcolm*; *New Black Poetry*; *New Black Voices*; *Poetry of Black America*; *Soulscript*.

SAUNDERS, DORIS EVANS. Librarian, Columnist, Editor, Teacher.
Born in Chicago, Ill., Aug. 8, 1921. *Education:* B.A., Roosevelt U., Chicago, 1951; M.S., 1977, M.A., 1977, Boston U.; further study, Vanderbilt U. *Family:* Married Vincent E. Saunders, Jr., Oct. 28, 1950 (div. Aug. 1963); children: Ann Camille Vivian, Vincent Ellsworth III. *Career:* Chicago Public Lib.: Lib. Asst., 1942-46; Principal Ref. Librn., 1946-49. Johnson Pub. Co.: Librn., 1949-66; Dir., Bk. Div., 1961-66. Information, Inc., Chicago: Pres., 1966-68. Chicago State Coll.: Dir. Community Relations, 1968-70; U. of Ill., Chicago Circle: Staff Assoc., Chancellor's Office, 1970-73; Johnson Pub. Co.: Dir., Bk. Div., 1973- . Prof., Journalism, Jackson State Coll. Columnist, *Chicago Daily Defender*, 1966-70, *Chicago Courier*, 1970-73; Assoc. Ed., *Negro Digest*, 1962-66. *Mailing address:* c/o Johnson Pub. Co., 820 S. Mich. Ave., Chicago, Ill. 60605.

Writings:
Nonfiction

The Day They Marched, ed. (Chicago, Johnson, 1963)

The Kennedy Years and the Negro, a Photographic Record, ed. (Johnson, 1964)

The Ebony Handbook (Johnson, 1974)

Black Society, with Gerri Major (Johnson, 1976)

The Life and Times of William L. Dawson (Johnson, 1978)

Sidelights: Doris Saunders was writer and producer of television program "Our People," 1968-70. She was host of radio program "The Think Tank," 1971-72.

Sources: *Books in Print*, 1979-80; *Contemporary Authors*, vols. 77-80, 1979; Pub. information.

SAVAGE, WILLIAM SHERMAN. History Professor, Historian.
Born in Wattsville, Va., Mar. 7, 1890. *Education:* Morgan State Coll., Baltimore; A.B., Howard U., 1917; M.A., Oregon U., 1925; Ph.D., Ohio State U., 1934. *Family:* Married Roena Muckelroy; children: Eloise Savage Logan, Inez Savage Allen. *Career:* Chairman, Dept. of Hist. & Govt., Lincoln U., Mo., 1921-60; Prof., Hist., & Chairman, Dept., Jarvis Christian Coll., 1960-66; Visiting Prof., Hist., Dept. of Hist. & Soc. Sci., Cal. State, L.A., 1966-70; Exchange Prof., Stephens Point, Wis.; Tchr., summers, Ala. State, Tuskegee, & Whittier Coll. (Cal.); Columnist, *Kansas City Call*, "Know Your History," 5 yrs. *Honors:* Emeritus Prof., Lincoln U., Jefferson City, Mo. Died May 23, 1980. *Mailing address:* (Roena Savage), 5063 Oaknoll Ave., L.A., Cal. 90043.

Writings:
Nonfiction

The Controversy over the Distribution of Abolition Literature 1830-1860 (Wash., D.C., ASNLH, 1938; N.Y., Negro Universities Press, 1968; reprint, Westport, Conn., Greenwood, n.d.)

The History of Lincoln University (Jefferson City, Mo., n.p., 1939)

Our Cause Speeds On—An Informal History of the Phi Beta Sigma Fraternity, with L. D. Reddick (Atlanta, Fuller Press, 1957)

Blacks in the West (Greenwood, 1978)

Sources: Author information; *Books in Print*, 1981-82.

SCHUYLER, GEORGE S. Editor, Journalist.
Born in Providence, R.I., Feb. 25, 1895. *Education:* Public schs. of Syracuse, N.Y. *Family:* Married Josephine Schuyler, Jan. 1928 (dec.); d. Philippa Schuyler (celebrated pianist & composer—dec.).

Career: 1st Lt., U.S. Army, 1912-18; Asst. Ed. & Managing Ed., *Messenger Magazine*, 1923-28; Ed., Illustrated Feature Section for Negro Press, Chicago, 1928-29; Publicity Dept., NAACP, N.Y.C., 1933-35; Bus. Manager, *Crisis* mag., NAACP, 1937-44; Assoc. Ed., *Pittsburgh Courier*, N.Y. office, 1942-64; Ed. Staff, *Plain Talk*, 1946- ; Columnist, Spadea Syndicate, 1953-61; Contrib., N. Amer. Newspaper Alliance. *Honors:* Citation of Merit, Outstanding Journalist, Sch. of Journalism, Lincoln U., Jefferson City, Mo., 1954. Died Aug. 31, 1977, in N.Y.C.

Writings:
Fiction

Black No More; Being an Account of the Strange and Wonderful Workings of Science in the Land of the Free, A.D. 1938-1940, novel (N.Y., Macauley, 1931; George Park, Md., McGrath, 1969; N.Y., Negro Universities Press, 1969; N.Y., Collier, 1971)

Slaves Today; A Story of Liberia, novel (N.Y., Brewer, Warren & Putnam, 1931; McGrath, 1969; N.Y., AMS Press, 1969)

Nonfiction

Fifty Years of Progress in Negro Journalism (Pittsburgh, Pittsburgh Courier, 1950)

Black and Conservative; The Autobiography of George S. Schuyler (New Rochelle, N.Y., Arlington, 1966)

Sidelights: "As a special correspondent for *New York Evening Post* investigated charges of slavery in Liberia in 1931, labor conditions in Mississippi Flood Control Project, 1932-33, labor unionism in 40 United States industrial centers in 1937, and civil rights compliance in state capitals across the nation...." (*Blackamerican Literature*)
"During twenties was a regular columnist for the black socialist monthly, *The Messenger*. But has since been conservative columnist on *Pittsburgh Courier*." (*Afro-American Writing*)

Sources: *Afro-American Writing*; *Blackamerican Literature*; *In Black and White*, 3rd ed., 1980; *Negro Caravan*; Pub. information.

SCHUYLER, PHILIPPA DUKE. Concert Pianist, Composer.
Born in N.Y.C., Aug. 21, 1932. *Education:* Manhattanville Convent of Sacred Heart; piano & composition with Herman Wasserman, Otto Cesana, Gaston Dethier. *Family:* Single. *Career:* Started touring as a child prodigy; 1st symphonic composition, *Manhattan Nocturne*, performed at Carnegie Hall (at age 12); her scherzo "Rumpelstiltskin" performed by Dean Dixon Youth Orchestra, Boston Pops, New Haven Symphony, N.Y. Philharmonic (at age 13); soloist, N.Y. Philharmonic (at age 14); debuted in dual role of composer & pianist with N.Y. Philharmonic, playing Saint-Saën's *Concerto no. 2 in A Minor* & her own "Rumpelstiltskin," written as part of her planned *Fairy Tale Symphony*. Concerts in over 80 countries, many under auspices of U.S. State Dept. Formerly foreign correspondent for United Press Features, *New York Daily Mirror*, *Manchester Union Leader*, & Spadea News Syndicate, Afro-Asian Educational Exchange, Secy. *Honors:* 27 music awards, including two from Wayne State U. for composition, and award for symphonic poem *Manhattan Nocturne* & for symphonic scherzo "Rumpelstiltskin," & three decorations from foreign governments. Killed in crash of U.S. Army helicopter in Da Nang Bay, S. Vietnam, May 9, 1967, while on concert tour.

Writings:
Nonfiction

Adventures in Black and White, autobiog. (N.Y., Speller, 1960)

Who Killed the Congo? (N.Y., Devin-Adair, 1962)

Jungle Saints; Africa's Heroic Catholic Missionaries (Roma, Herder, 1963)

Kingdom of Dreams (Speller, 1966)

Good Men Die (N.Y., Twin Circle, 1969)

Sidelights: "The only child of an interracial marriage.... Her progress was measured periodically by the Clinic for Gifted Children at New York University." (*Biographic Encyclopedia of Women*)

Sources: *Biographic Encyclopedia of Women*; *Negro Almanac*; *Negro Digest*, Sept. 1944.

SCOTT, JOSEPH WALTER. Sociology Professor.
Born in Detroit, Mich., May 7, 1935. *Education:* B.S. (Sociol., honors) Central Mich. U., 1957; M.A. (Sociol.), 1959, Ph.D. (Sociol.-Anthropology), 1963, Ind. U. *Family:* Married; five children. *Career:* Asst. Prof., Sociol., U. of Ky., 1965-67; Asst. Prof., Sociol., U. of Toledo, 1967-70; U. of Notre Dame: Assoc. Prof., Sociol., & Dir., Black Studies, 1970-75; Prof., Sociol.-Anthropology, 1976-78; Prof., Sociol., 1978- . *Honors:* Natl. Institutes of Health Fellow, 1962-63; John Hay Whitney Found. Fellow, 1960-61; Rockefeller Found. Prof. to Nigeria, 1972-73; Fulbright Grant Prof. to Argentina (summer), 1967 & 1969; Amer. Council in Educ. Fellow, 1975-76. *Mailing address:* 325 O'Shaughnessy, Dept. of Sociol., U. of Notre Dame, Notre Dame, Ind. 46556.

Writings:
Nonfiction

The Black Revolts: The Politics of Racial Stratification (Cambridge, Mass., Schenkman, 1976)

Sidelights: President-Elect of North Central Sociological Association, 1982-83.

Sources: Author information; *Who's Who among Black Americans*, 3rd ed., 1980-81.

SCOTT, NATHAN A., JR. Theologian, Priest, Critic, Essayist.
Born in Cleveland, Ohio, Apr. 24, 1925. *Education:* B.A., U. of Mich., 1944: B.D., Union Theol. Sem., 1946; Ph.D., Columbia U., 1949. *Family:* Married Charlotte Hanley (Asst. V. Pres., Fed. Reserve Bank); son Nathan A. Scott III, d. Leslie Kristin Scott. *Career:* Shailer Mathews Prof. of Theol. & Lit., U. of Chicago Divinity Sch., & Dept. of Eng. (Chairman, Theol. & Lit. Field); Priest of Episcopal Church; Canon Theol. of the Cathedral of St. James, Chicago; Co-ed., *Journal of Religion*; Fellow, Sch. of Letters, Ind. U., 1965-72; Adjunct Prof., Eng., U. of Mich., 1969; Walter & Mary Touhy Visiting Prof., Relig. Studies, John Carroll U., 1970. *Honors:* Litt. D., Ripon Coll.; L.H.D., Wittenberg U., 1965; D.D., Phila. Divinity Sch., 1967; S.T.D., Gen. Theol. Sem., 1968; Litt. D., St. Mary's Coll., Notre Dame, 1969. *Mailing address:* The Divinity Sch., U. of Chicago, Chicago, Ill. 60637.

Writings:
Nonfiction

Rehearsals of Discomposure; Alienation and Reconciliation in Modern Literature (N.Y., King's Crown, 1952, 1958)

The Tragic Vision and the Christian Faith (N.Y., Assoc. Press, 1957)

Modern Literature and the Religious Frontier (N.Y., Harper, 1958)

Albert Camus (N.Y., Hillary House, 1962; London, Bowes, 1962)

Reinhold Niebuhr (Minneapolis, U. of Minn. Press, 1963)

The New Orpheus; Essays toward a Christian Poetic (N.Y., Sheed & Ward, 1964)

The Climate of Faith in Modern Literature, ed. (N.Y., Seabury, 1964)

Samuel Beckett (Hillary House, 1965; Bowes, 1965)

Four Ways of Modern Poetry, ed. (Richmond, John Knox Press, 1965)

Man in the Modern Theatre, ed. (John Knox Press, 1965)

Forms of Extremity in the Modern Novel (John Knox Press, 1965)

Ernest Hemingway; A Critical Essay (Grand Rapids, Mich., Eerdmans, 1966)

The Broken Center: Studies in the Theological Horizon of Modern Literature (New Haven, Conn., Yale U. Press, 1966)

The Modern Vision of Death, ed. (John Knox Press, 1967)

Adversity and Grace: Studies in Recent American Literature (Chicago, U. of Chicago Press, 1968)

Craters of the Spirit: Studies in the Modern Novel (Wash., D.C., Corpus Bks., 1968)

Negative Capability: Studies in the New Literature and the Religious Situation (Yale U. Press, 1969)

The Unquiet Vision: Mirrors of Man in Existentialism (N.Y., World, 1969; paper, Nashville, Tenn., Abingdon, 1980)

Nathanael West; A Critical Essay (Eerdmans, 1971)

The Wild Prayer of Longing; Poetry and the Sacred (Yale U. Press, 1971)

Three American Moralists: Mailer, Bellow, Trilling (Notre Dame, Ind., U. of Notre Dame Press, 1973)

Legacy of Reinhold Niebuhr (U. of Chicago Press, 1975)

Sidelights: "Relatively unknown as a Negro, Nathan A. Scott, Jr., is a critic of modern literature who has written extensively, on the relationships between the literary and religious imagination." (*AFRO USA*)

Sources: *AFRO USA*; Author information; *Cavalcade.*

SEALE, BOBBY. Activist.
Born in Dallas, Tex., in 1937. *Education:* Attended Merritt Coll., Oakland, Cal. *Career:* Founded, with Huey Newton, Black Panther Party, 1966. *Mailing address:* c/o Times Bks., N.Y. Times Bk. Co., 3 Park Ave., N.Y., N.Y. 10016.

Writings:
Nonfiction

Seize the Time; The Story of the Black Panther Party and Huey P. Newton (N.Y., Random House, 1970)

A Lonely Rage: The Autobiography of Bobby Seale (N.Y., Times Bks., 1978)

Sidelights: In 1969 Seale was indicted in Chicago with seven others (group known as the "Chicago Eight") — for conspiracy to disrupt 1968 Democratic National Convention in Chicago. Seale was sentenced to four years in prison for contempt of court. Earlier had been arrested and charged with murder of an alleged Black Panther informer in New Haven, Connecticut. Charge was later dismissed. (*Encyclopedia of Black America*)

Sources: *Books in Print*, 1979-80; *Encyclopedia of Black America*; *Seize the Time.*

SÉJOUR, VICTOR (JUAN VICTOR SÉJOUR MARCON ET FERRAND). Playwright, Poet.
Born in New Orleans, La., in 1817 (father a Santo Domingoan Black; mother a quadroon). *Education:* Saint Barbe Acad., conducted by Michel Seligny. *Career:* One of three New Orleans poets who produced a collection called *Les Cenelles* (1845), 1st anthology of Amer. Negro poetry. "In France he was a very popular dramatist, twenty-one of his best plays being staged there, the first in 1844. In the 1850's at least three of his plays were produced in New Orleans." (*Early Black American Poets*) Died in a charity ward of a Paris hospital of tuberculosis in 1874.

Writings:
Fiction
Diegarias, 1st play (produced at Théâtre Français, 1844)

Les Cenelles, anthology, with Others (New Orleans, H. Lauve, 1845)

La Chute de Sejan, play (Paris, Michel-Lévy frères, 1849)

(Greatest)
Richard III, play (Paris, D. Giraud et J. Dagneau, 1852)

Les Noces Vénitiennes (Michel-Lévy frères, 1856)

Le Fils de la nuit, play (Michel-Lévy frères, 1856)

Les Grands Vassaux (Michel-Lévy frères, 1859; Lagny, 1860)

Les Volontaires de 1814 (Michel-Lévy frères, 1862)

Les Fils de Charles Quint (Michel-Lévy frères, 1864)

Sidelights: "... he was accepted in the literary circles of Paris, where he became acquainted with Alexandre Dumas and Emile Augier. Because of these friendships, he became intrigued with drama....

"His works were noted for the grandiose verse, the sumptuous costuming and spectacular settings — all of which were popular in Paris during the mid-19th century." (*Historical Negro Biographies*)

Sources: *American Negro Reference Book*; *Early Black American Poets*; *Historical Negro Biographies*.

SELLASSIE, BERHANE MARIAM SAHLE [Sahle, Sellassie Berhane Mariam]. (Ethiopian). Amharic and English Language Novelist, Short Story Writer, Journalist, Government Official. Born in Wardina, Ethiopia, in 1936; a Chaha. *Education:* Catholic Mission sch., Endeber; secondary sch., Addis Ababa; Law, Aix-en-Provence; M.A. (Polit. Sci.), UCLA, 1963. *Career:* Govt. Staff Training Officer, Addis Ababa; Writer. *Honors:* Fellow, Near Eastern Center & African Studies Center (both UCLA). *Mailing address:* c/o Heinemann Educ. Bks., 4 Front St., Exeter, N.H. 03833.

Writings:
(Partial Listing — English Only)
Fiction
Shinega's Village; Scenes of Ethiopian Life, novel, transl. from original Chaha-Amharic version by Wolf Leslau (Berkeley, Cal., U. of Cal. Press, 1964)

The Afersata: An Ethiopian Novel (London, Heinemann, 1969)

Warrior King, ed., novel (Heinemann, African Writers Ser., 1974)

Sidelights: Using Arabic script, Sellassie wrote the first work ever written in Chaha. "Dr. Leslau has praised (*Shinega's Village*) ... as a novel which started out to be a work of linguistic scholarship ... has ended up as charming literature." (*Reader's Guide to African Literature*)

Sources: *African Authors*; *Books in Print*, 1980-81; *Reader's Guide to African Literature*.

SENGHOR, LÉOPOLD SÉDAR. (Senegalese). President of Senegal, Philosopher, Poet. Born in Joal, Senegal, Oct. 9, 1906. (Serer tribe). *Education:* Libermann Coll. (classical lycée), Dakar, Senegal; French bachelor's degree, Lycée Louis-le-Grand, Paris, 1928; "aggrégation" (like Amer. Master's), Sorbonne, 1933; Diplôme d'Études Superieures (doctorate), Sorbonne, 1934; Licence-ès-Lettres, Sorbonne (teacher's certificate for French lycée); African lang., Ecole des Hautes Etudes, Paris. *Career:* Tchr., Greek & Latin classics, Lycée Descartes, Tours, 1935-38; Lycée Marcellin Berthelot, St. Maur-des-Fossés, 1938-40; Tchr., African Lang., Ecole Nationale de la France d' Outre-Mer, Paris & St. Maur; Socialist deputy for Senegal, French Natl. Assembly, 1946-60; Founder & Party leader of Parti du Regroupment Africain, 1958; 1st Pres., Republic of Senegal, 1960- . *Honors:* 1st African apptd. Prof. of Lycée of Tours, after being 1st African awarded aggrégation degree. "Senghor has been elected into the extremely exclusive French academic society, the Agrégés de Grammaire, the highest organization of intellectuals in France." (*African Authors*) *Mailing address:* c/o Cambridge U. Press, 32 East 57th St., N.Y., N.Y. 10022.

Writings:
(Partial Listing — English Only)
Fiction
Selected Poems, ed. by Reed & Wake (London, Oxford U. Press, 1964; N.Y., Atheneum, 1964)

Prose and Poetry, ed. & transl. by Reed & Wake (Oxford U. Press, 1965)

Nocturnes, poems, transl. by Reed & Wake (London, Heinemann, 1969; N.Y., Third Press, 1971)

Nonfiction

African Socialism; A Report to the Constitutive Congress of the Party of African Federation, transl. & ed. by Mercer Cook (N.Y., Amer. Soc. of African Culture, 1958)

Nationhood and the African Road to Socialism, transl. by Mercer Cook (Paris, Présence Africaine, 1962; N.Y., Praeger, 1965)

On African Socialism, transl. by Mercer Cook (London, Pall Mall, 1964; Praeger, 1964)

The Foundations of "Africantité" or "Négritude" and "Arabité," transl. by Mercer Cook (Présence Africaine, 1971)

Sidelights: The Negritude movement was originated by Senghor, Aimé Césaire of Martinique and Léon Damas of French Guiana, during Senghor's student days in Paris. Negritude argued for African pride and a recognition by Africans of their humanity and long cultural inheritance. Thus began a life-long effort to redeem the past and to elevate African art, ideas, and history into genuine pride for Black Africans and of intellectual concern to all others.

The vigorous Black cultural journal *Présence Africaine* was founded by Senghor with Alioune Diop in 1947. This journal, along with Présence Africaine publishing house, has printed many works by Black writers from all parts of the world, and become a major stimulus to creative writing throughout the continent.

The first World Festival of Negro Arts in Dakar, Senegal, in 1966, was sponsored by Senghor and organized by Alioune Diop. This event was of world-wide importance.

"... he remains more purely than any other African poet, the singer of nostalgia and African warmth. Yet, in many ways Senghor is the most thoughtful and forebearing critic of colonialism." (*African Authors*)

Sources: *African Authors*; *Books in Print*, 1981-82; *Emerging African Nations and Their Leaders*, vol. 2, 1964; *Selected Poems*.

SENGSTACKE, JOHN HERMAN HENRY. Newspaper Publisher.
Born in Savannah, Ga., Nov. 25, 1912. *Education:* B.S. (Bus. Admin.), Hampton Inst., 1933; Mergenthaler Linotype Sch.; Chicago Sch. of Printing; Northwestern U., Ohio State U. *Family:* Married Myrtle Picou, July 9, 1939; son John Herman, son Robert Abbott, son Lewis Willis. *Career:* With Robert S. Abbott Pub. Co., pub. of *Chicago Defender*, since 1934, V. Pres. & Mgr., 1934-40, Pres. & Gen. Mgr., 1940; Chairman, Bd. of Dirs., *Michigan Chronicle* (Detroit), *Louisville Defender*; Pres., *Tri-State Defender*, Defender Publ., Amalgamated Pub., Inc.; Pub., *Daily Defender*. *Mailing address:* (Office) 2400 S. Michigan Ave., Chicago, Ill. 60616.

Writings:
Nonfiction
Chicago Defender, newspaper (1905-)

Tri-State Defender, newspaper (Memphis, 1951-)

Sidelights: The *Chicago Defender* was founded by the present publisher's uncle, Robert Sengstacke Abbott, in 1905. Sengstacke is the founder of the Negro Newspaper Publishers' Association.

"... the *Chicago Defender* had the slogan 'American race prejudice must be destroyed,' and with a goal of 'opening up of all trades and trade unions to black as well as white,' 'representation in the President's cabinet,' 'Federal legislation to abolish lynching,' and 'full enfranchisement of all American citizens.' " (*Current Biography*)

Sources: *Current Biography*, 1949; *Negro Handbook*.

SHANGÉ, NTOZAKE [Paulette L. Williams]. Dancer, Teacher, Playwright.
Born in Trenton, N.J., Oct. 18, 1948. *Education:* B.A. (Amer. Studies) Barnard Coll.; M.A. (Amer. Studies), U. of S. Cal.; studied Contemporary Afro-Amer. Dance, San Francisco. *Family:* Single. *Career:* "Readings of poetry ... as well as readings organized by Poetry-in-the-Schools and readings in prisons. Performing dancer with Raymond Sawyer & Halifu ... [taught] in Humanities & Women's Studies at Sonoma College, Cal." (Author) *Mailing address:* c/o St. Martin's Press, 175 Fifth Ave., N.Y., N.Y. 10010.

Writings:
Fiction
For Colored Girls Who Have Considered Suicide, When the Rainbow Is Enuf, poems (San Lorenzo, Cal., Shameless Hussy Press, 1975; N.Y., Macmillan, 1977; N.Y., Bantam, 1980)

Nappy Edges: (Love's a Lil Rough/Sometimes) (N.Y., St. Martin's, 1978; Bantam, 1980)

Three Pieces, plays (St. Martin's, 1981; paper, N.Y., Penguin, 1982)

Sassafras, Cypress & Indigo, novel (St. Martin's, 1982)

Daughter's Geography (St. Martin's, 1983)

Nonfiction
North Ridge 127, photography of Jules Allen & poem-montage of Hunter's Point, San Francisco

See No Evil: Prefaces, Reviews & Essays (San Francisco, Momo's Press, 1984)

Sidelights: Shangé's other works are: *Invisible City, Anon., Third World Women, Time to Grease, Phat Mama,* and *The Gallery.*
Sassafras was presented by the Raymond Sawyer Afro-American Dance Company as a dance-drama in spring '75. "I write in English, French and Spanish cuz my conscious-nesses mingle all New World Afrikan experiences." (Author)

Sources: Author information; *Books in Print*, 1980-81, 1983-84.

SHARP, SAUNDRA. Actress, Singer, Poet, Theatrical Agent.
Born in Cleveland, Ohio, Dec. 21, 1942. *Education:* B.S. (Music/Radio-TV Production), Bowling Green State U., Ohio, 1964; TV/film production, L.A. City Coll., 1980- . *Career:* Actress on stage, TV, & films. Performed in *The Learning Tree, Black Girl, Hello Dolly, Black Quartet, Five on the Black Hand Side, Poetry Now, To Be Young, Gifted and Black, Our Street, Minstrel Man,* and *Hollow Image.* Poetry reading by others on record albums for Scholastic Magazine & on "The Black Experience" (radio ser. for N.Y.C. Bd. of Educ.). Heads Togetherness Productions, theatrical agency established to focus attention on young Black creative artists; Book Div.: Poets Pay Rent Too. Has performed as pop singer on TV and in clubs in the U.S., W. Indies, & Mexico. *Honors:* Outstanding Young Women of America, 1971, 1974; Cleveland Chap., PUSH-EXCEL Award, 1980. *Mailing address:* P.O. Box 75796, Stanford Station, L.A., Cal. 90075.

Writings:
Fiction
From the Windows of My Mind; Poems (N.Y., Togetherness Productions, 1970)

In the Midst of Change, poems (Togetherness Productions, 1972)

The Sistuhs, play (Togetherness Productions, 1975)

Soft Song, poems (Togetherness Productions, 1978)

Nonfiction
Women of the Wilmington 10 (Togetherness Productions, 1978)

Sidelights: Played "Netta" in J. E. Franklin's *Black Girl* (off-Broadway), and "Prissy" in Gordon Park's *The Learning Tree.* Wrote script for show "The Way It's Done," 1973. Appeared with Jimmy Owens Quartet, Sammy Benskin Trio, Danny Holgate, Jimmy Radcliffe, and Bob Cunningham Trio. Has made commercials on television and radio.

Co-author, co-editor, History of Blacks in Film Exhibit Catalog (William Grant Still Gallery, L.A.), 1983; Directory of Black Film/Television Technicians and Artists, West Coast (Togetherness Productions, 1980).

Sources: Author/Pub. information; *A Rock against the Wind: Black Love Poems.*

SHINE, TED. Playwright, Teacher.
Born in Baton Rouge, La. *Education:* Public schs. of Dallas, Tex.; Howard U.; M.A., U. of Iowa; U. of Cal. *Career:* Karamu Theatre, Cleveland, Ohio; taught & lectured at several colleges, including Howard U. & Dillard U.; Eng. Dept., Prairie View Coll., Tex. *Mailing address:* c/o Prairie View A&M U., Prairie View, Tex. 77445.

Writings:
Fiction

Cold Day in August, one-act play (1950)

Sho' Is Hot in the Cotton Patch, one-act play (1951)

Epitaph for a Bluebird (U. of Iowa, Drama Dept., 1958)

Morning, Noon and Night, play (1964)

Miss Weaver, play (1965)

Contribution, one-act play (Negro Ensemble Co., St. Mark's Playhouse, 1969)

Shoes, one-act play (Off-Broadway, 1969)

Comeback, after the Fire, play (1969)

Idabel's Fortune, one-act play (1969)

Flora's Kisses, play (1969)

Contributions; Three One-Act Plays (N.Y., Dramatists Play Service, 1970)

Plantation, one-act play (Off-Broadway, 1970)

Black Theatre, U.S.A. Forty Five Plays by Black Americans, 1847-1974, with James V. Hatch (N.Y., Free Press, 1974)

Sidelights: One-act plays performed while a student at Howard: *Cold Day in August* and *Sho' Is Hot in the Cotton Patch*. Others: *Epitaph for a Bluebird* and *Contribution* (1969). Has also written all-black soap opera about urban problems, produced by the Maryland Center for Public Broadcasting, Baltimore. Mr. Shine's *Contribution* was presented by Negro Ensemble Company at St. Mark's Playhouse on March 25, 1969, marking his New York debut. Directed by Douglas Turner Ward, this play won special praise from Walter Kerr of the *New York Times*. In March 1970, his three one-act plays, *Shoes, Plantation,* and *Contribution,* were presented off-Broadway. (*Black Drama*)

Sources: *Black Drama; Black Scenes; Books in Print*, 1979-80.

SHOCKLEY, ANN ALLEN. Librarian, Novelist.
Born in Louisville, Ky., June 21, 1927. *Education:* B.A., Fisk U., 1948; M.S.L.S., Case Western Reserve U., 1959. *Family:* Div.; son William L. Shockley, Jr., d. Tamara Ann Shockley. *Career:* Asst. Librn., Delaware State Coll., 1959-60; Asst. Librn. & Curator, Negro Collection, U. of Md., Eastern Shore, 1960-66, Assoc. Librn. & Curator, 1966-69; Assoc. Librn. for Spec. Collections & U. Archivist, Fisk U., 1969- ; Writer, Del. & Md. newspapers. *Honors:* Natl. Short Story Award, Amer. Assn. of U. Women, 1962; ALA Black Caucus Special Award for editing *Black Caucus Newsletter*, 1975; Hatshepsut Award for Lit., 1981; Interdenominational Ministers of Nashville, Martin L. King, Jr., Black Author's Award, 1982. *Mailing address:* 1809 Morena St., Apt. G-4, Nashville, Tenn. 37208.

Writings:
Fiction

Loving Her; A Novel (Indianapolis, Bobbs-Merrill, 1974; N.Y., Avon, 1978)

The Black and White of It, short stories (Wetherby Lake, Mo., Naiad Press, 1980)

Say Jesus and Come to Me (Avon, 1982)

Nonfiction

Living Black American Authors: A Biographical Directory, with Sue P. Chandler (N.Y., R. R. Bowker, 1973)

A Handbook of Black Librarianship, with E. J. Josey (Littleton, Colo., Libraries Unlimited, 1977)

Sources: Author information; *Books in Print*, 1980-81; *Contemporary Authors*, vols. 49-52, 1975.

SIMMONS, WILLIAM J. Educator.
Born in Charleston, S.C., June 29, 1849. *Education:* A.B., Howard U., 1873, A.M., 1881. *Family:* Married Josephine A. Silence in 1874; seven children. *Career:* Pres., Ky. State U., Louisville. Died in 1890.

Writings:
Nonfiction

Men of Mark: Eminent, Progressive and Rising, biog. (Cleveland, Ohio, George M. Rewell, 1887; Cleveland, Ohio, Baltimore, Rewell Pub., 1891; reprint, N.Y., Arno, 1968; Chicago, Johnson Ebony Classics Ser., 1970)

Sources: *Books in Print*, 1980-81; *Men of Mark*.

SIMS, JANET L. Librarian, Bibliographer.
Education: B.A. (Sociol.), N.C. Central U., Durham; M.A. (Lib. Sci.), U. of Med., Coll. Park. *Career:* Librn., Lib. of Congress, *Congressional Quarterly*; Ref. Librn. (Afro-Amer. Hist. Spec.), Moorland Spingarn Res. Center, Howard U. (present). *Mailing address:* c/o Moorland Spingarn Res. Center, Howard U., 2400 Sixth St., N.W., Wash., D.C. 20001.

Writings:
Nonfiction

The Black Family in the United States, with Lenwood G. Davis (Westport, Conn., Greenwood, 1978)

Black Women in the Employment Sector (Monticello, Ill., Vance Bibliographies, 1979)

Marcus Garvey, with Lenwood G. Davis (Greenwood, 1980)

Black Artists in the United States, with Lenwood G. Davis (Greenwood, 1980)

The Progress of Afro-American Women: A Selected Bibliography and Resource Guide, comp. (Greenwood, 1980)

Marian Anderson: An Annotated Bibliography and Discography, comp. (Greenwood, 1981)

Sources: *Black Artists in the United States*; *Books in Print*, 1981-82; *Freedomways*, vol. 21, no. 2, 1981; Pub. information.

SIMS, NAOMI RUTH. Fashion Model, Free-lance Writer, Columnist, Business Executive.
Born in Oxford, Miss., Mar. 30, 1949. *Education:* Fashion Inst. Tech., N.Y.; N.Y.U. *Family:* Married Michael A. Findlay (Art Dealer), Aug. 4, 1973; son John Phillip Sims. *Career:* Fashion Model, Ford Modeling Agency, 1967-73; Founder/Owner/Chief Executive, Naomi Sims Collection, 1973- ; Co-developer, synthetic hair fiber for wig making, 1972-73; Free-lance Writer, 1970- ;

Columnist, *Right On* mag. *Honors:* Model of Year Award, 1969; N.Y.C. Bd. of Educ. Award, 1970; Woman of Achievement, *Ladies Home Journal*, 1970; Intnl. Best Dressed List, 1971-73; Woman of Achievement, Amer. Cancer Soc., 1972; Naomi Sims Day, proclaimed Sept. 20, by Governor Walker, Ill., 1973; Top Hat Award, *New Pittsburgh Courier*, 1974. *Mailing address:* Naomi Sims Collection, 48 E. 21st St., N.Y., N.Y. 10010.

Writings:
<u>Nonfiction</u>

All about Health and Beauty for the Black Woman (N.Y., Doubleday, 1976)

How to Be a Top Model (Doubleday, 1979)

All about Success for the Black Woman (Doubleday, 1982)

All about Hair Care for the Black Woman (Doubleday, 1982)

Sources: *Library Journal*, Oct. 15 & Nov. 15, 1982; *Who's Who among Black Americans*, 1975-76; *Who's Who in America*, 1978-79, 1980-81.

SKINNER, BYRON R. Administrative Dean, Behavioral and Social Sciences Dean, University President.
Born Sept. 13, 1932. *Education:* B.A. (Hist.), W. Mich. Coll., Kalamazoo, 1956; M.A. (Hist. Educ.), Chicago State U., 1966; Ph.D., U. of Cal., Berkeley, 1978; Educational Management, 1974-80, Higher Educational Management Inst. *Family:* Married; two children. *Career:* Tchr., Chicago public schs., 1960-66; Tchr., Sequoia Union High Sch. Dist., Redwood City, Cal., 1968-75; Dir., Soc. Sci. Div., Canada Coll., Redwood City, 1975-77; Area Dean, Behavioral & Soc. Sci., Amer. River Coll., Sacramento, 1977-80; Admin. Dean, Academic Affairs (V. Pres.), San Bernardino Valley Coll., San Bernardino, Cal., 1980-82; Pres., U. of Maine, Augusta, 1983- . *Mailing address:* c/o Book Attic Press, 555 W. Base Line, San Bernardino, Cal. 92410.

Writings:
<u>Nonfiction</u>
Black Origins in the Inland Empire (San Bernardino, Cal., Book Attic Press, 1983)

Sidelights: *Black Origins* "describes the role Afro-Americans took in settling the San Bernardino, Redlands and Riverside areas (of California) 1850-1900." (Publisher)

Sources: Author information; Pub. information.

SMITH, ARTHUR L. [Molefi Kete Asante]. Communication Specialist (Interracial and Institutional), Editor, Speech Professor.
Born in Valdosta, Ga., Aug. 14, 1942. *Education:* Southwestern Christian Coll.; B.A., Okla. Christian Coll., 1964; M.A., Pepperdine U., L.A., 1965; Ph.D., UCLA, 1968. *Family:* Married Jean [Ngena] Smith; d. Kasina Eka. *Career:* Asst. Prof., Purdue U., Lafayette, Ind., 1968-69, Assoc. Prof. of Speech, 1971-73; Dir., Center for Afro-Amer. Studies, UCLA, 1970-73; Prof. & Chairman, Dept. of Speech Communication, SUNY, Buffalo. Bds. of Ed.: *Black Man in America*, reprint ser., N.Y., 1969-70; Ed. Assoc., *The Speech Teacher*, 1970-72, 1972-74; Ed., *Journal of Black Studies*, 1969- . *Honors:* Intnl. Men of Achievement, 1974; Christian Guild Writer's Award, 1965; Outstanding Young Men of America, 1970. Grants: Prin. Investigator, Martin L. King-Drew Medical Complex, Curriculum Evaluative Model for Pre-Sch. Instr., $30,000; Prin. Investigator, Black Colleges Commitment Program, Model Cities, Health, Educ. & Welfare, $113,000, 1971-72, renewed for 1972-73, $145,000. *Mailing address:* Dept. of Communication, State U. of N.Y., Buffalo, N.Y. 14221.

Writings:
<u>Nonfiction</u>
Rhetoric of Black Revolution (Boston, Allyn & Bacon, 1969)

Rhetoric of Revolution (Allyn & Bacon, 1969)

Toward Transracial Communication (L.A., Center for Afro-Amer. Studies, 1970)

The Voice of Black Rhetoric: Selections, with Stephen Robb (Allyn & Bacon, 1971)

How to Talk with People of Other Races, Ethnic Groups, and Cultures, with Others (L.A., Trans-Ethnic Found., 1971)

Language, Communication and Rhetoric in Black America, ed. (N.Y., Harper, 1972)

Transracial Communication (Englewood Cliffs, N.J., Prentice-Hall, 1973)

Sidelights: On-going research: Role of the Spoken Discourse in Development of Contemporary Black Leadership; Nature of Black Communication Experience as Expressed in Language Styles.

Source: Author information.

SMITH, JESSIE CARNEY. Library Administrator, Library Science Professor.
Education: B.S. (Home Econ.), N.C. A&T U., 1950; M.A. (Child Development), Mich. State U., 1956; M.A. (Lib. Sci.), George Peabody Coll. for Tchrs., 1957; Ph.D. (Lib. Admin.), U. of Ill., 1964. *Family:* Div., one son. *Career:* Head Cataloger & Instr., Tenn. State U., 1957-60; Tchg. Asst., U. of Ill., 1961-63; Coordinator, Lib. Serv., & Asst. Prof., Tenn. State U., 1963-65; U. Librn. & Prof., Fisk U., 1965- . *Honors:* Recipient, Fellowship, Council on Lib. Resources, 1969; Certificate of Achievement, Alpha Kappa Alpha Sorority, 1976; Natl. Urban League Fellow, 1968, 1976. *Mailing address:* 5039 Hissboro Rd., No. 146, Nashville, Tenn. 37215.

Writings:
Nonfiction
A Handbook for the Study of Black Bibliography (Nashville, Fisk U. Lib., 1971)

Black Academic Libraries and Research Collections: An Historical Survey (Westport, Conn., Greenwood, 1977)

Sidelights: Director, Inst. on Selection, Organization and Use of Materials by and about the Negro, 1970; Director, Inst. in Black Studies Librarianship, 1971; Tennessee Cordinator, African-Amer. Materials Project, 1971-74; Director, Res. Program in Ethnic Studies, Librarianship, 1975; Ed., Major Minorities Collection, Gaylord Professional Publications, 1976.

Sources: Author information; *Books in Print,* 1980-81; *Dictionary Catalog of the Negro Collection of the Fisk University Library, Nashville, Tennessee,* vol. 5.

SMITH, VERN E. Novelist, Correspondent.
Education: B.A., San Francisco State Coll., 1969; Grad. Sch. of Journalism, Columbia U. *Career:* Gen. Assignment Reporter, Long Beach *Independent-Press Telegram*; Correspondent, *Newsweek,* Atlanta bureau. *Honors:* Ford Found. Fellow, Columbia U.; Detroit Press Club Foundation's annual mag. writing award, *Newsweek* article entitled "Detroit's Heroin Subculture." *Mailing address:* c/o Warner Bks., 75 Rockefeller Plaza, N.Y., N.Y. 10020.

Writings:
Fiction
The Jones Men, novel (Chicago, Regnery, 1974; paperback, N.Y., Warner Brothers, 1976)

Sources: *Books in Print,* 1979-80; Pub. information.

SMITH, WILLIAM GARDNER. Novelist, Reporter, Editor.
Born in Phila. Pa., Feb. 6, 1927. *Education:* Temple U., Phila. *Family:* Div.; d. Michele, son Claude. *Career:* Novelist, News Ed., Eng. Lang. Serv., Agence France-Presse (French News Agency). Died Nov. 5, 1974.

Writings:

Fiction

Last of the Conquerors, novel (N.Y., Farrar, 1948)

Anger at Innocence, novel (Farrar, 1950)

South Street, novel (Farrar, 1954)

The Stone Face, novel (N.Y., Pocket Bks., 1963)

Return to Black America, novel (Englewood Cliffs, N.J., Prentice-Hall, 1970)

Sidelights: "Published his first book, *Last of the Conquerors*, at the age of 20 and followed this three years later with *Anger at Innocence*. He went to Paris in 1951 and wrote his third novel, *South Street*. He subsequently married a French lycée teacher and decided to stay in France." (*Black American Writer*)

Sources: *Black American Writer*, vol. I: *Fiction*; *Black World*, Feb. 1975; Pub. information.

SMYTHE, MABEL MURPHY. Economics Professor, Free-lance Writer, U.S. Ambassador.
Born in Montgomery, Ala., Apr. 3, 1918. *Education:* Spelman Coll.; A.B., Mt. Holyoke Coll., 1937; M.A., Northwestern U., 1940; Ph.D., U. of Wis., 1942. *Family:* Married Hugh H. Smythe (Sociol.), July 26, 1939; child: Karen Pamela. *Career:* Asst. & Assoc. Prof., Econ. & Bus. Admin., Lincoln U., Mo., 1942-45; Prof., Econ., Tenn. Agricultural & Industrial State U., 1945-46; Lect., Econ., Brooklyn Coll., CUNY, 1946-47; Free-lance Writer, 1948-51; Visiting Prof. of Econ., Shiga U., Japan, 1951-53; High sch. tchr. & Prin., N.Y.C., 1954-69; V. Pres. & Dir., Res. & Publ., Phelps-Stokes Fund, 1969- ; U.S. Ambassador to United Republic of Cameroon, 1977- . *Mailing address:* c/o Prentice-Hall, Inc., Englewood Cliffs, N.J. 07632.

Writings:

Nonfiction

Intensive English Conversation, with Alan B. Howes (Tokyo, Kairyudo, 1953)

The New Nigerian Elite, with husband, Hugh H. Smythe (Stanford, Cal., Stanford U. Press, 1960)

The Black American Reference Book, ed. (Englewood Cliffs, N.J., Prentice-Hall, 1976)

Sidelights: Mabel Smythe has traveled or lived in Cameroon, Japan, Syria, Malta, France, Spain, Thailand, Nigeria. An avocational interest is the piloting of light planes.

Sources: *Books in Print*, 1980-81; *Contemporary Authors*, vols. 37-40, 1st rev.

SNOWDEN, FRANK M., JR. Classics Professor.
Born in York County, Va., July 17, 1911. *Education:* A.B., 1932, A.M., 1933, Ph.D., 1944, Harvard U. *Family:* Married Elaine; children: Jane S. Lepscky, Frank III. *Career:* Instr., Latin, French, & Eng., Va. State Coll., 1933-36; Instr. in Classics, Spelman Coll., 1936-40. Howard U.: Prof., Classics, 1945; Dean of Coll. of Liberal Arts, 1940-42, 1956-68; Dir., Evening Sch. & Adult Educ., 1942-48; Chairman, Dept. of Classics. *Honors:* Fulbright Fellowship Res. Grant; Amer. Council of Learned Socs.; Howard U. Res. Fund; Medoglia d'ore, Italian govt. *Mailing address:* c/o Howard U., 2400 Sixth St., N.W., Wash., D.C. 20001.

Writings:

Nonfiction

Blacks in Antiquity: Ethiopians in the Greco-Roman Experience (Cambridge, Mass., Harvard U. Press, 1970)

Before Color Prejudice: The Ancient View of Blacks (Harvard U. Press, 1983)

Sources: *Books in Print*, 1983-84; *Freedomways*, vol. 17, no. 1, 1977; *Who's Who among Black Americans*, vol. 1, 1975-76.

SOLOMON, BARBARA J. (BRYANT). Social Work Professor.
Born in Houston, Tex., Sept. 10, 1934. *Education:* B.S. (Psychology, magna cum laude), Howard U., 1954; M.S.W., U. of Cal., Berkeley, 1956; D.S.W., U. of S. Cal., 1966. *Family:* Husband; four children. *Career:* Clinical Soc. Worker, Veterans Admin., Houston, Tex., 1957-61; Clinical Soc. Worker, Wadsworth Veterans Admin., L.A., Cal., 1961-63; Prof., Soc. Work, U. S. Cal., 1966- . *Mailing address:* 5987 Wrightcrest Dr., Culver City, Cal. 90230.

Writings:
  Nonfiction
    Black Empowerment: Effective Social Work in the Community (N.Y., Columbia U. Press, 1976)

Sources: Author information; *Books in Print*, 1980-81.

SOUTHERLAND, ELLEASE. Novelist, Poet.
Born in Brooklyn, N.Y., June 18, 1943. *Education:* B.A., Queens Coll., N.Y., 1965; M.F.A., Columbia U., 1974. *Career:* Caseworker, Dept. of Soc. Serv., N.Y.C., 1966-72; Instr., Eng., Community Educ. Exchange Program, Columbia U., 1973-76; Adjunct Asst. Prof., Black Lit., Manhattan Community Coll., CUNY, 1973- ; Poet-in-Residence, African Lit., Pace U. (present). *Honors:* John Golden Award, Queen's Coll., CUNY, for novella *White Shadows*, 1964; Gwendolyn Brooks Poetry Award from *Black World*, for "Warlock," 1972; Book-of-the-Month Club alternate selection, *Let the Lion Eat Straw. Mailing address:* Dept. of Eng., Pace U., 1 Pace Plaza, N.Y., N.Y. 10038.

Writings:
  Fiction
  The Magic Sun Spins, poems (London, Breman, 1975)

  Let the Lion Eat Straw, novel (N.Y., Scribner, 1979; Boston, G. K. Hall, 1979; N.Y., New Amer. Lib., 1980)

Sources: *Books in Print*, 1980-81; *Contemporary Authors*, vol. 107, 1983; *Let the Lion Eat Straw.*

SOUTHERN, EILEEN JACKSON. Music Professor, Editor.
Born in Minneapolis, Minn., Feb. 19, 1920. *Education:* B.A., M.A., U. of Chicago; Ph.D., N.Y.U.; (Piano), Chicago Musical Coll.; Boston U.; Juilliard. *Family:* Married Joseph Southern; d. April. *Career:* Prairie View Coll., 1941-42; Southern U., 1943-45, 1949-51; public schs., N.Y.C., 1954-60; Brooklyn Coll., 1960-68; Prof. of Music, York Coll., CUNY, 1968- . *Honors:* U. of Chicago Alumni Assn., Achievement Award, 1971; Natl. Assn. of Negro Musicians, Achievement Award, 1971; Voice of America, Citation, 1971; apptd. U.S. Bicentennial Com. of Amer. Musicology Soc., 1971-76; apptd. Com. of Examiners, Advanced Music Test, Grad. Record Examinations, Educ. Testing Serv., Princeton, N.J., 1971- ; Distinguished Woman Award, Delta Alpha Hon. Soc., U. of Mo., Kan. City, 1972; Outstanding Educator in Music Award, Chicago Chap., Phi Delta Kappa, 1973; ASCAP-Deems Taylor Award for excellence in nonfiction writing about music, 1973; Election: Council Amer. Musicological Soc., 1973; Bd. of Dir., Amer. Musicological Soc., 1974-76. *Mailing address:* 115-05 179th St., St. Albans, N.Y. 11434.

Writings:
  Nonfiction
  The Buxheim Organ Book (Brooklyn, Inst. of Medieval Music, 1963)

  The Music of Black Americans: A History (N.Y., Norton, 1971, 2nd ed., 1983)

  Readings in Black American Music, ed. (Norton, 1971)

  Black Perspective in Music (Journal), ed. & pub., vols. 1-7 (Cambria Heights, N.Y., Found. for Res. in Afro-Amer. Creative Arts, 1973-79)

  Biographical Dictionary of Afro-American and African Musicians (Westport, Conn., Greenwood, Greenwood Encycl. of Black Music Ser., 1982)

Sources: Author information; *Books in Print*, 1979-80; *Library Journal*, Jan. 1, 1982.

SOWELL, THOMAS. Economist, Economics Professor.
Born in Gastonia, N.C., June 30, 1930. *Education:* A.B. (magna cum laude), Harvard U., 1958; A.M., Columbia U., 1959; Ph.D., U. of Chicago, 1968. *Family:* Married Alma Jean Parr; two children. *Career:* Economist, U.S. Dept. of Labor, Wash., D.C., 1961-62; Instr., Econ., Douglass Coll., Rutgers U., 1962-63; Lect., Econ., Howard U., 1963-64; Econ. Analyst, Amer. Telephone & Telegraph, N.Y., 1964-65; Asst. Prof., Econ., Cornell U., Ithaca, N.Y., 1965-69; Assoc. Prof., Econ., Brandeis U., Waltham, Mass., 1969-70; Assoc. Prof., Econ., UCLA, 1970-72; Project Dir., Urban Inst., Wash., D.C., 1972-74; Prof., Dept. of Econ., UCLA, 1974- . *Mailing address:* c/o Dept. of Econ., UCLA, 405 Hilgard, L.A., Cal. 90024.

Writings:
Nonfiction

Economics: Analysis and Issues (Glenview, Ill., Scott, Foresman, 1971)

Say's Law: An Historical Analysis (Princeton, N.J., Princeton U. Press, 1972)

Black Education: Myths and Tragedies (N.Y., McKay, 1972)

Classical Economics Reconsidered (Princeton U. Press, 1974)

Affirmative Action Reconsidered: Was It Necessary in Academia? (Wash., D.C., Amer. Enterprise Inst. for Public Policy Res., 1975)

Race and Economics (McKay, 1975)

American Ethnic Groups, ed. (Wash., D.C., Urban Institute, paper, 1978)

Knowledge and Decisions (N.Y., Basic Bks., 1980)

The Fairmont Papers: Black Alternatives Conference, December, 6, 1980 (San Francisco, Inst. for Contemporary Press, 1981)

Markets and Minorities (Basic Bks., 1981)

Ethnic America: A History (Basic Bks., 1981)

The Economics and Politics of Race: An International Perspective (N.Y., Morrow, 1983)

Sources: *Encyclopedia of Black America;* L.A. Public Lib., card catalog; *Who's Who among Black Americans*, 2nd ed., vol. 1, 1977-78; *Books in Print*, 1983-84.

SOYINKA, WOLE [Akinwande Oluwole]. (Nigerian). Playwright, Drama Professor, Poet, Anthologist.
Born in Abeokuta, W. State, Nigeria; a Yoruba. *Education:* U. Coll., Ibadan, 1952-54; Honors (Eng.), U. of Leeds, Eng. *Career:* Resident Playwright, Royal Court Theatre, 1958 (Eng.); Lect., Extra-Mural Dept., U. of Ibadan (founded "The 1960 Masks"); Eng. Dept., U. of Ife, Ife, 1962; Acting Head, Eng. Dept., Lagos U., 1963; Lect., Cambridge U. Founded theatre group Orizan Theatre Co., 1964. *Honors:* Rockefeller grant, African dramatic arts, 1960. *Mailing address:* c/o Dept. of Literature, U. of Ife, Ife, Nigeria.

Writings:
Fiction

The Invention, play (Royal Court Theatre, Ibadan, n.d.)

Camwood on the Leaves, play (Nigerian Broadcasting Corp., 1960; London, Methuen, 1973)

A Dance of the Forest, play (London & Ibadan, Oxford U. Press, 1963)

The Lion and the Jewel, play (Oxford U. Press, 1963)

Three Plays: The Swamp-dwellers. The Trials of Brother Jero. The Strong Breed. (Ibadan, Mbari Publ., 1963; Evanston, Ill., Northwestern U. Press, 1963)

The Road, play (London, Oxford U. Press, 1965)

Before the Blackout, plays (Ibadan, Nigeria, Orisun Acting Ed., 1965?)

The Interpreters, novel (London, Audré Deutsch, 1965; N.Y., African-Amer. Lib., Collier, 1970; N.Y., African Pub. Corp., 1972)

Idanre and Other Poems (Methuen, 1967; N.Y., Hill & Wang, 1968)

Kongi's Harvest, play (Oxford U. Press, 1967)

The Forest of a Thousand Daemons: A Hunter's Saga, novel, transl. by Daniel Olorunfemi Fagumva (London, Nelson, 1968)

Three Short Plays (Oxford U. Press, Three Crowns Bks., 1969)

Poems from Prison (London, Collings, 1969)

Plays from the Third World, anthology (N.Y., Doubleday, 1971)

Palavar: Three Dramatic Discussion Starters (N.Y., Friendship, 1971)

The Man Died: Prison Notes of Wole Soyinka (N.Y., Har-Row, 1972)

A Shuttle in the Crypt, poems (Collings, 1972; Hill & Wang, 1972)

Madmen and Specialists, poems (Methuen, 1972)

Collected Plays, vol. 1, new ed. (Oxford U. Press, 1973)

The Bacchae of Euripedes: A Communion Rite (N.Y., Norton, 1974)

Collected Plays, vol. 2, (Oxford U. Press, 1975)

Poems of Black Africa, anthology (Hill & Wang, 1975)

Death and the King's Horseman, play (Norton, 1975)

Ogun Abibiman, poems (Collings, 1976)

Ake: The Years of Childhood (Collings, 1981)

Opera Wonyosi, play (Bloomington, Ind. U. Press, Midland Bk., no. 259, 1981)

Nonfiction
Myth, Literature and the African World, criticism (Cambridge U. Press, 1976)

Sidelights: "In Biafran War detained in 1965. In 1966 shared with Tom Stoppard the John Whiting drama prize. In 1967 appointed Director, School of Drama, University of Ibadan, but was arrested before could start work, for pro-Biafran activities. On December 18, 1968, was awarded the Jock Campbell Prize for Commonwealth Literature by 'The New Statesman' for his novel *The Interpreters* and his poems.

"On October 25, 1969, was released as part of an Independence Anniversary Amnesty. He resumed his post as Director of School of Drama at Ibadan and held it until April 1972 when he resigned." (*Who's Who in African Literature*)

Sources: *Bibliography of Creative African Writing*; *Books in Print*, 1980-81, 1982-83; *Who's Who in African Literature*; *Writing of Wole Soyinka*.

SPELLMAN, A. B. Poet, Editor, Jazz Critic, Historian.
Born in Elizabeth City, N.C., Aug. 7, 1935. *Education:* B.A. (Polit. Sci.), Howard U.; grad. work in Law & Eng. Lit. *Career:* Ed., *The Cricket* (mag. of Black music); Writer-in-Residence, Morehouse Coll. & Emory U., Atlanta. *Mailing address:* c/o Morehouse Coll., 223 Chestnut St., S.W., Atlanta, Ga. 30314.

Writings:
Fiction
The Beautiful Days, poems (N.Y., Poets Press, 1965)

Nonfiction

Four Lives in the Bebop Business (N.Y., Pantheon, 1966)

Black Music: Four Lives (original title: *Four Lives in the Bebop Business*, N.Y., Schocken, 1970)

Sidelights: *Four Lives in the Bebop Business* is concerned with the careers of musicians, Ornette Coleman, Herbie Nichols, Jackie McLean, and Cecil Taylor. (*Poetry of Black America*)

Sources: *Black Fire*; *Books in Print*, 1979-80; *Poetry of Black America*.

STACK, CAROL B. Anthropologist, Anthropology Professor.
Education: Ph.D. (Anthropology), U. of Ill., Urbana. *Career:* Dir., Center for Study of the Family and the State; Assoc. Prof., Anthropology & Inst. of Policy Scis., Duke U. *Mailing address:* Center for the Study of the Family and the State, Box 4875 Duke Station, Durham, N.C. 27706.

Writings:
Nonfiction

All Our Kin: Strategies for Survival in a Black Community (N.Y., Harper, 1974; Magnolia, Mass., Peter Smith, 1975; Harper, paper, 1975)

Sources: Author information; *Books in Print*, 1978-79, 1980-81.

STAPLES, ROBERT EUGENE. Sociology Professor.
Born in Roanoke, Va., June 28, 1942. *Education:* A.A., L.A. Valley Coll., 1958; B.A., Cal. State U., Northridge; M.A., San Jose U., 1965; Ph.D., U. of Minn., 1970. *Career:* Asst. Prof., Sociol., Cal. State U., Hayward, 1968-70; Assoc. Prof., Sociol., Howard U., 1970-72; Assoc. Prof., Sociol., U. of Cal., San Francisco, 1973-74; Prof., Sociol., Howard U., 1974- . *Mailing address:* c/o Black Scholar Press, Box 31245, San Francisco, Cal. 94131.

Writings:
Nonfiction

The Black Family: Essays and Studies, ed. (Belmont, Cal., Wadsworth, 1971, 2nd ed., 1978)

The Black Woman in America: Sex, Marriage, and the Family (Chicago, Nelson-Hall, 1973)

Introduction to Black Sociology (N.Y., McGraw Hill, 1976)

The World of Black Singles: Changing Patterns of Male/Female Relations (Westport, Conn., Greenwood, Contrib. in Afro-Amer. Studies, no. 57, 1981)

Black Masculinity: The Black Man's Role in American Society (San Francisco, Black Scholar Press, 1982)

Sources: *Books in Print*, 1979-80, 1982-83; *Contemporary Authors*, vols. 49-52, 1975.

STEPTO, ROBERT BURNS. English Professor, Critic.
Born in Chicago, Ill., Oct. 28, 1945. *Education:* B.A. (cum laude), Trinity Coll., Hartford, Conn.; M.A., 1968, Ph.D., 1974, Stanford U. *Family:* Married Michele Leiss (coll. tchr.), June 21, 1967; children: Gabriel Burns, Rafael Hawkins. *Career:* Asst. Prof., Eng., Williams Coll., Williamstown, Mass., 1971-74; Asst. Prof., Yale U., 1974-79; Assoc. Prof., Eng. & Afro-Amer. Studies, 1979- , & Dir., Afro-Amer. Grad. Studies, 1978- , Yale U. *Honors:* Woodrow Wilson Found. Fellow, 1966-67. *Mailing address:* Dept. of Eng., Yale U., New Haven, Conn. 06520.

Writings:
Nonfiction

Afro-American Literature: The Reconstruction of Instruction, ed. with Dexter Fisher (N.Y., Mod. Lang. Assn. of Amer., 1978)

From behind the Veil: A Study of Afro-American Narrative (Urbana, U. of Ill. Press, 1979)

Chant of Saints, ed. with Michael Harper (U. of Ill. Press, 1979)

Afro-American Literature: The Reconstruction of Literary History, ed. with John M. Reilly (Mod. Lang. Assn. of Amer., 1981)

Sources: *Books in Print*, 1981-82; *Contemporary Authors*, vol. 101, 1981.

STEPTOE, JOHN LEWIS. Artist, Juvenile Writer.
Born in Brooklyn, N.Y., Sept. 14, 1950. *Education:* Grammar sch., St. Benedict's Our Lady of Good Counsel; High Sch. of Art & Design (11th yr. completed). *Family:* Single; d. Bweela, son Javaka. *Career:* Artist; Juvenile Writer. *Honors:* ALA Notable Children's Bk. Award for *Stevie*; Soc. of Illustrator's Gold Medal for *Stevie*; *Stevie* illustrations reproduced in their entirety in *Life* mag., Aug. 29, 1970; Brooklyn Public Lib., Citation for children's bks.; Brooklyn Museum show, "Dreams and Delights at Christmas 1972." *Mailing address:* 840 Monroe St., Brooklyn, N.Y. 11221.

Writings:
Fiction

Stevie, juv. (N.Y., Harper, 1969)

Uptown, juv. (Harper, 1970)

Train Ride, juv. (Harper, 1971)

Birthday, juv. (N.Y., Holt, 1972)

My Special Best Words, juv. (N.Y., Viking, 1974)

Marcia, juv. (Viking, 1976)

Daddy Is a Monster ... Sometimes, juv. (Phila., Lippincott, 1980)

Jeffrey Bear Cleans Up His Act, juv. (N.Y., Lothrop, 1983)

The Story of Jumping Mouse, juv. (Lothrop, 1984)

Sidelights: John Steptoe was the recipient of Coretta Scott King Committee's Honorable Mention for his illustrations in *All the Colors of the Race* (by Arnold Adoff, Lothrop, 1982)

Sources: *American Libraries*, Apr. 1983; Author information; *Books in Print*, 1982-83; Pub. information.

STILL, WILLIAM. Abolitionist, Historian.
Born free in Burlington County, N.J., in 1821. *Career:* Clerk, Phila. Anti-Slavery Soc. (met & helped hundreds of Blacks who were fleeing to North via underground railroad; kept record of slaves' experiences, collected between 1850 and 1860). Died in 1902.

Writings:
Nonfiction

The Underground Railroad. A Record of Facts, Authentic Narratives, Letters, etc., Narrating the Hardships, Hair-breadth Escapes and Death Struggles of the Slaves in Their Efforts for Freedom as Related by Themselves and Others, or Witnessed by the Author; Together with Sketches of Some of the Largest Stockholders, and Most Liberal Aiders and Advisers, of the Road (Phila., Porter and Coates, 1872; rev. ed., Phila., Cincinnati, People's Pub., 1879; reprint, Salem, N.Y., Arno, 1968)

Sidelights: "Still not only forwarded numberless Negro passengers on the Underground but also aided the escape of several of John Brown's men after Harpers Ferry. Nineteen out of twenty fugitives stopped at Still's house on their way through Philadelphia." (*Negro Caravan*)
An early forerunner of Carter G. Woodson's Association for the Study of Negro Life and History was a "social, civil, and statistical association," organized by William Still in 1861. (*Cavalcade*)

Sources: *Cavalcade*; *Negro Caravan.*

SUTHERLAND, EFUA THEODORA (MORGUE). (Ghanaian). Playwright, Poet, Essayist, Teacher. Born in Cape Coast, Central Region, Ghana, June 27, 1924. *Education:* St. Monica's Training Coll., Mampong, Ashanti; B.A. (Educ.), Homerton Coll., Cambridge U., Eng.; Sch. of Oriental & African Studies, U. of London. *Family:* Married William Sutherland (Amer.) in 1954; three children. *Career:* Tchr., Secondary, Takoradi & St. Monica's Training Coll., Mampong (both Ghana); a founder, Writer's Workshop, Inst. of African Studies, U. of Ghana, Legon; Tchr., African Lit. & Drama, U. of Ghana, Legon; a founder, Ghana Society of Writers; Children's Theater, Kusum Agoromba. Playwright, Ghana radio; Photo-journalist. *Mailing address:* c/o Longman Group, 74 Grosvenor St., London WIX UA5 Eng.

Writings:
  Fiction
  Anansegora, play (Paris, Présence Africaine, Eng. lang. ed., no. 22, summer 1964)

  Edufa, play (London, Longman's, Green, 1967, 1969; Wash., D.C., Three Continents, 1979)

  Foriwa, play (Accra, Ghana, State Pub. Corp., 1967)

  Vulture! Vulture! Two Rhythm Plays (Accra, Ghana Pub. House, 1968)

  The Marriage of Anansewa: A Story-Telling Drama (Longman's, 1975; Three Continents, Sun-Lit. Ser., 1980)

  The Voice in the Forest: A Tale from Ghana (N.Y., Philomel Bks., 1983)

  Nonfiction
  Playtime in Africa, photo-journalism (London, Brown, 1960; N.Y., Atheneum, 1962)

  The Roadmakers, photo-journalism (Accra, Ghana Information Serv., 1961)

Sidelights: "Black Africa's most famous woman writer." (*African Authors*)
  "From 1958 to 1961 she founded a programme of experimental theatre, and with grants from the Rockefeller Foundation and the Arts Council of Ghana, built the 'Ghana Drama Studio' in Accra to house it." (*Who's Who in African Literature*)

Sources: *African Authors*; *African Writers Talking*; *Books in Print*, 1980-81; *Who's Who in African Literature.*

TARRY, ELLEN. Juvenile Writer, Social Worker.
  Born in Birmingham, Ala., Sept. 26, 1906. *Education:* Ala. State U.; Fordham U.; Bank St. Writers' Lab., N.Y.C. *Family:* Children: Elizabeth, Tarry Patton. *Career:* Journalist; assoc. with Catherine De Jueck, founder of Friendship House, Harlem, N.Y., 1929- ; established similar inst. in Chicago; Staff, Natl. Catholic Community Serv. (during World War II); Asst. to Regional Admin. for Equal Opportunity, Dept. of Housing & Urban Development. *Residence:* N.Y., N.Y.

Writings:
  Fiction
  Janie Bell, juv. (N.Y., Garden City Pub., 1940)

  Hezekiah Horton, juv. (N.Y., Viking, 1942, 1945, 1965)

  My Dog Rinty, juv. with Marie H. Ets (Viking, 1946)

  The Runaway Elephant, juv. (Viking, 1950)

  Nonfiction
  The Third Door, the Autobiography of an American Negro Woman (N.Y., McKay, 1955; reprint, Westport, Conn., Negro Universities Press, 1971)

Katherine Drexel; Friend of the Neglected, juv. (N.Y., Farrar, 1958)

Martin de Porres, Saint of the New World, juv. (N.Y., Vision Bks., 1963, 1973; London, Burns, 1963)

Young Jim: The Early Years of James Weldon Johnson, juv. (N.Y., Dodd, 1967)

The Other Toussaint: A Modern Biography of Pierre Toussaint, a Post-Revolutionary Black (Boston, St. Paul Editions, 1981)

Sidelights: Because Ellen Tarry was heavily involved in the Civil Rights Movement, she became one of the first authors to use Blacks as main characters in children's books.

Sources: *AFRO USA*; *Books in Print*, 1980-81, 1983-84; *Something about the Author*; *Young Jim*.

TATE, MERZE. History Professor, Historian.
Born in Blanchard, Mich. *Education:* B.A., W. Mich. U.; M.A., Columbia U.; B. Litt., Oxford U.; Ph.D., Radcliffe Coll. & Harvard U.; Litt.D., W. Mich. U.; D. Laws, Morgan State Coll.; further study: Geneva Sci. Intnl.; Berlin U. *Family:* Single. *Career:* Prof. of Hist., Howard U., 1942- ; holder of GS-18 U.S. Civil Serv. rating as historian in three areas of hist. *Honors:* Scholarship & honor student, W. Mich. U., elected to Pi Gamma Mu; recipient of 3rd Alpha Kappa Alpha Sorority foreign fellowship; 1st Amer. woman of color to matriculate at Oxford U. & 1st Amer. Negro to receive a higher degree there; Julius Rosenwald Found. Fellow, 1939 (yr.'s residence at Radcliffe toward Ph.D.); elected to Phi Beta Kappa; Rep. U.S., 1948 UNESCO Seminar on tchg. about UN & related agencies; Natl. Urban League Achievement Award, 1948; Fulbright Lect. in India, 1950-51; W. Mich. U. Distinguished Alumna Award, 1970; named Mich. Isabella County's most distinguished citizen, 1969; Amer. Council of Learned Soc. res. grant, 1959; *Washington Evening Star* res. grant, 1961; Rockefeller Found. res. grant, 1961; one time mem., Natl. Bd. of Radcliffe Coll.; mem. 1960 Screening Com. for United Kingdom of the Inst. of Intnl. Educ.; among "Two Thousand Women of Achievement," London, 1972. *Mailing address:* c/o Hist. Dept., Howard U., Wash., D.C. 20059.

Writings:
  Nonfiction

The Disarmament Illusion; The Movement for a Limitation of Armaments to 1907 (N.Y., Macmillan, 1942; reprint, N.Y., Russell, 1970)

The United States and Armaments (Cambridge, Mass., Harvard U. Press, 1948; reprint, Russell, 1969)

The United States and the Hawaiian Kingdom; A Political History (New Haven, Conn., Yale U. Press, 1965)

Hawaii: Reciprocity or Annexation (E. Lansing, Mich. State U. Press, 1968)

Diplomacy in the Pacific (Wash., D.C., Hist. Dept., Howard U., 1973)

Sidelights: As Fulbright Lecturer in India, assigned to Rabindranath Tagore's World University, lectured at 11 other Indian universities, in Burma for the USIS in Ceylon, Thailand, Singapore, Manila, Tokyo, and Honolulu. *The Disarmament Illusion, The United States and Armaments*, and *The United States and the Hawaiian Kingdom* all received a publication subvention from the Bureau of International Research, Harvard University and Radcliffe College.

Source: Author information.

TAYLOR, MILDRED. Juvenile Writer.
Born in Jackson, Miss. *Education:* U. of Toledo; U. of Colo. (Journalism). *Career:* Peace Corps, Ethiopia; Recruiter, Peace Corps, U.S.; Writer. *Honors: Song of the Trees* named Outstanding Book of the Year, *New York Times*; ALA Notable Bk., 1976, Natl. Bk. Award finalist, Newbery Medal, 1977, all for *Roll of Thunder, Hear My Cry. Mailing address:* c/o Bantam Bks., 666 Fifth Ave., N.Y., N.Y. 10019.

Writings:

Fiction

Song of the Trees, juv. (N.Y., Dial, n.d.; N.Y., Bantam, 1975)

Roll of Thunder, Hear My Cry, juv. (Dial, 1976; Bantam, 1978)

Let the Circle Be Unbroken (Dial, 1981)

Sources: *Books in Print*, 1979-80; *Something about the Author*, vol. 15, 1979.

TERBORG-PENN, ROSALYN. Historian.
Education: B.A. (Hist.), Queens Coll., CUNY, 1963; M.A. (Hist.), Howard U., 1977. *Family: d. Jeanna. Career:* Assoc. Prof., Hist., Morgan State U., 1969- ; Dir., Morgan State U. Oral Hist. Project, 1978- . *Honors:* Phi Alpha Theta grad. scholarship in Hist., 1965; Howard U. Grad. Fellow, Hist., 1973-74; Rayford W. Logan Grad. Essay Award, Hist., Howard U., 1973. *Mailing address:* 5484 Sleeping Dog Lane, Columbia, Md. 21045.

Writings:

Nonfiction

A Special Mission: The Story of Freedmen's Hospital, 1862-1962, with Others (Wash., D.C., Academic Affairs Div., Howard U., 1975)

The Afro-American Woman: Struggles and Images, ed. with Sharon Harley (Port Wash., N.Y., Kennikat, 1978)

The James Van Horn Kindred, 1800-1980 (Baltimore, Md., Morgan State U., 1982)

Sources: Author information; *Who's Who among Black Americans*, 3rd ed., 1980-81.

TERRELL, MARY CHURCH. Women's Rights Advocate, Lecturer.
Born in Memphis, Tenn., in 1863. *Education:* A.B. (Classical Lang.), Oberlin Coll., 1884. *Family:* Married Robert Terrell (Fed. Judge, D.C.); d. Phillis. *Career:* Tchr., Wilberforce U., 2 yrs.; Tchr., M Street Colored High Sch., Wash., D.C.; Mem., Dist. of Columbia Sch. Bd., 1884- ; Charter Mem., Natl. Assn. of Colored Women; Secy., Race Relations Com., Wash. Fed. of Churches, Treasurer, Interracial Com. *Honors:* Doctor of Humane Letters (hon.), Oberlin Coll. Died at Annapolis, Md., in 1954.

Writings:

Nonfiction

A Colored Woman in a White World (Wash., D.C., Ransdell, 1940; reprint, N.Y., Arno, Signal Lives Ser., 1980)

Sidelights: In 1953, Mrs. Terrell headed a committee of Washington citizens who demanded enforcement of a 75-year-old law prohibiting discrimination in restaurants. This paved the way for the beginning of integration in public accommodations of the nation's capital. She was also active in woman's suffrage and passage of the Nineteenth Amendment.

Sources: *Afro-American Encyclopedia*, vol. 9; *Books in Print*, 1980-81; *Negro Almanac*.

TERRY, LUCY. Poet.
Born in Africa in 1730. "Kidnapped as a child and brought to Rhode Island, where she was bought as a servant to Ebenezer Wells, who had her baptized in 1744 in his Deerfield, Massachusetts home. [The semi-literate slave] married the very capable Abijah Prince in 1756 ... six children later—their names were Cesar, Duroxa, Drucilla, Festus, Tatnai and Abijah, Jr...." (*Early Black American Poets*). Died in 1821.

Writings:
  Fiction
  "Bars Fight" (1746)

Sidelights: "Lucy Terry is generally considered to be the first Negro poet in America. In a ballad which she called 'Bars Fight,' she recreated an Indian Massacre which occurred in Deerfield, Massachusetts in 1746 during King George's War ... ('Bars Fight' has been hailed by some historians as the most authentic account of the massacre).

"... The Prince house served as a center for young people who gathered to listen to their hostess' story-telling." (*Negro Almanac*)

Sources: *Early Black American Poets*; *Negro Almanac*.

THOBY-MARCELIN, PHILIPPE. (Haitian). Poet, Novelist, Folklorist, Critic, Public Official. Born in Port-au-Prince, Haiti, Dec. 11, 1904. *Education:* Petit Séminaire Collège Saint-Martial, Port-au-Prince; Law, Paris. *Career:* Secy. Gen., Dept. of Public Works, Haiti; Official, Pan-Amer. Union, Wash., D.C. *Honors:* Winner, 2nd Latin Amer. Literary Prize Contest for *The Beast of the Haitian Hills*, 1946. Died Aug. 13, 1975, in Syracuse, N.Y.

Writings:
  (Partial Listing—English Only)
  Fiction
  The Beast of the Haitian Hills, novel, transl. from French by Peter Rhodes (London, Gollancz, 1951; N.Y., Rinehart, 1946)

  The Pencil of God, novel, transl. from French by Leonard Thomas (Boston, Houghton, 1951; Gollancz, 1951)

  All Men Are Mad, novel, transl. from French by Eva Thoby-Marcelin (N.Y., Farrar, 1970)

  Singing Turtle and Other Tales from Haiti (Farrar, 1971)

  Nonfiction
  Art in Latin America Today: Haiti (Wash., D.C., Pan-Amer. Union, 1959)

Sidelights: By 1926 Thoby-Marcelin was a leader of the "Nativist" group with Jacques Roumain, which began preaching against a European line and seeking a return to African and folk sources.

He helped found the Revue Indigène, 1927-29, the most important voice for the new generation. Pierre Thoby-Marcelin was a partner in all novels written by his brother Philippe. (*Caribbean Writers*)

Sources: *Caribbean Writers*; *Modern Black Writers*; *Resistance and Caribbean Literature*.

THOMAS, TONY. Writer, Black Nationalist. Born in Wash., D.C., May 29, 1949. *Education:* Amer. U., 1968. *Career:* Writer. *Mailing address:* c/o Pathfinder Press, 410 West St., N.Y., N.Y. 10014.

Writings:
  Nonfiction
  In Defense of Black Nationalism (N.Y., Pathfinder, 1971)

  Marxism vs. Maoism: A Reply to the "Guardian" (Pathfinder, 1974)

  Black Liberation and Socialism, comp. (Pathfinder, 1974)

  What Road to Black Liberation: The Democratic Party or an Independent Black Party, with Norman Oliver (Pathfinder, 1974)

  Angola: The Hidden History of Washington's War, with Ernest Harsch (Pathfinder, 1976)

Sources: *Books in Print*, 1978-79, 1980-81; *Contemporary Authors*, vols. 61-64, 1976.

THOMPSON, ERA BELL. Editor.
Born in Des Moines, Iowa. *Education:* U. of N.D. (2 yrs.); B.A., Morningside Coll., Sioux City, Iowa, 1933; grad. study, Medill Sch. of Journalism, Chicago; hon. doctorates: Morningside Coll., 1965; U. of N.D., 1969. *Family:* Single. *Career:* Interviewer, Ill. & U.S. Employment Services, Chicago (5 yrs.); Assoc. Ed., *Ebony* (4 yrs.); Co-Managing Ed., *Ebony*, 1951-64; Intnl. Ed., Johnson Pub. Co., 1964- . *Honors:* Wesleyan Serv. Guild scholarship; won Patron Saints Award for *American Daughter*, 1968; Fellow, Breadloaf Writer's Conf., 1949; Iota Phi Lambda's Outstanding Woman of the Year, 1965. *Mailing address:* c/o Johnson Pub. Co., 820 S. Mich. Ave., Chicago, Ill. 60605.

Writings:
Nonfiction
American Daughter (Chicago, U. of Chicago Press, 1946; reissued, Chicago, Follett, 1967; rev. ed., U. of Chicago Press, Midway Reprint Ser., 1974)

Africa, Land of My Fathers (N.Y., Doubleday, 1954)

White on Black, co-ed. (Chicago, Johnson, 1963)

Sources: *American Daughter*; Author information; *Books in Print*, 1980-81.

THORPE, EARL(IE) ENDRIS. History Professor, Historian.
Born in Durham, N.C., Nov. 9, 1924. *Education:* U. of Florence, Italy (U.S. Army Extension Program); B.A. (Soc.-Hist.), 1948, M.A. (Hist.-Educ.), 1949, N.C. Coll., Durham; Ph.D. (Hist.), Ohio State U., 1953. *Family:* Married Martha Vivian Branch; d. Rita Harrington, d. Gloria Earl. *Career:* Tchr., Stowe Tchrs. Coll., St. Louis, Mo., 1951-52; Ala. A&M Coll., Normal, Ala., 1952-55; Southern U., Baton Route, La., 1955-62; Prof. & Chairman, Dept. of Hist. & Soc. Sci., N.C. Central U., 1962- . *Honors:* Visiting Prof. of Hist., Duke U., 1969-70; Visiting Prof., Afro-Amer. Studies, Harvard U., 1971. *Mailing address:* 164 Oakmont Circle, Durham, N.C. 27713.

Writings:
Nonfiction
Negro Historians in the United States (Baton Rouge, La., Fraternal Press, 1958; reissued under title *Black Historians: A Critique*, N.Y., Morrow, 1971)

The Mind of the Negro: An Intellectual History of Afro-Americans (Westport, Conn., Greenwood, 1961; reprint, Greenwood, 1970)

Eros and Freedom in Southern Life and Thought (Durham, N.C., Seeman Printery, 1967; reprint, Greenwood, 1979)

The Central Theme of Black History (Seeman Printery, 1969; reprint, Greenwood, 1979)

The Old South: A Psychohistory (Seeman Printery, 1972; reprint, Greenwood, 1979)

Sidelights: "The Black Experience in America," gen. ed., ten-booklet ser. (Amer. Educ. Publ.)

Source: Author information.

THURMAN, HOWARD. Clergyman, Theologian.
Born in Daytona Beach, Fla., Nov. 18, 1900. *Education:* B.A., Morehouse Coll., 1923; B.D., Rochester Theol. Sem., 1926. *Family:* Married Sue E. Bailey, June 12, 1932; d. Anne Chiarenza, d. Olive Wong. *Career:* Pastor, Mt. Zion Bap. Church, Oberlin, Ohio, 1926-28; Dir., Relig. Life, & Prof., Relig., Morehouse Coll., Spelman Coll., 1928-31; Prof., Systematic Theol., & Dean, Rankin Chapel, Howard U., 1932-44; Pastor, Church for Fellowship of All Peoples, San Francisco, 1944-53 (1st completely integrated church in Amer. life); Dean, Marsh Chapel, Boston U., 1953-64, Emeritus, 1964- ; Prof., Spiritual Discipline & Resources, Boston U., 1953-65; U. Minister-at-Large, 1964-65; Vis. Prof., Sch. Relig., Earlham Coll., 1966; apptd. Ingersol Lect. on the Immortality of Man, Harvard U., 1947; Merrick Lect., Ohio Wesleyan U., 1953; Ratcliff Lect., Tufts U., 1957; Lect., Beech Quiet Hour, Bangor Theol. Sem., 1958; Earl Lect., Pacific Sch. of Relig., 1959; Smith Wilson

Lect., Southwestern U., 1960; Mendenhall Lect., De Pauw U., 1961; Wilson Lectures, Neb. Wesleyan U., 1961; Theme Lect., Gen. Council, United Church of Can., 1962; Quaker Lect., Earlham Coll., 1962; Visiting Prof., U. of Ibadan, Nigeria, 1963; Billings Lect., U. Hawaii, 1964; Oswald McCall Memorial Lect., Berkeley, Cal., 1964. *Honors:* Phi Beta Kappa; Gutenberg Award, Chicago Bible Soc.; (hon. degrees) D.D.: Wesleyan Coll., Conn., Lincoln U., Howard, Oberlin, Boston U.; H.H.D.: Va. State U., Ohio Wesleyan U.; LL.D.: Wash. U., Fla. Normal Coll.; Litt.D.: Tuskegee Inst. Died in 1981.

Writings:
  Nonfiction

  The Greatest of These (Mills College, Cal., Eucalyptus, 1944)

  Deep River; An Interpretation of Negro Spirituals (Eucalyptus, 1945; Richmond, Ind., Friends United, 1975)

  The Negro Spiritual Speaks of Life and Death (N.Y., Harper, 1947, 1969; Friends United, 1975)

  Meditations for Apostles of Sensitiveness (Eucalyptus, 1948)

  Jesus and the Disinherited (Nashville, Abingdon, 1949, 1969)

  Deep Is the Hunger; Meditations for Apostles of Sensitiveness (Harper, 1951; Friends United, 1973)

  Meditations of the Heart (Harper, 1953; Friends United, 1976)

  The Creative Encounter; An Interpretation of Religion and the Social Witness (Harper, 1954; Friends United, 1972)

  The Growing Edge (Harper, 1956; Friends United, 1974)

  Footprints of a Dream (Harper, 1959)

  Mysticism and the Experience of Love (Wallingford, Pa., Pendle Hill, 1961)

  The Inward Journey (Harper, 1961; Friends United, 1973)

  Temptations of Jesus (n.p., L. Kennedy, 1962; Friends United, 1979)

  Disciplines of the Spirit (Harper, 1963; Friends United, 1977)

  The Luminous Darkness: A Personal Interpretation of the Anatomy of Segregation and the Ground of Hope (Harper, 1965)

  Why I Believe There Is a God (Chicago, Johnson, 1965)

  The Centering Moment (Harper, 1969; Friends United, 1980)

  With Head and Heart: The Autobiography of Howard Thurman (N.Y., Harcourt, 1979)

Sidelights: In 1935 Dr. Thurman was the leader of a "pilgrimage of friendship" of students of religion to the colleges of Burma, India, and Ceylon.
  "Dr. Thurman was photographed in *Life* (April 6, 1955) as one of twelve 'Great Preachers' of this century." (*Current Biography*)

Sources: *Books in Print*, 1979-80, 1980-81; *Current Biography*, 1955; *Disciplines of the Spirit*; *Negro Caravan*; *Who's Who in America*, 37th ed., 1972-73.

THURMAN, SUE (BAILEY). Historian, Music Teacher.
  Education: Grad., Spelman Coll., Atlanta; Grad. (Music), Oberlin Coll., Oberlin, Ohio, 1926. *Family:* Married Howard Thurman (minister), June 12, 1932; children: Olive, Anne. *Career:* Tchr., Music, Hampton Inst., Va.; Natl. Traveling Staff, YWCA. *Mailing address:* 2020 Stockton St., San Francisco, Cal. 94133.

Writings:
Nonfiction

Pioneers of Negro Origin in California (San Francisco, Acme Pub. Co., 1952; reprint, San Francisco, R & E Assoc., 1971)

The Historical Cookbook of the American Negro, ed. & comp. for Natl. Council of Negro Women (Wash., D.C., Corporate Press, 1958)

Sidelights: *Pioneers of Negro Origin in California* first appeared as a series of articles in San Francisco *Sun Reporter*, in the Centennial Celebration of California Gold Rush, 1949. Based to some extent on Delilah Beasley's *Negro Trail Blazers of California*. (*Pioneers of Negro Origin in California*)

Sources: *Books in Print*, 1979-80; *Dictionary Catalog of the Schomburg Collection of Negro Life and History*, vol. 9, 1962; *Pioneers of Negro Origin in California*.

THURMAN, WALLACE. Novelist, Playwright.
Born in Salt Lake City, Utah, in 1902. *Education:* U. of S. Cal. *Career:* Served on ed. staffs of *The Messenger* & the Macaulay Pub. Co.; helped found the short-lived mags. *Fire & Harlem*. Died in 1934.

Writings:
Fiction

The Blacker the Berry; A Novel of Negro Life (N.Y., Macaulay, 1929; reprint, N.Y., AMS; N.Y., Arno, Amer. Negro—His Hist. & Lit. Ser., no. 2, 1969; Charles H. Larson, ed., N.Y., Macmillan, African-Amer. Lib., 1970)

Harlem, play with W. J. Rapp (1929)

Infants of the Spring, novel (Macaulay, 1932; reprint, Arno, Black Heritage Lib. Collection Ser.; AMS, 1975; Carbondale, S. Ill. U. Press, Los Amer. Fiction Ser., 1979)

The Interne, novel with A. L. Furman (Macaulay, 1932)

Sidelights: Best known for *The Blacker the Berry*, "Wallace Thurman was a leader among the young black intelligentsia who earned their literary reputations during the Harlem Renaissance." (*Black American Literature: Fiction*) He died of tuberculosis at age 32.

Sources: *Black American Literature: Fiction*; *Books in Print*, 1979-80, 1980-81; *Negro Caravan; Negro Novel in America.*

TOLSON, MELVIN BEAUNORUS. Poet, Educator, Playwright, Mayor, Poet Laureate of Liberia.
Born in Moberly, Mo., Feb. 6, 1900. *Education:* Fisk U.; M.A., Columbia U. *Career:* Taught at various S. colleges. Became assoc. with Langston U., Okla., where he was Prof. of Creative Lit. and directed campus Dust Bowl Theater. Became Avalon Prof. of Humanities at Tuskegee Inst. *Honors:* Poem "Dark Symphony" won Natl. Poetry Contest conducted by Amer. Negro Exposition in Chicago & was pub. in the *Atlantic Monthly*; designated Poet Laureate of Liberia for poem *Libretto for Republic of Liberia*, 1953; received Bess Hokin Prize of Mod. Poetry Assn. in 1952; received literary fellowship from both Rockefeller Found. & Omega Psi Phi. Arts & Letters Award, 1966. Died on Aug. 29, 1966.

Writings:
Fiction

The Moses of Beale Street, play (n.d.)

Southern Front, dramatizations of George Schuyler's novel *Black No More* & Walter White's *Fire in the Flint* (n.d.)

Rendezvous with America, poems (N.Y., Dodd, 1944)

Libretto for the Republic of Liberia, poems (N.Y., Twayne, 1953)

Harlem Gallery: Book I, the Curator, poems (Twayne, 1965, 1971)

A Gallery of Harlem Portraits, poems, ed. by Robert M. Farnsworth (Columbia, Mo., U. of Mo. Press, 1979)

Sidelights: "In an Introduction by Karl Shapiro, to *Harlem Gallery*, he said: 'A great poet has been living in our midst for decades and is almost totally unknown, even by the literati, even by poets. Can this be possible in the age of criticism and publication unlimited? It is not only possible but highly probable.' " (*Anger, and Beyond*)

Sources: *Anger, and Beyond*; *Black American Literature: Poetry*; *Black Voices*; *Books in Print*, 1981-82; *Cavalcade*; *Dark Symphony*; *Kaleidoscope*.

TOOMER, JEAN. Poet, Novelist.
Born in Wash., D.C., Dec. 26, 1894 (grandson of P. B. S. Pinchback, La. Reconstruction Lt. Governor). *Education:* U. of Wis.; City Coll. of N.Y. *Family:* Married 1st Margery Latimer (novelist), Oct. 30, 1931 (dec. 1932); married 2nd Marjorie Content (d. of prominent Wall St. broker). *Career:* Beginning in 1918, contrib. poems, sketches, & reviews to a variety of natl. mags. such as *Broom*, *Crisis*, *The Liberator*, *Little Review*, *Modern Review*, *Nomad*, *Prairie*, *Sun*, *Pagany*, *Bifur* (Paris), & *Adelphi* (London). Worked as sch. prin. in Ga. (1922). Died Mar. 30, 1967.

Writings:
Fiction
Cane, novel (N.Y., Boni & Liveright, 1923; rev., Liveright, 1975)

Sidelights: One of the voices of the Negro Renaissance of the 1920s. Associated with such white intellectuals as Hart Crane, Waldo Frank, Gorham Munson, and Kenneth Burke. Became a disciple of the Russian mystic Gurdjieff.
    Cane was his only book. This classic in Black American literature was a mosaic of poems, short stories, and intense sketches (which grew out of his Southern sojourn). In the introduction to *Cane* Arna Bontemps observed: "By far the most impressive product of the Negro Renaissance, it ranks with Richard Wright's *Native Son* and Ralph Ellison's *Invisible Man* as a measure of the Negro novelist's highest achievement."
    In Robert Bone's *Negro Novel in America*, he declared "*Cane* is an important American Novel." (*Cane*)

Sources: *Black American Literature: Poetry*; *Black Voices*; *Cane*; *Cavalcade*; *Negro Novel in America*.

TOPPIN, EDGAR ALLAN. History Professor, Historian.
Born in N.Y.C., Jan. 22, 1928. *Education:* B.A., 1949, M.A., 1950, Howard U.; Ph.D., Northwestern U., 1955. *Family:* Married Antoinette L. Lomaz (Educ. Instr., Va. State Coll.), Apr. 2, 1953; son Edgar Allan, Jr., d. Avis Ann, d. Antoinette Louise. *Career:* Chairman, Soc. Sci., Fayetteville State Coll., N.C., 1955-59; Asst. Prof., U. of Akron, Ohio, 1959-63; Prof. of Hist., Va. State Coll., Petersburg, 1964- ; Visiting summer prof.: N.C. Coll., 1959, 1963, Case Western Reserve U., 1962, U. of Cincinnati, 1964, San Francisco State Coll., 1969. Lect., CBS-TV "Black Heritage" ser. *Mailing address:* c/o Va. State U., Petersburg, Va. 23803.

Writings:
Nonfiction
Pioneers and Patriots: The Lives of Six Negroes of the Revolutionary Era, with Lavinia Dobler (N.Y., Doubleday, 1965)

The Unfinished March: The Negro in the United States, Reconstruction to World War I, with Carol Drisko (Doubleday, 1967)

A Mark Well Made: The Negro Contribution to American Culture (Chicago, Rand McNally, 1967)

Blacks in America: Then and Now (Boston, Christian Sci. Pub. Soc., 1969)

A Biographical History of Blacks in America since 1528 (N.Y., David McKay, 1971)

The Black American in the United States History (Boston, Allyn & Bacon, 1973)

Source: *Contemporary Authors*, vols. 21-22, 1969.

TROTTER, WILLIAM MONROE. Newspaper Publisher, Civil Rights Activist.
Born in Springfield Township, Ohio, Apr. 17, 1872. *Education:* A.B. (Phi Beta Kappa, magna cum laude), 1895, M.A., 1896, Harvard U. *Family:* Married Geraldine Pindell. *Career:* Established *Boston Guardian* newspaper (with George Washington Forbes), 1901; real estate & insurance broker; organizer (with others): Niagara Movement; NAACP. Died Apr. 7, 1934.

Writings:
Nonfiction
Boston Guardian, newspaper (1901-)

Sidelights: "He was articulate, fearless and idealistic and under his editorship the *Guardian* played an important role in reestablishing the Negro press as a dominant force in the fight for Negro rights." (*Negro Handbook*)

"He made five major contributions: 1. He ... challeng(ed) Booker T. Washington at the outset of his career; 2. He defied President Woodrow Wilson ... (on) segregation of Negroes employed in offices of the Federal Government in Washington; 3. He ... (protested) against racial discrimination on a world scale when he intervened at the Versailles Peace Conference in 1919; 4. He pioneered in the staging of picket lines to protest plays derogatory to Negro people; 5. He was the first ... leader to organize mass struggle on issues with national and international significance since ... Frederick Douglass and the abolitionists." (*Negro History Bulletin*)

Sources: *Afro-American Writing*; *Ebony*, June 1968; *Historical Negro Biographies*; *Negro Handbook*; *Negro History Bulletin*, Nov. 1947.

TROUPE, QUINCY. Poet, Anthologist, Teacher, Editor.
Born in N.Y.C. in 1943. *Education:* B.A., Grambling Coll., La.; UCLA. *Career:* Tchr.; UCLA; U. of S. Cal.; Ohio U.; Ed. & Founder, *Confrontation: A Journal of Third World Literature*, pub. by Black Studies Inst., Ohio U., Athens; Ed., *Mundus Artium* (lit.); Faculty, Richmond Coll., Staten Island, N.Y. *Mailing address:* c/o Warner Bks., 75 Rockefeller Plaza, N.Y., N.Y. 10020.

Writings:
Fiction
Watts Poets: A Book of New Poetry and Essays, ed. (L.A., House of Respect, 1968)

Embryo, poems (N.Y., Barlenmir House, 1972)

The Event, poems (N.Y., Crowell, 1975)

Giant Talk: An Anthology of Third World Writings, with Rainer Schutle, eds. (N.Y., Random House, 1975)

Snake-Back Solos: Selected Poems, 1969-1977 (N.Y., Reed Bks., 1978)

Nonfiction
The Inside Story of TV's "Roots," with David Wolper (N.Y., Warner Brothers, 1978)

Sidelights: Troupe was an original member of the Watts Writers Workshop. (*Poetry of Black America*)

Sources: *Books in Print*, 1979-80; *New Black Voices*; *Poetry of Black America*; *Watts Poets*.

TURNER, DARWIN T. English Professor, Literary Critic, Anthologist, Editor, Poet.
Born in Cincinnati, Ohio, May 7, 1931. *Education:* B.A. (Eng., Phi Beta Kappa), 1947, M.A. (Eng.), 1949, U. of Cincinnati; Ph.D. (Eng. & Amer. Dramatic Lit.), U. of Chicago, 1956; Litt.D., U. of Cincinnati, 1983. *Family:* Married Maggie Jean Lewis; d. Pamela T. Welch, son Darwin Keith, son

Rachon. *Career:* Asst. Prof., Eng., Clark Coll., Atlanta, 1949-51; Asst. Prof., Eng., Morgan State Coll., Baltimore, 1952-57; Prof. & Chairman, Dept. of Eng., Fla. A&M U., Tallahassee, 1957-59; Prof. & Chairman, Dept. of Eng., N.C. Agricultural & Technical Coll., Greensboro, 1959-70, Prof. of Eng. & Dean, Grad. Sch., 1966-70; Prof. of Eng., U. of Mich., Ann Arbor, 1970-71; Visiting Prof. of Eng., U. of Iowa, Iowa City, 1971-72, & Prof., Eng., & Dir., Afro-Amer. Studies, 1972- ; Advisory Ed., *CLA Journal*, 1960- ; Gen. Ed., Arno Press, Afro-Amer. Culture Ser., 1969; Charles E. Merrill Co.'s African-Afro-Amer. Ser., 1970- ; Advisory Ed., *Bulletin of Black Books*, 1971- ; Advisory Ed., *Amer. Lit.*, 1976- ; Advisory Ed., *Obsidian*, 1974- . *Honors:* Fellow, Cooperative Program in Humanities, Duke U., 1965-66; Amer. Council of Learned Socs. Grant, 1965; Rockefeller Found. Grant for Res., 1972; U. of Chicago Professional Achievement award, 1972; U. of Iowa Developmental Leave, 1978; George W. Carver Award, Simpson Coll., U. of Iowa Found. Distinguished Prof., 1981; Distinguished Alumnus Award: U. of Chicago & U. of Cincinnati. *Mailing address:* Afro-Amer. Studies, U. of Iowa, Iowa City, Iowa 52242.

Writings:
Fiction
Katharsis, anthology (Wellesley, Mass., Wellesley Press, 1964)

Images of the Negro in America, anthology, co-ed. (Boston, D. C. Heath, 1965)

Black Drama in America, an Anthology, ed. (Greenwich, Conn., Fawcett, 1971)

Voices from the Black Experience: African and Afro-American Literature, co-ed. (Lexington, Mass., Ginn, 1972)

Responding Five, co-ed. (Ginn, 1973)

The Wayward and the Seeking: A Collection of Writings by Jean Toomer, ed. (Wash., D.C., Howard U. Press, 1980, 1983)

Nonfiction
A Guide to Composition, ed. (Greensboro, N.C., Office Serv., Co., 1960)

Standards for Freshman Composition, ed. (Greensboro, N.C., Deal Printing Co., 1961)

Nathaniel Hawthorne's "The Scarlet Letter," essay (N.Y., Dell, 1967)

Black American Literature: Essays, ed. (Columbus, Ohio, Merrill, 1969)

Black American Literature: Fiction, ed. (Merrill, 1969)

Black American Literature: Poetry, ed. (Merrill, 1969)

Afro-American Writers, comp. (N.Y., Appleton, 1970)

Black American Literature: Essays, Poetry, Fiction, Drama, ed. (Merrill, 1970)

Theory and Practice in the Teaching of Literature by Afro-Americans, with Barbara D. Stanford (Urbana, Ill., Natl. Council of Tchrs. of Eng., 1971)

In a Minor Chord: Three Afro-American Writers and Their Search for Identity (Carbondale, S. Ill. U. Press, 1971)

The Teaching of Literature by Afro-American Writers: Theory and Practice, co-author (Natl. Council of Tchrs. of Eng., 1972)

The Art of the Slave Narrative: Original Essays in Criticism and Theory, co-ed. with John Sekora (Macomb, Ill., W. Ill. U. Press. 1982)

Sidelights: Dr. Turner entered the University of Cincinnati at age 13, was elected to Phi Beta Kappa at 15, received B.A. at 16, M.A. at 18. (Author)

Sources: Author information; *Black American Literature: Poetry*; *Black Voices*; *Books in Print*, 1979-80, 1982-83; *Galaxy of Black Writing*.

TURNER, LORENZO DOW. English Professor, Linguist.
Born in 1895. *Education:* B.A., 1914, M.A., 1917, Howard U.; Ph.D., U. of Chicago, 1926. *Career:* Prof. & Head, Eng. Dept., Howard U., 1917-29; Prof. & Head, Eng. Dept., Fisk U., 1929-46; Prof., Eng., Roosevelt U., Chicago, 1946-? *Honors:* Charles H. Smiley Prize, U. of Chicago. Died in 1972.

Writings:
Fiction
Readings from Negro Authors, anthology, collaborator (N.Y., Harcourt, 1931)

Nonfiction
Anti-Slavery Sentiment in American Literature prior to 1865 (Wash., D.C., Assn. for the Study of Negro Life & Hist., 1929)

Africanisms in the Gullah Dialect (Chicago, U. of Chicago Press, 1949; reprint, N.Y., Arno, 1969)

The Krio Language of Sierra Leone, West Africa, transl. & ed. with Others (Chicago, Roosevelt U. Press, 1963)

Sidelights: Dr. Turner has studied Gullah using scientific linguistic techniques. He is considered an authority in this field, and is noted for study and recording of speech of groups of people in both the United States and Brazil, in his search for African influences.

Sources: *In Black and White*, 3rd ed., vol. 2, 1980; *National Union Catalog*, 1963-67; *Negro in American Culture*; *Who's Who in Colored America*, Supplement, 7th ed., 1950.

TURNER, RUFUS P. Electrical Engineer, Technical Writer, English Professor.
Born in Houston, Tex., Dec. 25, 1907. *Education:* U. of R.I., 1927-28; Lewis Inst. (Ill. Inst. of Technology), 1930-31; B.A. (Eng.), Cal. State U., L.A., 1958; M.A., 1960, Ph.D., 1966, U. of S. Cal. (both in Eng.). *Family:* Married Mary J. Hayes, Dec. 25, 1928 (dec. Jan. 23, 1979). *Career:* (Tech.): Between 1928 & 1960 held positions as technician, engineer, tech. writer, & tech. ed. in electronic & aerospace industry in Mass., N.Y., Ill., & Cal. Licensed as professional electrical engineer in Mass. (1944-70) and Cal. (1948-80s). (Educ.): Tchr., part-time, of radio & electronics at New Bedford (Mass.) Vocational Sch. & U. of R.I.; Lect. in Eng. part-time at U. of S. Cal. (bus. communications); Assoc. Prof. of Eng. (principally Tech. Writing), Cal. State U., L.A., 1960-70 (retired 1970). Died in Mar. 1982.

Writings:
Nonfiction
Radio Test Instruments (N.Y., Ziff-Davis, 1945, 1946)

Basic Electronic Test Instruments; Their Operation and Use (N.Y., Holt, 1953, rev. ed. 1963; Spanish ed., Argentina, 1969)

Transistors: Theory and Practice (N.Y., Gernsback, 1954, 2nd ed., 1958; Spanish ed., Argentina, 1958)

Transistor Circuits (Gernsback, 1957)

Simplified Electronics (Hollywood, Cal., Trend Bks., 1957)

Basic Electricity (N.Y., Rinehart, 1957, 2nd ed., 1963; Chinese ed., 1971)

Electronic Hobbyists' Handbook (Gernsback, 1958)

Basic Electronic Test Procedures; A Practical Handbook for Electronic Technicians (Rinehart, 1959)

How to Use Grid-Dip Oscillators (N.Y., Rider, 1960, 2nd ed., 1969; Spanish ed., Argentina, 1964)

Semiconductor Devices (N.Y., Holt, 1961; reprint, N.Y., Krieger, 1976)

Diode Circuits Handbook (Indianap., Howard W. Sams, 1963, 2nd ed., 1967)

Transistorized Miniature Amplifier and Tuner Applications (Syosset, N.Y., Lafayette Radio-Electronics Corp., 1964, 2nd ed., 1967, 3rd ed., 1968)

Practical Oscilloscope Handbook, vols. 1 & 2 (Rider, 1964; Brit. ed., 1966; French ed., 1966; German ed., 1970)

Grammar Review for Technical Writers (Holt, 1964; rev., San Francisco, Cal., Rinehart, 1971)

Technical Writer's and Editor's Stylebook (Sams, 1964)

Photocell Applications (Lafayette Radio-Electronics Corp., 1965)

ABCs of Varactors (Sams, 1966)

Bridges and Other Null Devices (Sams, 1967)

FET Circuits (Sams, 1967, 2nd ed., 1977)

Integrated Circuits, Fundamentals and Projects (Chicago, Allied Radio Corp., 1968)

Waveform Measurements (Rochelle Park, N.J., Hayden, 1968)

ABCs of Thermistors (Sams, 1970)

ABCs of Voltage-Dependent Resistors (Sams, 1970)

Technical Report Writing (Holt, 1965, 2nd ed., Rinehart, 1971; Australian ed., 1971)

ABCs of FETS (Sams, 1970, 2nd ed., 1978)

125 One-Transistor Projects (Blue Ridge Summit, Pa., Tab Bks., 1970)

ABCs of Integrated Circuits (Sams, 1971, 2nd ed., 1977)

How to Make Electronic Tests without Specialized Equipment (Hayden, 1972)

ABCs of Electronic Power (Sams, 1972; Brit. ed., 1972)

ABCs of Zener Diodes (Sams, 1974)

ABCs of Resistance and Resistors (Sams, 1974)

Metrics for the Millions (Sams, 1974)

Solid-State Components (Sams, 1974)

ABCs of Calculus (Sams, 1975)

Electronic Conversions, Symbols & Formulas (Tab, 1975)

Frequency and Its Measurement (Sams, 1975)

MOSFET Circuits Guidebook (Tab, 1975)

Solar Cells and Photocells (Sams, 1975; reprint, Lafayette, 1976, 2nd ed., 1980)

Semiconductor Devices, paperback ed. (Melbourne, Fla., Krieger, 1976)

Impedance (Tab, 1976)

RC Circuits (Sams, 1976)

106 Easy Electronics Projects beyond the Transistor (Tab, 1976)

Getting Acquainted with the IC (Sams, 1978)

Antenna Construction Handbook (Tab, 1978)

Simple IC-Type Test Instruments You Can Build (Sams, 1979)

LC Circuits (Sams, 1980)

Illustrated Dictionary of Electronics (Tab, 1980)

Sidelights: "*Articles:* More than 3,000 in radio, electrical, electronic, and mechanical magazines; trade papers; house organs; *Encyclopedia Americana*; and *Grolier Encyclopedia*. Earliest publication date: November 1924." (Author)

Sources: Author information; *Books in Print*, 1979-80, 1981-82; *Directory of Professional Engineers and Land Surveyors*; *125 One-Transistor Projects*; *Technical Report Writing*; *Trojan Family*, July 1980.

TURPIN, WATERS EDWARD. Novelist, English Professor.
Born in Oxford, E. Shore, Md., in 1910. *Education:* B.A., Morgan Coll., Baltimore; M.A., Ph.D., Columbia U. *Career:* Eng. Tchr. & Football Coach, Storer Coll., Harper's Ferry, W. Va.; Eng. Tchr., Lincoln U. Died in 1968.

Writings:
Fiction

These Low Grounds, novel (N.Y., Harper, 1937)

O Canaan!, novel (N.Y., Doubleday, Doran, 1939)

The Rootless, novel (N.Y., Vantage, 1957)

Sidelights: "He set the locale of his first novel, *These Low Grounds* ... on his native Eastern Shore of Maryland where ... oysters (are processed) for market.
"*O Canaan!* ... is the story of Joe Benson's rise from a poor Mississippi field hand to a Chicago realtor and banker and his fall back to poverty and to life as a Pullman porter.
"*The Rootless* ... is a historical treatment of black slavery as practiced on a Maryland plantation in the late eighteenth century." (*Black Insights*)

Sources: *Black Insights*; *Negro Caravan*.

TUTTLE, WILLIAM McCULLOUGH, JR. History Professor, Historian, Biographer.
Born in Detroit, Mich., Oct. 7, 1937. *Education:* B.A., Denison U., 1959; M.A., 1964, Ph.D., 1967, U. of Wis. *Family:* Married Linda Stumpp, Dec. 12, 1959 (div.); children: William M. III, Catharine Terry, Andrew Sanford. *Career:* Historian, U.S. Hist., Study of Amer. Educ., Princeton, N.J., 1965-67; (U. of Kan.) Asst. Prof., 1969-70; Assoc. Prof., 1970-75; Prof., Amer. Hist., 1975- . *Honors:* Harry S. Truman Lib. Inst. res. grant, 1968, 1975-76; Senior Fellow, S. & Negro Hist., Johns Hopkins U., 1969-70; Award of Merit, Amer. Assn. for State & Local Hist., 1972; Res. Fellow, Harvard U., 1972-73; Guggenheim Memorial Found. Fellow, 1975-76. *Mailing address:* c/o Dept. of Hist., U. of Kan., Lawrence, Kan. 66045.

Writings:
Nonfiction

Race Riot: Chicago in the Red Summer of 1919 (N.Y., Atheneum, 1970, also paper)

W. E. B. DuBois, ed. (Englewood Cliffs, N.J., Prentice-Hall, 1973)

Sources: *Contemporary Authors*, vols. 29-32, 1972; *Writers Directory*, 1980-82.

TUTUOLA, AMOS. (Nigerian). Novelist, Short Story Writer.
Born in Abeokuta (Yoruba country), Nigeria, in 1920. *Education:* Salvation Army sch.; Lagos High Sch.; Anglican Central Sch., Ipose Ake, Abeokuta. *Family:* Married Victoria Alake, 1947; two children. *Career:* Coopersmith; Blacksmith; Writer (& in cooperation with prof. at U. of Ibadan, dramatic versions of stories produced). *Mailing address:* c/o Federal Radio Corp., Broadcasting House, New Court Road, Ibadan, Nigeria.

Writings:
Fiction

The Palm-Wine Drinkard and His Dead Palm-Wine Tapster in the Dead's Town, novel (London, Faber, 1952; N.Y., Grove, 1953 — 9 printings; Westport, Conn., Greenwood, 1970)

My Life in the Bush of Ghosts, novel (Faber, 1954; Grove, 1954; N.Y., Evergreen, 1970; Japanese ed., Tokyo, Shinchosha, 1962)

Simbi and the Satyr of the Dark Jungle, novel (Faber, 1956)

The Brave African Huntress, novel (Faber, 1958; Grove, 1958; Evergreen, 1970)

The Palm-Wine Drinkard and His Dead Palm-Wine Tapster in the Dead's Town, play, Eng. version, adapted with Prof. Collis (Ibadan, Nigeria, U. of Ibadan, 1962)

Feather Woman of the Jungle, novel (Faber, 1962, 1968)

Ajaiyi and His Inherited Poverty, novel (Faber, 1967)

Sidelights: Tutuola is a master storyteller. Bernth Lindfors believes "... he has come to be accepted as a unique phenomenon in world literature, a writer who bridges two narrative traditions and two cultures by translating oral art into literary art." (*Contemporary Novelists*)

Sources: *Books in Print*, 1979-80, 1980-81; *Contemporary Novelists*, 1972; *World Authors 1950-1970*.

U TAM'SI, GÉRALD FÉLIX TCHICYA [Tchicaya, Félix]. (Congolese). Poet, Folklorist, Radio Scriptwriter, Editor.
Born in Mpili, Congo-Brazzaville, in 1931 (son of a deputy in the French Natl. Assembly). *Education:* Orleans Lycée; Lycée Janson de Sailly, Paris. *Career:* Radio Scriptwriter (African folktales); Ed., *Congo* (a Zaire daily journal); UNESCO official; Poet. *Honors:* Grand Prize for Poetry, Festival of African Arts, Dakar, Senegal, 1966. *Mailing address:* c/o Oxford U. Press, 200 Madison Ave., N.Y., N.Y. 10016.

Writings:
(Partial Listing — English Only)
Fiction
Brush Fire, poems, transl. into Eng. by Sangodare Akanji (Ibadan, Nigeria, Mbari Press, 1964)

Selected Poems, transl. by Gerald Moore (from last four of U Tam'si's vols.) (London, Heinemann, 1970)

Sidelights: U Tam'si's poetry has been translated into Polish, Czech, and Hungarian. (*African Writers on African Writing*)
Gerald Moore called U Tam'si "a poet of some importance and the most prolific black poet of French expression to appear since Cesaire." (*Reader's Guide to African Literature*)

Sources: *African Writers on African Writing*; *Poems from Black Africa*; *Reader's Guide to African Literature*.

VAN DYKE, HENRY. Novelist.
Born in Allegan, Mich., Oct. 3, 1928. *Education:* M.A., U. of Mich. *Family:* Single. *Career:* Writer-in-Residence, Kent State U. (fall quarter, 1974); Assoc. Ed., U. of Mich., engineering res., 1956-58; Coordinator, Crowell-Collier-Macmillan, 1959-67. *Honors:* Guggenheim Fellow, 1971; Amer. Acad. of Arts & Letters Award, 1974. *Mailing address:* 40 Waterside Plaza, N.Y., N.Y. 10010.

Writings:
Fiction
Ladies of the Rachmaninoff Eyes, novel (N.Y., Farrar, 1965; Manor Bks., 1973; Old Greenwich, Conn., Chatham, 1975)

Blood of Strawberries, novel (Farrar, 1969)

Dead Piano, novel (Farrar, 1971)

Sources: Author information; *Books in Print*, 1979-80.

VAN PEEBLES, MELVIN. Actor, Composer, Playwright, Novelist, Filmmaker.
Born in Chicago, Ill., Aug. 21, 1932. *Education:* Grad., Ohio Wesleyan U. *Career:* Recording Artist; Filmmaker; Novelist; Short Story Writer; Actor. *Honors:* 1st Prize, Belgian Festival, for *Don't Play Us Cheap*. *Mailing address:* c/o Ballantine Bks., Div. of Random House, 201 E. 50th St., N.Y., N.Y. 10022.

Writings:
Fiction

Un Ours pour le F.B.I., novel (Paris, Buchet-Chastel, 1964); transl. as *A Bear for the FBI*

Un Américain en enfer (The True American: A Folk Fable) (Paris, Editions Denoël, 1965; N.Y., Doubleday, 1976)

Le Chinois du XIV, short stories (Paris, le Gardenet, 1966)

La Fête à Harlem, novel (Paris, Martineau, 1967)

A Bear for the FBI, novel (N.Y., Trident, 1968; N.Y., Pocket, 1969)

Watermelon Man, film (n.d.)

Sweet Sweetback's Baadasssss Song, film (1971)

The Making of Sweet Sweetback's Baadasssss Song, adapted from the film (N.Y., Lancer Bks., 1971)

Aint Supposed to Die a Natural Death, play (Bantam, 1973)

Don't Play Us Cheap; A Harlem Party, novel (Bantam, 1973)

Just an Old Sweet Song, novel (N.Y., Ballantine, 1976)

The True American: A Folk Fable (Doubleday, 1976)

Sidelights: "Writer, composer, director, film maker, producer, promoter, actor, singer and one-man conglomerate, he's the first black man in show business to beat the white man at his own game." (*New York Times*)
With $70,000, an amateur cast, a nonunion crew, and rented equipment, he filmed *Sweet Sweetback*, which grossed $12 million. (*1000 Successful Blacks*)

Sources: *Afro-American Writers*; *Contemporary Authors*, vols. 85-88, 1980; *Don't Play Us Cheap*; *New York Times*; *1000 Successful Blacks*.

VAN SERTIMA, IVAN. Anthropologist.
Born in Kitty Village, Guyana, Jan. 26, 1935. *Education:* B.A. (honors), London Sch. of Oriental & African Studies, London, 1969; M.A., Rutgers U., 1977. *Family:* Married Maria Nagy, Oct. 24, 1964; child: Lawrence Josef. *Career:* Press & Broadcasting Officer, Govt. Information Services (Guyana Civil Serv.), Georgetown, Guyana, 1956-59; Eng. Broadcaster, Central Office of Information, London, Eng., 1960-70; Instr., 1970-72, Asst. Prof., 1972-79, Assoc. Prof., African Studies, 1978- (all Douglass Coll., Rutgers U., New Brunswick, N.J.); Pres. & Ed., *Journal of African Civilizations*, Ltd. *Honors:* Nominated for Nobel Prize in Lit., 1976-80; Clarence L. Holte Prize from Twenty-First Century Found., 1981, for *They Came before Columbus*. *Mailing address:* 59 S. Adelaide Ave., Highland Park, N.J. 08904.

Writings:
Fiction

River and the Wall, poems (Miniature Poets, 1958)

Nonfiction

Critical Writers, Critical Essays (London, New Beacon Bks., 1968; N.Y., Panther House, 1971)

Swahili Dictionary of Legal Terms (Tanzania, 1968)

They Came before Columbus: The African Presence in Ancient America (N.Y., Random House, 1977)

Sidelights: *They Came before Columbus* was a Book-of-the-Month Club selection.

Sources: *Books in Print*, 1979-80; *Contemporary Authors*, vol. 104, 1982; *They Came before Columbus*.

VANN, ROBERT L. Newspaper Publisher, Attorney.
Born in Ahoskie, N.C., Aug. 29, 1879. *Education:* Va. Union U., Richmond; B.A., LL.B., U. of Pittsburgh. *Family:* Married Jessie Matthews, 1910. *Career:* Founder-Pub., *Pittsburgh Courier*, 1910; Lawyer; Asst. City Solicitor, Pittsburgh, 1918-22; Asst. U.S. Attorney Gen. *Honors:* Hon. degrees: Va. Union U., Wilberforce. Memorial tower named for him at Va. Union U. Liberty Ship named for him in Oct. 1943. Died in 1940.

Writings:
Nonfiction
Pittsburgh Courier, newspaper (1910-)

Sidelights: The publication of the *Courier* was a success. As a spokesman for the Republican Party, it became the news media for the Negro community in Pittsburgh. "By the 1930's, its circulation reached from coast to coast, with branch offices and outlets throughout the United States."

"During the ... thirties, Vann saw fit to change the support of the *Courier* from the Republican Party to that of the New Deal Democrats. For his support of the Roosevelt program, he was appointed assistant U.S. attorney general in the late thirties." (*Historical Negro Biographies*)

Sources: *Historical Negro Biographies*; *Negroes in Public Affairs and Government*; *Negroes Past and Present*.

VASSA, GUSTAVUS. Ship Steward, Abolitionist, Autobiographer.
Born in Benin, Nigeria, W. Africa, c. 1745. Thrust into slavery at age 11, 1st on a Va. plantation; then in illegal serv. of a Brit. naval officer (who gave him a fair educ.). Finally, slave on plantations and small trading vessels in W. Indies as property of Phila. merchant. (*Negro Author*). *Career:* Bought freedom, his master becoming his adviser & protector. Traveled extensively as ship's steward. Converted to Methodism; settled down in England; engaged in antislavery work. (*Negro Author*). Died c. 1801.

Writings:
Nonfiction
The Interesting Narrative of the Life of Olaudah Equiano, or Gustavus Vassa, the African (n.p., 1789, in 8th ed. by 1794)

Sidelights: *The Narrative* "regarded as highly informative account of the evils of slavery as it affected both master and slave." (*Negro Almanac*)

Although not actually an American Negro; he did spend "considerable time in bondage in this country and his book was so frequently reprinted in the United States that he might as well be considered in this connection." (*Early Negro American Writers*)

Sources: *Early Negro American Writers*; *Negro Almanac*; *Negro Author*.

VROMAN, MARY ELIZABETH. Short Story Writer, Novelist, Teacher.
Born in Buffalo, N.Y., in 1923. *Education:* Ala. State U. *Career:* Ala. tchr.; N.Y., Bd. of Educ. "Higher Horizons" Program, Music, Art Coordinator; Short Story Writer; Screenwriter. *Honors:* First Black woman to be granted membership in Screen Writers Guild; Christopher Award for inspirational magazine writing, 1952. Died in 1967.

Writings:
Fiction
Esther, novel (N.Y., Bantam, 1963)

Harlem Summer, juv. (N.Y., Putnam, 1967; N.Y., Berkley, 1968)

Nonfiction
Shaped to Its Purpose: Delta Sigma Theta, the First Fifty Years (N.Y., Random House, 1965)

Sidelights: Short stories "See How They Run" and "And Have Not Charity" were published in *Ladies Home Journal*. "See How They Run" was purchased by Metro-Goldwyn-Mayer and released in 1953 as the movie *Bright Road*.

Sources: *Afro-American Encyclopedia*, vol. 9; *American Negro Short Stories*; *Dictionary Catalog of the Schomburg Collection of Negro Literature and History*, 1st Supplement, vol. 2, 1962-67 (1974)

WADDY, WILLANNA RUTH. Artist.
Born in Lincoln, Neb., Jan. 7, 1909. *Education:* U. of Minn., 1927-28, 1930-31. *Family:* Married William Henry Waddy, Feb. 2, 1931 (div. June 1933); d. Marianna. *Career:* Exhibited on one-man shows at Jimmy Crawford's Frame Shop, L.A., 1963; Safety Savings & Loan Assn., 1969; Independence Square, 1966; Contemporary Crafts Gallery; Exhibited in group shows at Art W. Assoc., Inc., 1963- ; Graphic aus fünf Kontinenten, Leipzig, Germany, 1965; New Perspectives, Oakland, Cal. Mus., 1968; permanent collections include Oakland Mus., Golden State Mutual Life Insurance Co., L.A., & Metropolitan Mus. of Art. N.Y. *Mailing address:* 1543 S. Western Ave., L.A., Cal. 90006.

Writings:
Nonfiction

Black Artists on Art, vol. I, ed. with Samella S. Lewis (Pasadena, Cal., Ward Ritchie Press, 1969)

Black Artists on Art, vol. II, ed. with Samella S. Lewis (Ward Ritchie Press, 1971)

Sidelights: Ruth Waddy was founder of Art West Associates, Inc., 1962.

Source: *Who's Who in the West*, 14th ed., 1974-75.

WALCOTT, DEREK ALTON. (Saint Lucian). Poet, Playwright, Producer, Teacher, Journalist.
Born in Castries, St. Lucia, Jan. 23, 1930 (son of Warwick, Eng., watercolorist & a Soc. Worker & Dramatics Tchr.) *Education:* St. Mary's Coll., Castries, St. Lucia; B.A., U. Coll. of W. Indies, Mona, Jamaica, 1953. *Family:* Married; three children. *Career:* Feature Writer, *Public Opinion*, Kingston, Jamaica, & *Trinidad Guardian*, Port-of-Spain, Trinidad; Founding Dir., Trinidad Theatre Workshop, 1958- . *Honors:* Rockefeller Found. Fellow, 1957 (Amer. theater); Guiness Award in Poetry, 1961; Royal Soc. of Lit. Award, for *The Castaway*; Chalmondelay Award for *The Gulf*, 1969, 1974 Jack Campbell/New Statesman Prize, for his autobiographical *Another Life*, 1973; Eugene O'Neill Found.-Weseyan Fellowship for Playwrights; Heinemann Award, 1966; Order of the Hummingbird, Trinidad & Tobago, 1969; Obie Award for *Dream...*, for most distinguished foreign off-Broadway production, 1971. Walcott's musical, *Joker of Seville*, was commissioned by Royal Shakespeare Co. of Great Brit. in 1974; Hon. Doctorate of Letters, U. of W. Indies, 1972; decorated by St. Lucia. *Mailing address:* 165 Duke of Edinburgh Ave., Diego Martin, Trinidad.

Writings:
Fiction

Twenty-Five Poems (Port-of-Spain, Guardian Commercial Printery, 1948)

Epitaph for the Young, poems (Bridgetown, Barbados, Advocate, 1949)

Henri Christophe; A Chronicle in Seven Scenes, play (Advocate, 1950)

Henri Dernier; A Play for Radio Production (Advocate, 1951)

Wine of the Country, play (Mona, Jamaica, U. Coll. of W. Indies, 1953)

Poems (Kingston, Jamaica, City Printery, 1953)

The Sea at Dauphin; A Play in One Act (Mona, U. Coll. of W. Indies, 1954)

Ione, a Play with Music (U. Coll. of W. Indies, 1957)

Drums and Colors; An Epic Drama, played 1958 (Port-of-Spain, Caribbean Quarterly, 1961)

Ti Jean and His Brothers, play (U. Coll. of W. Indies, n.d.)

In a Green Night: Poems 1948-1960 (London, Cape, 1962)

The Selected Poems of Derek Walcott (N.Y., Farrar, 1964)

The Castaway and Other Poems (Cape, 1965)

Malcauchon, or Six in the Rain (U. Coll. of W. Indies, 1966)

The Gulf, Poems (Farrar, 1970)

Dream on Monkey Mountain and Other Plays (Farrar, 1970; U. Place, 1970)

Another Life (Farrar, 1973; Wash., D.C., Three Continents, 1982)

Sea Grapes, poems (Farrar, 1976)

The Star-Apple Kingdom, short story (Farrar, 1979)

Remembrance and Pantomine: Plays (Farrar, 1980)

Sidelights: According to Louis James: "Rejected by the young Walcott as a cliché, the vitality and colour of the Caribbean setting emerge in Walcott's mature verse to energise a vision at once intensely personal, Caribbean, and universal." (*Contemporary Poets*)

Robert Graves stated that Walcott handles English with a closer understanding of its inner magic than most—if not all—of his English-born contemporaries. George Lamming considered his work a formidable achievement.

He took part in the Poetry International Festival in London in 1969. *Dream on Monkey Mountain* was produced with great success at Eugene O'Neill Memorial Theatre at Waterford, in 1969. (*Caribbean Writers*)

Sources: *Books in Print*, 1981-82; *Caribbean Writers*; *Contemporary Poets*, 2nd ed., 1975; *Freedom-ways*, vol. 17, 1977; *Writers Directory*, 1980-82.

WALCOTT, RONALD. English Teacher.
Born in N.Y.C., July 22, 1946. *Education:* B.A., Hunter Coll.; M.A. & doctoral candidate, Columbia U. *Family:* Married; son Christopher, son Quentin. *Career:* Asst. Prof. of Eng., Kingsborough Community & Queens Colls. of CUNY (Afro-Amer. Thought & Lit. & other courses). *Mailing address:* c/o Random House, Inc., 201 E. 50th St., N.Y., N.Y. 10022.

Writings:
Fiction

Twenty-Eight Short Stories: An Anthology, Tchrs. Manual, co-ed. with Michael Timko (N.Y., Random House, 1975)

Sources: Author information.

WALKER, ALICE MALSENIOR. Teacher, Novelist, Short Story Writer, Poet.
Born in Eatonton, Ga., Feb. 9, 1944. *Education:* Spelman Coll., 1961-63; B.A., Sarah Lawrence Coll., 1965. *Family:* Married Melvyn R. Leventhal (civil rights lawyer), Mar. 17, 1967; d. Rebecca Grant. *Career:* Consultant, Black Studies, Friends of the Children of Miss., 1967-68; Tchr., Writing & Black Lit., Jackson State Coll., & Tougaloo Coll., Miss., 1968-70; Wellesley Coll., Mass. (Lect. in Writing & Lit.), 1972- ; Lect. in Lit., Yale U.; Contrib. Ed.: *Freedomways, Southern Voices, Ms. Honors:* Breadloaf Writer's Conf., scholar, 1966; Merrill Writing Fellow, 1966-67; McDowell Colony Fellow, 1967; NEA grant (for *Third Life of Grange Copeland*), 1969-70; Radcliffe Inst. Fellow, 1971-73; Rosenthal (Found.) Award, Natl. Inst. of Arts & Letters, 1973 (for *In Love and Trouble*); nomination for Natl. Bk. Award, 1973 (for *Revolutionary Petunias*); Lillian Smith Award (for *Revolutionary Petunias*), 1973; Guggenheim Found. Fellow, 1978; NEA Award; won both 1983 American Bk. Award & Pulitzer Prize for Fiction for *The Color Purple. Mailing address:* c/o Harcourt Brace Jovanovich, 757 Third Ave., N.Y., N.Y. 10017.

Writings:

Fiction

Once; Poems (N.Y., Harcourt, 1968, 1976; paper, HarBraceJ, 1976)

The Third Life of Grange Copeland, novel (Harcourt, 1970, 1977; paper, HarBraceJ, 1974)

Revolutionary Petunias, poems (HarBraceJ, 1973)

In Love and Trouble: Stories of Black Women (Harcourt, 1973; HarBraceJ, 1974)

Meridian, novel (Harcourt, 1976, 1981; N.Y., Pocket Bks., 1977; paper, N.Y., Wash. Square Press, 1981)

Good Night, Willie Lee, I'll See You in the Morning: Poems (N.Y., Dial, 1979; paper, N.Y., Doubleday, 1979)

You Can't Keep a Good Woman Down: Stories (HarBraceJ, 1981, paper also)

The Color Purple: A Novel (HarBraceJ, 1982; paper, Wash. Square, 1983)

Nonfiction

Langston Hughes, American Poet, juv. (N.Y., Crowell, 1974; N.Y., Har Row, Biog. Ser., 1981)

In Search of Our Mothers' Gardens: Womanist Prose (San Diego, HarBraceJ, 1983)

Sidelights: Alice Walker is an outstanding chronicler of the social and personal drama in the lives of the "folk," who struggle for survival in hostile environments. (*Dictionary of Literary Biography*)

Her latest, Pulitzer Prize winning *The Color Purple*, is "about women who, despite the lousy hands life deals them, survive, evolve and thrive through their love and support of each other." (*Los Angeles Times*)

Sources: Author information; *Best Short Stories by Negro Writers*; *Books in Print*, 1978-79, 1982-83; *Dictionary of Literary Biography* (American Novelists since World War II), 2nd ser., 1980; *Ebony*, Mar. 1974; *Good Night, Willie Lee, I'll See You in the Morning*; *Los Angeles Times*, June 8, 1983; *Poetry of Black America*.

WALKER, DAVID. Abolitionist, Activist.

Born in Wilmington, N.C., Sept. 28, 1785 (son of a slave father & a free mother). He resolved not to live in the South. Reaching Boston after many trials, he learned to read & write. *Family:* Married in 1828; his home became a shelter for the poor. *Career:* Opened a clothing store on Brattle St. and prospered, 1827. Died in 1830.

Writings:

Nonfiction

Walker's Appeal, in Four Articles; Together with a Preamble to the Coloured Citizens of the World, but in Particular and very Expressly to Those of the United States of America (Boston, David Walker, 1829; in 3rd ed. in a yr.; ed. by Henry H. Garnet with sketch of author's life, in 1848; reprint, Salem, N.Y., Ayer, 1969)

Sidelights: "Two states promptly 'enacted laws forbidding the circulation of incendiary publications and forbidding the teaching of slaves to read and write' [after copies of the *Appeal* were found on Blacks in Savannah]. In North Carolina a person found guilty of writing or circulating publications which might 'excite insurrection, conspiracy, or resistance in the slaves or free Negroes' was to be 'imprisoned for not less than a year and be put in the pillory and whipped at the discretion of the court.'... A reward of $1000 was placed on Walker dead, a reward of $10,000 on Walker alive." (*Negro Caravan*)

"... his wife and friends advised that he go to Canada, but he refused, saying, 'I will stand my ground. Somebody must die in this cause. ... it is not in me to falter if I can promote the work of emancipation.' Before the close of 1830 he died, and the belief was persistant that he met with foul play." (*Early Negro American Writers*)

Sources: *Early Negro American Writers*; *Negro Caravan*.

WALKER, JAMES LYNWOOD. Theologian, Religion Professor.
Born in Fayetteville, N.C., Dec. 19, 1940. *Education:* B.A., N.C. Central U., 1963; grad. study, Duke U., 1963-65; B.D., Pacific Sch. of Relig., 1966; Ph.D., Grad. Theol. Union & U. of Cal., Berkeley, 1970. *Family:* Married Joyce Moore, Dec. 19, 1958; married 2nd, Harmon Lamb, July 27, 1963; children: (1st wife), Michael Anthony; (2nd wife), David Edward, Angela Lynette. *Career:* Asst. Prof., Relig. & Personality Sci., & Asst. Dean, Grad. Theol. Union, Berkeley, Cal., 1970-73; self-employed counselor, consultant, & writer, 1978- . *Mailing address:* 3500 25th Ave., W., No. 424, Seattle, Wash. 98199.

Writings:
  Nonfiction
  Body and Soul: Gestalt Therapy and Religious Experience (Nashville, Abingdon, 1971)

Sources: *Body and Soul; Contemporary Authors*, vols. 37-40, 1st rev., 1979.

WALKER, MARGARET ABIGAIL. Poet, Novelist, English Professor.
Born in Birmingham, Ala., July 27, 1915. *Education:* Gilbert Acad.; B.A., Northwestern U.; M.A., Ph.D., U. of Iowa; hon. degrees: Fine Arts, Denison U., 1974; Dr. of Lit., Northwestern U., 1974. *Family:* Married Firnist James Alexander (interior decorator); d. Marion Elizabeth, d. Margaret Elvira, son attorney Firnist James, Jr., son Sigismund Walker. *Career:* Lecture Platform, Natl. Concert-Artists Corp., N.Y., 1943-48; U. of Iowa Rhetoric Program, 1962-64; at Jackson State Coll., Jackson, Miss. since 1949: Prof. of Eng. & Dir. of Inst. for the Study of Hist., Life, and Culture of Black People. *Honors:* Yale Award for Younger Poets, 1942; Rosenwald Found. Fellow, 1944; Ford Found. Fellow (Fund for Advancement of Educ.), Yale U., 1953-54; Houghton Mifflin Literary Fellow, 1966; apptd. as Fulbright Prof. to Norway, 1971 (postponed); NEH Fellow, 1972; Alumni Merit Award, Northwestern U., 1974. *Mailing address:* 2205 Guynes St., Jackson, Miss. 39213.

Writings:
  Fiction
  For My People, poems (New Haven, Conn., Yale U. Press, 1942; N.Y., Arno, Amer. Negro — His Hist. & Lit. Ser., no. 2, 1969; reprint, N.Y., AMS, n.d.)

  Jubilee, novel (Boston, Houghton Mifflin, 1966; N.Y., Bantam, 1975)

  Prophets for a New Day, poems (Detroit, Broadside, 1970)

  October Journey, poems (Broadside, 1973)

  Nonfiction
  How I Wrote Jubilee (Chicago, Black Paper Ser., Third World, 1972)

  A Poetic Equation: Conversation between Nikki Giovanni and Margaret Walker (Wash., D.C., Howard U. Press, 1974)

Sidelights: James A. Emanuel relates that in a speech to a National Urban League Conference, the author proclaims, "We are still a people of spirit and soul. We are still fighting in the midst of white American Racism for the overwhelming truth of the primacy of human personality and the spiritual destiny of all mankind." (*Contemporary Novelists*)

Sources: Author information; *Black American Literature: Poetry; Black Insights; Black Voices; Cavalcade; Contemporary Novelists; Dark Symphony; Kaleidoscope;* Pub. information.

WALKER, WILLIAM O. Publisher-Editor.
Born in Selma, Ala., Sept. 18, 1896. *Education:* Grad.: Wilberforce U., 1916; Oberlin Bus. Coll., 1918. *Career:* Secy. to Dir., Pittsburgh Urban League, 1918; City Ed., *Pittsburgh Courier*, 1919; City Ed., *Norfolk Journal & Guide*, 1920; Co-founder & Managing Ed., *Washington Tribune*, 1921-30; Advertising Mgr. to Asst. Mgr., Fair Dept. Store, downtown Wash., D.C., 1930, Mgr., 1932; took over, revived *Cleveland Call and Post*, 1932. *Honors:* Dir. campaign publicity for Senator Robert A.

Taft & Governor-Senator John W. Bricker. Elected to Republican State Central & Executive Com. from 21st Dist., 1956, 1958; Dir., Dept. of Industrial Relations for State of Ohio, 1963- . Died Oct. 29, 1981, in Cleveland, Ohio.

Writings:
Nonfiction

Cleveland Call and Post, newspaper (1932-)

Sources: *Contemporary Authors*, vol. 105, 1982; *Negro Handbook*.

WALKER, WYATT TEE. Clergyman.
Born in Brockton, Mass., Aug. 16, 1929. *Education:* B.S. (Chemistry & Physics), magna cum laude, Va. Union U.; M. Divinity, Va. Union U., Sch. of Relig.; D. Ministry, Colgate Divinity Sch.; L.H.D. (hon.), Va. Union U. *Family:* Married Theresa Ann; children: Ann Patricia, Wyatt, Jr., Robert, Earl. *Career:* Resident Minister, Canaan Bap. Church of Christ, 1967- , N.Y.C. Asst. to Governor of N.Y. on Urban Affairs; Chief-of-Staff to Martin L. King, Jr. Has conducted sensitivity seminars for: IBM, AT&T, N.Y. Bell Telephone & Consolidated Edison. *Honors:* Recipient of over 150 awards for excellence in the field of human relations. *Mailing address:* c/o Judson Press, Valley Forge, Pa. 19481.

Writings:
Nonfiction

Black Church Looks at the Bicentennial, with Harold A. Carter (Elgin, Ill., Progressive Natl. Bap. Pub. House, 1976)

"Somebody's Calling My Name": Black Sacred Music and Social Change (Valley Forge, Pa., Judson Press, 1979)

Sidelights: Canaan Baptist Church of Christ subsidizes Anti-Narcotics Center.

Sources: *Books in Print*, 1981-82; *1000 Successful Blacks*; *Somebody's Calling My Name*.

WALLACE, MICHELE. Writing Teacher.
Born in Harlem, N.Y., in 1952. *Education:* New Lincoln Sch.; Coll. of City of N.Y. *Career:* Staff of *Newsweek*; Tchr., Writing, N.Y.U. *Mailing address:* c/o Dial Press, One Dag Hammarskjold Plaza, N.Y., N.Y. 10017.

Writings:
Nonfiction

Black Macho and the Myth of the Superwoman (N.Y., Dial, 1979)

Sidelights: *Library Journal* states: "Wallace writes about the radical politics of the 1960's from the perspective of a black woman.... The aim of the black political movement became 'the pursuit of black manhood' and the open denigration of black women was its corollary." (*Book Review Digest*)

Sources: *Black Macho and the Myth of the Superwoman*; *Book Review Digest*, 1979; *Books in Print*, 1981-82.

WALLACE, SUSAN J. (Bahamian). Poet, Teacher.
Born in West End, Grand Bahama, c. 1935. *Education:* West End, Grand Bahama; St. John's Coll., Nassau; Nassau Tchr.-Training Coll., U. of Exeter, Inst. of Educ.; U. of Miami. *Family:* Married to (Officer, Dept. of Civil Aviation); five children. *Career:* Tchr., elementary sch., high sch.; Tchr., Nassau Tchr.-Training Coll.; Official, Bahamas Ministry of Educ., 1968-69. *Mailing address:* c/o Dorrance & Co., Cricket Terrace Center, Ardmore, Pa. 19003.

Writings:
Fiction
Bahamian Scene, Poetry (Phila., Dorrance, 1970; five printings by 1972)

Source: *Caribbean Writers.*

WALLACE, WALTER L. Sociologist, Sociology Professor, Consultant.
Born in Wash., D.C., Aug. 21, 1927. *Education:* B.A., Columbia U., 1954; M.A., Atlanta U., 1955; Ph.D., U. of Chicago, 1963. *Family:* Married Patricia Denton, Mar. 28, 1964; one son (previous marriage), Jeffrey Richard; d. Robin Claire, d. Jennifer Rose. *Career:* Instr., Spelman Coll., Atlanta U., 1955-57; Prof., Sociol., Northwestern U., 1963-71; Prof., Sociol., Princeton U., 1971- ; Staff Sociol., Russell Sage Found., N.Y.C., 1969-77, Visiting Scholar, 1968; Consultant, *World Book*, 1977- ; Fellow, Center for Advanced Study in Behavioral Sci., Stanford, Cal., 1974-75. *Mailing address:* Dept. of Sociol., Princeton U., Princeton, N.J. 08540.

Writings:
Nonfiction

Student Culture; Social Culture and Continuity in a Liberal Arts College (Chicago, Aldine, 1966)

Sociological Theory, an Introduction, ed. (Aldine, 1969)

Logic of Science in Sociology (Aldine, 1971)

Black Elected Officials: A Study of Black Americans Holding Governmental Office, with James E. Conyers (N.Y., Russell Sage Found., 1976)

Principles of Scientific Sociology (Aldine Pub., 1983)

Sources: *Books in Print*, 1980-81, 1983-84; *Who's Who in America*, 1978-79.

WALROND, ERIC. Essayist, Short Story Writer.
Born in Georgetown, Brit. Guiana, in 1898. *Education:* Columbia U.; City Coll. of N.Y. *Career:* Assoc. Ed., *The Negro World*, 1923. Died in 1966.

Writings:
Fiction
Tropic Death, novel (N.Y., Boni & Liveright, 1926)

Sidelights: "*Tropic Death*, his first and only book was published in 1926. It is a collection of stories depicting the contrast between the natural beauty of the American tropics and the poverty, disease, and death of its inhabitants." (*AFRO USA*)

Sources: *Afro-American Writers*; *AFRO USA.*

WALTON, HANES, JR. Political Science Professor.
Born in Augusta, Ga., Sept. 25, 1942. *Education:* B.A., Morehouse Coll., 1963; M.A., Atlanta U., 1964; Ph.D., Howard U., 1967. *Family:* Married Alice Walton. *Career:* Instr., Atlanta U., summer 1966; Assoc. Prof., Savannah State Coll., 1967- . *Honors:* Kappa Alpha Psi Scholarship & Achievement Award; Soc. Sci. Res. Council Fellow. *Mailing address:* c/o Scarecrow Press, 52 Liberty St., Metuchen, N.J. 08840.

Writings:
Nonfiction
The Political Philosophy of Martin Luther King, Jr. (Ann Arbor, Mich., U. Microfilms, 1967)

The Negro in Third Party Politics (Ardmore, Pa., Dorrance, 1969)

Black Political Parties; An Historical and Political Analysis (N.Y., Free Press, 1972)

Black Politics: A Theoretical and Structural Analysis (Phila., Lippincott, 1972)

The Poetry of Black Politics (London, Regency, 1972)

The Study and Analysis of Black Politics: A Bibliography (Metuchen, N.J., Scarecrow, 1973)

Political Theory and Political Broadcasting (n.p., William Frederick, 1973)

Black Republicans: The Politics of the Black and Tans (Scarecrow, 1975)

Source: Author information.

WALTON, ORTIZ MONTAIGNE. Teacher, Composer, Bassist.
Born in Chicago, Ill., Dec. 13, 1933. *Education:* B.S., Roosevelt U.; M.A., Ph.D., U. of Cal., Berkeley. *Family:* Married Carol Walton; son Omar Kwame. *Career:* Tchr., Sociol. of Afro-Amer. Music, Ethnic Studies, Lect. & Performer, Ellington Symposium, U. of Cal., Berkeley; Tchr., Mission Sch. of Music, San Francisco; Tchr., E. Bay Music Center; Master Classes in art of double bass performance; Solo Bassist, Cairo, Egypt. Symphony Orchestra: 1st Black & youngest, Boston Symphony Orchestra; Asst. Prin., Buffalo Philharmonic; Mem., Hartford, Conn., & Springfield, Mass., symphony orchestras; Prin. Bassist, Natl. Orchestra Assn., N.Y.C. *Honors:* Ford Found. Grant, 1972-73; Natl. Inst. of Mental Health Grant, 1968-71. *Mailing address:* 1129 Bancroft Way, Berkeley, Cal. 94702.

Writings:
Nonfiction

Coronation of the King: Contributions by Duke Ellington to Black Culture (Berkeley, U. of Cal. Press, 1969)

Music; Black, White and Blue; A Sociological Survey of the Use and Misuse of Afro-American Music (N.Y., Morrow, 1972)

Sidelights: Some of Walton's musical compositions are: "Night Letter to Duke" (an unaccompanied double bass sonata); songs with lyrics by Ishmael Reed, recorded by Black Box, 1972. (Author)

Source: Author information.

WARD, DOUGLAS TURNER. Actor, Playwright, Producer.
Born near Burnside, La., May 5, 1930. *Education:* Wilberforce U.; U. of Mich.; Paul Mann's Actors' Workshop, N.Y.C. *Career:* Made debut as actor in *The Iceman Cometh*; next, *Lost in the Stars*; *Raisin in the Sun.* Leading roles: *One Flew over the Cuckoo's Nest*; *Rich Little Rich Girl*; *The Blacks*; *Blood Knot*; *Coriolanus.* TV: "East Side, West Side"; "The DuPont Show of the Month"; "The Edge of Night"; & co-starred in CBS special "Look Up and Live." Founder, Negro Ensemble Co., 1968; Productions: Lonne Elder's *Ceremonies in Dark Old Men*; Wole Soyinka's *Kongi's Harvest*; plays by other Black writers; and Peter Weiss's *Song of the Lusitania Bogey.* In *The River Niger*, Ward took the lead. *Honors:* His 1st two plays, *Happy Ending & Day of Absence*, were produced at St. Mark's Playhouse on Nov. 15, 1965, and ran for 504 performances. They won both a Vernon Rice Drama Desk Award & an Obie Award. Ebony Black Achievement Award, 1980. *Mailing address:* 222 E. 11th St., N.Y., N.Y. 10003.

Writings:
Fiction

Happy Ending and Day of Absence, play (N.Y., Okpaku, 1966; N.Y., Dramatists Play Serv., 1968)

Two Plays (N.Y., Third Press, 1966, 1972; paper, Okpaku, 1971)

Brotherhood, play (Dramatists Play Serv., 1970)

The Reckoning, play (Dramatists Play Serv., 1970)

Sidelights: "Douglas Turner Ward ... called for the establishment of a Negro-oriented theater in New York. He envisioned it as combining both professional performances by a resident company, and an extensive training program for promising actors, playwrights, directors, and managerial and technical personnel. It is that vision which has been realized in the establishment of the Negro Ensemble Company." (*New Black Playwrights*)

Sources: *Black Drama*; *Black Scenes*; *Books in Print*, 1978-79; *Dictionary of Literary Biography*, Part 2: *Twentieth-Century American Dramatists*, 1981; *New Black Playwrights*.

WARD, SAMUEL RINGGOLD. Anti-Slavery Agent, Teacher.
Born in 1817. Parents escaped from slavery and brought him to N.Y. at age 3. Received some education. *Career:* Sch. tchr.; Minister; Anti-slavery agent (co-worker with Gerrit Smith). Died in 1864.

Writings:
Nonfiction

The Autobiography of a Fugitive Negro; His Anti-Slavery Labours in the United States, Canada, & England (London, J. Snow, 1855; reprint, Salem, N.Y., Ayer, 1968)

Sidelights: "In 1851, because of his inflamatory speechmaking ... he was forced to (flee) ... to Canada. He ... continued to lecture in Canada and England.... Frederick Douglass was the only Negro orator who was considered to be his superior. Douglass said of him: 'In depth of thought, fluency of speech, readiness of wit, logical exactness, and general intelligence, Samuel R. Ward has left no success among the colored men amongst us....' " He died in Jamaica. (*Negro Caravan*)

Sources: *Historical Negro Biographies*; *Negro Caravan*.

WARD, THEODORE. Playwright, Teacher, Actor.
Born in Thibodeaux, La., Sept. 15, 1902. *Education:* U. of Utah; U. of Wis. *Career:* "In 1940 he organized The Negro Playwrights Company in Harlem, in association with Langston Hughes, Paul Robeson and Richard Wright. He also aided in forming The Associated Playwrights, The Midwest People's Theatre, and The South Side Center of the Performing Arts, Inc." (*Black Scenes*). He wrote 22 plays. *Honors:* Zona Gale Fellow, U. of Wis.; Guggenheim Found. Fellow, 1948; *Our Lan'* won a Theatre Guild Award; Negro of the Year Award, 1947; DuSable Writers' Seminar & Poetry Festival Award, 1982. Died May 8, 1983, in Chicago.

Writings:
Fiction

Big White Fog, play (Chicago, T. Ward, 1937; produced by Fed. Theatre, Chicago, 1938)

Our Lan', play (produced off-Broadway in Henry St. Playhouse, 1946)

Sidelights: "One of the organizers of the Negro Playwrights Company, he is better known as the author of two powerful, enthusiastically acclaimed dramas—*Big White Fog* ... which critic Sterling Brown described as the most artistic production of the Federal Theater during the 1930's, and *Our Lan'*."

"A modified version [of *Our Lan'*] was produced on Broadway at the Royale Theatre in the fall of (1946)." (*Black Drama in America*)

Sources: *Black Drama in America*; *Black Scenes*; *Los Angeles Times*, May 14, 1983.

WASHINGTON, BOOKER TALIAFERRO. Educator, Statesman.
Born in Hale's Ford, Va., in Apr. 1856 (?). *Education:* Grad., Hampton Inst., Va., 1876; Wayland Sem., Wash., D.C. "The differences in the early experiences of [Frederick Douglass & Booker T. Washington] undoubtedly account for the differences in attitudes and approaches in their methods of attacking racial problems during their years of national leadership. While Douglass learned the hard way, through trial and error and bitter ideological battles with whites and blacks alike, Washington had the 'luxury' of a formal education in close association with white educators at Hampton Institute." (*Black Insights*). *Career:* Orator. Recalled to Hampton for study. Recommended to head new educ. project at Tuskegee, Ala. (which became Tuskegee Inst.); founded in 1881 with $2,000.

After 34 yrs., when he died Nov. 14, 1915, he left a coll. with 2,500 students, 111 buildings, and 3,500 acres of land. Considered the outstanding leader of his race; had written ten books, had delivered hundreds of speeches. *Honors:* Apptd. advisor to two Pres.; 1st Black to receive hon. degree from Harvard U.; 1st to dine at White House with a Pres. Died Nov. 14, 1915.

Writings:
Nonfiction

Black-Belt Diamonds: Gems from the Speeches, Addresses, and Talks to Students of Booker T. Washington (N.Y., Fortune & Scott, 1898; N.Y., reprint Negro Universities Press, 1969.)

The Future of the American Negro (Boston, Small, Maynard, 1899; reprint, N.Y., Haskell House, 1968)

The Story of My Life and Work, autobiog. (Toronto, Ont., Nashville, Ill., Nichols, 1900; reprint, Negro Universities Press, 1969)

A New Negro for a New Century: An Accurate and Up-to-Date Record of the Upward Struggle of the Negro Race (Chicago, Amer. Pub. House, 1900; facsimile ed., Arno, Black Heritage Lib. Collection)

Sowing and Reaping (Boston, L. C. Page, 1900; Freeport, N.Y., Bks. for Libs., 1971)

Up from Slavery; An Autobiography (Boston, Western Islands, 1901; N.Y., A. L. Burt, 1901; N.Y., Sun Dial, 1937; reprint, Williamstown, Mass., Corner House, 1971)

Character Building; Being Addresses Delivered on Sunday Evenings to the Students (N.Y., Doubleday, 1902; reprint, N.Y., Haskell, Studies in Black Hist. & Culture, no. 54, 1972)

Negro Problem: A Series of Articles by Representative American Negroes of Today (n.p., 1903; reprint, Arno, Amer. Negro—His Hist. & Lit. Ser., no. 2, n.d.)

Working with the Hands: Being a Sequel to Up from Slavery Covering the Author's Experience in Industrial Training at Tuskegee (Doubleday, 1904; reprint, Arno, Amer. Negro—His Hist. & Lit. Ser., 1969)

Tuskegee and Its People; Their Ideals and Achievements (N.Y., Appleton, 1905)

Frederick Douglass (Phila., G. W. Jacobs, 1906; N.Y., Greenwood, 1969)

The Negro in the South: His Economic Progress in Relation to His Moral and Religious Development; Being the William Levi Bull Lectures for the Year 1907, with W. E. B. DuBois (G. W. Jacobs, 1907; reprint, n.p., Metro Bks., 1972)

The Negro in Business (Boston, Chicago, Hertel, Jenkins, 1907; reprint, Metro Bks., 1969)

The Story of the Negro: The Rise of the Race from Slavery, 2 vols. (Doubleday, 1909; N.Y., Smith, 1940; reprint, Negro Universities Press, 1969)

My Larger Education; Being Chapters from My Experience (Doubleday, 1911)

Booker T. Washington's Own Story of His Life and Work Including an Authoritative Sixty-four Page Supplement by Albon L. Holsey ... the Original Autobiography Brought Up to Date with a Complete Account of Dr. Washington's Sickness and Death ... Containing the Only Photos of the Funeral and Burial (Nichols, 1915)

Selected Speeches of Booker T. Washington, ed. by E. Davidson Washington (Doubleday, 1932; Millwood, N.Y., Kraus Reprint, 1976)

Sidelights: "*Up From Slavery* ... has probably been reprinted more frequently than any other book by a Negro author and ranks in popularity with Benjamin Franklin's *Autobiography*." (*Cavalcade*)
"Booker T. Washington became a proponent of the belief that black people should help themselves through education rather than political demands." (*Afro-American Literature: Non-Fiction*)
"He was reviled by some Negroes who accused him of 'Uncle Tomism,' but he was venerated by an overwhelming majority of blacks as a modern savior." (*Black Insights*)

Sources: *Afro-American Literature: Non-Fiction*; *Black Insights*; *Books in Print*, 1981-82; *Cavalcade*; *Negro Almanac*; *Negroes Who Helped Build America*.

WASHINGTON, JOSEPH R., JR. Minister, Chaplain, Religion Professor.
Born in Iowa City, Iowa, Oct. 30, 1930. *Education:* B.A. (Sociol.), U. of Wis., 1952; B.D. (Soc. Ethics), Andover Newton Theol. Sem., 1957, advanced study, 1957-58; Th.D. (Soc. Ethics), Boston U. Sch. of Theol., 1961. *Family:* Married Sophia May Holland, Feb. 13, 1952; son Bryan Reed, son David Eugene. *Career:* 1st Lt., Military Police, U.S. Army, 1952-54; ordained to Bap. Church, 1957; Minister to students, First Bap. Church, Brookline, Mass., 1957-58; Assoc. Protestant Chaplain, Boston, Mass., 1958-61; Dean of Chapel & Asst. Prof. of Relig. & Philosophy, Dillard U., New Orleans; Chaplain & Asst. Prof. of Relig. & Philosophy, Dickinson Coll., Carlisle, Pa., 1963-?; Chairman, Afro-Amer. Studies, U. of Va. *Honors:* Iron Cross, U. of Wis. (contrib. to life of the universe); D.D. degree, U. of Vt., 1969; Danforth Assoc. *Mailing address:* B-12 Cocke Hall, U. of Va., Charlottesville, Va. 22901.

Writings:
   Nonfiction
   Black Religion: The Negro and Christianity in the United States (Boston, Beacon, 1964)

   The Politics of God (Beacon, 1967)

   Black and White Power Subreption (Beacon, 1969)

   Marriage in Black and White (Beacon, 1970)

   Black Sects and Cults (N.Y., Doubleday, 1972)

Source: Author information.

WASHINGTON, LEON H., JR. Newspaper Publisher.
Born in Kan. City, Kan., Apr. 15, 1907. *Education:* Sumner High Sch.; Washburn Coll., Topeka, Kan. *Family:* Married Ruth Washington. *Career:* Beginning in 1930 worked with *California News & California Eagle.* Started a throwaway weekly, *Shoppers News*; later founded the *Los Angeles Sentinel* (1934). Died June 17, 1974.

Writings:
   Nonfiction
   Los Angeles Sentinel, newspaper (1934-)

Sidelights: "*Sentinel* became known as the 'voice' of Black people west of the Rockies. For the past [fifty] ... years the *Los Angeles Sentinel* has constantly and consistently articulated the needs, hopes and aspirations of the Los Angeles Black community ... beginning in 1934 with the movement launched by Colonel Washington with the slogan: 'Don't Spend Your Money Where You Can't Work.' That campaign, along with many similar activities, put his paper in the forefront of the civil rights movement for equality in employment, education, housing and every phase of American life for all minorities." (Obituary)

Source: Obituary, June 1974.

WASHINGTON, MARY HELEN. English Professor, Anthologist.
Born in Cleveland, Ohio, Jan. 21, 1941. *Education:* B.A., Notre Dame Coll., 1962; M.A., 1966, Ph.D., 1976, U. of Detroit. *Career:* Eng. Tchr., high sch., Cleveland, Ohio, 1962-64; Instr., Eng., St. John Coll., Cleveland, 1966-68; Asst. Prof., Eng., 1972-75, Dir., Center for Black Studies, 1975- , U. of Detroit; Assoc. Prof., Eng., U. of Mass., Boston (present). *Honors:* Richard Wright Award for Literary Criticism, *Black World*, 1974; Bunting Fellow, Radcliffe Coll. *Mailing address:* c/o Eng. Dept., U. of Mass., Boston, Mass. 02109.

Writings:
   Fiction
   Black-Eyed Susans, anthology, ed. (N.Y., Doubleday, 1975)

   Midnight Birds: Stories of Contemporary Black Women Writers, anthology (N.Y., Anchor, 1980)

Sources: *Contemporary Authors*, vols. 65-68, 1977; *Freedomways*, vol. 21, no. 4, 1981.

WEAVER, ROBERT CLIFTON. Economist, Former Secretary of Housing and Urban Development, Urban Affairs Professor.

Born in Wash., D.C., Dec. 29, 1907. *Education:* B.S. (cum laude), 1929, M.A., 1931, Ph.D., Harvard U. *Family:* Married Dr. Ella Haith, July 19, 1935; son Robert. *Career:* Visiting Prof., Sch. of Educ., N.Y.U., 1947-51; Dir., Opportunity Fellowships, John Hay Whitney Found., 1949-54; N.Y., State Rent Admin., 1955-59; V. Chairman, N.Y.C. Housing & Redevelopment Bd., 1960-61; Admin., U.S. Housing & Home Finance Agency, 1961-66; Secy., U.S. Dept. of Housing & Urban Development, 1966-68; Pres., Baruch Coll., CUNY, 1969-70; Prof. of Econ., CUNY, 1970-71; Distinguished Prof. of Urban Affairs, Hunter Coll., 1971- . *Honors:* (Hon. degrees) LL.D., Litt.D., D.H.L., D.S.S., D.P.A. from 39 coll. & universities. (Awards) Spingarn Medal, 1962; Russwurm Award, 1964; Albert Einstein Commemorative Award, 1968. *Mailing address:* Dept. of Urban Affairs, Hunter Coll., 790 Madison Ave., N.Y., N.Y. 10021.

Writings:

Nonfiction

Male Negro Skilled Workers in the United States, 1930-36, monograph (Wash., D.C., Govt. Printing Office, 1939)

Negro Labor: A National Problem (N.Y., Harcourt, 1946; Port Wash., N.Y., Kennikat, 1969)

The Negro Ghetto (Harcourt, 1948; N.Y., Russell, 1967)

The Urban Complex; Human Values in Urban Life (N.Y., Doubleday, 1964; N.Y., Anchor, 1966; Spanish: Bibliografica Omeba, Buenos Aires, 1969)

Dilemmas of Urban America (Cambridge, Harvard U. Press, 1965; N.Y., Atheneum, 1967; Portuguese: Distribuidora Record, Rio de Janeiro, 1967; Spanish: Pax-Mexico, Mexico City, 1972)

Sidelights: He "served as member of the 'Black Cabinet' during Roosevelt's administration.... The group, with Mary McLeod Bethune as titular head, consisted of Ralph Bunche, William Hastie, James C. Evans and others. Weaver was considered the architect of the group and the most influential." (*Negroes in Public Affairs and Government*)

Sources: Author information; *Negro Handbook*; *Negroes in Public Affairs and Government*; Pub. information.

WEBB, SHEYANN. Autobiographer.

Born in Dallas County, Ala., Feb. 17, 1956. *Education:* Selma High Sch.; B.S. (honors, Soc. Work), Tuskegee Inst., Ala., 1979; grad. stud., Counseling. *Family:* Single. *Career:* Autobiographer. *Honors:* Stud. Govt. Assn., Stud. Coordinator, 1978-79; Dean's List, Tuskegee Inst.; Who's Who in Amer. Coll. & U.; Soc. Work Honors Assn. *Mailing address:* 312 E. GWC Homes, Selma, Ala. 36701.

Writings:

Nonfiction

Selma, Lord, Selma: Girlhood Memories of the Civil Rights Days, autobiog., with Rachel W. Nelson (University, U. of Ala. Press, 1980; paper, N.Y., Morrow, 1980)

Sources: Author information; *Books in Print*, 1980-81.

WELBURN, RONALD GARFIELD, Poet, Musician, Critic, Teacher, Editor.

Born in Bryn Mawr, Pa., Apr. 30, 1944. *Education:* B.A., Lincoln U. (Pa.), 1968; M.A., U. of Ariz., 1970. *Family:* Married Eileen Welburn. *Career:* Instr., Afro-Amer. Studies, Syracuse U., 1970-73; Asst. Prof., 1973- ; Creative Writing Consultant, Auburn Correctional Facility, Auburn, N.Y., 1972; Advisory Ed., *Open Workshop*, ed. by Gil Scot-Heron, 1967-68; Assoc. Ed., *Obsidian: Black Literature in Review*, 1974; Ed.-in-Chief, *Dues: An Annual of New Earth Writing. Honors:* Lincoln U.: Journalism Key, 1966-67; Edward S. Silvera Award for Poetry, 1967 & 1968; William Eichelberger Award for Prose, 1967; Amy T. Lockett Memorial Prize, Outstanding Serv. to Campus &

Community, 1968; Class of 1899 Prize for Eng. Studies, 1968; S. Grad. Study Fellow, 1968-70. *Mailing address:* c/o Lotus Press, P.O. Box 601, Coll. Park Station, Detroit, Mich. 48221.

Writings:
Fiction

Peripheries: Selected Poems, 1966-1968, vol. I (Greenfield Center, N.Y., Greenfield Review Press, 1972)

Dues: An Annual of New Earth Writing, anthology, nos. 1 & 2, ed. (N.Y., Emerson Hall, 1973)

Along the Estabon Way, poems (Emerson Hall, 1973)

Brown Up, and Other Poems (Greenfield Review Press, 1977)

Heartland: Selected Poems (Detroit, Lotus, 1981)

Sources: Author information; *Books in Print*, 1979-80, 1981-82; *New Black Voices*; *Poetry of Black America*.

WELLS (BARNETT), IDA BELL. Civil Rights Activist, Editor.
Born in Holly Springs, Miss., July 16, 1862. *Education:* Rust Coll., Miss.; Fisk U. (summers, 1884-91). *Family:* Married Ferdinand Lee Barnett (attorney), 1895; son Charles A., son Herman K., d. Ida B. Wells-Barnett, Jr., d. Alfreda M. Barnett Duster. *Career:* Writer, *The Living War* (newspaper); Part-owner, Ed., Memphis *Free Speech*; Assoc. (to T. Thomas Fortune), *New York Age*; Natl. Equal Rights League (with William Monroe Trotter); civic & polit. leader, Chicago. *Honors:* "The first Federal Housing Project in Chicago was named The Ida B. Wells Homes in 1940." (Alfreda B. Duster, daughter). Died March 25, 1931.

Writings:
Nonfiction

On Lynchings: Southern Horrors (N.Y., N.Y. Age, 1892; Wash., D.C., Amer. Negro – His Hist. & Lit. Ser., no. 2, 1969)

A Red Record (Chicago, Donahue & Henneberry, 1895; Wash., D.C., Amer. Negro – His Hist. & Lit. Ser., 1969)

Mob Rule in New Orleans (n.p., n.p., 1900; N.Y., Arno & N.Y. Times, 1969)

Crusade for Justice: The Autobiography of Ida B. Wells, ed. by Alfreda Duster (Chicago, U. of Chicago Press, 1970)

Sidelights: "In 1892, three Negro businessmen were horribly lynched in Memphis and Ida B. Wells charged, in the columns of *Free Speech*, that the murders had been instigated and planned by the white business community. She urged Blacks not to support these business establishments, but to migrate to new Oklahoma territory. Business suffered and they migrated by the scores. Fortunately she had left town, but her presses and equipment were destroyed by fire. She was threatened with execution, so she could not return." (*Negro Handbook*)

Sources: Information from author's daughter; *Negro Handbook*.

WESLEY, CHARLES HARRIS. College President, History Professor, Historian, Clergyman.
Born in Louisville, Ky., Dec. 2, 1891. *Education:* B.A., Fisk U., 1911; M.A., Yale U., 1913; Guild Internationale, Paris, 1914; Howard U. Law Sch., 1915-16; Ph.D., Harvard U., 1925. *Family:* Married 1st Louise Johnson, Nov. 25, 1915; d. Louise Johnson, d. Charlotte Harris; married 2nd Dorothy Porter, Nov. 30, 1979. *Career:* Howard U.: Instr. to Assoc. Prof., 1914-20, Prof. of Hist. & Head, Dept., 1921-42, Acting Dean, Coll. of Liberal Arts, 1937-38, Dean of Grad. Sch., 1938-42. Pres., Wilberforce U., 1942-47 (became Central State U.), 1942-65. Pastor & Presiding Elder, AME Church, 1918-37. Executive Dir., ASNLH, 1965-72. *Honors:* Hon. degrees: D.D., Wilberforce U.; LL.D., Allen U., Va. State Coll., Morris Brown U., Paul Quin Coll., Campbell Coll., Western U.; Litt.D., Morgan State Coll. Scholarships: Yale U., 1913, Harvard U., 1920-21. Guggenheim Found. Fellow, 1930-31. *Mailing address:* c/o ASNLH, 1538 Ninth St., N.W., Wash., D.C. 20001.

Writings:
Nonfiction

Negro Labor in the United States, 1850-1925: A Study in American Economic History (N.Y., Vanguard, 1927, reprint, 1967)

The History of Alpha Phi Alpha; A Development in Negro College Life (Wash., D.C., Howard U. Press, 1929, 1935; Wash., D.C., Foundation Pub., 1939, 1959, 1961)

Richard Allen, Apostle of Freedom (Wash., D.C., Assoc. Pubs., 1935)

The Collapse of the Confederacy (Assoc. Pubs., 1937; N.Y., Russell, 1968)

Ohio Negroes in the Civil War (Columbus, Ohio State U. Press, 1962)

Negro Americans in the Civil War; From Slavery to Citizenship, with Patricia W. Romero (N.Y., Pubs. Co., 1967, 2nd ed., 1968, rev. ed., 1969; Wash., D.C., ASNLH, 1976)

Quest for Equality; From Civil War to Civil Rights (Pubs. Co., 1968; ASNLH, 1976)

Neglected History: Essays in Negro History by a College President (ASNLH, 1969)

History of Sigma Pi Phi, First of the Negro American Greek-letter Fraternities (ASNLH, 1969)

The Fifteenth Amendment and Black America, 1870-1970 (Assoc. Pub., 1970)

In Freedom's Footsteps, from the African Background to the Civil War (Pubs. Co., 1970)

Afro-American Encyclopedia, ed. with Martin Rywell, 10 vols. (Miami, Educ. Bk. Publ., 1974)

Henry Arthur Callis: Life and Legacy (Chicago, Foundation Pub., 1977)

Prince Hall: Life and Legacy (Wash., D.C., U.S. Supreme Council, Prince Hall Affiliation, 1977)

Sources: *Negro Almanac*; *Negro Caravan*; *Negro Handbook*; *Who's Who in Colored America*, 7th ed., 1950.

WESLEY, RICHARD ERROL. Playwright, Editor, Teacher.
Born in Newark, N.J., July 11, 1945. *Education:* B.F.A., Howard U., 1967. *Family:* Married Valerie Wesley; d. Thembi Amala. *Career:* Passenger Agent, United Air Lines, 1967-69; Managing Ed., *Black Theatre*; Tchr., Wesleyan U., Conn., & Manhattanville Coll., Purchase, N.Y. *Honors:* Spec. playwriting, Samuel French Pub. Co., 1965; Drama Desk Award for Outstanding Playwriting, 1972. *Mailing address:* Nasaba Artists, Inc., Suite 910, 1860 Broadway, N.Y., N.Y. 10018.

Writings:
Fiction

Put My Dignity on 307, presentation on WRC-TV's "Operation Awareness," (May 1967)

The Streetcorner, play (prod. at Black Arts, W. Seattle, Wash., 1970)

Headline News, play (Black Theatre Workshop, Harlem, 1970)

Knock, Knock, Who Dat, play (Theatre Black, U. of the Streets, N.Y.C., 1970)

Getting It Together, play (Theatre Black, Bed-Sty Theatre, Brooklyn, 1971)

Black Terror, play (Howard U., Wash., D.C., 1971)

The Mighty Gents, play (N.Y., Dramatists Play Serv., 1979)

Sidelights: Other plays are: *The Sirens*, *The Past Is the Past*, and *Goin' Thru Changes*. Movies are: *Uptown Saturday Night* and *The Ernie Davis Story*.

Source: Author information.

WHARTON, CLIFTON REGINALD, JR. University President, Economist, Foreign Policy Specialist. Born in Boston, Mass., Sept. 13, 1926 (son of Clifton R. Wharton, Sr., America's 1st Black career diplomat & ambassador). *Education:* Boston Latin Sch.; B.A. (cum laude), Harvard U., 1947; M.A. (Intnl. Studies), Johns Hopkins Sch. of Advanced Intnl. Studies, 1948; M.A. (Econ.), 1956, Ph.D. (Econ.), U. of Chicago, 1958. *Family:* Married Dolores Duncan (writer); son Clifton R. III, son Bruce D. *Career:* Head, Reports & Analysis Dept., Amer. Intnl. Assn. for Econ. & Soc. Development, N.Y., 1948-53; Visiting Prof., U. of Malaya, 1958-64, & Stanford U., 1964-65; Agricultural Development Council, N.Y.; Council Assn. for Malaysia, Thailand, Vietnam, & Cambodia: 1964-66, Acting Dir., 1966-67, V. Pres., 1967-70; Pres. & Prof. of Econ., Mich. State U., E. Lansing, 1970-78; Chancellor, SUNY, 1978- . *Honors:* Named Boston Latin Sch. "Man of the Year," 1970; Amistad Award from Amer. Missionary Assn., 1970; D. Laws: U. of Mich., Johns Hopkins U., & Wayne State U., 1970; Dr. of Pub. Serv., Central Mich. U., 1970; Alumni Prof. Achievement Award, U. of Chicago, 1971; D.H.L., Oakland U., 1971; awarded Alumni Medal by U. of Chicago, 1980. *Mailing address:* Chancellor's Office, State U. of N.Y., State U. Plaza, Albany, N.Y. 12246.

Writings:
Nonfiction

U.S. Graduate Training of Asian Agricultural Economists (N.Y., Council on Econ. & Cultural Affairs, 1959)

Research on Agricultural Development in Southeast Asia (N.Y., Agricultural Development Council, 1965)

Subsistence Agriculture and Economic Development, ed. (Chicago, Aldine, 1969)

Sidelights: "... Chancellor of the 64-campus State University of New York. He was honored for his outstanding accomplishments as educator, economist, foreign policy expert, and crusader against the trauma of starvation." (*University of Chicago Magazine*)

Sources: *Contemporary Authors*, vols. 41-44, 1974; *Information Service*, Mich. State U., 1974; *University of Chicago Magazine*, Sept. 1980.

WHEATLEY, PHILLIS. Poet.
Born in Senegal, W. Africa, in 1753. Kidnapped on slave ship to Boston, c. 1761. Personal servant to wife of John Wheatley, who educated her liberally. Married John Peters (free Black), 1778; three children. Died in 1784.

Writings:
Fiction

An Elegiac Poem, on the Death of That Celebrated Divine, and Eminent Servant of Jesus Christ, the Reverend and Learned George Whitefield, Chaplain to the Right Honorable the Countess of Huntington, &c, &c (Boston, Esekiel Russell, 1770)

Poems on Various Subjects, Religious and Moral, only book (Boston, A. Bell, 1773; reprint of 1776 ed., N.Y., AMS, n.d.)

Memoir and Poems of Phillis Wheatley; A Native African and a Slave (Boston, G. W. Light, 1834; 2nd ed., Boston, Light & Horton, 1835; 3rd ed., Boston, Knapp, 1838; facsimile of 1838 ed., Salem, N.Y., n.d.)

Poems and Letters; First Collected Edition, ed. by Charles Frederick Heartman (N.Y., C. F. Heartman, 1915)

Nonfiction

Letters of Phillis Wheatley, the Negro-Slave Poet of Boston, ed. by Charles Deane (Boston, J. Wilson, 1864)

Phillis Wheatley and Her Writings, ed. by William H. Robinson (N.Y., Garland, 1984)

Sidelights: Miss Wheatley left 46 known poems, 18 of which were elegies. Exposed to typical New England education after alertness noted; able to read most difficult parts of classics and Bible, within 16 months of being in the country. High point of life, in 1773 when she received freedom, and was sent to London for health. Met distinguished Londoners, had book published. Returned to Boston.... Fortunes declined, her mentors died, she married, bore children; reduced to common domestic work and early death at age 31, when frail health completely gave way. (*Early Negro American Writers*)

Sources: *Afro-American Writers*; *Black American Literature: Poetry*; *Cavalcade*; *Early Black American Poets*; *Early Negro American Writers*; *Poetry of the Negro, 1746-1949*; *Who Was Who in America, Historical Vol., 1607-1896*, rev. ed.

WHITE, WALTER FRANCIS. Novelist, Essayist, NAACP Secretary, Civil Rights Leader.
Born in Atlanta, Ga., July 1, 1893. *Education:* B.A., Atlanta U., 1916; Coll. of City of N.Y.; LL.D. (hon.), Howard U., 1939. *Family:* Married 1st Leah Gladys Powell of Ithaca, N.Y.; d. Jane, son Walter Carl Darrow; married 2nd Poppy Cannon. *Career:* Atlanta Life Insurance Co.; NAACP: Asst. Executive Secy. (to James Weldon Johnson), Executive Secy., 1934-55. *Honors:* Guggenheim Found. Fellow, 1927, 1928; Spingarn Medal, 1937; Delegate, Second Pan-African Congress, 1921. Died in 1955.

Writings:
Fiction
Fire in the Flint, novel (N.Y., Knopf, 1924; reprint, N.Y., Negro Universities Press, 1969)

Flight, novel (Knopf, 1926; reprint, Negro Universities Press, 1969)

Nonfiction
Rope and Faggot: A Biography of Judge Lynch (N.Y. & London, Knopf, 1929; reprint, Salem, N.Y., Ayer, 1969)

A Rising Wind (N.Y., Doubleday, 1945; reprint, Negro Universities Press, 1971)

A Man Called White; The Autobiography of Walter White (N.Y., Viking, 1948; reprint, Ayer, 1969)

How Far the Promised Land? (Viking, 1955; reprint, N.Y., AMS)

Sidelights: "The NAACP under White's direction fought diligently and forcefully for equality in civil rights, focusing attention on the evils and horrors of lynchings and pushing relentlessly for an end to discrimination and segregation in travel and education."
One of the goals that Walter White set out to achieve was the famous 1954 decision of the Supreme Court against segregated schools. (*Historical Negro Biographies*)

Sources: *Current Biography*, 1942; *Historical Negro Biographies*; *Negro Caravan*; *The Negro Genius*.

WHITMAN, ALBERY ALLISON. Poet.
Born near Munfordsville, Hart County, Ky., May 30, 1851. *Education:* Intermittent; Wilberforce U., Ohio. *Career:* Poet-Evangelist, AME circuit, Ohio & Kan.; Sch. tchr. Died in 1901.

Writings:
Fiction
Leelah Misled, poems (Elizabethtown, Ky., Richard LaRue, 1873)

Not a Man and Yet a Man, with Miscellaneous Poems (Springfield, Ohio, Republic Printery, 1877; facsimile ed., Salem, N.Y., Ayer, n.d.)

The Rape of Florida (St. Louis, Mo., Nixon, Jones, 1884; facsimile ed., Ayer, n.d.)

Twasinta's Seminoles, or, Rape of Florida, poems (Nixon, Jones, 1885)

Drifted Leaves, poems (St. Louis, n.p., 1890)

The World's Fair Poems: The Freedmen's Triumphant Song (Atlanta, Halsey Job, 1893)

An Idyl of the South, an Epic Poem in Two Parts (N.Y., Metaphysical Pub., 1901)

Sidelights: *Drifted Leaves* was dedicated to Confederate veterans and "received wide circulation in the press throughout the country." Whitman was one of the many beneficiaries of Bishop Daniel Payne. (*Early Black American Poets*)

Sources: *Early Black American Poets*; *Negro Caravan*.

WIDEMAN, JOHN EDGAR. Novelist, Short Story Writer, Teacher.
Born in Washington, D.C., June 14, 1941. *Education:* B.A., U. of Pa., 1963; B. Philosophy, New Coll., Oxford U., 1966. *Career:* Assoc. Prof. in Eng. & Dir. of Afro-Amer. Studies Program, U. of Pa., 1967- . *Honors:* Rhodes Scholar, New Coll., Oxford U., 1963-66. *Mailing address:* c/o Avon Bks., 959 8th Ave., N.Y., N.Y. 10019.

Writings:
Fiction

A Glance Away, novel (N.Y., Harcourt, 1967; reprint, Old Greenwich, Conn., Chatham, 1975)

Hurry Home, novel (Harcourt, 1970)

The Lynchers, novel (HarBraceJ, 1973)

Hiding Place, novel (N.Y., Avon, 1981)

Damballah, short stories (Avon, 1981)

Sent for You Yesterday, novel (Avon, 1983)

Sources: *Books in Print*, 1978-79, 1981-82; *Freedomways*, vol. 21, no. 4, 1981; *Interviews with Black Writers*.

WILKIN, BINNIE TATE. Librarian, Lecturer, Specialist in Children's Literature and Services, Minority Services Coordinator.
Born in Greenville, N.C. *Education:* B.A., N.C. Central U., 1954; M.S.L.S., SUNY, Albany, 1957. *Career:* Librn.: Elementary schs., Wilson, N.C., Schenectady County Public Lib., N.Y.; Fla. Normal Coll., St. Augustine; Albion Public Lib., Mich.; Senior Children's Spec., Fed. Project, L.A. Public Lib., Cal.; Assoc. Prof., U. of Wis., Milwaukee; Lect., Cal. State U., Fullerton; Lect., UCLA; Minority Services Coordinator, L.A. County Public Lib., 1981-84; Lect. U. Cal., Berkeley. *Honors:* Graduated cum laude, N.C. Central U.; Certificate of Merit, L.A. Public Lib., 1970; Nominated Librarian of the Year, L.A. County Public Lib., 1984; Apptd. Co-Chair, ALA, President's Commission on Services to Minorities, 1984. *Mailing address:* 5006 Victoria Ave., L.A., Cal. 90043.

Writings:
Nonfiction

The Role of the Public Library as an Alternative Force in Early Childhood Education, commissioned paper (N.Y., Tchrs. Coll., Columbia U., Div. of Lib. Programs, Office of Educ., 1974)

Survival Themes in Fiction for Children and Young People (Metuchen, N.J., Scarecrow, 1978)

Sidelights: Conducts workshops in ethnicity and performance of stories with dance. (Consultant) Institute on Library Service to Disadvantaged, Washington State University; Right to Read Seminar, Systems Development Corporation, Los Angeles, California; A National Network for the Acquisition, Organizing, Processing and Dissemination of Materials by and about Blacks, Urban Resource Incorporated and Florida Agricultural and Mechanical University; Institute on Black Materials and Programs for Black Children, Alabama Agricultural and Mechanical University; Black Images in Literature, Alabama State University; Excellence in Children's Literature and Children and Computers, U. Cal., Berkeley; Master Plan Steering Com. and Task Force, State Library. (Author)

Sources: Author information; *Books in Print*, 1981-82.

WILKINS, ROGER. Lawyer, Assistant Attorney General of United States, Journalist (Pulitzer Prize Winner).

Born in Kan. City, Mo., Mar. 25, 1932. *Education:* B.A., 1953, LL.B., 1956, U. of Mich. *Family:* Married 1st Eve Tyler (div.); married 2nd Patricia King; children: Amy, David. *Career:* Attorney, N.Y.C., 1956-62; Foreign Aid Dir., State Dept., 1962-66; Asst. Attorney Gen., U.S. Justice Dept., 1966-69; Program Dir., Ford Found., 1969-72; Spec. Asst., Agency for Intnl. Development; Ed. Page Staff, *Washington Post*, 1972-74; Ed. Bd., *N.Y. Times*; Dir., Community Relations Serv., 1965- . *Honors:* Pulitzer Prize Winner, *Washington Post* (Watergate editorials); Bd. of Visitors, U. Mich. Law Sch.; Hon. LL.D., Central Mich. U., 1974. *Mailing address:* c/o Simon & Schuster, 1230 6th Ave., N.Y., N.Y. 10020.

Writings:
Nonfiction

A Man's Life; An Autobiography (N.Y., Simon & Schuster, 1982, also paper, 1984)

Sidelights: Nephew of Roy Wilkins, late Executive Director of National Association for the Advancement of Colored People. Both of his parents were college graduates: father (who died early) was a journalist; mother is presently a Young Women's Christian Association national board member.

A Man's Life is a sensitive, revealing portrait of the life of a middle-class Black, who has sat in the seat of power. (Compilers)

Sources: *Books in Print*, 1983-84; *A Man's Life*; *Negroes in Public Affairs and Government*; *Who's Who among Black Americans*, 1975-76.

WILKINS, ROY. Executive Secretary (NAACP), Civil Rights Leader.

Born in St. Louis, Mo., Aug. 30, 1901. *Education:* A.B., U. of Minn., 1923. *Family:* Married Aminda A. Bandeau, Sept. 15, 1929. *Career:* Managing Ed., *Kansas City Call*; Asst. Secy., Executive Secy., (Natl.) NAACP, 1931-77; Ed., *Crisis*, 1934-49. *Honors:* Outstanding Achievement Award, U. of Minn., 1960. Died Sept. 8, 1981.

Writings:
Nonfiction

Search and Destroy: A Report, with Ramsay Clark for Com. of Inquiry into the Black Panthers & the Police (N.Y., Metropolitan Applied Res. Center, 1973)

Talking It Over with Roy Wilkins: Selected Speeches and Writings (Norwalk, Conn., M & B, 1977)

Standing Fast: The Autobiography of Roy Wilkins, with Tom Mathews (N.Y., Viking, 1982)

Sidelights: In reviewing *Standing Fast*, David Bradley relates: "This intimate and often personal account provides a stiff backbone to Wilkins' often attacked position: 'We believed that citizenship had to be firmly secured in law, or it would become a whimsical thing, dependent on local or regional happenstance.' " (*Los Angeles Times Book Review*)

Sources: *Books in Print*, 1979-80; *Current Biography*, 1964; *Los Angeles Times Book Review*, Aug. 29, 1982; *Search and Destroy*.

WILKINSON, BRENDA S. Juvenile Writer.

Born in Moultrie, Ga., Jan. 1, 1946. *Education:* Hunter Coll., CUNY. *Family:* Separated; children: Kim, Lori. *Career:* Juvenile Writer. *Honors:* Natl. Bk. Award nominee, 1976. *Mailing address:* c/o Harper & Row Pub., 10 E. 53rd St., N.Y., N.Y. 10022.

Writings:
Fiction

Ludell, juv. (N.Y., Harper, 1975)

Ludell and Willie, juv. (Harper, 1977, also paper, 1981)

Ludell's New York Time, juv. (Harper, 1980)

Sources: *Books in Print*, 1980-81; *Something about the Author*, vol. 14, 1978.

WILKINSON, DORIS YVONNE. Sociology Professor, Sociologist.
Born in Lexington, Ky., June 13, 1938. *Education:* B.A., U. of Ky., 1958; M.A., 1960, Ph.D., 1966, Case Western Reserve U. *Career:* Instr., Sociol., Kent State U., Ohio, 1961-63; Asst. Dir., Intergroup Relations Workshop, Case Western Reserve U., summers 1963, 1965, 1966; Instr., Sociol., Carnegie Mellon U., Pittsburgh, Pa., 1966-67; Asst. Prof., U. of Ky., Lexington, 1967-70; Consultant, Natl. Com. on Causes & Prevention of Crime, 1968-69; Assoc. Prof., Macalester Coll., St. Paul, Minn., 1970- . *Honors:* Woodrow Wilson Found. Fellow, 1959-61; Delta Tau Kappa; Outstanding Woman Faculty Mem., U. of Ky., 1969. *Mailing address:* c/o Nelson-Hall Pub., 111 N. Canal St., Chicago, Ill. 60606.

Writings:
Nonfiction

Black Revolt: The Strategies of Protest, ed. (Berkeley, Cal., McCutchan, 1969)

Black Male/White Female: Perspectives on Interracial Marriage and Courtship (Cambridge, Mass., Schenkman, 1975)

The Black Male in America: Perspectives on His Status in Contemporary Society, ed. with Ronald L. Taylor (Chicago, Nelson-Hall, 1977)

Sources: *Books in Print*, 1978-79; *Living Black American Authors*.

WILLIAMS, CHANCELLOR. Historian, History Professor, Novelist.
Born in 1902. *Education:* Doctorate, Amer. U. *Career:* Prof., African Hist., Howard U.; Visiting Res. Scholar, Oxford U.; African Hist. Studies, U. of Ghana; Economist, U.S. Govt. *Mailing address:* 40 Carlton House, 91 Station St., Ajax, Ontario, Can. LIS 3H2.

Writings:
Fiction

The Raven, novel (Phila., Dorrance, 1943; reprint, N.Y., AMS, n.d.)

Have You Been to the River?, novel (Hicksville, N.Y., Exposition, 1952)

Nonfiction

The Rebirth of African Civilization (Wash., D.C., Public Affairs Press, 1961)

The Destruction of Black Civilization: Great Issues of a Race from 4500 B.C. to 2000 A.D. (Dubuque, Iowa, Kendall/Hunt Pub., 1971; rev. ed., Chicago, Third World, 1974)

The Second Agreement with Hell (Ontario, Can., Carlton House, 1979)

Sources: *Books in Print*, 1978-79; *The Destruction of Black Civilization*; *Dictionary Catalog of the Negro Collection of Fisk University Library*; *Dictionary Catalog of the Schomburg Collection of Negro Literature and History*; *In Black and White*, 3rd ed., 1980.

WILLIAMS, ERIC EUSTACE. (Trinidadian). Prime Minister (Trinidad and Tobago), Political Science Professor, Historian.
Born in Port-of-Spain, Trinidad, 1911. *Education:* Tranquillity Intermediate Sch. & Queen's Royal Coll. (both Port-of-Spain); B.A. (honors), Hist. & Polit. Sci., 1932, Ph.D., Oxford U., 1938. *Family:* Married three times; d. Erica. *Career:* Prof., Soc. & Polit. Sci., Howard U., 1939-53. Chief Minister; Minister of Finance, Planning, & Development; Prime Minister (all Trinidad & Tobago). *Honors:* In Jan. 1964 he was designated a Privy Councillor by Queen Elizabeth of Great Britain. Died Mar. 31, 1981.

Writings:
Nonfiction

The Negro in the Caribbean (Wash., D.C., Associates in Negro Folk Educ., 1942)

Capitalism and Slavery (Chapel Hill, U. of N.C. Press, 1944; N.Y., Russell, 1961)

Goon in the Block (London, Cape, 1945)

Education in the British West Indies, 1807-1833 (Port-of-Spain, Trinidad, Guardian Commercial Printery, 1952; N.Y., U. Place, 1968)

History of the People of Trinidad and Tobago (Port-of-Spain, Trinidad, PNM Pub. Co., 1962; N.Y., Praeger, 1964; London, Deutsch, 1964)

Documents of West Indian History, 1492-1655 (PNM Pub. Co., 1963)

British Historians and the West Indies (PNM Pub. Co., 1964; Deutsch, 1966; N.Y., African Pub., 1972)

Inward Hunger: The Education of a Prime Minister (Deutsch, 1969; Chicago, U. of Chicago Press, 1971)

From Columbus to Castro: The History of the Caribbean, 1492-1969 (Deutsch, 1970; N.Y., Har-Row, 1971)

Sidelights: "After founding Trinidad's first stable political party, the People's National Movement ... guided Trinidad and Tobago to independence within the British Commonwealth in 1962." (*Afro-American Encyclopedia*)

After publication of his dissertation by the University of North Carolina Press in 1944, "it was described by Henry Steele Commager in a review in the New York *Herald Tribune* ... as 'one of the most learned, most penetrating, and most significant [monographs] that has appeared in this field of history.' " (*Current Biography*)

Sources: *Afro-American Encyclopedia*; *Bibliography of the Caribbean*; *Complete Caribbeana, 1900-1975*; *Current Biography*, 1966; *International Who's Who*, 1965-66.

WILLIAMS, ETHEL LANGLEY. Librarian, Bibliographer.
Born in Baltimore, Md., July 13, 1909. *Education:* B.A. (Hist.), Howard U., 1930; B.S., Columbia U., 1933; M.L.S., 1950 (Lib. Sci.); Howard U., 1947-50. *Family:* Married Louis J. Williams; d. Carole Juanita Jones. *Career:* Process Filer & Order Searcher, Lib. of Congress, 1936-40; Supvr. at Howard U.: (WPA) Moorland-Spingarn Collection, 1939, Ref. Librn., Cataloger, 1941-47, Sch. of Relig. Lib., 1946- . *Mailing address:* 1925 Primrose Rd., N.W., Wash., D.C. 20012.

Writings:

Nonfiction

Biographical Directory of Negro Ministers, ed. (Metuchen, N.J., Scarecrow, 1965, 1970, 1974; Boston, G. K. Hall, Ser. Seventy, 1975)

Afro-American Religious Studies: A Comprehensive Bibliography with Locations in American Libraries, comp. with Clifton L. Brown (Scarecrow, 1972, 1974)

The Howard University Bibliography of African and Afro-American Religious Studies: With Locations in American Libraries, with Clifton L. Brown (Wilmington, Del., Scholarly Resources, 1977)

Sources: Author information; *Books in Print*, 1981-82.

WILLIAMS, GEORGE WASHINGTON. Historian, Lawyer, Minister, Editor.
Born in Bedford Springs, Pa., Oct. 16, 1849 (of German, Negro, & Welsh descent). *Education:* Howard U.; Newton Theol. Sem., grad. 1874; Cincinnati Law Sch. *Career:* Ed., *The Commoner* (Wash., D.C.) and *Southwestern Review* (Cincinnati); passed Ohio bar; practiced law; admitted to practice before Ohio Supreme Court; served in Ohio State Legis., 1879; Minister to Haiti, 1885; Pastor, Boston & Cincinnati. Developed interest in Congo & entered serv. of Belgian govt. there. Died in Blackpool, Eng., in 1891.

Writings:
Nonfiction

The History of the Negro Race in America from 1619 to 1880, Negroes as Slaves, as Soldiers, and as Citizens; Together with a Preliminary Consideration of the Unity of the Human Family, an Historical Sketch of Africa, and an Account of the Negro Governments of Sierra Leone and Liberia, 2 vols. (N.Y. & London, Putnam, 1882, 1883; reprint, N.Y., Arno, Amer. Negro—His Hist. & Lit. Ser., no. 1, 1968)

A History of the Negro Troops in the War of the Rebellion 1861-65, Preceded by a Review of the Military Services of Negroes in Ancient and Modern Times (N.Y., Harper, 1888; reprint, Atlantic Highlands, N.J., Humanities, 1968; Westport, Conn., Negro Universities Press)

Sidelights: "His histories were recognized in their day as the most authoritative accounts of the Negro that had appeared." (*Negro Caravan*)

Sources: *Books in Print*, 1980-81; *Cavalcade*; *Historical Negro Biographies*; *Negro Caravan*; *Negro Genius.*

WILLIAMS, JOHN ALFRED. Novelist, Essayist, Editor.
Born in Jackson, Miss., in 1925. *Education:* B.A., Syracuse U., grad. sch., 1951. *Family:* Married Lorrain Isaac; son Gregory, son Dennis (1st marraige), son Adam. *Career:* Ed. & Pub., *Negro Market Newsletter*, 1956-57; Asst. to Pub., Abelard Schuman, 1957-58; Co-ed., *Amistad* (Vintage), 1969-71; Ed. Bd., *Audience Magazine*, 1970-72; Contrib. Ed., *American Journal*, 1972-73; Lect., Black Lit., Coll. of the Virgin Islands, 1968; Lect., Creative Writing, City Coll. of N.Y., 1968-69; Guest Tchr., Writing, Sarah Lawrence Coll., Bronxville, N.Y., 1972-73; Distinguished Prof. of Eng., CUNY, LaGuardia Coll., 1973-75. *Honors:* Natl. Inst. of Arts & Letters, 1962; Centennial Medal for Outstanding Achievement, Syracuse U., 1970. *Mailing address:* 35 W. 92nd St., N.Y., N.Y. 10025.

Writings:
Fiction

The Angry Ones, novel (N.Y., Ace, 1960; N.Y., Pocket Bks., 1970; Old Greenwich, Conn., Chatham, 1975)

Night Song, novel (N.Y., Farrar, 1961; Pocket Bks., 1970; Chatham, 1975)

The Angry Black, anthology, ed. (N.Y., Lancer, 1962)

Beyond the Angry Black, anthology, ed. (N.Y., Cooper Square, 1962, 2nd ed., 1966; N.Y., New Amer. Lib., 1970)

Sissie, novel (Farrar, 1963; N.Y., Doubleday, 1969; Chatham, 1975)

The Man Who Cried I Am; A Novel (Boston, Little, Brown, 1967; New Amer. Lib., 1968, 1972)

Sons of Darkness, Sons of Light; A Novel of Some Probability (Little, Brown, 1969; Pocket Bks., 1970)

Captain Blackman, novel (Doubleday, 1972; Pocket Bks., 1974)

Mothersill and the Foxes, novel (Doubleday, 1975)

The Junior Bachelor Society, novel (Doubleday, 1976)

Click Song, novel (Boston, Houghton Mifflin, 1982)

Nonfiction

Africa, Her History, Lands and People, Told with Pictures (Cooper Square, 1962, 1965, 3rd ed., 1969)

The Protectors (Farrar, 1964)

This Is My Country Too (New Amer. Lib., 1966)

The Most Native of Sons; A Biography of Richard Wright (Doubleday, 1970)

The King God Didn't Save; Reflection on the Life and Death of Martin Luther King, Jr. (N.Y., Coward-McCann, 1970; Pocket Bks., 1971)

Flashbacks (Garden City, N.Y., Anchor, 1973)

Sidelights: Williams has commented, "I think art has always been political and has served political ends more graciously than those of the muses. I consider myself to be a political novelist and writer to the extent that I am always aware of the social insufficiencies which are a result of political manipulation." (*Contemporary Novelists*)

Sidelights: Author information; *Black Insights*; *Books in Print*, 1979-80, 1982-83; *Cavalcade*; *Contemporary Novelists*, 1972; *Dark Symphony*; *Negro Almanac*.

WILLIAMS, LORRAINE A. History Professor, University Administrator.
Education: B.A., M.A., Howard U.; Ph.D., Amer. U. *Career:* Prof. & Chairperson, Dept. of Hist., Howard U., & Dir., Afro-Amer. Inst. for Secondary Sch. Tchrs.; V. Pres. for Acad. Affairs, Howard U. *Mailing address:* Office of V. Pres. for Acad. Affairs, Howard U., Wash., D.C. 20059.

Writings:
Nonfiction
Africa and the Afro-American Experience: Eight Essays (Wash., D.C., Howard U. Press, 1977, 1981)

Sources: *Afro-American Encyclopedia*, vol. 10; *Books in Print*, 1978-79.

WILLIAMS, RUBY ORA. English Professor, Lyric Coloratura Soprano.
Born in Lakewood, N.J., Feb. 18, 1926. *Education:* B.A. (Eng.), Va. Union U.; M.A. (Eng.), Howard U.; further study: Columbia U.; N.Y.U.; Ph.D., U. of Cal., Irvine. *Family:* Single. *Career:* Instr., Eng. Dept., Southern U., Baton Rouge, La., 1953-55; Instr., Eng. Dept., Tuskegee Inst., 1955-57; Instr., Eng. Dept., Morgan State Coll., Baltimore, 1957-65; Program Advisor, Natl. Headquarters, Camp Fire Girls, Inc., N.Y.C., 1965-68; Assoc. Prof., Eng. Dept., Cal. State U., Long Beach, 1968- . Participant in N.Y.U. "Joy of Singing" Ser., Town Hall, 1967; occasional soloist, First Unitarian Church, Baltimore; recitals: Glassboro State Coll., N.J.; Cochran Bap. Church, L.A.; Triangular Church of Religious Sci., L.A.; Bethel AME Church, San Francisco. Reviewer, *Bibliographic Survey: The Negro in Print*, 1968. *Honors:* Danforth Found. Fellow, Relig. Perspectives in Higher Educ.; Vassie D. Wright Authors Award, Our Authors Study Club. *Mailing address:* c/o Eng. Dept., Cal. State U., Long Beach, Cal.

Writings:
Nonfiction
American Black Women in the Arts and Social Sciences: A Bibliographic Survey (Metuchen, N.J., Scarecrow, 1973; rev. ed., 1978)

An Alice Dunbar-Nelson Reader, ed. (Wash., D.C., U. Press of Amer., 1979)

Sources: Author information; *Books in Print*, 1978-79.

WILLIAMS, SHERLEY ANNE [Shirley Williams]. English Professor, Poet.
Born in Bakersfield, Cal., Aug. 25, 1944. *Education:* B.A. (Eng.), Fresno State U., 1966; Howard U. (grad. study), 1966-67; M.A. (Eng.), Brown U., 1972; additional study, L.A. City Coll.; Fisk U. *Family:* Son, John Malcolm. *Career:* Community Educator, Fed. City Coll., Wash., D.C., 1970-72; Dept. of Eng.: Assoc. Prof., Eng., Fresno State U., 1972-73; U. Cal., San Diego, La Jolla, Assoc. Prof. of Lit., V. Chair. & Grad. Advisor, 1975-76; Chairwoman, 1976-78; Prof., 1982- . Visiting Prof.: Dept. of Eng., Cornell U., 1979; Dept. of Eng., U. of S. Cal., 1981-82. *Honors: The Peacock Poems* nominated for Natl. Bk. Award, 1976; San Diego TV Emmy, 1978. *Mailing address:* 5595 56th Pl., San Diego, Cal. 92114.

Writings:
Fiction

The Peacock Poems (Middletown, Conn., Wesleyan U. Press, 1975)

Some One Sweet Angel Chile, poems (N.Y., Morrow, 1982)

Nonfiction

Give Birth to Brightness: A Thematic Study in Neo-Black Literature (N.Y., Dial, 1972)

Sidelights: Sherley Williams is also author of "Ours to Make," for television, and *Traveling Sunshine Show*, a play.

Sources: Author information; *Books in Print*, 1983-84; *Give Birth to Brightness*; *New Black Writing: Africa, West Indies, the Americas*; *Some One Sweet Angel Chile*.

WILLIE, CHARLES V. Social Scientist, Urban Studies Professor.
Born in Dallas, Tex., Oct. 8, 1927. *Education:* B.A., Morehouse Coll., 1948; M.A., Atlanta U., 1949; Ph.D., Syracuse U., 1957. *Family:* Married Mary Sue Conklin; d. Sarah Susannah, son Martin Charles, son James Theodore. *Career:* Instr., Dept. of Preventive Medicine, SUNY, 1955-60; Res. Dir., Wash., D.C., 1962-64; Visiting Lect., Dept. of Psychiatry, Harvard Medical Sch., 1966-67; Instr. to Prof., Dept. of Sociol., Syracuse U., 1967-71; V. Pres., Student Affairs, Syracuse U., 1972-74; Prof. of Educ. & Urban Studies, Grad. Sch. of Educ., Harvard U., 1974- . *Honors:* Phi Beta Kappa, Morehouse Coll., 1972; D.H.L., Berkeley Divinity Sch., Yale U.; D.D., Gen. Theol. Sem., N.Y.; Distinguished Alumnus Award, Maxwell Sch., Syracuse U., 1974. *Mailing address:* 41 Hillcrest Rd., Concord, Mass. 01742.

Writings:
Nonfiction

The Family Life of Black People, ed. (Columbus, Ohio, Merrill, 1970)

Black Students at White Colleges, with A. S. McCord (N.Y., Praeger, 1972)

Race Mixing in the Public Schools, with Jerome Beker (Praeger, 1973)

Racism and Mental Health: Essays, ed. with Others (Pittsburgh, Contemporary Community Health Ser., U. of Pittsburgh, 1974)

Oreo: A Perspective on Race and Marginal Men and Women (Wakefield, Mass., Parameter Press, 1975)

A New Look at Black Families (Wayside, N.Y., General Hall, 1976, 2nd ed., 1981)

Black-Brown-White Relations: Race Relations in the 1970s (New Brunswick, N.J., Transaction Bks., 1977)

The Sociology of Urban Education: Desegregation and Integration (Lexington, Mass., Lexington Bks., 1978)

Black Colleges in America, ed. with Ronald R. Edmonds (N.Y., Tchrs. Coll., 1978)

The Ivory and Ebony Towers: Race Relations and Higher Education (Lexington Bks., 1981)

Community Politics and Educational Changes: Ten School Systems under Court Order, with Susan L. Greenblatt (N.Y., Longman, 1981)

School Desegregation Plans That Work (Westport, Conn., Greenwood, 1984)

Sources: Author information; *Books in Print*, 1978-79, 1980-81, 1982-83.

WILMORE, GAYRAUD STEPHEN. Theologian.
Born in Phila., Pa., Dec. 20, 1921. *Education:* U. of Florence, Italy; B.A., Lincoln U. (Pa.); M. Divinity, Lincoln U. Theol. Sem.; S.T.M., Temple U.; Drew Theol. Sem. *Family:* Married Lee

Wilson; son Stephen, son Jacques, d. Roberta, son David. *Career:* Ed.; Lect.; Dir. Amer. Forum for Intnl. Studies, Ghana, 1971. *Honors:* D.D., Lincoln Coll., Ill.; D.D., Tusculum Coll.; L.H.D., Lincoln U., Pa. *Mailing address:* c/o Doubleday & Co., 245 Park Ave., N.Y., N.Y. 10017.

Writings:

Nonfiction

The Secular Relevance of the Church (Phila., Westminster, 1962)

Christian Perspectives on Social Problems, ed., 10 vols. (Westminster Press Ser., 1962-64)

Black Religion and Black Radicalism (N.Y., Doubleday, 1972; 2nd rev. & enlarged ed., Maryknoll, N.Y., Orbis, 1983)

Asians and Blacks, with C. S. Song (n.p., East Asia Christian Council, 1973)

Last Things First (Westminster, 1982)

Black and Presbyterian: The Heritage and the Hope (Phila., Geneva Press, 1983)

Sidelights: Professor Wilmore gave Cook's lectures in India, Thailand, Indonesia, Korea, Japan, and Taiwan in 1972, and in Guyana in 1974. (Author)

Sources: Author information; *Books in Print*, 1983-84.

WILSON, H(ARRIET) E. Novelist.

Born in Fredericksburg, Va., in 1808. Later lived in Phila. & Boston. Died about 1870.

Writings:

Fiction

Our Nig: Or Sketches from the Life of a Free Black, in a Two-Story White House, North. Showing That Slavery's Shadow Falls Even There, by "Our Nig" (Boston, George C. Rand & Avery, 1859)

Our Nig, ed. by Henry L. Gates, Jr. (N.Y., Random House, 1983)

Sidelights: H. E. Wilson not only wrote the first novel published by a Black person in the United States, but it was also the first published by a Black woman.

"But while there was a thriving market for stories about the evils of slavery in the South, 'Our Nig' was about the decidedly unpopular subject of racism in the North, and its publication was ignored by abolitionists and by a black person ordinarily eager to promote the writings of black authors." (*Los Angeles Herald Examiner*)

Sources: *Los Angeles Herald Examiner*, Nov. 9, 1982; *Our Nig*.

WILSON, WILLIAM JULIUS. Sociologist, Sociology Professor.

Born in Derry Township, Pa., Dec. 20, 1935. *Education:* B.A., Wilberforce U., 1958; M.A., Bowling Green State U., 1961; Ph.D., Wash. State U., 1966. *Family:* Married 1st Mildred, Aug. 31, 1957; married 2nd Beverly Huebner (an ed. asst.), July 31, 1971; children: Colleen, Lisa. *Career:* Asst. Prof., U. of Mass., Amherst, 1965-69, Assoc. Prof. of Sociol., 1969-71; Assoc. Prof. of Sociol., 1971-?, Prof. of Sociol. (present), U. of Chicago; Visiting Scholar-in-Residence, Concordia Coll. (Morehead, Minn.), 1968; Visiting Prof., Harvard U., summer 1972, Chairman of Five Coll. Black Studies Com., 1970; Assoc. of Inst. of Black World, 1971; Soc. Sci. Res. Com., Natl. Inst. of Mental Health, 1972-75; Res. Consultant, Russell Sage Found.; Mem. of Ed. Bd., Warner Modular Publ., 1972- . *Mailing address:* Dept. of Sociol., U. of Chicago, Chicago, Ill. 60637.

Writings:

Nonfiction

The Declining Significance of Race: Blacks and Changing American Institutions (Chicago, U. of Chicago Press, 1978, 2nd ed., 1980)

Say When (N.Y., Paulist, Emmaus Bks., 1978)

Sources: *Book Review Digest*, 1979; *Books in Print*, 1979-80; *Contemporary Authors*, vols. 45-48, 1974; *Freedomways*, vol. 18, no. 4, 1978.

WIMBERLY, EDWARD P. Theology Professor, Pastoral Counselor.
Born in Phila., Pa., Oct. 22, 1943. *Education:* B.A., U. of Ariz., 1965; S.T.B., Boston U. Sch. of Theol., 1968; S.T.M. (Sociol. of Relig.), Boston U., 1971; Ph.D. (Pastoral Psychology & Counseling), Boston U., 1976. *Family:* Married Anne Streaty. *Career:* Pastoral Consultant, Fuller Community Mental Health Center, Boston, 1973-75; Minister of Urban Affairs, Worcester Area Council of Churches, 1969-73; Pastor, St. Andrew's United Methodist Church, Worcester, Mass., 1968-74; Asst. Prof., Psychology of Relig. & Pastoral Care, Interdenominational Theol. Center, Atlanta. *Honors:* Exchange Minister to West Germany, Northeast Assn. for Church & Society, 1973. *Mailing address:* 671 Beckwith St., S.W., Atlanta, Ga. 30314.

Writings:
Nonfiction
Pastoral Care in the Black Church (Nashville, Abingdon, 1979, paper, 1982)

Sources: Author information; *Books in Print*, 1981-82, 1982-83.

WINSTON, HENRY. Communist Party Chairman.
Born in Miss. in 1911. *Career:* Natl. Chairman, Communist Party, 1966- . *Mailing address:* c/o New Outlook Pub., 239 W. 23rd St., N.Y., N.Y. 10011.

Writings:
Nonfiction
Build the Communist Party, the Party of the Working Class: Report to the 19th National Convention, Communist Party, U.S.A., April 30-May 4, 1960 (N.Y., New Outlook, 1969)

Black Americans and the Middle East Conflict (New Outlook, 1970)

Fight Racism—For Unity and Progress! (New Outlook, 1971)

Politics of People's Action: The Communist Party in the '72 Elections (New Outlook, 1972)

Africa's Struggle for Freedom, the USA and the USSR: A Selection of Political Analyses, Assembled and with an Introduction by Henry Winston, ed. (New Outlook, 1972)

A Marxist-Leninist Critique of Roy Innis on Community Self-Determination and Martin Kilson on Education (New Outlook, 1973)

Meaning of San Rafael (New Outlook, 1973)

Strategy for a Black Agenda; A Critique of New Theories of Liberation in the United States and Africa (N.Y., Intnl., 1973)

The Moynihan-Kissinger Doctrine and the Third World (New Outlook, 1975)

Class, Race and Black Liberation (Intnl., 1977)

Sidelights: Winston played a leading role in the struggles around the unemployed movements and the Scottsboro trial of the 1930s and the labor-organizing drives of pre-World War II and the post-war civil rights movement. "In 1956 he began an 8-year prison sentence under the Smith Act frameup. While in prison he became blind due to deliberate neglect of his health by prison authorities. Worldwide protests caused his release in 1961.... He also helped organize the movement around Angela Davis during her attempted frameup. This movement later led to her acquittal." (Publisher)

Sources: *Books in Print*, 1980-81; Pub. information; *Strategy for a Black Agenda*.

WINSTON, MICHAEL. Researcher, Consultant.

Born in N.Y.C., May 26, 1941. *Education:* B.A., Howard U., 1962; M.A., 1964, Ph.D., 1974, U. of Cal. *Family:* Married Judith Marianno; children: Lisa M., Cynthia A. *Career:* Instr., Howard U., 1964-66; Executive Asst. & Assoc. Dir., Inst. Serv. Educ., 1965-66; Asst. Dean, Liberal Arts, Howard U., 1968-69; Educ. Consultant, Educ. Assoc., Inc., 1966-68; Development Consultant, Langston U., 1966-68; Dir. Res., Hist. Dept., Howard U., 1972-73; Dir., Moorland Spingarn Res. Center, Howard U., 1973- . *Mailing address:* Howard U., Wash., D.C. 20059.

Writings:
Nonfiction

The Negro in the United States, with Rayford W. Logan (N.Y., Van Nostrand Reinhold, 1970-71)

The Howard University Department of History, 1913-1973 (Wash., D.C., Howard U. Press, 1973)

Dictionary of American Negro Biography, co-ed. (N.Y., Norton, 1983)

Sidelights: "It [*Dictionary of American Negro Biography*] is an essential reference work, one that contributes to our understanding of the integral role Negroes have played in the development of American society." (*Dictionary of American Negro Biography*)

Sources: *Crisis*, Feb. 1983; *Dictionary Catalog of the Schomburg Collection*, Supplement, 1974; *Dictionary of American Negro Biography*; Pub. information; *Who's Who among Black Americans*, 2nd ed., 1977-78.

WOODSON, CARTER GODWIN. Educator, History Professor, Historian, Executive Director (Association for the Study of Negro Life and History).

Born in New Canton, Va., Dec. 19, 1875. *Education:* Berea Coll., Litt.B., 1903; Sorbonne, Paris; U. of Chicago, B.A., 1907, M.A., 1908; Harvard U., Ph.D., 1912. *Family:* Single. *Career:* Tchr., high schs., Wash., D.C., 1908-18; Dean, Sch. of Liberal Arts, Howard U., 1919-20; Dean, W. Va. Collegiate Inst., 1920-22; Executive Dir., ASNLH: Chairman Bd., Assoc. Pub., Inc.; Founder/Ed., *Journal of Negro History*, 1916; Founder/Ed., *Negro History Bulletin*, 1937. *Honors:* LL.D., Va. State Coll., 1941; Spingarn Medal, NAACP, 1926. Died Apr. 3, 1950.

Writings:
Nonfiction

The Education of the Negro Prior to 1861; A History of the Education of the Colored People of the United States from the Beginning of Slavery to the Civil War (N.Y. & London, Putnam, 1915; reprint, N.Y., Arno, Amer. Negro—His Hist. & Lit. Ser., no. 1, 1968)

A Century of Negro Migration (Wash., D.C., ASNLH, 1918; reprint, N.Y., AMS; N.Y., Russell, 1969)

History of the Negro Church (Wash., D.C., Assoc. Pub., 1921)

The Negro in Our History (Assoc. Pub., 1922, 7th ed., 1941)

Free Negro Heads of Families in the United States in 1830, Together with a Brief Treatment of the Free Negro (ASNLH, 1925)

Free Negro Owners of Slaves in the United States in 1830, Together with Absentee Ownership of Slaves in the United States in 1830 (ASNLH, 1924; reprint, Westport, Conn., Greenwood, n d)

Negro Orators and Their Orations, ed. (Assoc. Pub., 1925; reprint, N.Y., Russell, 1969)

The Mind of the Negro as Reflected in Letters Written during Crises 1800-1860, ed. (ASNLH, 1926; reprint, Russell, 1969)

Negro Makers of History (Assoc. Pub., 1928, 2nd ed., 1938)

African Myths, Together with Proverbs; A Supplementary Reader Composed of Folk Tales from Various Parts of Africa, Adapted to the Use of Children in the Public Schools (Assoc. Pub., 1928)

The Rural Negro (ASNLH, 1930; reprint, Russell, 1969)

The Mis-Education of the Negro (Assoc. Pub., 1933; reprint, AMS, 1972)

The Negro Professional Man and the Community, with Special Emphasis on the Physician and the Lawyer (ASNLH, 1934; reprint, Negro Universities Press, 1969)

The Story of the Negro Retold (Assoc. Pub., 1935)

The African Background Outlined: Or, Handbook for the Study of the Negro (ASNLH, 1936; reprint, Negro Universities Press, 1968)

African Heroes and Heroines (Assoc. Pub., 1939)

The Works of Francis J. Grimke, ed. (Assoc. Pub., 1942)

Sidelights: "The 'father of Negro history,' Carter G. Woodson was for many years the lone voice of any consequence in American Negro historiography." (*Black Historians*)

A tremendous impetus to scholarship was given by ASNLH in the first 25 years of its existence. It published more than 30 volumes and the *Journal of Negro History*. Beginning in 1926, the Association made Negro History Week a success. (*Current Biography*, 1944)

"Dr. Woodson concluded after years of research, that the Negro 'taught the modern world trial by jury, music by stringed instruments, the domestication of the sheep, goat and cow, and the use of iron....' He was distressed to let generations of people continue to be ignorant about those facts." (*Negroes Who Helped Build America*)

Sources: *Black Historians: A Critique*; *Books in Print*, 1980-81; *Current Biography*, 1944; *Negro Almanac*; *Negroes Who Helped Build America*; *Who Was Who in America*, vol. III, 1951-60.

WORK, JOHN WESLEY, JR. Composer, Teacher.
Born in Tullahoma, Tenn., in 1901. *Education:* Fisk U.; Columbia U.; Yale U.; Inst. of Musical Art, N.Y. *Career:* Tchr., Fisk U.; Dir., Fisk Jubilee Singers, 1948-57. Died in 1967.

Writings:
Nonfiction

American Negro Songs; A Comprehensive Collection of 230 Folk Songs, Religious and Secular (N.Y., Bonanza Bks., 1940)

American Negro Folk Songs and Spirituals; A Comprehensive Collection of 230 Folk Songs, Religious and Secular (N.Y., Crown, 1940)

Sidelights: His phonodisc is *The Fisk Jubilee Singers*, published by Folkways, 1955.

Sources: *Black American Writers, 1773-1949*; *Dictionary Catalog of the Schomburg Collection of Negro Literature and History*, 1962; *Encyclopedia of Black America*.

WORK, MONROE NATHAN. Pedagogy & History Professor, Publisher.
Born in Iredell County, N.C., in 1866. *Education:* Chicago Theol. Sem.; B.A. (Philosophy), M.A., U. of Chicago. *Career:* Prof. of Pedagogy & Hist., Ga. State Industrial Coll., 1903-?; Dir., Dept. of Records & Res., Tuskegee Inst., Ala., 1908-38 (collected pertinent data & statistics on Negro). *Honors:* Harmon Award in Educ. for "scholarly research and educational publicity through periodic publication of the *Negro Yearbook* and the compilation of a *Bibliography of the Negro*." Alumni Citation, U. of Chicago Alumni Assn., 1942 (for 40 yrs. of public serv.). Died in 1945.

Writings:
Nonfiction

Negro Yearbook: An Annual Encyclopedia of the Negro, 1912-1919 (Tuskegee Inst., Ala., Negro Year Bk. Pub. Co., 1912-19)

A Bibliography of the Negro in Africa and America (N.Y., H. W. Wilson, 1928; reprint, N.Y., Argosy, 1965; N.Y., Octagon, 1966)

Sidelights: "Through his research in Europe and America, Dr. Work obtained important data for his compilation of the *Bibliography of the Negro*. ...a significant achievement ... the first effort of its kind. In one volume ... works of publications about Negroes in all parts of the world from ancient times to 1928." (*Historical Negro Biographies*)

Sources: *Books in Print*, 1978-79, 1980-81; *Historical Negro Biographies*.

WRIGHT, CHARLES STEVENSON. Novelist, Poet.
Born in New Franklin, Mo., June 4, 1932. *Education:* Public schs., New Franklin & Sedalia, Mo. *Career:* Free-lance Writer, *Kan. City Call. Honors:* Eunice Tietjens Memorial Award for *Blood Lines*, 1976. *Mailing address:* c/o Wesleyan U. Press, 55 High St., Middletown, Conn. 06457.

Writings:
Fiction
The Messenger, novel (N.Y., Farrar, 1963)

The Wig: A Mirror Image, novel (Farrar, 1966; London, Souvenir, 1967; N.Y., Manor Bks., 1977)

Private Madrigals, poems (Madison, Wis., Abraxas, 1969)

The Graves of the Right Hand, poems (original title: *Lost Displays*, Middletown, Conn., Wesleyan U. Press, Wesleyan Poetry Program, vol. 51, 1970)

Hard Freight, poems (Wesleyan U. Press, 1973)

Bloodlines, poems (Wesleyan U. Press, 1975)

China Trace, poems (Wesleyan U. Press, Wesleyan Poetry Program, vol. 88, 1977)

Dead Color, poems (Salem, Ore., Seluzicki Poetry, Fine Press Poetry Ser., 1980)

Nonfiction
Absolutely Nothing to Get Alarmed About (Farrar, 1973)

Sources: *Books in Print*, 1979-80; *Contemporary Authors*; *Interviews with Black Writers*.

WRIGHT, JAY. Poet, Playwright.
Born in Albuquerque, N. Mex., May 25, 1935. *Education:* B.A., U. of Cal., Berkeley; M.A., Rutgers U., 1966. *Career:* Playwright; Poet (plays produced in Cal. & pub.). *Honors:* Several fellowships, including Rockefeller Brothers Theol. Fellowship. *Mailing address:* c/o U. of Tex. Press, Box 7819, Austin, Tex. 78712.

Writings:
Fiction
Death as History, poems (Milbrook, N.Y., Kriya Press, 1967)

Balloons, a Comedy in One Act (Boston, Baker's Players, 1968)

The Homecoming Singer, poems (N.Y., Corinth, 1971)

Dimensions of History, poems (Santa Cruz, Cal., Kayak, 1976)

Soothsayers and Omens, poems (N.Y., Seven Woods, 1976)

Double Invention of Komo, poems (Austin, Tex., U. of Tex. Press, U. of Tex. Poetry Ser., no. 5, 1980)

Sidelights: "The Yale University literary critic Harold Bloom calls Wright the most important and permanent contemporary black poet he has read; a learned, mythological poet with a distinguished, difficult and absurdly neglected body of work." (*New Republic*)

Sources: *Black Fire*; *Books in Print*, 1980-81; *For Malcolm*; *Freedomways*, vol. 19, no. 2, 1979; *New Black Voices*; *New Republic*, Nov. 26, 1977; *Poetry of Black America*.

WRIGHT, NATHAN, JR. Educator, Civil Rights Activist, Consultant, Priest.
Born in Shreveport, La., Aug. 5, 1923. *Education:* B.A., U. of Cincinnati, 1947; B.D., Episcopal
Theol. Sch., Cambridge, Mass., 1950; S.T.M., Harvard U., 1951; Ed. M., State Tchrs. Coll.,
Boston, 1962; Ed. D., Harvard U., 1964; LL.D. (hon.), Upsala Coll., 1969. *Family:* Married Carolyn
Elliott May, July 18, 1969; two sons, three daughters. *Career:* Prof. of Urban Affairs & Former
Chairman, Dept. of Afro-Amer. Studies, SUNY, Albany, 1969- ; Assoc. Natl. Humanities Faculty,
1971- ; Consultant, Upsala Coll., E. Orange, N.J., 1967- ; Consultant, Orange, N.J., 1956-66;
Educ. Consultant, self-employed, Newark, N.J., 1964-69; Res., Newark Com. of Better Public
Schs., Newark; Tchr., Colgate-Rochester Divinity Sch., Rochester, N.Y.; Executive Dir., Dept. of
Urban Work, Diocese of Newark, N.J., 1964-69. *Honors:* 1st Prize (Intnl.) for *One Bread, One
Body*, Christian Res. Found.; Media Workshop Award for *Black Power and Urban Unrest*; nomina-
tion for Pulitzer Prize for *Let's Work Together*, 1969. *Mailing address:* c/o Hawthorn Bks., 260
Madison Ave., N.Y., N.Y. 10016.

Writings:
Nonfiction
The Riddle of Life, and Other Sermons (Boston, Bruce-Humphries, 1952)

The Song of Mary (Bruce-Humphries, 1958)

One Bread, One Body (Greenwich, Conn., Seabury, 1962)

Black Power and Urban Unrest; Creative Possibilities (N.Y., Hawthorn, 1967)

Ready to Riot (N.Y., Holt, 1968)

Let's Work Together (Hawthorn, 1968)

Let's Face Racism (Camden, N.J., T. Nelson, 1970)

What Black Educators Are Saying (Hawthorn, 1970)

What Black Politicians Are Saying (Hawthorn, 1972)

Sidelights: "A *Publishers Weekly* writer notes that Wright 'thinks the only way for the Negro to achieve
his rightful place in our society is through self-direction, even if that means separation....' "
(*Contemporary Authors*)

Sources: Author information; *Contemporary Authors*, vols. 37-40, 1973.

WRIGHT, RICHARD. Novelist, Essayist.
Born near Natchez, Miss., Sept. 4, 1908. *Education:* Seventh Day Adventist Sch. *Family:* Married
Ellen Wright; two daughters. *Career:* Fed. Writers Project, Chicago, 1935, N.Y.C., 1937; Contrib.
to "little" mags., *Daily Worker, New Masses. Honors:* Won $50 prize for *Uncle Tom's Children*
(*Story* mag.); received Guggenheim Found. Fellowship for *Native Son* (1st bk. by Afro-Amer. to
become Book-of-the-Month Club selection); also became successful Broadway prod. & filmmaker in
S. Amer.; *Black Boy* repeated as Book-of-the-Month selection; in decade and a half after *Native Son*,
nearly 50 transl. & foreign eds. of his works were pub. Died Nov. 28, 1960. *Agent:* c/o Paul R.
Reynolds & Son, 599 Fifth Ave., N.Y., N.Y. 10017.

Writings:
Fiction
Uncle Tom's Children, Five Long Stories (N.Y., Harper, 1938; N.Y., Modern Lib., 1942; N.Y.,
World, 1958; N.Y., Har-Row, 1965)

Native Son, novel (Harper, 1940, 1957, 1966, 1969; N.Y., New Amer. Lib., 1961, 1964)

The Outsider, novel (Harper, 1953, 1969)

Savage Holiday, novel (N.Y., Avon, 1954; Old Chatham, Conn., Chatham, 1975)

The Long Dream, novel (N.Y., Ace Bks., 1958; Chatham, 1969)

Eight Men, short stories (Avon, 1961)

Lawd Today, novel (N.Y., Walker, 1963)

Richard Wright Reader, ed. by Ellen Wright & Michel Fabre (Harper, 1978)

Nonfiction
12 Million Black Voices: A Folk History of the Negro in the United States (N.Y., Viking, 1941; N.Y., Arno, Amer. Negro—His Hist. & Lit. Ser., no. 2, 1969)

Black Boy, a Record of Childhood and Youth, autobiog. (World, 1945, 1950; New Amer. Lib., 1963; Harper, 1966, 1969)

Black Power: A Record of Reactions in a Land of Pathos (Harper, 1954; Westport, Conn., Greenwood, 1974)

The Color Curtain; A Report on the Bandung Conference (World, 1956)

Pagan Spain (Harper, 1957; London, The Bodley Head, 1960)

White Man Listen! (N.Y., Doubleday, 1957; Greenwood, 1978)

American Hunger (Har-Row, 1977, 1979, paper, 1983)

Farthings Fortunes (N.Y., Atheneum, 1979)

Sidelights: "Richard Wright has been described as the most influential Afro-American novelist who ever lived." (*Black American Literature: Fiction*)
An expatriate for 15 years, he died in 1960 and was buried in Père Lanchaise, Paris, France. (*Who Was Who in America*)

Sources: *American Negro Reference Book*; *Black American Literature: Fiction*; *Black Voices*; *Cavalcade*; *Dark Symphony*; *Richard Wright*; *Who Was Who in America*, vol. IV, 1961-68.

WRIGHT, SARAH ELIZABETH. Poet, Novelist.
Born in Wetipguin, Md. *Education:* Howard U.; U. of Pa.; New Sch. for Soc. Res. *Family:* Son Michael, d. Shelley. *Career:* Fiction Consultant, Creative Artists Pub. Serv. Program, N.Y. State Council on the Arts; Pres., Writers for Our Time (intercommunity creative writers' workshop). *Honors: This Child's Gonna Live* selected by the *New York Times* as one of the Outstanding Books of the Year, 1969; chosen by the *Baltimore Sun* for its Readability Award. *Mailing address:* 780 West End Ave., 1D, N.Y., N.Y. 10025.

Writings:
Fiction
Give Me a Child, poems (Phila., Kraft, 1955)

This Child's Gonna Live, novel (N.Y., Delacorte, 1969; N.Y., Dell, 1971, 1975)

Sidelights: Stuyvesant High School, Mini-Course Lecture Series Poetry Recitations: WBAI & WEVD-FM, New York City; Syndicated radio program "The Second Forty," produced by Information Center for Mature Women. Talk shows: WABC TV; WNBS; WLIB; WNYC; WPEN; Frank Ford Show, Philadelphia; WFIL TV (ABC), Philadelphia; WFLN.

Sources: Author information; *Books in Print*, 1978-79; *Poetry of Black America*.

WYNTER, SYLVIA [Wynter Carew]. (Jamaican). Critic, Playwright, Novelist, Dancer, Actress, Teacher.
Born in Cuba in 1932, of Jamaican parents. *Education:* Jamaica; London; Madrid. *Family:* Married Jan Carew (writer). *Career:* Tchr., U. W. Indies, Mona, Jamaica; Tchr. (U.S.). *Mailing address:* c/o Ohio U. Press, Scott Quadrangle, Athens, Ohio 45701.

Writings:
Fiction
Ssh ... It's a Wedding, musical (Jamaica, 1961?)

The University of Hunger, play, with Jan Carew (performed Georgetown Theatre Guild, 1966; broadcast BBC, 1961; televised BBC, 1962, as *The Big Pride*)

The Hills of Hebron: A Jamaican Novel (N.Y., Simon & Schuster, 1962; London, Cape, 1962)

Miracle in Lime Lane, play, with Jan Carew (Spanish Town, Jamaica, Folk Theatre, 1962)

Brother Man, play, adaptation of Roger Mais' novel of same name (produced Jamaica, 1965)

1865 Ballad for a Rebellion, play, epic story of Morant Bay Rebellion (produced Jamaica, 1965)

Rockstone Anancy, play, a magical morality (Jamaican Pantomime), with Alex Gradussov (produced in Jamaica, 1970)

Black Midas, adaptation for children of Jan Carew's novel (London, Longman's, 1970)

Nonfiction
Jamaica's National Heroes (Kingston, Jamaica, Natl. Commission, 1971)

Sidelights: She has translated and adapted several classical Spanish prose works for the British Broadcasting Company.

Sylvia Wynter's *The Hills of Hebron* documents the wide range of cults in the islands: a pocomania cult, corresponding to Haitian voodoo worshipers; "the Believers," like the break-away Baptist cults; and the "New Believers," a cross between Marcus Garvey's Black God religion and the Jamaican Ras Tafarians belief in the Emperor of Ethiopia's divinity. (*West Indian Novel and Its Background*)

"... more recently she seems to have been concentrating on criticism." (*Caribbean Writers*)

Sources: *Caribbean Writers*; *Complete Caribbeana, 1900-1975*; *Jamaican National Bibliography*; *Resistance and Caribbean Literature*; *West Indian Literature*; *West Indian Novel and Its Background*.

YERBY, FRANK. Novelist.
Born in Augusta, Ga., Sept. 5, 1916. *Education:* B.A., Paine Coll., Augusta, Ga., 1937; M.A., Fisk U., 1938; further study, U. of Chicago. *Family:* Married 1st Flora H. Claire Williams, Mar. 1, 1941 (div.); son Jacques Loring, d. Nikki Ethlyn, d. Faune Ellena, son Jan Keith; married 2nd Blanquita Calle-Perez, 1956. *Career:* War work, Ford Motor Co., Dearborn, Mich., 1942-44; Ranger Aircraft, Jamaica, N.Y., 1944-45; Writer. *Mailing address:* Avenida de America 37, Apt. 710, Madrid 2, Spain.

Writings:
Fiction
The Foxes of Harrow, novel (N.Y., Dial, 1946; N.Y., Dell, 1972; Cutchoque, N.Y., Buccaneer, 1976)

The Vixens, novel (Dial, 1947; London, Heinemann, 1948; Dell, 1976)

The Golden Hawk, novel (Dial, 1948; Heinemann, 1949; Dell, 1977)

Pride's Castle, novel (Dial, 1949; Heinemann, 1965; Dell, 1975)

Floodtide, novel (Dial, 1950; Dell, 1976, 1982)

A Woman Called Fancy, novel (Dial, 1951; N.Y., Garden City Bks., 1952; Dell, 1978)

The Saracen Blade, novel (Dial, 1952; Dell, 1976)

The Devil's Laughter, novel (Dial, 1953; Dell, 1977)

Benton's Row, novel (Dial, 1954; Dell, 1977)

Bride of Liberty, novel (N.Y., Doubleday, 1954; N.Y., Pyramid, 1964)

Treasure of Pleasant Valley, novel (Dial, 1955; Dell, 1976)

Captain Rebel, novel (Dial, 1956; Heinemann, 1957; Dell, 1975)

Fairoaks, novel (Dial, 1957; Dell, 1977)

The Serpent and the Staff, novel (Dial, 1958; Dell, 1976)

Jarrett's Jade, novel (Dial, 1959; Dell, 1976)

Gillian, novel (Dial, 1960; Dell, 1972)

The Garfield Honor, novel (Dial, 1961; Dell, 1978)

Griffin's Way, novel (Dial, 1961; Dell, 1978)

The Old Gods Laugh; A Modern Romance (Dial, 1964; Dell, 1978)

An Odor of Sanctity; A Novel of Medieval Moorish Spain (Dial, 1965; Dell, 1977)

Goat Song; A Novel of Ancient Greece (Dial, 1967; Dell, 1977)

Judas, My Brother; The Story of the Thirteenth Disciple, an Historical Novel (Dial, 1968; Dell, 1978)

Speak Now, a Modern Novel (Dial, 1969; Dell, 1975)

The Dahomean, an Historical Novel (Dial, 1971; Dell, 1977)

The Girl from Storyville; A Victorian Novel (Dial, 1972)

The Voyage Unplanned, novel (Dial, 1974; Dell, 1975)

Tobias and the Angel, novel (Dial, 1975; Dell, 1976)

A Rose for Ana Maria: A Novel (Dial, 1976; Dell, 1976)

Hail the Conquering Hero: A Novel (Dial, 1978; Dell, 1980)

A Darkness at Ingraham's Crest: A Tale of the Slaveholding South, novel (Dial, 1979; Dell, 1980)

Western: A Saga of the Great Plains, novel (Dial, 1982)

Sidelights: His twenty-nine best-selling novels have sold more than 50,000,000 copies; were translated into nearly a dozen languages. Three were successful movies: *The Foxes of Harrow*, starring Rex Harrison and Maureen O'Hara; *The Golden Hawk*, with Rhonda Fleming and Sterling Hayden; and *The Saracen Blade*, with Ricardo Montalban. *Pride's Castle* was a live television drama.

Frank Campenni's critique: "*The Dahomean* [a] moving chronicle of the making of an African chief ... is written with such sympathy, seriousness and control ... that *The Dahomean* emerges as his best work." (*Contemporary Novelists*)

Publishers Weekly said of *Western*: "highly entertaining ... a passionate love story ... a novel of revenge and counter-revenge, suspenseful ... full of satisfying surprises." (Publisher)

Sources: *American Negro Short Stories*; *Best Short Stories by Negro Writers*; *Black American Literature: Fiction*; *Contemporary Novelists*; Pub. information, *Who's Who in America*, 37th ed., 1972-73.

YETTE, SAMUEL F. Journalist, Journalism Professor.
Born in Harriman, Tenn., in 1929. *Education:* B.A. in Eng. & Speech, Tenn. State U.; M.A. in Journalism & Govt., Indiana U.; Doctor of Humanities (hon.), Prentice Inst., Miss. *Career:* Wash. Correspondent, *Newsweek*; Prof., Journalism, Howard U. *Honors: The Choice* was selected by Black Acad. of Arts & Letters as the Non-Fiction Work of Distinction, 1972. *Mailing address:* c/o Howard U., 2400 Sixth St., N.W., Wash., D.C. 20001.

Writings:
Nonfiction
The Choice: The Issue of Black Survival in America (N.Y., Putnam, 1971; paper, Silver Spring, Md., Cottage Bks., 1982)

Sidelights: "The extermination of the black man in America ... emerges from Samuel Yette's startling research as a genuine possibility.

"... Mr. Yette lets us see White America through the eyes of Black America ... we learn why Blacks feel that the issue facing them is one of survival." (Senator Birch Bayh in *The Choice*)

Sources: *Books in Print*, 1983-84; *The Choice*; "National Conference of Afro-American Writers," Nov. 1974.

YOUNG, AL. Poet, Novelist, Teacher, Musician.
Born in Ocean Springs, Miss., May 31, 1939. *Education:* U. of Mich., 1957-61; Stanford U. (fellow in creative writing), 1966-67; B.A., U. of Cal., Berkeley, 1969. *Family:* Married Arlin Belch (free-lance artist), Oct. 8, 1963; son Michael James. *Career:* Free-lance musician, playing guitar & flute & singing professionally throughout U.S., 1957-64; Disc Jockey, Radio Station KJAZ-FM, Alameda, Cal., 1964-65; Writing instr. & lang. consultant, Berkeley Neighborhood Youth Corps, 1968-69; Jones Lect. in Creative Writing, Stanford U., 1969- ; Founder, Ed., *Loveletter* (irregular review, late 1960s). *Honors:* Wallace E. Stegner Fellow, Creative Writing; Joseph Henry Jackson Award, San Francisco Found., 1969, for *Dancing*; NEA Grant (poetry), 1969-70; Natl. Arts Council Awards, 1968, 1969; Cal. Assn. of Tchrs. of Eng., Spec. Award, 1973. *Mailing address:* 390 Oxford Ave., Palo Alto, Cal. 94306.

Writings:
Fiction

Dancing; Poems (N.Y., Corinth Bks., 1969)

Snakes; A Novel (N.Y., Holt, 1970; N.Y., Dell, 1972; Berkeley, Cal., Creative Arts, 1981)

The Song Turning Back into Itself; Poems (Holt, 1971)

Earth Air Fire and Water, poems (N.Y., Coward, 1971)

Who Is Angelina? A Novel (Holt, 1974, 1975)

Geography of the Near Past: Poems (Holt, 1976)

Sitting Pretty: A Novel (Holt, 1976)

Zeppelin Coming Down, poems (Yardbird Wing, 1976)

Yardbird Lives!, anthology, ed. with Ishmael Reed (N.Y., Grove, 1978)

Calafia: The California Poetry (Berkeley, Cal., Reed & Young Quilt, 1979)

Ask Me Now, poems (N.Y., McGraw-Hill, 1980)

Bodies and Soul; Musical Memoirs (Creative Arts, 1981)

Quilt One, anthology, ed. with Ishmael Reed (Reed & Young Quilt, Quilt Ser., 1981)

The Blues Don't Change: New and Selected Poems (Baton Rouge, La. State U. Press, 1982)

Sidelights: "[*Snakes*] has been acclaimed by several reviewers, including Martin Levin and L. E. Sissman, as an authentic exploration of the experiences of a jazz-oriented black youth growing up in a middle American city." (*Contemporary Authors*)

Sources: *Books in Print*, 1979-80, 1982-83; *Contemporary Authors*, vols. 29-32, 1972; *Kirkus Reviews*, May 1, 1980; *New Black Voices*; *Poetry of Black America*.

YOUNG, BERNICE ELIZABETH. Juvenile Writer.
Born in Cleveland, Ohio, Oct. 7, 1931. *Education:* Vassar Coll.; Case Western Reserve U. *Family:* Single. *Career:* Asst. to Dir. of Advertising, Charles of the Ritz, 1961-64; Dir., BEATLES (U.S.A.) LIMITED (Amer. Rep. for The Beatles, Cilla Black, Gerry & the Pacemakers & Others under management of Brian Epstein), 1964-67; Protestant Advisor/Media Advisor, Girl Scouts of U.S.A., 1968; Account Executive, Addison, Goldstein & Walsh, 1969-70; "You and Your Money," daily WLIB radio ser., consumer educ. (26 weeks), 1970; Writer, 1970- . *Mailing address:* 333 E. 34th St., Apt. 17H, N.Y., N.Y. 10016.

Writings:
Nonfiction

Harlem, the Story of a Changing Community, juv. (N.Y., J. Messner, 1972)

The Picture Story of Hank Aaron, juv. (J. Messner, 1974)

The Picture Story of Frank Robinson, juv. (J. Messner, 1975)

The Story of Hank Aaron, juv. (Englewood Cliffs, N.J., Prentice-Hall, 1976)

Sources: Author information; *Books in Print*, Supplement, 1975-76.

YOUNG, MARGARET BUCKNER. Juvenile Writer, Teacher.
Born in Campbellsville, Ky., Mar. 20, 1922. *Education:* B.A., Ky. State Coll., 1942; M.A., U. of Minn., 1946; further study, Atlanta U., 1958. *Family:* Married Whitney Young, Jr., (Executive Dir., Natl. Urban League), Jan. 2, 1944; d. Marcia Elaine, d. Lauren Lee. *Career:* Instr. at Ky. State Coll., Frankfort, 1943, & Atlanta U., 1958; Inst. in Educ. & Psychology, Spelman Coll., Atlanta, 1958-60. *Mailing address:* c/o Franklin Watts, Inc., 730 Fifth Ave., N.Y., N.Y. 10019.

Writings:
Nonfiction
How to Bring Up Your Child without Prejudice (N.Y., Public Affairs Comm., 1965)

The First Book of American Negroes, juv. (N.Y., Watts, 1966)

The Picture Life of Martin Luther King, Jr., juv. (Watts, 1968)

The Picture Life of Ralph J. Bunche, juv. (Watts, 1968)

Black American Leaders, juv. (Watts, 1969)

The Picture Life of Thurgood Marshall, juv. (Watts, 1971)

Source: *Something about the Author*, 1973.

YOUNG, THOMAS WHITE. Lawyer, Newspaper Publisher.
Born in Norfolk, Va., Oct. 26, 1908. *Education:* B.S., LL.B., 1932, Ohio State U. *Family:* Married Marguerite J. Chisholm, Mar. 2, 1943; d. Millicent Marguerite. *Career:* Admitted to Norfolk bar, 1933; practiced in Norfolk, Va., 1933-36; War Correspondent, *Journal and Guide* (Norfolk), 1943-45; Pres., The Guide Pub. Co., Norfolk, 1947- . *Honors:* Wolfe Journalism Honor Medal, 1931. *Mailing address:* 719 E. Olney Rd., Norfolk, Va. 23504.

Writings:
Nonfiction
(Norfolk) *Journal and Guide*, newspaper (Norfolk, 1947-)

Source: *Negro Handbook.*

YOUNG, WHITNEY MOORE, JR. Social Work Professor, Educator, Executive Director (National Urban League), Civil Rights Leader.
Born in Lincoln Ridge, Ky., July 31, 1921. *Education:* B.S., Ky. State Coll., 1941; Mass. Inst. of Technology, 1942-43; M.A., U. of Minn., 1947; Harvard U., 1960-61; LL.D. (hon.): N.C. Agricultural & Tech. Coll., 1961; Tuskegee Inst., 1963. *Family:* Married Margaret Buckner, Jan. 2, 1944; d. Marcia Elaine, d. Lauren Lee. *Career:* Industrial Relations & Vocational Guidance Dir., St. Paul, Minn. Urban League, 1947-50; Executive Secy., Omaha Urban League, 1950-53; Instr., Sch. of Soc. Work, U. of Neb., 1950-58; Dean, Sch. of Soc. Work, Atlanta U., 1954-60; Executive Dir., Natl. Urban League, N.Y.C., 1961-71. *Honors:* Florina Lasker Award ($1,000 for outstanding achievement in field of soc. work), 1959; Outstanding Alumni Award, U. of Minn., 1960. Drowned while swimming off W. Coast of Africa, Mar. 11, 1971.

Writings:
Nonfiction
To Be Equal (N.Y., McGraw-Hill, 1964)

Beyond Racism; Building and Open Society (McGraw-Hill, 1969)

Sidelights: "Whitney Young, as executive secretary of the National Urban League, accepted the challenge of directing the organization into a more dynamic role in the struggle for civil rights...."

"He attempted to restore the League to the front rank of leadership in the revolution of the 1960's." (*Historical Negro Biographies*)

Sources: *Historical Negro Biographies*; *Negro Handbook.*

Bibliography of Sources

(Arranged alphabetically by title)

African Authors: A Companion to Black African Writing. Vol. 1: *1300-1973.* Edited by Donald E. Herdeck. Washington, D.C.: Black Orpheus Press, 1973.

The African Origin of Civilization. Cheikh A. Diop. Westport, Conn.: Lawrence Hill, 1974.

African Writers on African Writings. Edited by G. D. Killam. Evanston, Ill.: Northwestern University Press, 1973.

African Writers Talking. Edited by Dennis Duerden and Cosmo Pitterse. London: Heinemann, 1972.

African Writing Today. Ezekiel Mphahlele. Baltimore, Md.: Penguin Books, 1967.

Afro-American Authors. William Adams. Boston: Houghton Mifflin, 1972.

Afro-American Encyclopedia. N. Miami, Fla.: Educational Book Publisher, Inc., 1974.

Afro-American Literature and Culture since World War II. Charles D. Peavy. Detroit: Gale Research, 1979.

Afro-American Literature: Drama. Edited by William Adams, et al. Boston: Houghton Mifflin, 1970.

Afro-American Literature: Fiction. Edited by William Adams, et al. Boston: Houghton Mifflin, 1970.

Afro-American Literature: Non-Fiction. Edited by William Adams, et al. Boston: Houghton Mifflin, 1970.

Afro-American Writers. Compiled by Darwin T. Turner. New York: Appleton, 1970.

Afro-American Writing. Vol. 1. Edited by Richard A. Long and Eugenia W. Collier. New York: New York University Press, 1972.

AFRO USA: A Reference Work on the Black Experience. Edited by Harry A. Ploski and Ernest Kaiser. New York: Bellwether, 1971.

American Authors and Books: 1640 to the Present Day. 3rd rev. ed. Edited by W. I. Burke and Will D. Howe. Revised by Irving and Ann Weiss. New York: Crown, 1978.

American Book Publishing Record. Cumulative, 1876-1949, 1950-1977. New York: R. R. Bowker, 1980.

American Libraries. Monthly journal. Chicago: American Library Association.

American Literature by Negro Authors. Edited by Herman Dreer. New York: Macmillan, 1950.

American Men and Women of Science: Physical and Biological Science. 15th ed., vol. IV. Edited by Jacques Cattell Press. New York: R. R. Bowker, 1982.

American Negro Poetry. Edited by Arna Bontemps. New York: Hill & Wang, 1963.

American Negro Reference Book. Edited by John P. Davis. Englewood Cliffs, N.J.: Prentice-Hall, 1966.

American Negro Short Stories. Edited by John H. Clarke. New York: Hill & Wang, 1960.

American Women Writers: A Critical Reference Guide from Colonial Times to the Present. Edited by Lina Mainiero. New York: Frederick Ungar, 1979.

Amistad 1. Edited by John A. Williams and Charles Harris. St. Paul, Minn.: Vintage Books, 1970.

Anger, and Beyond. Herbert Hill. New York: Harper & Row, 1966.

Anthology of American Negro Literature. Edited by V. F. Calverton. New York: Modern Library, 1929.

An Anthology of Verse by American Negroes. Edited by Newman I. White and Walter C. Jackson. Durham, N.C.: Trinity College Press, 1924.

Authors and Writers Who's Who. London, Burke's Peerage, Ltd., 1971.

Authors in the News. Edited by Barbara Nykoruk. Detroit: Gale Research, 1976.

Authors of Books for Young People. Martha E. Ward and Dorothy A. Marquardt. New York: Scarecrow, 1964.

The Beautyful Ones Are Not Yet Born. Ayi Kwei Armah. Boston: Houghton Mifflin, 1968.

Best Short Stories by Negro Writers: An Anthology from 1899 to the Present. Edited by Langston Hughes. New York: Little, Brown, 1967.

Bibliography of Creative African Writing. Janheinz John and Claus P. Dressler. Millwood, N.Y.: Kraus-Thomson, 1973.

Bibliography of the Caribbean. Audine Wilkinson. Cave Hill, Barbados: University of W. Indies, 1974.

Biographic Encyclopedia of Women. World Biography Press, 1975.

A Biographical History of Blacks in America since 1528. Edgar A. Toppin. New York: David McKay, 1971.

Black American Literature: Essays. Edited by Darwin T. Turner. Columbus, Ohio: Charles E. Merrill, 1969.

Black American Literature: Fiction. Edited by Darwin T. Turner. Columbus, Ohio: Charles E. Merrill, 1969.

Black American Literature: Poetry. Edited by Darwin T. Turner. Columbus, Ohio: Charles E. Merrill, 1969.

Black American Playwrights, 1800 to the Present. Edited by Esther S. Arata and Nicholas J. Rotoli. New York: Scarecrow, 1976.

Black American Playwrights, 1823-1977: An Annotated Bibliography of Plays. Compiled and edited by James V. Hatch and Omani Abdullah. New York: R. R. Bowker, 1977.

Black American Writers: 1773-1949. Geraldine O. Matthews and African-American Materials Project Staff. Durham, N.C.: N.C. Central University, 1975.

Black American Writers Past and Present. Theressa Rush, et al. New York: Scarecrow, 1975.

Black American Writers. Vol. I: *Fiction*. Edited by C. W. E. Bigsby. Baltimore, Md.: Penguin Books, 1969.

Black American Writers. Vol. II: *Poetry and Drama*. Edited by C. W. E. Bigsby. Baltimore, Md.: Penguin Books, 1969.

Black Artists in the United States. Janet L. Sims and Lenwood G. Davis. Westport, Conn.: Greenwood Press, 1980.

Black Arts. Ahmed Alhamisi and Kofi Wangara. New York (?): Black Arts, 1969.

Black Books Bulletin. Irregular. Chicago: Institute of Positive Education.

Black Collegian. Bimonthly magazine. New Orleans, La.

Black Drama. Edited by William Brasmer and Dominick Consolo. Columbus, Ohio: Charles E. Merrill, 1970.

Black Drama Anthology. Edited by Woodie King and Ron Milner. New York: New American Library, 1971.

Black Drama in America. Edited by Darwin T. Turner. New York: Fawcett, 1971.

Black Enterprise. Monthly magazine. Mount Morris, Ill.: Earl G. Graves Pub. Co.

Black Expression. Addison Gayle. Weybright & Talley, 1969.

Black Fire: An Anthology of Afro-American Writing. Edited by LeRoy Jones and Larry Neal. New York: Morrow, 1968.

Black Heritage. Monthly magazine. Reston, Va.: Sylvestre C. Watkins Co., 1961-82.

Black Historians. Earl E. Thorpe. New York: Morrow, 1969.

Black Insights: Significant Literature by Black Americans—1760 to the Present. Nick Aaron Ford. Waltham, Mass.: Ginn, 1971.

Black Joy. Edited by Jay David. Chicago: Cowles Books Co., 1971.

Black Moses: The Story of Marcus Garvey. E. David Cronon. Madison, Wis.: University of Wisconsin Press, 1969.

Black Poets of the United States from Paul Lawrence Dunbar to Langston Hughes. Jean Wagner. Urbana, Ill.: University of Illinois Press, 1973.

Black Politicians. Richard Bruner. New York: McKay, 1971.

Black Power. Charles V. Hamilton and Stokely Carmichael. New York: Random House, 1967.

Black Scenes. Edited by Alice Childress. Garden City, N.Y.: Doubleday, 1972.

Black Scholar. Monthly magazine. San Francisco.

The Black Seventies. Edited by Floyd Barbour. Boston: Porter Sargent, 1970.

Black Voices: An Anthology of Afro-American Literature. Abraham Chapman. New York: New American Library, 1968.

Black World. Monthly magazine (discontinued).

Black Writers in French. Lilyan Kesteloot. Phila.: Temple University Press, 1974.

Black Writers in Los Angeles, California. (Pamphlet.) Hilda G. Finney. L.A.: Center for Extending American History, n.d.

Black Writers of America. Richard Barksdale. New York: Macmillan, 1972.

Blackamerican Literature. Edited by Ruth Miller. Beverly Hills, Cal.: Glencoe Press, 1971.

Blackness and the Adventure of Western Culture. George E. Kent. Chicago: Third World Press, 1972.

Book of American Negro Poetry. Rev. ed. Edited by James Weldon Johnson. New York: Harcourt, Brace & World, 1959.

Book Review Digest. 1966 ed., 1976 ed., 1978 ed. New York: H. W. Wilson, 1967, 1977, 1979, 1982.

Books in Print. New York: R. R. Bowker. Published annually.

Broadside Authors and Artists: An Illustrated Biographical Directory. Compiled and edited by Leonead P. P. Bailey. Detroit: Broadside Press, 1974.

Caribbean Writers. Edited by Donald E. Herdeck. Washington, D.C.: Three Continents Press, 1979.

Caricom Bibliography. 2 vols. Georgetown, Guyana: Caribbean Community Secretariat, 1977-78.

Caroling Dusk: An Anthology of Verse by Negro Poets. Edited by Countee Cullen. New York: Harper & Row, 1927.

Cavalcade: Negro American Writing from 1760 to the Present. Edited by Arthur P. Davis and Saunders Redding. Boston: Houghton Mifflin, 1971.

Chicago Daily Defender. Daily newspaper.

Chicago Tribune. Daily newspaper.

Complete Caribbeana, 1900-1975. Edited by Lambros Comitas. Kingston, Jamaica: Kraus, 1977.

Conference Notes (Recent Development in Black Literature and Criticism). L.A.: UCLA Center for Afro-American Studies, 1983.

Contemporary Authors: A Bio-Bibliographical Guide to Current Writers and Their Works. Detroit: Gale Research. Published quadrennially.

Contemporary Dramatists. Edited by James Vinson. New York: St. Martin's Press, 1977.

Contemporary Novelists. Edited by James Vinson. New York: St. Martin's Press, 1972; 2nd ed., 1976.

Contemporary Poets. 2nd ed. Edited by James Vinson. New York: St. Martin's Press, 1975; 3rd ed., 1980.

Crisis. Monthly magazine. New York.

Cumulative Book Index. New York: H. W. Wilson, 1898- .

Current Biography: Who's News and Why. New York: H. W. Wilson. Published annually.

Cyprian Ekwensi. Ernest Emenyonu. London: Evans Brothers, 1974.

Daddy King. Martin Luther King, Sr. New York: Morrow, 1980.

Dark Symphony: Negro Literature in America. Edited by James A. Emanuel and Theodore L. Gross. New York: Free Press, 1968.

Dictionary Catalog of the Negro Collection of Fisk University. Boston: G. K. Hall, 1974.

Dictionary Catalog of the Schomburg Collection of Negro Literature and History, 1962. Boston: G. K. Hall, 1962. 1st Supplement, 1962-67, 19 . 2nd Supplement, 1972. Supplement 1974, 1976.

Dictionary Catalog of the Vivian G. Harsh Collection of Afro-American History and Literature. Chicago Public Library. Boston: G. K. Hall, 1978.

Dictionary of American Negro Biography. Edited by Rayford W. Logan and Michael Winston. New York: Norton, 1983.

Dictionary of American Scholars, Vol. II: *English, Speech and Drama*. Edited by Jacques Cattell. New York: R. R. Bowker, 1969.

Dictionary of Literary Biography, Part 2: *Twentieth Century American Dramatists*. Edited by John MacNichols. Detroit: Gale Research, 1981.

Dictionary of Literary Biography, Yearbook: 1981. Edited by Karen L. Rood, et al. Detroit: Gale Research, 1982.

Dictionary of Literary Biography, vol. 33, Afro American Fiction Writers after 1955. Edited by Thadious M. Davis and Trudier Harris. Detroit: Gale Research, 1984.

Directory of American Poets and Fiction Writers. 1980-81 ed. New York: Poets & Writers, Inc., 1980.

Directory of American Scholars, Vol. I: *History*. 5th ed. Edited by Jacques Cattell. New York: R. R. Bowker, 1969.

Directory of Professional Engineers and Land Surveyors. Cal. Dept. of Consumer Affairs, 1929.

Drumvoices: The Mission of Afro-American Poetry. Eugene B. Redmond. Garden City, N.Y.: Doubleday, 1976.

DuBois: A Pictorial Biography. Shirley L. Graham. Chicago: Johnson Publishing Co., 1978.

Early Black American Poets. Edited by William H. Robinson, Jr. New York: William C. Brown, 1969.

Early Negro American Writers. Benjamin Brawley. Chapel Hill, N.C.: University of North Carolina Press, 1935.

Ebony. Chicago: Johnson Publishing Co. (Various issues)

Emerging African Nations and Their Leaders. Vol. 1. Edited by Lancelot Evans. Yonkers, N.Y.: Educational Heritage, Negro Heritage Library, 1963. Vol. 2, 1964.

Emperor Shaka the Great. Mazisi Kunene. London: Heinemann, 1979.

Encyclopedia of Black America. Edited by W. Augustus Low and Virgil A. Clift. New York: McGraw-Hill, 1981.

Encyclopedia of World Literature in the 20th Century. Edited by Wolfgang B. Fleischmann. New York: Frederick Ungar, 1967.

Facts on File. New York, 1984.

Famous American Negro Poets. Charlemae Rollins. New York: Dodd, Mead & Co., 1955.

Famous American Negroes. Langston Hughes. New York: Dodd, Mead & Co., 1954.

Famous Negro Athletes. Edited by Arna Bontemps. New York: Dodd, Mead & Co., 1964.

The First Time. Karl and Anne T. Fleming. New York: Simon & Schuster, 1975.

First World. Irregular magazine (discontinued).

For Malcolm: Poems on the Life and the Death of Malcolm X. Edited by Dudley Randall and Margaret Burroughs. Detroit: Broadside Press, 1969.

Forgotten Pages of American Literature. Edited by Gerald W. Haslam. Boston: Houghton Mifflin, 1970.

Forthcoming Books. New York: R. R. Bowker, Sept. 1975.

14th Annual Booklist, Young Adult Reveiwers of Southern California. California Library Association, 1979.

Freedomways. A quarterly. New York: Freedomways Associates, Inc.

From Slavery to Freedom. John H. Franklin. New York: Knopf, 1956.

From the Dark Tower: Afro-American Writers, 1900 to 1960. Arthur P. Davis. Washington, D.C.: Howard University Press, 1974.

A Galaxy of Black Writing. R. Baird Shuman. Durham, N.C.: Moore Publishing Co., 1970.

Great Negroes Past and Present. 3rd ed. Edited by Russell Adams. Chicago: Afro-American Publishing Co., 1969.

Harlem: Negro Metropolis. Claude McKay. New York: Dutton, 1940.

His Own Where. June Jordan. New York: Crowell, 1971.

Historical Negro Biographies. Wilhelmena S. Robinson. New York: Association for the Study of Negro Life and History, 1967.

A Humanist in Africa. Kenneth Kaunda. Nashville, Abingdon Press, 1966.

In Black and White: Afro-Americans in Print, 1916 to 1969. Edited by Mary M. Spradling. Kalamazoo, Mich.: Kalamazoo Library System, 1971.

International Authors and Writers Who's Who. 7th ed. Edited by Ernest Kay. Cambridge, Eng.: Melrose Press, 1976.

International Encyclopedia of Higher Education. Vol. 6. San Francisco: Jossey-Bass, 1977.

International Who's Who, 1965-66. London: Europa Publications, Ltd.

Interview with Six Nigerian Writers. John Agetua. Benin City, Nigeria: Bendel Newspaper Corp., 1976.

Interviews with Black Writers. Edited by John O'Brien. New York: Liveright, 1973.

An Introduction to West African Literature. Oladdele Tarivo. London, Nelson, 1967.

Jamaican National Bibliography. Kingston, Jamaica: Kraus, 1981.

Jet Magazine. Weekly. Chicago: Johnson Publishing Co.

Journal of African History. London: Cambridge University Press, 1960.

Jump Bad, a New Chicago Anthology. Gwendolyn Brooks. Detroit: Broadside Press, 1971.

Kaleidoscope: Poems by American Negro Poets. Edited by Robert Hayden. New York: Harcourt, Brace & World, 1967.

Kirkus Review Service. Semimonthly. New York: Kirkus Service, Inc.

Library Journal. Semimonthly. New York: R. R. Bowker.

Living Black American Authors. Edited by Ann A. Shockley and Sue P. Chandler. New York: R. R. Bowker, 1973.

The Lonesome Road. Saunders Redding. Garden City, N.Y.: Doubleday, 1958.

Los Angeles Herald Examiner. Daily newspaper.

Los Angeles Sentinel. Weekly newspaper.

Los Angeles Times. Daily newspaper.

Los Angeles Times Book Review. Weekly.

A Man of the People. Chinua Achebe. London: Heinemann, 1977.

Men of Mark. William J. Simmons. Chicago. Johnson Publishing Co., 1970.

Modern Black Writers. Edited by Michael Popkin. New York: Frederick Ungar, 1978.

More Black American Playwrights: A Bibliography. Edited by Esther S. Arata. New York: Scarecrow, 1978.

My Odyssey: An Autobiography. Nnamdi Azikiwe. New York: Praeger, 1970.

"National Conference of Afro-American Writers" Program. Boston: Howard University Institute for Arts and Humanities, Nov. 1974.

National Guardian (discontinued).

National Playwrights Directory. 2nd ed. Edited by Phyllis Johnson Kaye. Waterford, Conn.: Eugene O'Neill Theater Center, 1981.

The National Union Catalog. Pre-1956 Imprints; 1958-63; 1963-67; 1968-72; 1973-77. Compiled by Library of Congress. New York: Rowman and Littlefield.

A Native Sons Reader. Edited by Edward Margolies. Phila.: Lippincott, 1970.

Negro Almanac. 2nd ed. Edited by Harry A. Ploski and Ernest Kaiser. New York: Bellwether, 1971.

The Negro Author: His Development in America to 1900. Vernon Loggins. Port Washington, N.Y.: Kennikat Press, 1959.

Negro Builders and Heroes. Benjamin Brawley. Chapel Hill, N.C.: University of North Carolina Press, 1937.

Negro Caravan: Writings by American Negroes. Edited by Sterling A. Brown, et al. New York: Arno Press and N.Y. Times, 1969.

Negro Digest. Monthly magazine (discontinued).

Negro Genius: A New Appraisal of the Achievement of the American Negro in Literature and the Fine Arts. Benjamin Brawley. New York: Dodd, Mead & Co., 1937.

Negro Handbook. Compiled by editors of *Ebony*. Chicago: Johnson Publishing Co., 1966.

Negro History Bulletin. Quarterly journal.

Negro in American Culture. Margaret Just Butcher. New York: Knopf, 1956.

Negro Novel in America. Robert A. Bone. New Haven, Conn.: Yale University Press, 1958.

Negro Poets and Their Poems. 3rd rev. ed. Edited by Robert T. Kerlin. Washington, D.C.: Associated Publication, 1935.

Negro Vanguard. Richard Bardolph. New York: Random House, 1959.

Negro Voices in American Fiction. Hugh Gloster. New York: Russell, 1965.

Negroes in Public Affairs and Government. Edited by Walter Christmas. Yonkers, N.Y.: Educational Heritage, 1966.

Negroes Who Helped Build America. Madeline R. Stratton. Waltham, Mass.: Ginn, 1965.

New Black Playwrights. Edited by William Couch, Jr. New York: Avon, 1970.

New Black Poetry. Edited by Clarence Major. New York: International Publisher, 1969.

New Black Voices: An Anthology of Contemporary Afro-American Literature. New York: New American Library, 1972.

New Black Writing: Africa, West-Indies, the Americas. Tulsa, Okla.: University of Tulsa, 1977.

New Negro Poets, U.S.A. Edited by Langston Hughes. Bloomington, Ind.: Indiana University Press, 1964.

New Republic: A Journal of Opinion. New York: Republic Publishing Co.

New York Amsterdam News. Weekly newspaper.

New York Herald Tribune. Daily newspaper.

New York Times. Daily newspaper.

New York Times Book Review. New York: New York Times, Dec. 14, 1965; Apr. 19, 1981; May 3, 1981; Aug. 9, 1981; Jan. 9, 1983.

Newsweek. Weekly magazine. New York: Newsweek, Inc.

Nine Black Poets. Edited by Baird Shuman. Durham, N.C.: Moore Publishing Co., 1968.

No Sweetness Here. Ama Ata Aidoo. Garden City, N.Y.: Doubleday, 1970.

100 Years of Negro Freedom. Arna Bontemps. New York: Dodd, Mead & Co., 1961.

1000 Successful Blacks. Compiled by editors of *Ebony.* Chicago: Johnson Publishing Co., 1973.

Paul Robeson. Virginia Hamilton. New York: Harper & Row, 1974.

Paul Robeson, Citizen of the World. Edited by Stanley J. Kunitz and Vineta Colby. New York: H. W. Wilson, 1955.

Pillars in Ethiopian History. Edited by Joseph E. Harris. Washington, D.C.: Howard University Press, 1974.

Pittsburgh Courier. Weekly newspaper.

Poems from Black Africa. Edited by Langston Hughes. Bloomington, Ind.: Indiana University Press, 1963.

Poetry of Black America. Edited by Arnold Adoff. New York: Harper & Row, 1973.

Poetry of the Negro, 1746-1949. Edited by Langston Hughes and Arna Bontemps. Garden City, N.Y.: Doubleday, 1949.

Profiles of Negro Womanhood. Sylvia G. Dannett. Yonkers, N.Y.: Educational Heritage, 1964.

Protest and Conflict in African Literature. Cosmo Pieterse and Donald Munro. New York: Africana, 1969.

Publishers Weekly. Weekly journal. New York: R. R. Bowker.

Reader's Encyclopedia of American Literature. Edited by Max J. Herzberg. New York: Crowell, 1962.

A Reader's Guide to African Literature. Compiled by Hans M. Zell and Helene Silver. New York: Africana, 1971.

Resistance and Caribbean Literature. Selwyn R. Cudjoe, Athens: Ohio University Press, 1980.

Revolt of the Black Athlete. Harry Edwards. New York: Free Press, 1969.

Right On! Edited by Bradford Chambers. New York: New American Library, 1970.

A Rock against the Wind: Black Love Poems. Lindsay Patterson, comp. New York: Dodd, Mead, 1973.

School Library Journal. Monthly journal. New York: R. R. Bowker.

"Second Annual Authors Autography Party" (brochure). California Librarians Black Caucus, July 1975.

Selected Black American Authors: An Illustrated Bio-Bibliography. Compiled by James A. Page. Boston: G. K. Hall, 1977.

Selected Poems. Leopold Senghor. Cambridge, Eng.: Cambridge University Press, 1977.

Seven Black American Scientists. Robert C. Hayden. Reading, Mass.: Addison-Wesley, 1970.

$70 Billion in the Black. D. Parke Gibson. New York: Macmillan, 1978.

Slave and Freeman: The Autobiography of George L. Knox. Edited by Willard B. Gatewood, Jr. Lexington: University of Kentucky Press, 1979.

The Slave Girl. Buchi Emecheta. New York: Braziller, 1977.

Soledad Brother. George Jackson. New York: Bantam, 1970.

Something about the Author. Vols. 1-14. Edited by Anne Commire. Detroit: Gale Research, 1973-78.

Soon, One Morning: New Writing by American Negroes. Edited by Herbert Hill. New York: Knopf, 1963.

Soulscript: Afro-American Poetry. Edited by June Jordan. Garden City, N.Y.: Doubleday, 1970.

Sturdy Black Bridges. Edited by Roseann P. Bell. Garden City, N.Y.: Doubleday, 1979.

They Showed the Way. Charlemae Rollins. New York: Crowell, 1964.

13 against the Odds. Edwin R. Embree. New York: Viking Press, 1944.

Time. Weekly magazine. New York: Time Inc.

To Gwen with Love: An Anthology Dedicated to Gwendolyn Brooks. Edited by Patricia Brown, et al. Chicago: Johnson Publishing Co., 1971.

Today's Negro Voices. Edited by Beatrice M. Murphy. New York: Julian Messner, 1970.

Trojan Family. Quarterly. Los Angeles: University of Southern California.

Twentieth Century Authors: A Biographical Dictionary of Modern Literature. Edited by Stanley J. Kuniz and Howard Haycraft. New York: H. W. Wilson, 1942.

University of Chicago Magazine. Chicago: University of Chicago, Sept. 1980.

Washington Post Book Review. Washington, D.C.: Washington Post, May 24, 1981.

West Indian Literature. Jeannette B. Allis. Boston: G. K. Hall, 1981.

West Indian Novel. Michael Gilkes. Boston: Twayne, 1981.

West Indian Novel and Its Background. Kenneth Ramchand. London: Faber, 1970.

West Indian Poetry. Lloyd Brown. Boston: Twayne, 1978.

Who Was Who in America. Historical vol. and 4 vols. 1607-1968. Chicago: A. N. Marquis, 1942-68.

Who's Who among Black Americans. Edited by W. M. C. Matney. Northbrook, Ill.: Who's Who among Black Americans, Inc. Published biennially.

Who's Who in African Literature. Edited by Janheinz John. Tubingen, Germany: Horst Erdmann, 1972.

Who's Who in America. Chicago: A. N. Marquis. Published biennially.

Who's Who in American Art. Edited by Dorothy B. Gilbert. New York: R. R. Bowker, 1962.

Who's Who in Colored America. 7th ed. Edited by James Fleming and Christian E. Burckel. New York: Christian E. Burckel & Association, 1950.

Who's Who in the American Negro Press. Edited by Roy L. Hill. Royal Publishers, 1960.

Who's Who in the West. 14th ed., 1974-75. Chicago, A. N. Marquis, 1974.

The Worker. Semiweekly newspaper. New York.

World Authors 1950-1970. Edited by John Wakeman. New York: H. W. Wilson, 1975.

World Encyclopedia of Black Peoples, Vol. 1: *Conspectus*. St. Clair Shores, Mich.: Scholarly Press, 1975.

World's Great Men of Color. Edited by J. A. Rogers. New York: Macmillan, 1972.

Writers Directory. New York: St. Martin's Press. Published triennially.

Writing of Wole Soyinka. Eldred D. Jones. London: Heinemann, 1975.

Zambia Shall Be Free. Kenneth Kaunda. New York: Praeger, 1963.

African Writers Nationality Index _____

Cameroon
Bebey, Francis
Beti, Mongo
Oyono, Ferdinand

Congo — Brazzaville
U Tam'si, Gérald Félix

Ethiopia
Sellassie, Sahle

Ghana
Aidoo, Ama Ata
Armah, Ayi Kwei
Awoonor, Kofi
Nkrumah, Kwame
Sutherland, Efua

Guinea
Laye, Camara

Ivory Coast
Dadié, Bernard
Nokan, Charles

Kenya
Kenyatta, Jomo
Mbiti, John
Ngugi, James
Ogot, Bethwell A.
Ogot, Grace

Liberia
Henries, A. Doris B.

Malawi
Kayira, Legson

Nigeria
Achebe, Chinua
Azikiwe, Nnamdi
Clark, John Pepper
Ekwensi, Cyprian
Emecheta, Buchi
Nwapa, Flora
Obichere, Boniface
Okara, Gabriel
Okigbo, Christopher
Okpaku, Joseph
Soyinka, Wole
Tutuola, Amos

São Tomé
Espirito Santo, Alda de
Margarido, Maria M.

Senegal
Diop, Birago
Diop, Cheikh A.
M'Baye, Annette
Ousmane, Sembène
Senghor, Léopold S.

South Africa
Abrahams, Peter
Brutus, Dennis
Head, Bessie
Kgositsile, Keoropetse
Kunene, Mazisi
La Guma, Alex
Luthuli, Albert
Mphahlele, Ezekiel
Rive, Richard

Caribbean Writers Nationality Index _____

Bahamas
Wallace, Susan

Barbados
Brathwaite, Edward K.
Clarke, Austin C.
Lamming, George
Marshall, Paule

Costa Rica
Samuels, Wilfred

Cuba
Guillen, Nicolás

French Guiana
Damas, Léon
Jumniner, Bertène

Guyana
Braithwaite, E. R.
Dathorne, Oscar
Harris, Wilson
Mittelhölzer, Edgar
Van Sertima, Ivan

Haiti
Roumain, Jacques
Thoby-Marcelin, Philippe

Jamaica
Baugh, Edward
Bennett, Louise
Figueroa, John
Hearne, John
Mais, Roger
Palmer, C. Everard
Patterson, Horace Orlando
Reid, V. S.
Wynter, Sylvia

Martinique
Césaire, Aimé
Fanon, Frantz
Glissant, Edouard
Maran, René

Panama
Salkey, Andrew

Saint Lucia
Lewis, Sir William A.
Walcott, Derek

Trinidad
Anthony, Michael
Cartey, Wilfred
Guy, Rosa
Hodge, Merle
James, C. L. R.
Williams, Eric

Occupational Index _____

Abolitionists
Brown, William Wells
Douglass, Frederick
Forten, Charlotte L.
Garnet, Henry Highland
Grimké, Archibald
Harper, Frances Ellen Watkins
Still, William
Vassa, Gustavus
Walker, David
Ward, Samuel Ringgold

Activists; Revolutionaries
Baraka, Imamu Amiri [Everett LeRoi Jones]
Boggs, James
Brown, Claude
Bullins, Ed
Carmichael, Stokely
Cleaver, (LeRoy) Eldridge
Davis, Angela Yvonne
DuBois, David Graham
DuBois, William Edward Burghardt
Edwards, Harry
Fanon, Frantz
Giovanni, Nikki
Glissant, Edouard
Jackson, George
Lee, Don Luther
Lester, Julius
Lightfoot, Claude M.
Little, Malcolm [Malcolm X]
McKissick, Floyd Bixler
Neal, Lawrence P.
Nkrumah, Kwame
Robeson, Paul
Sanchez, Sonia
Seale, Bobby
Thomas, Tony
Trotter, William Monroe
Walker, David
Wells (Barnett), Ida B.
Winston, Henry

Actors; Actresses
Angelou, Maya [Marguerite Johnson]
Bailey, Pearl Mae
Bennett, Louise Simone [Mis Lou]
Branch, William Blackwell
Childress, Alice
Davis, Ossie
Gordon/E, Charles Edward
Mayfield, Julian
Poitier, Sidney
Robeson, Paul
Sharp, Saundra
Van Peebles, Melvin
Ward, Douglas Turner
Ward, Theodore
Wynter, Sylvia [Wynter Carew]

Anthologists
Bontemps, Arna Wendell
Braithwaite, William Stanley
Dathorne, Oscar Ronald
Figueroa, John (Joseph Maria)
Kaiser, Ernest Daniel
King, Woodie
Lane, Pinkie Gordon
Lee, Ulysses
Long, Richard
McElroy, Colleen J.
Neal, Lawrence P.
Patterson, Lindsay
p'Bitek, J. P. Okot [Okot, p'Bitek]
Randall, Dudley Felker
Redmond, Eugene Benjamin
Robinson, William Henry, Jr.
Roumain, Jacques (Jean Baptiste)
Salkey, (Felix) Andrew (Alexander)
Soyinka, Wole [Akinwande Oluwole]
Troupe, Quincy
Turner, Darwin T.
Washington, Mary Helen

Anthropologists
Davis, Allison
Drake, (John Gibbs) St. Clair
Dunham, Katherine
Fauset, Arthur Huff
Gwaltney, John Langston
Kenyatta, Jomo [Kamaua Ngengi]
Robeson, Eslanda Cardozo
Stack, Carol B.
Van Sertima, Ivan

Artists
Andrews, Benny
Burroughs, Margaret G.
Chase-Riboud, Barbara
Demby, William
Fax, Elton Clay
Feelings, Tom
Higgins, Chester Archer, Jr.
Joans, Ted
Johnson, Charles Richard
Lewis, Samella Sanders
Locke, Alain Leroy
Long, Richard Alexander
McGaugh, Lawrence Walter, Jr.
Parks, Gordon Alexander
Porter, James Amos
Steptoe, John Lewis
Waddy, Williana Ruth

Bibliographers
Arata, Esther Spring
Baldwin, Claudia A.
Davis, Lenwood G.
Perry, Margaret
Porter, Dorothy Burnett
Sims, Janet L.
Williams, Ethel Langley

Biographers; Autobiographers
Anderson, Jarvis
Angelou, Maya [Marguerite Johnson]
Azikiwe, Benjamin Nnamdi
Baker, Josephine
Bontemps, Arna Wendell
Clarke, John Henrik
Graham, Shirley Lola
Grimké, Archibald H.
Haley, Alex
Haskins, James
Henries, A. Doris Banks
Hughes, (James) Langston
Killens, John Oliver
Kaunda, Kenneth (David)
Kayira, Legson
Luthuli [Lutuli], Chief Albert John Mvumbi
Maran, René
Mphahlele, Ezekiel
Pickens, William

Quarles, Benjamin Arthur
Tuttle, William McCullough
Vassa, Gustavus
Webb, Sheyann

Black Nationalists
Garvey, Marcus
Lee, Don Luther
Little, Malcolm [Malcolm X]
Thomas, Tony

Broadcaster
Figueroa, John (Joseph Maria)

Business Persons
Davis, George B.
Gloster, Jesse E.
Holland, Jerome Heartwell
Morrow, Everett Frederic
Knox, George L.
Reid, V(ictor) S(tafford)
Sims, Naomi Ruth

Civil Rights Leaders & Advocates
Clark, Kenneth Bancroft
DuBois, William Edward Burghardt
Gregory, Richard Claxton (Dick)
Harding, Vincent
Hedgeman, Anna Arnold
Johnson, James Weldon
King, Coretta Scott
King, Martin Luther, Jr.
Moody, Anne
Morrow, Everett Frederic
Robeson, Paul
Rollins, Bryant
Rowan, Carl Thomas
Rustin, Bayard
Trotter, William Monroe
Wells (Barnett), Ida B.
White, Walter Francis
Wilkins, Roy
Wright, Nathan, Jr.
Young, Whitney

Columnists
Goodwin, Ruby B.
Lomax, Louis Emanuel
Mathis, Sharon Bell
Rodgers, Carolyn Marie
Rodgers, Joel Augustus
Rowan, Carl Thomas
Saunders, Doris Evans

Consultants
Damas, Léon Gontran
Figueroa, John (Joseph Maria)
Ford, Nick Aaron
Kaiser, Ernest Daniel

Kent, George Edward
Lincoln, Charles Eric
Molette, Carlton Woodard II
Murray, Albert L.
Wallace, Walter L.
Winston, Michael
Wright, Nathan, Jr.

Dancers
Angelou, Maya [Marguerite Johnson]
Baker, Josephine
Beckford, Ruth
Dunham, Katherine
Polite, Carlene Hatcher
Shangé, Ntozake [Paulette L. Williams]
Wynter, Sylvia [Wynter Carew]

Diplomats
Braithwaite, (Eustace) E(dward) R(icardo)
Bunche, Ralph Johnson
Cook, Mercer
Diop, Birago Ismaïl
Douglass, Frederick
Holland, Jerome Heartwell
Johnson, James Weldon
Oyono, Ferdinand Léopold
Smythe, Mabel Murphy
Wharton, Clifton Reginald, Jr.

Directors
(Drama)
Branch, William Blackwell
Childress, Alice
Davis, Ossie
Gordon/E, Charles Edward
King, Woodie
El Muhajir [Marvin X]

(Films)
Parks, Gordon Alexander
Poitier, Sidney

Economists
Bobo, Benjamin F.
Brimmer, Andrew Felton
Gibson, D. Parke
Harris, Abram Lincoln
Lewis, Sir William Arthur
Sowell, Thomas
Weaver, Robert Clifton
Wharton, Clifton Reginald, Jr.

Editors
(Journals)
Bullins, Ed
Clarke, John Henrik
DuBois, William Edward Burghardt
Johnson, Percy Edward
Lee, Don Luther

Low, W. Augustus
Major, Clarence
Mayfield, Julian
Mitchell, Loften
Murphy, Beatrice Campbell
Neal, Lawrence P.
O'Daniel, Therman Benjamin
Samuels, Wilfred D.
Smith, Arthur L. [Molefi Kete Asante]
Troupe, Quincy
Turner, Darwin T.
Welburn, Ronald Garfield
Williams, George Washington

(Magazines)
Allen, Robert L.
Atkins, Russell
Bennett, Lerone, Jr.
Blassingame, John W.
Bogle, Donald
Brown, Frank London
Cullen, Countee Porter
Dunbar, Ernest
Fauset, Jessie Redmond
Fuller, Hoyt W.
Gale, Addison, Jr.
Gillespie, Marcia Ann
Graham, Shirley Lola
Johnson, Charles Spurgeon
Johnson, Fenton
King, Helen H.
Lewis, Ida Elizabeth
McPherson, James Alan
El Muhajir [Marvin X]
Parks, Gordon Alexander
Patterson, Lindsay
Plumpp, Sterling Dominic
Poisett, Alex
Reid, V(ictor) S(tafford)
Saunders, Doris Evans
Schuyler, George S.
Spellman, A. B.
Thompson, Era Bell
Wesley, Richard Errol
Williams, John Alfred

(Newspapers)
Bass, Charlotta A. (Spears)
Cornish, Samuel E.
Dabney, Wendell Philips
Davis, Arthur P.
Davis, Frank Marshall
DuBois, David Graham
Fortune, Timothy Thomas
Grimké, Archibald H.
Hughes, (James) Langston
Jackson, Clyde Owen
Jones, Clarence B.
Major, Geraldyn (Gerri) Hodges
Martin, Louis E.

Editors (cont'd)
(Newspapers), cont'd
  Matney, William C., Jr.
  Miller, Loren
  Rollins, Bryant
  Russwurm, John B.
  Smith, William Gardner
  U Tam'si, Gérald Félix Tchicya
  Walker, William O.
  Wells (Barnett), Ida Bell

(Series or Publishing Co.)
  Cliff, Virgil Alfred
  Coombs, Orde
  Emanuel, James Andrew
  Goode, Kenneth Gregory
  Halliburton, Warren J.
  Johnson, John Harold
  Morrison, Toni [Chloe Anthony Wofford]
  Redmond, Eugene Benjamin
  Southern, Eileen

Educators; Educational Administrators
  Baugh, Edward
  Berry, Mary Frances
  Billingsley, Andrew
  Bond, Horace Mann
  Butcher, Philip
  Carter, Wilmoth Annette
  Cheek, Donald K.
  Davis, George B.
  Dett, Robert Nathaniel
  Garnett, Henry Highland
  Gary, Lawrence E.
  Gloster, Hugh Morris
  Goode, Kenneth Gregory
  Green, Robert L.
  Grimké, Archibald H.
  Harris, William M., Sr.
  Hill, Leslie Pinckney
  Holland, Gerome Heartwell
  Horne, Frank S.
  Johnson, Charles Spurgeon
  Langston, John Mercer
  Leonard, Walter J.
  Mays, Benjamin Elijah
  Miller, Kelly
  Moton, Robert Russa
  Page, James
  Payne, Daniel A.
  Phinazee, Annette Alethia (Lewis)
  Pickens, William
  Reid, Ira De Augustine
  Roberts, James Deotis, Sr.
  Rosser, James Milton
  Simmons, William J.
  Skinner, Byron R.
  Tolson, Melvin Beaunorus
  Washington, Booker Taliaferro
  Wharton, Clifton Reginald, Jr.

  Williams, Lorraine A.
  Woodson, Carter Godwin
  Wright, Nathan, Jr.
  Young, Whitney Moore, Jr.

Essayists
  Baldwin, James
  Bogle, Donald
  Chrisman, Robert
  Christian, Barbara
  Clarke, John Henrik
  Cleaver, (LeRoy) Eldridge
  Collier, Eugenia
  Coombs, Orde
  Dathorne, Oscar Ronald
  Ellison, Ralph Waldo
  Fax, Elton Clay
  Gayle, Addison, Jr.
  Gibson, Donald B.
  Hercules, Frank
  James, C(yril) L(ionel) R(obert)
  Johnson, James Weldon
  Kgositsile, Keoropetse (William)
  Killens, John Oliver
  Lacy, Leslie Alexander
  Lester, Julius
  Long, Richard A.
  Major, Clarence
  Mayfield, Julian
  Nyerere, Julius Kambarage
  p'Bitek, J. P. Okot [Okot p'Bitek]
  Redding, Jay Saunders
  Scott, Nathan A., Jr.
  Walrond, Eric
  White, Walter Francis
  Williams, John Alfred
  Wright, Richard

Filmmakers
  Ousmane, Sembène
  Price, Robert E. [Bashiri]
  Robeson, Susan
  Van Peebles, Melvin

Folklorists
  Bennett, Louise Simone [Mis Lou]
  Brewer, John Mason
  Bryan, Ashley F.
  Dance, Daryl Cumber
  Ekwensi, Cyprian Odiatu Duaka
  Fauset, Arthur Huff
  Guillen, Nicolás
  Hurston, Zora Neale
  Lester, Julius
  Morgan, Kathryn L.
  Nichols, Charles Harold
  Thoby-Marcelin, Philippe
  U Tam'si, Gérald Félix Tchicya
    [Tchicaya, Félix]

Free-lance Writers

Bennett, Hal Z. [George Harold]
Clarke, Austin Chesterfield
Cruse, Harold
Gardner, Carl
Goodwin, Ruby B.
Jackson, Jesse
King, Helen H.
King, Woodie
Meriwether, Louise
Mittelhölzer, Edgar Austin
Sims, Naomi Ruth
Smythe, Mabel Murphy

Genealogists

Blockson, Charles L.
Haley, Alex

Historians

Beasley, Delilah Leontium
Bennett, Lerone, Jr.
Berry, Mary Frances
Daniels, Douglas Henry
Diop, Cheikh Anta
DuBois, William Edward Burghardt
Franklin, John Hope
Goode, Kenneth Gregory
Greene, Lorenzo Johnston
Hansberry, William Leo
Harding, Vincent
Harris, Joseph E.
Hornsby, Alton, Jr.
Huggins, Nathan Irvin
James, C(yril) L(ionel) R(obert)
Johnson, Jesse J.
Lee, Ulysses
Logan, Rayford Wittingham
Mandel, Bernard
Nell, William Cowper
Obichere, Boniface Ihewunwa
Ogot, Bethwell Alan
Ottley, Roi Vincent
Painter, Nell Irvin
Quarles, Benjamin Arthur
Robinson, Wilhelmena Simpson
Rogers, Joel Augustus
Savage, William Sherman
Still, William
Tate, Merze
Terborg-Penn, Rosalyn
Thorpe, Earlie Endris
Thurman, Sue (Bailey)
Toppin, Edgar Allan
Tuttle, William McCullough
Wesley, Charles Harris
Williams, Chancellor
Williams, Eric Eustace
Williams, George Washington
Woodson, Carter Godwin

Illustrators

Brown, Margery
Fax, Elton Clay

Journalists

Abrahams, Peter Lee [Peter Graham]
Allen, Robert L.
Anderson, Jervis
Anthony, Michael
Armah, Ayi Kwei
Azikiwe, Benjamin Nnamdi
Bebey, Francis
Booker, Simeon Saunders
Cayton, Horace R.
Chalk, Ocania
Clark, John Pepper
Davis, George B.
Douglass, Frederick
Espirito Santo, Alda de
Fortune, Timothy Thomas
Guillen, Nicolas
Hayden, Robert C.
James, C(yril) L(ionel) R(obert)
Jourdain, Rose L.
Kimenye, Barbara
La Guma, (Justin) Alexander
Lomax, Louis Emanuel
Matney, William C., Jr.
Mphahlele, Ezekiel
Nelson, Alice Dunbar
Ottley, Roi Vincent
Price, Robert E. [Bashiri]
Reid, V(ictor) S(tafford)
Reynolds, Barbara A.
Robeson, Eslanda Cardozo
Rogers, Joel Augustus
Rollins, Bryant
Roumain, Jacques (Jean Baptiste)
Rowan, Carl Thomas
Salkey, Andrew
Schuyler, George S.
Sellassie, Sahle Berhane Mariam
    [Sahle, Sellassie Berhane Mariam]
Smith, Vern E.
Smith, William Gardner
Walcott, Derek
Wilkins, Roger
Yette, Samuel F.

Juvenile Writers

Baker, Augusta
Bambara, Toni Cade
Bontemps, Arna Wendell
Brown, Margery
Bryan, Ashley F.
Burroughs, Margaret G.
Clifton, Lucille T.
Cornish, Samuel James
Edet, Edna Smith

Juvenile Writers (cont'd)
Evans, Mari
Feelings, Muriel (Grey)
Feelings, Tom
Graham, Lorenz Bell
Graham, Shirley Lola
Greenfield, Eloise
Guy, Rosa Guthbert
Halliburton, Warren J.
Hamilton, Virginia Esther
Haskett, Edythe Rance
Haskins, James
Hunter, Kristin Eggleston
Jackson, Jesse
Jordan, June [June Meyer]
King, Helen H.
Lacy, Leslie Alexander
Lester, Julius
Mathis, Sharon Bell
Meriwether, Louise
Myers, Walter Dean
Palmer, C(yril) Everard
Perry, Margaret
Petry, Ann Lane
Rollins, Charlemae Hill
Salkey, (Felix) Andrew (Alexander)
Steptoe, John Lewis
Tarry, Ellen
Taylor, Mildred
Wilkinson, Brenda S.
Young, Bernice Elizabeth
Young, Margaret Buckner

Lawyers; Judges
Allen, Samuel W. [Paul Vesey]
Brooke, Edward William
Grimké, Archibald H.
Hamilton, Charles Vernon
Higginbotham, A. Leon, Jr.
Johnson, James Weldon
Jones, Clarence B.
Langston, John Mercer
Leonard, Walter J.
McKissick, Floyd Bixler
Miller, Loren
Murray, Pauli
Owens, Charles Edward
Oyono, Ferdinand Léopold
Vann, Robert L.
Wilkins, Roger
Williams, George Washington
Young, Thomas White

Librarians; Library Administrators
Baker, Augusta
Baldwin, Claudia A.
Bontemps, Arna Wendell
Chapman, Dorothy Hilton
Churchwell, Charles Darrett

Cunningham, William D.
Jackson, Miles Merrill, Jr.
Jones, Clara Stanton
Josey, E(lonnie) J(unius)
Lorde, Andre
Mapp, Edward
Page, James
Perry, Margaret
Phinazee, Annette Alethia
Porter, Dorothy Burnett
Randall, Dudley Felker
Rollins, Charlemae Hill
Saunders, Doris Evans
Shockley, Ann Allen
Sims, Janet L.
Smith, Jessie Carney
Wilkin, Binnie Tate
Williams, Ethel Langley

Literary Critics
Baker, Houston A., Jr.
Baugh, Edward
Bontemps, Arna Wendell
Braithwaite, William Stanley
Brathwaite, Edward Kamau [L. Edward]
Brawley, Benjamin Griffith
Brown, Sterling Allen
Cartey, Wilfred
Davis, Arthur P.
Davis, Charles T.
Emanuel, James Andrew
Figueroa, John (Joseph Maria)
Ford, Nick Aaron
Gates, Henry Louis, Jr.
Gayle, Addison, Jr.
Gibson, Donald B.
Greene, J. Lee
Harris, (Theodore) Wilson
Henderson, Stephen E.
Henries, A. Doris Banks
Kent, George Edward
Kgositsile, Keoropetse (William)
Lamming, George Eric
Locke, Alain Leroy
Long, Richard Alexander
Maran, René
Mphahlele, Ezekiel
Neal, Lawrence P.
Ngugi, James [Wa Thiong'o]
O'Daniel, Therman Benjamin
Okpaku, Joseph Ohiomogben
Patterson, Lindsay
Rampersad, Arnold
Redding, Jay Saunders
Robinson, William Henry, Jr.
Salkey, (Felix) Andrew (Alexander)
Samuels, Wilfred D.
Scott, Nathan A., Jr.
Stepto, Robert Burns

Poets

Abrahams, Peter Lee [Peter Graham]
Allen, Samuel W. [Paul Vesey]
Amini, Johari M. [Jewell Christine McLawler Latimore]
Angelou, Maya [Marguerite Johnson]
Atkins, Russell
Awoonor, Kofi [George Awoonor-Williams]
Baraka, Imamu Amiri [Everett LeRoi Jones]
Barrax, Gerald William
Bell, James Madison
Bennett, Louise Simone [Mis Lou]
Bogus, S. Diane
Braithwaite, William Stanley
Brathwaite, Edward Kamau [L. Edward]
Brawley, Benjamin Griffith
Brooks, Gwendolyn Elizabeth
Brown, Sterling Allen
Brutus, Dennis Vincent
Burrell, Evelyn (Patterson)
Césaire, Aimé Fernand
Chrisman, Robert
Clark, John Pepper
Clifton, Lucille T.
Coleman, Wanda
Cornish, Samuel James
Cortez, Jayne
Cotter, Joseph Seamon, Sr.
Cullen, Countee Porter
Dadié, Bernard
Damas, Léon Gontran
Danner, Margaret Esse
Davis, Frank Marshall
Diop, Birago Ismaïl
Dodson, Owen Vincent
Dumas, Henry
Dunbar, Paul Laurence
Emanuel, James Andrew
Espirito Santo, Alda de
Evans, Mari
Fabio, Sarah Webster
Faust, Naomi F.
Figueroa, John (Joseph Maria]
Giovanni, Nikki
Glissant, Edouard
Grimké, Angelina Weld
Guillen, Nicolás
Hammon, Jupiter
Harper, Frances Ellen Watkins
Harper, Michael Steven
Harris, (Theodore) Wilson
Hayden, Robert E.
Henderson, David
Henries, A. Doris Banks
Hill, Leslie Pinckney
Horton, George Moses
Hughes, (James) Langston
Jeffers, Lance
Joans, Ted

Johnson, Fenton
Johnson, Georgia Douglas
Johnson, James Weldon
Johnson, Percy Edward
Jones, Gayl Amanda
Jordan, June [June Mayer]
Kaufman, Bob Arnell
Kgositsile, Keoropetse (William)
Knight, Etheridge [Imamu Etheridge Knight Soa]
Kunene, Mazisi Raymond (Zulu poet)
Lane, Pinkie Gordon
Lanusse, Armand
Lee, Don Luther [Haki R. Madhubuti]
Lomax, Pearl Cleage
Lorde, Audre
McElroy, Colleen J.
McGaugh, Lawrence Walter, Jr.
McKay, Claude
McLlelan, George Marion
Madgett, Naomi Long
Major, Clarence
Maran, René
Margarido, Maria Manuela
Martin, Herbert Woodward
M'baye, Annette
Mbiti, John Samuel (Kikamba poet)
Miller, May
El Muhajir [Marvin X]
Murphy, Beatrice Campbell
Nelson, Alice Dunbar
Nokan, Charles
Okigbo, Christopher
Parks, Gordon
p'Bitek, J. P. Okot [Okot p'Bitek]
Plato, Ann
Plumpp, Sterling Dominic
Price, Robert E. [Bashiri]
Randall, Dudley Felker
Ray, Henrietta Cordelia
Redmond, Eugene Benjamin
Reed, Ishmael S.
Roumain, Jacques [Jean Baptiste]
Richardson, Nola M.
Rivers, Conrad Kent
Rodgers, Carolyn Marie
Salkey, (Felix) Andrew (Alexander)
Sanchez, Sonia
Séjour, Victor [Juan Victor Séjour Marcon et Ferrand]
Senghor, Léopold Sédar
Sharp, Saundra
Southerland, Ellease
Soyinka, Wole [Akinwande Oluwole]
Spellman, A. B.
Terry, Lucy
Tolson, Melvin Beaunorus
Toomer, Jean
Troupe, Quincy

Bradley, David Henry, Jr.
Brawley, Benjamin Griffith
Brown, Sterling Allen
Butcher, Margaret Just
Butcher, Philip
Collier, Eugenia
Dance, Daryl Cumber
Dathorne, Oscar Ronald
Davis, Arthur P.
Davis, Charles T.
Faust, Naomi F.
Ford, Nick Aaron
Gates, Henry Louis, Jr.
Gibson, Donald B.
Gloster, Hugh Morris
Greene, J. Lee
Hayden, Robert E.
Henderson, Stephen E.
Jackson, Blyden
James, Charles Lyman
Jeffers, Lance
Kent, George Edward
Lane, Pinkie Gordon
McElroy, Colleen J.
Madgett, Naomi Long
Mebane, Mary Elizabeth
Nichols, Charles Harold
Polite, Carlene Hatcher
Rampersad, Arnold
Redding, Jay Saunders
Robinson, William Henry, Jr.
Samuels, Wilfred D.
Stepto, Robert Burns
Turner, Darwin T.
Turner, Lorenzo Dow
Turner, Rufus P.
Turpin, Waters Edward
Walker, Alexander, Margaret Abigail
Washington, Mary Helen
Wideman, John Edgar
Williams, Ruby Ora
Williams, Sherley Anne [Shirley Williams]

(Ethnic Studies)
Bryant, Henry A., Jr.

(French)
Lewis, David Levering

(Health Care Management)
Rosser, James Milton

(History)
Bennett, Lerone, Jr.
Blassingame, John W.
Brathwaite, Edward Kamau [L. Edward]
Franklin, John Hope
Gilmore, Al-Tony
Greene, Lorenzo Johnston
Hansberry, William Leo
Harris, Joseph E.

Hornsby, Alton, Jr.
Huggins, Nathan Irvin
Logan, Rayford Whittingham
Low, W. Augustus
Morgan, Kathryn L.
Moses, Wilson Jeremiah
Obichere, Boniface Ihewunwa
Ogot, Bethwell Alan
Painter, Nell Irvin
Quarles, Benjamin Arthur
Robinson, Wilhelmena Simpson
Savage, William Sherman
Tate, Merze
Thorpe, Earlie Endris
Toppin, Edgar Allan
Tuttle, William McCullough
Wesley, Charles Harris
Williams, Chancellor
Williams, Lorraine A.
Woodson, Carter Godwin

(Human Relations)
Noble, Jeanne L.

(Humanities)
Johnson, Percy Edward

(Journalism)
Yette, Samuel F.

(Languages)
Cook, Mercer
Pickens, William

(Law)
Berry, Mary Frances
Higginbotham, A. Leon, Jr.

(Library Science)
Cunningham, William D.
Jackson, Miles Merrill
Smith, Jessie Carney

(Literature)
Cartey, Wilfred
Damas, Léon Gontran
Jackson, Richard L.
Ngugi, James [Wa Thiong'o]

(Mathematics)
Miller, Kelly

(Medical Science)
Jumniner, Bertène
Poindexter, Hildrus A.

(Music)
Roach, Hildred Elizabeth
Southern, Eileen Jackson

(Pedagogy)
Work, Monroe Nathan

(Physiology)
Just, Ernest Everett

Knox, George L.
Martin, Louis E.
Murphy, Carl
Sengstacke, John Herman Henry
Trotter, William Monroe
Vann, Robert L.
Walker, William O.
Washington, Leon H., Jr.
Young, Thomas White

Religious Leaders; Theologians
Carter, Harold A.
Cone, James H.
Crummell, Alexander
Fisher, Miles Mark
Garnet, Henry Highland
Griggs, Sutton E.
Hicks, H. Beecher, Jr.
King, Martin Luther, Jr.
King, Martin Luther, Sr.
Locke, Alain Leroy
Long, Charles Houston
McLlelan, George Marion
Mays, Benjamin Elijah
Mbiti, John
Mitchell, Henry H.
Muhammad, Elijah
Murray, Pauli
Payne, Daniel A.
Powell, Adam Clayton, Jr.
Powell, Adam Clayton, Sr.
Roberts, James Deotis, Sr.
Robinson, James Herman
Scott, Nathan A., Jr.
Thurman, Howard
Walker, James Lynwood
Walker, Wyatt Tee
Washington, Joseph R., Jr.
Wesley, Charles Harris
Williams, George Washington
Wilmore, Gayraud Stephen
Wimberly, Edward P.
Wright, Nathan, Jr.

Scientists; Engineers
Banneker, Benjamin
Byrd, Harold Eugene
Carwell, Hattie
Counter, S. Allen
Diop, Cheikh Anta
Ferguson, Lloyd N.
Harris, William M., Sr.
Hinton, William Augustus
Just, Ernest Everett
Miller, Kelly
Okpaku, Joseph Ohiomogben
Rosser, James Milton
Sampson, Henry T., Jr.
Turner, Rufus P.

Screenwriters; Scriptwriters
Davis, Nolan
Demby, William
Elder, Lonne, III
Fuller, Charles H., Jr.
Jefferson, Roland S.
Jones, Silas
Price, Robert E.
U Tam'si, Gérald Félix Tchicya
    [Tchicaya, Félix]

Short Story Writers
Abrahams, Peter Lee [Peter Graham]
Achebe, Chinua
Aidoo, Christina Ama Ata
Anthony, Michael
Bambara, Toni Cade
Chesnutt, Charles Waddell
Clarke, Austin Chesterfield
Colter, Cyrus
Diop, Birago Ismaïl
Dumas, Henry
Ekwensi, Cyprian Odiatu Duaka
Fair, Ronald
Gaines, Ernest J.
Head, Bessie
Hughes, (James) Langston
Jumniner, Bertène
Kelley, William Melvin
Kimenye, Barbara
Knight, Etheridge [Imamu Etheridge Knight
    Soa]
La Guma, (Justin) Alex(ander)
Laye, Camara [Kamara]
Lucas, Wilmer Francis, Jr.
McPherson, James Alan
Mais, Roger
Major, Clarence
Marshall, Paule
Moody, Anne
Nelson, Alice Dunbar
(Nwapa), Nwakuche Flora
Ogot, Grace Akinye
Okara, Gabriel Imomotimi Obaingaing
Oyono, Ferdinand Léopold
Petry, Ann Lane
Reid, V(ictor) S(tafford)
Rive, Richard
Roumain, Jacques [Jean Baptiste]
Sellassie, Sahle Berhane Mariam
    [Sahle, Sellassie Berhane Mariam]
Vroman, Mary Elizabeth
Walker, Alice Malsenior
Walrond, Eric
Wideman, John Edgar

Rive, Richard
Rivers, Conrad Kent
Robeson, Eslanda Cardozo
Rodgers, Carolyn Marie
Rollins, Charlemae Hill
Shangé, Ntozake [Paulette L. Williams]
Shine, Ted
Tenell, Mary Church
Thurman, Sue (Bailey)
Troupe, Quincy
Vroman, Mary Elizabeth
Walcott, Derek Alton
Walcott, Ronald
Walker, Alice Malsenior
Wallace, Michele
Wallace, Susan J.
Walton, Ortiz Montaigne
Ward, Samuel Ringgold
Ward, Theodore

Welburn, Ronald Garfield
Wesley, Richard Errol
Wilkin, Binnie Tate
Wynter, Sylvia [Wynter Carew]
Young, Al
Young, Margaret Buckner

Translators
Allen, Samuel W. [Paul Vesey]
Fauset, Jessie Redmond
Hodge, Merle
Nyerere, Julius Kambarage

Tribal Chief
Luthuli [Lutuli], Chief Albert John Mvumbi

Veterinarian
Diop, Birago Ismaïl

Title Index

Titles listed are of plays and radio, television, and motion picture scripts, as well as of books. See the main author entry for full information.

A B C of Color. W. E. B. DuBois.
ABCs of Calculus. Rufus P. Turner.
ABCs of Electronic Power. Rufus P. Turner.
ABCs of FETS. Rufus P. Turner.
ABCs of Integrated Circuits. Rufus P. Turner.
ABCs of Resistance and Resistors. Rufus P. Turner.
ABCs of Thermistors. Rufus P. Turner.
ABCs of Varactors. Rufus P. Turner.
ABCs of Voltage-Dependent Resistors. Rufus P. Turner.
ABCs of Zener Diodes. Rufus P. Turner.
A. Philip Randolph. Jervis Anderson.
An A to Z of African Writers. Oscar R. Dathorne.
An Absence of Ruins. Orlando Patterson.
Abraham Lincoln, Man and Statesman. William Pickens.
Absolutely Nothing to Get Alarmed About. Charles Wright.
Achievement Sketches of 100 Living Black Americans. Doris Innis.
Adam by Adam. Adam Clayton Powell, Jr.
Adam Clayton Powell. James Haskins.
The Adding Machine. Edgar Mittelhölzer.
"An Address to Miss Phyllis Wheatly (sic), etc." Jupiter Hammon.
"An Address to the Negroes in the State of New York." Jupiter Hammon.
An Address to the Slaves of the United States of America. Henry H. Garnet.
The Adventure of Catullus Kelly. Andrew Salkey.
Adventures in Black and White. Philippa Schuyler.
Adventures of Aku. Ashley Bryan.
The Adventures of Fathead, Smallhead, and Squarehead. Sonia Sanchez.

The Adventures of Jimmy Maxwell. C. Everard Palmer.
Adventurous Preaching. James H. Robinson.
Adversity and Grace. Nathan A. Scott.
The Afersata: An Ethiopian Novel. Sahle Sellassie.
Affirmative Action and Libraries. William Cunningham.
Affirmative Action Reconsidered. Thomas Sowell.
Africa and Africans as Seen by Classical Writers. William L. Hansberry.
Africa and America. Alexander Crummell.
Africa and the Afro-American Experience. Lorraine A. Williams.
Africa and the War. Benjamin Brawley.
Africa at the Crossroads. James H. Robinson.
Africa Dream. Eloise Greenfield.
Africa, Her History, Lands and People. John A. Williams.
Africa in Prose. Oscar R. Dathorne.
Africa, Land of My Fathers. Era Bell Thompson.
Africa Must Unite. Kwame Nkrumah.
Africa, My Africa. Margaret G. Burroughs.
Africa: Our History. A. Doris B. Henries.
Africa Reader, 2 vols. Wilfred Cartey.
The Africa Reader. Martin L. Kilson.
African Background Outlined. Carter G. Woodson.
The African Diaspora. Martin L. Kilson.
An African Frame of Reference. Johari M. Amini.
African Heroes and Heroines. Carter G. Woodson.
The African Image. Ezekiel Mphahlele.
African Journey. Eslanda Robeson.

The Amen Corner. James Baldwin.
America, Red, White, Black and Yellow. Arthur H. Fauset.
America, Their America. John P. Clark.
Un Américain en enfer. Melvin Van Peebles.
American Aesop: Negro and Other Humor. William Pickens.
American Argument. Eslanda Robeson.
American Black Women in the Arts and Social Sciences. Ruby Ora Williams.
American Culture in Literature. Nick A. Ford.
American Daughter. Era Bell Thompson.
The American Dream and the Negro. St. Clair Drake.
American Government. Charles V. Hamilton.
American History Series, 17 vols. Gen. ed., John H. Franklin.
American Hunger. Richard Wright.
American Journal. Robert E. Hayden.
American Negro Folk Songs and Spirituals. John W. Work.
American Negro Folklore. Ed. by John M. Brewer.
American Negro Musicians. Robert L. Green.
The American Negro: Old World Background and New World Experience. Rayford W. Logan.
American Negro Short Stories. John H. Clarke.
American Negro Songs. John W. Work.
American Revolution. James Boggs.
The American Shore. Samuel R. Delany.
American Society and Black Revolution. Frank Hercules.
America's Code of Caste a Disgrace to Democracy. Kelly Miller.
America's First Negro Poet. (Jupiter Hammon) Stanley A. Ransom, ed.
America's Majorities and Minorities. Warren J. Halliburton.
Amifika. Lucille Clifton.
Amongst Thistles and Thorns. Austin C. Clarke.
Amsterdam News. Clarence B. Jones.
Anabiosis. Charles E. Gordone.
An Analysis of Health Care and Delivery. James M. Rosser.
An Analysis of the Origins, Development and Structure of Negro Slave Society in Jamaica. Orlando Patterson.
Analytical Study of Afro-American Culture. Larry P. Neal.
Anancy Stories and Dialect Verse. Louise Bennett.
Anancy's Score. Andrew Salkey.
Anansegora. Efua Sutherland.
The Ancestors and the Sacred Mountain. Mazisi Kunene.
Ancestral Power and Lament. Kofi Awoonor.
Anchor Man. Jesse Jackson.

The Ancient Rain. Bob G. Kaufman.
And a Threefold Cord. Alex La Guma.
And Bid Him Sing. David G. DuBois.
"And Have Not Charity." Mary E. Vroman.
And Most of All Man. Roger Mais.
And Still I Rise. Maya Angelou.
And Then We Heard the Thunder. John O. Killens.
Andrew Young. Carl Gardner.
Andrew Young. James Haskins.
Angela Davis, an Autobiography.
Anger At Innocence. William G. Smith.
Angle of Ascent. Robert E. Hayden.
Angles. Samuel J. Cornish.
Angola: The Hidden History of Washington's War. Tony Thomas.
The Angry Black. John A. Williams.
The Angry Ones. John A. Williams.
Animals Made by Me. Margery Brown.
Annie Allen. Gwendolyn Brooks.
Another Country. James Baldwin.
Another Kind of Rain. Gerald Barrax.
Another Life: The Selected Poems of Derek Walcott.
Another Side of Tomorrow. Lee Hunkins.
Anowa. Ama Ata Aidoo.
Antenna Construction Handbook. Rufus P. Turner.
Anthem of the Decades. Mazisi R. Kunene.
An Anthology of African and Malagasy Poetry in French. Francis Bebey.
Anthology of Magazine Verse. William S. Braithwaite.
Anthology of Magazine Verse for 1958. William S. Braithwaite.
Anthology of the American Negro in the Theatre. Lindsay Patterson.
Anti-Slavery Harp. William W. Brown.
Antigone. Percy E. Johnston.
Any Place But Here. Arna Bontemps.
Apartheid: A Collection of Writings.... Alex La Guma.
Appalachee Red. Raymond Andrews.
An Appeal to Conscience. Kelly Miller.
Appearances, or Don't Judge by Appearances. Garland Anderson.
Apropos of Africa. Martin L. Kilson.
Arilla Sun Down. Virginia Hamilton.
Ark of Bones and Other Stories. Henry Dumas.
Arm Yourself or Harm Yourself. Imamu A. Baraka.
Army Life in a Black Regiment. T. W. Higginson. Ed. by John H. Franklin.
Arna Bontemps—Langston Hughes Letters, 1925-1967. Charles H. Nichols.
Around You. Rose Jourdain.
The Arrivants, trilogy. Edward K. Brathwaite.
Arrow of God. Chinua Achebe.
Art: African American. Samella S. Lewis.

Benjamin Banneker's ... Almanack and
Ephemeris ... 1792.
Beyond a Boundary. C. L. R. James.
Beyond Racism. Whitney M. Young.
Beyond the Angry Black. John A. Williams.
Bibliography of Negro History and Culture for
Young Readers. Miles M. Jackson.
A Bibliography of the Negro in Africa and
America. Monroe N. Work.
Big Doc Bitteroot. C. Everard Palmer.
Big Gold Dream. Chester Himes.
The Big Sea. Langston Hughes.
Big White Fog. Theodore Ward.
The Bigger Light, a Novel. Austin C. Clarke.
Bio-Bibliography of Countee P. Cullen, 1903-
1946. Margaret Perry.
Biographical Dictionary of Afro-American and
African Musicians. Eileen Southern.
Biographical Directory of Negro Ministers.
Ethel L. Williams.
A Biographical History of Blacks in America
since 1528. Edgar A. Toppin.
A Biography of President William V. S. Tub-
man. A. Doris B. Henries.
Biology of the Cell Surface. Ernest E. Just.
Birago Diop's Mother Crocodile. Rosa G. Guy.
Bird at My Window, novel. Rosa G. Guy.
Birthday. John L. Steptoe.
Black Abolitionists. Benjamin Quarles.
Black Academic Libraries and Research Collec-
tions. Jessie C. Smith.
The Black Aesthetic. Addison Gayle.
Black Africa on the Move. Leslie A. Lacy.
Black Africa: The Economic and Cultural
Basis for a Federated State. Cheikh A.
Diop.
Black Aged in the United States. Lenwood
Davis.
Black Almanac. Alton Hornsby.
"Black America." Charles H. Fuller.
The Black American: A Brief Documentary
History. Benjamin Quarles.
The Black American in the United States
History. Edgar A. Toppin.
Black American Leaders. Margaret B. Young.
Black American Literature: Essays. Darwin T.
Turner.
Black American Literature: Essays, Poetry,
Fiction, Drama. Darwin T. Turner.
Black American Literature: Fiction. Darwin T.
Turner.
Black American Literature: Poetry. Darwin T.
Turner.
Black American Music: Past and Present.
Hildred Roach.
Black American Playwrights, 1800 to the
Present. Esther S. Arata.
The Black American Reference Book. Mabel
Smythe.

Black American Scholars. Horace M. Bond.
Black American Writers Past and Present.
Esther S. Arata.
Black Americans and the Middle East Conflict.
Henry Winston.
Black Americans and the Political System.
Jesse J. McCorry.
Black Americans and the World Revolution.
Claude M. Lightfoot.
Black and Blues. Edward K. Brathwaite.
Black and Conservative. George S. Schuyler.
Black and Presbyterian. Gayraud Wilmore.
Black and White: Land, Labor, and Politics.
T. Thomas Fortune.
The Black and White of It. Ann Schockley.
Black and White Power Subreption. Joseph R.
Washington.
Black and White: Stories of American Life.
Donald B. Gibson.
Black Antisemitism and Jewish Racism. James
Baldwin.
Black Armed Forces Officers, 1736-1971. Jesse
J. Johnson.
Black Art. Imamu A. Baraka.
Black Artists in the United States. Lenwood
Davis.
Black Artists of the New Generation. Elton C.
Fax.
Black Artists on Art, Vols. I & II. Samella S.
Lewis.
Black Athletes in the United States. Lenwood
Davis.
Black Awakening in Capitalist America. Robert
L. Allen.
The Black B.C.'s. Lucille Clifton.
Black Back: Back Black. Sarah W. Fabio.
Black Belief. Henry H. Mitchell.
Black Belt Diamonds. Booker T. Washington.
Black Bird. El Muhajir.
Black Boogaloo. Larry P. Neal.
Black Bourgeoisie. E. Franklin Frazier.
Black Boy. Richard Wright.
Black-Brown-White Relations. Charles V.
Willie.
Black Child Care. Alvin Poussaint.
The Black Christ. Countee Cullen.
Black Church Looks at the Bicentennial. Wyatt
T. Walker and Harold A. Carter.
The Black Church since Frazier. C. Eric
Lincoln.
Black College Sport. Ocania Chalk.
Black Colleges in America. Charles V. Willie.
Black Community Development. William M.
Harris.
Black Dialectics. El Muhajir.
A Black Diplomat in Haiti. (Frederick Doug-
lass). Ed. by Norma Brown.
Black Drama Anthology. Ron Milner; Woodie
King.

Black Drama in America. Darwin T. Turner.

Black Drama: The Story of the Negro in the Theater. Loften Mitchell.

Black Education: Myths and Tragedies. Thomas Sowell.

Black Elected Officials. Walter L. Wallace.

Black Emergency Cultural Coalition (Attica Book). Benny Andrews.

Black Empowerment. Barbara J. Solomon.

Black Essence. Johari M. Amini.

The Black Expatriates. Ernest Dunbar.

"The Black Experience in America." Earlie E. Thorpe.

The Black Experience in American Politics. Charles V. Hamilton.

The Black Experience in Big Business. Harold E. Byrd.

Black Experience in Children's Books. Augusta Baker.

Black Expression. Addison Gayle.

Black Extended Family. Elmer P. Martin.

Black-Eyed Susans. Mary Helen Washington.

Black Families and the Struggle for Survival. Andrew Billingsley.

Black Families in the American Economy. John H. Clarke.

Black Families in White America. Andrew Billingsley.

The Black Family. Alvin Poussaint.

The Black Family: Essays and Studies. Robert Staples.

The Black Family in the United States. Janet L. Sims.

Black Feeling; Black Talk. Nikki Giovanni.

Black Feeling Black Talk/Black Judgment. Nikki Giovanni.

Black Films and Film-Makers. Lindsay Patterson.

Black Fire. Larry P. Neal.

The Black Flame. W. E. B. DuBois.

Black Folk: Then and Now. W. E. B. DuBois.

Black Folktales. Julius Lester.

Black Genealogy. Charles L. Blockson.

Black Girl. J. E. Franklin.

Black Girl: From Genesis to Revelations. J. E. Franklin.

Black Gods of the Metropolis. Arthur H. Fauset.

Black Government. Kenneth Kaunda.

Black Guide to Washington. William D. Cunningham and Ron Powell.

Black Heritage Books, 22 vol. ser. Ed. by Vincent Harding.

The Black Hermit. James Ngugi.

Black Historians: A Critique. Earlie E. Thorpe.

Black History's Antebellum Origin. Benjamin Quarles.

Black Humor. Charles R. Johnson.

The Black Image in Latin American Literature. Richard Jackson.

Black Image Syndrome. Silas Jones.

Black Images. Wilfred Cartey.

Black in America. Jesse Jackson.

Black Insights. Nick A. Ford.

Black Internal Migration, United States and Ghana. Benjamin Bobo.

Black Is a Panther Caged. Sarah W. Fabio.

Black Is the Color of the Cosmos. Henry L. Gates. Edited by Charles Davis.

The Black Jacobins: Toussaint L'Ouverture and the San Domingo Revolution. C. L. R. James.

Black Judgment. Nikki Giovanni.

Black Lawyers. Walter J. Leonard.

Black Leaders of the 20th Century. Gen. ed., John H. Franklin.

Black Liberation and Socialism. Tony Thomas.

Black Librarian in America. E. J. Josey.

The Black Librarian in the South. Annette Phinazee.

The Black Librarian in the Southeast. Annette Phinazee.

Black Life in Corporate America. George Davis.

Black Lightning. Roger Mais.

Black Literature in America. Houston A. Baker.

Black Macho and the Myth of the Superwoman. Michele Wallace.

Black Magic. Langston Hughes.

Black Magic ... Collected Poetry. Imamu A. Baraka.

The Black Male in America. Doris Wilkinson.

Black Male/White Female. Doris Wilkinson.

Black Man Abroad. James A. Emanuel.

Black Man, His Antecedents, His Genius and His Achievements. William W. Brown.

Black Man in the White House. E. Frederic Morrow.

Black Man Listen. El Muhajir.

Black Manhattan. James W. Johnson.

Black Manifesto for Black Education. Jim Haskins.

Black Manifesto in Jazz, Poetry and Prose. Ted Joans.

Black Man's America. Simeon Booker.

Black Man's Burden. John O. Killens.

Black Man's Verse. Frank M. Davis.

Black Marsden. Wilson Harris.

Black Masculinity. Robert Staples.

A Black Mass. Imamu A. Baraka.

Black Men in Chains. Charles H. Nichols.

Black Messiahs and Uncle Toms. Wilson J. Moses.

Black Metropolis. St. Clair Drake and Horace R. Cayton.

Black Midas. Sylvia Wynter.

The Black Mind: A History of African Literature. Oscar R. Dathorne.

The Black Mood. Lerone Bennett.
Black Music. Imamu A. Baraka.
Black Music: Four Lives. A. B. Spellman.
Black Music Resource Book. Hildred Roach.
The Black Muslims in America. C. Eric Lincoln.
Black New Orleans: 1860-1880. John W. Blassingame.
Black No More. George Schuyler.
Black North in 1901. W. E. B. DuBois.
Black Odyssey. Nathan Huggins.
Black Odyssey. Roi V. Ottley.
Black on Black. Chester B. Himes.
Black Opportunity. Jerome Holland.
Black Origins in the Inland Empire. Byron Skinner.
Black Pearl and the Ghost. Walter D. Myers.
Black Perspective in Music, Vols. 1-7. Ed. by Eileen Southern.
Black Poetry. Dudley Randall.
Black Poetry in America. Blyden Jackson.
The Black Poets. Ed. by Dudley Randall.
Black Poets and Prophets. Woodie King.
Black Political Parties. Hanes Walton.
A Black Political Theology. James D. Roberts.
The Black Politician. Mervyn Dymally.
Black Politics. Hanes Walton.
The Black Position. Gwendolyn Brooks.
Black Pow-Wow. Ted Joans.
Black Power. Richard Wright.
Black Power and Liberation. Claude M. Lightfoot.
Black Power and the World Revolution. Floyd McKissick.
Black Power and Urban Unrest. Nathan Wright.
Black Power; Gary Style. Alex Poinsett.
Black Power: The Politics of Liberation in America. Charles V. Hamilton and Stokely Carmichael.
Black Power USA. Lerone Bennett.
Black Preacher in America. Charles V. Hamilton.
Black Preaching. Henry H. Mitchell.
The Black Presence in American Foreign Affairs. Jake C. Miller.
Black Pride. Don L. Lee.
Black Profiles. George R. Metcalf.
Black Psychology. Reginald Jones.
Black Quartet. Ed Bullins.
Black Quartet. Woodie King.
Black Rage. William Grier.
Black Religion and Black Radicalism. Gayraud Wilmore.
Black Religion: The Negro and Christianity in the United States. Joseph R. Washington.
Black Republicans. Hanes Walton.
Black Resistance, White Law. Mary F. Berry.
Black Revolt: The Strategies of Protest. Doris Wilkinson.

The Black Revolts. Joseph W. Scott.
Black Rituals. Sterling Plumpp.
Black Scenes. Alice Childress.
Black Sects and Cults. Joseph R. Washington.
Black Short Story Anthology. Woodie King.
The Black Situation. Addison Gayle.
Black Skin, White Masks. Frantz Fanon.
The Black Soldier Documented 1619-1815. Jesse J. Johnson.
Black Spirits. Woodie King.
Black Students. Harry Edwards.
Black Students at White Colleges. Charles V. Willie.
Black Studies Debate. James M. Rosser.
Black Studio: Threat or Challenge? Nick A. Ford.
Black Terror. Richard E. Wesley.
Black Theater. Lindsay Patterson.
Black Theater in America. Jim Haskins.
Black Theatre, U.S.A. Forty Five Plays by Black Americans, 1847-1974. Ted Shine.
Black Theology. James Cone.
Black Theology and Black Power. James Cone.
A Black Theology of Liberation. James Cone.
Black Think. Jesse Owens.
Black Thunder. Arna Bontemps.
Black Titan: W. E. B. DuBois. John H. Clarke.
Black Troubador: Langston Hughes. Charlemae Rollins.
The Black Unicorn. Audre Lorde.
A Black Value System. Imamu A. Baraka.
Black Voices from Prison. Etheridge Knight.
The Black Wine. Hal Bennett.
The Black Woman. Toni C. Bambara.
Black Woman. Chester A. Higgins.
The Black Woman in America. Robert Staples.
Black Woman in American Society. Lenwood Davis.
Black Women in the Employment Sector. Janet L. Sims.
Black Women Novelists. Barbara Christian.
The Black Worker. Michael Harper.
Black Workers and the New Unions. Horace Cayton.
Black Writer in America. Charles L. James.
Black Writers in Latin America. Richard Jackson.
Black Writers of America: A Comprehensive Anthology. Richard K. Barksdale.
Blacks in Classical Music. Raoul Abdul.
The Blackamericans. C. Eric Lincoln.
The Blacker the Berry. Wallace Thurman.
A Blackman Speaks of Freedom. Peter Abrahams.
Blackness and the Adventure of Western Culture. George E. Kent.
Blacks and Criminal Justice. Charles E. Owens.
Blacks in America: Then and Now. Edgar A. Toppin.

History of the Negro Troops in the War of the Rebellion 1861-65. George W. Williams.

History of the People of Trinidad and Tobago. Eric Williams.

A History of the Southern Luo. Bethwell A. Ogot.

History of the World War and the Important Part Taken by Negroes. Kelly Miller.

History of Tuberculosis in the Black Community. Lenwood Davis.

The Hit. Julian Mayfield.

Hog Butcher. Ronald Fair.

Hollow Image. Lee Hunkins.

Home; Social Essays. Imamu A. Baraka.

Home to Harlem. Claude McKay.

Homecoming. Sonia Sanchez.

Homecoming: Essays. James Ngugi.

The Homecoming Singer. Jay Wright.

Homesteader. Oscar Micheaux.

Honey, I Love and Other Poems. Eloise Greenfield.

Honorary White: A Visit to South Africa. E. R. Braithwaite.

Hoodoo Hollerin' Bebop Ghosts. Larry P. Neal.

Hoops. Walter D. Myers.

Hope of Liberty. George M. Horton.

Horn of My Love. J. P. Okot p'Bitek.

House behind the Cedars. Charles Chesnutt.

House by the Sea. Kofi Awoonor.

The House of Blue Lightning. Wilfred Cartey.

House of Dies Drear. Virginia Hamilton.

The House of Falling Leaves. William S. Braithwaite.

House of Slammers. Nathan C. Heard.

House on Hay. Hal Bennett.

House under Arcturus; An Autobiography. William S. Braithwaite.

Houseboy. Ferdinand Oyono.

How Far the Promised Land? Walter White.

How God Fix Jonah. Lorenz Graham.

How I Got Ovah: New and Selected Poems. Carolyn Rodgers.

How I Write/2. James A. Emanuel.

How I Wrote Jubilee. Margaret Walker.

How the Leopard Got His Claws. Chinua Achebe.

How to Be a Top Model. Naomi Sims.

How to Bring Up Your Child without Prejudice. Margaret B. Young.

How to Eat to Live. Elijah Muhammad.

How to Make Electronics Tests without Specialized Equipment. Rufus P. Turner.

How to Talk with People of Other Races. Arthur L. Smith.

How to Use Grid-Dip Oscillators. Rufus P. Turner.

Howard Street. Nathan C. Heard.

The Howard University Bibliography of African and Afro-American Religious Studies. Ethel L. Williams.

The Howard University Department of History, 1913-1973. Michael Winston.

Howard University: The First Hundred Years, 1867-1967. Rayford W. Logan.

Howdy Honey Howdy. Paul L. Dunbar.

Hue and Cry. James A. McPherson.

Human Rights U.S.A.: 1948-1966. Pauli Murray.

Human Rights U.S. Style. Claude M. Lightfoot.

Humanism in Zambia and a Guide to Its Implementation. Kenneth Kaunda.

A Humanist in Africa. Kenneth Kaunda.

Hummingbird People. C. Everard Palmer.

Humorous Folktales of the South Carolina Negro. John Brewer.

The Hundred Penny Box. Sharon B. Mathis.

The Hungered One. Ed Bullins.

Hurricane. Andrew Salkey.

Hurry Home. John E. Wideman.

Hurry Up, America, and Spit. Pearl Bailey.

Hymn for the Rebels. Pearl C. Lomax.

I Am a Black Woman. Mari Evans.

I Am the American Negro. Frank M. Davis.

I Can Do It by Myself. Eloise Greenfield.

I Greet the Dawn: Poems of Paul Laurence Dunbar. Ashley Bryan.

I Have a Dream. Lenwood Davis.

I Have Changed. Jesse Owens.

I Know Why the Caged Bird Sings. Maya Angelou.

I Look at Me. Mari Evans.

I Love Myself When I Am Laughing.... (Zora Neale Hurston). Ed. by Alice Walker.

I Love You. June Jordan.

I Remember Ruben. Mongo Beti.

I Sing Because I'm Happy. Jesse Jackson.

I Sought My Brother. S. Allen Counter.

I Want a Black Doll. Frank Hercules.

I Will Try. Legson Kayira.

I Wonder as I Wander. Langston Hughes.

Idabel's Fortune. Ted Shine.

Idanre and Other Poems. Wole Soyinka.

Idu. Flora Nwapa.

An Idyl of the South. Albery Whitman.

Idylls of the Bible. Frances Harper.

If Beale Street Could Talk. James Baldwin.

If He Hollers Let Him Go. Chester B. Himes.

If They Come in the Morning. Angela Davis.

Ignoring Hurts, Poems. John Figueroa.

Ikolo the Wrestler and Other Ibo Tales. Cyprian Ekwensi.

Illustrated Dictionary of Electronics. Rufus P. Turner.

My Bondage and My Freedom. Frederick Douglass.
My Bones and My Flute. Edgar Mittelhölzer.
My Brother Fine with Me. Lucille Clifton.
My Dog Rinty. Ellen Tarry.
My Face Is Black. C. Eric Lincoln.
My Father, Sun-Sun Johnson. C. Everard Palmer.
My Green Hills of Jamaica. Claude McKay.
My House. Nikki Giovanni.
My Larger Education. Booker T. Washington.
My Life in the Bush of Ghosts. Amos Tutuola.
My Life, My Country, My World. Hugh Gloster.
My Life of Absurdity. Chester B. Himes.
My Life with Martin Luther King, Jr. Coretta S. King.
My Lives and How I Lost Them. Countee Cullen.
My Lord What a Morning. Marian Anderson.
My Name Is Afrika. Keoropetse Kgositsile.
My Name Is Black. Chester A. Higgins.
My Odyssey: An Autobiography. B. Nnamdi Azikiwe.
My Own Thing. Sarah W. Fabio.
My People of Kikuyu and the Life of Chief Wangombe. Jomo Kenyatta.
My Southern Home, or the South and Its People. William W. Brown.
My Special Best Words. John L. Steptoe.
My World of Reality. Hildrus A. Poindexter.
The Mystic Female. Pinkie G. Lane.
Mysticism and the Experience of Love. Howard Thurman.
Myth, Literature and the African World. Wole Soyinka.
Myth Makers. Frank L. Brown.
Myths and Symbols: Essay in Honor of Mircea Eliade. Charles H. Long.
Myths That Mire the Ministry. Harold A. Carter.

The Nail. Russell Atkins.
Naked Genius. George M. Horton.
Nappy Edges. Ntozake Shangé.
Narrative of Hosea Hudson. Nell I. Painter.
Narrative of William W. Brown, a Fugitive Slave.
The Narrows. Ann Petry.
Nathanael West. Nathan A. Scott.
Nathaniel Hawthorne's "The Scarlet Letter." Darwin T. Turner.
Nationhood and the African Road to Socialism. Léopold Senghor.
Native Daughter. Leslie A. Lacy.
Native Son. Richard Wright.
"Native Son" (Richard Wright). Darwin T. Turner.

Natives of My Person. George Lamming.
Nature Knows No Color Line. J. A. Rogers.
Nebula Winners Thirteen. Samuel R. Delany.
Negative Capability. Nathan A. Scott.
Neglected History. Charles H. Wesley.
Negrito, Negro Dialect Poems of the Southwest. John Brewer.
Negritude: Essays and Studies. Richard A. Long.
The Negro. W. E. B. DuBois.
The Negro. Saunders Redding.
Negro Almanac. Ernest D. Kaiser.
Negro American. Kenneth B. Clark.
The Negro American: A Documentary History. Benjamin Quarles.
The Negro American Artisan. W. E. B. DuBois.
The Negro American Family. W. E. B. DuBois.
Negro Americans in the Civil War. Charles H. Wesley.
Negro Americans, What Now? James W. Johnson.
The Negro and His Music. Alain Locke.
Negro Art—Past and Present. Alain Locke.
The Negro Artisan. W. E. B. DuBois.
Negro as Business Man. Carter G. Woodson.
Negro as Capitalist. Abram L. Harris.
Negro Authors and Composers of the United States. W. C. Handy.
Negro Builders and Heroes. Benjamin Brawley.
The Negro Caravan. Sterling A. Brown.
The Negro Caravan. Ulysses Lee.
The Negro Church. W. E. B. DuBois.
The Negro Church in America. E. Franklin Frazier.
Negro College Graduate. Charles S. Johnson.
Negro Digest/Black World. John H. Johnson.
Negro Doctor. Warren J. Halliburton.
Negro Education in Alabama. Horace M. Bond.
Negro Education in America. Virgil A. Clift.
The Negro Family in the United States. E. Franklin Frazier.
The Negro Freedom Movement. A. Philip Randolph.
The Negro Genius. Benjamin Brawley.
The Negro Ghetto. Robert C. Weaver.
Negro Historians in the United States. Earlie E. Thorpe.
The Negro Immigrant.... Ira D. A. Reid.
The Negro in American Cities. Dorothy Porter.
Negro in American Civilization. Charles S. Johnson.
The Negro in American Culture. Margaret J. Butcher.
The Negro in American Fiction. Sterling A. Brown.
The Negro in American Life and Thought.... Rayford W. Logan.
The Negro in Art.... Alain Locke.
The Negro in Business. Booker T. Washington.

The Negro in Business. W. E. B. DuBois.
Negro in Colonial New England. Lorenzo
    Greene.
The Negro in Literature and Art. Benjamin
    Brawley.
The Negro in Music and Art. Lindsay Patterson.
Negro in New York. Roi V. Ottley.
Negro in Our History. Carter G. Woodson.
The Negro in Politics. T. Thomas Fortune.
Negro in the American Economic System.
    Ira D. A. Reid.
The Negro in the American Rebellion....
    William W. Brown.
The Negro in the American Revolution.
    Benjamin Quarles.
The Negro in the Caribbean. Eric Williams.
The Negro in the Civil War. Benjamin Quarles.
The Negro in the Making of America. Benjamin
    Quarles.
The Negro in the South. Booker T. Washington.
The Negro in Twentieth Century America.
    John H. Franklin.
The Negro in the United States. Dorothy
    Porter.
The Negro in the United States. E. Franklin
    Frazier.
The Negro in the United States. Rayford W.
    Logan.
The Negro in Third Party Politics. Hanes
    Walton.
Negro Labor: A National Problem. Robert C.
    Weaver.
Negro Labor in the United States, 1850-1925.
    Charles H. Wesley
Negro Legislators of Texas and Their Descendents. John Brewer.
Negro Makers of History. Carter G. Woodson.
The Negro Mood. Lerone Bennett.
Negro Mother. Langston Hughes.
Negro Orators and Their Orations. Carter G.
    Woodson.
Negro Pilgrimage in America. C. Eric Lincoln.
Negro Poetry and Drama. Sterling A. Brown.
The Negro Population of Denver, Colorado.
    Ira D. A. Reid.
Negro Problem. Booker T. Washington
The Negro Professional Man and the Community. Carter G. Woodson.
The Negro Protest. Kenneth B. Clark.
Negro Protest Pamphlets. Dorothy Porter.
The Negro Revolt. Louis E. Lomax.
Negro Slave Songs in the United States.
    Miles M. Fisher.
The Negro Spiritual Speaks of Life and
    Death. Howard Thurman.
Negro Tales. Joseph S. Cotter.

Negro Trail Blazers of California. Delilah
    Beasley.
Negro Voices. Beatrice Murphy.
Negro Voices in American Fiction. Hugh
    Gloster.
Negro Wage Earner. Carter G. Woodson.
Negro Yearbook. Monroe N. Work.
The Negroes in America. Claude McKay.
Negroes in Science. James M. Jay.
The Negro's Church. Benjamin E. Mays.
The Negro's God. Benjamin E. Mays.
Neo-Colonialism. Kwame Nkrumah.
New African Literature and the Arts.
    Joseph Okpaku.
New Americans: Cuban Boat People. James
    Haskins.
New Americans: Vietnamese.... James Haskins.
The New Black Poetry. Clarence Major.
New Day. V. S. Reid.
New Days. June Jordan.
New Dimensions in Academic Library Service.
    E. J. Josey.
New Directions in Special Education. Reginald
    Jones.
New England Black Letters. William H.
    Robinson.
New Kind of Joy. James Haskins.
New Lafayette Theatre Presents. Ed Bullins.
New Life: New Room. June Jordan.
A New Look at Black Families. Charles V.
    Willie.
The New Negro: An Interpretation. Alain
    Locke.
A New Negro for a New Century. Booker T.
    Washington.
The New Negro; His Political, Civil and
    Mental Status and Related Essays.
    William Pickens.
New Negro of the South. Wilmoth Carter.
New Negro Renaissance. Arthur P. Davis.
New Nigerian Elite. Mabel Smythe.
The New Orpheus. Nathan A. Scott.
New Perspectives of Man in Action. Roscoe C.
    Brown.
New Perspectives on Black Studies. John W.
    Blassingame.
New Plays from the Black Theatre. Ed Bullins.
A New Song. Langston Hughes.
New Space: Critical Essays on American
    Culture. Larry P. Neal.
New States in the Modern World. Martin L.
    Kilson.
New Survey of English Literature. Benjamin
    Brawley.
New Testament Eschatology in an African
    Background. John Mbiti.
New World A-Coming.... Roi V. Ottley.
New Worlds of Literature. Warren J. Halliburton.

One Love. Andrew Salkey.
One Scene from the Drama of Early Days.
    Pauline Hopkins.
One Way Ticket. Langston Hughes.
One Way to Heaven. Countee Cullen.
Opera Wonyosi. Wole Soyinka.
Operation Burning Candle. Blyden Jackson.
Opportunities for Minorities in Librarianship.
    E. J. Josey.
An Ordinary Woman. Lucille Clifton.
Oreo: A Perspective on Race and Marginal Men
    and Women. Charles V. Willie.
Organic Chemistry. Lloyd N. Ferguson.
Organic Molecular Structures. Lloyd N.
    Ferguson.
"Original Poetry" (Darwin Turner).
Orphee Noir. Samuel W. Allen.
Other American Revolution. Vincent Harding.
Other Exiles. Edward K. Brathwaite.
The Other Side of the Wall. Clarence Major.
The Other Toussaint. Ellen Tarry.
The Other Woman. Grace A. Ogot.
Our Cause Speeds On. William S. Savage.
Our Lan'. Theodore Ward.
Our Nig. H. E. Wilson.
Our Nig. (Harriet E. Wilson). Ed. by Henry L.
    Gates, Jr.
Our Sister Killjoy or Reflections from a Black-
    Eyed Squint. Ama Ata Aidoo.
Un Ours pour le F.B.I. Melvin Van Peebles.
Out of the Dead City. Samuel R. Delany.
Out of the House of Bondage. Kelly Miller.
Outline for the Study of the Poetry of American
    Negroes. Sterling A. Brown.
The Outsider. Richard Wright.
"The Outsider" (Richard Wright) Darwin T.
    Turner.
Overhead Costs. Sir William A. Lewis.
Overshadowed. Sutton E. Griggs.
An Overview of International Studies. John R.
    Howard.
The Owl Answers. Adrienne Kennedy.
The Ox of the Wonderful Horns and Other
    African Folktales. Ashley Bryan.
Oxherding Tale. Charles R. Johnson.
Ozidi. John P. Clark.
The Ozidi of Atazi, film. John P. Clark.
The Ozidi Saga. John P. Clark.

Pagan Spain. Richard Wright.
Paid Servant. E. P. Braithwaite.
Palace of the Peacock. Wilson Harris.
Palaver: Dramatic Discussion Starters from
    Africa. Wole Soyinka.
Palaver: Modern African Writings. Wilfred
    Cartey.
Palestine, and Saints in Caesar's Household.
    Adam C. Powell, Sr.

The Palm-Wine Drinkard. Amos Tutuola.
Pan-Africanism. Robert Chrisman.
Pan-Africanism Reconsidered. Samuel W.
    Allen.
Panther and the Lash. Langston Hughes.
Panther Man. James A. Emanuel.
Paper Soul. Carolyn Rodgers.
Part Two, Sounder. Lonne Elder.
Passing. Nella Larsen.
Passion: New Poems 1977-1980. June Jordan.
Passport of Mallam Illia. Cyprian Ekwensi.
Past and Present Condition. Henry H. Garnet.
Pastoral Care in the Black Church. Edward P.
    Wimberly.
Patent Leather Sunday. W. F. Lucas.
Path of Dreams. George McLlelan.
The Path of Thunder. Peter Abrahams.
Pathos of Power. Kenneth B. Clark.
Patria o Muerte: The Great Zoo and Other
    Poems by Nicolas Guillen, 1928-1970.
Patriotism and the Negro. Adam C. Powell, Sr.
Patternmaster. Octavia Butler.
Patterns of Negro Segregation. Charles S.
    Johnson.
Paul Laurence Dunbar, a Singer of Songs.
    Herbert W. Martin.
Paul Laurence Dunbar: Poet of His People.
    Benjamin Brawley.
The Paul Laurence Dunbar Reader. Ed. by Jay
    Martin.
Paul Robeson. Eloise Greenfield.
Paul Robeson. Virginia Hamilton.
Paul Robeson, Citizen of the World. Shirley
    Graham.
Paul Robeson, Negro. Eslanda Robeson.
Paul Robeson: The Great Forerunner. Ernest D.
    Kaiser.
Paul Robeson, Tributes, Selected Writings.
    Paul Robeson.
Paul Vesey's Ledger. Samuel W. Allen.
Pauline E. Hopkins Papers.
The Peacock Poems. Sherley A. Williams.
Pearl's Kitchen. Pearl Bailey.
Pecko Poems. Sherley A. Williams.
Pele. Jim Haskins.
The Pencil of God. Philippe Thoby-Marcelin.
Pennsylvania's Black History. Charles L.
    Blockson.
People and Music. Alice D. Nelson.
People of the City. Cyprian Ekwensi.
People beneath the Window. Samuel J.
    Cornish.
The People Who Came. Edward K. Brathwaite.
Perchance to Dream, Othello. Conrad K.
    Rivers.
The Perfect Party. Charles H. Fuller.
Peripheries: Selected Poems, 1966-68. Ronald
    Welburn.

The Poetic Year for 1916. William S. Braithwaite.

Poetical Works. George M. Horton.

Poetical Works of James Madison Bell.

Poetry for My People. Henry Dumas.

Poetry of Black Politics. Hanes Walton.

The Poetry of Derek Walcott. John Figueroa.

Poetry of the Negro. Langston Hughes.

A Poet's Mind. James A. Emanuel.

Pointing the Way. Sutton E. Griggs.

Police. Imamu A. Baraka.

Political Awakening of Africa. Martin L. Kilson.

Political Change in a West African State. Martin L. Kilson.

The Political Philosophy of Martin Luther King, Jr. Hanes Walton.

The Political Status of the Negro in the Age of FDR. Ralph Bunche.

Political Theory and Political Broadcasting. Hanes Walton.

Politics in West Africa. Sir William A. Lewis.

The Politics of God. Joseph R. Washington.

The Politics of Literary Expression. Donald B. Gibson.

Politics of People's Action. Henry Winston.

The Poor Christ of Bomba. Mongo Beti.

Popo and Fifina, Children of Haiti. Arna Bontemps.

Portable Soul. Sterling Plumpp.

Portfolios on Contemporary American Artists. Samella S. Lewis.

A Portion of That Field. Gwendolyn Brooks.

Portraits Americains. Mercer Cook.

A Possible Reality. Kenneth B. Clark.

The Potter's Field in Public Opinion. Roger Mais.

Powerful Long Ladder. Owen V. Dodson.

Practical Oscilloscope Handbook, Vols. 1 & 2. Rufus P. Turner.

Praisesong for the Widow. Paule Marshall.

Prayer Tradition of Black People. Harold A. Carter.

Prayers for Dark People. W. E. B. DuBois.

The Prayers of African Religion. John Mbiti.

Precision Bridge. Frank M. Davis.

Preface to a Twenty-Volume Suicide Note. Imamu A. Baraka.

Preface to Racial Understanding. Charles S. Johnson.

Prejudice and Your Child. Kenneth B. Clark.

The Prescriber. John H. Clarke.

The Present Is a Dangerous Place to Live. Keoropetse Kgositsile.

Prides Castle. Frank Yerby.

The Prime Minister, a Novel. Austin C. Clarke.

Primer of Facts Pertaining to the Early Greatness of the African Race.... Pauline Hopkins.

The Primitive. Chester B. Himes.

Prince Hall. Charles H. Wesley.

Principia of Ethnology. Martin Delany.

Principles of Economic Planning. Sir William A. Lewis.

Principles of Scientific Sociology. Walter L. Wallace.

Printer's Measure. Warren J. Halliburton.

Prisoners of Honor: The Dreyfus Affair. David L. Lewis.

Private Line. Clarence Major.

Private Madrigals. Charles S. Wright.

The Problem and Other Poems. Benjamin Brawley.

Problems and Issues in the Education of Exceptional Children. Reginald Jones.

The Proceedings of the Free African Union Society.... William H. Robinson.

The Prodigal Sister. J. E. Franklin.

Profile Trinidad. Michael Anthony.

Profiles in Black. Doris Innis.

Profiles in Black Power. James Haskins.

Progress of Afro-American Women. Janet L. Sims.

Progress of Liberty. James M. Bell.

The Progressive Era. Nell I. Painter.

The Promised Land. Grace A. Ogot.

Prophets for a New Day. Margaret Walker.

Prose and Poetry. Léopold Senghor.

The Protectors. John A. Williams.

Protest and Beyond. Silas Jones.

Protestants against Poverty. Nathan Huggins.

Proud Shoes, the Story of an American Family. Pauli Murray.

Psychology in the World Today. Robert Guthrie.

Psychology of Black Language. Jim Haskins.

Psychology of the Child in the Middle Class. Allison Davis.

Psychovisualism. Russell Atkins.

The Public Image of Henry Ford. David L. Lewis.

Public Library Information and Referral Service. Clara Jones.

Puerto Rican Perspectives. Edward Mapp.

Purlie (musical). Ossie Davis.

Purlie Victorious. Ossie Davis.

Put My Dignity on 307. Richard E. Wesley.

Quality of Hurt. Chester B. Himes.

A Quality of Violence. Andrew Salkey.

Quark, nos. 1, 2, & 3. Samuel R. Delany.

Quartet: New Voices from South Africa. Alex La Guma.

Quartet: New Voices from South Africa. Richard Rive.

Quest for a Black Theology. J. Deotis Roberts.

Quest for Equality. Charles H. Wesley.

Samuel Beckett. Nathan A. Scott.
Samuel Gompers. Bernard Mandel.
Sandra Street and Other Stories. Michael
    Anthony.
"Sanford and Son." Nolan Davis.
Sapphire's Sampler. S. Diane Bogus.
Saracen Blade. Frank Yerby.
Sassafrass, Cypress & Indigo. Ntozake Shangé.
Savage Holiday. Richard Wright.
Say Jesus and Come to Me. Ann Shockley.
Say When. William J. Wilson.
Say's Law. Thomas Sowell.
Scarifications. Jayne Cortez.
The Scholar Man. Oscar R. Dathorne.
School Desegregation Plans That Work.
    Charles V. Willie.
School on 103rd Street. Roland Jefferson.
"School Teacher." Ossie Davis.
Science Fiction of Samuel R. Delany.
Scott Joplin. James Haskins.
Scottsboro Limited. Langston Hughes.
Scuse Me While I Kiss the Sky. David
    Henderson.
The Sea Birds Are Still Alive. Toni C.
    Bambara.
Sea Grapes. Derek Walcott.
The Sea at Dauphin. Derek Walcott.
Sean Pendragon Requiem. Percy E. Johnston.
Search and Destroy. Roy Wilkins.
The Search for Talent. Horace M. Bond.
Search for the New Land. Julius Lester.
A Season in the Congo. Aimé Césaire.
Season of Adventure. George Lamming.
The Second Agreement with Hell. Chancellor
    Williams.
Second Book of American Negro Spirituals.
    James W. Johnson.
Second Class Citizen. Buchi Emecheta.
The Second Stone. Margery Brown.
The Secret Ladder. Wilson Harris.
Secret Lives. James Ngugi.
The Secular Relevance of the Church. Gayraud
    Wilmore.
"See How They Run." Mary E. Vroman.
See No Evil. Ntozake Shangé.
Seeking to Be Christian in Race Relations.
    Benjamin E. Mays.
Seize the Time. Bobby Seale.
A Select Bibliography of the Negro American.
    W. E. B. DuBois.
Selected Black American Authors. James A.
    Page.
Selected Poems. Claude McKay.
Selected Poems. Gérald Félix U Tam'si.
Selected Poems. Gwendolyn Brooks.
Selected Poems. Langston Hughes.
Selected Poems. Robert E. Hayden.
Selected Poems. William S. Braithwaite.
Selected Poems of Claude McKay.

The Selected Poems of Derek Walcott.
Selected Poetry. Imamu A. Baraka.
Selected Speeches of Booker T. Washington.
Selected Writings of C. L. James.
Selections from the Papers of the Accra
    Assembly. Julian Mayfield.
Self Determining Haiti. James W. Johnson.
Selma, Lord, Selma. Sheyann Webb.
The Semi-Centenary and the Retrospection of
    the African Methodist Episcopal Church.
    Daniel A. Payne.
Semiconductor Devices. Rufus P. Turner.
The Senate and the Versailles Mandate System.
    Rayford W. Logan.
Sent for You Yesterday. John E. Wideman.
Sentry of the Four Golden Pillars. Eugene
    Redmond.
Sequel to the "Pied Piper of Hamelin...."
    Joseph S. Cotter.
Seraph on the Suwanee. Zora Neale Hurston.
Serpent and the Staff. Frank Yerby.
Serowe: Village of the Rain-Wind. Bessie Head.
Services of Colored Americans in the Wars of
    1776 and 1812. William C. Nell.
Seven Black American Scientists. Robert C.
    Hayden.
The Seven Sleepers of Ephesys. Benjamin
    Brawley.
Seventeen. Samuel R. Delany.
Seventeen Black Artists. Elton C. Fax.
Seventh Heaven. Hal Bennett.
The Seventh Son: The Thoughts and Writings
    of W. E. B. DuBois. Julius Lester.
$70 Billion in the Black. D. Parke Gibson.
Sewing for the Outdoors. Hal Bennett.
Sex and Race. J. A. Rogers.
Sex and Racism in America. Calvin C. Hernton.
Shades and Shadows. Randolph Edmonds.
Shadow and Act. Ralph Ellison.
Shadow of the Plantation. Charles S. Johnson.
The Shadow That Scares Me. Dick Gregory.
Shadows Move among Them. Edgar Mittel-
    hölzer.
Shaker, Why Don't You Sing. Maya Angelou.
Shakespeare in Harlem. Langston Hughes.
The Shame of America. Archibald H. Grimké.
Shannon. Gordon A. Parks.
Shaped to Its Purpose; Delta Sigma Theta.
    Mary E. Vroman.
Shaping of Black America. Lerone Bennett.
Shaping of Education for Librarianship.
    Charles Churchwell.
Share My World. Georgia Johnson.
Sharecroppers All. Ira D. A. Reid.
The Shark Hunters. Andrew Salkey.
She Come Bringing Me That Little Baby Girl.
    Eloise Greenfield.
She Walks in Beauty. J. A. Rogers.

The Story of Hank Aaron. Bernice E. Young.
The Story of Jesus. Lorenz Graham.
Story of Jumping Mouse. John L. Steptoe.
The Story of My Life and Work. Booker T. Washington.
The Story of Phillis Wheatley. Shirley Graham.
The Story of Pocahontas. Shirley Graham.
Story of Stevie Wonder. James Haskins.
The Story of the Great War. William S. Braithwaite.
Story of the Negro. Arna Bontemps.
Story of the Negro Retold. Carter G. Woodson.
The Story of the Negro: The Rise of the Race from Slavery. Booker T. Washington.
"Storyline." Nolan Davis.
Storytelling Art and Technique. Augusta Baker.
Storytelling Techniques for Children. Augusta Baker.
Strains. Dennis Brutus.
Stranger and Alone. Saunders Redding.
A Stranger at the Gate. John Hearne.
Strategies for Freedom. Bayard Rustin.
Strategy and Tactics of a Pan African Nationalist Party. Imamu A. Baraka.
Strategy for a Black Agenda. Henry Winston.
The Street. Ann Petry.
Street Gangs. Jim Haskins.
A Street in Bronzeville. Gwendolyn Brooks.
Street Scene. Langston Hughes.
The Streetcorner. Richard E. Wesley.
Streets. Samuel J. Cornish.
Streets of Conflict. Michael Anthony.
The Streets of Oakland. Henry A. Bryant.
Strength of Gideon. Paul L. Dunbar.
Strength to Love. Martin L. King, Jr.
Stride toward Freedom. Martin L. King, Jr.
Structural Organic Chemistry. Lloyd N. Ferguson.
The Struggle That Must Be. Harry Edwards.
Stubborn Hope: Poems. Dennis Brutus.
The Stubborn Old Lady Who Resisted Change. Loften Mitchell.
Student Culture. Walter L. Wallace.
Student Dissent in the Schools. Reginald Jones.
Student Unrest at Tuskegee Institute. Chester A. Higgins.
A Student's Guide to Creative Writing. Naomi L. Madgett.
Studies in a Dying Colonialism. Frantz Fanon.
Studies in Child Protective Services. Andrew Billingsley.
Studies in Southern Nigerian History. Boniface Obichere.
The Study and Analysis of Black Politics. Hanes Walton.
Sturdy Black Bridges: Visions of Black Women in Literature. Roseann Bell.
Subsistence Agriculture and Economic Development. Clifton Wharton.

Success in Language and Literature. Naomi L. Madgett.
Sudan Rajul Samia. El Muhajir.
Suffering without Bitterness. Jomo Kenyatta.
Sugar Ray Leonard. James Haskins.
Sula. Toni Morrison.
The Sun Salutes You. C. Everard Palmer.
Superfight No. 11. Joseph Okpaku.
The Suppression of the African Slave Trade. (W. E. B. DuBois). Ed. by John H. Franklin.
The Suppression of the African Slave Trade to the United States of America, 1638-1870. W. E. B. DuBois.
The Survey Graphic "New Negro." Alain Locke.
Survival Themes in Fiction for Children and Young People. Binnie T. Wilkin.
Survive the Peace. Cyprian Ekwensi.
Survivor. Octavia Butler.
The Survivors. Kristin Hunter.
Survivors of the Crossing. Austin C. Clarke.
Susie King Taylor, Civil War Nurse. Simeon Booker.
Swahili Dictionary of Legal Terms. Ivan Van Sertima.
Swallow the Lake. Clarence Major.
A Swarthy Boy. Edgar Mittelhölzer.
Sweet Billy and the Zooloos. Silas Jones.
Sweet Sweetback's Baadasssss Song. Melvin Van Peebles.
Sweet Whispers, Brother Rush. Virginia Hamilton.
Symptoms and Madness. Clarence Major.
The Snycopated Cakewalk. Clarence Major.
Syphilis and Its Treatment. William A. Hinton.
The System of Dante's Hell. Imamu A. Baraka.

Take a Sad Song. Mary E. Mebane.
Take Care of Business. El Muhajir.
A Tale of Three Places. Edgar Mittelhölzer.
Tale of Time and Toilet Tissues. Eugene Redmond.
Tale of Two Toms. Eugene Redmond.
"Tales." Imamu A. Baraka.
Tales and Short Stories for Black Folks. Toni C. Bambara.
Tales of Amadou Koumba. Birago Diop.
Tales of Darkest America. Fenton Johnson.
Tales of Momolu. Lorenz Graham.
Tales of Neveryon. Samuel R. Delany.
Talk about a Family. Eloise Greenfield.
Talking It Over with Roy Wilkins. Roy Wilkins.
Talking to Myself. Pearl Bailey.
Talking Tree. Augusta Baker.
Tambourines to Glory. Langston Hughes.
Tan. John H. Johnson.
Tar Baby. Toni Morrison.

"West Indian Festival of Arts" (record).
    Louise Bennett.
West Indian Poetry 1900-1970. Edward Baugh.
West Indian Stories. Andrew Salkey.
West Indies: Islands in the Sun. Wilfred Cartey.
Western: A Saga of the Great Plains. Frank
    Yerby.
What Black Educators Are Saying. Nathan
    Wright.
What Black Librarians Are Saying. E. J. Josey.
What Black Politicans Are Saying. Nathan
    Wright.
What Do the People of Africa Want? Eslanda
    G. Robeson.
What Manner of Man. Lerone Bennett.
What Road to Black Liberation. Tony Thomas.
What Shall I Tell My Children Who Are Black.
    Margaret G. Burroughs.
What the Negro Thinks. Robert R. Moton.
What the Negro Wants. Rayford W. Logan.
What the Wine Sellers Buy. Ron Milner.
What We Must See. Orde Coombs.
What's Happening. Dick Gregory.
When Harlem Was in Vogue. David L. Lewis.
When He Was Free and Young and He Used to
    Wear Silks. Austin C. Clarke.
When I Know the Power of My Black Hand.
    Lance Jeffers.
When Love Whispers (novelette). Cyprian
    Ekwensi.
When Malindy Sings. Paul L. Dunbar.
When One Loves. Nola Richardson.
When Peoples Meet. Alain Locke.
When Rain Clouds Gather. Bessie Head.
When Shadows Fall. Nathan C. Heard.
When the Marching Stopped.... Andrew
    Brimmer.
When the Rattlesnake Sounds. Alice Childress.
When the Word Is Given. Louis E. Lomax.
Where Do We Go from Here: Chaos or
    Community? Martin L. King, Jr.
Where Does the Day Go. Walter D. Myers.
Where Is All the Music. Mari Evans.
Where It's At. John Howard.
Where the Hummingbird Flies. Frank Hercules.
Whichever. Russell Atkins.
Whip Me Whop Me Pudding. Margaret G.
    Burroughs.
Whispers from a Continent. Wilfred Cartey.
White Man Listen! Richard Wright.
White Marble Lady. Roi V. Ottley.
White on Black. Era Bell Thompson.
White Papers for White Americans. Calvin C.
    Hernton.
The White Rat. Gayl Jones.
A White Song and a Black One. Joseph S.
    Cotter.
Witherspoon. Lance Jeffers.
Who Are the Handicapped? James Haskins.

Who I Am. Julius Lester.
Who Is Angelina? Al Young.
Who Killed the Congo? Philippa Schuyler.
Who Look at Me. June Jordan.
The Whole Armour. Wilson Harris.
The Whole World in His Hands. Susan
    Robeson.
Who's Got His Own. Ron Milner.
Who's Who among Black Americans. William
    C. Matney.
Whose Town? Lorenz Graham.
Why Are We So Blest? Ayi K. Armah.
Why Blacks Kill Blacks. Alvin Poussaint.
Why Have the Youth of Today Not Heard
    about This Man—Paul Robeson.
    Margaret G. Burroughs.
Why I Believe There Is a God. Howard
    Thurman.
Why We Can't Wait. Martin L. King, Jr.
Wife of His Youth. Charles Chesnutt.
The Wig: A Mirror Image. Charles Wright.
Wild Conquest. Peter Abrahams.
The Wild Prayer of Longing. Nathan A. Scott.
Wild Seed. Octavia Butler.
A Wilderness of Vines. Hal Bennett.
William Lloyd Garrison, the Abolitionist.
    Archibald Grimke.
The William Stanley Braithwaite Reader.
William Styron's Nat Turner. Ed. by John H.
    Clarke.
The Wind from Nowhere. Oscar Micheaux.
Wind Thoughts. Pinkie G. Lane.
Wine of the Country. Derek Walcott.
Wings of Oppression. Leslie P. Hill.
Winona. Pauline Hopkins.
"A Winter Piece." Jupiter Hammon.
Winterkill. Xavier Jefferson.
Winters. Samuel J. Cornish.
Winters without Snow. Colleen J. McElroy.
Wisdom's Call. Sutton E. Griggs.
Witchcraft, Mysticism and Magic in the Black
    World. James Haskins.
With Head and Heart: The Autobiography of
    Howard Thurman.
Witherspoon. Lance Jeffers.
Witness. Silas Jones.
A Woman Called Fancy. Frank Yerby.
Woman in the Moon. Diane S. Bogus.
Woman—Man's Best Friend. El Muhajir.
Woman, Race and Class. Angela Davis.
The Women and the Men. Nikki Giovanni.
Women of Achievement. Benjamin Brawley.
Women of the Wilmington 10. Saundra Sharp.
Won't Know till I Get There. Walter D. Myers.
The Wooing of Beppoo Tate. C. Everard
    Palmer.
The Word Is Here. Keoropetse Kgositsile.
The Word on the Brazos. John Brewer.

Words in the Mourning Time. Robert E. Hayden.

A Working Bibliography on the Negro in the United States. Dorothy Porter.

Working with the Hands. Booker T. Washington.

The Works of Francis J. Grimké. Carter G. Woodson.

The World and Africa. W. E. B. DuBois.

The World of Black Singles. Robert Staples.

The World of Gwendolyn Brooks.

World of Nothing. Ronald Fair.

The World of Work.... Walter D. Myers.

World Revolution, 1917-1936. C. L. R. James.

A World View of Race. Ralph Bunche.

Worldwide News. Ida E. Lewis.

The World's Fair Poem: The Freedmen's Triumphant Song. Albery Whitman.

World's Great Men of African Descent. J. A. Rogers.

World's Great Men of Color. J. A. Rogers.

The Wounded and the Worried. Edgar Mittelhölzer.

A Wreath for Udomo. Peter Abrahams.

A Wreath for Udomo. William Branch.

The Wretched of the Earth. Frantz Fanon.

The Wright Poems. Conrad K. Rivers.

Write Me In. Dick Gregory.

Writers in Politics. James Ngugi.

Writing in Cuba since the Revolution. Andrew Salkey.

Writings of W. E. B. DuBois.

Xala. Sembène Ousmane.

Yaba Roundabout Murder (novelette). Cyprian Ekwensi.

Yardbird, vol. 1, no. 1. Ed. by Ishmael Reed.

Yardbird Lives! Ed. by Ishmael Reed.

Yardbird Reader. Vols. I & II. Ed. by Ishmael Reed.

The Year in San Fernando. Michael Anthony.

Year the Yankees Lost the Pennant. Warren J. Halliburton.

Yellow Back Radio Broke-Down. Ishmael Reed.

Yesterday I Climbed a Mountain. Margery Brown.

You Can't Keep a Good Woman Down: Stories. Alice Walker.

You Can't Pet a Possum. Arna Bontemps.

Young and Black in America. Julius Lester.

Young Commonwealth Poets '65. Oscar R. Dathorne.

Young Jim: The Early Years of James Weldon Johnson. Ellen Tarry.

Young Landlords. Walter D. Myers.

Young People's History of the United States. Bernard Mandel.

The Young Warriors (novelette). V. S. Reid.

Youngblood. John O. Killens.

Your Hand in Mine. Samuel J. Cornish.

Your Most Humble Servant. Shirley Graham.

Your Rights, Past and Present. Jim Haskins.

Zamani: A Survey of East African History. Bethwell A. Ogot.

Zamani Goes to Market. Muriel Feelings.

Zambia Shall Be Free. Kenneth Kaunda.

Zeely. Virginia Hamilton.

Zeppelin Coming Down. Al Young.

Zik, a Selection from the Speeches of Nnamdi Azikiwe.

Zooman and the Sign. Charles H. Fuller.

The Zulu Heart. Shirley Graham.

Zulu Poems. Mazisi R. Kunene.